Byzantium and the Papacy 1198–1400

Byzantium and the Papacy 1198–1400

Joseph Gill, S.J.

Rutgers University Press
New Brunswick, New Jersey

Library of Congress Cataloging in Publication Data

Gill, Joseph, 1901–
Byzantium and the papacy, 1198–1400.

Bibliography: p.
Includes index.
1. Orthodox Eastern Church—Relations—Catholic Church. 2. Catholic Church—Relations—Orthodox Eastern Church. 3. Byzantine Empire—History. 4. Christian union. I. Title.
DF548.G5 949.5 78-23971
ISBN 0-8135-0864-9

Manufactured in the United States of America

Contents

	Preface	vii
	Abbreviations	xi
I	The Twelfth Century	1
II	The Fourth Crusade	9
III	The Capture of Constantinople	24
IV	The Resurgence of the Greeks	48
V	The Decline of the Latin Empire	78
VI	The Greeks Regain Constantinople	97
VII	The Second Council of Lyons	120
VIII	Greeks, Latins, and the *Filioque*	142
IX	The Reaction to the Council of Lyons	161
X	Instability in Both East and West	182
XI	The Decline of Byzantium	200
XII	The Fourteenth Century: Occasional Contacts	233
XIII	Epilogue	244
	Notes	256
	Bibliography	311
	Index	332

Preface

Several years ago I published two books on the history of Greco-Latin relations during the last fifty years of the Byzantine Empire, with a detailed account of the Council of Florence. Thereby I recorded the end of an epoch, which itself was the result and culmination of a beginning and a middle. The beginning and much of the middle had been briefly but adequately covered by G. Every in his *Byzantine Patriarchate 451–1204*. S. Runciman in his racy *The Eastern Schism* examined again, but more in detail, the eleventh and twelfth centuries. That left the two centuries before A.D. 1400 in need of closer examination. That gap I am filling in this volume.

I am not the first who has set his hand to this task. In 1903 W. Norden published his *Das Papsttum und Byzanz* with the subtitle *Die Trennung der beiden Mächte und das Problem ihrer Wiedervereinigung*. It was a scholarly work covering the relations between the papacy and the Eastern Church from the second half of the eleventh century to 1453, though the period from the early fourteenth century to the end is sketched rather than examined in detail. The book has lately been reprinted, but, although a very great deal of new and relevant information has come forth in the last seventy years, it was not brought up to date as it deserved to be. It remains, however, a valuable work in spite of its age and of its noticeable bias against the papacy. There is no other general survey of church relations during the last centuries of the Byzantine Empire, though there have been several excellent monographs and many instructive articles on individuals and particular situations. Most of the books treat primarily of political history. Many of the articles, especially those of V. Grumel, A.A., and V. Laurent, A.A., deal directly with ecclesiastical affairs.

Most outstanding events have occasioned a significant monograph. The thirteenth century opened with an episode of primary importance, the Fourth Crusade. Its instigator, Pope Innocent III, has been studied from every aspect and in many languages, and his character variously assessed, with a tendency, as the years have passed, towards a more sympathetic appraisal.[1] Inevitably he figures also in the general histories of the crusades, of which there have been several in the last few years,[2] and in other studies confined to discussing in particular the part he played in the Fourth Crusade.[3] The political history of the Latin Empire of Constantinople has been told by J. Longnon,[4] and the events that ensued when the Greeks recovered their empire are narrated in two excellent studies, published almost simultaneously, the one, S. Runciman, *The Sicilian Vespers* (Camb., 1958), viewing the history more from a Western viewpoint, the other, D.J. Geanakoplos, *Emperor Michael Palaeologus and the West* (Cambridge, Mass., 1959), rather with an Eastern eye. Very recently M. Angold has published his researches into *A Byzantine Government in Exile* (Oxford, 1974), i.e., the Kingdom of Nicaea, but, though he has a long chapter on relations within it between Church and State, he makes no mention of the Church's relations with the papacy. On the other hand, a little more than a decade ago B. Roberg produced a work of ecclesiastical history on the Council of Lyons very relevant to the subject-matter of this book.[5] A. Laiou (*Constantinople and the Latins: The Foreign Policy of Andronicus II (1282–1328)* [Cambridge, Mass., 1972]), U. Bosch (*Andronicus III. Palaeologus* [Amsterdam 1965]), G. Weiss *(Johannes Kantakuzenos—Aristocrat, Staatsmann, Kaiser und Mönch—in der Gesellschaftsentwicklung von Byzanz im 14 Jahrhundert* [Wiesbaden, 1969]), D. Nicol *(The Last Centuries of Byzantium 1261–1453* [London, 1972]), and J.W. Barker *(Manuel II Palaeologus [1391–1435]: A Study in Late Byzantine Statesmanship* [New Brunswick, N.J., 1968]) in their political histories include naturally some reference to Church relations. O. Halecki's study, *Un Empereur de Byzance à Rome* (Warsaw, 1930), is purely church history. It is an excellent book and has left little for later enquirers to add to the story of John V's direct contacts with the papacy.

The ecclesiastical history of the thirteenth century and of the first half of the fourteenth century is not lacking in published sources. For the Greeks, George Acropolites described the events of most of the thirteenth century, but he rarely mentions ecclesiastical matters. George Pachymeres wrote the histories of Michael Palaeologus and his son Andronicus, and, being a cleric, he dilated on the fortunes of the Church, but of the Church at home rather than abroad, and he says little about relations with Rome. In the fourteenth century Nicephorus Gregoras was closely involved in Church events, but as a protagonist in the purely Greek hesychastic controversy. John Cantacuzenus, emperor then monk, is mainly concerned to defend his own actions. But if these writers say little about relations with the papacy, they are generous in their descriptions of the home background of their Church against which the contacts with the papacy occurred.

Much might have been hoped for from imperial and patriarchal archives, but they no longer exist.[6] The political *Regesten* published by F. Dölger for the thirteenth and fourteenth centuries and the *Actes des Patriarches* of the thirteenth century edited by V. Laurent have each less than two thousand entries. On the other hand, the registers of the letters of the popes of the period have all been published and they are very rich—e.g., for Gregory IX (1227–41) there are 6,183 items and for John XXII (1316–34) no less than 64,421.

So, it is not surprising that more information can be gleaned about negotiations for Church union, even those initiated by Constantinople, from papal archives than from Greek archives. The papal archives still have the originals of a few of the more solemn documents received from Byzantium. The registers of papal letters preserve, but only very occasionally, translations of communications from the emperor or patriarch of Constantinople. The same registers, however, contain—with the few exceptions of when a whole volume has been lost—copies of all letters sent out by the Curia. These letters are very valuable, not only because they give papal replies, but because they preface each reply with a résumé of the letter that is being answered. Such records are nearly as useful as the original Greek documents, for the standard of accuracy of the résumés is very high, to judge from the rare examples of originals still extant for comparison. It is, therefore, inevitable that in this book papal documents are quoted or referred to very frequently. This may give the impression that the point of view of the Latin Church is being presented more often or more urgently than that of the Greeks. That is not really the case. Papal documents, in fact, are frequently the only source in existence and they are often as much a record of Greek diplomacy as of Latin.

It is, then, from documents of various sorts, enriched by the many insights furnished by learned books and articles written about them, that this history has been written. But, it should be noted, this study is not a political history of the thirteenth and fourteenth centuries. It is not even a history of the Latin Church or a history of the Greek Church during that period. It is a history of the relations between the two Churches and, since these almost always were concerned with the union of the two Churches, it may be said to be a history of the negotiations about ecclesiastical union from 1198 to 1400. Union of the Churches, however, though eminently desirable in itself and indeed desired by both East and West for its own sake, was usually a live issue only when political circumstances brought it into prominence. The conquest of Constantinople seemed to Innocent III, but not to the Greeks, to have united the Churches, and he acted accordingly. When Michael VIII Palaeologus regained the Byzantine capital in 1261, union of the Churches was his best bargaining counter to restrain Latin projects of reconquest. In the fourteenth century union was inevitably linked with requests for Latin aid to check the advance of the Turks. So, political considerations cannot be excluded from this ecclesiastical history, and they are introduced insofar as they seem necessary to portray the relations between the Churches within their historical context.

Joseph Gill, S.J.

Campion Hall
Oxford

Abbreviations

ArchHP	*Archivum Historiae Pontificiae*
ArchOFM	*Archivum Franciscanum Historicum*
ArchOP	*Archivum Fratrum Praedicatorum*
BBTS	Golubovich, G., *Biblioteca bio-bibliografica della Terra Santa e dell'Oriente francescano,* 5 vols. (Quaracchi, 1906–1927)
BChartes	*Bibliothèque de l'Ecole des Chartes*
Bess	*Bessarione*
BForsch	*Byzantinische Forschungen*
Bslav	*Byzantinoslavica*
Byz	*Byzantion*
BZ	*Byzantinische Zeitschrift*
CMH	*Cambridge Medieval History,* IV^2 (Cambridge, 1966)
Dölger *Reg*	Dölger, F., *Regesten der Kaiserurkunden des östromischen Reiches*
DOP	*Dumbarton Oaks Papers*
EEBS	*Epeteris Hetaireias Byzantivon Spoudon*
EO	*Echos d'Orient*
Greg	Nicephorus Gregoras, *Byzantina Historia,* ed. L. Schopen–I. Bekker, 3 vols. (Corpus Scriptorum Historiae Byzantinae XIX) (Bonn, 1829–1855)
JOBG	*Jahrbuch der österreichischen byzantinischen Gesellschaft*
Halecki	Halecki, O., *Un Empereur de Byzance à Rome* (Warsaw, 1930)
Laurent *Reg*	*Les regestes des actes du patriarcat de Constantinople.* Vol. I, *Les actes des patriarches,* fasc. IV, *Les regestes de 1208–1309,* ed. V. Laurent (Paris, 1971)
Mansi	*Sacrorum conciliorum nova et amplissima collectio*
MGH	*Monumenta Germaniae historica*

MM	*Acta et diplomata graeca medii aevi sacra et profana,* 6 vols. (Vienna, 1860–1890)
MPG	Migne, *Patrologiae cursus completus,* ser. *graeco-latina*
MPL	Migne, *Patrologiae cursus completus,* ser. *latina*
Norden	Norden, W., *Das Papsttum und Byzanz* (Berlin, 1903; reprinted 1958)
OCP	*Orientalia Christiana Periodica*
Pach I	Pachymeres, G., *De Michaele Palaeologo,* ed. I. Bekker (Bonn: CSHB, 1835)
Pach II	Pachymeres, G., *De Andronico Palaeologo,* ed. I. Bekker (Bonn: CSHB, 1835)
Pont. Comm.	Pontificia Commissio ad redigendum codicem iuris canonici orientalis
Raynaldus	Raynaldus, O., *Annales ecclesiastici*
REB	*Revue des Etudes Byzantines*
RHSE	*Revue historique du sud-est européen*
SBN	*Studi bizantini e neoellenici*
Spec	*Speculum*
ST	*Studi e Testi*
Trad	*Traditio*
TT	Tafel, G.L.F. and Thomas, G.M., *Urkunden zur älteren Handels- und Staatsgeschichte der Republik Venedig,* pts. I-III *(Fontes Rerum Austriacarum,* abt. II, vols. XII-XIV) (Vienna, 1856–1857)

Byzantium and the Papacy 1198–1400

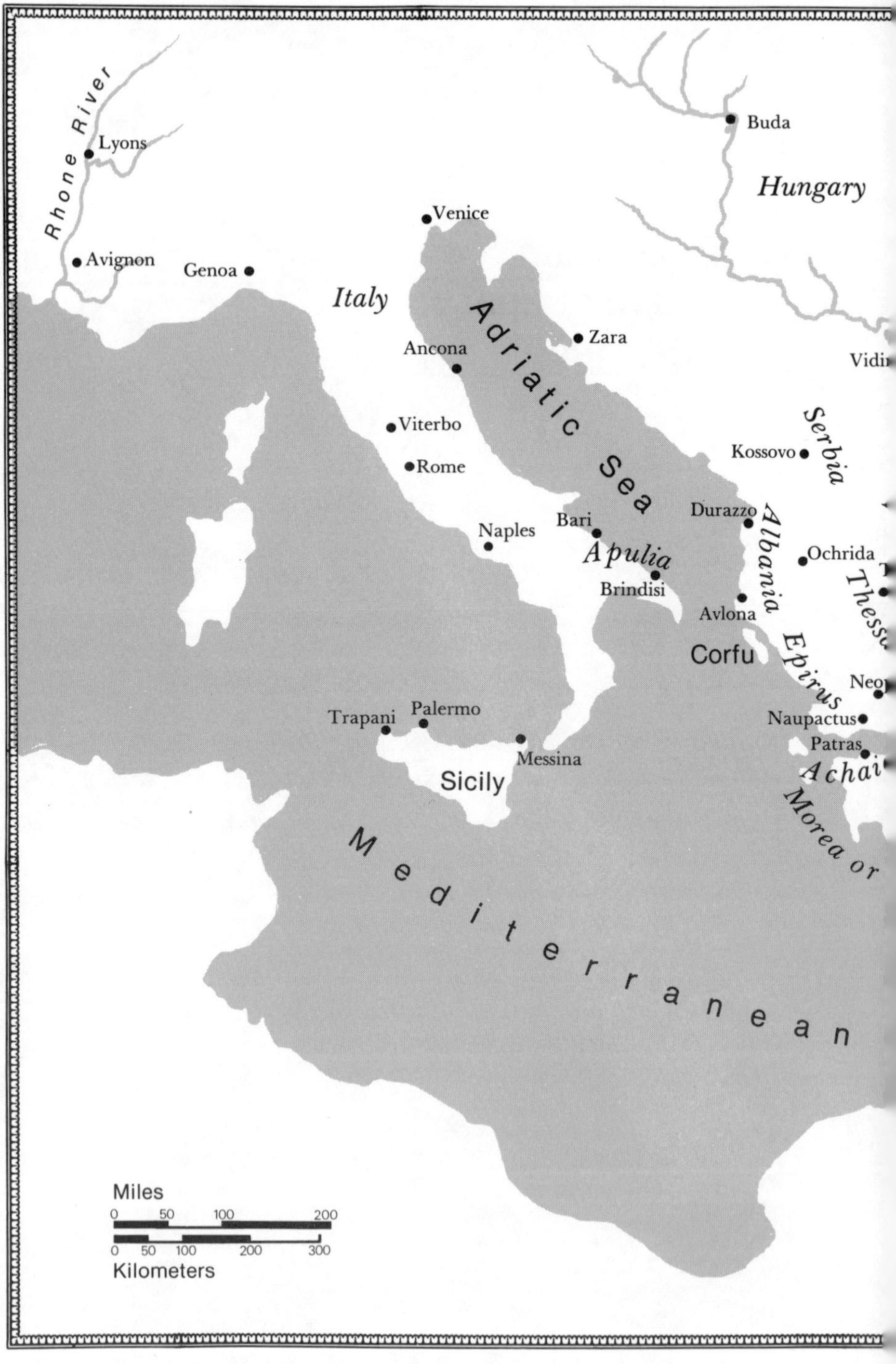

Rhone River
Lyons
Avignon
Genoa
Venice
Italy
Adriatic Sea
Zara
Ancona
Viterbo
Rome
Naples
Bari
Apulia
Brindisi
Buda
Hungary
Serbia
Kossovo
Durazzo
Albania
Ochrida
Avlona
Corfu
Epirus
Naupactus
Patras
Trapani
Palermo
Messina
Sicily
Mediterranean
Miles
0 50 100 200
0 50 100 200 300
Kilometers

Black Sea
Cherson
Danube River
Bulgaria
Sozopolis
Trebizond
Adrianople
Thrace
Didymotichus
Constantinople
Gallipoli
Nicaea
Sangarios River
Brusa
Aegean Sea
Tenedos
Asia Minor or Anatolia
Chios
Smyrna
Nymphaeum
Philadelphia
Meander River
Armenia
Antioch
Rhodes
Cyprus
Nicosia
Tripoli
Crete
Acre
Jerusalem
Alexandria
Damietta

Chapter I

The Twelfth Century

By the beginning of the twelfth century both the Roman Church and the Byzantine state had attained stability after a period of weakness. If it seems strange to compare the eastern *state* with the Western *Church,* it should be borne in mind that the Byzantine Church and the Byzantine state were much more of a single entity than was the Western Church, personified as it was in the papacy, and the many independent and often hostile kingdoms of the West.[1] The firmness of the reforming pope Gregory VII (1073–85) bore fruit in the Concordat of Worms (25 September 1122) and relieved the church of much of the heavy weight of secular domination. Emperor Alexius I Comnenus (1081–1118) by heroic efforts checked the rapid decline of the Byzantine Empire. He repelled a determined Norman attack on Corfu and the Greek mainland launched from Italy, defeated the Pechenegs to the north, and checked the advance of the Turks in Asia Minor. In the process he took two steps in his relations with the West whose baleful consequences he did not foresee. To withstand the Norman attack of Robert Guiscard, in return for the support of its fleet, Alexius gave Venice a series of commercial privileges in Byzantine ports that could never be rescinded. This debilitated the commercial activity of Byzantium itself, and ultimately, when Genoa enjoyed at least equal privileges, led to the utter decline of the Byzantine fleet and to Constantinople's dependence on foreign ships for its food. The other fateful step was Alexius's request for aid from Pope Urban II which occasioned the crusades, in consequence of which contacts and accompanying frictions between East and West were suddenly multiplied enormously.

The very first crusade illustrated the danger. As soon as the crusading armies reached Constantinople, Alexius and the western leaders differed before Alexius could induce them to agree to restore to him all territories they might capture that had previously been parts of the Byzantine Empire. Bohemond, the son of Alexius's old enemy Guiscard, took Antioch (1098) and, claiming that the imperial forces had betrayed him by leaving him at the time of his greatest need during the siege, refused to surrender the city to the emperor. Some years later Bohemond returned to the West where he toured the courts of Europe disseminating stories of Byzantine perfidy and laying the foundations for western distrust of the Greeks. Bohemond then directed another Norman attack on the empire but was easily defeated and, according to the terms of the Treaty of Devol (1108), was forced to acknowledge Alexius as his suzerain and to hold Antioch as an imperial fief. But Bohemond never returned to the East.

The presence of Latin crusaders in Syria and Palestine also brought the churches into contact. Of the five patriarchates, three—Alexandria, Jerusalem, and Antioch—were situated within the territories occupied by the Saracens. Except during one short period, the Muslims had not molested the Christians' organization and practice, and the Greeks with their patriarchs and the other Christian bodies continued in their normal peaceful existence. The arrival of the Latins brought a new element. Alexandria came into western hands only spasmodically during short periods of active warfare, so there was little occasion for religious contact. When the crusaders took Jerusalem, the patriarchal throne was vacant and they filled it with a Latin. Antioch's Greek patriarch, John, remained in residence when Bohemond occupied the city, and for a few years the papal legate Adhemar and John both resided there. After the legate's death, the Greek patriarch was thought too sympathetic with the Greek emperor whom Bohemond was defying. Tension increased until John left the city and took refuge in Constantinople. There he and his successors, elected and consecrated in the Greek capital, remained except for short periods of détente, as a reminder of Latin intransigence more stringent than the fanaticism of the Muslims. In their stead Latin patriarchs were installed. The offense the Greeks felt at the presence of a Latin patriarch in Antioch can be gauged from the fact that a clause of the Treaty of Devol between Alexius and Bohemond stipulated that the patriarch of Antioch should be "one whom your Majesties shall appoint from among [the personnel of] the Great Church of Constantinople."

After a long and successful reign Alexius I died and was succeeded by his son John (1118–43), whom "the verdict of contemporaries and posterity has proclaimed as the greatest of the Comneni."[2] Like his father, John was always aware of the Norman danger from Sicily; he cultivated friendship with the Hohenstaufen princes of Germany and, in spite of his endeavor to lessen the privileges of Venice in Byzantium, in 1126 he had to renew the old treaty. Nevertheless John put an end forever to the attacks of the Pechenegs, imposed himself on Serbia, and was on the point of attacking Antioch at the time of his death. His son Manuel I (1143–80) energetically continued and extended the same general policies. To strengthen the alliance with Germany against Sicily, he married the sister-in-law of the Hohenstaufen Conrad III, a tie which confirmed his personal admiration for many western chivalrous institutions, so that his court took on a western aspect. In addition he filled high posts, especially in the army, with westerners. But the Second Crusade took Conrad to an inglorious campaign in the East and left the field open for King Roger II of Sicily to attack Corfu and mainland Greece. Then, due to Roger's diplomacy, Europe became divided into pro- and anti-Byzantine factions. Tension momentarily relaxed when Frederick I Hohenstaufen ("Barbarossa") succeeded Conrad († 1252). When two years later Roger II of Sicily also died, Emperor Manuel, inspired by the traditional Byzantine aspiration for world hegemony and intending to eliminate danger from the West once and for all, attacked Italy in 1255 and was soon in command of the area from Ancona to Taranto in the south. Manuel's triumph did not last long, however, for King William I of Sicily inflicted a convincing defeat on his forces. His expedition was also a failure in other respects. Venice, afraid of the presence in its home waters of a power capable of interfering with its shipping, moved towards friendship with Sicily. And Barbarossa, who had been crowned holy Roman emperor in 1155 and who considered himself the Christian emperor par excellence, looked on Manuel's action as an attack not only on his imperial territory but also on his imperial claims. Thus the friendship between Byzantium and Germany was ended.

Elsewhere, however, the Greek emperor was eminently successful. Manuel accomplished what his father had been about to do at his death when he made the Latin ruler of Antioch acknowledge Byzantine suzerainty. He first brought Armenia to heel and then advanced on Antioch, which quickly yielded. In 1159, arrayed in all his imperial insignia, Manuel rode into the city on horseback while the Latin prince of Antioch walked beside his horse holding the imperial stirrup. And the king of Jerusalem without any insignia followed on horseback far behind. Once more the Byzantine emperor insisted on the restoration of the Greek patriarch.

Manuel never gave up the idea of expansion in the West. His attempt at conquest having failed, he resorted to diplomacy to foil Frederick I's plans by encouraging Barbarossa's enemies and generously supplying them with money. Furthermore, he invited the papacy, France, and Sicily to join with him in an anti-German alliance.

The Latin Church at that time was in disarray because of a contested papal election in 1159. Frederick had supported Victor IV against Alexander III in the election. In consequence Alexander had to take refuge in France where he resided for several years; he regained peaceful possession of Rome only in 1177. Naturally it was to Alexander that Manuel made his overtures, first in 1163–64 and later in 1166 and 1167. Manuel proposed himself as emperor of a united East and West and Alexander pope of a united church. So as not to seem to dismiss the imperial proposal too lightly, the pope sent two cardinal legates to accompany the Greek envoys on their return to Constantinople in both 1166 and 1167. But Alexander was too prudent to give an enthusiastic welcome to Manuel's proposal, which would have negated all his endeavors to restore peace to Christian Europe.

In 1176 two decisive military engagements occurred: the defeat of Frederick Barbarossa at Legnano and the annihilation at Myriokephalon of a Byzantine army under Emperor Manuel I. At Legnano the League of Lombard Cities, supported by Pope Alexander III and encouraged (and to some extent financed) by Manuel, broke the German Emperor's hold on northern Italy. In consequence, peace between the holy Roman emperor and the pope was effected in the following year by the Treaty of Venice. The success of the Seljuk Turks at Myriokephalon was at once a severe blow to the power of the Eastern Empire in Asia Minor and an end to Manuel's dream of a single vast Christian empire taking in both East and West. Indeed all his many intrigues in the West, on which he had spent immense sums of money that would have been used to better advantage in strengthening his eastern frontiers, failed. Manuel's efforts to displace Barbarossa had only made that monarch lay firmer claim to the headship of the whole of Christendom and induced him to make contact with the Greeks' eastern neighbors and rivals, the Turks. Manuel's plots with Norman nobles of the Two Sicilies against their king, William II, even though backed by a Byzantine army, came to nothing; but they created for him still another enemy in William. Manuel also insulted William by repudiating without a word of explanation the marriage between his daughter Mary and William that had been arranged in 1170. Here Manuel was outwitted by Frederick, who, to upset the Sicilian marriage project with its political prospects, proposed his own son Henry for Mary's hand and then refused to receive the Greek ambassadors when they came to settle the terms of the arrangement. Manuel disliked the Venetians for their firm grip on eastern commerce, their arrogance, and their opposition to some of his political aims. In 1171 he suddenly had all the Venetians in his empire arrested and their goods confiscated. At the time the Signoria could do little to redress the wrong.

Manuel died in 1180 leaving only one son, Alexius II, age eleven, who had just married eight-year-old Agnes-Anna, daughter of the king of France. Power passed to the boy's mother, challenged by his much older stepsister. Constantinople was split into a pro-Latin party supporting the queen mother and an anti-Latin party centering on the princess. Both nobles and populace were involved in the ensuing fighting; the well-disciplined troops of the crown finally checked but did not utterly quell the mob. Manuel's cousin Andronicus, with bribes, promises, and treachery, profited by the situation and made himself master of the capital. He won the favor of the populace by allowing it to vent its pent-up hatred of the Westerners without restraint. In April 1182 Latins were massacred in Constantinople. They were mostly Pisans and Genoese because the Venetians had not reorganized their quarter of the city after the coup of 1171. The mob, without hindrance from the city's authorities, raged through the streets murdering men, women, children, the sick in the hospitals, and the clergy as well as layfolk. The papal legate John was beheaded and his head was dragged through the dirt at the tail of a dog. Some four thousand Westerners were sold into slavery to the Turks.[3]

The reign of Andronicus was a disaster. Filled with a fierce dislike of the noble families, he imprisoned, exiled, or executed them in numbers. Fear of rivals made him murder the boy emperor, Alexius, and contrive the death both of the queen mother and of the princess, Manuel's only daughter. At the age of about sixty-three, Andronicus married Agnes-Anna, the eleven-year-old widow of the boy he had murdered. Though there were many plots against him, none succeeded and the plotters paid the price of failure. Moreover, the empire was assailed on many sides by external foes. Though he fought to hold them off, the emperor dared not let any general have too big a command, for a successful general was a potential aspirant to the throne. Thus Andronicus' divided armies achieved little and allowed the Bulgarians to gain independence, the start of a new Bulgarian empire.

Some of the Italians who had escaped the massacre of 1182 by flight took their revenge—and to some degree compensated themselves for their financial losses—by raiding Byzantine settlements and monasteries around the coast. As the years passed there were many others who, with or without a like excuse, followed their example, so that piracy became a chronic, devastating menace to all commerce and to the security and possessions of the seaboard.[4] In 1185 William II of Sicily sent an army to capture Constantinople. It had already reached Thessalonica before serious measures were taken to check it. In consequence the city was captured and mercilessly sacked. Eustathius, metropolitan of Thessalonica and an eyewitness, wrote a long, rhetorical account: houses were pillaged, priests beaten, women—even maidens—assaulted. Churches were robbed of the precious metals adorning the icons; filthy actions were performed in the churches; and monuments and tombs were smashed and despoiled. The people fled in panic, mothers were separated from their daughters, fathers from their sons. Many threw themselves down from the roofs or into wells, and so added to the already great mortality of the citizens.[5] Fearful of a popular reaction in Constantinople, the emperor determined to suppress possible leaders of revolt. An agent of his sent to arrest Isaac Comnenus was killed in a panic by his would-be victim, who, fleeing for refuge to St. Sophia, to his amazement and horror found himself hailed as emperor. Andronicus fled, was captured, and despatched with the utmost barbarity as a spectacle for the mob.

Isaac II Angelus (1185–95) was a better emperor than Andronicus who preceded him and than Alexius who followed him. But he was too mild, pliable, and pleasure-loving to be a good emperor. He was not lacking in sound sense. He united the armies opposed to the Sicilians under one general, Branas, who checked the Norman advance. So undisciplined were the Norman troops that the check developed into a defeat, the defeat into a panic, and the army hastened back to Durazzo in disorder and even there was defeated again. Then Branas, the successful general, led the most serious of the many revolts against the emperor. With his army he also had the support of the magnates—but he failed. The mob that had put Isaac on the throne ran riot in the city, but when the disorders began to turn into another anti-Latin pogrom, it was found that the would-be victims had learned from their experiences of 1182: they had provided themselves with means of self-defense, which on this occasion as on subsequent ones were effective.

Branas was not the only rebel. In Asia Minor there were several pretenders to the throne or magnates striving for independence. In 1186 there began the incessant raids of the Vlach and Cuman allies of the Bulgarians that drained the empire's resources of men and money. In each of the years from 1187 to 1191 Isaac took the field in person against the raiders—and there were other campaigns entrusted to his generals—but there was little real success. In 1188 Frederick Barbarossa announced his crusade to free the Holy Land, and sent ambassadors to request from Isaac free passage and facilities for buying food for his troops. Isaac was desperately afraid. By a series of embassies he conceded all the holy Roman emperor's requests and promised friendship, yet at the same time he imprisoned the German envoys at his court and confirmed a treaty with Saladin guaranteeing to delay and destroy the German forces. He succeeded in deceiving Barbarossa for a time until Byzantine guerrilla warfare and indeed formal military opposition opened his eyes. Thereupon the German monarch, who until then had no desire to injure the Greeks, took the offensive. He plundered Byzantine lands and occupied Adrianople. With that city as a center of operations he planned to capture Constantinople with the aid of a fleet which he instructed his son Henry to make ready. Only then did Isaac regret his perfidy and grant Frederick's requests. Constantinople was saved by his compliance, but Isaac's devious actions confirmed the Latin conviction that Greeks were unreliable and treacherous, and strengthened the idea that possession of Constantinople was a necessary preliminary for the freeing of the Holy Land.

The German king Henry VI had in 1186 married Constance, daughter of Roger II, king of Sicily. On 18 November 1189, Roger's successor, William II, died childless at the age of thirty-six, and Constance was next in line for the throne. Frederick Barbarossa drowned on 10 June 1190. Thus within the space of less than a year Henry became king of the Germans and, through his wife, claimed the throne of Sicily. He succeeded in establishing himself in Germany, was crowned holy Roman emperor in 1191 by Pope Celestine, and by 1194 had made good his claims in Sicily. In Palermo he found Irene, daughter of the Byzantine emperor Isaac II and widow of Roger III, son of Tancred. Henry had her marry his brother Philip of Swabia and so brought to the House of Hohenstaufen an indirect claim to the throne of Byzantium. He, had, however, no immediate intention of campaigning against Constantinople, for he was planning a crusade to the Holy Land. But he meant to impose a certain dominion over the Greek capital and to make the Greeks pay for their peace and his wars. In 1195 Henry sent an embassy to demand aid for his forthcoming crusade and the cession of the provinces between Durazzo and Thessalonica that King William had won (and lost) in the expedition of a decade before. Emperor Isaac did not think of resisting. Henry agreed to accept money instead of territories and even to reduce to 1,600 pounds of gold the original sum stipulated at 5,000.

Isaac II Angelus received the demand of Henry VI, but it was Alexius III Angelus who bargained about it. Alexius was the only one of Isaac's brothers who had not been blinded by Andronicus I. Trusted completely by Isaac, Alexius plotted against him, deposed him, and blinded him. Constantinople lost by the exchange. The empire was crumbling on all its frontiers. Pretenders with Turkish patrons appeared in Asia Minor; Alexius gained temporary security by buying off the Turks. The usual Vlach-Cuman raids continued. Several small principalities were founded by successful leaders, at least two of whom were disposed of when the emperor broke his oath of safe conduct to entrap the leaders. In the south Leo Sgouros, starting from Nauplion, made himself the master of Argos, the Isthmus of Corinth, and Thessaly; but Athens resisted him. Alexius was fortunate when Kalojan, who had succeeded his brothers as prince of the Bulgars, made peace in 1202. Apart from this success Alexius's "advent [to the throne] proved a disaster for Byzantium. The circumstances of his accession left him a prisoner of the nobles who had conspired with him: he could deny them nothing, nor did he have the will to resist them. The wealth, offices, and lands of the crown fell into their hands, and their greed was supplemented by that of other powerful groups, the monasteries and the Latins."[6]

By 1200 the Venetians, Pisans, and Genoese who had been robbed and their compatriots massacred in 1171 and 1182 were back in force, occupying and extending their old quarters of the city. Manuel had done little to placate the Venetians for the events of 1171. But Andronicus I, whose reign had been inaugurated by the massacre of 1182, had soon made overtures of peace to them. He agreed to pay as compensation for their losses up to 1,500 pounds of gold, to restore all their old privileges, and to increase their quarter. His successors were still paying the compensation in irregular annual installments when Constantinople fell to Venetian arms in 1204. Genoa and Pisa were likewise conciliated. However, the measures that appeased the Latins enraged the Greeks, because they granted privileges to foreigners at the expense of the natives. Between Latins, therefore, and Greeks there was always tension, and, with the threat of a popular rising against them never far away, the Italians in Constantinople lived in an atmosphere of insecurity.

On the eve of the Fourth Crusade relations between Eastern and Western Christendom were not happy. On both sides there was a deep-seated antagonism. The Greeks fiercely resented the privileged position of the Latins within their empire, and on more than one occasion showed their feelings violently: the massacre of 1182 was but the most successful outburst. To the Latin mind the Greeks were perfidious. The First Crusade had implanted the idea; Barbarossa's experience confirmed it: far from being a help, Greeks in Constantinople were a hindrance to the liberation of the Holy Land. For the mercantile Italian states—conscious from firsthand knowledge of the internal debility of the empire, its maladministration and political instability—the Greeks were a constant threat to the security of their citizens and an obstacle to wider commercial activity. Normans and Germans both cast covetous eyes from Sicily on the Eastern Empire. There was, then, little that could act as a bond of peace between Christian East and Christian West, not even religion, because the churches were in schism. All that was needed was an apt occasion to lead to open war. That occasion came with the new crusade that was being prepared.[7]

Chapter II

The Fourth Crusade

In 1187, after annihilating the Christian forces in Outremer, Saladin captured Jerusalem and the relic of the Holy Cross. Europe was aghast and outraged. The result was the spontaneous movement of the Third Crusade encouraged by the church but directed by the laity. Frederick Barbarossa left Germany at the head of his army in 1189, only to perish in a river in Armenia in 1190. Conrad of Montferrat, Philip Augustus of France, and Richard Lionheart of England reached Palestine, where they managed to secure a strip of coastline from Acre to Jaffa, but failed to take the Holy City (1191–92). Saladin died in 1193, and his sixteen sons divided his kingdom among them; in the ensuing rivalries lay an opportunity for the Christians to reconquer the kingdom of Jerusalem. A leader was at hand, Henry VI Hohenstaufen, son of the dead Barbarossa, who by 1197 was holy Roman emperor and king of Germany, king of the Two Sicilies, and liege-lord of England, Cyprus, and Armenia. Henry was strong in character like his father, and had aspirations to the Byzantine throne like his Norman predecessors in Sicily. In August of 1198 he was in Messina organizing his army's departure for Palestine. On 28 September he was dead, and the crusade collapsed.

At least two people felt a sense of relief at his death. One was the emperor of Constantinople, who feared another attack on his empire launched from Sicily. The other was Pope Celestine III, sandwiched between Henry's possessions in the north and his Sicilian kingdoms in the south. Within four months Pope Celestine also was dead (8 January 1198) and a new pope had been elected.

Innocent III was born in 1160 or 1161 in a period when the church was striving with all its might on three fronts—to regain the Holy Land, to oppose heresy, and to purify itself. As pope, he tried as few before him to attain all three ends. By training he was well prepared. Connected by birth with an ancient family and with the Roman nobility, he studied theology in Rome and Paris and canon law in Bologna under famous masters. Back in Rome, he was soon created cardinal by his uncle Clement III. He was unanimously elected pope on 8 January 1198, the very day of the death of his predecessor.

He was a man who believed in and practiced the ascetical life and who had a ready sympathy for the unfortunate. An ardent defender of the rights of the church on the lines of Gregory VII, Innocent had a high esteem for his office of vicar of Christ; nevertheless, he did not infringe customary civil law or deviate from the canons. In spite of his high qualities, he achieved none of the great aims that motivated him. Many historians attribute his failure to ambition and devious diplomacy which, they say, vitiated his action. He is said to have aimed at world domination in the wide sense, covering the political as well as the ecclesiastical world.[1]

Innocent claimed complete authority, *plenitudo potestatis,* in the ecclesiastical and spiritual spheres on the grounds that he was vicar of Christ, successor of St. Peter, and holder of the power that Christ had given to St. Peter for his office of vicar and through him to his successors.[2] Hence the pope alone had the *plenitudo potestatis* of all the churches: others—bishops,[3] and even patriarchs[4]—had only a partial *solicitudo* of the churches dependent on him. This dependence was to be shown by metropolitans receiving the "pallium taken from the body of St. Peter" (i.e., from the tomb of St. Peter),[5] which they were to wear at the solemnities of certain feasts within their own jurisdictions. All major causes were to be referred to Rome and that not by reason of church law only, but by divine ordinance.[6] On the other hand, papal authority even in the ecclesiastical sphere also had severe limitations. It applied only to what was man-made in the Church, not to what was of divine mandate.

Innocent did not claim supreme political power over all the Christian world. Over the Papal States, of course, he did, and so on occasions he compared himself to Melchisedech the priest-king.[7] He followed a tradition first clearly enunciated by Pope Gelasius in holding that both swords, the spiritual and the temporal, derive from God, the one to the pope, the other to princes and in particular to the holy Roman emperor.[8] The swords were complementary and should work together in harmony.[9] Complementary though they were, the spiritual nevertheless was superior to the temporal as the sun is to the moon.[10] A pope could interfere in political questions, not because he held universal temporal power, but only *casualiter* and *ratione peccati. Casualiter* applied to cases where there was no competent temporal judge.[11] *Ratione peccati* opened a wider field, for many a political action involved a moral problem.

In all this Innocent was no innovator. He followed traditional canonistic teaching, influenced by St. Bernard and much more by his master at the University of Bologna, the famous canonist Huguccio.[12] What is more, he applied the canons and his own principles rigorously, risking the enmity of princes and remaining undeterred by the resentment of bishops and their protectors.[13] Innocent looked on the Greek Church as a part of the universal Church like any big metropolitanate and, when occasion came, he treated it in the same way or very nearly in the same way as he did, say, the Church of France. The results were unfortunate.

The death of Henry VI put an end to the immediate danger to the eastern empire from Sicily. Nevertheless Emperor Alexius III still pursued relations with Rome. A letter from Innocent III to him dated early August 1198 is the reply to an embassy from Constantinople.[14] Presumably Alexius had asked for papal support. Innocent's answer did little more than keep the diplomatic door open, while making his conditions for future fruitful collaboration known. Innocent wrote that Alexius should put his trust in Christ, should use his great power and wealth for the freeing of the Holy Land and should "see that the Church of the Greeks return to the unity of the Apostolic See and the daughter to her mother"; otherwise Innocent advised that he would have no choice but to do his duty and pass just judgment.[15] A similar letter was addressed to the patriarch; it lay just a little more stress on the primacy of the Roman See over the Greek Church, "which (if indeed what is in addition to the one [Church] should really be called a Church) has left the unity of the Apostolic See."[16]

In February 1199 by the emperor's messengers the patriarch sent a reply courteously but firmly rebutting Innocent's main points by proposing that if there was any mother church it was that of Jerusalem, and that responsibility for the rending of the seamless garment of Christ lay not with the Greek Church but with the Latin because of its innovation in the doctrine of the Procession of the Holy Spirit. The Scriptures and the Doctors of the church had always referred this to the Father. The Eastern Church, following them, still did.[17] The emperor answered also. On the question of church union he told Innocent that there would be no difficulty if men would subordinate their wills to God's and that, if the pope would call a council, "the most holy Church of these parts would not be slow to respond."[18]

More than half of Innocent's answer to Alexius dated 13 November 1199 is devoted to explaining why the emperor should fight for the Holy Land. In the remainder of the letter, the pope broached the question of ecclesiastical union and informed the emperor that for a variety of reasons he did actually intend to call a council, "to which, if on our invitation [the patriarch] shall come and pay due reverence and obedience to the Roman Church. . . . We shall receive him graciously and gladly as our most dear brother and the chief member of the Church. . . . Otherwise . . . in that council We shall have no choice but to act in this matter on the advice of our brethren."[19] The emperor also received a copy of the pope's answer to the patriarch, in which at very great length Innocent expounded scriptural and other proofs for the primacy of the See of Peter. Moreover, having informed the patriarch of the future council as he did in the letter to the emperor, Innocent added that if the Greek Church did not act as indicated, "which We do not credit, We shall be compelled to proceed both against the Emperor himself, who can if he wishes do what We require, and against you and the Church of the Greeks."

To this letter Camaterus sent a long reply, though whether it ever reached Innocent is doubtful, for there is no answer to it recorded in the registers of the pope, who seemed never to have failed in a correspondence. The patriarch was most concerned to rebut the Latin claim to primacy. Neither Gospel, he asserted, nor council ever proclaimed Roman primacy; other cities were evangelized by Apostles; why, then, he queried, should Rome be distinguished from them as the "mother," when five are the sees called patriarchal, which like fingers on the hand or strings on a lyre act in harmony and no one of them is over the others? The patriarch continued that all the Apostles were taught by the Holy Spirit; all were sent by Christ; to all, the words of Christ apply when he made them the foundation of the church and bade them feed the flock. Peter had a special mission to the Hebrews; Paul to the Gentiles; James was bishop of Jerusalem. We declare, he wrote, that Peter was honored by Christ above the other Apostles and that the Church of Rome is first in rank and honor among equal sisters, not, however, because Peter was ever bishop of Rome, but because Rome at that time was the residence of the emperor and of the senate. The Roman Church calls itself "catholic"; in that way it makes a part the equal of the whole, for only the whole Church is catholic, i.e., universal, and it has not two heads but one only, who is Christ. The faith began in Jerusalem; the name "Christian" originated in Antioch; Rome may have many baptisms, but the size of a church cannot make it universal.[20]

This preliminary correspondence between Rome and Constantinople was largely academic and had little sense of urgency. However, it clearly manifested Innocent's attitude towards the Greek Church. He had no doubt whatsoever that the Greek Church had left the unity of the Church of Christ, that it was its duty to return to the Western Church "as a daughter to a mother," that it owed to the pope of Rome a reverence and obedience different in no essential from that owed by the metropolitan churches of the West, and that apparently it was completely subservient to the Byzantine emperor.

The patriarch of Constantinople obviously saw things in a different light. To Rome he could concede no more than that it was the first among five equal patriarchal sees, which together constituted the Church. There was no question of mother and daughters, but of sister churches. Three of these five, Alexandria, Antioch, and Jerusalem, were in lands that had been overrun by the Arabs and that, with diminished importance, had come to depend largely on Constantinople. At the beginning of the thirteenth century, they were in a worse plight than ever; they were being contended for politically by pagans and Christians, and ecclesiastically by the Greek Church and the Latin. Further, the See of Rome was held in condemnation for having added to the Creed the *Filioque* clause, which in the judgment of easterns embodied a doctrine that was heretical. Union with such a church, let alone submission, was impossible as long as the charge of heresy subsisted. So the Church of Constantinople felt itself to be the bastion of orthodoxy, which was as it should be, for it was the embodiment of the religious and ecclesiastical aspirations of the Byzantines, the people of God, who politically were ruled by the God-given emperor. Emperors certainly were the protectors of orthodoxy and they interfered not a little in the day-to-day affairs of the church, but they were not priests and could not dictate doctrine. Innocent's letters, therefore, to the Patriarch made little impression on him. Camaterus was unmoved by his arguments and his veiled threats.

Events, however, were moving rapidly to make East-West relations more meaningful. Innocent's exhortations to Alexius to defend the Holy Land were not a mere formality. He honestly believed that the Byzantine emperor could dispose of rich resources and a powerful army,[21] and he himself was promoting a crusade from the West with ever more vigor. The crusade should have started in March 1199,[22] but circumstances were unfavorable. England and France were at war, and Philip Augustus was antipapal because the church would not countenance his divorce. Germany was involved in civil war, and England after the death of Richard (6 April 1199) was rent by factions. Innocent himself was embroiled in wars over Sicily, the March, Romagna, and other areas of the Papal States, hardly any part of which was he then holding in peaceful possession.

Innocent did not, however, allow these adverse conditions to distract him from the policies he thought right. He sent legates to press for peace between England and France. In Germany Otto of Brunswick had been elected (9 April 1198), and crowned king on 12 July. Two months afterwards, on 8 March, the late king's brother, Philip of Swabia, was elected king; he was crowned on 8 September. Innocent, though he was appealed to and threatened by both claimants, for some years did nothing. He claimed no power over the Germans' election of their king; however, as he was empowered to crown the holy Roman emperor he held that he had the right, and indeed the duty, to approve the candidate proposed as emperor, i.e., the elected German king. Finally in a dispassionate document of 5 January 1201 weighing the qualifications of both claimants, he rejected Philip and conditionally approved Otto. Otto, of course, swore to fulfill each and every condition proposed, and on 3 July 1201 was proclaimed king of the Romans by the papal legate at Aix-la-Chapelle. Philip's fortunes sank, but he did not give up and the war in Germany continued.

With all the monarchs thus too occupied with their own affairs to listen to appeals for the Holy Land, the pope turned to the bishops and the knights. The response was generous, especially in France. There Thibaut of Champagne was elected as head of the crusade, and a deputation was sent to Venice to arrange transport for the voyage to Outremer. The price was fixed at 85,000 marks "of pure silver of the weight of Cologne" and the half of everything acquired by the expedition. Innocent gave his approval on 8 May 1201.

In autumn of that same year Prince Alexius, son of Isaac (who had been deposed from the Byzantine throne and blinded by his brother the emperor Alexius III), escaped to Ancona.[23] The prince first went to his sister, wife of Philip of Swabia, and later visited the pope. He was in search of western assistance for his attempt to overthrow his uncle and to restore his father to the throne. Innocent returned a noncommittal and discouraging answer. Thereupon Prince Alexius, through his brother-in-law Philip, contacted the crusade leaders, promising large gifts, generous contributions to the crusade, and his endeavors to satisfy the desires of the pope and the Roman Church.[24] Meantime Thibaut had died and in September 1201 Boniface, Marquis of Montferrat, was elected to head the crusade in his stead. He visited Philip Augustus, king of France, who was an ally of Philip of Swabia, and then probably Philip himself. Later Boniface went to the pope, whom he sounded on Prince Alexius's proposal, only to meet with a negative attitude.[25]

The French crusading army began to gather in Venice in the summer of 1202; but it was not as large as had been expected, partly because some of the knights went directly to Syria by sea and others betook themselves to Apulia as being more in a direct line for their goal. The result was that the army in Venice, lodged on the island of St. Nicolo de Lido, could not find the requisite 85,000 marks to pay the Venetians, even after some of the barons surrendered their gold and silver plate to swell the funds. As a solution to the difficulty the doge proposed that the crusade should sail and payment of the deficit be deferred, provided that en route to the east the French assist the Venetians to reduce the city of Zara to submission. Zara, the doge claimed, belonged to Venice, but was being unjustly held by the king of Hungary. After serious and genuine hesitation, the leaders of the pilgrims acquiesced. Thereupon, with every show of piety, Doge Dandolo took the Cross and a throng of enthusiastic Venetians followed his example.

The decision was indeed a serious one, for it diverted the crusade from its one main purpose in order to use its arms against Christians, subjects of a monarch who had himself taken the Cross and who was therefore protected in his person and possessions by the church. It was a decision that caused very great dissatisfaction within the French army and occasioned many desertions. It also brought the leaders into conflict with the pope.

Innocent had sent Peter Capuano, cardinal of St. Marcello, to Venice as his apostolic legate in order to have a voice in the direction of the crusade. But the Venetians refused to accept him in that capacity; they would recognize him only as preacher.[26] Capuano arrived in Venice on 22 July, preached to the troops, encouraged them, and some time later departed again.[27] Montferrat joined the army on 15 August,[28] and only after his arrival could there be real discussion and decision about the expedition to Zara. Contingents from various places continued to arrive. With a German one came Conrad, archbishop of Helmstadt, who, disturbed at the diversion of the crusade to Zara, consulted Capuano and was urged not to leave on the grounds that the pope certainly would not want the crusading army to be dissolved.[29] Abbot Martin of Pairis was given the same advice.[30] But was Capuano really reflecting Innocent's mind? As regards the maintenance of the crusade—unquestionably, yes. As regards the expedition to Zara (Capuano had not had occasion to discuss this with the pope), it is more than doubtful. It is quite certain that Innocent forbade the expedition to Zara under pain of excommunication and that the crusaders were aware of the prohibition before the siege began. Writing later to the French, Innocent reminded them that Capuano himself had notified some among them of his ban and later "our letters were publicly put before you."[31] Other sources give similar evidence.[32] Nevertheless Zara fell to the crusaders' arms on about 17 November,[33] and its walls were razed to the ground by the Venetians a little while before their departure for their next exploit towards the end of April.

Meanwhile Philip of Swabia had been active. He had been in communication with Boniface of Montferrat and the other leaders of the crusade, and also probably with the Venetians soon after his brother-in-law Prince Alexius had reached him. Certainly by the autumn of 1202, Emperor Alexius III in Constantinople had heard that an attack was being planned against him to restore ex-Emperor Isaac. He sent an embassy to seek the pope's protection. This, with other interesting information, is furnished by Innocent's answer, dated 17 November 1202, possibly the very day of the fall of Zara. Alexius III had denied any right on his nephew's part to the imperial throne since succession in Byzantium depended on election, not heredity. Also, the emperor had asked the pope not to favor the dangerous Philip for the German throne. By way of answer Innocent recounted his meeting with the young prince, asserted that Philip had immediately communicated with the leaders of the crusading army in Prince Alexius's favor, and that the leaders had sent Cardinal Peter, the legate, to him to know his will in the matter. According to Innocent, in spite of the opinion of some that he should "welcome their request since the Church of the Greeks shows little obedience and devotion to the Apostolic See," his decision would please the emperor: Philip was being held in check by Otto, a fact for which Alexius should be grateful since he little deserved it, for had Philip obtained the empire, Constantinople would have had much to endure. Furthermore, for a long time only words, not deeds, had emanated from Constantinople: "We ask Your Imperial Excellency, therefore, . . . to see that you reply to Us in deeds and not only in words, because We have in fact shown the love We bear you in deed and affection."[34] What Innocent wanted was practical help with the crusade and union of the churches, which was precisely what young Alexius was then promising to all and sundry in the most generous terms.

When Innocent dispatched this letter he cannot have known that despite his prohibition, Zara was as good as taken. After the capture the attackers found themselves excommunicated. In the course of the winter the French, but not the Venetians, sent to the pope for absolution.[35] Innocent replied with two letters, the one "To the Army of the Crusaders," the other "To the Counts, Barons, and other Crusaders," both without the customary benediction by way of salutation and both full of reproach for their crime of turning Christian arms against Christians. Nevertheless, provided they were penitent—which implied restoring to Hungary the spoils they had taken—he wrote he would empower his legate to absolve them. To the barons he repeated his prohibition under pain of excommunication against "the invasion or damage of the countries of Christians unless they should maliciously impede your passage or there should arise some other just, that is, necessary, reason for which after recourse to the counsel of the Holy See you may act otherwise."[36] If Gunther's account is trustworthy these letters left Rome only in the beginning of April.[37]

While the Bishop of Soissons in Rome was persuading the pope, though with difficulty,[38] to be understanding about the army's predicament in respect to Zara, the crusaders were involving themselves in another momentous question. On 1 January 1203 messengers from Philip of Swabia and Prince Alexius had presented themselves before the doge and the barons in Zara. A decision was finally taken to divert the crusade still again, this time to Constantinople, but it was very unpopular with the French. Villehardouin wrote: "I must tell you here that only twelve persons in all took the oath on behalf of the French; no more could be persuaded to come forward." And he described the discord in the army, the preaching against the proposal by some abbots and the preaching to keep the army together by others, desertions in various ways, the departure of a leading baron with all his contingent of knights and soldiers to join the king of Hungary, and leaves sought and given for other knights to go for a time direct to Outremer.[39]

The pope, of course, knew of the activity of Prince Alexius and Philip of Swabia, but he thought he had the situation well in hand because the barons in the autumn of 1202 had sent the apostolic legate, Capuano, to him in order (as he wrote to Emperor Alexius on 19 November 1202) "to learn our will, since in so difficult an undertaking they could not and should not act without our command and authority."[40] This, however, is precisely what they did when, in January 1203 without consulting the pope further, they made the solemn pact to help the prince.

Whether Innocent was officially informed of the decision is not certain. In a letter to Capuano of 21 April 1203 he is still referring to it as hearsay. Innocent responded to Capuano's request for directives on three matters: the Venetians' refusal to seek absolution from the censure; Capuano's status with the crusade; and what action to take "if, as you [Capuano] have been told for certain, they wish to go to Greece with the son of the exemperor of Constantinople, whom they mean to take with them." Innocent's answers are categorical—if the Venetians would not receive the absolution in the precise form laid down, promising at the same time not to take up arms against Christians, and would not agree to accept him as legate, he should abandon the army and make his way to Syria.[41] Capuano did abandon the army, which left Zara razed to the ground by the Venetians, towards the end of April 1203.

Before the last ship set sail, however, Prince Alexius arrived in Zara and was generously provided with transport by the doge. Meantime the French barons had received the pope's letters and answered them. They renewed their expression of penitence and, as had been stipulated by Innocent, bound themselves and their heirs by oath to the satisfaction imposed.[42] Montferrat, too, wrote with the same sentiments, but he had a further action to explain. He had withheld from the Venetians the papal letter promulgating their excommunication. The letter had been brought by the messenger of Capuano who had come with delegated power to absolve the penitent in the legate's name. He explained the reason for his action: "Expecting, nay! being quite certain that your letter at that time and place could not possibly have been disclosed without the immediate dissolution of the army and the dispersal of the fleet." The barons' letter, seeking to exculpate the marquis, gave the same explanation: "That very day the fleet would have been dispersed and the army dissolved." So, as Innocent himself had earlier counseled Montferrat to dissimulate where necessary if the Venetians should aim at breaking up the fleet, they asked for further instructions, at the same time declaring themselves ready to deliver the document if the pope insisted.[43]

The pope did insist, and on 20 June he wrote to tell them so. But he had also another purpose in writing, since he had meantime learned that they were on their way to Constantinople. In the beginning of May, the fleet in fact reached Corfu, where it stayed for three weeks. During this time there was a very serious movement of dissidents determined to go from there to Brindisi and thence to Syria. They were prevailed on to remain with the army only when the others had sworn to send them on their way whenever they requested.[44] From Corfu, on 24 May, the expedition went to Constantinople, arriving within sight of the city on 23 June.

There is no good reason for doubting the sincerity of the penitence of the French nobles for their action at Zara or the truth of their plea that they had no alternative. In honor they were bound to pay the Venetians 85,000 marks for the fleet built and equipped specially for them. They could not have left Venice for Apulia trusting only to luck to find transport for the East. They were in reality prisoners on the island of St. Nicolo.[45] The number of defections from the host and the deep dissatisfaction pervading it are proof enough of their real desire to fulfill their crusaders' vow of going to the Holy Land. The second diversion of the force to Constantinople does not disprove this. At least the French unhesitatingly believed that when the citizens of Constantinople saw their rightful prince they would open their gates and all would be peacefully settled, with aid for the crusade, wealth for themselves, and union of the churches, just as Alexius had promised. Innocent III may have been less sanguine. Gunther records his bitter opposition to the project, anticipating that it could be effected only at the cost of serious bloodshed.[46] By his letters of June, when he could no longer stop the pilgrims going to Constantinople, the pope tried to limit their involvement and to bring them back to their true objective, the succor of the Holy Land.

The letter to Montferrat and the barons began without salutation: "We were grieved and We are grieved." Innocent grieved for himself, for them, and for the people at the exultation of the Saracen and for their own disillusionment. The barons had repented of their previous fault—sincerely, he hoped. They should not, like dogs, return to their vomit. "Let no one deceive himself into thinking that he may possess himself of territory of the Greeks on the ground that it is little submissive to the Holy See and that the emperor of Constantinople usurped the imperial throne when he deposed, and indeed blinded, his brother." It was not theirs to judge and avenge that crime, but rather the crime against the Crucified to whom they had specially dedicated themselves. "They should make the passage to the aid of the Holy Land and avenge the injury done to the Cross, getting from the spoils of the enemy what perhaps, were they to linger on in Greek territory, they might have to extort from brethren." They must bear in mind the prohibition with its sanction against harming Christian territory and, lest the guilt of the Venetians recoil on them, they must deliver the document they had held back.[47]

The letter addressed "To the Crusaders" explains at length why, until they "disembark on land of the Saracens or in the Province of Jerusalem," they may hold necessary communication with the excommunicated Venetians, but why, once they had arrived, they should not fight alongside of them; rather, "as occasion offers, they should as far as is expedient suppress their malice." Strangely and out of context, there is a sentence of more practical import. "So that you may not lack for provisions, We shall write to our most dear son in Christ, the Emperor of Constantinople, so that in accordance with the promise he gave Us in writing he will have provisions ready for you." If he refuses, they could justly use a right like his of living off the land as far as might be necessary, harming no individual and being ready to make compensation.[48]

The Greeks did not open the gates of Constantinople to their prince, even when he was paraded around the walls to incite them to loyalty. Recourse had to be had to arms. The crusaders were outnumbered ten to one, were running short of food and were continually being harassed by the defenders. There was fighting, but, had Alexius III been a man of greater courage, he could hardly have lost. As it was, he fled. The blinded Isaac was brought from prison and put again on the throne in the palace of Blachernae, where on 17 July the crusaders found him with the empress, magnificently arrayed. Only when Isaac had ratified by oath the bargain his son had made did the barons let Prince Alexius out of their hands. He was crowned emperor on 1 August. Isaac and Alexius prevailed on the crusaders to remain for another full year to help them stabilize their reign. The hostile populace had been persuaded by the fugitive Alexius III that the whole purpose of the western expedition was to subjugate their empire to the Latins and their church to the pope. That is what Alexius IV and the crusaders told Innocent in letters dated 25 August 1203. Alexius IV also assured Innocent that he would show the same devotion to him and his successors as the emperors before him had shown to Innocent's predecessors and that, as occasion offered, he would earnestly try to induce the Oriental Church to do the same.[49] He hired the fleet for another year from the Venetians, "paying them enough to make it worth their while," and gave 100,000 marks to the host. Of this the Venetians took the half in virtue of the original pact, and also 36,000 of the rest to balance the deficit owed by the French for the fleet. These were left with only 20,000 marks to share among themselves.[50]

Innocent did not reply to Alexius and the crusaders until February 1204. The gist of his answer to the emperor can be seen in one sentence. Having repeated from Alexius's letter the imperial promises of acknowledgement of papal primacy he continued: "Indeed, if your deeds measure up to your words and you carry out in action what you promise in theory," you will have the support of God and the Holy See.[51] He was equally reserved in his letters to the crusaders. What they had written about Alexius's promise of submission was interpreted by many, he said, as a mere excuse for their own disobedience; their sincerity would appear if they produced results, that is, if the emperor sent his profession in writing and if he prevailed on the patriarch to recognize the Roman primacy, to promise obedience, and to request from the Holy See the "pallium taken from the body of St. Peter, without which the patriarchal office cannot rightly (*rite*) be exercised."[52] In this letter to the leaders, as in those to the bishops of Soissons and Troyes and to the crusaders, Innocent hesitatingly "fears that they are excommunicated once more" for turning their arms against Christians, and he bids the bishops have recourse again to the legate Capuano, who was empowered to absolve them. They could show their sincerity by their zeal that "the Greek Church should return to the Roman, and the member to the head, and the daughter come back to the mother, and that there should be one fold and one shepherd and no longer any distinction between Latins and Greeks, but that they should be united both in the Catholic faith and in ecclesiastical unity.[53] However, he ends his letter to Montferrat and the barons by urging them to fulfill their true purpose: great though his desire is for the union of the churches, greater still is his desire to help the Holy Land. Hence, he presses and commands all of them to receive forgiveness for their sins so as to pursue with purity of heart their primary aim: "Therefore strive with all your might for the recovery of the Holy Land since that will be for you what is most vital, before God most meritorious, and in the eyes of men most glorious."[54]

To judge from his letters and actions, Innocent III thoroughly disapproved of the attack on Zara both beforehand and afterwards. He disapproved also of the diversion of the pilgrims to Constantinople, doubtless for a variety of reasons—distrust of the glib promises of the young Alexius, disinclination to strengthen the hand and further the designs of Philip of Swabia, a faint hope of persuading Alexius III to join the crusade. But most of all Innocent vehemently desired to see the crusaders pursue their chief and only genuine purpose—to free the Holy Land. In his letter to Alexius

III, union was always mentioned in the second place, perhaps because he considered that it was less urgent or in the circumstances less practicable; or, it may be, because, convinced as he was of the supremacy of the Western Church, the pope thought that the return of "the daughter to the mother" was bound to come about sooner or later.

Innocent's belief in the oneness of the Church and his deep desire that all Christians should be members of the one Church were genuine. All Christians entertained them. He, of course, had no doubt that the Roman Church was that one Church of Christ; therefore, he followed up any overtures that promised a union of Christians with Rome. Of these there were not a few. The king of Serbia and his brother had asked for legates to help them: Innocent sent his secretary John and received the sincere thanks of the king for the good he had done.[55] A closer tie was formed with the czar of Bulgaria. Kalojan had continued the struggle begun by his brothers for Bulgaria's independence from Constantinople. He turned to Rome to procure a non-Byzantine sanction for both his crown and his church, asking "that we may be established within the Roman Church with, as it were, a sonship of a mother" and from that church receive "the crown and honor, as a beloved son, such as was had by our emperors of old.[56] Innocent replied graciously on 27 November 1202, but, reminding Kalojan of how the emperors of old had later abandoned Rome for Constantinople, he said he would not send a cardinal as legate, but rather John, his secretary, with powers to regulate for the church and authority to discuss with the king the question of the crown. Kalojan put his kingdom and the church within it in the hands of the pope by a solemn document which he entrusted to the returning legate John.[57] The pope thereupon on 25 February 1204 nominated Leo, Cardinal of St. Croce, his solemn delegate "to anoint by our authority and in our stead [Kalojan], to bestow the royal sceptre and impose the crown." He was empowered also to confirm Archbishop Basil as primate of all Bulgaria and Vlachia, "it being understood that with Us these two names, primate and patriarch, mean practically the same, since primate and patriarch have one formula, though the names are different,"[59] and he bestowed on him the right of crowning future Bulgarian monarchs. The pallium was given again to the new primate in a solemn rite and also to the other two archbishops constituted previously by the papal secretary. In future, after canonical election, they would seek it from Rome. Innocent had been surprised to learn that in the oriental rite of episcopal consecration, priestly ordination, and baptism there was no anointing. Since, however, "the Catholic Church maintains this [practice] not only by divine precept but also from the example of the Apostles," he directed that the primate of Bulgaria should receive the anointing omitted from his consecration from the apostolic legate; the primate should then anoint the metropolitans (and they their bishops), and that in future anointing should not be omitted.[60] Kalojan was crowned on 8 November 1204 and was solemnly presented by the cardinal with the papal banner displaying the Cross and the Petrine keys "that you may employ this same banner in humility of heart and be not unmindful of the Lord's Passion in the midst of war."[61]

Innocent's correspondence with Bulgaria is instructive because all his basic ideas about the church are here illustrated—the primacy of the Apostolic See, the pope as vicar of Christ possessed of the *plenitudo potestatis* over all churches whereas others had some *solicitudo* for a part, and the need for these to seek the pallium "from the body of St. Peter." The privileges of the archbishop of Trnovo as primate were such that he could confirm the canonical elections of metropolitans, who would make their oaths of obedience to the pope through him and would also make one to him; he could consecrate the sacred chrism; he could have the Cross carried before him in his own territory; and, as being of oriental rite, he could carry a staff.[62]

Kalojan's enthusiasm for the Latin Church was not unconnected with his political aspirations. The king of Armenia, Leo, had felt the need of a like support. When Barbarossa undertook his journey to the Holy Land, Leo hastened to put his kingdom under Barbarossa's protection and, on Barbarossa's death, under that of his son and successor, Henry VI. He also asked for coronation from the pope and on 6 January 1195 was crowned by Celestine's legate. On Innocent's accession to the papal throne Leo wrote professing his obedience and his determination to lead all Armenians everywhere to acknowledge the Holy See.[63] The catholicos, Gregory V,[64] wrote in a like sense. Innocent replied to them both, encouraging them to fidelity.[65] The situation soon became more complicated, for King Leo became involved in war with the prince of Tripoli, Bohemond, in defense of the rights to the throne of Antioch of the infant Rupinus. He appealed to Rome.[66] Innocent, unable to decide without knowing both sides of the question, promised to send legates and urged Leo meanwhile to war only against the Saracen, for which he sent him a papal banner.[67] The legates took a long time to arrive, and Leo wrote again complaining that Bohemond of Tripoli, on whom Innocent had equally imposed peace, far from obeying the papal mandate, was himself invading Armenian territory and also inciting the Saracen to do likewise. Leo asked for a speedy intervention and the favor that Armenia should be immune from any ecclesiastical censure save one emanating from the Apostolic See.[68] The pope replied on 1 June 1202 granting the favor requested; at the same time he informed Catholicos Gregory that his legates would bring for him the pallium and the miter he had asked for.[69] Both king and prelate should have courage and "await help, effective from heaven and speedy from earth," for "by God's grace the greater part of the crusaders' army has reached Venice, whence soon they will board ship to cross the seas and bring help to the Holy Land."[70]

Chapter III

The Capture of Constantinople

The hopes that King Leo and Catholicos Gregory set in Innocent's encouraging news of 1202 were doomed to disappointment. The crusaders did indeed board their ships and sail, but they sailed first to Christian Zara and then to Christian Constantinople. And from there they never sailed again to carry to Jerusalem the succor that was the whole aim and object of their pilgrim expedition. Neither did they achieve the other religious purpose—which, though outside their original plans, had it been gained might have compensated for their primary failure—the healing of the ecclesiastical schism. It was indeed one of Pope Innocent's principal goals, second only to the freeing of the Holy Land. Prince Alexius had promised it,[1] the crusaders were sincerely set on it,[2] and in the first flush of victory they thought they had achieved it.[3] But their reception at Constantinople ought to have warned both them and the pope of the futility of their hopes. Prince Alexius and the crusaders in their first letters from the captured capital gave as the reason for the hostility of the Greeks their belief that the western army "had come to deliver over to the Roman Pontiff their place and nation and to subject the Empire to the laws of the Latins."[4] Had the citizens opened the gates to Alexius and peacefully restored his father, their fears could have proved unfounded. By refusing him entry they started a chain of events that ended with their worst forebodings being completely justified.

The conditions that Prince Alexius had sworn to observe as the price for the crusaders' help were, as his father Isaac said, "very hard and I do not really see how we can put them into effect."[5] They were mainly concerned with the payment of money and the provisioning of the troops. The crusaders insisted that the conditions should be fulfilled. The emperors found their resources dwindling. In spite (according to Nicetas, though not, one suspects, without a deal of exaggeration) of their having had "not only the holy icons of Christ hacked down with axes and thrown on the ground and their ornamentation wrenched off without care or reverence and cast into the melting pots, but also even the venerated and holy vessels brazenly carried off from the churches and melted down and delivered over to the enemy forces just like common silver and gold,"[6] they could pay less and less until, yielding also to public opinion, they refused to pay any more. The pilgrims, who were encamped outside the city walls, delivered an ultimatum which was not met. A kind of guerilla warfare followed and on 1 January 1204 Alexius had sixteen fireships floated down onto the Venetian fleet in the hope of destroying it. Only superhuman efforts saved it and with it the crusaders who, already short of food,[7] without the fleet would have been at the mercy of their enemies. Within the city there was growing unrest that culminated in seizure of the throne by one of the palace officials, Alexius Murtzuphlus. Isaac died of fright. Alexius IV was strangled. The crusaders had little choice left but to take the city again by force, and the bishops with them justified their action.

Before launching their coordinated attack (they were rarely free from skirmishes), the Venetians and the barons made a solemn pact concerning the division of the spoils after the capture. All booty was to be collected together and shared. Six Venetians and six of the others would elect the new emperor, and the party that lost should have St. Sophia and the patriarchate. The emperor should have one-quarter of all territories acquired, the rest to be divided between the Venetians and the barons. The clergy of each party should administer the churches in the territories of their party and should be allowed property enough for their decent maintenance. The rest of the church property should be divided like any other.[8] One can hardly fail to see the hand of Dandolo in this businesslike contract which was signed and sealed before ever the goods were delivered. At about this time another momentous step was taken unwittingly. Kalojan, czar of the Bulgars and leader of the Vlachs and the Cumans, offered to help the crusaders if they would recognize him as king of the areas he held. They refused.[9]

On Friday, 9 April, the first combined assault on the city was made and failed. On the following Monday it was renewed and an entry forced. On Tuesday, 13 April, the Latins moved forward cautiously to stabilize their position only to find that Emperor Alexius V had fled and that the city was theirs. There followed three days of brutal sack and pillage, of which the Latin reports say hardly a word. But Nicetas Choniates has left a long and moving account. The conquering soldiers, he wrote, raged through the city looking for booty, which they piled on their horses. Nothing was spared, nothing was safe from their hands. They snatched everything of value that they could find, from private houses and from churches. There they tore the silver and gold from altars and icons, smashed it into bits and carried it off. To load up more easily they rode into the Church of St. Sophia, where the horses fouled the pavement and slipped on the marble floor. A harlot sat herself on the patriarchal throne, and danced to amuse the raiders. In the streets there was panic, men and women running here and there, seeking to escape the soldiers' hands, abused by them, fearing for their lives. He breaks into a lament: "O city, city! light of all cities, famed the wide-world over, a sight not of this earth, mother of Churches, leader of religion, guide on the way of right, darling of oratory, abode of all this is good. . ."—and that had been desolated by the barbarous Latins.[10]

Baldwin was elected and on 16 May 1204 was crowned emperor. He wrote, probably in late May, to announce to the West the victory and his accession. He narrates the events that culminated in the capture, attributes the victory to the providence of God and, elected emperor by the representatives of the pilgrims (who were all ecclesiastics) and of the Venetians, records his coronation, "the Greeks also in their own way approving to the honor of God and of the holy Roman Church and to the help of the Holy Land." What follows in the letter was an ill omen for future happy relations with the conquered Greeks. Constantinople, the letter continues, can now cooperate in devotion to the Holy Land; hitherto for so long it was its opponent and adversary, aiding its enemies, execrating the See of Rome and despising all Latins.[11] The pope is asked to encourage people of every condition and sex "to flock to Constantinople"[12] and in particular to send worthy preachers to instruct the Greeks. Praise and gratitude are owed to the clerics with the host for their labors and to all others, but especially to the doge, Dandolo.[13]

The crusaders proceeded quickly to carry out the rest of the pact they had made. They divided the empire between them, Baldwin getting five-eighths of Constantinople, with the territory all around it, and Asia Minor; the Venetians three-eighths of the capital, the west coast of the Greek mainland, the Morea, and various islands in the Aegean; Montferrat the kingdom of Thessalonica. But they soon had two major opponents: Theodore Lascaris who installed himself first at Brusa and then in Nicaea in Asia Minor, and Michael (Doucas Angelus) Comnenus, who established himself in Epirus on the western seaboard of Greece. Also they had still to make good their claims against the inhabitants elsewhere. While the forces thus engaged were dispersed over Asia Minor and Greece, Kalojan attacked. He defeated Baldwin near Adrianople, took him prisoner, and with him most of his knights who had not been slain in the battle (14 April 1205). The emperor was not heard of again. Dandolo died soon after (May 1205). Montferrat was killed in a skirmish in September 1207, and the formidable Kalojan followed him a month later.

These events, being in the future, were of course unknown to Innocent when he read Baldwin's letter. He did not know in any detail even what had happened in Greece in the immediate past, because the letter, his only source of information, was designed to solicit approval and not necessarily to give a full account. He wrote back to the emperor on 7 November with no excessive display of enthusiasm, but congratulating, promising to take the kingdom under his protection, ordering the army to remain in Constantinople to consolidate the victory, exhorting Baldwin to keep the Greek Church in obedience to the Holy See and reminding him to have ecclesiastical property preserved intact until the Curia should make its will known about it.[14]

A few days later he wrote a more exultant letter "To the Bishops, Abbots, and Other Clerics in Constantinople with the Crusaders' Army." The prophet Daniel's declaration that it is God who transfers kingdoms "with gladness We see fulfilled in the kingdom of Greece in our day . . . and the bringing back of the daughter to the mother." Confidently he wrote of expected union. Saints Peter and John both ran to the tomb at Our Lord's resurrection. Peter, typifying the New Testament and the Latin Church, arrived second but entered; John stayed outside, symbolizing the Old Testament and the Greek Church, which hence does not believe in the full doctrine of the Blessed Trinity. But the Greeks will learn and enter in. God predestined the Latin Christians of Constantinople to achieve this and to produce one fold with one shepherd.[15]

Nearly a month later, when he still knew nothing of the circumstances of the capture of the eastern capital, Innocent wrote again to the ecclesiastics telling them not to leave churches abandoned by the Greeks without religious services, but to organize them and to elect among themselves an overseer to coordinate their ministries.[16]

His solicitude was unnecessary, as he shortly learned. Baldwin and Dandolo sent him letters with a copy of the pact they had made before the assault on the city, which they had already implemented. In fact, a patriarch for Constantinople had been elected in the person of Thomas Morosini, a subdeacon and a Venetian then resident in Venice. The messengers who brought the letters doubtless gave an account of the general situation of the new empire: that there had very nearly been civil war between Baldwin and Montferrat over who should rule Thessalonica, that in October the final partition of lands had been made and within them fiefs distributed, and that the various lords had marched to establish themselves in their assigned territories, where they so far had met with success. In other words, the empire, still in the making, was in a situation when it could only with difficulty have survived a major divisive setback, such as a drastic ecclesiastical reaction against those articles of the pact that referred to the church.

On 21 January Innocent dispatched three letters to Constantinople, the longest of them to the clerics. Half of it (and it is very long) consists of an analogical exegesis of the incident when Christ preached from Simon's boat—the Latin Church. Innocent wrote that his predecessors had labored hard but had taken nearly nothing. "But when I let down the nets at the will of the Lord we enclosed, I and my brethren, a great shoal of fish, both in Livonia . . . and in Bulgaria and Vlachia . . . as well as in Armenia. . . ." Thereupon they beckoned to their partners in the other ship. "The other ship was the Church of the Greeks which made itself other when it rashly dared to separate itself from the unity of the universal Church." Innocent described how the Latins beckoned to them by letters and by envoys to return

> to take up again part of Our solicitude as helpers in the providential task allotted to Us. But by God's grace they came because after the Empire of Constantinople was in these days transferred to the Latins, the Church also of Constantinople came back to obedience to the Apostolic See like a daughter to a mother and a member to the head, so that for the future there might reign between us and them an undivided partnership. Truly We proclaim them brethren, partners, friends, because, though We have the office of government over them, it is a government that leads not to domination but to service. . . . In Constantinople the crusaders have elected a French Emperor and a Venetian, Thomas Morosini, as patriarch, and both the Emperor with his barons and the Doge have petitioned Us to confirm the patriarchal election as being necessary also for the maintenance of their political partnership which is essential for the continuance of the Latin Empire. We examined the election and, finding it uncanonical both because of lay interference and because the so-called canons of St. Sophia have not been instituted by the Holy See, We have had it declared null in open consistory. But in view of the petitions of the authorities of Constantinople and the circumstances in which they are placed, We Ourselves elected and confirmed the same Thomas Morosini as patriarch.[17]

Few of Innocent's letters give so clear an insight as does this one into his views about the Greek Church, views which governed all his action towards it. He had no doubt that on the eve of the Fourth Crusade the two churches were not united and that the division was the fault of the Greek Church, the daughter church, which had left the universal Church and its truth. Unity could be achieved only by the return of the daughter to the mother.[18] The emperor could bring that about if he wished.[19] The military conquest of Constantinople had indeed effected precisely that return. It was manifestly the action of God,[20] and the victory that made the Eastern Empire subject to Latin domination simultaneously made the Greek Church subject to the Latin Church.[21] Union of churches was synonymous with obedience to Rome,[22] and obedience was the prelude to unity of faith.[23] The patriarchate of Constantinople was of very great importance, second only to Rome,[24] and the union of empires and churches would lead to that most desirable of goals: the freeing of Jerusalem.[25] Such were the axioms that Innocent accepted without reserve and which directed his actions.

The establishment of the Latin Empire of Constantinople took Innocent by surprise, but the first news of it left him optimistic. However, the terms of the pact, which reached him towards the end of 1204 and which he was asked to ratify, made him pause. It clearly eliminated as far as it could all church influence in the empire, for, without reference to the Holy See, the contracting parties allotted territories, divided ecclesiastical jurisdictions, distributed benefices, appointed canons who elected the patriarch, and appropriated all church property, allowing at their discretion some to the ecclesiastics. Had anything like that been perpetrated in the West, Innocent would have reacted with drastic measures—warnings, excommunications, and finally interdict. In the Eastern Empire, after consultation with cardinals and very many archbishops and bishops,[26] he acted differently. The circumstances were different. Severe ecclesiastical penalties might have endangered the existence of the as yet unstable empire, which, however unfortunate its beginnings, was already a fact, and, as such, opened up very desirable prospects of unity of the churches and of enlarged aid to the Holy Land.

The situation in Greece was not a purely political issue. The conquering army and all its leaders were pilgrims under vow to go to the Holy Land. They obviously could not leave immediately after the capture, but Innocent intended that after a brief interval of stabilization they should go. On 29 January 1205 he refused to dispense the ancient doge from his crusader's vow, but shortly afterwards he acceded to a request from Baldwin to encourage laymen and clerics to go to build up the new empire, taking breviaries and missals so that "the Eastern Church might not sing out of harmony with the Western."[27] After the news of Baldwin's capture and the grave situation created by it, he proposed help to Constantinople as a way of working for the liberation of the Holy Land, and he enriched this with crusading indulgences.[28] He wrote also both to Kalojan and to Henry, Baldwin's brother and newly appointed regent, urging them to make peace, but the victorious Bulgar refused. The French knights suffered another serious defeat from his Cumans in early February 1206.[29]

Innocent's great concern for the empire did not outweigh his greater solicitude for the Holy Land. Writing to the doge on 5 August 1206, he blamed the Venetians for the diversion of the crusade to Constantinople and added: "Granted indeed that We were gratified by the return of Constantinople to the obedience of the holy Roman Church, We should have been far more gratified if Jerusalem had been brought back into the hands of Christian people."[30] Capuano, at the news of the capture of Constantinople (and perhaps summoned by Baldwin),[31] hastened from Syria to Greece with Soffredo, the other legate, and the bishop of Tyre. Hearing of this, Innocent sent him a reprimand but, since Capuano was in Constantinople, the pope appointed him temporary legate there.[32] Later, when he learned that the legate had released from their pilgrim's vow all those who helped in the defense of Constantinople for an additional year from March 1205, and when he also had been informed of details of the sack and pillage of the Byzantine capital on its capture, the pope wrote again. His letter reflects his deep disappointment and bitter wrath on both counts.

> Since We sent you not to amass worldly riches but to merit eternal ones, you should have attended to the business of your legation and have given all your thought to it, that We did not deem you empowered to capture the Empire of Constantinople but to defend what is left of the Holy Land and, if God grant it, to recover what has been lost. We cannot help but be incensed at your dispensing from the oath. . . . How will the Church of the Greeks return to the unity of the Church and devotion to the Apostolic See? . . . now rightly it abominates [the Latins] like dogs. We are sending the Cardinal of St. Susanna as legate. You We enjoin to return to the Holy Land forthwith.[33]

Sending Benedict, cardinal of St. Susanna, was a measure intended to moderate the unacceptable terms of the pact and to introduce order into the ecclesiastical situation. The doge, by the pact, had appointed canons of St. Sophia and through them a patriarch, all of them Venetians. In fact the canons had to swear to admit only Venetians to any church office; furthermore (as Innocent learned afterwards), the authorities in Venice had not let Morosini, the new patriarch, set sail for his see until he had taken an oath to the same effect and had even agreed to limit all archiepiscopal sees to Venetians. Susanna as legate was superior to the patriarch. Innocent bade him install non-Venetian canons if Morosini would not,[34] and time and again the pope pressed the patriarch to accept individuals proposed by the emperor or by the legate.[35] Aware at last of Morosini's oath in Venice, he first condemned it and later insisted that the patriarch repudiate it as illicit and null publicly from the pulpit of St. Sophia, which was done on 14 December 1209.[36]

Another frequent cause of friction was the question of the church property that the leaders of the army had appropriated. Innocent naturally refused to acquiesce, and protested both to the Venetians and to the French. A settlement was made with the emperor Henry for his territories in 1206, giving the church one-fifteenth of all property outside Constantinople, besides all monasteries and monastic properties, which were to remain in the possession of the church.[37] This, however, proved ineffective, because

Morosini was not content with the one-quarter of the proceeds apportioned to him by the cardinal legate: he claimed one-half.[38] In the kingdom of Thessalonica, Montferrat did not seize church property, but after his death the Lombard barons did, and it was not until the parlement held at Ravennica in 1210 that an agreement covering the empire, Thessalonica, and the Venetian areas (but not the Morea) gave the church one-twelfth of all properties.[39] But local magnates often refused to implement it, and only after Innocent's death was a stable solution reached, confirmed by the emperor Robert in 1222 and by the Venetians in 1223, giving the church one-eleventh.

Those local magnates, from Emperor Henry downwards, were often in conflict with the church because of their violent seizure of church lands. The *Regesta Innocentii* contain letter after letter of advice to complaining bishops or of remonstrance to offending barons. The pope warned the emperor Henry that he was reducing the Church of St. Anastasis to destitution by refusing to relinquish the farms that belonged to it.[40] A few months later he had to bid the chamberlain of Thessalonica to restore church property and not to extort illicit taxes.[41] The prince of Athens, Othon de la Roche, who had been given the fief by the Venetians, was guilty of so many attacks on the church that the archbishop of Athens, with two other bishops, went in person to Rome to seek redress.[42] The Morea had been occupied by a nephew of the chronicler Villehardouin, who was also called Villehardouin. He and his barons were the object of various censures including interdict for taking property by violence, for haling ecclesiastics before secular courts, and for disposing of benefices and abbeys to laymen or ecclesiastics at their whim.[43] There was constant friction between secular and ecclesiastical authorities over legacies which the former forbade being made for pious purposes;[44] over the tenths payable to the church which they would not themselves pay or let their subjects pay;[45] as to whether Latins were liable to the traditional Greek tax due from the church to the lay lords;[46] and whether the sons of Greek priests were bound to military service. At the Parlement of Ravennica (1210) these last two questions were decided in favor of the barons.[47]

Such frequent frictions between the lay and the ecclesiastical authorities in the Latin Empire could not have helped promote peaceful relations or union between the Latin and the Greek churches. Pope Innocent's attitude towards the Greek Church was quite clear. Its bishops were to take an oath of obedience to him and—after the election of a Latin patriarch—also to the Latin patriarch of Constantinople. If they did that, they were to be left in peace and to enjoy parity of right and privilege with Latin bishops. Innocent had indicated this principle in his earliest letters to Constantinople when he informed Patriarch John Camaterus that, if he was to take part in a projected general council, he would have to show due obedience to the Church of Rome.[48] Likewise the pope had proposed a solemn act of obedience from the patriarch as the proof of the sincerity of Prince Alexius and the crusaders after their first capture of Constantinople.[49] There is no document extant where Pope Innocent dictates such obedience from the Greek prelates after the second conquest of Constantinople, but it is perceptible as the background of all the Greco-Latin ecclesiastical relations of the time. It was on the question of submission to the See of Rome that the meeting in December 1204 between the legate Peter Capuano and the Greek ecclesiastics turned. The discussion did not last long, for the Greeks, incensed by the brusqueness of the interpreter, brought it to a speedy end by leaving the hall, though not before their spokesman, John Mesarites, had stated their position: "We are under the rule of the Emperor as regards the outer man, but in respect of the inner and hidden man we are subject to our Patriarch, John."[50]

Benedict, Cardinal of St. Susanna, who replaced Capuano as legate, was commissioned by the pope "to form the Greek Church more completely in devotion and purity of faith according to the institutions of the most holy Roman Church, which the Lord appointed to be the mother and mistress of all Churches."[51] Benedict was a man of gentle character who tried to fulfill his mission by persuasion. He held several meetings with the Greeks. The archbishop of Athens, Michael Choniates, went to talk with him in Thessalonica in late summer 1205 when he first arrived.[52] Benedict also had conversations to promote unity elsewhere as he moved about on his legatine business. He was again in Thessalonica in late 1206:[53] he received the act of obedience to the pope of Theodore, Bishop of Negroponte, probably on the island of Euboea itself,[54] and a year later Benedict probably visited Achaia.[55] His interpreter, Nicholas of Otranto, speaks of him as having held theological disputations with learned Greeks in Thessalonica and Athens, as well as in Constantinople.[56]

It is only of these last meetings that there is any detailed record and even that is not very satisfactory. Some years after Innocent's death, the interpreter for the Latins, Nicholas of Otranto, who was Greek in faith although he acknowledged the pope, wrote three tractates based on the discussions at which he had assisted in Greece, turning into theological instruction what had been a debate.[57] More contemporary is the account written by Nicholas Mesarites, at that time a deacon of Constantinople, later metropolitan of Ephesus. He and his brother John were spokesmen for the Greeks in the discussions held on 30 August, 29 September, and 2 October 1206, Nicholas in that of August and John in the other two. John died on 5 October 1207, and his brief report on the two discussions he directed are reproduced in the panegyric his brother Nicholas wrote for his funeral.

However, before the arrival of Cardinal Benedict in Constantinople, Latin Patriarch Morosini held a meeting with the Greeks. The occasion was his refusal to allow them to celebrate their usual weekly service in veneration of the icon of Our Lady Hodegetria, which he had placed in his cathedral, the Church of St. Sophia, unless they prayed also for him. They refused, not being willing to give that degree of recognition to his claims. Nicholas and John Kontotheodorou, who were both deacons, headed the Greeks in the discussion, if, indeed, the occasion can rightly be called a discussion. According to the report Mesarites later wrote, Morosini and the Latins said no more than forty-one lines in short questions to prompt the Greek to expound his answers over some 278 lines. But, although the account is clearly unbalanced, it indicates the topics that were raised.

Morosini opened the debate by asking, "Do you agree to accept me as Patriarch?" Mesarites replied, insisting that the ministers, and especially the chief minister, who dispense the sacraments to the Greeks should be Greek. The functions of an archbishop were to teach, to ordain, and to bind and loose. That could not be done through an interpreter as the patriarch suggested. Would Greeks have to confess their sins, and to participate in the Liturgy, through an interpreter? Latin ordinations were to a dead sacrifice in unleavened bread. St. Peter was but one among the Apostles, the Apostle to the Jews, while to St. Paul was entrusted the apostolate of the gentiles. St. Peter, therefore, was never bishop of Rome: if he was a bishop anywhere, he was bishop of Antioch. In any case, Jerusalem was the first see, and Andrew taught in Constantinople years before Peter reached Rome. The See of Rome acquired preeminence only from its being the capital city of the empire and the abode of the senate. The promise to St. Peter, "On this rock, etc.," was not to him personally but a response to the faith he expressed, and neither Rome, nor Constantinople, nor Jerusalem, nor any other individual see, but the whole wide world, was the seat of the promise, the foundation.[58]

The papal legate, Cardinal Benedict, was the instigator of the meetings of 29 September and 2 October. He was assisted by Patriarch Morosini. The Greeks in the debate were monks of Propontis and Mt. Auxentius for whom John Mesarites was the spokesman. The cardinal opened the proceedings by asking why they would not acknowledge the patriarch sent by the pope and commemorate him in the Liturgy. They replied that they had commemorated John Camaterus until he died and, after that, being without a patriarch, they had commemorated no one. When the legate insisted that the patriarch appointed by Rome was a legitimate one, the discussion turned to the question of St. Peter and the See of Rome, and ranged over the same ground as that traversed in the August meeting with Morosini. Further, although it was true that a patriarch unjustly condemned could appeal to Rome as Athanasius did, that did not mean that the bishop of

Rome was judge of the world or could interfere outside his own province. The thirty-fourth canon of the Apostles and canons of the first and later councils limited the powers of bishops outside their own areas. So the pope could not canonically consecrate a bishop for Constantinople. Thereupon Benedict is said to have inveighed against the Greek condemnation of Rome and to have given them two days to withdraw their refusal to commemorate the Latin patriarch.

On the following Monday they met again and, to the demand that they recognize Morosini they replied, "Yes, if he was consecrated canonically," implying that he had not been so consecrated. The discussion returned to the canons they had quoted in the previous meeting. When they asked, "What can we do if you do not observe the canons?" Benedict replied, "Rome never errs. All heresies have originated in Constantinople," instancing Nestorius and others, to whom the Greeks wryly added the name of Honorius. As they still loudly refused to accept Morosini, Benedict exclaimed, "All of you, I see, are disobedient, stiff-necked, impudent, and not yet humbled to realize what is to your profit." The Greeks replied, "Not so. We, like so many, could have fled to Nicaea, to Trebizond, to barbarian lands or even to the Turk, to escape from our daily miseries. Instead we have stayed to endure what the Lord sent us. Our only treasure is our holy orthodox faith, which you will never be able to take away from us, even if you devise against us afflictions by the thousand, for we shall never be found traitors to the holy faith as long as there is breath in us." The cardinal and patriarch retired from the hall for a time, and on their return Morosini exclaimed, "You should accept me. You are disobedient and we shall treat you for what you are."[59]

Such were the discussions as described by John Mesarites. When they had ended with satisfaction for neither side, the Greeks petitioned the emperor to allow them to elect a patriarch for themselves, since John Camaterus had died at Didymotichus in Thrace on 20 June 1206. Henry reminded them of the ancient custom of commemorating the pope in the Liturgy, and would permit the election they asked for only if the pope agreed. So the Greeks composed a letter to Innocent requesting his permission and at the same time suggesting that he send representatives to Constantinople to discuss with them the differences between the churches, with a view to union. Quoting the thirty-fourth of the Apostolic Canons, they pleaded that, as long as their church had no patriarch, they could not effect anything; that they were like the Alexandrians after the deposition of Dioscorus. Then they suggested that the pope summon a council, since the differences between the churches sprang from ignorance, which he would readily forgive in the spirit of the Gospel. Whether this letter ever reached Innocent cannot be said; no answer is recorded.[60]

The letter to the pope was probably written towards the end of 1206. About a year later—perhaps after waiting for an answer that never came and being still without an acceptable successor to John Camaterus—the Greeks of Constantinople took other steps. Nicholas Mesarites went to Nicaea to ask Theodore Lascaris to arrange for the election of a Greek patriarch. He was the bearer of three letters, one to Theodore himself, one to his queen, Anna, and the third to their son, Nicholas. The letter to Lascaris was from "The People of Constantinople"; but it was written by Mesarites. After a long encomium on the person of Theodore, the letter asked him to come to their aid, bereft as they were of a religious head, and to have a patriarch elected according to the canons and local custom. For their part they would recognize him as the glorious king (Basileus) of the whole world, and they prayed "that the Lord may fulfill all your desires and protect you, the *Pantocrator* protecting the *autocrator.*"

There was, probably, nothing that Theodore desired more than to be *autocrator.* John Camaterus had never left Thrace for Nicaea to give him that patriarchal crowning that would have completed his official accession to the imperial throne and enormously increased his claims to the loyalties of the Greeks. He lost no time in complying with Mesarites' request for the patriarchal election. Mesarites' letter (Lascaris wrote in the official convocation of the synod) had moved him to put into effect a purpose of his own, of filling the vacancy caused by the late patriarch's death. He, therefore, summoned all bishops with their synods to meet in Nicaea in the third week of Lent so as to elect a patriarch in time to bless the Holy Chrism at the accustomed ceremonies of Holy Week. "Let all come who can and let others be present by their written votes."[61] Mesarites took the royal answer to Constantinople and then returned to Nicaea for the synod. There Michael Autorianus was enthroned as patriarch on 20 March 1208. In the beginning of April he crowned Theodore emperor. Thereafter Nicaea possessed an emperor approved by both state and church, and a Greek patriarch elected "according to the canons and to local custom." Nicaea had become a more serious rival than ever to Latin-held Constantinople.

Some months before his coronation, Theodore wrote to Pope Innocent. His letter is not preserved but its content is known because the papal reply dated 16 March 1208 begins with a précis of it. At great length he had accused the crusaders of apostasy for turning Christian arms against Christians, of sacrilege during the sack of Constantinople, and of perjury for breaking various truces. The charges were a prelude to a request for papal intervention to effect a permanent peace, establishing the sea as the boundary between the Latin Empire and the kingdom of Nicaea. In his reply Innocent did not excuse the Latins, "whom We have often reproved for their excesses," but repeated verbatim to Lascaris the excuses that

Montferrat had sent to Rome some time before.[62] However that may be, Innocent continued, the fall of Constantinople was a judgment of God on the Greeks for rending the seamless garment of Christ by schism, and for never, though rich and near the Holy Land, helping to liberate it. Lascaris should acknowledge Emperor Henry and show due reverence to the See of Rome. A legate would shortly be sent to the East to mediate in charity.[63]

The number of Greek bishops who met in Nicaea to elect the new patriarch is not known. How many remained in the territories conquered by the Latins cannot be determined, but they must have been few. No incumbent of the more important sees stayed,[64] but incidental references indicate the presence of some suffragans. A papal letter to Morosini speaks of "certain Greek bishops returning to your obedience."[65] Four years later Innocent assured the bishop of Rhodesto, who had lately made his submission, that he would "enjoy a liberty equal to that of the Latin bishops" and suggested that he "encourage other bishops, monks, and clergy" to emulate his example.[66] Queen Margaret, regent of the kingdom of Thessalonica, baptized in the Latin rite and converted to the Greek rite on her marriage to Emperor Isaac, had reverted to the Latin rite when she married Boniface of Montferrat. She was accused (and more than once) not only of "detaining abbots, abbeys, and priests from the Latin bishops," but also of encouraging Greek bishops not to obey the pope.[67] Margaret did not amend. Two years later Innocent appointed three bishops who were to use if necessary ecclesiastical censures against her for still retaining Church property and still encouraging Greek suffragan bishops to refuse due obedience to their metropolitan, the Latin archbishop of Larissa. "Already," he wrote, "once, twice, and three times have We directed missives" to the Queen.[68]

In 1213 the province of Thessalonica had a Latin archbishop and at least five Greek suffragans; the latter sat with Duke George Frangopoulus, a Greek, as judges in ecclesiastical cases. Their decisions were not questioned even after the province's return into Greek hands.[69] Corinth retained a Greek prelate until the city fell into Latin hands when, because he would not take the oath, he was replaced by Innocent's nominee. The Greek bishop of Zante was to be admonished for disobedience and unbecoming conduct.[70] Theodore, bishop of Negroponte, was a Greek. The Latin archbishop of Patras sought advice from the pope on how to act, since at the conquest of Achaia, "certain Greek suffragan bishops fled from their dioceses, of whom some took no notice of canonical injunctions to return, [and] others could no longer be found."[71] Several years later Innocent's successor Honorius complained that Greek bishops in Achaia were indiscriminately ordaining priests for money.[72]

Not all the sees vacated by the Greeks were filled by Latins. Some were left vacant and others were combined under one bishop; but the latter were not suppressed "so that if need be in the future a change back may be easy."[73] Suffragan sees were taken from one metropolitan see and given to another. Some metropolitan sees lost their high rank; other sees were raised to be metropolitan. The reason given for many of these alterations in the diocesan structure was that dioceses were numerous, small, and very poor,[74] their poverty on occasion increased by the rapacity of a Latin incumbent.[75]

Towards the middle of 1206 Morosini addressed a number of queries to the pope. Innocent's answer of 2 August 1206 was designed (as he wrote) to ease for the Greeks as much as he could the difficulties inevitably accompanying a period of transition. In dioceses of mixed Latin and Greek population, the pope directed that Morosini should appoint Latin prelates; for those that were purely Greek, Greeks if he could find suitable candidates "who are devoted and faithful to Us and to you and willing humbly and devoutly to accept consecration from you." There were absent Greek bishops still taking revenues from their dioceses and others who had abandoned their sees for more than six months. In respect of such the pope warned Patriarch Thomas "in view of the changed state of things and the upheaval of the Empire you must proceed with the greatest deliberation. You must have them cited not once only, but often, that is, once, twice and thrice, and, if they then will not present themselves but persist in their contumacy" Thomas should bring pressure to bear by suspension and excommunication. If that is ineffective, Innocent wrote that the cardinal legate would remove them from office, but, to provide for the possibility of mercy in the future, he should not promulgate a sentence of degradation. With regard to rite, the Greeks are not to be forced to change; they should be allowed to retain their rite "if they cannot be dissuaded, until such time as the Apostolic See after more mature consideration may think fit to decide otherwise."[76] On the question of the use of chrism in the consecration of bishops, Innocent's ruling was milder for Greece than for Bulgaria. In Greece anointing was not to be insisted upon in the case of existing bishops and abbots prepared to accept pope and patriarch but unwilling to be anointed, though the Latin rite was to be used for those being newly consecrated.[77] When the Latin archbishop of Athens deposed the Greek bishop of Negroponte for refusing to accept supplementary unctions, Innocent appointed a commission of two bishops and one abbot to restore him to his see.[78]

Monasteries were not to be converted into secular canonries as long as regulars, whether Greek or Latin, could be found for them.[79] Monks and nuns were to be exhorted to live faithfully according to their rule.[80] Monasteries that before the conquest had been exempt from the local bishop were to remain so afterwards, whether they were "imperial" or patriarchal. Innocent took monks under his own protection[81] and had a particular regard for the monastic communities of Mount Athos. The legate Benedict had with papal sanction appointed the bishop of Sebaste custodian "of the monasteries of the Holy Mountain which are said to belong directly to the Apostolic See." Sebaste committed "enormities" and Innocent had him removed.[82] A few years later the monasteries were despoiled by some bandit "with the aid of the secular arm," and the monks appealed to Innocent to take them under his protection. To this request from that "house of God and gate of heaven" he willingly acceded and confirmed their privileges.[83]

A large proportion of the monks stayed in their monasteries and did not leave the new empire. The archbishop of Athens, Michael Choniates, who had taken refuge in Ceos, through correspondence remained involved in the affairs of his old diocese. He encouraged the monks not to abandon their monasteries, and on occasion confirmed the election of a new abbot.[84] In 1206 monks of Propontis and Mount Auxentius held discussions with the legate in Constantinople, and references to monasteries suffering depredation occur in most of the complaints made against voracious landowners. On the other hand, the curial clergy of dioceses occupied by Latin incumbents were apparently replaced by Latin canons that were often few in number because of small diocesan revenues and not always well disciplined.[85] The lower clergy with their families for the most part remained in their parishes, paying as before the "crustica" tax to the secular authorities; but their sons, as long as they had not been ordained, were now liable to the various obligatory services. Once ordained, "they enjoy the same privileges as clergy who are under the obedience of the Roman Church."

The village clergy were nearly all Greeks. The request by the lord of Athens for a Latin priest (in addition to the Greek priests) in any of his villages with more than twelve well-to-do Latin inhabitants was exceptional.[86] The proportions of Greek priests over the empire in general can be gathered from the preamble of a letter of Pope Honorius III, dated 4 September 1223, introducing the text of the convention arrived at in the Parlement of Ravennica of 1210 about church property and taxation of the clergy. "In a village of between twenty-five and seventy households there should be two priests with their wives, children and household" free from lay jurisdiction, and each priest may have one servant also free. A village with more than seventy households should have four priests with similar privileges; with more than 125 households, six priests. A hamlet of less than twenty-five households should be joined with other similar ones until it is big enough to have its two priests. Other rural priests shall be liable to all services to the landlords to which layfolk are liable, except that temporal lords shall not dare to lay hands on them or allow them to celebrate against the will of Latin clerics. Priests of the cathedrals and cities shall have like privileges. Bishops should not ordain priests in excess of the numbers indicated.[87]

The country clergy were often the victims of lay rapacity. The clergy of Thessalonica appealed to the pope for protection. Innocent commissioned two bishops to use ecclesiastical censures if necessary to preserve for "the clergy of the Greeks of the diocese of Thessalonica who have returned to the obedience of the holy Roman Church that liberty which they enjoyed in the time of the Greeks and which the legate Benedict accorded them, together with suitable maintenance from the churches."[88] On the other hand, they were sometimes rebellious and upheld in their opposition by the lay power, especially by Queen Margaret of Thessalonica and the lay lords of Achaia. With the advent of the Latin Church the Greeks also had to pay tenths to the church (later reduced to one-thirtieth), but the large number of papal letters answering complaints from bishops—either that they did not pay or that the lords of the land retained the tenths for themselves—testifies to continuing friction in spite of the agreement of Ravennica of 1210.

Patriarch Thomas Morosini died in 1211. Rival parties elected two successors. Appeals went to Rome. Innocent appointed a judge to decide, but he was detained in Venice and prevented from sailing to Constantinople. So in 1213 the pope sent as his legate Cardinal Pelagius, bishop of Albano. Pelagius was less mild and accommodating than his predecessor, Cardinal Benedict. George Acropolites, the Greek chronicler, in fact, asserts that he threw monks into prison, priests into chains, that he shut all Greek churches and even threatened death (a manifest exaggeration) for those who would not accept papal supremacy and commemorate the pope in the Liturgy. The Greeks appealed to Emperor Henry who, despite the legate, freed the prisoners and opened the churches. But, before the Latin emperor had restrained the legate's tempestuous zeal, many clerics had abandoned Constantinople for Nicaea. Acropolites continues: "Many of the monks left Constantinople and went to Emperor Theodore. On his orders monasteries were assigned to them for their habitation. Priests too went to Nicaea, some of whom were enrolled among the patriarchal clergy, others finding attractive sanctuaries lived there in peace."[89]

That pressure was brought to bear on the Greeks and that Henry found a compromise to solve at least a part of the difficulty appear in a letter from the leading Greek ecclesiastics of Constantinople addressed to the pope. There it is recorded that for the commemoration of the pope normally made during the Liturgy there was substituted an acclamation after the Liturgy: "Long live Lord Innocent, Pope of ancient Rome."[90] Pelagius also evicted as rebels the monks from the ancient monastery of Ruffiano, but in this he was upheld by later legates and Pope Honorius.[91]

Meanwhile in Nicaea Patriarch Michael Autorianus had died on 26 August 1214 and on 28 September Theodore Irenicus was enthroned in his place. Letters from Constantinople informed him of the pressure the legate was exercising to exact obedience to the pope and commemoration of him in the Greek Liturgy. Thereupon the new patriarch wrote a letter to the Greeks of Constantinople and elsewhere exhorting them to remain true to their traditional faith. The word *faith,* he warned, can have two meanings. "You may believe as absolutely true that the cardinal is representative of the Pope, that the Pope holds the first See and that he is the bishop of Rome, but to have faith in his teaching, a teaching that alienates you from the truth, that casts you into the pit and to spiritual death—that is better said to be the opposite of faith. Therefore, drive far from you anyone who slyly proposes this to you and asks your acceptance." If they were untrue to their faith, no matter what their rank or dignity, they were expelled from the church and excommunicated. They were not to take the oath of obedience, "for how would your orthodox faith be preserved and safeguarded, if you should agree to be one of the Pope's faithful?" Such people would be "pistoápistoi." They could, therefore, submit to the Latins in things temporal, but not in things divine.[92]

The bishop of Albano, however, was capable also of milder counsels. As part of his mission he entered into negotiations with Theodore Lascaris. Soon after the election of Patriarch Theodore in Nicaea, two of the legate's messengers arrived at the court of the emperor to treat of both political and religious peace. Lascaris, after two days of conversations, sent them back with an embassy of his own to meet Cardinal Pelagius. Nicholas Mesarites, now metropolitan of Ephesus and exarch of all Asia, led the Greek mission. In Constantinople he was well housed and fed and was treated in a princely manner, but at the first meeting Pelagius saluted him only by stretching out his arms to him, kissing him and putting him on a throne like his own. The bishop of the minor see of Albano and cardinal legate of the pope did not go to meet the exarch of all Asia and envoy of the emperor as he entered, and so Mesarites considered himself slighted.

The Greek opened the discussion by demanding why the Latins persecuted Greeks for not taking the oath when they allowed toleration to Jews and other kinds of heretics. What benefit was it to them, Mesarites asked, to force into conformity pious and unlettered monks? Such action only strengthened the position of Lascaris. Why were Latin clerics so richly dressed? They should look to the monks, withdrawn from the world, poor, laborers. Sumptuous attire did no honor to the pope. If there was question of honor, their emperor Theodore deserved it for his prowess in arms. To this diatribe Pelagius replied mildly that all he desired was unity, and that if the Greek emperor would become a true son of the church his subjects could remain forever undisturbed and his clergy tranquil in their churches.

A second meeting was held on the feast of St. Cecilia, 22 November, when at the cardinal's request the subject discussed was the Eucharist in leavened or unleavened bread. According to the account written later by Mesarites (the only account that exists of all these discussions), after the opening question put to him by the legate, he spoke for the rest of the session, expounding an interminable exegesis on the meaning of the Pasch in the Old Testament with every detail of the story of the Exodus explained with analogical applications, all of it except for the beginning and the end taken verbatim from St. Gregory (*MPG* 36 640C–648C). When finally Mesarites said, "That the abundance of my discourse may not tire your ears, I will lay down my pen," Pelagius ended the session, saying, "It is time for dinner."[93]

Three days later Mesarites bade farewell and, accompanied by a Spanish jurist as envoy of the cardinal and the interpreter, Nicholas of Otranto, he sought the Greek emperor first in Nicaea and then in Paphlagonia. The jurist treated in private with Lascaris on political questions—probably peace with the Latin Empire—but there is no record of what passed between them. The emperor also favored ecclesiastical peace, so at his suggestion Mesarites engaged the Latin envoy in theological discussions. The Latin put forward the Roman claim to primacy and Mesarites propounded again his views on Rome, Antioch, and Jerusalem in respect of St. Peter and their dignity as sees. Asked then why the Greek Church was separated from the Latin, he replied that Rome had sown darnel among the wheat—the *Filioque* that had infiltrated a duality into the oneness of God. So the doctrine of the *Filioque* was introduced and the rest of this long debate consisted of short reasons put forward by the Latin to prove its orthodoxy and long answers from the Greek to demonstrate the inadequacy of his arguments.

The Latin quoted John 16:15, "Whatever the Father has is mine." The Greek denied that production of the Holy Spirit, which, he claimed, is a property of only the Father, was included in that. In John 16:14, the Spirit "shall receive of mine" is not, he said, the same as "of me"—the former refers to the Father, the latter would refer to the Son if the text said it but it does not say it. This explanation is not challenged, he considered, by St. Paul's "God has sent the spirit of his Son into our hearts" (Gal. 4:6), because this phrase declares his nature without reference to the mode of his Procession. Mesarites conceded to the Latin that the Third Person is certainly called the Spirit of Truth, and that the Son is Truth, but denied that this necessarily implied origin. When the Latin said that the Greeks had changed the Creed by inserting into it the word "only" ("from the Father only''), the Greek denied the change flatly but accused him (more justly) of adding the *Filioque* clause. After these thrusts and parries, the Latin explained more at length that his doctrine did not make the Spirit the fruit of generation but of Procession. Mesarites would not hear of it, for he declared that the western doctrine would bring inequality into the Blessed Trinity. So the discussion returned to individual arguments, the Greek rebutting the Latin's suggestions that ''being sent by the Father'' and ''being sent by the Son'' meant origin for Son and Spirit respectively, and that the Father's double relationship to the other Persons was paralleled by two relationships for the Son. He rejected, also, analogies like the sun with rays emitting light; substance with power leading to action; the point, the line, and the surface; the finger of the hand of the Father. Time put an end to the discussion and, the Emperor unable to judge who was the winner, left the decision to the audience. They gave the result as a draw.

The debate over, the Latin mission returned to Constantinople with imperial gifts, and Mesarites went to Nicaea, where he met with a cool reception from the new patriarch, because Pelagius, in spite of Mesarites' insistence, had addressed him in a letter only as ''Archbishop of the Greeks.''[94]

So another theological debate had taken place without result. Indeed, at that time it was most unlikely that any debate of the sort would have produced agreement. The arguments put forward on both sides were not new. Both Latins and Greeks were firmly entrenched in their own positions and, after the treatment that they had received from the crusaders and the crusaders' church, the Greeks were less inclined than ever to give ground. More or less contemporaneously, perhaps, with the conversations in Paphlagonia there was circulated ''The Latin Atrocities in Constantinople after the Capture,'' under twenty-four heads—desecration of churches and icons, rape, thefts, etc.—most of them true.[95]

On the Latin side the pope insisted on obedience not only to himself but also to the Latin patriarch of Constantinople, which meant in effect an acceptance of both the ecclesiastical and the political status quo, and a rejection of the national aspirations centered on Theodore Lascaris and the patriarch in Nicaea. Most prelates and many monks preferred to take refuge in Nicaea or Epirus rather than to submit. For those who remained, the Latin lay lords were harsh masters, especially in the early years of the Latin Empire. Their aim was their own enrichment, and church property, both Greek and Latin, was easy booty.

While Pelagius and Mesarites were discussing the theology of union, the pope was engaged in preparing for a council. Its purpose was to strive ''for the recovery of the Holy Land and for the reform of the universal Church.'' There was no mention of union with the Greeks in the bull of convocation, though copies of it were dispatched also to the East "to the patriarch, archbishops, bishops, abbots, both Latin and Greek of the Province of Constantinople" and elsewhere.[96]

The pope had long realized that the Latin Empire of Constantinople needed all its energies for self-preservation and that he could expect little help from it for his consuming desire to free the Holy Land.[97] He, therefore, determined to launch a new crusade, this time to be kept out of lay control and so out of danger of diversion. The council convoked to meet on 1 November 1215 in the Lateran Palace of Rome was the beginning of his new project. To this council, with its aims limited to zeal for the Holy Land and internal church reform, only those were summoned who in Innocent's view were members of the church. In respect of the East it meant the Latin prelates and those Greek bishops who had made their profession of obedience to pope and Latin patriarch. Only one Greek bishop, Theodore of Negroponte, accompanied Gervasius of Constantinople with eight Latin archbishops and seven bishops to the Lateran. The patriarch of Jerusalem and three prelates of the province of Tyre, a delegate of the ailing patriarch of Antioch, all Latins, were present, as well as the patriarch of the Maronites lately reconciled with Rome, and probably the Jacobite patriarch John XIV and a delegate of the Melchite patriarch of Alexandria. Cyprus sent two Latin prelates.

In many debates and three sessions the council treated of western affairs. In the last session on 30 November 1215, seventy-one *constitutiones* or *capitula* were solemnly promulgated. The first was a statement of faith repeating the substance of the Nicene Creed but augmented and adapted to meet the heresies that had been discussed in the sessions, one of which, that of Joachim of Flora, was concerned with the Blessed Trinity. The council's affirmation of trinitarian doctrine was directed solely at him, but inevitably it reflected on relations with the Greeks, as it formed another step in the formulation of the official teaching of the Latin Church on the *Filioque*. It declared: "There is one only and true God, Father, Son, and Holy Spirit, three Persons indeed, but one essence, substance, or nature altogether simple . . . the Father from no one, the Son from the Father, the Holy Spirit from the one and the other." The second *capitulum,* treating specifically with Joachim's error, asserted among other things: "There is one supreme *res,* which is truly Father, Son, and Holy Spirit, being at one and the same time three Persons and each one of these separately . . . each of the Three Persons is that *res*—i.e., substance, essence, or divine nature—but it is the Father who begets, the Son who is begotten, and the Holy Spirit who proceeds, so that the distinctions are in the Persons and the unity in the nature."[98]

Other *capitula* dealt directly with the Greeks. The fourth, entitled "On the Pride of the Greeks against the Latins," begins: "Whereas we wish to cherish and honor the Greeks, who in our day return to obedience to the Holy See, by maintaining as far as we can in the Lord their customs and rites, yet we neither wish nor ought to yield to them in matters which are the cause of danger to souls and are detrimental to the fair name of the Church." Of such a nature is the practice which the Greeks had of washing their altars before celebrating on them if a Latin had used them, and of rebaptizing those baptized by Latins—which, it had been reported, was still done by some. Such practices should cease, and delinquents be punished by excommunication and deprivation of office.[99]

The fifth *capitulum* established the rank of the patriarchates. Rome, as "mother and mistress of all the faithful of Christ, is first, and in order after her come Constantinople, Alexandria, Antioch, Jerusalem."[100] This canon had practical application only for Latin patriarchs. It is, however, interesting for the order it establishes among the patriarchates—the order proposed by the Council of Chalcedon and rejected by Pope Leo I—and it indicates also the western evaluation of a patriarch. It gives to patriarchs more or less the same privileges that Innocent had granted to the primate of Bulgaria.

Another of the *capitula* probably had the Greeks in view. It certainly was applicable to many parts of the East: "IX. About Different Rites within the same Faith. Seeing that in many places within the same district and diocese there are mingled people of diverse languages with many rites and customs within the one faith, we strictly enjoin that the prelates of such districts or dioceses should provide suitable men to minister divine service to them according to the diversities of rites and languages, instructing them by word and example." No diocese, however, should have several prelates, "a body with many heads, like a monster." Where there was the need, the bishop should appoint a vicar, subordinate to himself in all things, some one of the same nation and rite as those to be served.[101]

The fourteenth *capitulum* "On Punishing the Incontinent," was addressed primarily to the Western Church. But it acknowledged the custom of married clergy that obtained in areas of oriental rite. "But those who according to the custom of their countries have not renounced the marriage bed should be more severely punished, should they lapse, since they may legitimately avail themselves of matrimony."[102]

In this same last session there was read the constitution *Ad liberandam* that determined the detailed arrangements for the projected crusade. It announced that the Kingdom of Sicily was chosen for the rendezvous of the host, with Brindisi and Messina as the ports of departure. Innocent himself would be there to direct the enterprise.[103] But Pope Innocent died on 16 July 1216.

In spite of his repeated assertion that the Church of the Greeks had returned to the obedience of the Apostolic See, Innocent's endeavors and hopes for union of the churches were still unfulfilled at his death.[104] Many consider that he had only himself to blame for this because of his insistence on the oath of obedience and his failure to summon a council of the two churches. But the issue is not so simple. The oath signified acceptance of papal primacy, a doctrine that was not invented by Innocent III to impose himself on the Greeks, but was Catholic teaching. Taking the oath was the sign of adherence to that teaching and a witness to the individual's personal belief. If there was to be union of churches, there should be union of faith. This was one way of achieving it, even if not the best way. But the fact remains that Innocent saw union too much as a jurist. Fulfillment of the canons—the external adherence to set forms—was made to be the essence of union, seemingly without regard to the inner spirit.[105]

An alternative might have been a general council, but it is unlikely that Innocent ever seriously contemplated this as a solution of the problem of union. With a Latin patriarch in Constantinople and Latin prelates in the major sees, he thought that union was already an accomplished fact. It was for the Greeks to accept it by the external act of submission, which implied also recognition of the Latin claim to orthodoxy of doctrine. If they did not accept it, it was their loss and condemnation. Doctrinal truths were to be believed, not debated. The Fourth Lateran Council that met in 1215 had no mention of theological discussion with Greeks on its agenda.

Innocent has also been accused of subordinating the spiritual good of the church to the temporal success of the Latin Empire, and persuasive arguments can be adduced in support of this contention. This judgment, however, is more alluring when one reads history backwards than when one follows the actual sequence of events as they occurred. The first announcement of the capture of Constantinople opened up an attractive prospect of greater help for Jerusalem and of church union. Innocent, convinced of the riches and power of the Byzantine Empire, was confident that the conquest would greatly benefit the Holy Land, and so for some time he supported the new empire.[106] But as soon as he realized that his hopes were unfounded, he gave the empire no more help and began to mature his plans for a new crusade.[107] The union of the churches he apparently at first took for granted as an automatic consequence of the capture. In that he was grossly mistaken, but he showed no sign of recognizing that fact. There was obvious resistance. He did not resort to force, but continued to insist only on what he held to be necessary for unity of faith. Would it, in the long run, have made any difference if he had not accepted the fait accompli of a Latin patriarch in the person of Morosini? Even if he had rejected Morosini for the office, sooner or later a Latin patriarch in Constantinople would have been inevitable. John Camaterus had fled. No Greek of merit would have sincerely accepted the dignity with its concomitant obligation of professing and enforcing obedience to Rome. With emperor, local princes, large landowners, and masses of their soldiers and dependents all Latins in a Latin Empire that was thought to be stable and lasting, the Latin Church had to be established everywhere with all the chief dioceses in Latin hands.

The capture by the Latins of the capital and center of the empire resulted in the strengthening of national sentiment among the Greeks. The fugitives from the conquered territories did not all leave in the first moments of panic, but they continued to go in the following years. With the timid went many men of talent who were rebellious against a foreign domination and desirous of putting an end to it. Most migrated to Epirus and Nicaea, each of which was ruled by an energetic leader bent on recovering the lost empire. The common disaster and common purpose threw leaders and led into close contact. Enthusiasm was kindled for a national cause: to eject the intruding Latins and to regain by their own efforts their queen city and empire. This new spirit is reflected, for example, in the letters of the prelates of Epirus, letters that ring with exultation at the prowess and successes of Theodore Doucas and reject every hint of criticism of him. Victory and conquest, after defeat and disaster, threw their minds back to the ancient history of their country. They began to write of themselves, and doubtless also to think, as Hellenes. Greeks, wherever they were, were of their race. Vatatzes from Nicaea helped the revolt in Crete against the Venetians (1230). New schools promoted the ideological return to the past, which brought fresh vigor to the present. So it turned out that the event of 1204 produced a growing sentiment of nationality among the Greeks, which showed itself immediately in fierce hostility to the Latins, and which in the course of time led to a kind of literary and artistic renaissance, a revival of the past.[108]

The church shared in the national renewal. Naturally the bishops, priests, and monks in exile nurtured a fierce resentment against those responsible for their plight and longed to be able to eject the Latin intruders, to repossess themselves of their old homes, and to restore to their church what belonged to it. Latin retention was pollution of what was Greek. (They washed altars where Latins had celebrated.) Official measures were not lacking. Patriarch Michael, shortly after his election, issued several documents with his synod in support of Emperor Lascaris and his aims. One was directed to all citizens and soldiers of the emperor. God, they were told, after punishing them for their sins by the savagery of their enemies, had taken pity of them again by giving them a good emperor; soldiers, therefore, were to fight valiantly and the clergy to pray. To encourage the army (and presumably as a counter-attraction to the Latin crusaders' indulgence) the patriarch granted pardon of sins to all "whom death shall overtake risking their lives for the fatherland and the salvation and redemption of the people." Another letter was an encomium addressed to Lascaris, with the concession also to him of forgiveness of his sins. A third (issued at the emperor's orders) was a proclamation of loyalty to Emperor Theodore Lascaris, to his queen, and to his son, Emperor Nicholas, and a repudiation of any other claimant, whether Greek (i.e., the line of Alexius III at that time residing at the court of the Seljuq Sultan on Lascaris' frontier) or non-Greek. Those present in the synod signed the document on the spot; those absent, and other notables, were to sign it later.[109] Clearly church and state were at one in the determination to achieve a triumphant return to Constantinople, with the Greek emperor to rule the Greek Empire and the Greek patriarch to direct the Greek Church.

Chapter IV

The Resurgence of the Greeks

In the decade that followed the capture of Constantinople, the situation of the kingdom of Nicaea had steadily improved. Faced with a multitude of enemies, Lascaris had reduced to submission local landowners aiming at becoming independent rulers, had parried the attacks of the Latin Emperor, partly by his own arms and partly by diversionary attacks by his ally Kalojan, and had held at bay the Seljuq Turks on his southern borders. Since the election of the Patriarch and his own coronation as Emperor, his kingdom was becoming more than ever a rallying point for the loyalties of the Greeks, especially as in 1211 he inflicted a decisive defeat on the Turks, and in 1214 the Latin Emperor Henry, after a victorious campaign in Asia Minor against Lascaris, had been forced by his other commitments to make a treaty with him, conserving for himself only the northwest coast and leaving the rest to the Greek. This was a notable success for Lascaris, for in effect it recognized him as head of a stable power. It also left him free to lead an attack on the kingdom of Trebizond that had been set up just before the capture of Constantinople (April 1204) by the brothers David and Alexius Comnenus, who early on had become vassals of the Latin Emperor. But Lascaris' prestige among the Greeks and his ambitions for the throne of Constantinople were seriously challenged by another Greek rival.

Michael Doucas, by the diplomacy of a treaty with the emperor Henry, submission to the pope, and a pact with Venice—all of which he observed just as long as it suited him[1]—had made himself master of Epirus. In 1212 he occupied Thessaly and by 1215, when he was murdered, he had evicted his Venetian patrons from the territories he was theoretically ruling in their name. His ambitious plans were continued by his half brother, Theodore Doucas, who in 1218 began a campaign to capture Thessalonica, the second city of the empire, then ruled by Montferrat's widow Margaret as regent for her son. Theodore's eye ranged beyond Thessalonica to Constantinople, and his loyal clergy enthusiastically supported him.

John Apocaucus, who had been appointed metropolitan of Naupactus in about 1200, before the empire was divided, was the leading prelate of Epirus. Full of admiration for the successes first of Michael and then of Theodore, he was a wholehearted supporter of their plans. So too were Demetrius Chomatianus, elected in 1217 to the See of "Justiniana and All Bulgaria" (that is, to be metropolitan of Ochrida), and George Bardanes, made bishop of Corfu in 1219. The ruler Michael had appointed bishops in Larissa (1212) and in Durazzo (1213) without reference to Nicaea. Soon after his election Patriarch Manuel of Nicaea protested but ratified the appointments, though with a warning against any similar action in the future. But Theodore Doucas, Michael's successor, continued to nominate with only the approval of the local synods. It may be that this sign of independence, combined with Theodore's success in the early stages of his campaign against Thessalonica, induced Lascaris to adopt other means of acquiring Constantinople. Ties with Constantinople could be strengthened by ties with Rome. In 1219 by a letter addressed to the metropolitan Apocaucus, the patriarch of Nicaea announced the convocation of a synod of all the prelates of the four eastern patriarchates, "which by common determination and vote should send envoys to the Pope of the elder Rome with a view to eliminating scandals, to giving peace to the Churches and to bringing all Christians for the future to one mind." Apocaucus replied for Theodore Doucas and the hierarchy of Epirus. He expressed their astonishment and distress at the idea of having relations with the Latins who were guilty of so many outrages against their church. Apocaucus wrote that if there should be a synod (though the best thing by far would be to let the whole project drop), it would be better to hold it in Epirus. It was not held at all. However, to counteract Latin influence in the Church of Serbia and perhaps to put up a rival to the pretensions of Chomatianus of Ochrida, autocephaly was granted by the emperor and the synod of Nicaea to the archbishop of Peć and all Serbia.[2]

The political rivalry continued under the cover of canon law. The patriarch, roused by a (false) rumor of a new appointment to Larissa, wrote against it, declaring that the consecration of Chomatianus was invalid and he threatened sanctions for breaches of patriarchal rights in the future. Apocaucus replied bidding the patriarch to be sure of his facts before protesting. He defended the validity of the appointment of the metropolitan of Ochrida, "who had been elected by our ruler whom we regard as sent from God and acknowledge as king of our country," and who had been confirmed in office by the synod. When Theodore took Thessalonica, the synod approved his coronation as emperor and requested Chomatianus to perform the ceremony, since the metropolitan of Thessalonica refused to officiate. Chomatianus willingly did so, justifying his action by appealing to antique (and long forgotten) privileges granted to his see by Justinian the Great. The new emperor wanted independence for his church. With this in view he summoned the bishops of his territories to meet in his presence in Arta. The conclusions of the synod were sent to Patriarch Germanus as "A Memorandum of All the Prelates to the Patriarch, written by the Metropolitan of Naupactus." Germanus was told that the emperor did not want eastern bishops for his western sees; he should, therefore, agree to accept candidates elected locally and acquiesce in those already appointed: he was still commemorated in the Liturgy with Theodore's approval, but he should be careful, for "there is fear that from necessity our mighty Emperor may put into effect what he already has in mind, namely, the establishment of an ecclesiastical supervision of the Pope of the older Rome also in this country." Germanus was allowed three months to decide, and Apocaucus demanded of him: "Why do you not call our God-given Despot and sovereign 'Emperor,' since by his many and varied qualities he is entitled to the imperial rule and name?"

Germanus could not call Theodore Doucas emperor because his own prince in Nicaea had been crowned by his predecessor as "faithful Emperor and sovereign of the Romans," which was what Theodore also claimed to be. Nor could he acquiesce in an independent western Greek Church such as Theodore wanted without at once denying his own position and conniving at Theodore's aspirations. Answering a letter from the metropolitan of Ochrida in very firm language, he derided the claims that Chomatianus had made for his see and reproved him for having dared to anoint and crown Theodore emperor, which was an office that belonged only to the patriarch. Germanus sent this letter by the metropolitan of Amastris, his envoy to the western Greek Church. The metropolitan met the bishops in a synod in Thessalonica. His message was uncompromising: Patriarch Germanus would allow no independence. On the other hand, Emperor Theodore was unyielding. His bishops in synod reflected his attitude. Their decision was put into writing by George Bardanes, metropolitan of Corfu. The threats hinted at by the synod of Arta became real. Canonical relations with Nicaea were broken off and the name of Germanus was deleted from the diptychs. There was schism between the two parts of the Greek Church.[3]

Though John Apocaucus in his letters time and again held up his prince as the champion of orthodoxy, Doucas, to achieve his political aims, was thoroughly capable of pitting the pope against Lascaris. That pope was Honorius III who, on 16 July 1216 already advanced in years, succeeded Innocent on the papal throne. His first interest was to promote the crusade that Innocent had had so much at heart and that had been promulgated at the Lateran Council of 1215. He soon wrote exhorting various princes to go to relieve the Holy Land, and he reminded bishops to implement the decision of the council whereby clerics should give one-twentieth of their revenues for the expenses of the crusade.[4]

Soon events closer at hand gave him another cause for concern. The Latin emperor of Constantinople, Henry, had died on 11 June 1216. To succeed him the barons elected his brother-in-law, Peter of Courtenay, who was then in France. Peter came to Rome and in April 1217 was crowned by Honorius in the Church of St. Lawrence-outside-the-walls.[5] On his way from Venice to Constantinople with 160 knights and 5,500 soldiers, he attacked Durazzo, but without success. Proceeding then through the mountain passes of Albania, he was ambushed. The whole expedition—emperor, army, and John Colonna, cardinal of St. Prassede and papal legate—was captured by Theodore Doucas.

Honorius wrote in haste to several princes urging them to use their influence for the release of the Latin emperor and the cardinal.[6] When these appeals were fruitless he sent his own envoys to Epirus. Not only were they well received, but Theodore was ready to swear to release the legate and to be obedient to the Holy See. Thereupon the pope received him "among the special sons of the Church," took his territories into papal protection and empowered the bishop of Cotrone, when once the legate had "been restored to liberty and arrived in Brindisi or some other safe place," to absolve the offending duke.[7] The papal legate was eventually freed in the middle of 1218, but Peter and his troops were never heard of again. With the imperial throne thus vacant, until the summer of 1219 Constantinople was ruled as regent for the infant Baldwin by Yolanda, Peter's widow, who had reached the city by sea. To ease relations with the Greeks of Nicaea, she married one of her daughters to the Nicene emperor, Theodore Lascaris, who thereby gained for himself an indirect claim to the Byzantine throne. After the coronation on 25 March 1221 of Yolanda's son Robert as emperor, Lascaris tried to arrange a marriage between Robert and his own daughter, but the opposition of the Patriarch Manuel, and his own death, rendered the project abortive.

Theodore Doucas's return to grace did not last long. Within two years he was excommunicated by the pope for attacking the kingdom of Thessalonica, and the archbishop and the commune of Brindisi were warned to prevent his receiving help in men and materials for his nefarious enterprise.[8] Nevertheless, Theodore captured the city of Thessalonica in late 1224 and proclaimed himself emperor of Constantinople.

Pope Honorius did very little to help the Latin Empire of Constantinople, apart from trying to secure the release of Emperor Peter and taking the young prince of Thessalonica, Demetrius, under his special protection. His chief interest was the crusade that reached Acre in September 1217. After a few uncoordinated forays the Hungarian contingent departed for home and, when the King of Cyprus died, there remained only a remnant with the king of Jerusalem, John of Brienne. This small army, reinforced by some new arrivals, sailed in 1218 to Egypt to take Cairo. After a preliminary success in capturing Damietta, which led them to refuse very favorable terms of peace offered by the sultan, in 1221 they attacked, were repulsed, and, to secure a safe retreat, had to surrender Damietta. During the course of this campaign Honorius wrote letter after letter to bishops, princes, and especially to Frederick II of Germany, pressing for aid in men, money, and materials for the crusaders. The failure of the enterprise was due in large measure to Cardinal Pelagius, the papal legate with the crusade, and Frederick II, crowned Holy Roman Emperor on 22 November 1222. Against the advice of Brienne, Pelagius had insisted on rejecting the peace terms and on attacking. Frederick had taken the cross in 1215 but, alleging a variety of excuses, time and again he had persuaded the gentle pope, who had once been his tutor, to let him defer his departure for the East, while in fact he was consolidating his power in Sicily and Italy with the final object of making himself a Roman emperor in the style of Caesar Augustus, ruling a worldwide empire both of state and church from Rome.[9] To the crusade he sent a contingent of five hundred knights, but before the death of Honorius on 19 March 1227 he had made no move to go himself.

After the death of Emperor Henry, while the political situation of the Latin Empire of Constantinople deteriorated under the regency of Yolanda and the incompetent rule of her eldest son, Robert of Courtenay, the fortunes of the church sank too. In the time of Pope Honorius there is no record of any conference of Latin and Greek theologians aimed at healing the breach between the churches. The papal letters of the period directed to Constantinople are mostly concerned with the organization and discipline of Latin ecclesiastics and the misdemeanors of Latin princes. Honorius followed the line laid down by Innocent III. He favored Greek monasteries that had accepted papal obedience. On 6 August 1217 he acceded to a request of the monks of Mt. Sinai to be taken under papal protection, and confirmed them in possession of their properties in various countries.[10] He renewed his protection on 4 December 1223;[11] and after legal process, he upheld the appeals of the monastery against impositions by the Latin archbishop of Crete and the bishop of Troyes. After a delegate from the Mt. Sinai monastery voyaged to Rome to see him in person, Honorius even quashed a decision of the papal legate.[12] A few days later a new bull of papal protection was issued recording the same list of localities that belonged to the monastery and the same exemption from tithes.[13] Similarly the pope confirmed a number of Greek monasteries in their legitimate privileges and customs and exempted them from the payment of tithes, because before the General Council (1215) they had never paid tithes: that custom, too, should be observed with the rest.[14]

On the other hand, the pope confirmed possession by Latin monks of Greek monasteries. In Constantinople the Latin Chapter of St. Michael of Buccaleon received the gift of the monastery of St. Focard, presumably because it had been abandoned by its former inmates.[15] When Monte Cassino was given the monastery of Our Lady of Virgiotti (Evergetis), it was expressly laid down that any Greek monks still there should not be disturbed.[16] St. Paul's-outside-the-walls, Rome, was to receive an annual payment from a monastery near Constantinople,[17] and a Cistercian abbey in Greece was given the ancient monastery of Ruffiano (Rufinianae). The legate Pelagius had given its Greek monks until the General Council (1215) to promise obedience to the Holy See. When the council was over, since they were still recalcitrant, the new Latin patriarch Gervasius (1215–19) invested the Cistercian abbot with the headship of the Greek monastery. Finally, the new legate John Colonna again exhorted the Greeks to obedience and, when they preferred to abandon their monastery, handed it over to the Cistercians.[18] Other monasteries that had been taken over by lay lords for secular purposes were brought back into monastic use and given to the Latins.[19] The Latin abbots of such monasteries, because a papal legate had installed them, were not therefore withdrawn from the jurisdiction of the patriarch.[20]

A reply sent by Pope Honorius to his legate in Constantinople, Cardinal Colonna, who had asked for directions to help him to meet the local situation, indicates some of his problems. Greeks were being secretly ordained by bishops who were not their Ordinaries. Others, excommunicated, in defiance of the bishops were celebrating the Liturgy according to the Greek rite in churches under interdict. Both Greek and Latin bishops were ordaining priests and collecting tithes in dioceses not their own. Laymen were dismissing their wives and taking others "at their own whim." Barons and knights, both Latin and Greek, were possessing themselves of abbeys and churches with all their lands and dependents, not paying tithes and encouraging others not to do so, with no regard for ecclesiastical censures of excommunication. The archdeacon of Negroponte was trafficking with Alexandria in defiance of the decree of the late council.

Honorius in answer reminded the legate that canon and civil law dealt with all these cases and he should apply them. But, in view of the state of the empire and the large number of delinquents, he could try to use persuasion with individuals and to mitigate the rigor of the law, except when there was question of what was for both Latins and Greeks a sacrament, namely matrimony. In respect of that, canon law should be exactly observed. "In matters not regulated by law proceed with equity as you perceive that the cases demand, keeping in mind the persons involved, the nature of the cases, places and times, always inclining to the side of clemency, particularly in view of the state of the Empire which is still weak."[21] Such a "tendency to clemency" and a refusal to give precise directions are characteristic of Honorius's letters. When Colonna inquired about pretensions of the Constantinopolitan clergy over various churches, in this following the example of their Greek predecessors, he was told to use his own judgement. The same letter states that some Greek monks and hermits refused to take an oath of obedience to the pope but were willing to give a "manual obedience," i.e., the feudal-like "hominium," putting their hands within those of the bishop: "for the time being you can receive them with a manual promise, since for some while, in view of the circumstances of places and times, there should be some relaxation of severity."[22]

The excesses of the clerics of Constantinople were led by the patriarch himself. No sooner had Gervasius returned from the Council of the Lateran as patriarch than he began to claim all the powers that he imagined a Greek patriarch would enjoy. He excommunicated and absolved from excommunication subjects of other metropolitans and appointed to churches within their areas.[23] In the duchies of Achaia and Athens he claimed as his monasteries those where any Greek patriarch had in the past planted a cross.[24] He sent officials of his church as "legates *a latere*" with powers equal to those of a papal legate; they then set up courts in other metropolitanates, heard cases, condemned, absolved even in crimes reserved to the Holy See, and went as far as placing an interdict on Geoffrey of Achaia and Othon of Athens, with strict injunctions to the local bishops to observe it exactly. Gervasius was warned: "No matter how great the prestige of your office, realize that you are subject to Us . . . and that . . . if you continue to usurp what belongs to others, you may be deprived of what is rightly yours."[25] The legate was to restrain the patriarchal ambitions without,[26] however, denying him certain rights and privileges.[27] Nevertheless the pope confirmed what the legate had tentatively conceded, that the metropolitan of Patras should be independent of Constantinople, in this claiming not to introduce any innovation but to restore the ancient situation of a vicariate of Thessalonica, dependent directly on Rome.[28]

The Latin patriarchate of Constantinople was steadily dwindling in size, as Theodore Doucas from the west occupied large tracts of Thessaly and Thrace, and Vatatzes from the east drove the Latins from Asia Minor and conquered towns of importance in Europe. In 1218 the bishop-elect of Nicomedia was recommended by Honorius to the good offices of the patriarch. He had resigned his see because most of his territory was in enemy hands: if adequate provision could not be made for him, his resignation should be accepted and the patriarch should arrange for the care of his diocese as best he could.[29] Some years later the patriarch was asked to help the bishop of Serres, "whose church had lately been overrun by the belial Theodore."[30] In October of the same year the metropolitan of Larissa, another victim of Theodore Doucas's victorious campaign, was given "until he could safely return" three dioceses from the metropolitanate of Athens.[31] A year later he gave them back.[32] Other dioceses were combined, usually because "their revenues were so meager that they could not support a bishop in a manner fitting his episcopal office"[33] or, rarely, because they were suffragans of a "rebel" metropolitanate.[34] In each case the local papal legate proposed the transfer and Pope Honorius issued the necessary document confirming the decision.

When Thessaly and most of Thrace came back into Greek hands, many of the exiled Greek bishops, like Constantine Mesopotamites, the metropolitan of Thessalonica, returned to their sees. They found the parochial organization much as they had left it. For the rest, though the leaders of the crusade had intended to treat church property as they did lay property, the vigorous intervention of Innocent III prevented this, and despite the numerous confiscations of church property by the rulers of the new states, the church managed on the whole to retain much of its property and many of its privileges. This was important for the later history of Byzantium, for with the recovery of most of the territories lost to the Latins, the Greeks again took possession of their churches and monasteries and applied once more, as a matter of course, the practices and institutions which concerned their properties before 1204. Indeed, these practices and institutions had been hardly altered by the political changes of 1204. What applied to church lands was true also of the monasteries. As Latin monks were driven out, Greek monks, either the original inhabitants or others, returned and "resumed their ancient ways—the exaction of additional privileges from the government and the acquisition of more and more property."[35] But the new situation was also different. The returning clerics and monks had lived through the events of 1204 and the subsequent years, and their attitude against the Latins had hardened into a triumphant, but bitter, hostility.

The papal registers record only two occasions when Honorius directed that troops or money destined for the crusade in the Holy Land be diverted to Constantinople. One was of very little importance and the papal injunction was probably never acted on. In the first moment of panic on hearing of the capture of Peter of Courtenay the pope wrote to the archbishop of Sens bidding him preach a crusade for the rescue of the prisoners. The second occasion was after the failure of the crusade in the

East when Constantinople was being pressured, particularly by the victorious arms of Theodore of Epirus. To help William of Montferrat recapture Thessalonica, crusading indulgences were promised to his helpers,[36] and he was given 15,000 marks collected for the crusade.[37] Honorius seems to have had a bad conscience about that, for he carefully explained that a strong empire in Latin hands would be a great advantage to the Holy Land. However, the empire, which would be the first beneficiary of a successful expedition, was also to help itself. All ecclesiastics within the kingdom of Thessalonica and to the south of it were to pay one-half of the revenues of the year and of their movable property to William of Montferrat; those in the rest of the empire were to give a like contribution to the emperor, except that these latter were enjoined to pay only one-quarter of their movable property and one-tenth of their revenues of the year, seeing that "there are said to be among them many who, established on the other side of the Bosphorus, have lost all their resources and whose needs have to be relieved by others."[38]

The expedition that Montferrat led to Thessaly in 1225 failed and William himself died in Greece. How much he and Robert of Constantinople received from the ecclesiastical tax is not known. By 1224, when the tax was levied, the controversy about church property, which resulted from the pact made by the crusaders in 1204 before taking Constantinople, had been settled for all the conquered territories, at least in theory. The new legate, sent in 1217, was instructed to look into the working of the arrangement drawn up at Ravennica for the imperial territories.[39] In the next year the Church of Constantinople was lamenting that its clergy "were being forced almost to beg" because neither the fifteenth (as arranged in 1206) nor the twelfth (as in 1210) of the revenues was being paid.[40] Shortly afterwards a papal letter to the metropolitans of Thessalonica and the Morea confirmed the charter of ecclesiastical immunities that had been agreed upon at Ravennica in 1210. Honorius acceded to a request from the same metropolitans that he should "lend his support to the excommunication fulminated against the princes of Achaia and Athens and their agents, who were seriously contravening that agreement."[41] There must have been legitimate complaints also from the clergy of Constantinople and the area, for in 1222, with additions in detail as to how the one-eleventh allotted to the church should be raised, the Ravennica agreement was repeated in a solemn document furnished with the seals of the Emperor and the chief barons. This concordat made with Emperor Robert was accepted also by the Baillie of Thessalonica, the Venetians, and the princes of the Morea.[42]

Honorius, like Innocent III, applied to the Greek Church the principles of Latin canon law. The Latin metropolitan of Crete was to correct and reform, even by ecclesiastical censure, bishops, abbots, and clerics, both

Greek and Latin where necessary,[43] but he was not allowed to infringe on the immunities of the Greek monastery of Mt. Sinai. Greek monks of the bishopric of Nicomedia who, after having submitted to the Holy See, had then "gone after the Greek who calls himself Patriarch of Nicaea," were to be made to return to their canonical obedience. If necessary their obedience was to be secured by invoking the aid of the secular arm.[44] A strong action of the same sort was ordained against Ruthenians of oriental rite who were entering Livonia and there causing difficulties among recent converts by execrating Latin baptism, dissolving marriages among them, and generally flouting the Latin Church. The intruders were to be made to conform to Latin observances wherever their activities were seen to lead men away from the Roman Church.[45]

In Cyprus a new situation had arisen after its capture by Richard Lionheart. He had sold it first to the Templars and then to Guy de Lusignan (1192). The population of the island was very mixed, but was predominantly Greek; their church was organised into fourteen dioceses with the metropolitan see at Famagusta. Guy's successor appealed to Pope Celestine to establish a Latin hierarchy. This was done in 1196; it consisted of a metropolitan at Nicosia and three suffragan bishops. Though the political authorities wanted to support the Latin Church by grants from the state, Celestine insisted on an independent provision being made for it from the start. The fourteen Greek bishops were not dispossessed, but remained in their sees. At King Hugh's death in 1218, his heir, Henry, was only a few months old. The queen mother, Alice, became regent and associated herself with a leading baron, Philip d'Ibelin. They took the occasion of the legate Pelagius's presence in the East to discuss and regulate the financial provision for the Latin Church, about which discord had risen. The bishop of Famagusta took the resulting agreement to Rome for papal approval, which was given in a document dated 17 December 1221.[46]

The convention was designed to meet the demands of the church, of the barons, and to some extent of the Greeks, on the lines of the arrangements obtaining in the kingdom of Jerusalem. The lay powers were to pay tithes to the Latins. The crown remitted certain taxes to the *"rustici"* of the archbishop and bishops of Cyprus (presumably only the Latin hierarchy). Greek priests and deacons were to be free of the poll tax and forced labour, but should give canonical obedience to the Latin bishop of their area. As the number of Greek priests and deacons in the island was very large, the barons' rights were safeguarded by insisting that they remain in their own villages, that candidates for ordination need permission from their lay lord, and that anyone ordained surreptitiously should not enjoy clerical immunities. At the election of abbots in monasteries the feudal superior should have right of canonical assent and the election should be confirmed by the local Latin Ordinary. Abbots were in all things to be obedient to their Latin bishops and should not be moved without their consent. The churches and abbeys of the Greeks should be left in undisturbed possession of whatever properties they had acquired after the Latin domination by permission or gift of the Latin lords.[47]

The bishop of Famagusta had, it seems, been commissioned by Queen Alice to induce the pope to leave within the Latin dioceses (which, of course, covered the whole of Cyprus) the Greek bishops, functioning as bishops, even though they would not yield obedience to the Latin Church. Honorius, despite his desire "to cherish and honor Greeks who return to the obedience of the Apostolic See by upholding as far as, with God, We can the customs and rites of those Greeks," could not fall in with her request, as being also against a canon of the late Lateran Council forbidding two bishops in any one see—a monster with two heads. Indeed, he commissioned the patriarch of Jerusalem to go with two archbishops to Cyprus to examine the situation. He told them that he had been informed that a Greek archbishop and some Greek bishops, without any apostolic warrant or consent of the local Latin hierarchy, had been established there; they paid obedience neither to the Roman Church nor to the prelates there and, "what was worse, [they] continued the former errors of the Greeks, granting permission to people separated on account of fornication to contract new marriages and secretly, since they dared not do it openly, repeating sacraments conferred by Latin priests and bishops." In virtue of the canon of the council, and because their action could lead to the loss of Cyprus to the Roman Church and even to the Latin power, the commissioners were to eject the Greek bishops as intruders and not to allow them for the future to remain in the dioceses with any function of authority (*velut praesides ullatenus commorari*). Greek abbots and other clerics should render canonical obedience to the Latin prelates. The recalcitrant should be constrained to obey by ecclesiastical censures.[48] A few weeks later the same commissaries were bid to bring certain dissident Syrians, Jacobites, and Nestorians into obedience.[49]

The agreement about tithes and the rest did not put an end to the tensions even between the Latin Church in Cyprus and the Latin barons. Owing probably to representations from the Latin hierarchy of the island, on 8 March 1222 the pope wrote to the queen and the barons insisting that all properties that had previously belonged to the Greek Church pertained by right to the Latin clergy.[50] In consequence, when Pelagius was in Cyprus on his return from Egypt, a meeting of the political and ecclesiastical authorities was held in Famagusta in the late summer of 1222 with him, a Knight Templar, and a Knight Hospitaller as assessors. They issued a new form of agreement acceptable to both sides. It was the old convention, with three additional clauses. Presumably because the monasteries were becoming a refuge of many who wanted to avoid labor-service to their lords, it was decreed that a delegate of the Latin bishops, together with a baillie appointed by the crown, should assess how many monks each monastery should reasonably have, and this number should not be exceeded. The secular authorities were guaranteed peaceful possession of the church lands they held, without recrimination from the clergy. Finally, the number of Greek bishops was reduced to four (that is, equal to the number of the Latin); they should be obedient to the Latin bishops "according to the custom of the kingdom of Jerusalem," and should reside in small towns on the periphery of the Latin sees.[51] Even this new agreement did not produce harmony, for the barons, in opposition to the queen, were averse to paying tithes to the church. To encourage her, Queen Alice was the recipient of two letters from the pope exhorting her to observe the pact and not to be discouraged by difficulties.[52] In fact, the payment of tithes had caused a serious rift between the two regents, with Philip d'Ibelin refusing flatly to pay them.[53] Alice fled to Syria and married Bohemond of Tripoli in 1225.

The reduction of the number of Greek dioceses was effected and the Latin bishops insisted on obedience from the Greek clergy. Archbishop Neophytus refused to ask for confirmation of his election and was banished from the kingdom. Thereupon the bishop of Solia and the abbot of Apsinthi (both named Leontius), in the name of the Cypriot Church, went to ask the patriarch of Nicaea how they should act. The Latin archbishop, they said, demanded obedience as a prerequisite for ministering to the flock. The demand would imply that they promise obedience with their hands in the archbishop's hands, that Greek bishops and abbots give notice to the Latin Ordinary before entering into office, and that there be a right of appeal for Greeks to the Latin archbishop from the judgments of Greek ecclesiastical courts. If they obeyed the Latin injunctions, they would seem to be unfaithful to their own church; if they did not, their flocks would soon be without pastors. The first decision of the patriarch with his synod was that none of these demands was against the faith, and that all could by "economy," or rather "pretense," be complied with without blame. A turbulent crowd of exiles from Constantinople then intervened, shouting that such action would play into Latin hands. Whereupon the synod modified its first decision. Approval was not given for the act of "*hominium,*" but the notice of election and the right of appeal were assessed as morally "indifferent" and in the circumstances excusable.[54]

Archbishop Neophytus, in the course of the journeys of his exile, went also to Nicaea. There he received from Emperor Vatatzes his official nomination as head of the Church of Cyprus.[55] He then returned to his archdiocese and, presumably with the emperor's approval (and, as he mistakenly thought, with that also of the patriarch and his synod), he and his bishops did all that was necessary to comply, at least externally, with Latin regulations in their regard. Letters of complaint from some of their faithful reached the patriarch in Nicaea. Incensed, in 1229 he directed an encyclical letter to the Cypriots censuring, though without mentioning specific names, Neophytus and the clergy that had conformed.

The greater part of this forceful letter was an attack on Rome and its pretensions—Rome wanted to make the five patriarchates into one; its greatest act of effrontery had been to add to the creed; modern popes had thus broken continuity with the popes of the seven councils in innovating new dogmas and canons; it was, therefore, an enormity to obey the Roman See of the day. He enjoined on all the laity of Cyprus to boycott priests who had accepted obedience to Rome; they should not frequent their churches or accept their blessings—indeed, it was far better to pray at home than in their churches. The patriarch continued that if any priest yielded, before he was let into their church, he should declare before the Latin archbishop and bishops: "It shall not be so; but let the synodical excommunications be enforced." Such priests should have recourse to the synod and patriarch of Nicaea. Clergy, he insisted, who wished to abide in the church must not yield obedience to bishops who submitted to Rome; that those bishops were a scandal to the church, and that the faithful should endure anything to preserve their faith.[56]

Not content with that one letter, Patriarch Germanus continued to send orders and advice to various people on the island. Finally Neophytus appealed to Vatatzes to intervene. He complained that, though Cyprus was autocephalous and outside patriarchal jurisdiction, Germanus was leaving no one in peace. He claimed that patriarch and synod had consented to his gesture of corporal submission, done so as to keep together the church and the numerous inhabitants of Cyprus. He had been accused, he wrote, of responsibility for the deaths of the thirteen martyrs condemned for their faith, a charge he rebutted, for they had brought the death penalty on themselves for their insulting language about Latin doctrines in the course of their trial. He ended by asking Vatatzes whether he should leave the island or stay.[57] Actually he stayed until about the year 1238.

Honorius III died on 18 March 1227. At the end of his reign the situation of the Latins in the East was much worse than when he ascended the papal throne. The territory of the empire had been reduced to Constantinople and a restricted area around it. Although the Greek Church was to some degree divided within itself, it had not yielded ground to the Latin. Every new Greek military victory brought former Greek dioceses once more into Greek hands; the Latin bishops were ejected and Greek bishops took their places.

The only bright spot in the East was the Morea, where the court of the Villehardouins was rapidly becoming a center of culture and chivalry, unassailed by enemies, and a reliable aid to Constantinople in its most perilous moments.

To succeed Honorius III, Gregory IX was elected on 19 March 1227. He was an octogenarian with a long experience of public activity behind him. His age did not imply any diminution in his intellectual faculties or in his power of will. He was a canonist of note who appreciated to the full the new power that had accrued to the church with the rise of the recently formed mendicant orders of Dominicans and Franciscans. Like his immediate predecessor on the papal throne, he was intent on promoting the crusade for the liberation of the Holy Land. The greatest obstacle in this regard was Frederick II, Holy Roman Emperor and King of Germany and of Sicily, who had twice solemnly taken the cross. Frederick had played on the weakness of Honorius, forever making new promises to fulfill his vows and forever putting off their execution. One of Gregory's first acts was to give Frederick a sharp reminder to delay no longer. In the summer of 1227, therefore, Frederick sailed with a large army from Brindisi (8 September), but on a plea of illness two days later he left the fleet at Otranto and returned home. Gregory immediately excommunicated him and, when the pope, refusing to accept his excuses, put him under interdict, Frederick counteracted with an encyclical letter and instigated rebellion in Rome which forced Gregory to flee the city. Next year he did go to the Holy Land, but with a fleet of only forty ships and he had more reasons than merely to fulfill his crusader's vow. In 1225 he had married the fourteen-year-old queen of Jerusalem, daughter of John of Brienne, who gave birth to a son, Conrad, on 25 April 1228 and died six days later. Frederick was now legally regent of Jerusalem. By feudal law he was also regent of Cyprus, since in 1196 the first king of Cyprus, Amalric, had accepted Henry VI Hohenstaufen of Sicily as his suzerain. Frederick meant to enforce both regencies and by doing so to rule both countries. In Cyprus he failed, but only after severe fighting. But when, on 1 May 1229, less than a year after his arrival, he departed from the Holy Land, he left as king of Jerusalem. Negotiations with the Saracens, begun before ever he set off from Italy, had been carried through to success without consulting the council of barons. By this means he regained possession of the Holy City and access to it, but had to guarantee a ten years' truce, during which time there should be no western attack. As all this time he was excommunicated, he received no help from the Orders of Knights, was denounced from church pulpits from Jaffa to Acre, and the patriarch of Jerusalem would not set foot in the Holy City while he was there. When, therefore, he was crowned King in the Church of the Holy Sepulchre on 18 March, he put the crown on his own head. His diplomatic mission finished—it was hardly a crusade—he departed.

On his return to Italy Frederick placated the pope, who recognized him as king of Jerusalem. For several years there was, if not peace between them, at least not war, an interval that Frederick employed in securing his position in Germany and Sicily and in getting ready to impose his domination on Italy. In anticipation of this the pope issued an encyclical letter, claiming possession of "both swords," i.e., universal power in both the spiritual and temporal spheres, on the strength of the Donation of Constantine. Frederick opened his campaign to acquire Italy by attacking the Lombard cities in 1237 with success, but he did not achieve a complete victory. He was excommunicated, carried on a pamphlet war to parry Gregory's, captured a hundred bishops and three papal cardinal legates traveling by sea to the council the pope had called in Rome, and was just outside the walls of the city with an army when Gregory died on 21 August 1241. Frederick's significance for the Latin Empire of Constantinople was that, though he was Holy Roman Emperor and so should have been a protagonist in every noteworthy endeavor of his church, he did nothing to help the Empire in its difficulties; this was partly because he had no intention of advancing papal projects, and partly because he did not want any Latin ruler firmly secured there unless it was himself. Indeed, Frederick's influence was not merely negative. In 1238 he actually impeded the passage of the troops that Baldwin had managed to raise in Europe, so that very few of them ever reached Greece to help resist the assaults of Asen and Vatatzes on Constantinople.

John Vatatzes, who in 1222 had succeeded Theodore I Lascaris on the throne of Nicaea. was prepared to use any and every means to get possession of Constantinople. During all of Gregory's reign that city was in a parlous state, and it survived in Latin hands as long as it did only because it had too many enemies. In 1229 Theodore Doucas, crowned emperor in Thessalonica, ruled over most of Greece north of the Gulf of Corinth and of the Duchy of Athens as far as Adrianople (situated northwest of Constantinople), which he had taken from his Nicene rival. Theodore offered the most dangerous threat to Constantinople. In 1230 he set his army in motion. But instead of assaulting the Latin Empire he attacked John Asen, who had been firmly established as czar of Bulgaria since 1218, presumably because he felt he had to consolidate his lines of communication before embarking on his final assault on the heavily fortified city on the Bosphorus. Surprisingly Theodore was defeated at Klokotnica and captured. Immediately Asen overran the northern part of Theodore's domain from Durazzo to Adrianople, but he allowed Manuel Doucas, Theodore's brother and John's own son-in-law, to retain Thessalonica and to rule over what was left of its empire. The archbishop of Thessalonica was subordinated to the See of Trnovo, still held by Basil, who had been made "Primate of All Bulgaria" by Innocent III. Constantinople now had a new principal enemy, for John Asen, not altogether untruly, ended an inscription to record his triumph: "The Franks hold only the cities in the vicinity of Constantinople and Constantinople itself; but even they are under the authority of my Empire since they have no other Emperor but me, and it is thanks to me that they survive, for thus has God decreed."

At that moment, in fact, Constantinople was without a Latin emperor. Robert of Courtenay had died and his brother Baldwin was only eleven years old. John Asen offered his daughter in marriage to the young heir, aiming at the regency of Constantinople for himself. The barons first accepted and then changed their minds.[58] They chose instead the octogenarian John of Brienne, who had been king of Jerusalem till he was tricked out of the title by Frederick II. After Robert's nerveless reign they wanted a warrior. Brienne accepted in 1229 and received papal approbation; but he was in Italy. After a journey to France to raise money and troops he arrived in Constantinople in the autumn of 1231. It was presumably his arrival and coronation that moved Asen, and the Bulgarian Church with him, to break off the relations with Rome that had begun in the time of Kalojan and Pope Innocent III.

Meanwhile Manuel of Thessalonica, adapting himself to the then pro-Latin religious affinities of his father-in-law, Asen, had sent an embassy to the papal court. It arrived shortly before 1 April 1232.[59] Gregory's answer is extant. The pope graciously acknowledged Manuel's recognition of the Roman Church as his mother and his submission to the pope's person, and promised to accede to his request to take his territory under papal protection as far as he could, but without first consulting the emperor and the patriarch in Constantinople he could not be more precise.[60] However, it did not much matter, for Manuel changed his policy. When Asen broke with Rome, Manuel turned to the patriarch of Nicaea. He wrote to Germanus recognizing his patriarchal right of confirming episcopal elections in Greece but alleging practical difficulties. The patriarch answered dismissing the difficulties and declaring that he would send his plenipotentiary to deal with all matters.[61] Thereupon Manuel held a synod and all the bishops present, including Bardanes, enthusiastically professed their allegiance to the patriarch of Nicaea. Christopher, metropolitan of Ancyra, the patriarchal envoy, arrived. He announced the end of the schism, and then toured the monasteries of Thessaly and Epirus asserting patriarchal privileges. He tried also to establish the patriarch's position in Bulgaria when archbishop Basil of Trnovo retired (or was dismissed) to a monastery on Mount Athos. But Asen would not acquiesce. He appointed a new primate himself and even subordinated to him the See of Thessalonica. Two years later, as part of a political alliance, Asen ceded ecclesiastical authority in Thessaly to Nicaea, and Nicaea, after consultation with the other three oriental patriarchates, granted autocephaly to the Church of Bulgaria and the title of patriarch to its primate, Joachim. Later there was a certain controversy. The Bulgarians claimed that the independence of their church was complete; the Greeks claimed that taxes and commemoration in the first place were still owed to the patriarch of Constantinople.[62] Nevertheless, the Church of mainland Greece was once more under the Patriarch of Nicaea, and the last traces of schism within the Greek Church were eliminated.

A few years later during the winter of 1235–36, Bardanes went to Italy on a political mission for his prince. He arrived there very ill and was nursed by a friend, John Grasso, in Otranto. While he was there, Fra Bartholomew, a Franciscan, visited him, anxious to learn what the Greek Church taught about Purgatory. He asked Bardanes, "I want to learn from you Greeks where the souls of those go who die without doing penance or who have not had time to fulfill the penances that their confessors have imposed on them." Bardanes was shocked because his church had no concept of temporal punishment attaching to sin, either in this world or in the next, but thought rather in terms of purification begun on earth and continued hereafter through the Liturgies, prayers, and almsgivings of the faithful on earth. He denied that there was any "place" or "fire" or "expiating penalties," and declared that the Latin teaching was tainted with Origenism, according to which even the devils in Hell are slowly purified and finally will enter Paradise. He wrote post haste to Patriarch Germanus to acquaint him of this new aberration and to put him on his guard, for until now the question of Purgatory had not figured on the long list of defects attributed by the Greeks to the Roman Church.[63]

In 1229 Germanus in his letter to the Cypriots had fiercely attacked the Church of Rome. In 1232, however, he wrote in a different spirit to the pope, sending his messenger with five Franciscan friars returning to Italy after a pilgrimage to the Holy Land. Edified by their evangelical poverty, Germanus had also been encouraged by their words to make an overture to the pope and the cardinals about ecclesiastical unity. The message of the letter to Gregory was: "But even if we or an angel from heaven should preach to you a gospel contrary to that which we preached to you, let him be accursed"; Latins and Greeks—each accuses the other of error; neither church is capable of passing an unbiased judgment on itself; there is need of a third party; and there exists, indeed, a third party—the Gospels, the epistles, and the Fathers. He also wrote to the cardinals in the same pacific spirit, reminding them of the relation of charity that once reigned between the churches. If the Greeks were at fault, Germanus wrote, let the Latins help them; if the Latins were at fault, they should remember that Paul withstood Peter to his face, and besides, Peter was overthrown by a servant-maid in the courtyard of Caiphas. Many other races agree with the Greeks in faith. He concluded, "May Almighty God . . . bring us together again in unity of faith and may He grant that the Church of the Greeks, together with her first sister, the elder Rome, glorify the Prince of Peace, Christ, by unity of faith in the restoration of the orthodoxy wherein in days of old they were agreed."[64]

Gregory replied on 26 July 1232, promising to send specially chosen envoys to treat of the proposal made by the patriarch. "So," he wrote, "that your letter might not seem to be treated with disdain, if it were not answered," he proceeded to comment on at least part of it. Courteously but firmly he asserted the primacy of St. Peter and laid the blame on the Greeks for the schism and on the schism for their loss of empire, which he regarded as a penalty for their sins. If they would return to the fold they would be received with joy and would find there what Germanus had proposed as a standard: the faith of the Gospels, of the epistles, and of the Fathers, and, in addition, a welcome as to a son and not a hired servant.[65]

Without undue delay the pope asked the generals of the Dominicans and the Franciscans to provide suitable personnel for the mission to Greece, but it was nearly a year before they were ready. They were four—two Dominicans, both probably Frenchmen, a certain Hugo and Peter of Sézanne, and two English Franciscans, Haymo of Faversham and Ralph of Rheims. The letter of credence they carried with them was curiously composed. The introduction and the recommendation of the messengers were wedged between a declaration that the Roman pontiff possesses both swords (of spiritual and temporal power) and a list of quaint Old Testament figures meant to prove that the Church of Christ is one. Then came mention also of the Eucharist—the Greeks celebrate with fermented bread more materially, the Latins with unfermented bread more spiritually, "but assuredly simple bread before the sacrifice is bread, but when transubstantiation has been effected by the Lord's words, it is not bread and so cannot be said to be either fermented or unfermented, but rather He is believed to be the real Bread that descends from heaven and gives life to the world."[66]

The four envoys reached Nicaea on Sunday, 15 January 1234, and were received with great cordiality by the emperor and the patriarch, a church being put at their disposal for their religious offices. They insisted that they were simple messengers and not legates, and only when pressed by the Greeks did they agree to open the debate. They asked why the Greek Church, having once like all other churches been subject to the Roman, had withdrawn its obedience. Somewhat disconcerted, the Greeks offered two reasons, the Procession of the Holy Spirit and the Eucharist. The friars wanted to start with discussion on the latter, but as their hosts insisted on the former,[67] they reluctantly gave way. Meetings were held on Thursday, Friday, and Saturday on the *Filioque* as an addition to the Creed, when the Latins parried the arguments from the prohibition enacted by the Council of Ephesus against changing the Nicene Creed by stressing the additions to that creed made in the Constantinopolitan Creed: if those two creeds were one because the doctrine was the same, as the Greeks said, then the Latin Creed was equally one with them both because again the doctrine was the same. Naturally they were challenged to prove their last statement and the discussion turned to the doctrine involved in the *Filioque* clause.

Towards the end of Friday's meeting and after a late start on Saturday, the discussion continued until "nearly the second watch of the night." The Latins had brought with them many Greek codices which they had used copiously on Friday. On Saturday a Greek "philosopher" spoke at length and tried to trip them with captious questions.[68] In the end, when it was agreed that "the Spirit of truth" of St. John's Gospel meant "the Spirit of Christ" and that Christ was such from eternity, the Latins asked why that was so, and suggested three possible reasons: because the Spirit is consubstantial with the Son (a reason previously advanced by Karukes); or, because the Son sends the Spirit to creatures; or, because the Spirit proceeds from the Son. The first two reasons they rejected, giving their arguments. That left only the third reason, which was Latin doctrine. They had been bidden by the emperor to put their case simply, but this statement of it was not so simple as it seemed, and it was not until the next evening that the Greeks had a reply ready. A long written document drawn up by Karukes was read by the patriarch, but "there were more ludicrous things in it than true," and by the time the parties met again the Greeks had a new statement prepared. This was from the pen of Blemmydes, who by general consent was the most learned and most acute Greek thinker of his day. The friars managed to translate it before being called on to reply at short notice.

Blemmydes' answer, after questioning whether the Spirit is the Spirit of Christ *from eternity,* tackled the friars' proposition. He argued that the reason for the truth of the assertion was that the Son and the Spirit are consubstantial and he supported his claim with quotations from St. Basil,[69] St. Cyril,[70] and again St. Basil.[71] Patristic proofs, he said, being the words of the most Holy Spirit, were far preferable to syllogisms. But to refute the Latin argument that, if the Spirit is the Spirit of Christ because He is consubstantial with God, then the Father also should be said to be the Spirit of Christ since he also is consubstantial, Blemmydes had recourse to syllogisms. He treated the friars' proposition as a syllogistic argument (which it was not and was not meant to be) and showed how it failed to follow the rules of logic. Then he proceeded to deal with their conclusion, that only Procession could be the grounds that the Spirit is the Spirit of Christ. This is said (he claimed) because the Spirit is always associated with Christ, but the distinction in the Trinity of common substance and personal properties must be remembered and maintained. Procession is a property and therefore of one; hence to "emit" is of one, that is, of the Father. If the Son also emitted the Spirit, Procession would not be a property, but of the substance and so of all three Persons, or the Father and the Son would be reduced to one Person, or there would be two Spirits, since there would be two sources.[72]

After the Greek defense had been read, the emperor (so records the Latin report) "when he heard that they could not defend their own writings, wishing to cover their disgrace, said: 'That will do for that document, because it produces nothing but disputes. Let us continue with your [the Latins'] proposal and do you prove the truth of your assertion from the works of the Fathers.' Thereupon one of our Friars, to whom the Lord had given a gift in the literature of the Greeks, opened a book of St. Cyril on the Ninth Anathema and began to read in Greek."[73] The passages called the Spirit "proper to" and "consubstantial with" the Son,[74] which, said the Friar, was the same as "proceed." The Greeks were in some confusion how to reply and the session closed.

On Thursday, 26 January, in the next session, since the emperor was to depart on the following day, the Latins asked that the subject of the Eucharist should be discussed. The patriarch avoided that subject on the grounds that the other three patriarchs should be consulted. These he would call to a council, and he pressed the Friars to participate in it with them. They repeated their lack of status and proposed instead that the Greeks in council should formulate their ideas on the peace and the reformation of the church and send them to Constantinople, where the friars would await them until the middle of March.

On Friday the envoys went to take leave of the emperor and found the patriarch with him. The emperor asked how the patriarch and the Church of the Greeks could be reconciled with the Roman Church. They replied: "It could be reconciled in this way, if it would believe and profess what the Roman Church believes and obey it in the same way as, and in those matters in which, it obeyed before the schism." The emperor rejoined, "If my Lord the Patriarch were willing to obey the Roman Church, would the Pope give the Patriarch back his rights?" "If," replied the friars, "the Patriarch would give obedience and what is due to his mother, we are convinced that he would find greater mercy than he expects from my Lord the Pope and the whole Roman Church."

With that the friars returned to Constantinople to await the patriarch's report. Instead, in mid-March they received a pressing invitation to attend a synod in Leschera. When they expostulated, a second request arrived, supported by a letter from the emperor and a letter of the patriarch to their local Franciscan superiors. What turned the envoys' decision in favor of accepting was the miserable state of the Latin Empire. The emperor John of Brienne, the chapter of St. Sophia, the prelates of the empire, all of whose advice was asked, were of one accord that they should go and try to persuade Vatatzes to concede a truce of one year.

> Besides, the land of Constantinople was almost without any protection. My Lord, the Emperor, was poor. All the mercenary soldiers had left. The ships of the Venetians, the Pisans, the merchants of Ancona and of other nations were on the point of departing, and some had already gone. Seeing then that the country was stripped bare, we were intimidated by the danger, because the land was set in the midst of enemies—Asen, King of the Vlachs on the north, Vatatzes on the east and south, Manuel on the west.[75]

So it came about that they left Constantinople on 26 March, and from Leschera, which they reached on *Laetare* Sunday, 2 April, they advised the emperor and the patriarch of their presence. Vatatzes was in Nymphaeum and asked them to come to him there. They arrived on 12 April, and the patriarch came the next day. But Germanus was without his prelates and, in spite of the friars' annoyance at the delay and their insistence on starting discussions, they were forced to yield to the emperor's request to defer all activity until after Easter.

The first meeting took place on Easter Monday, when the Greeks wanted to revert to discussion of the *Filioque* on the grounds that it was a more solemn and important subject than the Eucharist, and because the patriarchs and prelates present had not assisted at the meetings in Nicaea. The Latins refused and went on refusing, demanding that Germanus fulfill the promise he had made in Nicaea to answer the question as to whether the Eucharist can be celebrated in unleavened bread or not. Finally the Greeks yielded, but needed a day for consideration. In the next meeting (Wednesday, 26 April), by the sixth hour (the session had begun about the first hour) no progress whatever had been made and the Latins, weary and irritated, declared,

> We see you are wasting time and are trying to avoid our question and do not dare openly profess your beliefs. So we will now disclose our mind without reserve and will tell you what we think of you. We conclude that you condemn our Sacrament in unleavened bread: 1. because of your writings which are full of this heresy, 2. because you dare not reply to the question put to you for fear that your heresy should be obvious, 3. because your deeds prove it—

> for you wash your altars after a Latin has celebrated at them, 4. because you force Latins who approach your sacraments to apostatise and to abjure the sacraments of the Latin Church, 5. because you removed the Lord Pope from your diptychs and we know that you remove none but the excommunicated and heretics, 6. because once a year, as certain people who have heard it have told us, you excommunicate him.

The Chartophylax replied denying that they excommunicated the pope and excusing other practices on the grounds of the execrable behavior of the Latins on the capture of Constantinople.

That evening the friars spoke with the emperor, who had not been present at the debate, to complain about the broken promise and to ask leave to depart. Vatatzes said that he did not want them to go away dissatisfied, because he wished to send his envoys with them to the pope as bearers of rich presents, to gain his good will. The friars did not encourage him; they told him his gifts would avail nothing if the most important thing were lacking—unity of faith. "The Pope does not receive men because of their gifts, but gifts because of men." Vatatzes objected that "emperors Manuel, Theodore,[76] and many others had friendship with the pope in time of schism." The friars answered: "Be assured that we shall not take your envoys with us unless there is a prospect of peace resulting." "If you will not take them, I shall not send them," replied the emperor, but he promised to see that the friars should have the satisfaction in the next session of having their point discussed.

Two days later, Friday, 28 April, there was a gathering in the imperial palace. To the question, "Can the Eucharist be celebrated in unleavened bread?" the archbishop of Amastris replied that it was in no way possible; that St. Peter had established the tradition of leavened bread in Antioch, John in the churches of Asia, Andrew in Achaia, James in Jerusalem; and Peter had taught it to Clement so that in the beginning it was celebrated in that way also in Rome. The Latins asked each patriarch and prelate separately if that was his belief and each one agreed. "We beg you to put that belief in writing and sign it and to give it to us in writing." "And do you," replied Germanus, "write down for us that the Holy Spirit proceeds from the Son and that whoever disbelieves this is on the road to perdition?"

On Saturday the Greek document was duly read and presented. Then the friars delivered their profession of faith about the Procession, which also was read out aloud. It began,

> In the name of the Lord. Amen. The Father is perfect God in Himself; the Son is perfect God born of the Father; the Holy Spirit is perfect God proceeding from Father and Son, and the Spirit proceeds immediately from the Son but from the Father with the Son as medium. That the Holy Spirit proceeds from the Son—the Son has this from the Father. Hence whoso

believes that the Holy Spirit does not proceed from the Son is on the road to perdition.

The document went on to support these statements by quotations from St. Athanasius,[77] St. Gregory Thaumaturgus,[78] and St. Gregory of Nyssa,[79] and each quotation was explained with a little argumentation. Then, after mention of only the names of the Latins—Ambrose, Augustine, and Jerome—recognised as Doctors by the Greeks and upholders of the *Filioque,* a whole series of quotations from St. Cyril followed.[80] The profession ended: "All the holy Fathers, who were in subsequent synods held this [third] synod in veneration and believed the same as it did. And the holy Fathers who went before it had the same mind as it."

Having finished the reading of the statement, the Latin orator reverted to the question of the Eucharist. He told the audience that the Roman Church holds as heretics any who believe according to the Greek document, and he attributed such heresy either to ignorance or to obstinacy. To inform the ignorant and to confirm the obstinate in their sin, he appealed to the Bible and the Fathers. No copy of the Bible was to be found in the conference hall, but the Greeks had quoted St. Paul[81]—Christ took "artos," said to be ordinary, leavened bread. The friars challenged this translation and indicated cases in the Bible and the Fathers where "artos" meant unleavened bread. In other words, they held that the word specified neither leavened nor unleavened. On the other hand, the Latins continued, the Gospel narratives and many a commentary on them show that what Christ actually used at the Last Supper was unleavened bread—and the disciples were bidden to do what he did. At that stage, the Saturday discussion ended.

Sunday was a day of rest. On Monday, Tuesday, and Wednesday the papal messengers waited, expecting to be summoned to a session. No summons came. So they sent asking the emperor's leave to depart. He sent various proposals back to them, and asked them to come to his palace. He suggested a compromise. The Latin Church should give way, omitting the *Filioque* clause from its creed, and for their part the Greeks would recognize the Latin Eucharist. The friars stood firm: "Be sure of this, that my Lord the Pope and the Roman Church will not omit one iota of its faith and nothing that is recited in its Creed." To Vatatzes' despairing query: "How then are we going to make peace?" they gave the answer, "If you really wish to know, we now tell you briefly. About the Body of Christ, you must firmly believe and preach to others that the Body of Christ can be effected both in unleavened and in leavened bread, and all your books written against the faith should be condemned and burned. As regards the Holy Spirit we say that you must believe that the Holy Spirit proceeds from the Son as from the Father, and that you must preach this to the people. But, when once all the books that are contrary to this article are condemned and burned, my Lord the Pope will not insist on your chanting it in your Creed unless you want to yourselves." To this the emperor replied, "What I have heard is no formula of peace; but I will summon the prelates and inform them of what you say."

On Thursday, 4 May, there was a more crowded session than usual. The patriarch opened it by asking the Latins if they still stood by their profession of faith before it was promulgated over the Greek world. "We do," they replied. "It is, indeed, our desire that you and everyone of the Oriental Church should know, acknowledge, and faithfully hold the faith of the Roman Church which we delivered to you in writing." Some discussion followed, becoming gradually more uncontrolled, until Germanus called for silence. But before he could make his own announcement (which the friars thought would be an incitement to the crowd to maltreat them), the Latins burst in: "Do you believe that the Holy Spirit proceeds from the Son or not?" The patriarch answered; "We believe that He does not proceed from the Son." "Then," rejoined the friars, "since St. Cyril anathematized those who do not believe that, you are anathematized; and by denying that the Eucharist can be celebrated in unleavened bread, you are heretics. We separate ourselves from you as heretics and anathematized." With that, they left the conference hall, determined not to eat again that day until they had the permission of the emperor to depart. He gave it, albeit reluctantly, since they were leaving in an atmosphere of discord.

Their return journey was eventful. Towards the end of the second day, 7 May, they were overtaken by a messenger of the emperor chiding them for not having saluted the patriarch before their departure, and by the chartophylax as messenger of the patriarch offering to return to them their written profession of faith and requesting the return of the Greek statement on the Eucharist. The friars refused either to accept or to give. Thereupon they were not allowed to proceed, but in the afternoon they determined to defy the prohibition. The chartophylax retaliated by excommunicating the carriers as they prepared to load the cases of books. This temporarily blocked their departure, but, after some time, in spite of warnings of the dangers of an unprotected journey, the friars set off with what they could carry themselves, leaving the rest in the charge of the imperial escort (8 May). After some hours, the officer of the escort caught up with them and promised them that if they returned he could and would arrange everything. They compromised by waiting in a nearby village and sending friars back for the books. Then, in their presence though not with their consent, the chartophylax opened the packages they had left, found the written statement he wanted and was satisfied. (The friars, however, still had the translation they had made of it.) He then presented them with a letter for the pope (which seems not to have been preserved) and a lengthy statement of Greek belief about the Blessed Trinity. The excommunication was lifted and the papal messengers could continue on their way.

The profession of faith that the Greek synod had produced is imposing.[82] It begins:

> We believe in one Godhead, which is adored and glorified by every creature, in the Father, the Son, and the Holy Spirit; without beginning in respect of a beginning in time; uncreated, creator of all creatures; omnipotent, with power over everything; and without end. We profess that the Father is the natural principle of the Son and of the Holy Spirit, and that the Son and the Holy Spirit shone forth from the Father before all ages without movement or change, not the one first and the other afterwards, but at once Father, at once Son, at once Holy Spirit, the Son and the Holy Spirit proceeding with equal dignity from the Father, the Son by generation, but the Holy Spirit by procession. In the Trinity there are not two sources or two roots or two principles, and we do not profess two Gods. Hence for us whatever is adored is one God, because only the Father is principle and source and root of the Son and the Holy Spirit, as witness the two great luminaries who are above all criticism, St. Gregory Thaumaturgus and St. Gregory the Theologian. That only the Father is principle and root and source of the Son and of the Holy Spirit irreproachable witnesses are the aforesaid saints and the great Athanasius with the whole of the first general council of Nicaea, John Chrysostom, and, above all and especially, the great Denis.

The rest of this long profession (17½ columns of Mansi) is taken up with quotations from the Fathers with an occasional insertion of dogmatic statement or explanation. Of Greek Fathers, Athanasuis, Chrysostom, Gregory of Nyssa, Gregory of Nazianzen, Gregory Thaumaturgus, Basil, Cyril (and Theodoretus), Denis, Maximus Confessor, and John Damascene; of Latin Fathers, Celestine, Damasus, and Gregory Dialogus, are all cited, most of them several times. The document was drawn up by the chartophylax in the names particularly of the patriarchs of Nicaea and Antioch.

Thus, the attempt of the emperor of Nicaea to cultivate closer relations with the pope came to nothing.[83] He had probably been motivated by apprehensions caused by Brienne's taking charge in Constantinople—his prowess as a fighter and the attraction of his name to bring crusaders to the help of the Empire. Vatatzes need have had no fear on either count, for Brienne, practically speaking, did not fight and the troops he brought, unused and ill-paid, melted away. Following the failure of his western diplomacy with the pope, Vatatzes made an alliance with Asen of Bulgaria, affiancing his son to Asen's daughter. He attacked Gallipoli and massacred the inhabitants. Then the combined Greek and Bulgarian forces assailed Constantinople. John of Brienne, with only one hundred and fifty knights, defeated the land-forces; the Venetians destroyed a Greek fleet. In 1236 the attack was renewed, but Constantinople was saved again, this time by an army from Achaia led by Geoffrey II Villehardouin and by Italian ships which broke the blockade. In 1237 Asen, realizing that victory over Constantinople would benefit Vatatzes more than himself, broke off his treaty with Nicaea, but the death of his wife and of his son within a short time of each other, seen as a punishment of God, made him renew it. John of Brienne died in March 1237,[84] while the heir, Baldwin II, was in France trying to raise money and men for the defense of the empire, by then reduced almost to the city of Constantinople itself.

All these vicissitudes of the eastern empire are reflected in Pope Gregory's letters, despite his preoccupation with the political situation in Italy, where Frederick II's plans of domination were maturing in an atmosphere of uneasy peace. The emergency of 1235-36 caused a spate of letters from the Curia to obtain military and financial help for the empire. On 26 January 1236 all the archbishops of France and Hungary were urged to encourage crusaders to commute their vows and to help Constantinople, "for they will gain a double reward of divine recompense, since in that Empire they will be helping also the Holy Land."[85] On 22 November of the same year the clerics of the Morea were to support the patriarch of Constantinople, who was reduced to poverty.[86] A month later the clergy were to give one-tenth of a year's revenue to the emperor,[87] and on 18 January 1238 (repeated in 1239)[88] as much as one-third.[89] To relieve the poverty, the barons of the empire pawned their most sacred relic, the Crown of Thorns. When they were unable to redeem it, King Louis bought the relic for France, where to house it he built the exquisite Church of Sainte-Chapelle. Baldwin, with the support of numerous papal letters,[90] raised troops, but Frederick blocked their passage by sea, in spite of Gregory's request for cooperation.[91] When in 1239 Baldwin, with 700 knights and 30,000 horse, returned to Constantinople, he journeyed overland, passing through Bulgaria by permission of Asen.

John Asen's benevolence towards Baldwin was only one of his changes of policy. When he broke with Vatatzes in 1237, Asen wrote to the pope asking for a legate to treat about the situation of Constantinople. Gregory complied with the request enthusiastically. He appointed the bishop of Perugia, and recommended him to the good offices of the king of Hungary,[92] and, of course, to Asen,[93] who, as a "devoted and faithful son," was encouraged to assist Constantinople and its emperor soon to be aided by a large army of crusaders. But within a few months a papal letter to Bela, king of Hungary, called Asen "treacherous," a renegade and a supporter of heretics, and Gregory was commissioning the bishops of Hungary to preach a crusade against Asen to be rewarded with crusading indulgences.[94] Bela asked that he personally be appointed papal legate of Asen's territory with full power over division of dioceses, the appointment of bishops, etc., so as not, by arriving with an episcopal legate, to give the impression of subjecting the land to the Roman Church.[95] The pope replied, and praised his zeal; he did not, however, make Bela legate but let him nominate for that office any one of his bishops.[96] On the same day Gregory sent out seven letters to further the crusade against Asen.[97] Asen, suitably impressed, returned to the Latin side and facilitated Baldwin's return.

Baldwin, crowned in 1240, ruled over a diminished and poverty-stricken empire, whose church shared in the decline. By 1245 its patriarch lamented that there remained to it only three of its earlier thirty suffragan sees.[98] These apart, only the dioceses in the territories of the princes of the Morea and Athens were still in Latin hands. All the rest had been captured by Greeks or Bulgarians, and Greek or Bulgarian bishops held the sees. In consequence there is little in the registers of Pope Gregory that refers to the Latin-Greek relations. What is there shows that he had not changed the general principles laid down by Innocent III and enshrined in the *capitula* of the Fourth Council of the Lateran—obedience to the Roman See and its representatives, and toleration in respect of rite. But to Prince Daniel of Galicia who, perhaps for protection against a repetition of a Mongol attack, had made overtures to Rome, the pope proposed adoption of the Roman rite. Daniel, he wrote, "was a Christian prince, but was following the customs and rite of the Greeks and Ruthenians and having them observed by others in [his] realm." Gregory, having dilated on the unity of the church and on the primacy of St. Peter within it, exhorted the prince, besides embracing sound doctrine, "devotedly to adopt and observe the rite and customs of Latin Christians," and to put his kingdom under the protection of the Roman See.[99]

Shortly afterwards, answering queries proposed by the archbishop of Bari, Gregory declared that the Greek formula of baptism, not being evangelical, was invalid and that those baptized with it should be baptized afresh according to the Roman form. The sacrament of confirmation, he wrote, was reserved to bishops, and confirmation by simple priests was invalid and should be repeated by bishops. Clerics in major or minor orders who had been baptized according to the Greek form should, "to follow what is safer," be baptized again and have their orders repeated.[100] There was obviously a lively reaction among the Greeks of Apulia and Calabria to this decision, because on 20 February of the next year Gregory wrote again to the archbishop of Bari, bidding him absolve those who had been excommunicated for resisting it, and asking him to send "some of the more learned, with books," to discuss the question, since (apparently) there were various forms of the Greek baptismal rite. Meantime, since it might not prove to be necessary, they could cease rebaptizing, but for children and those coming to baptism for the first time the Roman rite should still be used.[101] "The more learned" from Apulia unfortunately were not able to state their case theologically.[102] Gregory, writing again to Bari on 8 June, said that capable theologians might have to be sought from Greece to debate the question, but five days later in still another letter he wrote that a full discussion would take considerable time; meanwhile the Greeks should "not be disturbed in the use of their rite in this regard." Gregory's doubts, it seems, about the validity of Greek baptism had been banished, and the man responsible for that was the Abbot of Casole in Taranto. Summoned to the papal court, he gladly and successfully defended the rite to which he belonged. In the words of George Bardanes, "he so brilliantly and fearlessly dealt with his adversaries that he was there not as one to be judged, but rather as one to judge and to condemn the foul errors of the heretics."[103]

In conformity with the fourth canon of the Council of the Lateran, Gregory had a bishop of their nation and rite appointed for the Vlachs, since in Hungary there was a great mixture of Cumans, Vlachs, and other peoples among whom Dominicans in number were working.[104] The Vlachs there would not submit to the Latin bishop of the Cumans (a Dominican), but would "receive all the sacraments from some pseudo-bishops following the rite of the Greeks: and others, Hungarians and Germans, dwelling among them were joining in with them." They were, therefore, to have their own bishop but, as laid down by the council, he was to be subject to the Latin bishop of the Cumans. King Bela, in accordance with the solemn promise he had made some few months before to impose obedience to the Roman See on all Christians in his realm,[105] was bidden to enforce acceptance by the Vlachs of the bishop when consecrated.[106]

The same kind of regulation was enforced against Christians of oriental rite in the East. The patriarchs of Antioch and Jerusalem and the archbishop of Nicosia were directed not to allow any Greek priest in the dioceses subject to them "to celebrate at all unless first he had sworn in the presence of his subjects obedience to the Roman Church and had abjured every heresy, and especially that by which they falsely say that Latins by reason of celebrating with unleavened bread are heretics."[107] The sequence in Cyprus is recorded in another papal letter addressed to the archbishop of Nicosia, repeating information received from him. Archbishop Eustorgius had called the Greek archbishop and bishops together and informed them of the instruction he had received. They persuaded him to give them a few days' grace to consider their action. Before, however, the time was up, "with the abbots, monks, and the more important priests, they stripped the monasteries and churches where they lived of all their goods and secretly left the province and [went], it is said, to Armenia, threatening with a sentence of excommunication the rest of the abbots, monks, and Greek priests who [were] left in the province, if they should obey the apostolic order." Gregory told Eustorgius to expel any who refused compliance, to fill the derelict churches with Latin priests or other suitable persons, and to make his excommunication of the recalcitrant Greeks and their abettors effective, if necessary, with the aid of the secular arm.[108]

What the reaction to the order was in the patriarchates of Antioch and Jerusalem is left unrecorded. Antioch at that time had its own problems. The catholicos of the Armenians refused to recognize the Latin patriarch's authority over him. The catholicos was at fault, wrote Gregory, for "there cannot be two heads like a monster in one patriarchate."[109] In the pope's view, all Greek, Armenian, and Georgian abbots and priests within the old bounds of the patriarchate should show obedience and respect to the Latin patriarch.[110] Prince Bohemond V gave the worst example. On mounting the throne he had refused to observe the usual ceremonies of investiture or to swear loyalty to the patriarch and the church of Antioch. Instead, he and his minions contravened every liberty of the church and pitted Greeks against Latins, intruding undesirable people into benefices, not paying tenths, and scorning all admonitions and ecclesiastical censures.[111]

From the very beginning of the Latin patriarchate of Constantinople the popes attempted to restrain the power of the patriarchs in an effort to prevent Venice's acquiring and consolidating its grip on the church of the empire and using it for its own secular ends. Innocent made Morosini withdraw his promise to appoint only Venetians. Both Innocent and Honorius, to dilute the Venetian monopoly in patriarchal elections, gave rights of participation to the prelates of the conventual churches, and these were put in the grant of the emperor. As a result, the first two patriarchal elections after Morosini's death resulted in strife, and each time the Holy See appointed the patriarch. Both of these, Gervasius (1215–19) and Matthaeus (1221–26), were Venetians; both were ambitious and avaricious, and were called to order by serious reprimands from the Holy See. From 1206 almost continuously until 1226 there was an apostolic legate in Constantinople, whose authority was higher than that of the patriarch and who was the pope's spokesman. However, after 1226 Gregory IX presumably felt that he had the situation in hand when he appointed Simon of Tyre (c. 1229–33). The new patriarch was almost certainly not a Venetian, for Gregory took from the emperor the right of nominating prelates to the thirty-two conventual churches and gave it to the patriarch, whom he also made apostolic legate with wide powers. The Holy See seemed to be no longer decreasing, but to be building up patriarchal prestige in the empire which had been sadly reduced in size by the conquests of Theodore Doucas, who had been crowned Emperor in Thessalonica c. 1228.[112]

Simon's successor as patriarch was Nicholas of Santo Arquarto (1234–51). He was from Piacenza and, like Simon, was also nominated legate. It seems that his predecessor (or predecessors) had held Greek priests in prison who refused to commemorate the pope in the Liturgy, and that Nicholas, on his arrival, had not immediately liberated them. In consequence, Patriarch Germanus of Nicaea sent him a letter of reproof and exhortation. He told him that he had hoped for clemency for the incarcerated priests from the new patriarch, but in vain. He exhorted Nicholas to obey St. Peter's admonition to lead the flock "not by constraint but willingly." He himself, Germanus wrote, had been bound to excommunicate Greeks who submitted to Rome or joined in Roman services. Either it should be proved that Greek priests, by not yielding to a church that had changed the creed, had contravened the canons, or they should be released. They are either orthodox or heretics; if heretics, they should be treated kindly; if they observe the canons, they should be set free.[113] It is, however, doubtful whether as late as 1234 Greek priests were held in prison merely because they did not submit to the Latin Church. One suspects that, if there were any priests confined, it was for some other reason.

Chapter V

The Decline of the Latin Empire

The first successor to Gregory IX died sixteen days after his election. More than eighteen months then passed before Innocent IV was chosen on 25 June 1243. Frederick, who had twice tried to capture Rome during the interregnum, placed high hopes of achieving his domination of the papacy in the new canonist pope, who had a great reputation as a diplomatist with an inclination towards policies of peace. But Frederick was destined to be disillusioned, for Innocent IV entertained ideas equally ambitious as any of his predecessors on the powers of the Roman See. St. Peter, he wrote in an encyclical letter, before there ever was any Donation of Constantine, was given the keys (plural): "As Vicar of Christ, by the one he received the power to exercise his jurisdiction on earth for things temporal, by the other in heaven for things spiritual."[1] When Frederick's envoys met Innocent, they were told that there could be no solution of the conflict between the Curia and the empire before the meeting of the council summoned by Pope Gregory—in other words, before the emperor's submission. While further parleys were still in progress, Innocent fled in disguise, first to Genoa (he was a Genoese), and then to Lyons (2 December 1244) in the kingdom of Arles and near the protection of King Louis of France. From there he issued a new convocation of a council, to be held in Lyons, starting on 24 June 1245. One hundred and forty bishops attended it, and in it on 17 July, Frederick was deposed from his thrones and excommunicated. Needless to say, Frederick did not acquiesce. He retired to Sicily, where he lived another five years striving to retain his hold on his territories in Germany and on the Lombard cities. Until 13 December 1250, when Frederick died in Sicily, Innocent did not dare return to Rome.

In the first two years of his reign, that is, until the Council of Lyons,

Innocent actively supported the Latin Empire of Constantinople. Within a few weeks of his election, he wrote to all clerics of "Romania" that they were to give 10,000 hyperpers for the support of the empire on which "our situation depends," and whose loss would be a serious blow to the good name of religion; he was appealing to them, he said, since the Holy See was in a grave financial position.[2] Eleven days later he directed all the clerics in the Morea, Negroponte, and the islands in Latin hands to give a tenth of the revenues of the following year to the support of the Church of Constantinople which "formerly was most opulent and, like a queen among the neighboring provinces, was outstandingly glorious with a certain unique quality, but now, when the Empire of Constantinople is disrupted, it is wretchedly and pitiably reduced almost to a complete extinction."[3] In September he bade his collectors scattered over Europe to scrape together as much money as they could and to send it to Constantinople.[4] In the following year, writing to Geoffrey of Achaia, he declared his "firm intention to be constantly at hand with efficacious counsel and help for the Empire . . . to secure that it should be completely freed from the enemy's yoke." Geoffrey, with others, was to cooperate powerfully for that end with one hundred soldiers for one year, or be deprived of the concession of enjoying the revenues of certain properties of the Church of Constantinople and other churches in his kingdom—a concession that had been granted him for a period of twenty years by Pope Honorius.[5] To see that Geoffrey complied, Innocent sent his own representative, who was also to make the clerics of all the dioceses still in Latin hands, including those in Crete, give one-third of all their incomes of the present year (two-thirds if the incumbent was absent) and half of quadrupeds and birds and other moving creatures, all of which was to go to Baldwin to save his empire.[6] Baldwin was indeed in dire need of money. He was selling what he could to raise funds; from 1444 to 1448 he was in France begging for help.

That the Latin emperor could leave Constantinople for so long a time meant that his enemies were more occupied with each other than with him. Theodore Doucas (crowned emperor of Constantinople in Thessalonica in 1225 or 1228 and prisoner since 1230 in Bulgaria) had been set free by Asen who, on the death of his wife in 1237, married the Greek's daughter. Theodore soon replaced his brother Manuel on the throne of Thessalonica with his own son, John. Manuel took refuge in Nicaea, and, with aid from Vatatzes, won back a part of Thessaly. Meantime, Epirus had come into the hands of Michael Angelus. In 1241 both John Asen and Manuel died. Michael of Epirus marched into Thessaly and took it. John Asen's heir, the child Koloman, sent ambassadors to Vatatzes. There were again three contenders for the throne of Constantinople, and, while he settled with the other two, Vatatzes made a truce with Baldwin.

Vatatzes soon forced Michael Angelus to renounce the ambitious title of emperor for the more modest one of despot of Epirus, but fears of a Mongol invasion on his eastern flank took Vatatzes back to Nicaea before he could make his ascendancy in Thrace complete. In 1246 the young Bulgarian czar Koloman died. From Epirus, Michael took over Albania, and Vatatzes, having occupied southern Bulgaria, got possession of Thessalonica. The marriage of his granddaughter to Michael's son was meant to eliminate rivalry from Epirus, but Michael, at first compliant, suddenly attacked Thessalonica (1251). In the campaign that followed, however, he declined battle and had to sue for peace (1252). The despotate of Epirus was no longer a serious threat.

The Council of Lyons took place while Baldwin was in France. He was actually seated next to the pope when Innocent in his opening discourse at the first formal session dilated on his "five wounds"—the abuses to be corrected in the church, the capture of Jerusalem by the Saracens, the plight of Constantinople, the savageries of the Tartars, and, finally, the persecution of the church by the emperor Frederick. Remedies were applied by the council. Frederick was deposed. It was counseled that the obvious routes of entry into Christian states by the Tartars should be blocked and fortified speedily, and the Holy See would try to help those attacked. Constantinople must be helped, and "the chief reason for this is that by giving aid to the Empire one can by that very fact succor the Holy Land." Hence the half of all revenues of persons nonresident in their benefices for more than six months (with certain exceptions) should go to Constantinople over a period of three years, and one-tenth of the revenues of the Roman See would be given to the same purpose, besides the tenth already earmarked from the same Roman See for the Holy Land.[7] The constitution of the Council of Lyons about the crusade repeated almost verbatim that of the Fourth Lateran Council under Innocent III. But, unlike its model, it did not impose any fixed payments on anyone, apart from the tenth of the revenues of the Holy See.

Subsequently Innocent made up for this lack of pecuniary clauses in favor of the crusades. Jerusalem had been captured by the Khwarismian Turks on 23 August 1244, and, at the very time that the council was being held, Louis IX of France was organizing a crusade to retake it. The pope was unremitting in sending letters throughout western Christendom to encourage men to take the cross, to insist that those who had taken it should fulfill their vow, to demand a monetary equivalent from those who should be legitimately excused, and to solicit legacies and gifts. The papal registers for the years after 1245 do not record any appeals for aid in men or money for Constantinople. They abound in appeals for the Holy Land. It almost seems as if Innocent, having arranged a generous measure of help for the

Latin Empire in the council of 1245, decided that in reality there was little prospect of salvaging it, and so concentrated his efforts on other projects and adopted other, more pacific methods to win the East.[8] He had the wisdom to utilize the religious fervor and single-minded dedication of the two new religious orders—the Dominicans and Franciscans. His predecessor had shown the way. Innocent was not slow to follow. The self-sacrificing and untiring zeal of the friars was more potent than armies.

Even before the Council of Lyons, when the pope's attention was concentrated almost exclusively on the conflict between the ecclesiastical and the secular powers, he was encouraging an ever-growing missionary activity. On 22 March 1244 he gave the Dominicans wide faculties, and a year later he repeated them in more detail to the Franciscans. The Dominicans were invited to evangelize Jacobites, Nestorians, Georgians, Greeks, Armenians, Maronites, and "Mossolini" (dwellers in Mosul? Mussulmans?). The Franciscans were to work with most of these peoples, and, in addition, in the lands of the Saracens, the Alans, the Chazari, the Goths, the Zichi (northwest shores of the Black Sea), the Ruthenians, the Nubians, and the Indians. To achieve so vast a task, they were empowered to do most things a bishop could do except ordain and confirm. They could eat, talk, and communicate with the excommunicate—and absolve them; they could allow clerics who had married after ordination to retain their orders, dwell with their own families, and still enjoy clerical privileges of exemption. They could dispense, absolve, and build churches. If they were not yet priests, they could get themselves ordained by any bishop, and "do other things, which, as best suited the circumstances of time and place, seemed to them to conduce to the exaltation of the divine Name, the spread of the Catholic faith, and the rebuke and frustration of those who opposed sacred traditions."[9] To recommend the efforts of the indefatigable missionaries, Innocent wrote a long letter to the czar of Bulgaria, Koloman, inviting him to unity: the church is one, as many figures of the Old and the New Testaments show; within it Christ is head and Peter is his viceregent. Furthermore, Innocent wrote, it is said that Greeks and Bulgarians are separated from the church; if, in fact, the czar thought a council necessary to restore unity, "We reply that We offer Ourselves ready and prepared to bring a council together at your request and at that of the prelates of Greece and Bulgaria," where the czar's representatives will be welcomed with the fatted calf and the first robe: so give these friars a courteous reception or, if you demand a more honorific embassy, the Pope will send prelates. A slightly abbreviated form of this liberal letter was addressed to "Our Venerable Brethren, All the Patriarchs, Archbishops, Bishops" in the lands of the various peoples to whom the friars were to go.[10]

The friars' labors bore fruit, for various groups of Nestorians and Jacobites wrote to the pope making professions of faith that had no trace of Nestorianism or of monophysitism, and acknowledging the primacy in the Church of St. Peter and of his successors. One urged Innocent to forgive the emperor Frederick. Another asked that his church should be independent of the local Latin patriarchs and archbishops and not have to pay them taxes, and that those of his faithful who married Latins should not be reconfirmed, since they had been confirmed at their baptisms. All acclaimed the merits of the friar missionaries.[11]

King Daniel of Galicia, having once experienced the might of the Tartars, turned to the Latin Church for protection and indicated his readiness for union. Innocent wrote back enthusiastically welcoming him and announcing the arrival of a legate. It seems that the pope expected the Russians to follow the Roman rite, though "in [their] region there have prevailed the customs and rite of the Greeks who superstitiously and culpably have left the unity of the Church," and he authorized his legate to consecrate for them Latin bishops.[12] Later, at the request of King Daniel, he allowed the clerics of Russia "licitly to celebrate the Eucharist according to their own custom with fermented bread and to observe their other rites, provided that these were not contrary to the Catholic faith which the Roman Church holds."[13] In September Innocent appointed a special legate to solemnly preside at the act of union, and he took the possessions of Daniel and his brother Basil under papal protection.[14]

A like mellowing, indeed almost a reversal of policy, was discernible in Innocent's relations with Christians of oriental rite in the East, especially those of Cyprus. On 7 July 1246 he appointed Brother Lawrence, a Franciscan, "Our penitentiary," to be his legate and "an angel of peace" in Armenia, Iconium, Turkey, Greece, and the kingdom of Babylon, and over all Greeks, as well as Jacobites, Maronites, and Nestorians, in Asia Minor, in the patriarchates of Antioch and Jerusalem, and in the kingdom of Cyprus. He was to protect the "Greeks of those parts by whatsoever name they go," not to allow them to be harassed, to redress injuries inflicted by Latins, and to impose on those same Latins amendment, if necessary by the use of ecclesiastical censures.[15] He advised the Greek patriarch of Antioch, the catholikos of the Armenians, and the patriarch of the Maronites, with their suffragans, of the appointment and invited their cooperation with his legate. Lawrence interpreted his commission too widely. He forbade the (Latin) patriarch of Jerusalem to have any dealings at all with his Greek subjects, and led these to believe that they were exempt from patriarchal jurisdiction. Consequently he received a mild correction from the pope[16] but not a cancellation of his faculties; two months later a letter addressed to patriarchs, archbishops, and bishops "in eastern parts" insisted that all censures imposed by the legate on both Latins and Greeks—except on prelates—were to be strictly observed and upheld.[17] A few days later Innocent fanned the flame of Brother Lawrence's zeal. He was to be particularly earnest in trying to win to devotion to the Holy See the Greek patriarch of Antioch and his suffragans. As a general policy he was to observe the demands of justice, so that any schismatics who had once been subject to the patriarch of Jerusalem or other prelates were to remain such after conversion, but others should be subject directly and only to the Holy See. In particular Lawrence should persuade the Greek Patriarch to come in person or by representative to Rome (and Lawrence should pay the expenses if necessary), with the assurance that both "he [the patriarch of Antioch], if he is not already the subject of some patriarch or prelate, and such of his suffragans as enjoy a similar liberty, would be subject to no one else but only to the Apostolic See."[18] The friar was also told to immediately correct cases of minor and obvious injustice suffered by orientals at the hands of Latins, but to refer to the pope issues of major importance.[19]

No more letters addressed to Brother Lawrence as legate are to be found in the papal registers. It seems, then, that his commission lapsed after 1247. But the pope had not let the idea drop or changed his policy. On 22 June of the next year he appointed the cardinal bishop of Tusculum, Eude de Châteauroux, as legate for the East. He informed all the relevant authorities, both ecclesiastical and secular, of the appointment as well as King Louis of France, who was then in the east, and gave the legate ample faculties.[20] The spirit with which Châteauroux was to perform his office is described in the opening paragraph of a papal letter dealing with Cyprus, addressed to him. Châteauroux should show to the orientals "inner bowels of paternal charity" and "a flowing breast of motherly sweetness" to win them from "the hateful schism of oriental separation." Lawrence, the letter continues, had recalled from exile the Greek archbishop of Cyprus; the archbishop with his suffragans had of his own free will presented himself before Eude and made a manual profession of obedience to the Roman Church. Subsequently the Greek hierarchy of the island had sent a list of petitions directly to the Holy See, which amounted to a restitution of the situation as it had been before the making of the agreements under Cardinal Pelagius. They asked to have their former fourteen episcopal sees, and that these should not be subordinate to the local Latin hierarchy but directly dependent on Rome. They requested free jurisdiction over their faithful with application of their own canon law; the payment to them of the one-tenth tithe on monastic revenues and on free Greeks and Syrians; traditional power over the Greek laity with right of appeal, not to Nicosia, but to the pope or his local legate, who also as delegate should receive their profession of obedience to the Holy See; and finally, they asked that the penalties enacted by Cardinal Pelagius for disobedience to his regulations be abolished. Innocent did not immediately reject this proposed reversal of previous papal policy, radical as it was. He recommended it "and their other just requirements" to the earnest consideration of the legate, as the local authority, who should consult unbiased advisers and enact with papal authority "what [he thought was] most to their purpose for the salvation of souls, the lasting peace of the Church, and the wholesome increase of Catholic obedience."[21]

It was perhaps too much to expect that the Latin hierarchy of Cyprus would take happily to the new policy. There is extant the list of excommunications that the Latin archbishop, Ugo da Fagiano, read publicly in "the great cemetery of the church of Nicosia on Palm Sunday of 1251"—the annual proclamation of excommunications common in the West and indeed in the East. Among other proscriptions, all Greeks who had received the sacraments of confirmation and matrimony in the Roman rite were to follow the Roman law of churchgoing, annual confession, etc., and to adhere to the Roman rite only, under pain of bann. "Those are excommunicated who say that the Roman Church is not the head of all Churches and do not obey her." Under a similar penalty were all Greek priests and deacons "who have not made and will not make the act of obedience to the Roman Church and the church of Nicosia," and those who did not pay their tenth honestly to the church of Nicosia. This fairly long list of punishable crimes sounds more hostile to the Greeks than in fact it was. It was no more than a repetition or the application of the regulations enacted in 1220 and 1222.[22]

The Greek archbishop of Cyprus died in 1251, and his suffragan bishops petitioned Rome for leave to elect a successor, which was granted even though the canonical interval for filling the see was past.[23] Cardinal Eude was instructed to deal with any opposition.[24] Opposition there was from the Latin hierarchy and Innocent bade his legate restrain the local Latin archbishop and his suffragans from harassing the Greek bishops. These elected a certain Germanus, and went themselves to Rome to the pope for confirmation of their candidate. But the election was judged invalid and was quashed. Innocent, however, gave them leave to reelect either the same person or another, but this time canonically, and wrote telling the legate to confirm the election without more ado if it should be rightly done. To avoid unnecessary complications, he empowered the Dominican and Franciscan superiors of the area to act, in case the cardinal was absent. The pope, canonist though he was, was riding roughshod over canon law to satisfy and please the Greeks, as the end of his letter showed: "Notwithstanding the aforesaid election which was null, or the constitution of the council [IV

Lateran, against two bishops in one diocese] or any contrary enactment issued, it is said, by Pelagius, Bishop of Albano of happy memory, then legate of the Apostolic See in those parts, even though they were later confirmed by the same See."[25]

Greeks and Latins facing each other in Cyprus on equal terms brought all the doubts and difficulties that Latins harbored about the Greek rite into open expression. The Latin hierarchy, it seems, had formulated their reserves, the Greeks had answered, and the legate, seeking advice, had forwarded both queries and answers to the Holy See. Innocent based his decisions on a broad principle: "Indeed, many of the Greeks have been returning to devotion to the Apostolic See and pay it reverence and attentive obedience. It is, then, lawful and fitting that by allowing their customs and rite as far as with God We can, We should retain them in the obedience of the Roman Church, though We neither can nor wish to defer to them in what might occasion danger for souls or tarnish the Church's good name." On this principle he decided that at baptism unctions as used in the Roman rite should be employed, although the Greek custom of anointing most of the body (which—though apparently he did not realize it—for them constituted the sacrament of confirmation) may be permitted as having little reference to the sacrament of baptism. Confirmation, he declared, should be reserved to a bishop, who can consecrate his own chrism or, if he prefers, obtain it from his patriarch or metropolitan. In the Eucharist, the pope advised that the custom of putting hot water in the chalice is in order, but the sacrament for the sick should not be reserved for more than fifteen days, lest the species of bread deteriorate. In the celebration of mass, provided the form of words used by Christ was retained, Innocent wrote that Greeks might follow their own custom. Candidates for the priesthood should be sufficiently instructed. Altars, chalices, and vestments should be suitable and clean. The Greek customs of Lenten fasting and of married priests acting as confessors should not be made into a source of difficulty. No doubt should be left that fornication between the unmarried is a grave sin. The pope "wishe[d] and expressly order[ed]" that Greek bishops confer the three minor orders that they omitted to so comply with Roman practice. He allowed, however, that "those who [were] already ordained by them in their way, owing to their very great number, might be left in their orders." He was aware that Greeks did not condemn but rather approved of second and third marriages; a second marriage, however, the pope declared, should not be (solemnly) blessed. Marriage between parties in the Greek eighth, or Latin fourth degree of consanguinity or affinity was declared illicit, but such marriages already performed could be considered dispensed and valid. The pope had been led to believe that Greek doctrine about the hereafter coincided with the Latin, but that the orientals did not employ the name "Purgatory" for the place of temporal punishment; thinking it a patristic name, he wished them to use it.[26]

In these decisions Innocent was making no innovations. His decretal, however, was more detailed than any previous papal assessment of Greek customs and, in spite of restrictions in favor of Latin usage in points that later would not be thought fundamental, it has a tone of sympathy with the Greeks, and judges many more customs as unessential and indifferent, and so permissible, than did, say, the Latin hierarchy of Cyprus. The document was to be explained to the Greek bishops of the island, and they were to observe it. The Latin bishops, too, were to observe it, in the sense that they were forbidden to bring pressure to bear on the Greeks in violation of its regulations. This document was destined to form a precedent of legislation and to serve as a model for future directives concerning Greco-Latin regulations.

One of the five wounds that Pope Innocent complained of in his opening discourse at the Council of Lyons was the devastation caused by the inroads of the Tartars. The great westward movement of the Mongols had begun as early as 1223. In 1237 they captured Moscow and Kiev, and in 1241 they attacked separately both Poland and Hungary. The Poles and Germans were crushed on 9 April; the Hungarians on 11 or 14 of the same month. King Bela took flight and appealed despairingly to the pope and to Emperor Frederick for aid. Frederick was too intent on taking Rome. Gregory had no means to help. In 1240, since western arms were engaged fighting the Saracens in Syria and Spain, he had had to plead in anguished terms his inability to aid the queen of Georgia who had begged succor for her ravaged country.[27] So the Mongols reached the Adriatic, and the way into Europe lay open.

Fortunately the death of the great khan led them to retire from Poland and Hungary, and in Europe to retain their hold on Russia only, but their presence there was a constant threat of possible future incursions. The council had urged Christian princes to fortify the likely routes of access and to acquaint the Holy See of impending movements. Pope Gregory had already taken action against the invaders. On 21 July 1241 he ordered the organization of a crusade against them in defense of Hungary and Germany. In 1245, on the eve of the council, Innocent adopted another method—of Christian mission and diplomacy. On 5 and 13 March he signed two bulls. One is a short exposition of faith and the notification that he was sending missionaries to impart that faith. The other is the expression of his indignation and horror at the savageries of the invaders, wherein he also threatens them with the wrath of God, and bids them treat his messengers well and give them safe guides for their return.[28]

It is possible that four separate missions were sent at this time, two missions of Franciscans and two of Dominicans, each with copies of the two letters. One Franciscan, John of Pian Carpino, left Lyons in April 1245. Taking a route through Poland, on 23 February 1246 he met Khan Batu twenty days' journey beyond Kiev. Batu sent him on to the Tartar capital, Karakorum, in eastern Transcaucasia, where he had to await the election of a new great khan. He arrived on 22 July, and it was only on 17 November that he could start home again carrying a missive from the great khan in answer to the papal letters. The pope was told that he should come in person to serve the khan, that his exhortation about baptism was not understood, and that his reproof about the destruction of Christians was not understood for they obeyed neither the khan nor God, and so God had slain them. Furthermore, the great khan asked Innocent how he knew that he was speaking with God's sanction, when God had made the world subject to the khan? He said the Pope must come and seek peace, otherwise he was an enemy. That was not the answer that Innocent had hoped for when Brother John of Pian Carpino reached him again towards the end of 1247.

The Dominicans, Andrew of Longjumeau and Ascelin, made their expeditions separately from Syria. Andrew went via Mosul; Ascelin went first to Tiflis in Georgia and then roughly east. His mission nearly ended in his death when, at the end of May 1246, on entering the camp of Khan Baichu, he refused to make the three genuflections that were customary and insisted that the pope was the greatest man on earth, that is, greater than the great khan. Baichu was only with difficulty placated; he told Ascelin to go to the great khan, but Ascelin refused (the Pope had instructed him to present his letters to the first Mongol chieftain he met), and would neither be persuaded nor forced, thereby risking his life again. Finally Baichu himself sent the papal letters to the great khan. Only on 25 July 1247 could Ascelin start back. With him were two Mongol envoys to the pope, with a general letter from the great khan on the treatment of foreigners, and a letter from Baichu, which was practically the same as that delivered by Pian Carpino. Ascelin reached the coast too late for the autumn sea passage and had to await the first of the next year.

These journeys of the friars were heroic undertakings performed in obedience to the Holy See at the risk of their lives. The results were negative. The Mongols had no terms to offer other than submission to themselves or devastation. When Louis IX, thinking that the Tartars wanted an alliance, sent envoys with rich presents, he got in answer only a demand for submission as an alternative to extermination.

Innocent sent his answer to the great khan by the two Mongol envoys who had accompanied Ascelin to Lyons. He told the khan that, in accordance with his duty to evangelize all creatures, he had sent his missioners to the Mongols "still in the darkness of ignorance," and that their rejection of the message endangered the salvation of their souls. The pope continued that the khan should not glory in his victories, but rather should humble himself before the patience of God; if in the future he desisted from slaughter, possibly he could still experience God's mercy.[29]

To the end of his life Innocent maintained his zeal for bringing the Tartars into the church. Letters from King Louis in the Holy Land had informed him of conversions among them. The pope wrote to his legate in those parts to consecrate bishops from the Dominicans and Franciscans and send them to instruct the new converts.[30] On the other hand, when warned by King Daniel of Galicia of an impending attack by the Mongols for which help was urgently needed, he wrote to all Christians and to all prelates of "Bohemia, Moravia, Serbia, and Pomoravia" bidding them arm and assist—also for their own sakes—and promising them crusaders' indulgences.[31] King Daniel was successful for a time, but finally he had to accept Tartar suzerainty and to agree to break all ties with the Western Church.[32] A year later the pope had the joy of believing that a large group of Tartars had been converted. An Armenian priest posing as a messenger of Khan Sartach reported that leader's conversion following the miraculous cure of his son by Christian prayers: some 50,000 Tartar subjects were supposed to have imitated their chief. Innocent wrote a letter to express his joy and felicitations at so happy an event.[33]

William of Rubruck, King Louis's envoy to the Mongols, had found ambassadors from Nicaea in the court at Karakorum when he arrived there. The emperor Vatatzes, like everyone else in the east, had reacted to the new danger. Besides sending envoys to the great khan, he had made an alliance with the Seljuq sultan, his eastern neighbor. In the West he had found an ally in Frederick II.[34] There had been communication between them in 1238,[35] which led in 1244 to Vatatzes marrying Frederick's bastard daughter (whom he treated abominably) who was only twelve years old. But that did not prevent Vatatzes from renewing his efforts to acquire Constantinople by agreement with the pope. At the end of 1248 he got in touch with Franciscans in Constantinople, asking them to request the pope to send to him John of Parma, the Franciscan minister general, as papal legate. The occasion for this step might have been the mediation of Mary, wife of King Bela of Hungary and daughter of Theodore I Lascaris of Nicaea, who asked papal permission to communicate with Vatatzes and persuade him to union. Innocent replied enthusiastically on 30 January 1247, and gave her every encouragement, though whether in fact she later took any steps is not known.[36] Innocent was so pleased with Vatatzes' request and so optimistic of results that he could not get John of Parma on his way quickly enough. He provided him with letters directing him "to see that you hold careful parleys with the Greeks and especially with the noble Vatatzes and the prelates, that they may wisely return to the obedience and the reverence of the Roman Church, mother and mistress of all the faithful, from which they have for long withdrawn themselves."[37] In another letter of the same date he gave his legate more detailed instructions. A prerequisite of unity (he wrote) was orthodoxy in respect of the Procession of the Holy Spirit. "We wish and by the authority of these present We enjoin that . . . you warn and exhort them effectively to think, believe and hold, confess with their voice and write in their Creed, precisely what the same [Roman] Church thinks, believes, observes and expressly professes in its Creed." Also Pope Innocent authorized John of Parma to summon and preside at a council in the East, in order to have the *Filioque* clause inserted in the Greek Creed "because some sagacious persons among the Greeks themselves assert (what is true) that the Roman Pontiff (whose alone is the power of convoking councils) can, when a council has met, by his own and the council's authority, harmonize our Creed with that of the Greeks." Warned perhaps by the events at Nymphaeum in 1234, he limited his legate's powers to the sole question of the *Filioque*: "But We wish that nothing else shall be decreed by apostolic authority in that council and that you should not give authority or consent or favor in the making of any other decisions or lend your presence thereto."[38]

John of Parma and his companions (two of whom, Dreux of Bourgogne and Bonaventure of Iseo, he chose in Constantinople for their knowledge of Greek and the Greeks) met the emperor, Patriarch Manuel, and the Greek prelates in Nymphaeum. Privately with Vatatzes they tried to cool his friendship with Frederick II,[39] but without success. At some time in the winter of 1249–50, they held discussions with the Greek bishops. No Latin report of these has been preserved, but Blemmydes in his *Curriculum Vitae* tells of his part in them, and incidentally indicates, though very briefly and only to refute it, the kind of argument the Latins used. These asserted that "the Father acts through the Son, and the Son through the Spirit; hence the Son is from the Father and the Spirit from the Son." Blemmydes replied that the Gospels record that the Father acts through the Son, but that the Son acts in the Spirit. But (the remainder of his argument ran) even if it were true that the Son acts through the Spirit, it would not follow that the Spirit is from the Son. The hand acts through the fingers—these are connatural—but it is not the cause of the fingers; hand and fingers have a common cause. So the Son acts through the Spirit as being connatural with Him; the Father through the Son as connatural and substantial cause; the Son through the Spirit as connatural, but not as principle of the Spirit, which the Father alone is. Similarly, the Son is the image of the Father as caused by Him and because the Father is beheld in the Son. The Spirit is the image of the Son as beheld in the Spirit, but not as caused by Him. It is characteristic of the image to reflect, not to possess, the archetype. The Latins apparently replied by quoting from St. John's Gospel, "He will take what is mine."[40] The meaning of this (retorted Blemmydes) is shown by Christ's next words: "All that the Father has is mine." As the Son receives all from the Father, so does the Holy Spirit; this quotation from St. John proves rather the Greek doctrine than the Latin. "So none of these arguments would in any way be proof that the Son is principle of the Spirit."[41]

The discussions once again, it seems, reached no conclusion and failed to foster ecclesiastical unity. Nevertheless, Vatatzes sent back with John of Parma a numerous embassy of his own, though at the same time he was sending a contingent of troops to swell the army of Frederick II.[42] Vatatzes needed Frederick's cooperation to get his envoys to the pope. He asked Frederick to transport them. Frederick wrote in answer denouncing the pope, who had excommunicated the Greeks as heretics and had condemned Vatatzes' own marriage as that of a Latin princess with a heretic. Frederick sadly remonstrated with the Greek emperor for receiving papal emissaries at his court; Vatatzes should first have consulted Frederick, who knew the western situation better. Nevertheless (Frederick wrote), he would send ships to Durazzo, though the representatives of the pope would have to wait there for their passage until he had first interviewed the Greek embassy.[43]

Both the Greek and the Latin envoys were in due course transported from Durazzo to Apulia. The friars were allowed to continue their journey to the pope at Lyons. The Greeks had to stay in Italy,[44] detained first by Frederick until his death in December 1250, and then by Manfred, who assumed the government after him. The friars arrived at the papal court with their news of the coming of Greek ambassadors; this news probably prompted Innocent to write a letter of welcome to them, a letter full of joy and of hope that union of the churches was on the way. It is addressed to "Our venerable brethren, archbishops and bishops and dear sons, the noblemen . . . . Great Interpreter and . . . kalithito, legates of the Greeks, coming to the Apostolic See."[45] But Innocent had to wait a year and a half before he could learn if his hopes were well founded. He had left Lyons and was resident in Perugia (where he arrived on 5 November 1251) when at last the imperial envoys came into his presence. They were bearers of a letter addressed to "the most holy and most wise and most blessed Pope of the Elder Rome, Lord Innocent, bishop of the most exalted Apostolic throne" from "Manuel by the mercy of God Archbishop of Constantinople, New Rome, and Ecumenical Patriarch, with my most holy brethren and bishops."

The letter is a very long and wordy disquisition on the desirability of ecclesiastical peace, and praise of the pope for his efforts to achieve it. Towards the end it becomes more precise: "Hence we approve with all our hearts and desire in Christ the healing of the long-standing schism; indeed we seek rather the complete union of the one Church of Christ and an unbreakable bond of communion, or, it would be more fittingly said, of a unity of nature of the separated parts to last for all ages." The Greeks were grateful for the humble and learned envoys the pope had sent. So they in return had chosen and sent spiritual and learned men,

> ambassadors of peace, and had entrusted them with the inquiry into and settlement of all relevant questions, whether concerned with the divine and holy ecumenical council or with the honor of Your Holiness or with the just requests on our part from your great Holiness and Majesty. Wherefore we know and believe that Your Holiness will show them great benevolence and will inspire them with courage and grant them freedom of speech, imbued as you are by very love and adorned with the sum total of virtues. Whatsoever Your Holiness together with our envoys shall conclude and ratify will be accepted by them as by all of us; and whatsoever they with Your Holiness shall conclude and ratify, do you accept as [agreed to] by us all.[46]

This apparently complete recognition by the patriarch of Nicaea-Constantinople and his prelates of papal primacy must have delighted and encouraged Pope Innocent. Unfortunately and surprisingly there is no official record of what more detailed proposals the Greeks made by word of mouth, of the Latin reaction to them, of negotiations, or even of a papal answer to the letter of the eastern hierarchy. Theodore Lascaris, heir to the throne of Nicaea but not yet emperor, wrote to Nicephorus Blemmydes referring either to this mission of Greek prelates to the pope or to the later one of 1254. (His letter is undated; it mentions the archbishop of Sardis, who was certainly a member of the second mission and only probably of the first. Nevertheless, Lascaris was probably commenting on the first mission.) He concludes that the papal conditions "amount to obedience on our part," though the pope promised the Greeks all their rights, and at a convenient time, a council. Sardis, he says, was optimistic, but Lascaris thought that his enthusiasm was due in part to papal generosity and he, Lascaris, "from certain words and signs [thought] it difficult to see much result."[47] Our only other information on the Greek mission comes from the diarist, Nicholas of Curbio: "They [the Greeks] were received with honor by the Pope in person. After conversations on various matters between them and the Sovereign Pontiff, they betook themselves back home to take counsel on those matters with the aforesaid Vatatzes, their master"[48]—probably in the spring of 1252.

The sequel seems to suggest that their verbal message fell far short of the promise expressed in the letter of the patriarch and his synod, because for some three years after the departure of the embassy nothing more was done.

Innocent, for all his real enthusiasm for union of the churches, sent no group of friars to the East to continue and settle the negotiations. Vatatzes (the power behind a willing patriarch) took no further diplomatic action. To counter any more direct move on the part of the Greek to achieve his ambition, and perhaps to make sure that Constantinople—the essential bargaining asset in all negotiations—remained in Latin hands, Innocent instructed the bishops of Negroponte and Olene to pay 1,000 silver marks from the resources of their churches (or, if these were not sufficient, from the possessions of Latin clerics in "Romania") to the doge of Venice and the prince of Achaia, provided that these "shall see to the protection for a full year of war of the city of Constantinople, enough for its maintenance and defense against the assaults of Vatatzes."[49]

The Latin patriarchate had been vacant since the death of Nicholas in the middle of 1251, a circumstance that could have favored a compromise with the Church of Nicaea. That Innocent filled the see on 15 February 1253 by nominating Pantaleon Giustiniani implies that he saw no immediate prospect of church unity. Pantaleon, as was usual, became apostolic legate and was given the revenues of vacant benefices for the support of the empire and of his see. He was allowed also to sequestrate revenues of absentee beneficiaries to force them to return to their cures.[50] The situation seemed to be static, except that the city was becoming ever poorer,[51] and Vatatzes had by now no dangerous rival to thwart his ambition to regain the empire.

Nevertheless, Vatatzes hesitated to assail the formidable defenses of the city on the Bosphorus, and at the same time to defend himself against both the troops that would inevitably come to Constantinople's support from Achaia and against the power of a Venetian fleet. It would certainly be less costly in men and money to secure the city by diplomacy with the pope. So in early 1253 he sent a new embassy to the Holy See. It consisted of the archbishops of Cyzicus and Sardis, Count Angelus, and Great Interpreter Theophylactus, with a suitable entourage. When they arrived in Apulia they were detained for several months by Conrad, son of Frederick II, and did not reach the papal Curia until the late summer. Innocent was at that time in Assisi. He went to Rome on 6 October 1253 and from there to Anagni in the spring of 1254. The envoys went with him. Then, "having asked and received leave from the Sovereign Pontiff, they returned with my Lord's written answer to their own Lord, Vatatzes."[52]

This Greek embassy brought specific and far-reaching proposals.[53] A document from the reign of Pope Alexander IV (Innocent's successor) reads as follows:

> These are the clauses of the acknowledgment and request, which earlier the Archbishops of Cyzicus and Sardis and Count Angelus and the Great In-

terpreter Theophylactus proposed on behalf of the Emperor Kalojan and the Church of the Greeks to our predecessor Innocent P.P. of happy memory and to the Apostolic See:

1. Namely, the complete acknowledgment and profession of the primacy in the Catholic Church over the other patriarchal Sees [as belonging] to the Roman See and its Supreme Pontiff;
2. canonical obedience to be given to the aforesaid predecessor [Innocent IV] and his successors canonically entering into office;
3. faculty of appealing to the Roman Church when sacred persons of the Church of the Greeks deem themselves oppressed by their superiors;
4. free recourse to the Roman See in questions which may arise between prelates and other Greek ecclesiastics;
5. obedience also in decisions which the Roman Pontiff shall promulgate, if not opposed to the sacred canons;
6. further, in councils the first place and the first signature, if signatures are to be given, to belong to the same Pontiff;
7. in questions of faith, if such should arise there, to give his opinion before others and to have precedence in proposing his judgment to its will (*suaeque voluntati praeferre iudicium*) which, provided it does not oppose gospel and canonical precepts, the rest will obediently adopt and follow;
8. in other causes and affairs of ecclesiastical persons which shall be dealt with in councils, the rest will acquiesce in the decisions which the authority of the Roman Pontiff shall dictate, provided these do not conflict with decrees of the sacred councils.
9. Besides this, the same envoys requested that the sovereignty of the city of Constantinople should be restored to the oft-mentioned Kalojan, and the rights of the patriarchal Sees both there and elsewhere to the [Greek] patriarchs, and that the Latin Emperor and Patriarchs should be removed from the same city and Sees, the Patriarch of Antioch being left in that city for his lifetime.

Such were the proposals presented to Innocent IV by the Greek envoys. The document goes on to record something of his reaction to them:

> Assuredly, with the counsel of his brethren (when I was of lesser rank than I am now), Our predecessor of happy memory, Pope Innocent, approved the aforesaid offer and declaration (*oblationem professionemque*) in order that, through acceptance of such goodwill for the welcome progress resulting from so great a reconciliation, the whole community of the faithful might be rejoiced, hoping that, once the aforesaid Church had by God's grace returned to the embrace of maternal peace, by a spontaneous dilatation of its love it would widen the bounds of its offer and declaration.

Innocent, then, agreed to the Greek proposals—they were far too complete and favorable to refuse—but with some reservations, which he hoped further negotiations would render unnecessary. One reservation was in respect of the controversial *Filioque*. While the Greeks in clause seven had promised obedience and submission to the opinion of the Holy See on doctrinal matters moved in councils, "provided they were not in conflict with gospel and canonical precepts," they expressly excepted the *Filioque* clause. Pope Alexander wrote:

> Our predecessor considered it very illogical, that in a council that article alone of the Nicene Creed, in which the Greek Church seems to differ somewhat from the Roman about the Procession of the Holy Spirit, was excepted by the aforesaid orators from the judgment of the Roman Pontiff, because the Greek Church would not agree to its definition in a council, unless this should establish what was defined by the witness of authentic scripture or a divine utterance (*divinum oraculum*). For the grounds on which the Greek Church was moved to refuse him in this one article the power of defining that it does not deny to him in the other articles of the faith did not seem reasonable.

But provided the Greek Church in its faith in the Blessed Trinity agreed in every respect in a Catholic manner with the Roman, Innocent saw no need to make any change in its traditional creed.

He did, however, foresee difficulties in respect of the *quid pro quo*, the restoration of the Greeks to power in Constantinople, and that from the legal standpoint of justice:

> Further, in regard to the aforesaid sovereignty, the same envoys received this reply from the same predecessor: that on that count, if the Latin Emperor has not been cited, right given by law does not allow of anything being settled, because a settlement would seem to be voided unless it were a process against one who either had pleaded guilty or been convicted. But so as not to omit anything that might conduce to the reconciliation of the Greek Church, he offered his earnest services to bring about a composition between Kalojan and the Emperor, confident that by his efforts he would succeed.

If he failed in that, Innocent proposed a procedure at law wherein he would do all he could in favor of the Greek cause and that the greater would be his zeal the more Vatatzes should be "a most dear and exalted son." The situation of the patriarchal sees could not be changed without a judicial decision, and so they should be left as they were unless the council, on which both Vatatzes and Innocent were agreed, should find a solution. With regard to the patriarch of Constantinople in particular, Innocent, to meet the emperor's request as much as he could, suggested that Manuel should immediately enjoy the title, "Patriarch of Constantinople," and as soon as the emperor in any way got possession of the city, should return to his ancient seat and there rule his subjects, the Latin Patriarch continuing to rule his own.

There is no reason to think that this *oblatio et professio* of the Greeks was anything but genuine and sincere. Vatatzes had already shown his willingness more than once to effect a compromise between church and state to secure the prize of Constantinople. Patriarch Germanus had made overtures of union to Rome but nothing came of them. His successor Manuel was more forthcoming. His letter to Innocent IV clearly indicated his readiness at least to discuss Roman terms and his acknowledgment in advance of Roman primacy. But the conditions proposed *viva voce* by the envoys who carried the letter (accepting the date of the letter as 1251) must have been either far too vague and imprecise or to have fallen far too short of what Rome demanded as a minimum; otherwise there would not have been the period of complete inactivity that followed.

But even the proposals offered in 1254, though they seemed to be a complete acceptance of what the popes had been repeatedly demanding over the last half century, did not mean that the schism was ended. The reluctance to let the *Filioque* question be settled except by a "divine utterance" still left the main theological obstacle to unity unresolved, and the phrases in three of the clauses about conformity with the canons would need a deal of good will and ingenuity to prevent them giving rise to new difficulties. Whether, and how, the Greeks should show their recognition of papal primacy (there is no mention recorded on either side of an "oath of obedience"), and what degree of papal interference in the organization and administration of the patriarchate the Greeks would bear, were still matters to be settled. Further, the central purpose of the Greek action, essential to the whole project—the restoration of imperial and ecclesiastical power to them—was doubtful of execution. Innocent could not (and probably would not have been allowed to) dismiss the Latin emperor and patriarchs against their wills, if no crime could be alleged and proved against them. Emperor Baldwin was not another Frederick, an avowed enemy of the Church who had been excommunicated many times and was thought to be even heretical.

All the same, the *oblatio* as it stood was the most promising opportunity of restoring unity to the church in the long years of schism. Innocent meant to utilize it to the full. His attitude to the Greeks of the East, particularly to those of Cyprus and to the Greek patriarch of Antioch, through his legates Brother Lawrence and the Cardinal of Tusculum, shows that a policy of reconciliation and of minimizing obstacles was no new impulse of the moment, but one of settled conviction, long-standing and sincere. Not to let delay in following up the negotiations lessen the promise of the situation, he commissioned Constantine, Bishop of Orvieto, to go to Nicaea.[54]

But Patriarch Manuel died in August 1254 and Emperor Vatatzes died on 3 November 1254. Pope Innocent IV died on 7 December 1254, and the commission of the Bishop of Orvieto lapsed.

On 28 May 1249 Innocent IV wrote to the general of the Dominicans that in the midst of all the strife that characterized his reign he had no other purpose "than to protect the Catholic faith with God's help, and to gain souls for Him . . . . For there is a most weighty reason for sorrow when We see many perish from blindness, some indeed because they know nothing of the way of salvation, many, however, because they have left the way to their loss."[55] These words sum up fairly Innocent's attitude to the East. The faith he was concerned to preserve was the faith of the Latin Church of which he was the head. That and that only was for him the true faith, which everyone should acknowledge, and, in the tradition of that day, acknowledgment was to be shown by canonical obedience. Also, he probably could hardly believe that schismatics (those who "have left the way to their loss") could be in good faith, at least not their hierarchies and leaders. In these respects he was not in advance of his time. But in many other respects he was. He had a great sympathy for the Greeks,[56] and allowed many things that his predecessors and most of his successors for many years to come would not consider. In his day there were a Maronite, an Armenian, and in Antioch even a Greek patriarch, with their rights (even though they were charged to be receptive of advice from papal legates). There were two archbishops in Cyprus in spite of the enactment of the Fourth Lateran Council; there was freedom to function for married clergy; use of the oriental liturgy, and protection from Latin oppression. Nevertheless, like all his coreligionists, he held the Latin rite in higher esteem than the Greek, and would have liked to see all Christians adopt it.[57]

For their part the Greeks despised the Latin rite. Both Latins and Greeks were intolerant, but the Latins less than the Greeks. At least, they did not deny the validity of the Eucharist in leavened bread; they condemned only the rejection by the Greeks of the Latin use of unleavened bread; they did not rebaptize or wash altars where Greeks had celebrated and their lists of ecclesiastical grievances had less in them of the petty than the Greek. Intolerant they both were, but even in that, they should be judged within the context of their day and compared with one another, not (as is too often done) with the liberality of modern ecumenism.

Chapter VI

The Greeks Regain Constantinople

When Frederick II died in 1250, Innocent IV had taken steps to gain control of Sicily, which was a papal fief. Conrad, Frederick's heir, invaded Italy to retain possession of it for the German crown, but on 21 May 1254 he died in Apulia, leaving as his heir a two-year-old son, Conradin, in Germany. Innocent, who had thought of offering the crown of the kingdom of Sicily (comprising southern Italy with its chief city of Naples and Sicily proper) to some non-German prince, desisted on Conrad's death and allowed Manfred, an illegitimate son of Frederick II, to act as baillie. But Manfred got possession of Frederick's treasure and Saracen troops, challenged the papal army, and soon made himself master of southern Italy. At this point Innocent died; he was succeeded five days later by Rinaldo Conti, cardinal-archbishop of Ostia, who took the name *Alexander IV*. Without the strength of character of his predecessor, he was less capable of facing the growing challenge from Manfred.

Engaged in meeting this situation, Alexander did not follow up the negotiations with the Greeks. The initiative in reopening them came from the new emperor of Nicaea, Theodore II Lascaris. Unlike his father, Theodore was interested as much in philosophy and theology as in politics; he thought himself a master of both, capable of ruling not only the state but the church as well, and indeed of deciding also about its doctrine. Only on his father's death did he become emperor. Vatatzes, while he lived, thought his son too immature and capricious to associate him with himself on the throne. Since Patriarch Manuel had died shortly before Vatatzes, Theodore had to find a successor to perform his coronation. He passed over Nicephorus Blemmydes, a very learned monk greatly favored for the office, in favor of a simple monk, Arsenius Autorianus, not yet in sacred orders, a man of holiness of life but of little education.[1] Once crowned, Theodore was called immediately to face hostilities from Bulgaria and Epirus. In this he was successful. He then turned his attention to the negotiations his father had started and which had been interrupted by his death. He sent two envoys, Theodore Dokianus and Demetrius Spartenus, with letters couched in obscure diction to the pope and to some cardinals, and doubtless a verbal message that was clearer than his letters.[2] His request was urgent. He wanted the appointment of some competent person on the Latin side to continue the negotiations. The pope hastened to meet the request. Alexander nominated as his legate Bishop Constantine of Orvieto, who had been selected for the same office by Innocent in 1254, and bade him present himself at the Curia within ten days, to accompany the Greek envoys on their return to Nicaea.[3]

Constantine also received another letter which contained, besides the terms of union proposed by Vatatzes to Innocent, Alexander's report of his predecessor's reaction to them,[4] which ended with instructions on how to conduct the negotiations in various possible contingencies. The pope instructed that if Constantine could get concessions more useful and honorable to the Roman Church and more conducive to the reconciliation of the two churches, he should not incontinently put forward the Greek proposals either by expounding them or by accepting them; but, if there was no such prospect, he could accept them in the name of the pope and of the Roman Church. Furthermore, if the Greeks wanted to arrive at a conclusion, but on conditions that as legate he had not the power to grant, he could, provided he was confident of a final reconciliation, receive their acts of canonical obedience (if they wished to make them) and leave the rest to future negotiation. Alternatively he could arrange for a Greek embassy with plenipotentiary powers to return with him to the pope to settle matters. If, finally, he should succeed in his negotiations according to his commission, he could fix a convenient time and place and summon a council "in those parts."[5] In other words, as a good ambassador, if he could get a better bargain for his principal than that offered by the Greek proposals, he should do so; otherwise he should act on them as they stood.

Bishop Constantine carried with him letters for the emperor and the patriarch. The papal missive to Theodore was one of warm congratulation and encouragement. The pope, with his brethren's (the cardinals') agreement, was sending a prudent envoy "to renew the reply given *viva voce* by Our Predecessor to the proposals" of the earlier imperial messengers, which Pope Alexander, like Innocent IV, accepted for the sake of peace. So he had given plenary power to the bishop of Orvieto to bring the negotiations to a successful conclusion. Peace between the churches (Alexander wrote) would be Lascaris' greatest claim to honor and would recommend his imperial dignity to kings and princes, and give his throne the stability of unwaning strength.[6]

The letter "to the Patriarch, archbishops, bishops and all dear sons, the totality of the clergy within the Empire of the Greeks," was more theological. Alexander dilated first on unity of the church and on the position of St. Peter within it—and hence of the Roman See—before recording, in the same words as to the emperor, the story of Vatatzes' action and his own mandate to the Bishop of Orvieto to accept the imperial propositions and to continue and conclude the negotiations.[7]

Constantine set out armed with these letters and with a sheaf of safe-conducts. Among others, the Latin emperor and the Latin patriarch of Constantinople were bidden to assist, if need be, "the legate of the Apostolic See commissioned to go to the region of the Empire of the Greeks for the reconciliation of the Oriental Church." As legate he was empowered to receive "into the bosom of the Universal Church" the emperor Theodore and others who so wished, and to absolve from all kinds of irregularities clerics who had received Holy Orders in schism, and to permit them to retain their dignities and benefices. He could commandeer the assistance of any friar or religious that he wished.

The bishop of Orvieto departed on his mission in the spring of 1256 and met the Greek emperor, not in Nicaea, but in Thessalonica. Theodore was there for a double purpose, to conduct a campaign against the Bulgars and to celebrate the marriage of his daughter, Mary, to Nicephorus, the son of Michael Doucas, despot of Epirus. For this latter reason, there were also gathered in Thessalonica thirty Greek bishops. George Acropolites mentions the papal legation in his *Annals,* but not as an event of major importance: "So the Emperor went off to the east, while I was detained by affairs in the west. Leaving Thessalonica, I arrived at Verroia, for in that town were also the legates of the Pope, whom I was by order of the Emperor to dismiss. Having remained there for a short time on account of the dismissal of the envoys and of other business, I went from there and struck the road leading to Albanum."[8] This very brief mention gives the impression that the papal mission was detained outside Thessalonica and finally was sent back unheard. So contemptuous an action on the part of the emperor towards the pope was in itself most unlikely, and in fact it did not occur. Theodore was in the neighborhood of Thessalonica between 14 September and 23 October, and in the general area until 6 December, when he returned to Nicaea. When and for how long he spoke with the papal envoys is not known, but speak with them he did. After the negotiations the patriarch Arsenius sent a letter to the pope. The first two-thirds of it is a wandering disquisition on peace, unity, and schism. The last third deals with the legate's mission. The Latins were "received, welcomed, and worthily honored by the most mighty and holy King and God-crowned Emperor'' and by the patriarch also. Lascaris wanted a quick and positive conclusion. But the legate could not give what the emperor demanded: ''He had a part of the power of Your Holiness—nay, rather not even a part, for to receive he was the perfect legate, but to give back in exchange he had no authority at all, not the slightest.'' So the legate went back to Rome to seek authorization. When he should return, five hundred bishops could be gathered in council with the utmost speed and the negotiations completed.[9]

Constantine, in other words, was empowered to do everything except the one thing that emperor and patriarch wanted: he could not give them immediate possession of Constantinople. With that, the promising negotiations ended. There is no record of any further communication between pope and emperor. The project of union foundered on the question of political possession of the Queen of Cities. But the failure of the attempt came not from the Greek Church but from the Greek emperor, for many of the highest-ranking metropolitans, together with their patriarch, were in favor of union.[10] Some few years later George Metochites summed up his account of this whole incident: ''Whoso reflects on the full story of these negotiations will assuredly perceive that whatever was then done in respect of the Church was the action of the whole body of the churchmen of that time and had their approval, and that there was no other obstacle [to success] except what arose from the political condition and controversy.''[11]

Emperor Theodore Lascaris died in August 1258.

Pope Alexander early in his reign had done something to support the Latins in Greece. On 2 February 1255 he had commissioned certain clerics of the empire to organize help for the Morea, ''which,'' he wrote, ''is so beset by necessity that unless help is quickly forthcoming through the foresight of this same [Holy] See, more serious dangers can overtake them.''[12] His help was also required farther east. The little territory left to Christians in Syria was torn by internal strife—Hospitallers fighting against Templars and, more destructively, Venetians, with Pisan help, against the Genoese. The pope's intervention in 1258 came too late to prevent the destruction of a Genoese fleet of thirty-two ships at Acre and the expulsion of all Genoese from the city, to the benefit of their enemies, who divided their quarter between them. The patriarchate of Jerusalem was vacant and disordered; Alexander nominated James Pantaléon, bishop of Verdun, first as patriarch and then also as apostolic legate. The properties of the patriarch of Antioch were so ravaged by frequent invasions that he had been promised by Innocent IV the revenues of the next see to fall vacant in his patriarchate or in Cyprus. Alexander gave him the See of Limasol, 21 February 1256.[13] Alexander continued the work of his predecessor in other respects by renewing the commission to the friars to work in various countries with the same ample faculties as of yore, and by providing for the maintenance of the ten poor clerical students that Innocent had sent to the University of Paris to learn Arabic and other oriental languages.[14]

Alexander had not the strength of character of his predecessor. When controversy over the Greek Church of Cyprus erupted once again, he ordered a thorough inquiry, but the result was the reintroduction of the old Latin domination. The insistence of the Latin hierarchy on their status prevailed. The vision of Innocent IV was lost. It will be recalled that in the last years of his reign Innocent IV, notwithstanding the ninth canon of the Fourth Council of the Lateran (1215) and other regulations, had allowed the Greek bishops of Cyprus to reelect Germanus as their archbishop and metropolitan after his first election had been quashed as uncanonical, and had made him exempt from the local Latin hierarchy, subject only to the Holy See. The Latin archbishop of Nicosia, Hugh, nevertheless summoned Germanus to appear before him to answer various charges. The Greek claimed his papal protection and did not obey. In consequence, he was excommunicated by Hugh, who subjected Germanus and many of his faithful to other oppressions. Germanus went to Anagni to complain to the pope, who appointed the bishop of Tusculum, late apostolic legate in Cyprus, to hear the case between the Greek archbishop and some procurators of the archbishop of Nicosia then by chance at the Curia.

The Latin plea was that Germanus's election was invalid since the bishops who elected him, being excommunicated, had no right to do so; that Pope Celestine had ejected the Greek bishops from their sees and had established a Latin archbishop with three suffragans as the official hierarchy for the whole of the island, with the rights to tenths, etc., formerly of the Greek Church; and that the legate Pelagius had limited the number of Greek bishops to four and made them subject to the Latin bishops, an arrangement subsequently confirmed by Rome. The legal process dragged on in interminable argument, until Germanus, pleading poverty, begged the pope to impose a settlement, "so that under obedience to the Roman Church the Greeks might live at peace with the Latins."

This is in brief what Alexander decreed: (1.) For the future there should be only four Greek bishops and they should reside in the towns allotted to them by the legate Pelagius. (2.) When a See was vacant, a successor should be elected and the Latin bishop of the area should approve the election, summon the other Greek bishops to perform the consecration, and give jurisdiction to the newly consecrated prelate when he had received from him an oath of obedience to the Holy See and to the archbishop of Nicosia. (The formula of the oath was added.) (3.) Only the pope should condemn, depose, or translate Greek bishops. (4.) The Greek bishops should have jurisdiction over their Greek institutions and faithful, and in legal actions between Greeks, but if a Latin were involved it should be decided by the Latin bishop of the region; there should be right of appeal from the Greek court to the local Latin bishop and, if necessary, thence to the archbishop of Nicosia. (5.) In any diocese there should be only one consistorium of ordinary jurisdiction for the Greeks. (6.) Greek bishops and abbots with their priests should once a year attend the diocesan synod (but not the provincial one) summoned by the Latin bishop and obey its regulations, unless these clashed with their rite. The Latin bishop could make a visitation of the Greeks with rights similar to those of a metropolitan, but only five, four, or three times a year (according to diocese), and they should be entitled to a fixed stipend of three hundred solidi from the Greeks. (7.) If the needs of the Greeks necessitated other visitations, these should be done gratis, since the goods of the church are given to bishops for the expenses of their pastoral office. (8.) The right to tenths in the island belonged to the churches of the Latins, and all men should pay them. Though the Church of the Greeks would not in future possess a metropolitan, the existing archbishop was to retain that dignity for his lifetime and to have his abode in Soli, whose present bishop will be transferred to Famagusta. (9.) Germanus should retain metropolitan rights over the Greek bishops of consecrating and making visitations, but on his death there should be no other Greek archbishop. (10.) As bishop of Soli, Germanus should take the oath of obedience to the Latin archbishop, but in practice remain exempt from his jurisdiction. Over all other Greeks, the Latin hierarchy was to have jurisdiction. (11.) Appeal from the Greek archbishop should be to the Latin archbishop. After the Greek archbishop's relinquishing of office, the Latin metropolitan making his visitation of any city or diocese should receive once annually sixty solidi from the Greek community. The Syrians of the island were to be under the same obligations as the Greeks.[15]

Such was the settlement that Pope Alexander IV gave to the ecclesiastical situation in Cyprus. Apart from the exceptions made for Archbishop Germanus for as long as he retained office, it was a complete return to the regulations obtaining before Innocent IV introduced his new ideas of toleration. Innocent, it is true, was in that respect out of step with current thought in both the Latin and the Greek churches, for in both the broader views that unexpectedly made their appearance in the negotiations of 1252–54 between Rome and Nicaea faded out with the deaths of their chief promoters. They had been very short-lived in Cyprus. Alexander's bull sounded their knell, especially as a new piece of legislation, fruit of a local synod held under Raphael, archbishop of Nicosia, still further extended Latin influence over the Cypriot Church. The regulations and instructions of this "Constitution," as it was called, are based on the legislation of Pope

Celestine, of the Fourth Lateran Council, and of the legate Pelagius, on the judgment that Innocent IV had given on 6 March 1254 of what was legitimate and what illegitimate in the practice of the Greek Cypriot Church, and on the settlement issued in 1260 by Alexander IV.[16]

After a preamble about the unity of the church and variety of rite ("as the canons testify, diversity of custom within the unity of the same faith raises no difficulty"), the Constitution treated a number of matters in twenty-seven paragraphs. These for the most part did no more than repeat the enactments found in the sources. The four bishops subject to the Latin hierarchy were to teach their Greek faithful by word and example. In respect of the seven sacraments, the use of unctions at baptism, confirmation only by a bishop, liberty to use either leavened or unleavened bread in the Eucharist, the prohibition of reservation for the sick beyond twenty-five days (fifteen days in Innocent's regulations), a penalty against those who deny the validity of the sacrament consecrated in unleavened bread, the conferring of the three minor orders, prohibition of marriage between parties in the fourth Latin (eighth Greek) degree of relationship, Pope Innocent's remarks on purgatory—the regulations on these are all repetitions. However, an added tendency to Latinization was introduced when the Constitution treated the preparation of the holy oils by bishops, the application of the Lateran canon imposing yearly confession, the prohibition against giving Holy Communion to sick persons who had not confessed, and the imposition of a sacramental penance in confession proportioned to the guilt of the penitent. Banns were to be called for marriage. Monks were to observe the rule of Saint Basil exactly, sleeping in a common dormitory and refraining from various works. The penalty of excommunication was to be imposed on any who hindered the baptism of Saracens or other pagans who desired it. There was also a list of excommunications to be published frequently by proclamation (very like the one that is recorded as having been proclaimed "in the great cemetery of the church of Nicosia" in 1251). This Constitution was to be drawn to the attention of the faithful and explained by the Greek bishops four times a year. At the end of the document there is a paragraph that deals with the burial of religious and bears the name of Pope Boniface VIII (1294–1303). If this is really a part of the original, the date for the whole must be brought back at least to the end of the thirteenth century. It is more likely, however, that this is a later interpolation, particularly as it seems to have no reference to Cyprus or Greeks.

It is most likely that the Latin bishops did not fail to ensure that the Greeks clergy and laity were regularly informed of the new ecclesiastical settlement. Poor Germanus, when he asked Pope Alexander to intervene, had hoped that "the Greeks might live at peace with the Latins under obedience to the Roman Church." What the settlement effected was a renewal of the old division between Greeks who acknowledged dependence on the archbishop of Nicosia and those who did not. Alexander's successor, Urban IV, was constrained to reprimand the regent of Cyprus for not supporting the church against "Greeks and Syrians, laymen of the kingdom of Cyprus," who rendered life impossible for Greek priests and clerics who accepted Roman authority. They dubbed the priests and clerics heretics, refused them the accustomed contributions for their maintenance—even wrecked their houses and ravaged their vineyards—and reduced them to such a pitch of destitution that the archbishop of Nicosia for pity's sake felt forced to take them into his own house and feed them. The regent (who obviously sympathized rather with the recalcitrant Greeks) was admonished, under pain of penalty, to assist the Latin archbishop to make the regulations of Pope Alexander's settlement prevail.[17] The papal reproof cannot have been very effective, for it was repeated less than a year later,[18] and still again shortly before Urban's death in October 1264.[19]

Alexander IV was an unfortunate pope. His settlement failed to give tranquility to the Christians of Cyprus and his negotiations with the Church of Nicaea achieved nothing. In Italy he was unable to stem the ambitions of Manfred of Sicily, who by 1257 had subjugated not only southern Italy but also the island of Sicily, and on 10 August 1258 had been crowned king in Palermo. Then, like other rulers of Sicily, Manfred began to cast his eye further afield. He occupied the island of Corfu and some towns on the mainland of Epirus which, when he married the daughter of Michael, the despot of Epirus, in 1259, he retained in peaceful possession as constituting her dowry. In Italy he disastrously defeated Florence, his chief opponent, at Montaperti (1260). Thus, "by 1261 all Italy was subject to Manfred's power, and the Pope was isolated, nervous and powerless in uncertain possession of Rome and nothing else."[20] On 25 May 1261 Alexander IV escaped from it all by dying.

The situation in the East was as unsettled as that of Italy. Theodore II Lascaris died in August 1258. He made his confidant George Muzalon (with perhaps also the patriarch, Arsenius) regent of his eight-year-old son and heir, John. A conspiracy among the nobles, who had been treated harshly and capriciously by Theodore, resulted in the murder of Muzalon within a few days. Michael Palaeologus, a successful general, was by common consent made regent, was named despot soon after, and, with his wife Theodora as empress, was crowned emperor at the end of 1258 by the patriarch Arsenius; the boy John rode in the cavalcade wearing a diadem, but not a crown.[21]

The despot of Epirus, Michael II Doucas, saw an opportunity in the confusion in Nicaea to try to retake the kingdom of Thessalonica, once in the possession of his family. Some years previously, to balance the growing might of Nicaea, he had married two of his daughters to powerful neighbors, the one to Manfred of Sicily, the other to William Villehardouin, prince of Achaia, and had made treaties with them. Attacked in 1259 by Nicene armies, he persuaded both his sons-in-law to assist him. Four hundred German cavalry from Sicily and all the feudal power of the Morea under William Villehardouin himself joined Michael and his two sons, Nicephorus and John the Bastard with his Vlachs. Treacherously deserted on the eve of battle by all the Greeks, Villehardouin and the Germans were left alone to face the forces of Nicaea under the sebastocrator, John Palaeologus, Michael's brother. They were utterly defeated in the summer of 1259 at Pelagonia. Villehardouin and nearly all his knights who had not been slain were taken prisoner and delivered to the Nicene emperor. Epirus was overrun and the Morea was rendered harmless. Michael Palaeologus by that one battle was relieved of all anxiety from Greece, and Constantinople was left isolated as never before. But its fortifications were still intact and it continued to present a formidable problem to any enemy.[22]

Early in 1260 the emperor Michael made a progress through Thrace and encamped just outside the walls of the capital, hoping to gain entry with the aid of a Latin traitor. He did not succeed. Later in the same year, Venice belatedly proposed a pact between the Latins of Greece and the islands to maintain a permanent force of a thousand soldiers in Constantinople.[23] Towards the end of 1260 Michael began negotiations with Genoa for a treaty. If he was ever to try to take Constantinople by assault he would need a fleet. So, in return for generous trading conditions (and the exclusion of Venice from all privileges in Byzantine ports), Genoa promised to provide fifty ships.[24] But it was really not necessary. For on 25 July 1261 a Nicene general with a small force,[25] en route for a campaign to impress the Bulgars, was enabled by the connivance of local Greek inhabitants to effect entry into Constantinople. At that time what military strength the city had was away attacking an island in the Black Sea. Panic, caused by the burning of the Venetian quarter of the city, drove the Latins to take refuge in their ships and to sail away. The city was Greek again, and Michael VIII Palaeologus, asleep some two hundred miles away and when he least expected it, had become in reality emperor of Byzantium.

He made his official entry into his new capital on 15 August on foot as a suppliant, thanking God for his mercy. Michael was to be crowned again, this time in Saint Sophia; but there was no patriarch to crown him. Arsenius, who had performed that office for him in Nicaea, indignant at the way Palaeologus was treating the boy John when he was under oath to respect all his rights, had left his patriarchal throne some time before and retired to a monastery. A successor had been elected but had died. To meet the need on so glorious an occasion as the recapture of the capital—and to truly be patriarch of Constantinople in Constantinople—Arsenius consented to return to office, and Michael was crowned. His son, Andronicus, was declared his heir. The boy John was not mentioned, nor was he commemorated in the Liturgy after Emperor Michael. He had been left behind in Asia Minor but, wherever he was, he remained a threat to the new dynasty. He was blinded on Christmas Day 1261. Patriarch Arsenius in turn excommunicated the emperor and maintained the excommunication, refusing to accept a token penitence.

Michael had now two aims in life, the one to keep his throne and empire, the other to regain all territories that had been lost since 1204. At home he won popularity with the nobles by donating residences to them in the capital, and with the ecclesiastics by restoring churches and enriching monasteries.[26] The bigger problem was to forestall an attempt from the west to reinstate Baldwin on his lost throne. If the western powers combined their military forces, he could not resist them. By diplomacy and intrigue he might achieve what he could not do by war.

In such circumstances Palaeologus was naturally intensely interested in the situation in Italy when Urban IV was elected pope on 29 August 1261. Danger from the west could be expected from the papacy that had been a consistent supporter of the Latin Empire, and from Manfred, king of Sicily, who for strategic reasons had possessed himself of and still held Corfu and important towns in Epirus. Either or both of these could help Baldwin. Fortunately for Michael, the popes were nearly as apprehensive of Manfred as was Michael; for several years they had been looking for someone to take over rule in Sicily, a papal feud, in his stead. In a first reaction to the capture of Constantinople, Pope Urban had a crusade preached in France, Poland, and Aragon for the restoration of the Latin Empire,[27] and was persuaded to threaten the Genoese government with excommunication if it did not cease to help the church's enemies—the Greeks.[28] The crusade did not materialize and the Genoese were not greatly impressed. Urban's attention was concentrated mostly on his own most pressing need, to restrain the power of Manfred of Sicily. He renewed in earnest the offer of the crown to Charles of Anjou.[29] By the end of July 1263 Charles was accepted as the champion of the church.

Palaeologus wasted no time in opening relations with the papacy. As soon as he had gained his throne on 1 January 1259, he sent two envoys to Pope Alexander IV, but they never arrived. Again, after the recapture of Constantinople, Palaeologus sent two more envoys, who also probably never reached the Apostolic Curia from Apulia, for they were Greeks, exsecretaries of the Latin emperor Baldwin, and were regarded in the kingdom of Sicily as traitors now that they were in the service of Baldwin's victorious rival.[30] So Emperor Michael sent still a third embassy, which arrived at the Curia probably towards the end of spring 1262.[31]

The heads of the letter they carried to the pope are repeated in Urban's answer dated 18 July 1263.[32] Michael had opened his letter by saluting the pope as successor on the apostolic throne and spiritual father of his empire, and by referring to himself as the pope's most devoted son. He extolled the earlier unity of the church, and expressed surprise that the Holy See, by excommunicating the Genoese for their alliance with the Greeks, preferred war to peace among Christians. The emperor then described the injuries suffered by the Greeks at the hands of the Latins but, as son to father, he said that he would forget them, and offered peace and concord. "Concerning dogmas, faith, and customs, that is, ecclesiastical rites, you declared you were saying nothing in that letter since, if in these points there was any discord, once peace and concord between Latins and Greeks had been attained, these would more easily be solved and more quickly settled." Michael asked urgently for the dispatch of envoys with a reply.

Pope Urban showed no haste in replying. He sent a verbal message back with the returning Greek messengers in the spring of 1263,[33] but sent no envoys of his own. His formal answer to the messages from the Greek emperor is dated about a year later, 18 July 1263. The reason for his delay was (so he wrote) his being thrust suddenly in the beginning of his reign into so many other matters of high importance that occupied all his attention.[34] It was also probably because he did not know what was best to do. On 16 May 1262 Venetians of Negroponte and William of Villehardouin had signed a treaty in Thebes for combined action against the "Greek usurper." A little later, in July 1262, i.e., shortly before,[35] or shortly after,[36] the arrival of Palaeologus's second embassy in Viterbo, the pope, Baldwin, the Venetians, and the Moreote barons and prelates agreed on similar measures. Besides, Urban doubted the sincerity of the emperor's talk about union of the churches,[37] a doubt substantiated by the actions of Palaeologus, for in 1262 he had opened an offensive in Epirus; and, in the spring of 1263, with the aid of a new Genoese fleet, he attacked the Latins in the Morea. Hence Urban sent him no delegation. On the contrary, he appealed in the West for help for Achaia,[38] and renewed his threats to Genoa.[39] Both of Palaeologus's military enterprises failed, and perhaps that, coupled with the papal reaction, accounted for his declaration of submission to papal judgment in the late spring of 1263.

On the other hand, Urban might have thought that any serious weakening of the position of Palaeologus would encourage Manfred in his eastern ambitions and at that time the pope was doing his best to repress Manfred. On 20 April 1262 Urban warned James, king of Aragon, against favoring

Manfred and implementing a proposal to marry his son to the Sicilian's daughter.[40] In November Urban summoned Manfred to appear before him.[41] He was greatly annoyed later, when Baldwin, who had taken refuge at the Sicilian court, tried his very hardest to persuade him to let Manfred be the church's champion against the Greek emperor. But apprehension at Manfred's growing strength should not be pressed too much as a motive of the benevolent papal reply to the Greek emperor's pacific feeler. Urban was at that time consolidating another line of defense. He was pressing vigorously his negotiations with Charles of Anjou, and on 17 June 1263 he had proposed a draft treaty to Charles which Charles had accepted. On the other hand, no pope rejected out of hand a proposal of church union. Urban welcomed that of the Greek emperor, but with caution and conditions, just as his predecessors had.[42]

The pope's long-delayed answer to Palaeologus's letter, when it was at last written, was long and friendly. It is dated 18 July 1263. In it he told Palaeologus that he rejoiced that "so great a prince had been illuminated to see the way of Catholic truth, by which the daughter would be restored to the mother, the part to the whole and the member to the head." He wrote he had wished to send his messengers, four Franciscans, with Michael's returning legates, but they were too distant from the Curia to arrive in time, and besides he had heard that the territories of Villehardouin in Achaia were being molested by Greek troops, which suggested that Palaeologus had abandoned his desire for peace.[43] He reminded the emperor that the Roman pontiff is the viceregent of Christ and in his name Urban strongly urged Michael to return to Catholic unity, for the church is one, wherein Peter, who as vicar of Christ was head of the Apostles, holds the primacy of the keys, and that the Doctors of the church venerated Peter's successors and, both Latins and Greeks, looked to them for guidance. Michael had professed his high regard for "the successor on the apostolic throne and spiritual father"; how happy it would be if these words were reduced to deed and how advantageous a spiritual unity would be to temporal power. Popes acted to restore peace between warring kings, and between princes and their vassals, and to protect the rights of minors. Therefore, Michael's empire could expect more help of that sort in his own defense and in that of his heirs, the more securely the church could await his conversion to unity, and that not only from the Genoese, but from all princes; but the Holy See could not endure that Genoese or any other "sons of obedience should consort with sons of disobedience in any treaty relationship." He also reminded Michael that the Roman Pontiff is vicar of the Truth, that those who refuse his obedience sin grievously; and it is the pope's office to warn and to chide. Division among Christians brings woeful ills, as the Greek have learned to their cost. Michael desired peace. Urban firmly approved, praying that it be a peace based on Christian charity and faith. "But because it would not be a true and firm peace if it did not rise from a solid foundation of unity and faith, Your Magnitude should not relegate the dogmas of faith and ecclesiastical rites to second place." So Urban was sending his envoys for both purposes—to treat of faith and ecclesiastical rites as well as of peace and concord. He reminded Michael that the popes have always striven for unity of the churches, and expressed his desire that Michael should welcome the envoys and treat with them. So that no untoward incident should mar the negotiations, Urban directed Michael to cease altogether from war against Achaia.[44]

Before the pope had completed this very long answer to the Greek emperor, the Curia received another letter (spring 1263) from Michael, in which he expressed his readiness to submit to the judgment of the Holy See all questions that might arise between his empire and the Latins. Urban added as a kind of postscript to his already long letter his congratulations on Michael's prudence and assured him of receiving justice.

Ten days later, Urban gave the usual extensive faculties enjoyed by papal emissaries to four Franciscans, Simon of Auvergne, Peter of Moras, Peter of Cresta, and Boniface of Ivrea. They were to go first to William of Villehardouin in Achaia to inform him of the papal wish for a truce with Palaeologus, and were thence to proceed to Constantinople to deliver the pope's letter and to "treat of both questions, namely about dogmas of faith and ecclesiastical rites as well as about peace and concord."[45] They set off on their mission in early August 1263, but took a very long time to reach their journey's end. By May 1264 the Curia had had no word from them and did not even know if they had yet arrived in Constantinople.

The four friars cannot have been long on their way before another embassy from Constantinople reached Orvieto; it had certainly left before the Franciscans arrived there, since there was no mention of the friars in the documents the Greek envoys carried. The Greek embassy was led by no less a person than Nicholas of Durazzo, appointed by Innocent IV on 2 September 1254 to be bishop of Cotrone in southern Italy, who was also an official of the papal Curia. Equally proficient in both Latin and Greek and very zealous for the union of the churches, he had produced a book, probably between 1254 and 1256, purporting to prove on the authority of the Greek and the Latin Fathers of the church that the *Filioque* doctrine was no obstacle to union. He had brought his work to the attention of Theodore II Lascaris in Nicaea. Lascaris had not been persuaded by it but had written in reply his own "On the Procession of the Holy Spirit," upholding extreme Greek opinion on the subject.[46] How Nicholas of Cotrone came to be Michael's messenger is recounted in the imperial letter of which he was the bearer, now preserved in its Latin translation in the papal archives.[47]

This letter opens with a paean of praise and reverence for the Holy See: "To the venerable father of fathers, most blessed Pope of Old Rome, father of Our Majesty, Lord Urban, supreme pontiff of the sacrosanct and apostolic See, great by the divine will and providence, worthy of reverence for his character, life, and doctrine before God and man, Michael, etc." It goes on in the same strain, calling the pope "prince of all priests" and the channel of grace for all members of the church. The emperor then noted how in the past messages of all sorts had traveled east and west to effect union of the churches, but instead of union, discord had increased, because the exposition of the Scriptures and of the Fathers had been distorted by lack of knowledge of each other's languages and the limitations of non-theological interpreters. However, Michael declared, "in the fourth year of our reign" (i.e., 1262) a voice of joy from the West, that had originated, however, in the land and nation of the Greeks, sounded in the imperial ears, replete with knowledge of the Scriptures and the Fathers. It was Nicholas, bishop of Cotrone. In the third year of his reign Palaeologus had invited Nicholas to come secretly to Constantinople and Nicholas had arrived on Christmas Eve 1262. "He revealed all things, one after another, that pertain to the true faith, and all this we perceived rightly and, with our heart and mind illuminated, we found that the holy Roman Church of God was not different from us in the divine dogmas of the faith, but understands and chants them almost with us." Nicholas had expounded the doctrines of the Latin Doctors and Palaeologus had found them in agreement with the teaching of the Greek Doctors. The emperor then declared that those doctrines

> with complete and undefiled faith we perceive, venerate, believe, and hold, and we venerate all the sacraments of the same Roman Church, believing that they have their effect in the souls of the just which are united together, conjoined and confirmed with God. . . . For the rest, we ask Your Holy Paternity that, as prince of all priests and universal Doctor of the Catholic Church, you would henceforward strive with unflagging solicitude for the reunification of the same Church, over which God has set you eminently in the place of Blessed Peter, because now Your Holiness has Our Serenity ready [to cooperate] for this object. To the very Mother of our Church, above all and in all Mother of my Church, that surpasses the whole body of the Catholic Church, all peoples and patriarchal Sees within the wide area embraced by our power and all nations will be subjected to devotion, obedience, and love of the same Church by the power of our Serene Highness.

The letter ended with an assertion of good faith and an urgent request for papal legates to accompany Nicholas back to Constantinople to complete the reunion of the churches. "Hence the whole matter is left to the judgment of Your most pious Holiness, and henceforward no accusation can be preferred against our Majesty in the sight of God."

This letter must have come as something of a shock to the papal Curia, especially as Cotrone unhesitatingly vouched for the emperor's sincerity.[48] But perhaps it was not so surprising to the recipients of that day as it is to the historians of today, who read it in the light of later events. That Palaeologus in all his dealings with the papacy had the political motive of using papal protection first against Manfred and later against Charles of Anjou is beyond question. The Latins were not unaware of it. Palaeologus did not try to conceal it from his own subjects when they proved recalcitrant—in fact, he used it as an argument to persuade them to play the same game. But at this stage in the progress of events he almost certainly had not yet approached his church about it. He was following a policy tried before by his two immediate predecessors, though in different circumstances—they to acquire, he to retain Constantinople. He was doing no more than Vatatzes, who had made a similar offer in 1254, or than Theodore II, who had considered doing the same. He had no reason to suspect that his church would behave differently in 1263 than it had done in 1253, when it had approved the imperial plan and cooperated in it. In fact, he was surprised and angry that ten years later the very prelates who for Vatatzes had discussed in synod and had signed the relevant document accepting papal supremacy obstructed his wish to do precisely the same. He had that document brought from the archives and showed them their own signatures.[49] Why the difference of behavior? Patriarch Joseph in 1273 was neither more learned nor more strong-willed than Manuel in 1254. But in 1273 the Arsenite schism had embittered a large section of the Greek Church, and that perhaps was the telling factor.

It is said that Michael was no theologian.[50] Neither was Vatatzes. But Michael claimed that the array of Greek Fathers expounded to him by the bishop of Cotrone had convinced him of the concordance in the doctrines of the two churches.[51] He must have been educated enough to follow the argument, which was one of Greek texts and one that was not by then unknown in the Greek Church. Earlier, Nicephorus Blemmydes († 1272) had written several treatises leading up to, but not quite concluding to, agreement in the meaning of "from the Son" and "through the Son." Nicetas of Maronea, archbishop of Thessalonica († c.1145), had argued in the same way and had actually drawn the conclusion. Shortly, Beccus would do the same and, as he suffered fourteen years of imprisonment and died in prison (March 1297) because he would not change his opinion, presumably he was sincere in his conversion.[52] The Council of Florence two and a half centuries later would endorse that conclusion in a solemn definition.

The pope answered Palaeologus's letter on 23 May 1264. The usual précis of the correspondent's missive that opens most papal replies is here nearly a verbal repetition of the whole. There follow expressions of joy at various sentiments and phrases of the Greek letter, and then Urban tells

Palaeologus that, though the four Franciscans presumably then at the Greek court were capable of dealing with the situation, to show the deep satisfaction of the papal Curia and to meet Palaeologus's urgent request, he would return the bishop of Cotrone as his apocrisiarius, with two more Franciscans, Gerard of Prato and Raniero of Siena. They, together with the earlier four Franciscans, if they were still in Constantinople, would be enabled to understand better the emperor's mind in respect of his letter and of Cotrone's oral communication, would encourage him, and would pave the way for a definitive conclusion of the whole business. But Palaeologus should not delay, for delay was always fraught with danger. He should not keep his "Mother" anxiously waiting, but should hasten to the maternal embrace and trustingly put himself in a father's arms.[53] The tone of the whole letter was warm, but it put forward no new proposals and added nothing to Urban's previous communications on the subject.

The four Franciscans who left Orvieto for the east in early August 1263 had been commissioned to arrange a truce between Villehardouin of Achaia and Palaeologus. It would be interesting to know exactly when they reached Constantinople, whether before the Greeks opened another campaign in the Morea (and so in spite of the pope's request for peace) or after. In the spring of 1264 a Greek army did, in fact, try to consolidate Byzantine rule over Achaia. After being checked several times, the army was seriously defeated at Makryplagi and a large number of generals and nobles were taken prisoner. That campaign must have been initiated and waged while the bishop of Cotrone was in the Curia presenting Michael's most conciliatory letter to the pope, and it suggests that the Greek emperor did not intend that his pacific policy in Italy should be an obstacle to his warlike aims in Greece. He could not expect others to take the same view.[54] The pope's reaction to the news of the Achaian fighting was to have a crusade preached in aid of Villehardouin.[55] He was having other crusades preached as well. In early 1263 and again at the end of that year, he issued more than a score of letters to foster help for the Holy Land.[56] Early in 1264 Manfred tightened his grip on central Italy by taking Lucca. The pope threatened his abettors and launched a crusade against him.[57] Urban's growing anxiety about the security of Rome let Charles of Anjou pressure the pope to gain for himself more favorable and lucrative conditions for his enterprise in Italy. After granting Charles on 3 May a tenth to be collected over several ecclesiastical provinces of France,[58] Urban sent to his legate in France, the cardinal bishop of Albano, the text of a new treaty satisfying Charles's demands.[59] Charles accepted, but the pope did not live long enough to endorse it. He died on 20 October 1264.

He was followed on the papal throne by another Frenchman, Clement IV, who had little choice but to continue the policy of his predecessor. On 7

March he authorized the diversion to Sicily of crusaders enrolled for the Holy Land or the campaign against Palaeologus, "since these are known to depend for the most part on events in the kingdom of Sicily."[60] Twelve days later he wrote telling the apostolic legate in France to levy a tenth from the prelates and the monasteries in his territory in favor of the Sicilian policy.[61]

Charles of Anjou arrived in Rome on 23 May 1265. His French army joined him in the middle of January 1266 and, having been crowned with his wife Beatrice on 6 January, he marched south on 20 January. He met Manfred at Benevento on 16 February and defeated and killed him. With his queen he entered Naples on 7 March. His success was complete, for Sicily accepted him. With the death of the Ghibelline protector Manfred, the Guelf factions in the cities of northern Italy revived, and a great parliament held in Milan hailed Charles. There was, however, a cloud on the horizon. In Germany, Conradin, now in his middle teens, was not content to see the kingdom of Sicily be lost so easily. Encouraged by partisans of the Hohenstaufen who had taken refuge from Italy in Germany (though Charles took no repressive measures against them), he began organizing an invasion of Italy, announcing his plans at a diet in Augsburg in October. Pope Clement was already becoming nervous. On 18 September and again two months later he announced censures against any who should support Conradin.

Such was the situation in Italy when an embassy arrived in Viterbo from the emperor Michael of Constantinople.[62] In his reply, after congratulating his illustrious correspondent on his zeal for union and professing his own, Pope Clement recalled the history of the negotiations about union between the Curia and the Greek emperor. He noted that Pope Urban, at the emperor's wish, had sent four Franciscans as envoys, not primarily to discuss concord, but rather doctrine and rite first, and then concord with other questions. If the negotiations went well and promised success, Palaeologus was to have sent plenipotentiaries to the Curia to settle the final arrangements. The pope recalled that the friars had not in fact succeeded in getting all they wanted and, "so it is said,"[63] agreed on certain written proposals, which they promised to recommend to the Holy See. This latest Greek embassy, received first in private audience by the pope at their own request, then heard by the College of Cardinals, refused even to speak about doctrine. They finally produced the written proposals, indicated above, not for discussion but simply for confirmation. Yet they were not empowered to accept them on behalf of Palaeologus and his people, even after a confirmation by the pope. Indeed, when pressed, they had to admit that they had no authorization at all in writing even to propose them—an extremely strange situation for an imperial embassy. The four Franciscan envoys, continued Clement, had been given power only to discuss and to refer back to Rome. The screed in question was unacceptable for various reasons, not only for some parts of its contents, but also because the Greek envoys had no authority from Palaeologus and the Greek nation to treat of it; in addition, the emperor, in the nearly three years' interval that had elapsed since the document was supposed to have been drawn up, had never in spoken word or written document brought it to the notice of the Holy See, even by means of the later papal embassy which stayed for some time at his court.

What pertains to the faith and the truth (the letter continued) should be exposed plainly and not be covered over. "Therefore We put before you clearly and set forth in detail what We believe firmly in our hearts and profess openly with our mouths, and We do not cover our dogmas in the wrappings of riddles, but the profession of the faith which We hold We want to be known to all the world in completely explicit and unambiguous terms." If the emperor and his people wished, as Pope Clement hoped they did, to return to unity with the Western Church, then emperor, clergy, and people must profess this same faith and also openly admit the primacy of the Church of Rome.

The papal document then gives the text of a long and detailed profession of faith, covering the theology of the Trinity (including, of course, the *Filioque* doctrine), the Incarnation, the Redemption, the inspiration of Scripture, the Latin doctrine of purgatory and the hereafter, and the seven sacraments. It ends with a paragraph asserting the primacy of the Holy See in respect of preserving and defining truths of the faith, of being a universal court of appeal, and, since it alone has the "plenitude of power," of being the source of power and privilege of all others, including patriarchs.

This most unerring exposition of the faith, the letter goes on to say, "it is neither fitting, nor do We wish, to submit afresh to discussion and definition." Though it had earlier been proposed to summon a council, Clement wrote that he would no longer consider one, not for fear of the Greek Church but because it would be quite unsuitable, even wrong, to call in question the purity of the true faith, supported as it is by the Scriptures, by the writings of the Fathers, and by the authority of the Roman pontiffs. To furnish proofs for all its statements would go beyond the bounds of a letter. The pope wrote he would send envoys capable of expounding them and, if there were points particularly hard to accept, Palaeologus could send some of his most erudite theologians for instruction to the papal Curia, where they would be received with great benevolence. Michael should press on with union which, if achieved, would add glory to his name. When once he, his clergy, and his people had professed the faith as proposed, and had accepted obedience to the Holy See, he could petition for a council to confirm the bond of charity, to be called when and where the pope wished.

The letter ends on a more threatening note. Clement directed that Michael should eliminate discord. But he should know "that on the occasion of a negotiation of this sort We do not intend, as We ought not to do, to fail in justice towards those who complain that they suffer oppression at the hands of Your Magnificence, nor shall We cease from pursuing so great a work by such other ways as the Lord shall provide for the salvation of souls."

A letter was sent also to the patriarch. Pope Clement wrote of his own most intense desire for union, which would heal so many ills. He recommended his solution to the problem and referred the patriarch to the emperor for the text of the profession of faith. He begged him to induce the emperor and as many others as he could to accept it.[64]

To judge from this papal reply, there was a great difference of tone between the Greek emperor's letter it was answering and the other that, infused with fire and enthusiasm, had been brought by Cotrone a few years before.[65] One can only guess at the reasons for this difference. It may be that Urban's noncommittal answer to the most effusive of all Michael's communications on church union had filled the latter with disappointment. Also, with a change of popes, a change of tactics might have seemed indicated, especially since in the interval between the two embassies the political situation in Italy had been greatly altered by the battle of Beneventuom, and since Manfred, the refuge of ex-Emperor Baldwin and avowed enemy of the Byzantine Empire, had disappeared from the scene. His place had been taken by Anjou, whom the popes had bound by treaty to a restricted exercise of rule, and who, in any case, had not yet had time to do more than take the first steps in establishing himself in his kingship of Sicily.

It was, however, not long before Charles began to show his hand. He held prisoner Manfred's widow, daughter of Michael II of Epirus, and meant to possess himself of the dowry of towns on the Albanian seaboard that she had brought to the throne of Sicily at her marriage. On 17 January 1267 he appointed a captain general for Corfu,[66] which action, if not immediately effective, was at least indicative of his plans. At about the same time Pope Clement, though he did not at all want to attract Charles north of Rome, felt constrained to ask him to send an army to repress the Ghibellines of Tuscany. Charles did and came himself, remaining for the rest of the year. While he was there, he began his diplomatic activity in favor of Emperor Baldwin and his son, Philip, who lived as pensioners at his court. Charles made a treaty with William of Villehardouin whereby he received the overlordship of Achaia and his son, also called Philip, would marry Villehardouin's daughter and heiress on the condition that at William's death the principality would pass to Philip and his heirs or, failing such, to Charles himself.[67] Three days later he signed another and more important treaty, an agreement between himself, Baldwin, and Villehardouin with the approval of Pope Clement[68] to restore "the noble limb severed by the schismatics from the body of our common Mother, the holy Roman Church," that is, to reconquer the Byzantine Empire. Charles would provide troops and would in return have one-third of any recovered territories, suzerainty over Achaia and the areas belonging to Queen Helena's dowry with other rights, and, if the line of Baldwin failed, the House of Anjou should be heir to its rights, i.e., the throne of Constantinople. In addition, Philip of Courtenay would marry Charles's daughter, Beatrice, when she was of marriageable age.[69]

This treaty adds point to the veiled threat contained in the closing paragraph of Clement's letter to Palaeologus dated some two and a half months previously. But it does not convict the pope of insincerity or duplicity. He was being assailed from two sides. Emperor Michael in various letters to the Curia was blowing hot and cold—rather, very hot and cool—on union of the Churches. And, while pleading for peace between Christians, that is, immunity for Constantinople from Italian attack, Michael was at the same time, despite papal recommendations, himself attacking Latin possessions in Greece at every opportunity. Not unnaturally, he was accused of trickery. Pope Clement observed a neutral stance. He adhered strictly to the policy of his predecessors. He insisted on spiritual union first and political concord afterwards just as they had done, but—and this they had not done—he spelled out what spiritual union meant. He proposed the profession of faith with the acknowledgment of papal primacy to be accepted by emperor, hierarchy, and people. He had put his cards on the table. It was for Michael to cover them. To the Latins, who badgered him to act in a hostile manner against the Greek emperor, Clement observed the same neutrality. He let them (he could not stop them) make their pact and he approved it. But that did not prevent his still pursuing the purely religious way of achieving church union which, if it had succeeded, would have reduced the pact to nonsense. There would no longer have been any "noble limb severed from Mother Church" to be restored by arms.

Two weeks after the signing of the anti-Greek pact (9 June 1267), the pope asked the master general of the Dominicans to find him three friars to go to Greece. He directed the master general not to waste time fetching men from distant parts, but to allot three from his Curia or at least from inside Italy. He asked for them "in order that either by their labors, if it please God, the Greeks, who formerly were wandering in inaccessible places, may now acknowledge the truth and, professing it when acknowledged, return to the unity of the Apostolic See; or, with their deceits and lies exposed, We may preserve our hands unstained lest their blood either now or hereafter be required of Us by the Lord."[70] The friars were not going in order to engage in argument, "for the Greeks [were] not offering themselves for discussion, but . . . [said] that they [were] ready to accept the truth shown to them."[71] Clement had laid down in clear terms the conditions for union that the Latin Church deemed essential and he had done it intending thereby to put an end to possible Greek evasion. It was to be "Take it or leave it," and according as they took or left, he would know what answer to return to Charles and Baldwin who were alleging Greek duplicity and demanding wholehearted approval for military action.

Clement had not sent his long letter of 4 March with the profession of faith by his own legates, but rather by Michael's returning messengers.[72] One of these messengers, the logothete, had stayed behind at his own desire in order to accompany the Latin envoys whenever they should set out. The latter had not left—indeed, they had not yet been recruited for the task—before Palaeologus sent another embassy, to which the pope replied on 17 May 1267.[73] In this letter Palaeologus made no mention of the profession of faith, so probably it had not arrived before he dispatched his messengers.[74] In this communication he adopted a new tactic guaranteed to appeal to a pope of that day. He lamented the defeat of the king of the Armenians by the Saracens and intimated his own desire to resist the enemies of the Cross. Clement's reply was brief and slightly acid. He commended the emperor's sentiments, "which We should certainly praise more wholeheartedly if your actions were to correspond to your feelings."[75] Louis IX, with his sons and a vast concourse, was just then preparing for a crusade—an apt occasion for Palaeologus if indeed he wanted one. Clement informed Michael that the danger (which Michael had alleged) that his territories would lie open to Latin incursions if he led his army elsewhere could easily be eliminated by returning to unity with the Roman Church. The pope continued, "Nor can what you wrote be of any use to you as an excuse, that it is to the prelates and the clergy, not to you and your people, that it must be attributed if they do not pay due obedience to Us, since there is no doubt whatsoever that you possess a far greater power over your prelates than is right." Clement advised Michael that he should not yield to them but, if he cannot succeed in forcing them, he should shun them as schismatics.

The popes consistently, from Innocent III to Nicholas III, greatly overestimated the power of the Greek emperors over their church. They had some little excuse for this mistake, because it was always emperors who led in negotiations for union. Clement in this answer seems to have suspected an attempt at the kind of Greek evasion that he was trying to render impossible by his profession of faith, and he gave it short shrift.

In this Pope Clement was less than just, for Palaeologus at this period was having great difficulties with a large section of his church. Patriarch

Arsenius had obstinately refused to lift the excommunication that in 1262 he had laid on him for blinding John Lascaris, unless Michael showed his repentance by renouncing the throne in favor of the boy, which of course he would not do. The emperor complained to the synod. The bishops interceded for him with the patriarch, as did also his spiritual father, the monk Joseph; but their pleas were in vain. So in 1264 Palaeologus had the synod depose Arsenius on a specious charge, hoping that his successor would be less adamant. Germanus was elected (28 May 1265) without any intervention from the emperor. He was a prelate, learned, affable, and generous; and he was generally liked until he became patriarch. Then those who regarded the deposition of Arsenius as uncanonical (as it was, in fact, unjust), and a few others from personal motives, fomented opposition to him. The Arsenites were mainly monks led by one Hyacinth, but they found supporters among the laity and even from members of the imperial family. When Michael realized that Germanus was not going to absolve him from his excommunication, he prevailed on him to abdicate (14 September 1266). The monk Joseph had been the emperor's agent in this, and the monk Joseph was the next patriarch (28 December 1266); his first official act was to absolve the emperor which he did on 2 February 1267, a few months before Pope Clement's letter mentioned above. The election of still another—to them illegitimate—patriarch and the absolution infuriated the Arsenites. Their number increased and bands of "unstable and peripatetic" monks swelled the ranks of those already under Hyacinth's leadership. Monks poured out of the monasteries of Constantinople and set up various factions. The grand logothete, George Acropolites, tried to restore order by force and succeeded only in increasing the unrest.[76]

In the midst of all this confusion Palaeologus pursued other lines of defense besides his correspondence with the popes. Venice was still hesitating on what course to pursue. On the one hand it had not yet confirmed the treaty with Constantinople negotiated in 1265, and on the other it resisted the combined efforts of the pope, King Louis of France, and Charles of Sicily to make peace with Genoa.[77] So, as Venice vacillated, in 1267 Palaeologus renewed his treaty with Genoa. In return for commercial advantages and a stable establishment across the Golden Horn, Genoa would provide a fleet. Venice had refused to enter the anti-Greek pact of May 1267 with Charles, Baldwin, and Villehardouin. It was becoming apprehensive of the grip that Anjou, with possessions on both sides of the Adriatic, was acquiring over the sea routes leading in and out of its harbors. For this reason and because its commerce in the Aegean was suffering serious depredations from pirates operating with at least the connivance of the Greeks,[78] on 1 November 1267 the Signoria made overtures to Palaeologus for a treaty, which was ratified in Venice on 30 June 1268. In this manner Charles was losing the cooperation of the two great naval centers of Italy. Yet he would need a fleet if he was to launch his expedition to the East.

Charles's future was, however, by no means secure at that moment. While he was still in Tuscany reducing the Ghibelline cities, and while the pope was beginning to feel safe—Clement wrote to Charles on 16 September expressing the opinion that Conradin would never invade Italy[79]—Conradin had in fact left Bavaria and by 21 October was already in Verona. In mid-September Sicily revolted in Conradin's favor, and on 18 October Hohenstaufen supporters made themselves masters in Rome. In spite of eloquent and anxious pleas from the pope that he should go south and restore order, Charles continued with his campaign in the north, and in Viterbo, Clement, now completely dependent on him, made Charles imperial vicar of Lombardy for ten years. Only in March 1268 did Charles begin his return south. Conradin went south too. He was received in Pisa on 7 April and, bypassing the pope in Viterbo, was enthusiastically welcomed in Rome on 24 July. Charles moved towards Apulia, a center of Hohenstaufen loyalites, to await the young king's arrival. They met at Tagliacozzo on 23 August, and Charles, at first beaten, rallied and won. Conradin fled, was captured, arraigned, and, at the age of sixteen, beheaded in Naples on 29 October. That was the end of the Hohenstaufen threat. The method of its extermination shocked the world. But it was final.

A month later Pope Clement IV was dead.

Chapter VII

The Second Council of Lyons

The conclave that followed the death of Clement IV was the longest in the church's history. Though Clement had died on 29 November 1268, his successor was not elected until 1 September 1271. The fifteen cardinals gathered in Viterbo, nearly equally divided between French and Italians, could not agree to give any candidate the necessary two-thirds majority. It was not until the civil authorities of the city removed the roof from over their heads and reduced their food to the minimum that they accepted a compromise. The result was that Teobaldo Visconti, archdeacon of the church of Liège, at that moment on pilgrimage in the Holy Land, was chosen. He took the name of Gregory X.

The long interval of nearly three years with no pope to gainsay him, which coincided also with a vacancy on the throne of Germany, gave Charles of Anjou a free hand to prepare for his eastern expedition. So as to have a fleet at his disposal, he continued his efforts to secure an alliance with Venice and Genoa, but without success. He began, therefore, to build ships for himself. Secure in Italy after Tagliacozzo, he turned his attention eastward. When in 1269 he got possession of the castle of Valona in Albania, he unified the command in that area and strengthened his hold on it by sending quantities of food and money from Apulia. Ambassadors who passed between Sicily and Hungary in 1269 arranged a treaty,[1] which was confirmed by a double marriage between the royal houses. To make it more stable, Charles asked the conclave to strengthen the pact with ecclesiastical sanctions. He was on terms of friendship with both of the heirs of Michael II Doucas, despot of Epirus, who had died in 1266 or 1267. Charles also renewed his friendly relations with Serbia and Bulgaria which were hostile to Greece.

For the emperor of Constantinople, on the other hand, the long conclave spelled danger. He had no pope to appeal to with overtures of church union, so he did the next best thing. He sent embassies to King Louis of France, whose saintly reputation had given him a prestige in the Western Church second only to that of a pope. Louis had been very hesitant about his brother Charles accepting the crown of Sicily and he favored still less Charles' plans to recapture Constantinople. He could not approve of Christians warring on Christians, especially when the Holy Land was still in the hands of the infidel. All Louis's enthusiasm was for the crusade for which his preparations were at that time nearing completion. Charles would be unlikely to directly oppose his brother's wishes.

Michael's first embassy to Louis passed through Genoa on 27 August 1269. Louis returned the courtesy by an embassy that traversed Sicily in December. In the spring of 1270 a new Greek embassy reached France, led by John Parastron, O.M., which conveyed as a present to the French king a magnificently illuminated New Testament.[2] As there was a question of union of churches, Louis disclaimed any competence to act and referred the whole business to the conclave. The cardinals after consideration appointed the apostolic legate in France (as Louis had suggested) to apply the conditions they laid down in a long letter which they addressed to him.[3]

It opens with a paragraph in praise of the king and then records the reason for its being written: King Louis through two Dominicans had informed the conclave of the Greek emperor's requests. Palaeologus, to fulfill his own, his clergy's, and his people's intense desire for union of the churches (so he had written) had often approached the Holy See to obtain it, but had not received satisfaction. He had then several times appealed to Louis asking him to act as arbiter and promising to "observe fully and inviolably whatever the same king should say about it"; and he had warned Louis that he would have to answer to God if he refused his cooperation. Louis had prudently and rightly referred the petition to the Holy See — in the circumstances, to the conclave of cardinals, who had given it serious attention. The letter also recounts in detail the contacts between the Greek emperor and popes Urban IV and Clement IV, with a résumé of the relevant papal letters.[4] "Whereupon, weighing so wholesome a business with due consideration," they decided that there was need, not of a change of policy, but of perseverance in the policy already adopted by the Holy See. Therefore, they reaffirmed as conditions for union, acceptance of the profession of faith and recognition of the primacy of the Roman Church in the form determined by Pope Clement. But, whereas Clement had been content to set out in precise terms the formula of the profession without determining any mechanism for its use, the conclave asserted: "We want the emperor, the patriarch of the Greeks, archbishops, bishops, archimandrites, abbots and other prelates of churches, the clergy and the people aforesaid in a general synod of the Greeks'' to make the profession and to make it on oath. The formula of the oath, very precise and exacting, followed. However, even the oath was not enough. The cardinals felt that prelates should also make the manual act of obedience, giving assurance of permanent fidelity on oath, promising also never to advocate in public or in private anything to the contrary. The legate was to send agents to various Greek centers to receive the oaths; certificates with seals attached were to be made to attest them and they were to be noted in registers provided for that purpose in cathedrals, churches, and monasteries where the professions were made so ''that the events of today may be known to posterity.''

Nothing came of all this, for the legate who was to impose it went to Tunis with Louis and died there on 7 August 1270. It is, however, worth noting for the insight it provides of the Latin mentality and its incomprehension of the Greek Church.

The brief that was sent to King Louis with the letter to the legate indicates the reason for the added stringency of the proposed measures. The cardinals' ''due consideration'' of the gravity and vast importance of union had been tempered by their realization that ''though attempts to achieve it had been made on many occasions, the intention of the Holy See was being frustrated by the devious device of long procrastination.'' Furthermore (the cardinals wrote) they believed that ''as the event shows, the Greeks were not really intending to proceed [toward union] with the simplicity of truth but to spin out time in precautions and pretenses.'' So they were trying to establish whether ''the Greeks really do wish to proceed in the business.'' They asked for Louis's cooperation ''to avoid the strategem of the usual dissension'' by the application of suitable safeguards and conditions.[5]

Nevertheless Palaeologus's diplomacy during the conclave was successful, for Charles had been meaning to mount his expedition to Greece in 1270. After his diplomatic successes of 1269 Charles started active military preparations. On 22 January 1270 he issued orders that all ships should be ready for the summer. On 5 February all ships in Apulian ports were to stand by ready for 15 March. Diplomatic activity in Achaia was multiplied. The marriage contract between Charles's son Philip and Villehardouin's daughter Isabella was signed on 17 June. On 31 March he appointed Hugh of Conches to command the squadron that was to help in the Morea and on 11 May the fleet of twenty-five ships sailed. But on 1 July 1270 King Louis departed on his crusade. He went, however, not to Egypt but to Tunis and — significantly for the Greek — his brother Charles could not refuse to take part in the expedition with him. Legates from Palaeologus, John Beccus, and Constantine Meliteniotes reached Tunis and spoke with the king shortly before he died on 25 August. Charles arrived just after his death — but he had gone to Tunis and not to Greece, which was a relief to Palaeologus. That a large portion of his fleet was wrecked on its way back to Sicily gave Palaeologus still another reprieve. But it was a reprieve, not a complete release, for Charles was not to be put off by minor mishaps. In 1271 he continued with his warlike preparations. On 5 February he issued an order from Capua to the barons and vassals of the province of Brindisi to prepare to go to "Romania." On 22 August he sent a force to the Morea. At Pentecost of the same year the marriage of his son Philip to the heiress of William of Villehardouin was solemnized in Trani, but already the year before (17 August 1270) Charles had sent his plenipotentiaries around to the castles of Achaia to receive the oaths of the barons that they recognized his suzerainty.

Gregory X reached Brindisi on 1 January 1272. Accompanied by the king of Sicily he arrived in Viterbo on 10 February to meet the cardinals who had elected him. In the beginning of March he was in Rome for his consecration and coronation, which took place on the 27th of the month. On 31 March he announced to the world a general council to meet on 1 May 1274. Its purpose was threefold: "to deal with the withdrawal of the people of the Greeks which has withdrawn itself from devotion and obedience to the Holy See, with the complete overwhelming and fearsome destruction of the Holy Land, and with the decadence of morals."[6] Of these the most important for Gregory was the second. Union with the Greeks, good though it was in itself, was for him more a means than an end. It would enormously facilitate a grand crusade.

The new pope, an Italian, though he had had very friendly relations with King Louis of France, was in no way tied to the House of Anjou. He had not been rescued from the threat of a Manfred or a Conradin by Charles and, not having been a cardinal, he was not involved in the political tensions of the College. He showed his freedom of spirit by communicating with Byzantine Emperor Michael before ever he reached the shores of Italy. According to the Greek historian Pachymeres, Gregory informed Palaeologus of his election, declared his intense desire to see peace restored between the churches and told the emperor that, if he cherished the same purpose, he could have no better occasion of procuring it than during his papacy.[7] When he reached Italy he was no doubt soon informed of the history of the negotiations with Greece and sensed the scepticism of the Sacred College.[8] Besides, Charles was often at his elbow to restrain his enthusiasm.[9] So he took no further step to continue relations with the Greek emperor, since the cardinals advised him to await an answer from Michael to Pope Clement's letter with its profession of faith.[10]

Meanwhile he invited bishops and other well-informed persons to send in reports and suggestions that would help in the preparation of the council.[11] But probably before this, the ex-master general of the Dominicans, Humbert de Romanis, submitted his ideas.[12] Humbert, a man of broad and sagacious mind, produced a profound analysis of the schism although as far as is known he had never set foot in Greece.[13] The first nine of the nineteen sections into which his observations are divided are devoted to showing that the church should be one, that it should have a supreme head, and that this head should be the pope. He worked chiefly through common sense arguments, though to prove Roman supremacy he appealed freely to the New Testament. Humbert's reasoning ran along these lines: there is a schism, and the Greeks rather than the Latins should be said to be the schismatics, indeed even heretics. But his solution of the ecclesiastical problem was practical. Latins should learn Greek and acquaint themselves with Greek theology and learning, and there should be more frequent intercourse between individuals of both churches. To overcome the three main obstacles to peace, he advocated that by diplomacy or marriage, certainly not by bloodshed, the emperor on the Greek throne should be one who would accept the primacy, that Rome should not be exacting but very broad minded in respect of Greek rites and customs, and that the pope should not insist on receiving a complete and total obedience but be content if the Greek patriarch was confirmed in office by him and if Roman legates were received in Constantinople with due honor.

Gregory shared in Humbert's spirit of pacific moderation and soon had a chance of showing it. An embassy from Palaeologus arrived at the Curia in the early summer of 1272 — nearly a year after the spontaneous message of the pope-elect. Both the delay in answering and the nature of the answer did nothing to clarify the situation, for the imperial message was no more than the usual declaration of affection and devotion to the Holy See (enhanced in this case by the expression of Michael's regret that Gregory had not visited Constantinople on his way from Acre to Italy), of his deep desire for union of the churches, and of his zeal against the enemies of the Cross. There was no reference to Pope Clement's letter or to the profession of faith. Perhaps Palaeologus hoped from so enthusiastic a pope as Gregory to get protection at a lesser cost. His envoy, John Parastron,[14] was to amplify and supplement the expression of the emperor's sentiments contained in the letter. No doubt he vouchsafed also for his sincerity.[15]

The letter and Parastron's optimism were enough for the pope. He wrote a long reply dated 24 October 1272.[16] In it he asserted at length his own most profound desire for union, to effect which, as well as to provide help for the Holy Land and to procure reform in the church, he had summoned a council to meet on 1 May 1274. He informed Michael that he had not written earlier to him of the council because the Curia was still awaiting an answer to Pope Clement's letter. Then, after a brief résumé of the imperial message, he recalled the history of Palaeologus's contacts with King Louis. This prompted him to exhort and encourage the Greek emperor not to desist from his efforts for peace. Negotiations, he declared, should begin with faith and dogmas (as his predecessor's letters had rightly insisted), and so Pope Clement had sent by the emperor's own envoys a statement of faith to be accepted, a copy of which (in case the earlier one had miscarried en route or been lost sight of) Gregory included in his letter. Four friars, Jerome of Ascoli, Raymond Berengario, Bonagrazia of San Giovanni in Persiceto and Bonaventure of Mugello, would come from the Holy See. The Emperor was asked to make the profession of faith in their presence and to sincerely accept the primacy of Rome, and finally to have his clergy and people do the same. When this has been done, the pope informed Palaeologus, it would be fitting—and very much according to his desire—for Palaeologus to attend the forthcoming council in person or by suitable representatives. With union thus proclaimed, discord between Latins and Greeks would be at an end and mutual goodwill restored.

Thus far in his letter Gregory followed exactly the proprosals of his predecessors, which were indeed harsh. They amounted to a complete and immediate submission of the Greek nation as a precondition of peace. Gregory realised that the Latin conditions were severe, so he offered a modification that softened the demand. He wrote he would be content if, either before or during the council, the emperor sent fully empowered representatives "so that there everything might be totally and securely completed in their right order, in respect both of the profession of faith with the acceptance of the primacy of the Roman Church, and of the unity of Latins and Greeks in mutual charity by the removal of all cause for discord between them."[17] By this the Pope meant (as he explained in the next paragraph) that the emperor and the patriarch with at least some of the higher prelates should assure the papal envoys in writing, using a form of words prescribed by himself, first that through representatives sent to the Curia they would make the profession of faith and of the primacy of the Roman Church, and later, if and when called on to do so, they would repeat it in person. Meanwhile negotiations could be in progress to bring about political peace and concord.

That was not the end of Gregory's concessions. His private directions to his legates repeated in much the same words the alternative he had allowed in the brief and included the formula that emperor and prelates should use. According to this formula, the emperor (or prelate) declares that "having heard the truth of the Catholic faith clearly read out and faithfully exposed," he acknowledges it and promises that "after peace has been restored, in the general council that you have summoned, or before it or after it, between Us, our clergy and people on the one hand and the Latins on the other in regard of differences that have arisen from one side or the other, without fail we will acknowledge that faith'' and will freely recognize the Roman primacy — first by representatives at the papal Curia and afterwards personally when the Apostolic See shall request — and will procure a similar action from the clergy and the people. But the word ''acknowledge'' (*recognoscere*) might be too strong for the Greeks. In that case, the legates could substitute for it ''agree in'' (*convenire*): ''we agree with you and the same holy Roman Church, our Mother, in that truth of the Catholic faith.'' If ''agree in'' should be unacceptable, they could be content with ''We wish to acknowledge, receive and profess. . .'' or ''We wish to be united in the profession of the same faith. . . .'' All these concessions were applicable not only to the emperor but to the patriarch and the individual prelates also.[18]

Pope Gregory certainly tried to make union easier for the Greek bishops and the clergy. Palaeologus had warned Pope Clement about their opposition, but Clement had been sceptical. Parastron probably repeated the warning to Gregory, and Gregory tried to understand. While he offered no concession in respect of faith and the position of the Roman See, he said no word about rite or customs and he demanded no oath; the word of emperor or bishop would suffice. He foresaw that some, perhaps many, of the Greek bishops might refuse even such conditions of union. He allowed for that, insisting only on the cooperation of the patriarch and some of the higher prelates, who should at least ''wish'' to profess the proposed faith and accept the Roman primacy. That was not a substantial demonstration of unity, but if it was the honest expression of the prelates' minds, it betokened good will and promised a better hope for the future. They were to make their written promise to the papal legates before the council. Not until political peace was established or was on its way, whether that was before or after the council, did they need to send their solemn embassy to the Curia to formally make the profession of faith; still less had they to repeat it personally themselves.

These were, indeed, liberal conditions of union. They gave the Greek emperor a certain freedom to maneuver with his clerics. But (so the papal letter ended) Gregory wanted a settlement between Latins and Greeks at least by the time the council was sitting; so he urged Palaeologus to expedite matters and to send back the papal envoys with his positive answer well before the council began. He ended with a note of warning: ''But We want you to know that if, in spite of our desire, the envoys should be delayed, We, left in ignorance of your reply, do not mean either to let drop or to delay the prosecution of so salutary an affair by ways that the Lord may deign to open up for the salvation of souls.''

A letter was sent also to the Greek patriarch urging him to cooperate to the utmost in procuring the union proposed in the papal brief to the emperor. It was fitting that, when union was achieved, the patriarch and other Greek prelates should, according to ancient custom, take part in the council with Latin princes and prelates. Gregory cordially invited them and promised them an honorable and warm welcome.[19]

These papal documents gave both the protagonists a formidable task to perform. Palaeologus was to be ready to agree to conditions of peace and to contrive to induce the Greek patriarch and at least some of the more outstanding prelates to sincerely favor union. Pope Gregory had to persuade the ex-Emperor Baldwin and Charles of Anjou to forgo their expedition to reconquer Constantinople. By the treaty of 1267 they were to launch the attack in 1273 or 1274, and they were nearly ready for it and impatient to begin. To dissuade them would be no easy task.

The pope needed Charles's cooperation also in respect of the safe passage of envoys, both Latin and Greek, through his territories. So while he was still preparing his answer to the Greek emperor,[20] he wrote to the Sicilian king to tell him he was sending four legates to treat of union. To deprive Palaeologus of all excuse for refusing negotiations about union, Gregory asked Charles to agree to a short truce with Palaeologus when there should be no movements of troops in the Balkans, and he suggested that such a truce could lead to a more stable peace, to union, and to the end of the schism. He appealed to Charles in the name of Christ to lend his help and even to send his own representatives secretly with the four friars.[21]

Charles did not fall in with the suggestion that there should be no movements of troops in the Balkans during the truce, and with some justification. Towards the end of 1271 a Greek army had defeated the Venetians of Negroponte, and in 1272 Licario, the Italian freebooter turned Greek admiral, was starting on his victorious campaign both there and at sea. In that same year he defeated Charles's general, Dieux de Beaumont, who was replaced on 8 July by William of Barres. At this time Palaeologus was pressing Venice to renew the treaty due to end in 1273. Gregory was very much opposed to this and at least three times he expressed his strong disapproval to the Signoria, "because Emperor Michael was excommunicated." In spring 1273, however, the treaty was prolonged for another two or four years. Nevertheless Charles accorded a safe-conduct to the four papal messengers en route for Constantinople. Encouraged by this, Gregory went a step further. On 7 November he asked Charles to grant a safe-conduct for Greek envoys; Charles could not honestly accuse the Greek emperor of duplicity if he refused him the possibility of communication.[22] Whether Anjou responded to this appeal or not is uncertain. In spring 1273 he sent reinforcements to Achaia. No Greek envoys, it is true, came for a long time. But it was not Charles who was responsible for that.

Pope Gregory, like his predecessors, negotiated with the emperor of the Greeks, not with the church, because overtures for parleys always came from the emperor. The Greek hierarchy must have been aware of what was going on, but union of the churches had been talked of so often and nothing had come of it, so they were content to take no notice, especially as it was manifestly more political than ecclesiastical.[23] However, to fulfill the conditions laid down for union (and for protection from Anjou) Palaeologus had to persuade his church.

Unfortunately for him a great part of the Greek Church was already hostile to him for his treatment of the boy John Lascaris and of Patriarch Arsenius.[24] On this account he had hardly left Nicaea when he had to suppress a rebellion of peasants in that area. The dissension pervaded all ranks of society, even splitting families into factions. By the time that Palaeologus was to bring the hierarchy to face up to the papal conditions of union, the schism was even more widespread and bitter. Many troublemakers of no religious zeal had joined it and others were influenced by a rumor (probably false) among the pious that long before his election Patriarch Joseph had been excommunicated by Arsenius, and so his election must have been invalid on that ground, too.[25]

Michael began in earnest to woo the synod after the arrival at his court of the four Latin ambassadors with Parastron at the turn of the year 1272. According to Pachymeres, the emperor, to avoid war and the shedding of blood in another devastating Latin attack on the empire, was set on his unionistic policy, whereas the bishops were determined to resist any theological innovation. However, the bishops, thinking that the project of union would in time die a natural and ineffective death and not wishing openly to oppose the imperial wishes, gave a false impression of acquiescence.[26] With the support of Archdeacon Meliteniotes and George Cyprius and their friends, as well as of Holobolus (though perhaps less sincerely), Palaeologus tried to persuade the Greek hierarchy that union was necessary and inoffensive. He reminded them that they had not hesitated to agree to it in the time of Vatatzes as the synodical document with their signatures showed. He argued that in the most important points of doctrine there was no difference between Latins and Greeks, that it was not uncanonical to commemorate the name of the pope in the Liturgy, and that, as regards appeals to him, he was so far away that any concession in that respect would have no practical meaning. The patriarch put the onus of replying on John Beccus, the chartophylax. He, torn between loyalty to his faith and fear of the emperor, finally answered: "Some people are heretics without being called so. Such are the Latins." His fears were fulfilled. He was cast into prison on a trumped-up charge.[27]

The emperor then tried another tack. His theologians wrote for him a little tractate to prove from documents and church history that the Latins were not tainted with heresy. This he sent to the patriarch. Joseph discussed it with members of the synod and others (including Eulogia, sister of the emperor himself), who produced a reply which was sent to the imperial court. But Joseph was of a pacific disposition. To prevent him from yielding under pressure, he was persuaded to circulate an encyclical letter, the work of one of the most intransigent monks, Job Jasites. This declared it impossible to acknowledge any papal right of appeal or primacy — still more any commemoration of a pope in the Liturgy — because "the Latins are guilty of having corrupted the word of Christ." The patriarch was prevailed on to affirm his adherence to this statement by oath. Most of the synod signed the document. When the emperor read it, he felt frustrated.[28] But another event at the moment gave him hope.

John Beccus, recognized by all as a man of outstanding ability and patent honesty, was given tractates on the Procession of the Holy Spirit to read while he was in prison. Among them were some from the pen of Nicephorus Blemmydes, protagonist for the Greeks against the Latin friars in the discussions of 1234 and 1250. He had written a number of essays stressing that the great doctors of the church taught, not that the Spirit proceeds from the Father only, but that He proceeds from the Father through the Son. Beccus procured copies of the patristic works from which Blemmydes had culled his quotations. He studied them and concluded that the difference between the Latin "from" and the Greek "through" did not warrant a schism of the churches. His "conversion" was a potent force in favor of union.[29]

While all this was going on, the four friars, papal envoys, were in Constantinople, and Pope Gregory was awaiting an answer to his letter and news whether Greeks would come to his council or not. At last, in the summer of 1273 Emperor Michael dispatched two Greek envoys with a letter to the pope. With them he sent back two of the four friars, whose word would more readily be believed when they assured Gregory of his sincerity. Addressed to the "Supreme Pontiff of the universal Church and successor of St. Peter," his letter mentioned the difficulties that union caused the Greeks, spoke at length of his labors to promote it, extolled the blessings that would come from it, and expressed his readiness to accept it and what it involved. It ended with a promise that his ambassadors would soon be on their way with the other two friars, for which they would need security for a safe journey.[30]

Pope Gregory wasted no time. On 20 November 1273 he asked Charles to provide safe-conducts for Greeks coming to the council, according to a formula which he himself suggested, and that, "not only for a full assurance for them, their suites and goods in coming, remaining and returning, but also that you take them under your protection for the whole of the territories subject to you, having them conducted by suitable persons, appointed by you, in all those territories."[31] The tone of this request to Charles is calm and assured. Nevertheless Gregory betrayed his anxiety by seeking the advocacy with Anjou of the archbishop of Palermo and of the chaplain, Boncelli.[32] He also directed the abbot of Monte Cassino to meet the Greeks at their port of arrival and to counter with ecclesiastical censures any obstacles that might arise to their safe journey.[33] Charles found the papal request most unpalatable,[34] but he did not refuse (7 January 1274), though he limited the validity of the safe-conduct to one month. He also agreed to delay the departure of the projected eastern expedition until 1 May 1275, but without prejudice to the obligations imposed by the treaty of Viterbo of May 1267 on its signatories. Perhaps Charles was amenable to these papal demands because in September 1273 the vacant throne of Germany was filled by the election of Rudolph of Hapsburg, whom Gregory recognized in 1275, and because his troops fighting the Genoese were meeting with reverses. Genoa joined forces with the Ghibellines of the north and opened its harbor to Alfonso of Castile, a friend of Palaeologus and a promoter of union. All these events lowered Sicilian prestige in northern Italy and encouraged opponents.

Gregory's answer to Michael's embassy was dated 21 November 1273. By this time he was already in Lyons, where the council was to be opened the following 1 May. He told Michael how much he was gladdened by his zeal, but warned him that "very many persons of high condition and status assert that on the Greek side the negotiations for union have been drawn out to great length with specious talk and deceit," and that the same people continously tried to dissuade him from sending ambassadors and to prevail on him to follow another way which was ready at hand. The emperor, therefore, should look to his reputation; he was bound in honor to carry things through, so that his action might silence those who accused him of insincerity and rob them of the opportunity of saying: "What we feared has happened; we told you so; your embassies were a waste of time." Michael should persevere and indeed intensify his efforts to send ambassadors armed with all the powers necessary to fulfill what the last papal letter had proposed. Gregory would provide them with safe-conducts.[35]

Whether Gregory fully understood the difficulties that Palaeologus faced may be doubted, but his letter was friendly and breathed a spirit of trust. It also disclosed how much pressure he had been subjected to from Charles of Anjou, who had been with him in Orvieto from 27 May to 9 June and in Florence during June and July. Baldwin, doubtless, and his son, Philip, who on 15 October married Charles's daughter Beatrice, must have pleaded their cause frequently and eloquently, and the French party among the cardinals have lent its support. Gregory, as he himself wrote, did not "lend an ear of belief" to their words. But he looked to the emperor to justify his trust.

At home, with Beccus on his side, Palaeologus tried to make progress with the bishops. He kept telling them of the ruin that threatened the empire from the king of Sicily and insisted that his project of union in no way endangered their church. The patriarch was, of course, bound by the oath that the cunning Job Jasites had got him to take. It posed a problem to the emperor who, perhaps because it was Joseph who had freed him from his excommunication, had a particular affection for him. They agreed together on a compromise. Joseph would retire to a monastery, retaining, however, the title, honor and emoluments of patriarch. If union was achieved, he would abdicate; if not, he would resume his old functions. On 11 January 1274 he went to the monastery of Peribleptos. The bishops, however, could not be persuaded by Beccus's array of patristic quotations, or by the cajoleries of the emperor. Palaeologus asserted that the whole question between Rome and Constantinople lay in three points: the primacy, the right of appeal, and the commemoration of the pope in the Liturgy. These really meant nothing. When would a pope come to Constantinople to take the first seat? Who would cross oceans to appeal to Rome? What does it matter if the patriarch in Saint Sophia prays for the pope? Here was a case for the "economy"[36] so often exercised by the Fathers. But the bishops were still hesitant, though some boggled only at the commemoration of the pope, on the grounds that it admitted to their communion one who differed in faith as expressed in the Creed. The example of the bishops reacted on the monks and the populace, and resulted in great confusion, the people splitting up into many small factions, each boycotting the others.

Persuasion failing, Michael proceeded to exert pressure of another kind. Beccus had been only imprisoned. Holobolus, head of the Patriarchal School and orator, earlier a supporter of the emperor's scheme of union, was exiled when at a public meeting of all the clergy, in a fit of pique, he opposed it. Less than a year later, the emperor decided to use him to warn others to be more accommodating. He had him brought back in chains to the city. The prisoner was first scourged and then, roped together with nine others and his own niece, and with the intestines of a freshly killed sheep draped round his neck, he was paraded through the streets and particularly in the environs of the Great Church, being all the time beaten over the head with the animal's liver. It was meant to impress especially the clergy.[37] Lay opponents found themselves suddenly obliged to pay rent with all arrears for the mansions bestowed (as they thought) on them by the emperor after the recovery of the city; Palaeologus now proclaimed them his property by right of conquest. The clergy begged Michael to hold his hand until the outcome of the Council of Lyons was known. But he continued to insist, and at length the bishops agreed to accept a union with Rome limited precisely to the three points that the emperor had always been stressing: the primacy of the Holy See, the right of appeal for everyone who felt himself unjustly treated in a local ecclesiastical tribunal, and commemoration of the pope in the diptychs. Afraid that the three points might be stretched to include much else, they asked the emperor for a chrysobull setting out clearly these terms of agreement and guaranteeing that no point of their rite and customs should be changed. Michael willingly consented. Thereupon the bishops in synod, in a written document which each of them signed, recorded their acceptance of the chrysobull and decreed excommunication for any who should contravene the undertaking. The document is dated 24 December 1273.[38] This allayed misgivings, and even those who had gone into exile "returned and were united with the Church, no one of the clergy being excepted."[39]

Under these new circumstances it was not difficult to get a letter from the synod to send to Lyons. It was in the name of thirteen metropolitans with their synods, thirteen metropolitans (with no mention of synods), and nine archbishops. It was, however, not the full profession of faith proposed in the papal briefs. Michael and his son, Andronicus, on the other hand, made no difficulty about accepting and suscribing to the texts as sent from the Roman Curia. Ambassadors were appointed to take the documents to the Pope.[40] They were the ecclesiastics: ex-Patriarch Germanus, Theophanes, archbishop of Nicaea, and the metropolitan of Philippi (who died before he could set out); with the lay officials George Acropolites, the Grand Logothete, Panaretus, the Grand Chamberlain, and the chief interpreter, Berrhoiotes. Loaded with gifts for the pope, they set sail on *Laetare* Sunday, 11 March 1274. A violent storm sank the ship carrying two of the nobles and the presents. The other ship with the two ecclesiastics, Acropolites, and the Franciscans, Jerome of Ascoli and Bonagrazia, reached Cape Leuca, near Brindisi, on 5 April.

From Leuca the friars wrote to the pope. The letter gives some interesting information. Emperor Michael had made the prescribed profession of faith and acknowledged the primacy of Rome in their presence; and he had subscribed to the formula testifying to this. The Greek envoys are described — Germanus, a unionist for the last thirty years; the archbishop of Nicaea, pro-Roman; two others of the envoys had gone down with the 214 men on the sunken ship; and another, the metropolitan of Philippi, had died before the departure from Constantinople. The emperor would not take any oath, it being against Greek custom. He had in his keeping the signatures of the other bishops,[41] and these counted as oaths. "But the Patriarch, who now has the seat, an underhand (*subversus*) kind of man, would agree neither to the faith, nor to peace, nor to obedience, though we frequently requested it of him. But he writes a letter to Your Holiness, which we have in our keeping. It is closed and in a sealed envelope. He told us the gist of it, however, and we shall report it to you *viva voce.*"[42]

Michael's ambassadors were met in Italy by the Abbot of Monte Cassino, passed safely through the kingdom of Sicily, and made their way to Lyons.

The Council of Lyons opened 7 May 1274 in the cathedral church. The papal court had fasted in preparation for three days at the pope's command. When Gregory entered the church for the opening ceremony there were present fifteen cardinals, James, King of Aragon, the Latin patriarchs of Constantinople and of Antioch, some two hundred bishops, the masters of the Hospitallers and the Templars, abbots, representatives of cathedral chapters, barons, and others — 1024 mitred prelates, so it is said, with innumerable laymen, come even from the outskirts of Latin Christianity, Poland, Bohemia, and Norway, Ireland and Portugal, Greece and Palestine. The usual ceremonies were performed — the litanies, a chanting of the gospel, the invocation of the Holy Spirit. Then the pope preached on the text: "With desire I have desired to eat this pasch with you before I suffer." The sermon finished, he paused a little and then addressed the congregation again, "describing the purpose and desire of his heart and the reasons why and for which he had summoned the council, namely, for aid for the Holy Land, for union with the Greeks, and for the reformation of morals."[43] He then announced the date of the next session, 18 May.

"Between the first and the second sessions, my Lord the Pope with the cardinals summoned to his chamber separately all archbishops of one kingdom after another in turn, each with one bishop and one abbot of his province; also bishops and abbots who were immediately subject to the Roman Church. From these he demanded and obtained the tenths of all incomes, products and revenues of their churches for six successive years, beginning from the feast of St. John the Baptist A.D. 1274 till the end of six successive years, as is enacted in the constitution."[44] The constitution, *Zelus fidei,* to provide the financial support for the crusade that Gregory was bent on launching, was read in the second session. Then, having achieved the first and chief purpose of the council, Gregory dismissed to their homes all procurators of chapters, nonmitred abbots, priors, and all lesser prelates except such as had been summoned by name to attend the council. The next session was fixed for 28 May. Before it Gregory interviewed the prelates privately and won their approval for thirteen decrees, mainly concerned with episcopal elections. They were promulgated when the session met, actually on 4 June.

In the interval before the third session, the letter reached Lyons that

Jerome of Ascoli, on his way from Greece, had dispatched from near Brindisi. Only then did Gregory know that his unionistic policy with Palaeologus was bearing the fruit he hoped for. Such was his joy at the news that he called the council to a special meeting in the cathedral. St. Bonaventure preached a sermon, then Jerome's letter was read.

As the time of the arrival of the Greek ambassadors was uncertain, no date for the fourth session was set. The pope gave the congregated fathers permission to leave Lyons, provided they remained within a radius of six leagues. They had all returned before 24 June, the day the Greek embassy arrived. It was composed of ex-Patriarch Germanus; Theophanes, metropolitan of Nicaea; and George Acropolites, the great logothete; with the two Franciscan papal envoys, Jerome of Ascoli and Bonagrazia of San Giovanni in Persiceto; accompanied by John Parastron, O.M.; and doubtless by many Greeks of the suite. "All prelates who were in the council with their households, the Camerarius (Treasurer) with all the papal household, the Vice-Chancellor and all notaries, and all the households of the cardinals, went out to meet them and escorted them with honor to the palace of My Lord the Pope. The same Lord Pope, standing in the hall of the same palace, with all the cardinals and many prelates, received them with honor to the kiss of peace. And they presented the letter of the Emperor of the Greeks with its golden seal, and another letter of the prelates, and they said in the presence of my Lord the Pope that they were coming to offer complete obedience to the holy Roman Church, acknowledgement of the faith that that Church holds and of the primacy itself. Afterwards they went to their lodgings."[45]

Gregory, it seems, remembered Humbert's suggestion that Greek ambassadors should be treated with great respect and honor. He received Germanus and the others, not seated, but standing, and exchanged with them the kiss of peace — on the cheek — surrounded by all the sacred college and many others. The imperial chrysobull was their letter of credence.[46]

The Latin text of the letter of credence was the work of a translator not well versed in both languages. It betrays its Greek origins, is halting and even ungrammatical. But its message is clear. After an obsequious salutation to the pope, Palaeologus dilated at length on his personal passion for church union, something that had gripped him even before he had ascended the imperial throne. Hence his repeated letters to a line of popes. He wrote he was convinced of the identity of faiths of the two churches and had tried to bring others to his point of view.[47] "Now all those, who earlier seemed of an obstinate mind, We have made bend their necks with Us to Your obedience and to submissiion under the spiritual yoke of Your Holiness; We have had them enter Your fold and We have decreed that all the Christians of our Empire should be fed by one shepherd. We have ordered that all prerogatives and privileges which of old belonged to Your Holiness, which before the schism were its right, should be accorded by everybody here, namely, that Your Holiness should be for all of us, and should be entitled, first and supreme Pontiff and head of all the Churches, that ecclesiastical lawsuits should be referred to it so that they might receive a moderator in accordance with the ecclesiastical and canonical regulations and constitution.''[48] All this, Michael wrote frankly, they have accepted under compulsion, making reservation only of legitimate customs that do not offend against right faith. The obstinate (he continued) he had exiled, and in future he would exile any others. After this he presented his five ambassadors, Germanus, Acropolites, Theophanes, Nicholas Panaretos and George Berrhoiotes (these last two drowned off Negroponte), and asked the pope to receive them graciously.

This credential letter, dated ''March,'' like the letter from the prelates, was carried by the Greek envoys and presented by them to the pope. At the same time they perhaps delivered another imperial letter asking the pope to grant audience to Germanus and Acropolites, men in the intimate confidence of the emperor and specially empowered to treat of nonecclesiastical questions.[49] The profession of faith that the emperor had made and signed in the presence of the papal envoys in Constantinople, and sealed with his golden seal, and the corresponding letter of his son and heir, Andronicus, were probably in the keeping of the friars. They duly delivered them together with the letter sent through them unofficially by the patriarch, Joseph. They must, also, have reported privately to the pope on their mission and have given him their impressions of the situation in Greece.[50]

On 29 June, the feast of Sts. Peter and Paul, Pope Gregory celebrated a pontifical mass. When the Creed had been sung in Latin, ''the Patriarch with all the Greeks, the archbishops of Calabria, Brother William of Morbecca, O.P., and Brother John of Constantinople, O.M., penitentiary of my Lord the Pope, all of whom knew Greek, sang solemnly in a loud voice the same Creed, and when they reached the article, 'Who proceeds from the Father and the Son,' they sang it three times solemnly and devoutly. After the end of the Creed the same Patriarch, archbishop and the Logothete with all the rest chanted in Greek solemn acclamations to my Lord the Pope. Then the Pope continued and finished the Mass with the Greeks standing near the altar.''[51]

On 4 July envoys of the Persian sultan, Abaqa il-Khan, arrived and were met with the same solemnity as the Greeks. They had come to propose peace between their master and all Christians.

The fourth session of the council was held on 6 July. The Greeks were located "in the place where my Lord the Pope sat with the cardinal-deacon, on the right side, behind the cardinals." After the sermon

> my Lord the Pope addressed the council, recalling the three reasons why he had summoned it and noting that, contrary to the opinion of nearly everybody, the Greeks were coming of their own free will to the obedience of the Roman Church, professing its faith and acknowledging its primacy, and, despite the widespread scepticism, they were asking for no temporal return. He related also that he had written to the Emperor of the Greeks that, if he was unwilling to come spontaneously into the obedience and faith of the Roman Church, he should send solemn ambassadors to negotiate about the requests he wished to make; but that he, with the help of God, omitting all such preliminary negotiation, spontaneously and freely had in Greece professed and acknowledged the faith of the Roman Church and its primacy, and had sent his ambassadors to profess and acknowledge them in his [the Pope's] presence, as is declared expressly in the letters addressed to him by the Emperor.[52]

The emperor's profession of faith, the letter from the Greek metropolitans and archbishops, and the letter of Andronicus (all chrysobulls) were then read in Latin to the council.[53] The emperor's profession was addressed, not to the council but to the pope. It was the one formulated by Pope Clement.[54] It affirmed the *Filioque,* the Latin doctrine of purgatory "as explained by Brother John Parastron," and papal primacy. To this the emperor added an asseveration of his beliefs more reminiscent of the formula proposed by the Conclave than of that suggested by Pope Gregory. There was still another paragraph:

> Professing, indeed, and approving and accepting all this and promising to observe it, as has been said, We ask Your Majesty that our Church may recite the Holy Creed as it did before the schism and up till today, and that we may abide in our rites, which we used before the schism, which rites are not contrary to the faith laid down or the divine commandments or the Old and New Testaments or against the teaching of the general councils and the Holy Fathers approved by the sacred councils which were convoked by the spiritual sovereignty of the Roman Church. This, then, is not a serious matter for Your Holiness nor is it unusual, but to Us at this moment it is difficult because of the vast multitude of the people.[55]

The emperor's profession of faith was unambiguously the profession demanded by Rome. The document that was given to Gregory in the name of twenty-six metropolitans with their synods and nine archbishops (with two proxies), also of (apparently) all the curia of the Great Church, was of another kind.[56] It declared that now, as in the past, they were distressed at the division among Christians and desired nothing so much as unity. The document explained that the emperor had expended superhuman labors to bring unity about, and that as a result some of them were in immediate agreement with him. Others, however, were more obdurate and needed time for more thought; "but the pertinacity of the Emperor won in the end and now has all of one accord in this single union, in which we agree to attribute to the Apostolic See of ancient Rome the primacy attributed to it from of old." This they wished to come to the notice of the pope and of their emperor.

They also wanted Gregory to know that "almost the whole college of bishops with all the venerable imperial clergy and all the officials, priests, deacons and lectors of the Great Church of God has met and they attribute without hesitation to Your Holiness and the Apostolic See what pertains to its honor, among other things that you are and are called the first and supreme pontiff of all Churches, in accordance with the ancient canons, which also our fathers in all past time and up to this schism always observed." They wrote that they and the emperor had striven hard to persuade the patriarch to adhere to the union, but in vain. So they and the emperor had bid him retire to a monastery until the Greek envoys should return from the West with peace. If the pope were to accept the proposals of the Greeks, the prelates informed him, they would urge the patriarch to acquiesce; otherwise they would depose him and elect another.

> This is what we propose to you, God-honored Lord, we bishops who are subject to the patriarchal See of Constantinople, with all the venerable clerics in our curias. From this short statement you can conclude that, if only Your Magnitude will piously accept the message of the legation, there is now no obstacle between us, and we yield readily and we submit to the Magnitude of Your Highness, and we offer most willingly what is of total spiritual subjection, and without hesitation we attribute whatever before the schism our fathers showed to those who ruled the Apostolic See.

The communication concluded by informing the pope that envoys would propose other matters, both spiritual and temporal, and that they begged for a gracious hearing.

This letter, "written in the month of February, in the second indiction, 6782 [i.e., 1274]," was sealed and signed by the chartophylax, J. Beccus. The Latin text as it has come down to us bears no signatures at the end. Jerome of Ascoli in his letter to the pope from Cape Leuca reported that the bishops had consigned their letter to the emperor and that he had retained "their signatures in his archives." It is probable that he had their document engrossed by his officials, and possibly translated, for delivery to the pope.

The third letter that was read was a short missive of the coemperor, Andronicus, who associated himself completely with his father. "Whatever, therefore, shall be professed and agreed to by my Lord, the

Emperor, my father, and confirmed and ratified by Your Great Holiness, We also with all our heart and soul profess, agree to, acknowledge and heartily accept it all, as it pleases God and the decision and will of my father the Emperor, and We pledge ourselves by this present letter to observe it undiminished and inviolate."[57]

As the emperor sent no form of oath and as Acropolites declared that it was "by word of mouth" that he had been empowered to swear in the monarch's name, the Latin jurists apparently demanded some written guarantee of the validity of the procedure. Therefore, Germanus, Acropolites, and Theophanes signed a document declaring that "we . . . prelates, in accordance with our custom, by our signatures, and we laymen members of the senate, in accordance with our custom by oral oaths, which are within our competency when we have a commission from our Lord the holy Emperor for this given personally by word of mouth, are prepared to do this whenever it shall be ordered us by the most holy our Lord the universal Pope so to do, namely, to sign and to swear, with a pure and true conscience."[58]

In the council it was the logothete who gave the oral oath:

> When these letters had been read, one of the envoys, namely, the Logothete, declaring that he had by word of mouth from the Emperor authority to swear on his soul, if it so pleased my Lord the Pope, publicly professed the faith of the Roman Church and acknowledged its primacy, affirming that the Emperor declared that he held the faith of the Roman Church as it had been read out in the council, and that the aforesaid Emperor and Empire would retain it for ever and would never depart from it, as is contained more at large in the form of the oath.[59]

The form of the oath that Acropolites then recited in the emperor's name to attest to his sincere acceptance of the faith and primacy of the Roman Church has been preserved.[60] It was not the oath proposed by the Conclave in 1270, or that put out by Gregory, or even the same as the asseveration appended to the end of the emperor's profession of faith. It was, seemingly, one concocted for the occasion. Perhaps the bishops added their signatures to the document when the logothete had read it aloud.

When this public recital of the oriental letters was ended, the pontifical mass continued. Once more the Creed was sung in Greek as well as in Latin, and once more "the patriarch of the Greeks, the archbishop of Nicaea and the other Greeks who had come with them, as well as other archbishops and Greek abbots from the kingdom of Sicily" sang "who proceeds from the Father and the Son" and repeated this article. The ambassadors of the Persian Sultan were present, in front of the pope. The letters they had presented were read in the council. At the end of the session the pope "had read out some words from all the ancient councils."[61] The author of the

Ordinatio does not indicate what the extracts from the councils were about or why the pope had them read in this particular session. They might have been the professions of faith of the different councils and the decrees peculiar to each. Whatever they were, the action would have pleased the Greeks, for it was an outward expression of the identity and the continuity of the ancient and the contemporary church. One hundred and fifty years later, at the Council of Florence, a similar thing was done at their insistence.

Before the next session Gregory had the difficult task of introducing new legislation designed to avoid any repetition of papal conclaves lasting as long as the one of Viterbo that had elected him. Again he saw prelates privately and, in order to counter his actions, so did the cardinals, for they were opposed to any limitation of their rights. Gregory, however, prevailed and had the prelates sign and seal, nation by nation, copies of the constitution he meant to promulgate. Only when this process was complete could he determine the date of the next session, 16 July. On 15 July the Franciscan, St. Bonaventure, died in Lyons and was buried with solemn rites the same day.

The fifth session was preluded by the baptism, at the hands of Peter, cardinal-bishop of Ostia (who would be the next pope), of one of the Tartar envoys with two of his companions. The pope then entered the cathedral and after the usual ceremonies fourteen decrees were promulgated, including the one regulating the conduct of future conclaves. Gregory had meant this session to be the last, but the baptism and a papal allocution on the dead cardinal, Bonaventure, had taken so long that it ended very late. So another session was decreed for the next day.

On 17 July, as soon as the pope entered the church, two decrees were read from the pulpit. One of them, the only dogmatic decree of the council, defined the Procession of the Holy Spirit as being also from the Son.

> Since the sacrosanct Roman Church which by God's design is the mother and mistress of all the faithful firmly holds, professes and teaches that the Spirit proceeds eternally from the Father and the Son, not as from two principles but as from one principle, not by two spirations but by one spiration alone, and since it is manifest that this is the teaching of orthodox Fathers and Doctors, Latin as well as Greek, and since because of this, from ignorance of this irrefragable truth, some people have fallen into a number of errors of one kind or another, we, desirous of closing the roads leading to these errors, condemn and reject all who dare to deny that the Holy Spirit proceeds eternally from the Father and the Son or who rashly dare to assert that the Holy Spirit proceeds from the Father and the Son as from two principles and not as from one.[62]

After the reading of the two decrees the pope addressed the bishops, telling them that they were the bane of the whole church and that, if they would not reform themselves (if they did there would be no need of new reform measures), he would act firmly. With that the session, and the council, ended.

The decree defining the Procession of the Holy Spirit was never discussed in the sessions of the council — nor was anything else. Whatever discussion there was took place between the pope and the interested parties in the intervals between the sessions. Whether the Greek envoys, or at least the two bishops, were consulted before the publication of the dogmatic decree is not known, but the probability is that they were. Its content would have caused them no difficulty, for they had concurred in the emperor's profession of faith, and their own chanting and repeating of the *Filioque* in the Creed were a public declaration of their belief in it. The union of the churches was, in fact, effected in the fourth session, not in the sixth. The sixth was only to confirm unity in faith and officially to reassure the Greek Church that the Latin Church did not hold and profess in respect of the Procession of the Holy Spirit a double causality, which antiunionists persisted in alleging against it. This decree was inspired by someone who was familiar with the Greek polemic against the Latin doctrine and who intended to meet it by showing that it had no justification.

Two of the Greek envoys, Germanus and Acropolites, were specially authorized to conduct political talks with the pope. There is no record of any audiences, but Gregory must have interviewed them, and more than once. On some occasion they discussed Greek participation in the forthcoming crusade and delivered a document signed by all three envoys pledging Greek aid "in troops, in money, in victuals and in every other provision" when the pope should so wish, but on condition of "having peace with Latin neighbors."[63]

There is also extant another document listing proposals that they were to make to the pope.[64] Gregory was asked to send the abbot of Monte Cassino with plenipotentiary powers to negotiate all matters affecting the Greeks. In respect of help with the crusade, the emperor asked to have "peace with all Latin princes and kings . . . in such a way that he should have no fear for his cities and territories." The pope was to arrange marriages for Michael's sons and daughters "to the honor of His Imperial Majesty, obedience to the Holy See, and the advantage of the Empire of the Greeks." He was to write letters both to the "College of Clergy" and to the Greek senate, explaining the ecclesiastical situation so "that they should remain in their pious customs" as requested by the imperial letter; Gregory was to "write also to them words of exhortation and encouragement, as he thinks fit." The pope was not to give refuge to, or let any Latin prince give refuge to, anyone owning lands or castles who was an enemy of the Greek Empire. And the pope and his successors were to protect and help any future heir to the Greek throne who was a minor, and should not favor Latin arms in such a case. The document expressed a desire for peace between Latins and Greeks in Antioch, Cyprus and Jerusalem, a Latin ruling the Latins, a Greek the Greeks, and that on the death of a prelate or abbot he should be succeeded by one of the same church. To bring order into the ecclesiastical confusion of the time, the churches of Bulgaria and Serbia should be subordinated to Ochrida.[65] Lastly, Gregory was asked to write to the Latins serving in Palaeologus's army, bidding them serve the emperor faithfully in accordance with their oath.

How many of these proposals were acted on by the pope is not known. In the short letters he wrote on 28 July to Emperor Michael and his son, the coemperor Andronicus, he does no more than express his profound joy at the event that had taken place and, bidding them also exult, exhorted them to carry on the good work of strengthening union and eradicating schism.[66] On the same day he wrote also to "Our venerable Brethren" (there follow the titles of thirty-three metropolitans and nine archbishops and various functionaries of the Great Church). He thanked them for their letter and rejoiced at its content, namely that, "with the ancient schism cast aside, there should be one dove of the Lord,[67] beauteous, perfect; one Church indeed equally of Latins and Greeks, united in the unity of the same faith and head — with this your inmost desires, as you wrote, were in accord." Herein was the power of God, the kindly Spirit of Wisdom, that inspired your souls and your emperor's. To God be praise, who has reserved this grace to this day. Now they should pursue with all their strength what had been begun and "strive to do away with all traces of the old schism, casting out sheep that are diseased lest they bring infection into the Lord's flock or attaint the purity of the faith that in your hearts you have newly acknowledged." Such action was particularly befitting prelates.[68]

Pope Gregory, though he would have been content with the adherence of "some of the higher prelates," clearly believed that the great majority of the Greek hierarchy was solidly behind the union and that the letter from the metropolitans was a genuine testimony of this support. The Greek ambassadors to Lyons and his own returned envoys, the friars, cannot have told him very much.

Chapter VIII

Greeks, Latins, and the *Filioque*

If Pope Gregory did not appreciate the difficulties that in Byzantium would face the implementation of the union of Lyons, Emperor Michael at least should have had no illusions. He had not merely to meet the objections that his Church and people might entertain against the Council of Lyons and its decisions. He had also—and this was a harder task—to persuade them, if they could not forget, at least to disregard a prejudice against the Latins that was the result of centuries of history and the accumulation of innumerable, mainly minor but still irritating, differences of custom and of thought. For their part, the Latins knew little about the Greeks and what little they knew they did not particularly like. These antipathies must be taken into account when one considers the sequel to the Council of Lyons. To help the reader do this is the purpose of this chapter.

One of those papal envoys who accompanied the Greek ambassadors to Lyons, Jerome of Ascoli, submitted to Pope Gregory at His Holiness's request a list of "The things in which I found the Greeks to be in error, especially their priests and monks." Jerome details only doctrinal errors, or what he takes to be such. Other lists exist, both Latin about the Greeks and Greek about the Latins, that include an interminable series of other complaints besides.[1]

Such catalogues of accusations witness to the estrangement, even dislike and hostility, that characterised Latin-Greek relations, a phenomenon that was not new in the thirteenth century; it had its roots in Christian antiquity. Leo Tuscan, writing about the year 1170, gave a dozen reasons for the split between East and West, beginning with Rome's support of Flavian against Paulinus as bishop of Antioch (A.D. 398) and, following the course of history through the first Council of Constantinople, Pope Leo's rejection of the twenty-eighth canon of Chalcedon and various other temporary schisms and frictions, ending with Pope Alexander III's non-acceptance of the proffered union of crown and Church by Leo Tuscan's patron, the Emperor Manuel of Constantinople. The writer of this list, a Latin layman, held for some twenty years a respected position in Manuel's court and doubtless here he is reporting what he heard from Greek Church leaders of the day. It is interesting that his list does not mention Photius directly but refers only to the rival evangelisation of Bulgaria in the Photian era. Also it says no word about Cerularius or about Charlemagne.

That is not true of another assessment of causes. The writer of the *Tractatus contra errores Graecorum,* composed in Constantinople in 1252, attributes the schism to four main reasons—the division of the Empire in A.D. 800; that the Greeks were not invited to the council in the West when the *Filioque* was added to the Creed; the pride of papal legates who, when yearly they took chrism to Constantinople, would not leave till they were given eighty pounds of gold by the clergy and the people; and, most important, the deposition and excommunication of Photius and of other prelates and abbots. The historical inaccuracy of some of these statements does not matter. What does matter is that they were believed to be true by the leaders of eastern thought. They show that from early times there had been a tension between East and West that led to a growing estrangement, and that this ultimately issued in schism. By the thirteenth century there was a set disposition on both sides which (as Humbert of the Romans wrote to Gregory X) was "traditional and irrational, like the hostility between Ghibelline and Guelf entertained by people who knew nothing of its origins and the reasons for it, but who continued it because they found it so."[2]

One such idea had characterised Byzantine thought from its beginning, namely, the divine mission of the Byzantine Empire. The *Vita Constantini* of Eusebius of Caesarea had laid a solid basis for it within a few years of the foundation of Constantinople. It was by the power of God that Constantine had established the Christian Empire which was the earthly counterpart of the heavenly, through which all men were to reach salvation. As there was only one heavenly kingdom, so there could be only one on earth, composed politically of the Empire, spiritually of the Church, these two not separate but aspects of the same. Also there could be only one head, vice-gerent of Christ, appointed by God, crowned by God, the "divine" Emperor, who was over both State and Church, though, not being a priest, incapable of performing purely sacerdotal offices. "The Emperor's reign on earth is a replica of God's reign in heaven and his function a replica of that performed by the unique *Soter* and Logos."[3] All those who accepted the Christian Emperor and the Christian God were subjects of the Empire, no matter their race or country, and so the Empire was coterminous with the *oikoumene.* Constantine had transferred the government of the Roman Empire from Old Rome to the New Rome, Constantinople. It was still the Roman Empire and its citizens were Romans: "Greek" took on the meaning of "pagan."

This "faith"[4] in one State-Church Empire under one Holy Emperor was general in both East and West, though it sank deeper roots in the more congenial soil of the East. In the West Ambrose of Milan did what no eastern prelate of that day would have dared to do. He forbade the Emperor Theodosius to enter his church till he had done penance, and declared: "The Emperor is within the Church, not over it." But till the middle of the eighth century the popes sought confirmation for their election from the Byzantine Emperor. Shortly afterwards, when he had asked in vain from Constantinople for protection against the Lombards, Leo III in the year 800 crowned the King of the Franks, Charlemagne, as Emperor. The Christian East was shocked and angry and, even though twelve years later it grudgingly and with reservations accepted what had been done, it never forgave the injury to the very foundation of its political thought. While the East brooded, the West forgot. Pope John XIII in 968 addressed a letter to "the Emperor of the Greeks" to recommend the German "Otto, the august Emperor of the Romans." The Byzantine court exploded, inveighed against the "poor, barbarous creature" Otto,[5] and imprisoned the messengers who had presented the letter. In the East the idea never died. Emperor Manuel I Comnenus in a very long inscription introducing a theological decree called himself among other things: "heir to the crown of Constantine the Great and in his spirit holding sway over all his [Constantine's] rightful possessions, inasmuch as some have broken away from our Empire."[6] In c.1393, when the Byzantine Empire was tottering to destruction, the Patriarch of Constantinople, Antony, admonished the Grand Duke of Moscow: "It is not possible for Christians to have a Church without an Emperor, for the imperial sovereignty and the church form a single entity and they cannot be separated from each other."[7]

The Latin Church had a very different history. Europe had been devastated by Goths, Vandals, Huns and others, and hardly had it begun to recover when Northmen, Moslems and Magyars overwhelmed it again. The Church survived and, as the situation slowly sorted itself out, it was involved in and subordinated to the political power grasped by the hands of a multitude of local rulers. Bishops were imposed on dioceses by landowners either just for profit or to reward clerics who had served in their administrative offices or to have trusted supporters in charge of the extensive church properties or for other reasons. The situation evoked movements of reform within the Church, which demanded liberty—liberty of church appointments and of administration and liberation from the secular yoke. It turned into a struggle between the ecclesiastical and the political authorities, between *sacerdotium* and *imperium*. In the event, though late, the Church prevailed—both powers were from God, but the spiritual was of its nature superior to the secular, and a pope could *ratione peccati* or *casualiter* override the secular prince. The papacy grew in prestige and authority. It was the antithesis of the eastern attitude.

The recurrent barbarian invasions of western Europe had played havoc with scholarship and culture. During the short existence of Charlemagne's Empire there had been a brief renaissance, but its effects were lost or buried till peace came again only centuries later. Byzantium had been spared that scourge. It was able to cherish and to preserve the patrimony of the classical culture it had inherited from the glorious past of Greece. But the accent should be put on "preserve," though also for this, posterity must be intensely grateful that so many texts of poetry, history, philosophy, theology, medicine, astronomy, were saved for us from oblivion. The preservation, however, became static and artificial—literature, a pursuit of grammar and a lifeless imitation of the ancient tongue with no new inspiration. Philosophical speculation was stifled. Nevertheless, the Byzantines were intensely proud of their cultural superiority to all the rest of the world, who were barbarians. Before the tenth century they were justified; after it they were not. "What, then, in brief recapitulation, were the dominant and permanent elements in Byzantine and post-Byzantine thought? First and foremost, an unquestioning *faith* in the postulate of exclusive supremacy, both in religious orthodoxy and in material sovereignty, and in cultural eminence. Second and consequentially, an inbred, instinctive hatred of the West of Europe, whose inhabitants were abhorred as heretics and contemned as barbarians." Third, the universal belief that the Empire would yet in God's good time regain its old prestige and fulfil its political and spiritual destiny.[8]

In Byzantium theology, like other scholarly activities, was subject to the general influences. It is noteworthy that when in the ninth century Photius first attacked the Latin doctrine of the *Filioque* he supported his charge with reasoning based on metaphysics. After that same question had been unhappily resurrected from oblivion two centuries later by Cardinal Humbert in his squabble with Cerularius, Greek polemics forsook almost entirely metaphysical argument and relied only on tradition. Their tractates on the Procession of the Holy Spirit were little more than catenae of quotations from the Fathers. Syllogistic argumentation was held to be quite inappropriate in questions of the Blessed Trinity.[9] The Byzantine Church had become the "Church of the Seven Councils and the First Eight Centuries."

While the intellectual life of the Byzantine Empire was slowing down, that of the West was developing at an ever increasing pace. Eminent theologians attracted groups of students and produced manuals of enduring merit, like Peter Lombard's *The Sentences* (completed c.1157) or Gratian's *Decretum* (completed c.1140). From this kind of beginning there sprang the universities which received their charters in the course of the next century when no country was without its important centres of learning, and certain cities—Paris, Bologna, Montpellier, Salerno, Oxford—enjoyed special and international fame. Into these new *Studia Generalia,* through the Moslems of Spain (less from Byzantium) there entered the treasures of ancient Greek philosophy, which were rapidly translated into Latin and lit a new intellectual flame. The same period was "the age of the flowering of medieval knighthood (1150 - 1300), of uniformly constituted values, which were binding on the knights of all lands of Christendom. . . . God's fighter (*miles christianus*) protected the Church and her goods, fought against the heathen, shielded the weak, widows and orphans, and unselfishly established God's order on earth."[10] The practice did not always accord with the theory, but the theory was there and exercised an ennobling influence, giving inspiration to and being developed by the crusades. Almost analogous to the feudal knights were the new Mendicant Orders of Dominicans and Franciscans, approved by the Holy See in 1219 and 1223 respectively. Their early fervour raised the standard of Christian practice, brought new genius to the study of theology (e.g., St. Thomas Aquinas and St. Bonaventure) and sent Friars in obedience to the popes' wishes as missioners to the ends of the earth.

It was when the West was in the full vigour of this cultural development in the arts of peace no less than in those of war, in an increasing number of lively cultural centres and in the use of the vernacular as a means of expression to a wider audience, that the Fourth Crusade and the Latin Empire of Constantinople brought it face to face with the East.

These fundamental ideological differences between East and West were felt rather than analysed by their contemporaries. Each side was convinced of its own superiority, despised the little that it knew of the other and was ready to condemn the least variation from its own self-righteous norm. This gave rise to a mutual malaise, which manifested itself largely in querulous complaints on matters of small importance.

Hugo Aetherianus (brother of Leo Tuscan and, like him, resident for a score of years in the eastern court) wrote in 1176 that Greek love of liberty came from pride and in their pride the Greeks thought themselves better than the Latins. That the Latins should have added "From the Son" to the Creed without consulting them was, they considered, an insult. Union with the Latins, they thought, would mean odious subjection. The last point at least was exemplified in 1204. Alexius III in 1203 rallied the inhabitants of

Constantinople not to open their gates to Prince Alexius, come with the crusaders, for the fear of the rule of Rome and the loss of liberty. Nevertheless the crusaders took the city. Whereupon the Latin Church insisted on obedience to the Pope and to the Latin Patriarch of Constantinople (which justified the Greeks' worst fears), and the Latin Empire was inaugurated by the capture and the savage sacking of their city. This made an impression on the Greeks that they could never forget, for their pride in the Queen of Cities, before it was disfigured by Latin insensibility, brutality and rapacity, was immense. Nicetas Choniates wrote pages of heart-broken lament on the senseless devastation. Innocent III berated the crusaders: The Church of the Greeks "has beheld in the Latins nothing but an example of perdition and the works of darkness, so that now rightly it abominates them more than dogs." While the soldiers snatched what gold and silver they could find in the churches, the prelates stole the relics of the saints. Abbot Martin of Pairis, having terrified the venerable monk-custodian of the church of the Pantocrator monastery by shouting at him *terribili voce,* made him open up the relics, "which, when the abbot saw them, he plunged both his hands in hurriedly and graspingly and, belted as he was, he filled his bosom with the holy sacrilege, as did also his chaplain, taking what seemed to them most precious, and then, cunningly hiding their booty, they went out."[11] The conquered Empire was divided among various lords, who were hard taskmasters, imperious and exacting with their new subjects. These, naturally, if they could not flee, bore their lot as best they could, but with no love for their masters. "The most accursed Latins liken the lands that have fallen to us to inhabit and cultivate to paradise, and, covetous to a degree of our good things, they are always ill-disposed to our race and devise all kinds of mischief for it. Even if for some occasion they put on a show of love, they really hate us and are our worst enemies. If their speech is gracious and flows out as smoothly and soundlessly as oil, still even such words of theirs are arrows, more trenchant than the two-edged sword."[12] A century and a half later (1339), Barlaam told Pope Benedict XII in Avignon: "It is not so much difference of doctrine that divides the hearts of the Greeks from you as the hatred against the Latins that has entered their souls from the many great evils that in different periods the Greeks have suffered from the Latins and still suffer every day. Unless this hatred is first dispelled, union can never be brought about."[13]

Despite the military successes of the Latins, the Greeks despised them as barbarians, the poverty of whose language perhaps excused them for not knowing the difference between "From the Father" and "From the Father and the Son." The Latins on their side believed that "serious scholarship has in great measure perished among them [the Greeks], and so they do not understand arguments from reason, but they cling to certain councils and to opinions that they have received from their forebears, just like heretics for whom reason has no value."[14] It is not surprising that Michael of Epirus, who tortured and killed Latin prisoners and beheaded all Catholic priests that fell into his hands, should call Latins "dogs,"[15] but even the exiled archbishop of Athens, the mild Michael Choniates, exhorted Theodore Lascaris to "drive the raving dogs out."[16]

On the other side, an unknown Franciscan of the thirteenth century described the Greeks as "divided from the Roman Church, cunning men, little practised in arms; they wear long beards and err in the faith and in the articles of the law."[17] "They treat Latins like dead bodies and despise them like cracked pots,"[18] or like "dead dogs."[19] If, with difficulty a Greek could be prevailed upon to give a thirsty Latin a drink of water, he would afterwards break the vessel or throw it away.[20] The chronicler of the Catalan Grand Company, Ramon Montaner, was contemptuous of the Greeks as soldiers. "God," he wrote, "had sent down so much pestilential evil on the Greeks that anyone could defeat them," and that for two sins of theirs: "One, that they are the most arrogant people in the world; there is no people on earth they esteem and value but only themselves, yet they are worthless people. The other is that they are the least charitable people to their neighbours to be found in all time."[21] Andronicus II paid the Catalans for their victorious services in a specially debased coinage that had only five parts gold to nineteen of alloy; and the Catalan chief, Roger de Flor, was murdered at a banquet given by the Emperor's son and heir, Michael, to get rid of the Company that had shown up his incapacity as a general (1305).

Byzantine diplomacy was notoriously devious, as was remarked on by a Russian chronicler of the eleventh or twelfth century, who bitterly recorded that "the Greeks have remained deceivers to the present day."[22] In the West, belief that the Byzantines were treacherous was current at least since Bohemond of Antioch after the first crusade had toured Europe rousing sentiment against the Emperor Alexius I Comnenus, who, he alleged, had withdrawn his army at the most crucial moment in the campaign for the capture of Antioch. The succeeding crusades tended to confirm that belief. Frederick Barbarossa, being bidden welcome by the imperial ambassadors of Emperor Isaac while his army was being harassed by imperial guerillas, nearly attacked Constantinople in 1189. Meanwhile, Emperor Isaac, continuing negotiations begun by his predecessor, was writing feverishly to press Saladin to confirm the treaty against the crusaders. He assured him that "They were so exhausted [i.e., Frederick's troops after Byzantine harassment] that they cannot reach your dominions; and even if they should succeed in reaching them, they could be of no assistance to their fellows, nor could they inflict any injury on Your Excellency."[23] Pachymeres attests that the Latins called his countrymen "white Saracens."[24] In the West the conviction was growing that no crusade would succeed till its lines of communication were safeguarded by possession of Constantinople.

The commercial privileges enjoyed by western merchants in eastern ports were a long-standing source of rankling resentment for the Greeks. In Constantinople, for instance, Genoese and Venetians in particular, as well as Pisans and others (some 80,000 in number in c. 1171), possessed special quarters in the city. They paid little or no tax on their commerce and had their own courts and various other prerogatives, while the native Greeks paid heavy taxes with diminishing returns.[25] In 1171, and again in 1182, popular indignation burst out in the massacre of Italians in the city. For a time western competition was lessened. But Michael VIII's treaties with Genoa and Venice gave back to the foreigners their old dominance and more, and ultimately involved the Empire in their fratricidal wars, wherein it always lost.

Despite, however, the ubiquity of Italian commercial activity in the east and especially in the ports of the Byzantine seaboard, seemingly few Latins learnt Greek and not many Greeks knew Latin. Even after the sixty years of the Latin Empire established on Greek soil, the papal Curia possessed no one proficient in Greek when Michael VIII began sending his embassies.[26] The Byzantine court, at any rate, had a department or at least an official court-translator for Latin documents, who on occasion was sent with an embassy to the West to interpret.[27]

It was only towards the end of the thirteenth century that some of the treasures of Latin theology were turned into Greek and so made available to eastern scholars. Maximus Planudes translated St. Augustine's *De Trinitate,* parts of Boethius and even some secular literature like Ovid's *Metamorphosis.* It was, however, not till the middle of the next century that the theological revival of the West made any notable impact on the East and then it was late: Barlaam and the Palamite controversy had deepened the prejudice against it. Demetrius Cydones, intent on learning Latin for practical uses, encountered the writings of St. Thomas Aquinas and was lost in admiration at "the loftiness of his thought." He hastened to share his discovery with his friends. He and his brother, Procorus, translated the *Summa contra Gentiles,* the *Summa theologica* and other works, as well as excerpts from St. Augustine, St. Jerome, and Boethius. Though St. Thomas († 1274) obviously had never heard of Gregory Palamas, his writings, chiefly his *De ente et essentia,* inspired many of the scholars who opposed Palamism, like Procorus Cydones, Isaac Argyrus, Theodore Dexius and John Cyparissiotes, and provoked others such as Nilus Cabasilas, Matthaeus Angelus Panaretos and Joseph Bryennius to compose refutations. Not all Latins could any longer be said to be barbarians, but they could still be heretics.

So, apart from this late contact in theology, over the centuries there had been no communication between East and West of patristic writings, theology, history, astronomy, literature and all the other vehicles of thought and taste that would have fostered friendly relations and mutual respect. Instead, Greeks and Latins lived in mental worlds apart. What material contact there was generated hostility and contempt. Humbert of the Romans was wise in pressing for the cultivation of relations of all kinds—scholarly, recreational, marital—with easy access to each other's literature, so as to bridge the chasm of estrangement that separated East and West.

Such mutual ignorance fostered misunderstandings. This was nowhere illustrated so fully as in the lists of ecclesiastical "errors" drawn up by both sides. The Greeks complained that in the Latin Church Mass was celebrated by the same priest more than once a day and that more than one Mass was said at the same altar on the same day; that baptism was by one immersion with the trinitarian formula, which meant confusion in the three Persons of the Trinity; that ordinations were confined to the *Quattuor tempora,* thereby setting limits to the power of the Holy Spirit; that priests were celibate and that they shaved like soldiers; that the popes and bishops wore silk, not wool which was a living material from which Christ's seamless garment had been woven; that the sign of the Cross was made with five fingers; that fasting was enjoined even on Saturdays; that Our Lady was called only St. Mary; that monks ate meat, and so on and so on. A list, composed probably in the middle of the thirteenth century, comprises sixty items, the last asking how people with such practices can be deemed orthodox and not heretical.

The Latin lists are shorter and deal somewhat less with trifles. They accuse the Greeks of simony in church appointments; of fasting only on one Saturday of the year and on only seven days in a year; of eating meat on Fridays. Greek monks are said to eat outside the cloister and to wear their hair long without the tonsure: divorce among Greeks is easy, a mere application to a city official. "Also they do not believe that simple fornication is a mortal sin."[28] Greek baptism, according to the lists, is strange, for the whole of the body of the candidate for the sacrament is anointed with oil, lest the water touch the skin; their bishops are chosen from monks, which is a mistake for monks are fanatics; they wash their altars if it happens that a Latin has celebrated there; and if a Latin marry a Greek woman, he must give up all his Latin traditional practices and adopt Greek ones. Greek women married to Latins often have their children rebaptised secretly in the Greek Church, thereby repeating the sacrament.

These lists with all their absurdities witness to a complete lack of understanding and sympathy between the Churches. They do not mention any of the large number of points believed and practised in common. They are all negative, and it is manifest that each Church, convinced of its own dogmatic and ritual superiority, condemned and despised the other for its supposed shortcomings and aberrations.

But besides the trifles already mentioned, in all the lists, both Greek and Latin, certain more fundamental questions figured. The two Churches had different regulations on the forbidden degrees of kinship for marriage and different ideas about the state of the just and the unjust immediately after death. The Latin Church conferred four minor orders; the Greek Church did not. The Greeks rejected outright as invalid the use of unleavened (dead) bread in the Eucharist, whereas the Latins allowed equally leavened and unleavened bread, but stigmatised as heretics those who denied validity to the sacrament in unleavened bread. For the Latins, the pope was successor of St. Peter and head of the whole Church. The Greeks declared that the Latins elevated him above St. Peter and nearly made him God. The greatest controversy raged round the *Filioque*—lawful or unlawful addition to the Creed, doctrinally true or false? For the Latins it was lawful and true; for the Greeks unlawful and false. It had been introduced into the Creed by the Roman Church acting alone. In Greek eyes no single patriarchate—indeed, because of the prohibition of the Council of Ephesus, not even the whole Church—could alter the Creed even by a syllable. At the least, for so serious a step, all the patriarchates should have been consulted in a general council. The Roman "Church" was no more than one of them, even though it was the first, the *primus inter pares*.

It was, of course, inevitable that as the centuries went by there should have been different developments in East and West, and even in theology. One such was in the approach of the two Churches to Trinitarian doctrine. "For the sake of describing things ineffable," wrote St. Augustine in his *De Trinitate* (vii, 4 [7]), "that we may be able in some way to express what we are in no way able to express fully, our Greek friends have spoken of one essence and three substances, but the Latins of one essence or substance and three persons." Both Greeks and Latins realized that these expressions of the mystery were inadequate and attempts at describing the indescribable, and that each in its own way was true. The harmony of tolerance continued for centuries till it was shaken when the East reacted to the inclusion by the West in the Nicene Creed of the word *Filioque* — the Spirit proceeds from the Father *and the Son*. This focused attention on the theology of the phrase. In the ninth century Photius, Patriarch of Constantinople, denounced it as heretical. It then dropped out of sight till Cardinal Humbert in 1054 accused the Greeks of omitting it from the Creed. Anselm of Havelberg, ambassador of the German King Lothar III to Constantinople in 1136, defended the Latin doctrine against Nicetas of Nicomedia. Some forty years later Hugo Aetherianus, domiciled for a score of years in Constantinople, wrote a long treatise, *De sancto et immortali Deo,* issued in both Greek and Latin, to prove the orthodoxy of the *Filioque,* which showed that the subject was then still alive in the eastern capital. It figured again, and in the first place, in every theological encounter of Latins and Greeks in the thirteenth century. It was (at least ostensibly) the chief obstacle to Emperor Michael's plans for Church union, even though the conversion of Beccus influenced some eastern theologians to moderate their condemnation of the western doctrines.

Beccus's change of front was the result of his reading the tractates of Blemmydes and others, whose treatment of the controversial question approached the Latin position. There were, in fact, in the thirteenth century among Greek writers on the Holy Spirit two schools of thought. Some, the majority perhaps, asserted flatly that the Spirit proceeds from the Father only. Others insisted (quite rightly) that no Doctor of the Church taught "only" and that most of them wrote of the Spirit as proceeding from the Father through the Son. But what was the significance of "Through"? For a few theologians it was the same as "From": Latin doctrine, therefore, was in itself orthodox. Others attributed to the word no more than a connotation of "consubstantiality," not of origin. For these, Latin doctrine was wrong. The material, as it were, from which these diverse conclusions were drawn was the same for all. With one or two notable exceptions, writers did not have recourse to metaphysical reasoning. A few scriptural texts, and chiefly — almost exclusively—quotations from Greek Doctors were the staple of the proofs.[29] Latin controversialists met their Greek counterparts on Greek ground. Hugo Aetherianus, the Friars at Nymphaeum, the author of the *Tractatus contra errores Graecorum* of 1252[30] and Bishop Nicholas of Cotrone relied upon abundant quotations from Greek Fathers to vindicate the orthodoxy of the Latin Creed.

Beccus claimed that other Greeks before him had written in favor of the *Filioque* clause—Peter, Patriarch of Antioch in the time of Cerularius; Nicetas, Archbishop of Thessalonica, who, though he fought shy of saying "From" and adhered to "Through," also held that Latin doctrine implied no double Procession but a single Procession from Father and Son, and that "by the grace of that Spirit . . . we agree with one another in saying 'the Procession of the Spirit is from the Father through the Son' ";[31] and chiefly Nicephorus Blemmydes.

Blemmydes modified his views certainly once, possibly twice, before his death in c. 1172. The replies that he made to the Latin arguments propounded in Nymphaeum (1234) and Nicaea (1250) have already been recorded. In them he granted that between the Son and the Spirit there was a real relationship of consubstantiality, of possession (the Spirit of the Son), of donation (the Spirit given by the Son), of mutual likeness and even of a certain dependence (like fingers [Spirit] on the hand [Son] which is of the person [Father]).[32] But he rejected outright the Latin co-causality. Only the Father is cause of both Son and Spirit: the action of fingers is not strictly caused by the hand but only by the person: water and water-vapor issue forth together, both equally and only from the one source. The same definite refusal to countenance the *Filioque* is contained in a reply he wrote to the Emperor Vatatzes: "Whoso says that the Spirit proceeds from the Son but that the Son is not cause of the Spirit is a liar."[33] For Blemmydes the *Filioque* necessarily implied two causes of the Spirit and that was blasphemy.

Obviously it was not these writings of Blemmydes that led Beccus to approve the *Filioque,* but two short treatises that he had written, the one addressed to James, archbishop of Bulgaria, composed c.1253,[34] the other to the Emperor Theodore II Lascaris of between 1254 and 1258.[35] Blemmydes's purpose in these essays was not to counter Latin doctrine but to oppose and correct some Greek writers. Several of these, he says, carried their polemics against the Latin "From the Son" to such excess that they denied that the Spirit proceeds from the Father through the Son, referring any use of the word "Through" in the Fathers to the temporal mission of the Spirit to men.

"Through the Son," asserted Blemmydes, is the common teaching of the Doctors and even of more recent writers, and no Father ever denied it. In proof he refers his reader to a big collection of texts that he had earlier produced, from which in these two treatises he repeats a certain number, quoting Athanasius, Basil, Gregory of Nyssa, Epiphanius, and Cyril, to show that "Through" was the common teaching and that "Through" in the Fathers meant a relation between Son and Spirit not of appearance only or of mission to creatures, but a reality, namely, that the Spirit proceeds by his essence from the Father through the Son.

Against this position adversaries appealed to St. John Damascene, who had written: "We do not say that the Spirit is from the Son but that the Father is the sole cause." Blemmydes cut the ground from under their feet by hailing this, not as an objection, but as a further proof of his own contention. The Damascene did not deny "Through." He was only affirming, and rightly affirming, that the Father is the prime source of divinity. "We profess one only principle without principle of both creation and divinity, of creation by activity, of divinity by essence, namely, the Father. Whoso then speaks of the Spirit as being from the Son gives rise to the suspicion that he is professing that the Son possesses the power of emitting, as the Father has of generating. . . . Whoso says that the Spirit is from the Father through the Son manifestly professes that the Father is sole cause of the Procession of the Spirit. For all that the Son has, he has as having received it from the Father, substantially that is and by essence, as true Son from true Father."[36]

In his solution of objections Blemmydes covers ground he had traversed in his controversies with the Latin Friars, but, as it were, in the opposite direction. His later answers reflect his change of thought. In self-defense he now answers objections he had put to them. In 1234 he had defended that the consubstantiality of the Son and the Spirit was sufficient explanation of the "Spirit of Truth" being the "Spirit of Christ," which the Latins had said demanded Procession. In 1253, faced with a like objection apropos of the Spirit being sent by the Son, he replied that consubstantiality was not enough, for otherwise the Spirit would equally send the Son: there was need of the more fundamental relationship of "Through the Son." His "Through," he declared against other difficulties, did not imply inequality between the Second and the Third Persons: "If one were to say that the Spirit is from the Son as from a first principle, the Son would then assuredly be conjoined with the Father in respect of the dignity of principle—but then how would he be Son? [i.e., he would be Father]. But if the Procession of the Spirit from the Father is clearly declared, as well as that whatever the Son has [he has from the Father], then the adversaries are fighting shadows."[37] This answer might well have come from the mouth of one of the Friars.

Another difficulty he had to face repeated what he had himself objected in Nymphaeum. It was based on the internal economy of the Blessed Trinity. "Whatever is said of God is either common to the three Persons or is the property of one of them. We know nothing that is half-way between an essential and an hypostatical property. But the Spirit admittedly proceeds from the Father; he cannot proceed from himself; hence not from the Son. So Procession will be proper to the paternal hypostasis." To this Blemmydes answered by insisting, first, that he was not asserting that the Spirit proceeds from the Son, but only through the Son: second, that the Spirit cannot be sent by himself, but he is sent by both Father and Son. "So then you have the mission of the Spirit half-way between an hypostatic and an essential property," which destroys the grounds of the objection. "Further, what are we to say when from the very name of the Spirit a medium is known where a medium is not descried, for the Holy Spirit is said to be Spirit of the Father and Spirit of the Son, and he is so; but he is not, nor is he said to be, Spirit of himself, just as the Father is not Father of himself nor is the Son Son of himself."[38]

In the discussion with the Franciscan, John of Parma, in 1250, Blemmydes roundly rejected the Latin *Filioque* and said nothing about the essential consubstantiality of Spirit and Son with the relevant Latin-sounding arguments. In 1253-8 his two treatises were full of this. In 1264 (the year in which he finished his *Curriculum vitae*) again there is no mention of it. Was he in 1253 leaning towards the *Filioque*? It is most unlikely. Certainly he nowhere professed it. The most he affirmed was "Through the Son." Even in the treatises to the Archbishop of Bulgaria and to Lascaris, where he was insistent on the "Through" in essence, he denied the "emitting power" to the Son and declared that its possession would have made the Son no Son at all, but Father. He followed the general line of Latin thought, but not to the end. With them he agreed that between Son and Spirit a more basic relationship than mere consubstantiality was needed to accord with the words of the Fathers, and one founded in the essential Procession. Both Churches taught that the Father is the prime source of divinity within the Blessed Trinity and that all is common in the Trinity except the individuating properties. The Latins argued that Fatherhood, Sonship, and Procession were the sole individuating properties. Blemmydes followed Greek thought—uncaused cause, caused by generation, caused by Procession. While using in the exposition of his own view the Gospel text, "All that the Father has is mine" (John XVI 15), Blemmydes could not, as did the Latins, accept that within that "All" there could be included also the power productive of the Holy Spirit, and therefore that Father and Son could be one sole cause of the spiration of the Spirit, with the Father still remaining prime source of all divinity. So, when in the writings of the Fathers he came across phrases like this one of St. Cyril: "When, then, the Holy Spirit being in us shows that we are conformed to God, and since He comes forth both from Father and Son, it is obvious that He is of the divine substance, coming forth substantially in it and from it." Blemmydes—but not Cyril—immediately added: "'He comes forth,' he says, 'from the Father and the Son,' that is, from the Father through the Son."[39]

When Beccus read the treatises addressed to the Archbishop of Bulgaria and Theodore Lascaris and studied the excerpts from the Fathers there quoted in their original contexts, unlike Blemmydes, he added no qualifying and negating comment of his own, but followed their thought logically to the end. In that way he became convinced that "From the Son" and "Through the Son" had the same substantial meaning and that schism between the Churches because of a supposed Latin heresy about the Holy Spirit was unjustifiable.

The first treatise that Beccus produced to vindicate the orthodoxy of his conversion and to persuade his colleagues to follow his example is entitled "On Union and Peace of the Churches of Old and New Rome."[40] He leaves the reader in no doubt as to his position: "As regards the purpose of this essay, I want straightway to sum up the scope of the essay in these two points: the one, specifically to expose in the essay all written testimonies in which the various theologians who have written on the Trinity manifestly state plainly and clearly that the Holy Spirit has his existence from the essence of the Father and the Son, which is what the Church of the Romans professes when it says that he proceeds from both: the other, by argumentation, with God's grace to prove that the opposition of the authors of the schism and the trend of their successors towards the same were not sufficient motives for their great extension of the schism, so disastrous to the Churches."[41] This is a clear commendation of Roman doctrine. Shortly after he repeats his approval. The Roman Church "founding itself on the teaching of the great saints and following their opinions proclaims that the Son is from the Father alone and says that the Holy Spirit is also from the Son. Nevertheless it clearly professes and confesses one principle in the Blessed Trinity, having learnt from the teaching of the Fathers that everything of the Spirit leads back to the Father, the first cause. To affirm that the Spirit is from the Father and the Son without at the same time professing two causes of the Spirit comes clearly from nowhere else than from the dictum that whatever is the Son's leads back to the Father, the first cause,"[42] as say Sts. Basil and Gregory and other saints (whose words he quotes at length).

In his day, Beccus asserts, St. Athanasius was accommodating over the penury of expression of the Latins but approved what they meant. The Greek saints have used a variety of phrases in respect of the Holy Spirit—"comes forth from," "flows from," "proceeds from"—and all of them in a substantial sense: they all mean the same thing, "that the Spirit is substantially from the Father." More recent theologians, "in their own estimation safer exponents of the faith than the Fathers, manufacture differences from these expressions and, basing themselves on these fabricated differences, they reject all steps leading to reconciliation with the Roman Church,"[43] which asserts the equivalence in meaning of the phrases. Hence they accuse the Romans of teaching two causes in the Trinity, in spite of Athanasius, Basil and others of the Fathers.

Beccus goes on to show by quotation after quotation that the great Doctors used "be poured out," "come from," "emanate from," and such like phrases to express the essential origin of the Spirit and that they employed them in respect both of the Father and of the Son, which showed that the Fathers and the Latin Church were in harmony. With more quotations he rebuts the objection that such words apply only to gifts outside the Trinity. "To be poured forth," "to issue forth," "to emanate," "to come forth," etc., "from the Father" clearly express the essential existence of the Spirit from the Father. There can be no reason to alter their meaning when they are applied to the Son, especially as the Doctors often link Father and Son together in them, e.g., "come forth from Father and Son" etc. To prove his point Beccus quotes among others the text from St. Cyril[44] which Blemmydes, having cited, had hastily rendered inoffensive by adding that, when the saint wrote "From," he meant "Through." For Beccus he meant what he wrote—"From"—and he goes on to demonstrate that in respect of the Holy Spirit "Through" is equivalent to "From." This he does once more by quotations from the Fathers where either they expressly assert the legitimate use of either word or where they employ consecutive phrases as synonyms, one with "From," another with "Through," to express the origin of the Holy Spirit. St. Cyril, for example, wrote "essentially from both, namely from the Father through the Son." Hence Beccus concluded: "There is no difference at all between saying that the Spirit flows forth essentially from the Father and the Son and flows forth from the Father through the Son."[45]

With such an assertion Beccus went further than Blemmydes. Without mentioning him specifically, he proceeded to justify himself. "There are people who say: 'Here we have something new, if the Spirit is said to be through the Son and to proceed from the Father through the Son, for we will not grant that here "through" is to be understood in the sense of ministry or essence: perhaps in neither of these ways.' What are we to say?"[46] Beccus answered at length. "Through," as all agree, implies a medial position of the Son between Father and Spirit—but of essence, not of ministry only. "The Spirit is said to be from the Father through the Son and from the substance of the Father and, since he is from the substance of the Father, who will not admit that the substance is of the hypostasis? So then, with the Spirit essentially and in hypostasis proceeding from the substance of the Father through the Son, who will affirm that 'Through the Son' is to be accepted as an expression with a non-essential meaning and not as an affirmation of an essential intermediatorship? For what is essentially from the essence of the Father and is not from the Father immediately has the Son as a medium, in every sense substantially, in harmony with his being from the Father."[47] In fact, to assert both "Immediately from the Father" and "Through the Son" is to affirm a contradiction. Sayings of the saints, like St. Gregory's "The son, the prototype of the Spirit" and "The Spirit, the image of the Son," all show this clearly.

But, continued Beccus, it is objected that a medium means an order—first, second, third. Agreed, he replied. That is precisely what Gregory of Nyssa and Basil taught—not an order in time, but a logical order of Son to Father and of Spirit to Father and Son. Then, to clinch the arguments for his position, Beccus discusses a number of ambiguous phrases found in the Fathers (but without mentioning St. John Damascene) and ends the first part of the treatise with quotations from Sts. Basil, Athanasius,

Chrysostom, Cyril and Epiphanius where they employ the preposition "From" to express the essential relationship of Spirit to Son.

Writers of note in the past had defended the proposition that the Spirit proceeds from the Father only. Beccus takes the more influential of them one by one, beginning with "the first inventor and father of the propositions devised against the Roman Church," and in his criticism "makes a start with the syllogisms that he disseminated in order to ignite the flame of battle." That was Photius.[48] After him, he deals with John Phurnes, Nicholas of Methone and Theophylactus of Bulgaria. He ends his treatise confident that "he had made peace with the Roman Church while adhering completely and in every detail without change to our own customs and ways, to the glory of Father, Son, and Holy Spirit of the consubstantial Trinity."[49] Adherence to "our own customs and ways" did not mean that Beccus rejected the Latin *Filioque.* He believed the doctrine it contained but would not insist on outward expression of it as often as the Creed was recited. As he wrote in his *Apology,* what he meant was that, "while for the sake of union he was acting as advocate for the Roman Church," like Athanasius he set more importance on the meaning than on the word, and so would not be a cause of dissension by undue insistence.[50]

Beccus wrote a number of other treatises in defence of his and the Latin doctrine of the *Filioque.* They cover the same ground though in different styles. In his "On the Procession of the Holy Spirit" he took specific texts or difficulties that were objected against him and offered solutions. The Bishop of Sugdaea received three short essays answering queries that he had proposed. One long treatise was entitled "Against Andronicus Camaterus." Camaterus had produced between 1170 and 1175 at the suggestion of Emperor Manuel Comnenus a volume with a large collection of quotations from the saints and the Fathers with comments of his own on them, to attack the Roman Church and the *Filioque* in particular. Beccus took them one by one, first quoting then answering each in turn.

Amid the general and inevitable repetition involved in so many writings on the same subject, here and there a phrase or a paragraph stands out and illustrates more clearly Beccus's thought and theological acumen. To Theodore of Sugdaea he explained why the *Filioque* does not confuse the Persons of the Son and the Spirit within the Blessed Trinity. "The very names, Father, Son and Holy Spirit, denote exactly the individuating properties of the Trinity. That the Father is neither Son nor Spirit is the precise property of the hypostasis of the Father," and similarly with the Son and the Spirit[51]—which is just what Latin theologians taught. Against Camaterus he complained that his adversaries triumphantly propounded arguments founded on so-called axioms that were nothing but fabrications of their own, and false at that. "There are fictitious doctrinal axioms asserting 1° that to produce the Spirit is the property of the Father; 2° whatever is affirmed of the Trinity is of one or three; 3° whatever is asserted about the divine Persons is either of a Person or the nature; 4° the Father is the cause of what is from him by reason of his hypostasis, not of his nature; 5° the Spirit is, without any medium, immediately from the Father. None at all of these, even if one were to read right through the writings of the God-directed Fathers a thousand times, would he ever find said by any of them. The promoters of schism made them all up."[52]

While able when necessary to argue metaphysically about the internal economy of the Blessed Trinity, Beccus, like the other theological writers of his day, relied mainly on the authority of tradition contained in the writings of the Fathers to support his case. That he had read them not merely in *catenae* or collections of quotations but had studied the complete treatises for himself is apparent from his handling of them and because normally he gives a clear indication of his source—the writer's name, the title of the treatise and the number or sub-heading of the section—to introduce each quotation. Blemmydes had sent "a tome full of very many quotations" to Lascaris (so he told the Emperor in the essay addressed to him), doubtless the collection of texts he had made as the arsenal for his treatises. Beccus too had written much and made full use of the words of the Fathers. He also produced a book of excerpts—the *Epigraphae.* He did better. He classified his quotations and arranged them in such a way that they built up into a powerful proof of his theological conviction. The line of argument is similar to that of his "On the Union of the Churches," but supported by much more numerous and ample quotations. The book has altogether thirteen sections, each with a paragraph of introduction and each containing apt excerpts from the Fathers, anything from a dozen to three dozen in number. It was a rich mine of patristic learning that would serve many an advocate of Church union in the years to come. But it failed to persuade the bishops of his day or to make any impression on the dogged opposition of the monks.

The theologians of the Eastern Church rejected the *Filioque,* not merely because it was an addition to the Creed, but because they were convinced that it was doctrinally erroneous. Anchored in the old truth enunciated by so many of the Doctors of the Church that the Father is the sole source of divinity, they saw in the *Filioque* a derogation from that fundamental principle and an undermining of the whole economy of the Blessed Trinity. Hence their opposition. In the West the *Filioque* had been introduced into the Creed to safeguard the full divinity of the Son, and, for their part, the Latins saw in the Greek exclusion of it a diminution of that divinity and a threat to the perfect Trinity in Unity.

So it was not surprising that, when Michael, with Beccus's support, and

Pope Gregory strove to bring the Churches to union, they came up against the built-in resistance of the mass of the Greek nation. The theological motives of the learned were bolstered up by the instinctive sentiments of the populace. The age-long tradition that the Latin Church was heretical defied argument. To have accepted Latin orthodoxy would have implied that the Greek Church had been wrong in its condemnation. It would have seemed to justify the arrogance of the Latins and their flouting of the other four patriarchs of the Pentarchy in adding to the Creed without the approval of a general council. It would have strengthened the influence of the barbarous Franks, with whom they wanted the least possible contact, for contact with them led to domination. They were the *Rhomaioi,* the genuine citizens of the Empire divinely established through the agency of Constantine the Great and, after its desecration by the impious barbarians, restored to them in 1261 by Providence, so that under the protection of the Virgin it might fulfill its destiny to the glory of orthodoxy and the confusion of heresy.

Chapter IX

The Reaction to the Council of Lyons

The Greek envoys to Pope Gregory in Lyons set off home in the autumn of 1274, bearers of the various papal letters. With them went John Parastron, commissioned specially by the Pope to continue to exercise in Constantinople the zeal for union he had shown in Lyons.[1] The Abbot of Monte Cassino was also of the party, entrusted with the task of arranging yet another truce between Philip of Courtenay and Charles of Anjou, the Latin contenders for power in Byzantium, and the Greek Emperor Michael. In this he succeeded and was back in Italy before 29 April 1275. So the Angevin expedition against the Greek capital was deferred again, this time till at least 1 May 1276. Anjou's acceptance of this proposal was not due entirely to religious motives. In 1274 he was engaged in defending Guelf interests in northern Italy. There, faced by a combination of Ghibelline cities headed by Genoa and supported by Alfonso of Castile, claimant for the kingship of the Romans, he was losing ground. Also the Genoese fleet dominated the waters round Sicily. Pope Gregory, after the election of Rudolf of Habsburg as King of the Romans, was bent on persuading Alfonso of Castile to withdraw his candidature and he looked, not to Charles, but to Rudolf, to settle the Ghibelline-Guelf strife in Italy. By the summer of 1276 Charles possessed only a few towns and villages in Piedmont.[2] He could then give more attention to his other projects. In the meantime he had not altogether neglected them; in fact, he had not been allowed to. Palaeologus did not consider that wars in Greece fell within the limits of the truces he had agreed to and, even during the council, he attacked towns held by Charles in Albania, capturing Butrinto and threatening Durazzo and Avlona. Charles had to send reinforcements to hold the Byzantine troops off.[3] But like Anjou, Emperor Michael accepted the truce proposed by Bernard of Monte Cassino, perhaps because he saw in it what the Pope meant it to be, the beginning of a permanent peace with the West and also, he hoped, liberty to pursue his plans in Greece.

When he wrote to Gregory to announce the success of his mission, the Abbot of Monte Cassino informed him that the Emperor Michael intended to send an embassy. At Gregory's request King Charles not only issued for it a safe-conduct, but assigned one of his officials to accompany it.[4] Not long afterwards Palaeologus sent another embassy. One of these two embassies was composed of two persons only, George Metochites and Theodore the Grand Dispenser. The other had four envoys, the Metropolitan of Serres, Theodore Monomachus and two others. Which came first and which second is not clear. Both figure in the same safe-conduct for the return-journey, given by Charles and dated Rome, 19 May 1276,[5] and this is the sum total of what we know of the existence and purpose of the larger mission. In respect of the smaller mission, Metochites has left an account of the task allotted to him by the Greek Emperor.[6] It was nothing less than, among other things, to suggest that the crusade that was to Gregory "as the breath of life" should make its way to Palestine, not by sea, but by land through Asia Minor. This was said to offer many advantages. The march would be safer, for Michael would arrange with his son-in-law, the Sultan of Turkey,[7] for safe passage. There would be less risk of dispersal of the army, and *en route* it would bring back into the hands of believers so many places famous and venerable for their past Christian associations. Gregory, reports Metochites, was ravished at the thought and declared that "either before or after the restoration of the Holy Places" it should be done. As, however, he was on the point of departing for Italy, he sent the ambassadors on to Rome to await him there. When he reached Rome in the winter, he would send one of his cardinals to Constantinople with them, and after Easter he would himself go to Brindisi and either there or in Avlona on the mainland of Epirus he would meet the Emperor Michael and arrange details.

The envoys waited in Rome, but Gregory never came. He had died on 10 January 1276 a few days' journey away from the city. Another important object of Metochites' mission (and perhaps the main one of that headed by the Archbishop of Serres) was to enquire about the Latin crusade—its personnel, prospective strength, time-table—and to renew certain requests previously made by the Greek Emperor—censures against "apostates" and security of inheritance to the throne for his descendants.[8]

Gregory's successor was the first Dominican to become Pope. He was Pierre de Tarentaise, archbishop of Lyons, then cardinal bishop of Ostia, elected on 20 January 1276, who took the name of Innocent V. To him it fell to deal with the two embassies sent to his predecessor. In answer to the political enquiries made through Metochites, he informed the Emperor that the kings of the Romans, of France and of Portugal, with a multitude of knights and nobles had taken the Cross and would set out when arrangements were concluded. Palaeologus himself should help generously, despite his treaty with the "Sultan of Babylon" (Baibars of Egypt), from which the Pope released him. In respect of the request for excommunications, "since certain princes of the Latins have petitioned and still petition with great insistence for what is diametrically opposite to your demands, in order that injury may not seem to be done to either of the two parties urging such contrary requests, We of set purpose have decided to comply with neither of them in these matters, thinking not without reason that such an attitude will do much to promote the negotiations for peace between you and those princes, negotiations whose success We have very much at heart."[9]

This letter he delivered to the Greek envoys. At the same time he commissioned four Franciscans, headed by Jerome of Ascoli, to take to the Greek Emperor other letters dealing with the spiritual situation. The two parties left for Constantinople in company. When they reached Ancona they learned that Innocent had died on 22 June 1276. The Greeks continued their journey. The Franciscans turned back.

The Greek legation that had assisted at the Council of Lyons had reached Constantinople towards the end of autumn 1274 with its tidings of success. But Patriarch Joseph made no move to abdicate from the patriarchal throne, and it needed a decision of the synod, that in the circumstances the agreement he had made in the previous January amounted to an abdication. He ceased to be commemorated in the Liturgy on 11 January 1275 and was lodged comfortably in the Lavra (the monastery of St. Michael) near Anaplous. A few days later, on 16 January, a solemn Liturgy was celebrated in the church of the Blachernae palace by Nicholas of Chalcedon. The epistle[10] and the gospel were read in both Greek and Latin, and Pope Gregory was commemorated in the appropriate place. The union was thus proclaimed, but the Greek Church was more than ever split into parties, some composed of people "whose knowledge was confined to the hoe and the axe . . . others with knowledge but far too vehement in their advocacies".[11]

As successor to Joseph, Beccus was elected patriarch (26 May) and enthroned (2 June 1275). Joseph at Anaplous was too near Constantinople to be left in peace. He became the centre of anti-unionist resistance and, in answer to the Emperor's expostulations, replied that he could not in conscience refuse his counsel no matter who asked for it. As a result, he was removed to Chele, a harsh place in winter, and Job Jasites was sent to Cabaia, a fort on the Sangarios river. The unrest in Constantinople continued. Michael's own favourite sister, Eulogia, was strongly anti-unionist. Her daughter, the Czarina of Bulgaria, at her mother's instigation conveyed to her by monks, even invited the Sultan Baibars to ally with her husband, the Czar, against her uncle Michael.

Michael must have had early news of the death of Pope Innocent from George Metochites and the other returning ambassadors. At some time, perhaps to felicitate the late Pope on his election, perhaps also as bearers of the new Patriarch's letter of enthronisation, he had "sent still another embassy to the Pope, both to make known the successful conclusion of the business and to learn whether Charles had desisted from the expedition and had restrained his ambitions." The envoys had found Charles at the papal court, biting his sceptre in paroxysms of frustrated rage as the Pope blandly turned a deaf ear to his protests and demands for freedom of action.[12]

Metochites would also have informed the Emperor and the new Patriarch, Beccus, that Pope Innocent had meant to send four nuncios to the court of Constantinople and, as he had been very friendly with the head of that embassy, Jerome of Ascoli,[13] he may have had a hint that the purpose of the Latin embassy was to press for a more general and palpable implementation of the union. It may have been this information that excited the anti-unionists to manifest their opposition more openly, and impelled the ecclesiastical authorities to take steps to restrain them. In February 1277 the Holy Synod met for the purpose and produced a *tomographia*—a Statement in Writing—that was signed by all the bishops present, imposing severe penalties on the opponents of the union. The document describes the situation it was intended to meet. It makes it clear that the opposition was both widespread and deeply felt, for among the anti-unionists were members of the imperial family, bishops, senators, ecclesiastical dignitaries, monks and laymen (among whom there were many women), whose propaganda was undermining the goodwill of the simple. So they were summoned to appear before the synod, and the impenitent were condemned, if they were clerics, to deprivation of office and excommunication; if laymen, to excommunication.[14]

All the officials of St. Sophia had to subscribe to the Statement, and there is extant a document bearing forty-one of their signatures witnessing that they accepted papal primacy, right of appeal, and commemoration of the pope in the union of the Churches.[15] Likewise the unsettled state of affairs prompted the Emperor to exact a declaration of loyalty from the officials of the palace.[16] Perhaps it was also in this same period of intense upheaval that an accurate translation of the dogmatic definition of the Council of Lyons was issued.[17]

At about the same time as the great synod was meeting in Constantinople to approve and confirm the union of the Churches, in Thessaly John

Doucas was convening an assembly for precisely the opposite purpose—to condemn it. He gathered together eight bishops, several abbots and about a hundred monks, who excommunicated Pope, Emperor, Patriarch and all who supported them in their nefarious work of union. Palaeologus sent an emissary to reason with John and his brother Nicephorus who also dubbed all unionists heretics. Thessaly, Epirus and even Trebizond were becoming refuges to which anti-unionists fled from Constantinople and the power of the Emperor. Their rulers saw a chance not only of vindicating their own orthodoxy but of making political capital out of the ecclesiastical unrest. Nicephorus of Epirus and John Doucas, the "Bastard," of Thessaly were both of them liege-vassals of the Emperor Michael, the one with the title of Despot, the other of Sebastocrator. They did not abate their opposition even when the Emperor sent them copies of two excommunications against opponents of union, the one promulgated by the great synod, the other issued by Rome.[18]

Beccus informed the Pope of the positive action that the Greek Church had taken when it decreed the punishment of anti-unionists in a letter which must date from very shortly after the meeting of the synod.[19] In it he affirms the acceptance by his Church of all papal prerogatives and privileges, and as evidence of the synod's zeal for union he sent also a copy of the *tomographia.* The letter ends with a profession of faith as a testimony to the Pope of the Patriarch's personal orthodoxy.[20] It was entrusted for delivery to the papal nuncios who had already arrived in Constantinople, probably at the end of February 1277.

The Pope who had sent them was John XXI. No sooner had he been elected on 8 September 1276 than he began to organise an embassy to Greece. It was composed of four Dominicans, two of them bishops.[21] They were the bearers of letters identical with those prepared by Innocent, apart from a change in the names of the nuncios, a small amendment in their faculties since two of them were bishops, and a permission to enlist interpreters. They set out for Constantinople early in December 1276.[22]

The spiritual letters they carried were short. They announced to the Emperor, to his son Andronicus, and to the Patriarch with his hierarchy John's accession to the throne, his rejoicing over the union and his desire that it should be brought to completion. To the hierarchy nothing more specific was said, except to recommend his nuncios to them. To the two Emperors a further hint was given, that "considering the situation together with our brethren, We find that what was done by you stands in need of the stability that comes from a greater firmness":[23] the nuncios would help them to remedy the defect.

The political situation was dealt with in the Bull, *Pacis aemulus.* The spiritual union that had been achieved ought not to be jeopardised by political dissension. Though what the Emperor had done in the spiritual sphere "still stands in need of the stability that comes from a greater firmness," nevertheless the Pope will proceed to deal with the temporal. Strife, disorder, rapine (he writes) are almost tangibly present, because Philip claims Constantinople as his own, Charles vindicates rights over some parts of it, and both declare themselves set on making good their titles.[24] The Pope fears that it will result in an appeal to arms. Palaeologus should not put his trust in his might or the uncertain fortunes of war but rather, on reflection, adjust his mind to thoughts of peace and communicate his conclusions to the papal nuncios. He should send his own plenipotentiaries to the Apostolic See within five months of the receipt of this papal Bull. "There is no doubt that it is to your advantage not to delay in this matter, for unless an effective and speedy answer is forthcoming concerning it, the aforesaid princes, thinking that they are being played with, will not (so they affirm) patiently let themselves be cheated of the ripeness of the present moment, on which they set great value. Nor can We without doing violence to their rights prevent them from pursuing those rights by such remedies as are permitted." Therefore to avoid incidents that could seriously interfere with the negotiations, Palaeologus should agree to a truce, as the nuncios would propose, "for We have already managed to incline the minds of the Emperor and the King to a truce."[25]

This letter has a very threatening tone, and the claims of the Latin contenders for the Greek Empire are expressed in blunt, almost violent, words. And it was addressed to "Michael, Emperor of the Greeks"[26] while Philip was described as Emperor of Constantinople. Innocent had already won Charles to accept yet another truce. The chief aim of the letter to Palaeologus with its ominous ending was to induce him to co-operate and, in addition, to take steps to establish a permanent peace. The Latin princes were already tired of his dilatoriness, construed by them as a policy. Alexander and then John XXI gave him five months in which to make a move. If he did not, they accepted no responsibility for the consequences.

What the Pope meant by the "stability that comes from a greater firmness" was indicated in the instructions given to the nuncios. When they met the Greek Emperors they were to salute them in the Pope's name, express his joy over the union and his affection for their imperial persons. Then in respect of spiritual requirements they were to ask 1) Michael to sign the original copy of his profession of faith (which they had with them) and to testify to it by oath, and 2) publicly to abjure the schism, which would be a demonstration of his sincerity and give him a greater claim on the gratitude of the Roman Church. 3) Andronicus was to be asked to do the same, and several copies on parchment and paper, sealed, were to be made of these public acts. 4) The Emperor was to be persuaded to induce the bishops who had not yet made a profession of faith and acceptance of the primacy to do so. 5) He should agree to abstain from what would impede the negotiations for peace and to agree to a truce covering the period known to be agreeable to Philip and Charles. 6) To meet the Emperor's request, the Roman Church "means as far as with God it can favourably to uphold them [the Greeks] and to support them in those of their rites which in the eyes of the Apostolic See do not infringe the integrity of Catholic faith and in no way transgress the enactments of the sacred canons." 7) The prelates and the clergy, singly, should unconditionally profess and recognise the truth of the faith, and accept the primacy of the Roman Church as Pope Gregory had enacted through Jerome of Ascoli, and should take an oath to that effect. The formula for that oath was included in the letter of instructions. (It was not the one proposed by Gregory, but the more rigid formula enacted by the Conclave in 1270, which included also a promise of canonical obedience with the act of obedience. Not only that. Other requirements set by the Conclave were added.) 8) Clerics were not to preach anything against that faith and in the Creed they were to chant also "And from the Son," "because that was treated of specially and acknowledgement of the true faith ought not to be hidden but rather to be publicly preached." 9), 10), 11) The envoys themselves were to go to the bigger cities to witness the professions. These were to be made in several copies and sealed, one of which was to be preserved locally in the archives for the information of posterity.[27]

The above *Memoriale* sets the maximum that the Pope hoped for. Other instructions to the envoys mitigated somewhat its demands.[28] If the Emperor would not abjure the schism publicly, he should do it at least in the presence of some notables; if not with an oath, he should repeat personally all that the Logothete had affirmed in his name and sign at least two copies or, at any rate, one. If the prelates refused manual obedience, it could be omitted and the envoys should get as many copies of their professions as was possible. As the Holy See was most anxious to maintain and to strengthen the union, the legates should fulfill all the requirements of the *Memoriale* if they could. If they could not, they should get as much as was in the circumstances possible, but they should also indicate to the Greeks their dissatisfaction at any deficiency.

Innocent V and after him John XXI in this letter suggest that they are imitating Pope Gregory when they propose their formula of acceptance of the faith and primacy of the Roman Church. That is not true, even verbally. The formula they proposed, of the Conclave of 1270, was devised in an atmosphere of distrust to pin down the Greeks and to eliminate all possibility of evasion. Gregory had introduced into the negotiations a new tone of trust, of sympathy, of elasticity in practical application. Though he hoped for more, he insisted only on a minimum—good will on the part of the Patriarch and of some eminent prelates. With that he was satisfied. He allowed variations in the formula and did not insist on an oath. He was content to get the union going in the hope that it would grow from strength to strength.

Innocent plunged it back into the old cast-iron mould. He would have it complete and immediate and, to demonstrate that it was so, he insisted that the *Filioque* should be publicly recited in the Liturgy. Presumably he did not realise how fatal a step that was, that it would seriously disconcert the unionists in Greece, antagonise the waverers and rally all the anti-unionists to a more implacable opposition. But if he did not, perhaps someone else did. Charles of Anjou, fully persuaded that Michael's unionistic fervour was purely political and expedient, and, from his contacts in Epirus and Thessaly, aware of the strength of the opposition to it in Constantinople, possibly urged Innocent to prove the sincerity of the ecclesiastical union by applying the acid test, the *Filioque.* Charles had some reason for his scepticism about Michael. The Greek Emperor, though pressed by successive popes, never did enter into serious negotiations for a stable peace, for that might have tied his hands in Greece and the Balkans. Gregory would have countered Charles's insistence with "The fortunes of war which once gave Constantinople to the Latins had now restored it to the Greeks."[29] Neither Innocent nor John had the breadth of mind to be so impartial.

The Greek Emperors, Michael and Andronicus, raised no difficulty about complying with the religious requirements of the Pope, in so far as they were concerned personally. In a long letter of April 1277 Michael reaffirmed his adherence to the union and his obedience to the Holy See.[30] This he sent to the Pope by a solemn embassy, bearers also of several copies of his profession of faith and of the oath he signed to accompany it. Andronicus also sent a long letter and copies of his profession and oath.[31]

Beccus was stimulated by their example to make a similar profession of faith. He wrote another and longer letter to the Pope.[32] Like the former one, this letter also began with union, that the Greek Church accepted wholeheartedly the primacy, the right of appeal and commemoration of the Pope. Again the penalties they had imposed on opponents were mentioned to show that the Church had accepted the union sincerely.[33] Then, he continued, because it had been said that "there was some difference in dogmas between the two Churches, the Greek and the Latin, by reason of the addition to the Creed, We certainly should set forth the formula of our faith."

The letter then becomes a profession of the Patriarch's faith, a paraphrase rather than a copy of the Clementine formula. Schism we abhor; we accept ecclesiastical concord and the unity and the primacy of the Holy See, and we promise to preserve inviolate the prerogatives recognised by previous patriarchs of Constantinople and the obedience and rights acknowledged by our emperors and our God-inspired Fathers as belonging to that See—"namely, that that sacred and holy Roman Church possesses supreme and complete primacy and sovereignty over the whole Catholic Church. We sincerely and humbly acknowledge that she received this, together with the plenitude of power, granted to her by the Lord in Blessed Peter, prince or head of the Apostles, whose successor is the Roman Pontiff. We likewise acknowledge that just as, more than others, she is held to defend the faith, so if questions about the faith arise they ought to be settled by her decision." To her all may appeal: to her all Churches should be subject and obedient. Whatever privileges other Churches may have acquired were confirmed by her and could be confirmed by no other.[34] There is no difference of faith between what is read in the Nicene Creed, in the Constantinopolitan Creed, and in the Roman Creed with the addition.

Then, beginning "We believe in one God," the patriarchal profession very verbosely expresses the Christian doctrine of the Trinity, including the Procession of the Holy Spirit from the Father and the Son as from one source.[35] The Latin doctrine about the hereafter comes next, expressed in the words of the Clementine text; then belief in the seven sacraments, with comments both to affirm the legitimacy of eastern practices regarding confirmation conferred by simple priests and the Eucharist celebrated with leavened bread and to admit third and even later marriages. "To sum up in a word: since the said holy Roman Church reverences and preaches all these tenets, we believe and say that that same Holy Roman Church teaches and preaches them with sound faith, orthodoxy and truth, but even so we must abide without change in the customs that have obtained in our Church from the beginning." This document is to prove our rejection of schism, our obedience to the Roman Church and that our Church is in complete agreement in the orthodoxy of its faith with the "holy, apostolic mother of all Churches, the Roman Church" (April 6785 [= 1277]).

The last document that the Greek envoys carried was a letter of credence dated 24 July 1277 authorising six named ambassadors to proceed to the papal Curia as plenipotentiaries to arrange a truce with Philip of Constantinople and Charles of Anjou.[36] When they arrived in the autumn of 1277 they found the papal throne vacant, for still another pope was dead. John XXI had succumbed on 20 May 1277.

All these new conditions required by the Holy Sea "to add stability" could not but render the task of Palaeologus and Beccus more difficult—indeed should they really try to implement them all, impossible. They did their best. On 16 July 1277 Patriarch Beccus excommunicated Nicephorus and John Doucas by name according to the formula drawn up by him and his Great Synod on the previous 19 February against all schismatics and disturbers of the union who would not recognise the Roman Church as "mother and head of all other Churches and mistress of the orthodox faith," and acknowledge the pope as "first pontiff and pastor of all Christians."[37] For his part, Emperor Michael sent an army under four generals, who were all relatives of his, to subjugate Thessaly. The generals, "knowing that the Emperor was united with the Pope and therefore deeming him a heretic," turned traitor and refused to engage, letting the Bastard occupy certain imperial strongpoints. They were brought back and imprisoned. Other commanders were sent, who disobeyed orders and were defeated. On the other side of Constantinople, the Emperor of Trebizond set himself up as an orthodox rival for the imperial throne "occupied by a heretic." John Doucas entered into an alliance with him. At home, women of the imperial and of noble families were plotting against the crown. Many magnates, men and women, were in prison for their anti-unionism. In Thessaly the bishop of Trikkala, because he stood by his word given in the Great Synod held by Beccus, was imprisoned by John for more than a year, until he escaped to Lepanto. The bishop of Kitros, suffragan of Thessalonica, was maltreated for the same reason. Those enemies of union were being constantly aided by the Latin lords of Thebes, Athens, Negroponte and the Morea. That is why Negroponte (so ends the *aide-memoire* of Ogerius) had been attacked and, by God's grace, successfully.[38]

Palaeologus readily fulfilled all the demands made on him by Pope John to implement the union. He wanted something in return. The nuncios nominated by Popes Innocent and John had been given faculties to impose ecclesiastical censures on those who impeded the union. Michael had asked Innocent for the excommunication of Nicephorus of Epirus and, particularly, of John of Thessaly. Innocent had refused, maintaining neutrality, for those two rulers, though admittedly they were fomenters of anti-unionist activity, were political allies of Charles of Anjou and political enemies of the Greek Emperor. Michael exerted great pressure on the four nuncios sent by John XXI to make them use their faculties against the two Despots and, one would say, not without reason in view of the Bastard's local synod that denounced all unionism as heretical. The nuncios probably promulgated in general terms the excommunication of all those who impeded union. They did not excommunicate anyone by name. On returning to the papal court they told the new Pope, Nicholas, about the insistent demand of the Emperor, with the consequence that when later Nicholas sent ambassadors of his own he laid down for them very detailed criteria on which to base their action.

So the embassy of Pope John XXI only laid new burdens on Palaeologus and released him of none. Yet the tale of woe, all of it true, recounted in the *aide-mémoire* of Ogerius demonstrates the difficulties in which he was placed, and the intensity and the ubiquity of the opposition to the union. It could not, however, adequately convey to Latin minds the magnitude of the danger threatening him. Their Emperor was, for the Greeks, the divinely appointed guardian of orthodoxy. If he were to lapse from the true faith, he could not be fulfilling his office.[39] As a heretic he could easily be regarded as having forfeited his imperial throne. That was precisely what John of Thessaly and Alexius Comnenus of Trebizond were saying openly and the Arsenite faction of monks, whose aims were as much political as ecclesiastical—to restore the Lascarid Dynasty to power—was whispering covertly when they claimed that Michael was a heretic.

As a result Constantinople was seething with unrest.[40] The populace—nobles and commoners alike—kept in a ferment by the ever-busy monks was divided into Arsenites and Josephites but united as anti-unionists. Forbidden to voice their protests publicly, they had recourse to pamphleteering. Leaflets, anonymous and so irresponsible, made the most outrageous statements. Beccus was the target of many. The hierarchy also was opposed to him. Michael was irritated by his insistence in pleading for clemency for condemned prisoners. He lent a ready ear to accusations made against him by the clergy and, to show his displeasure, he withdrew all patriarchal monasteries outside of the diocese of Constantinople from patriarchal jurisdiction, alleging an abuse. Beccus resigned his office on 2 March 1279.[41]

That the patriarchate should have been vacant at that moment was unfortunate for the Emperor, since papal nuncios arrived just then. He met them at Adrianople and, while escorting them to Constantinople, sent to beg Beccus to take up office again. The papal envoys had been dispatched by the new Pope. Giovanni Gaetani Orsini, an Italian, elected on 25 November 1277 as Pope Nicholas III, had announced his election both to Palaeologus and to Beccus and had received back from them in the course of 1279 replies expressive of their devoted affection.[42] The Greek Emperor utilised the returning papal messengers as envoys of his own and entrusted them with a *viva voce* communication for the Pope, whose content was outlined in the *aide-mémoire* of Ogerius already referred to. Palaeologus asked the Pope to give them a gracious hearing and begged him, "now that you know the truth, with aid, benedictions, counsel and favour, to assist me, the devoted son of Your Apostolic Holiness, to perform with profit for the heavenly Caesar what pertains to the earthly Caesar, that by Your help the works of the impious may be confounded." It was another plea for papal action against "apostates."

Before the year was ended Nicholas reopened contact with Constantinople. Meantime he had despatched a group of Franciscans to the Tartar kingdom in Persia ruled over by Abaga, who had sent an embassy to Pope Gregory in Lyons and another to Italy to Pope John.[43] By another letter he transferred to the vacant See of Corone the Latin bishop of Lacedaemon, who had never been able to, and still could not, have access to his See of Lacedaemon, which was in the hands of the Greeks.[44] In Hungary, the Tartar invasion had wiped out the Christian mission of the Franciscans. Nicholas took steps to restore it and he encouraged the Dominicans working among the Cumans, "allowing them to baptize those who wish to be converted to the faith according to the rite which in such cases the Roman Church observes."[45]

In October 1278 Pope Nicholas prepared an embassy for Constantinople, composed of four Franciscans, Bartholomew, bishop of Grosseto, with Bartholomew, Franciscan superior in Syria, Philip and Angelo. They were armed with a sheaf of letters and safe-conducts.[46] In the Brief presenting his nuncios Pope Nicholas praises Michael and his son for their zeal for union and thanks them for having sent the signed copies of the professions of faith. He encourages them to persevere. Report, statements from papal envoys, the truth and Palaeologus himself all declare that "this business [of union] and its perfect completion depend entirely on you" and so he should see to it and promptly. The papal ambassadors will ask the Emperor "to hear with good will what should suitably be done both by you and by others to lead to a more perfect completion, establishment, and a firmer strengthening, of this business." Nicholas apologises that Palaeologus's messengers had been detained for so long at the Curia (from the previous year) and ends: "In respect of the requests [for excommunications] made in your name to Our predecessors . . . and recently repeated in Our . . . presence, We know that . . . Innocent returned to you in a special letter a reply that sufficiently met the facts of the case, and, as no new circumstance has arisen to change these, neither have We thought that his answer should be changed."[47] In other words, no excommunication of Palaeologus's political enemies, the two Greek Despots who were patrons of the anti-unionists, or of the Latin lords in Greece who assisted them.

Accompanying this letter was another addressed to Emperor Michael, which, largely in the words of Pope Innocent, urged him to send within five months plenipotentiaries to conclude a truce with Philip of Constantinople and Charles of Anjou. Nicholas told Palaeologus openly that he had done nothing to comply with a similar request made by Pope John.[48] Herein is a mystery, for the papal archives contain a letter of credence from the Greek Emperor dated 24 July 1277 presenting envoys precisely to treat of a truce.[49] But clearly Pope Nicholas knew nothing of it.

Nicholas wrote also to the co-Emperor Andronicus a letter of thanks and congratulation. But he warned him that "for the more perfect completion of the union . . . there were some other things still to be done," for which reason he was sending his four Franciscan nuncios. A letter went also to the Patriarch and the prelates, praising them for the steps they had taken in the union. It held up to them as models the professions of faith of their Emperors and finally intimated that each and every one of them should do what they had done and fulfill all the requirements that his envoys would propose to them.[50]

What those requirements were, and what the Emperors should do "for the more perfect completion of the union," were contained in the *Memoriale* that Nicholas delivered to the Bishop of Grosseto.[51] It repeated almost *verbatim* large sections of the *Memoriale* of his predecessor—spiritual matters first; the papal purpose of procuring peace; more copies of the professions of faith on parchment with seals but addressed now to Nicholas. The prelates should make the profession of faith and should chant "And from the Son" in the Creed, "because unity of faith does not allow of diversity in its adherents either in the profession, the chanting or any other manifestation of the faith and especially in the chanting of the Creed, which, the more frequently it is used in the churches, the more ought it to be seen to be completely uniform. Therefore, the Roman Church has decided and wishes that it should be chanted uniformly by both Latins and Greeks with the addition of the *Filioque,* both because there have been special negotiations about that addition and because acknowledgement of the true faith ought not to be hidden but rather to be revealed and to be proclaimed publicly." Nicholas allowed the same conditional use of the Greek rite as Innocent, and like him recommended a truce with the Latin powers. All clerics of all towns, fortresses, villages, and localities were to accept the Roman faith and (once more using Gregory's name) sign a certificate to that effect according to the 1270 formula. They were also to confirm their word by oath, any custom to the contrary being merely an abuse, and they should preach that faith including the *Filioque.* The envoys were to go to towns and monasteries, etc., to witness the abjurations, which were to be recorded in several copies and preserved in local archives.

So far this *Memoriale* is like that of John, except that it is harsher in tone and more uncomprehending of the Greek mentality and situation. In it Nicholas repeats his conviction about Palaeologus, "who admits and affirms that this whole business [in reference to the professions of the prelates] depends on him and that his power in it all is paramount." This, when the Emperor was being defied by the greater part of the citizens of Constantinople precisely because of his policy on union. So Nicholas is more insistent on the *Filioque* and adamant on the bishops taking an oath. This was not owing to any special subservience to Philip and Charles for, though he consulted them, he deliberately limited Anjou's influence in Italy as part of his policy of making the Papal States independent of outside powers. While he asked Rudolph, the King of the Romans, to remove his officials from Romagna, he requested Charles to resign the senatorship of Rome (which he had been granted for ten years in 1268) and to give up his vicariate of Tuscany. Charles asked only for a few months' delay of execution, and then complied without difficulty.[52]

Nicholas displayed his logical, canonical mind and his complete ignorance of the broad situation even more in the concluding part of his *Memoriale.* The nuncios were to bring to the attention of the Greek prelates the surprise felt by the Roman Church that, after the union, they had taken no steps to obtain absolution from the censures incurred by their schism and had not sought from the Holy See any confirmation of the offices they held. These considerations, the document suggests, would give the nuncios a neat opportunity to intimate to the Emperor that he should ask for a cardinal Apostolic Legate, who with full papal powers could settle all outstanding questions on the spot. Nicholas meant to send one. The envoys should make discreet inquiries as to what treatment papal legates (if there had been any) had been accorded in the past and to suggest what would be suitable. If possible, they were to get Michael to put a request into writing or at least they were to note carefully whatever information they could gather on this topic.

The last point of the *Memoriale* was the vexed question of the censures on the enemies of the union. Nicholas repeats here the reply of Innocent and the refusal of Pope John's envoys to comply with Palaeologus's request. He bade his envoys use the utmost discretion. They were not to excommunicate any, just because they had withdrawn themselves from submission to the Greek Emperor and had allied themselves with the Latin Philip and Charles against him, but only "if they directly oppose the union and directly prevent Greeks and Latins from being united under obedience to the Roman Church in mutual charity, unity of faith and acknowledgement and acceptance of the primacy of that Church." Nicholas told his envoys that "above all things, they were to be careful not to say or do anything that could cause a breakdown in the business [of union] or give occasion, as far as in them lay, for such a rupture." All the same, he wanted not a superficial answer (as others had produced in the past), but a clear Yes or No to the various items of the commission entrusted to them.

The Pope had foreseen, however, that he might be disappointed in some respects. Like the four popes before him, he gave further instructions to the nuncios, mitigating somewhat the rigours of his *Memoriale,* in almost the same words as Innocent and John. Also, he armed them with faculties for censuring, absolving and dispensing—the copy, after a new introduction, of those first conceded by Innocent.[53] From Charles of Anjou in somewhat peremptory terms he asked on behalf of his own envoys and of the present and future Greek envoys, with their suites, safety both on their journeys and during the period of their negotiations.[54]

Such was the drastic and uncomprehending commission given to the four Franciscans who left the Curia some time after 7 January 1279.[55] Michael's task, when he met them in Adrianople, was, somehow or other, to make them believe that the union of the Churches was a reality. Certainly he had done his part. He had fallen in with every wish that the Popes had expressed for his personal execution. He had also employed every available means to obtain obedience from his people. Where persuasion had failed he had used force.

When the papal envoys reached Constantinople and Pera, where there were Franciscan convents, their confrères doubtless told them something of what was going on and opened their eyes to the real situation in respect of the union. Indeed, records Pachymeres,[56] their informants were Greeks involved in the ecclesiastical dissension, who asserted that the union was a farce and, with the *Filioque* in mind, bade them judge for themselves when they heard the Greek Creed. In that way they hoped to face the Emperor with a dilemma. If he refused the Friars' demands to insert the *Filioque* into the Creed, he would seriously jeopardise the union already achieved; if he accepted, he would palpably contravene his own guarantee to preserve inviolate their rite and customs, and so clearly justify the inveterate opposition.

Michael countered by summoning all the clergy, and only the clergy, to a meeting. In a long speech he reminded them of the harsh measures he had used against many people, among them persons most dear to him, not a few being relatives of his own, to impose the union, for such was its importance. In St. Sophia there was still exhibited the chrysobull of his solemn promise not to change one jot or tittle of the Creed. Some among them had told the Friars that the union was all make-believe, and so these were now demanding new and more stringent conditions. He was forewarning them, to prepare them. So he reaffirmed his guarantee given before on oath and asked them to meet the papal envoys graciously and peaceably.

They did. With Beccus back in the Mangana monastery, they met there and listened quietly to the legates explaining their demands. To impress the envoys still further, Palaeologus had his spiritual father, Isaac, bishop of Ephesus, conduct them round some of the prisons where anti-unionists were confined. They visited the cell where the four treacherous generals, his relatives, were chained by the neck, each in a separate corner.

Beccus resumed his patriarchal functions on 6 August 1279. Some little time after, a declaration on the faith was prepared for the Pope. It contained a great many citations from Greek Fathers, and, in regard to the Procession, professed that the Spirit "pours forth from, goes forth from, is given by, shines forth from, appears from, the Son." Signatures in abundance were appended, many of them of fictitious persons and fictitious Sees. The Emperor must have been cognizant of what was being done, though whether Beccus was or not Pachymeres did not know.[57] In September the Emperor Michael and his son Andronicus repeated once again their professions of faith and their oaths, signed and sealed.[58] The papal envoys, armed with these documents, returned to the Curia. They took with them also two Greeks, who had been condemned for their opposition to the union, to be submitted to the Pope's good pleasure. Nicholas received them kindly and sent them back with a letter recommending them for their blameless lives.

Opposition to the union hardened. There were many who, because of the traditional condemnation of the Latins, though they themselves had no personal knowledge of them, could not believe that the Western Church retained any vestige of the ancient faith and practice.[59] The Emperor again addressed the clergy—bishops, monks and certain known leaders of the anti-unionist faction whose security from arrest was guaranteed for the occasion. Without ever mentioning any doctrinal point in particular, he exhorted them not to damage their own Church by their divisive activity. To such a general appeal there was no immediate opposition.

At some time Beccus, who earlier had wisely decided not to condescend to enter into the pamphleteering-lists, could contain himself no longer. He began to write, and having begun went on, arguing forcibly that in respect of the Procession of the Holy Spirit, "Through" and "From" were synonymous and that the Latin faith, therefore, was sound. His action only drove his adversaries to write more answers. It also angered many of the bishops, especially the imperial confessor, Isaac, by "making dogma a subject of dispute," when they were managing to tolerate the union and so escape the monarch's wrath by avoiding any dogmatic issue. Besides, what he was doing was strictly forbidden to others. Appeal was made to the Emperor, whose reply was evasive.[60]

The obdurate opposition to the union roused the Emperor to fury and his cruelty increased. He had the three surviving imprisoned generals (one had died in chains) brought to him. Two were blinded for persisting in their refusal to agree to his union, the third yielded. He tortured and mutilated innocent people suspected of being cognizant of a plot. Many monks practised fortune telling. They were prophesying the Emperor's death. When they fell into his hands they lost eyes (like Galaction) or nose or tongue (like Meletius) or they were sent into exile. Pamphlets were written anonymously and distributed under cover of night. In defect of the author, the finder who read one, who passed one on, who did not straightway burn it, was to be punished by death. A most praiseworthy official of the queen's household caught with one, through her intercession had his punishment commuted to the loss of his sight. All clerics were summoned to be present. The victim was blinded by having a cap of burning pitch pressed on his head down to his eyes. His nose was then cut with a knife and "he was left half-dead and half-blind."[61]

Meanwhile the papal envoys had taken back to the Curia the professions of faith of Michael and Andronicus, and had given the Pope their impressions of the state of things in Constantinople. In the west the situation had developed. William of Villehardouin died on 1 May 1278, a year after the death of his son-in-law, Philip. Charles of Anjou, therefore, became lord of Achaia. This was not an unmixed blessing for him. It meant that the defence of the Morea was now his responsibility. For this he had to spend money and send troops, who were not very successful against the sporadic Greek attacks. At the same time he was strengthening his bases in Epirus and Albania. A formal treaty with Nicephorus put him in possession of the towns and ports that had once formed the dowry that Queen Helena had brought on her marriage to Manfred. One of these was Butrinto, nearly opposite Corfu, which was the port serving the fortress of Berat, which in turn was the key to the gateway leading to Macedonia. In 1279 and 1280 a strong force under Hugo le Rousseau de Sully was sent to Epirus, which in late 1280 laid siege to Berat. The situation was serious for Palaeologus, since Venice after renewing its treaty with him in 1275 and again in 1277 refused to do so in 1279. Licario, Michael's Italian admiral, was being too successful in Negroponte and other islands of the Aegean for the peace of mind of the Signoria, and the ravages on Venetian trade by pirates in the Aegean was going on unabated despite treaty obligations. In view of the growing danger from the west, public prayers were ordered in Constantinople and an army was sent to relieve Berat. The almost accidental capture of General Sully caused panic in the Angevin army (3 April 1281) and the Greeks not only retained Berat but occupied also much of Epirus. That event was more important than a mere victory and a triumph in Constantinople with Sully paraded before the citizens. It checkmated Charles's plan to launch his attack on the Bosphorus by land. Now to fulfill his dream he would have to get control of a fleet and mount a naval expedition.

While these events were taking place Nicholas III died on 22 May 1280. He was, however, probably still Pope when the Greek Emperor sent an ambassador, named Mandas or Mercurius, who on reaching Apulia was detained by Charles and was freed only after papal protests.[62]

Nicholas's successor was Martin IV, elected on 22 February 1281. He was a Frenchman who did not disguise his partisanship for the House of Anjou. One of his first measures after his election was to give back to Charles the senatorship of Rome and with it control of the city. The Emperor Michael, when he learnt that there was still another new Pope, sent the Metropolitan of Heraclea, Leo, and the one-time ambassador to Lyons, Theophanes of Nicaea, to proffer his congratulations and homage. They were very coldly received. They had to wait a long time before being admitted to an audience and, when they were, it was to hear the good faith of their Emperor impugned. Finally they were dismissed without the honours and courtesies usually shown to official ambassadors.[63] According to Pachymeres the reason for this was that the Curia had come to learn the truth about the situation in Byzantium, that the union was a make-believe and that "apart from the Emperor, the Patriarch and those immediately connected with them, everybody looked on the union with disfavour and that the Emperor was trying to preserve it by dealing out extravagant penalties."[64] That was, indeed, the situation and the stories brought back by the Friars, as well as the diplomatic note of Ogerius, made it all too plain. Besides, Palaeologus had not yet made the permanent peace that the Holy See had so often asked from him. Doubtless Charles of Sicily drummed his protests into the ears of the sympathetic Pope. Martin was not the one to restrain him. On 3 July 1281 in Viterbo where the papal court then was, Philip de Courtenay, Charles and Venice signed a pact for a common expedition "for the exaltation of the orthodox faith, the restoration of the apostolic authority in respect of the withdrawal from it of the Empire of Romania . . . and the recuperation of the Empire of Romania." The armament was to be ready not later than April 1283.[65]

Pachymeres recounts that it was the archbishop of Nicaea who on his return from Italy (the archbishop of Heraclea had meantime died) told Emperor Michael that he was excommunicated by the Pope. That was done on 18 November 1281 by Martin IV: "With the advice of Our brethren We, in the presence of a great concourse of the faithful, formally declare that Michael Palaeologus, who is called Emperor of the Greeks, as patron of the Greeks who are inveterate schismatics and fixed in the ancient schism, who are therefore also heretics, patron too of their heresy and schism, has incurred a sentence of excommunication and will be held bound by that sentence." Everyone, individuals and communities, were forbidden to help him or to communicate with him under pain of censure and interdict. The excommunication was promulgated by being affixed to the doors of the chief church in Viterbo.[66]

This ban was added to the list of excommunications renewed publicly every Maundy Thursday (in 1282, on 26 March), when it was also specified that any one who supplied the Greeks with warlike materials—horses, iron, timber, ships, etc.—on any pretext whatsoever were also excommunicated. The original excommunication with the later specifications was renewed on 7 May because "the Roman Church, mother and mistress of the faithful, having this very much at heart, is most anxious that nothing should be attempted to the detriment of the Christian faith."[67]

So Michael Palaeologus, who was making himself execrated at home by his own subjects for his harsh imposition of the "Christian faith" of the Roman Church, since he could not be assailed as a heretic or even as a schismatic when he had at least twice in his own person made the prescribed profession of faith, was excommunicated as a promotor of schism. The excommunication was, perhaps, directed as much against his friends in the west as against Palaeologus himself, for all excommunications, and specifically this one against him, involved in the ban all those who aided and abetted the excommunicated. By the end of 1281 Charles had, perhaps, begun to suspect that intrigues were going on between the Greek Emperor and some western powers. Certainly there were grounds for disquiet. Perhaps as early as 1279 Michael was in communication with the court of Peter of Aragon, whose wife, Constance, the daughter of Manfred of Sicily, was still looked on as a patroness of Hohenstaufen refugees. Of these, one in particular, John of Procida, and the Genoese Zaccaria, were the agents that moved between the two courts. Peter began to build a fleet in 1280, ostensibly to protect his interests in Africa. Towards the end of 1281 Palaeologus was sending money and an offer of marriage for his son.[68] The intrigue was widespread and active also in Sicily.

Charles's preparations for his long-deferred expedition were quickly coming to completion. He had the good will of Bulgaria and Serbia and the promise of assistance from John of Thessaly. Nicephorus of Epirus was not only Charles's vassal, but he was also a party to the treaty between him, the Latin Emperor Philip and Venice.[69] The Angevin fleet was being collected together at Messina and was said to amount to 400 vessels. The Pope had granted Charles a dime on Sardinia and Hungary for six years and the proceeds from the redemption of vows in Sicily, Provence and elsewhere for the same period.[70] To the Sicilians, restive under the heavy taxes imposed on them, it was forbidden to carry arms.

The stage was thus set for the great event, when Sicily exploded in revolt. A trifling incident was the occasion. An Angevin soldier molested a Sicilian woman in the square outside the church of the Holy Spirit near Palermo after the vespers of Easter Monday, 30 March 1282. Her husband stabbed the soldier. The crowd joined in. Soon all the island was in arms and

Frenchmen everywhere were being massacred. On 28 April the fleet at Messina was destroyed and the town, the last Angevin stronghold, also fell. Peter of Aragon, intimidated by threats from France, made a pretence of sailing to Tunis before directing his fleet towards Sicily. It was only when Charles's efforts to retake Messina failed that Peter left Algeria to land in Trapani on 30 August 1282. He entered Palermo on 2 September, and Messina on 2 October and even carried the war against Charles into southern Italy.[71] Nothing that Charles and the excommunications of Martin IV against him and Palaeologus[72] could do availed to change the situation. Sicily was finally lost to Charles. His expedition against Constantinople was rendered utterly impossible. The union of the Churches was at an end.

When the Emperor Michael had first heard of the papal excommunication against him he had been very angry. As an immediate reaction he had forbidden any further commemoration of the Pope in the Liturgy and had felt inclined to drop the union altogether. But second thoughts, that with the restoration of Joseph to the patriarchal throne the ecclesiastical situation would be easier, checked any hasty action.[73] The "Sicilian Vespers" relieved him of his great anxiety from the West. He did not survive his triumph long. While on a campaign in Thrace he fell ill at Allage. He received Holy Communion just before he died on 11 December 1282, excommunicated by the Roman Church with which he was united and execrated (and, as it will appear, forbidden the rites of Christian burial) by the Greek church of his birth. That same night he was hastily interred in a nearby monastery by his son Andronicus.

Michael was an astute politician in his dealing with political powers, less clear-sighted when dealing with his own people. He entered on the project of Church union unquestionably from political motives. He achieved it and maintained it for the same ends in spite of opposition. But it seems to me that in the course of his negotiations he became sincerely convinced that it was justified also from the theological point of view. Writing to Pope Urban IV he had asserted that the thesis of Nicholas of Cotrone had opened his eyes to the real unity in faith and practice of the two Churches. There is no good reason for doubting that statement, especially when men of undoubted integrity like Beccus, Metochites, Meliteniotes and various bishops like Theophanes affirmed precisely the same. Both Pachymeres and George Metochites portray even the Patriarch Joseph as a unionist at heart, restrained from showing his mind openly by the oath he had taken. Palaeologus's fury with his opponents may have come in part measure from his sense of frustration, not so much that they could not, as that they would not, face the evidence and draw the right conclusion. Or rather, they had drawn the conclusion in the time of Vatatzes, and even during his own reign the Great Synod (i.e., all the bishops), had signed the "tome" that was sent to Pope John XXI and had approved the solemn excommunication of opponents of union, dated 16 July 1277, both of which documents unconditionally acknowledged the orthodoxy of the Roman faith and admitted papal primacy. The most open and effective enemies of the union of Lyons were the monks. The vast majority of these had no theological formation at all and very many of them were Arsenites for whom, union or no union, Palaeologus was a usurper. The laity was very much under the influence of the monks. The combination of bishops, monks and laity was a formidable opposition that Michael held in check by fear. His death removed the restraint. Andronicus's interment of his father's body, hastily performed to avoid any untoward incident, was a significant indication of the reaction that was to come.

Chapter X

Instability in Both East and West

No sooner had Andronicus returned to Constantinople than his fanatically anti-unionist aunt, Eulogia, with her partisans urged him to reject the ecclesiastical union. He himself was already inclined to that. So the necessary decree was issued and those exiled for reasons of religion were recalled.[1] On Christmas Day the Liturgy in the palace chapel usually celebrated by the patriarch in the imperial presence was omitted to avoid participation with Beccus in the sacred function and in the public prayers he would have recited for the dead Emperor. Eulogia with an exaggerated show of grief declared that they would be useless, since Michael had died in heresy. Beccus was asked to retire and so on 26 December he went to a monastery. Four days later, carried in a litter "more dead than alive,"[2] Joseph was escorted to the patriarchal palace by a singing and bell-ringing throng. But, when the clerics went to the church of St. Sophia afterwards to chant vespers, they found it locked and barred, and so it remained till it had been purified, not by a bishop, but by the monk Galaction, who had been blinded by order of Emperor Michael. The monks, too, claiming to act for Patriarch Joseph, took charge of reconciliations of unionists, allotting bigger or smaller penalties as they thought fit. Bishops and clerics were suspended from office for three months; the archdeacons Meliteniotis and Metochites were permanently degraded for having assisted in Rome at the celebration of Mass by the Pope.

The general hatred was concentrated on Beccus, as if he alone had been responsible for the union. A trial was organised. Joseph could not be present—he was dying. George the Cypriot (unionist under Michael, anti-unionist under Andronicus), Holobolus and others who had suffered mutilation or exile for their faith acted as judges. If anyone had written about doctrine, he was judged not for what he wrote but because he wrote, and his screed was burnt. That was to set the stage for Beccus who, besides "having tried to delve into sacred mysteries more deeply than man should," had written to vindicate the orthodoxy of Latin doctrine about the Holy Spirit. The mob was summoned by the ringing of church bells. Beccus was brought to trial and made to sit in the lowest place. Challenged on his opinions, he realised the complete futility of attempting any justification before so hostile an audience. He replied, therefore, by demanding that they should first face the question whether they who had elected him as patriarch should not rightly treat him as such. Taken aback, they contented themselves with persuading him to visit Joseph, to sign a profession of faith with a rejection of errors[3] and to renounce the priesthood. The excommunication that followed was a synodal decision taken by prelates who had served under him. He was then sent into exile to Brusa with a pension for his sustenance granted by the Emperor, who, for his part, under pressure from the monks consented not to hold any religious services or public prayer for his dead father.

By weakly yielding in this way, Andronicus thought he had restored peace to the Church. But he was wrong. The old Arsenite faction, swollen in numbers by those returned from exile and no longer absorbed in the anti-union campaign, had leisure again to pursue its hatred of Joseph and his followers. They soon outnumbered the Josephites. Andronicus let them have a free hand in the hope of placating them. They were, in fact, as much a threat to him as they were to the Patriarch, for their aims were both political and ecclesiastical, to restore the Lascarid dynasty overthrown by the usurping Michael VIII[4] and to humiliate and dethrone Joseph, usurper in the See of Constantinople. They did, in fact, effect Joseph's abdication and he died shortly afterwards (March 1283), much to the relief of the Emperor.[5]

As successor Andronicus chose George the Cypriot, neither Arsenite nor Josephite, who was given all holy orders and consecration as Patriarch with the name, Gregory, privately behind closed doors by prelates not stained with Josephitism, in churches which neither Josephites nor unionists had used. To soften the anger of the faction at not having a patriarch of their number, the Arsenite monk, Athanasius, was restored to his old See of Sardis by the Emperor and named imperial confessor, but at the same time, so as to stifle any doubts about his own coronation as Emperor, Andronicus with Gregory issued a chrysobull attesting to Joseph's orthodoxy and to the legitimacy of his patriarchate.

Another trial of unionists was staged with Patriarch Gregory, the Archbishop of Sardis and various Arsenite notables as judges. The accused were brought in one by one, railed at by the monks, maltreated and led off in chains.[6] Many bishops and very many priests were deposed. Others were condemned *in absentia*. The dowager Empress Theodora had to present a written renunciation of the union and to promise not to procure religious rites for her dead husband. Athanasius, Patriarch of Alexandria, had to exculpate himself. Theodosius of Antioch secretly left for Syria and resigned his See.

The Arsenites were bitterly divided among themselves, and a meeting held just before Easter 1284 with the Emperor in Adramyttium that lasted for forty days did not succeed in healing the schism. Controversies, squabbles and rivalries went on, with Andronicus vainly trying to mediate peace. He sought to appease them by allowing them to bring the body of the dead Arsenius from Proconnesus (the island where he had died) to be buried in the capital city. Escorted to the church of St. Sophia by the Emperor and the Senate, by clerics with torches and incense and by a throng of layfolk, the corpse clad in patriarchal vestments was seated on the patriarchal throne before being buried with all liturgical pomp in the sumptuous chapel of the monastery of St. Andrew. This ceremony tacitly acknowledged that Arsenius was still Patriarch when he died and his successors, including Joseph who had crowned Andronicus as Emperor, were by implication stigmatised as impostors.

The most formal of the unionist trials took place in the Blachernae palace in early 1285. Before Patriarch Gregory, Patriarch Athanasius of Alexandria, the Emperor with his senate, the Great Logothete, clerics and eminent laymen, Beccus, with Meliteniotes and Metochites, was to answer a charge of heresy. It was he who had deliberately provoked this confrontation so as to be able publicly to vindicate the orthodoxy of his beliefs, which in the travesty of the trial of 1283 he had been unable to do. All three of the accused openly professed acceptance of the *Filioque* clause and quoted in proof St. John Damascene's words that the Father is "the emitter through the Word of the revealing Spirit," where "emitter" manifestly means "cause." The Chartophylax of the Great Church, Moschabar, declared the words spurious.[7] The Great Logothete, who was conducting the trial, rebuked him and, to rebut the conclusion of the unionists, he claimed that in the quotation "emitter" in respect of the Father certainly means "cause," but in respect of the Son, only "revealer." Beccus pilloried him for giving the same word in the same context two different meanings and continued, daring his accusers to reject the phrase "Through the Son," which was approved by the Fathers and the seventh council, and finally telling the Emperor that he would never achieve his hoped-for ecclesiastical harmony as long as Gregory was patriarch. After four sessions in which his opponents could find no answer to Beccus's arguments, the trial was postponed for six months. A last session was held in July, when the Patriarch of Alexandria tamely ended the embarrassing ordeal by declaring that dogma should not be debated. For his success in confounding the synod Beccus with his two companions was relegated, this time without any pension from the Emperor, to an isolated fortress, guarded by ferocious "Celts."

Unless Beccus was to be left moral victor on the field of battle, some answer to his arguments had to be found. Patriarch Gregory decided to produce one. He wrote a "tomos"—a statement on the Procession of the Holy Spirit interpreting the disputed passage of the Damascene, "The Father is the emitter (*proboleus*) through the Son of the revealing Spirit,"[8] by proposing that by this phrase the Father is said to be emitter, not of the being of the Spirit, but only of his eternal revealing.[9] The "tome" was promulgated from the pulpit. All were urged to sign it. The Emperor did so first in imperial cinnabar ink, then Patriarch Gregory, then various bishops and officials. Beccus learnt about it, wrote an answer and had it circulated covertly through his friends. He had no difficulty in demonstrating that, as the word "emitter" was, in the context of the Holy Spirit, generally used by the Fathers to mean "cause," Gregory either denied paternal causality or attributed causality to the Son and so supported Beccus's (and the Latins') case: to give the word two different meanings, as Gregory advocated, was completely unpatristic, untheological and unsound.

The lower clergy refused to sign the "tome" partly from fear of another purge if it should turn out to be unorthodox, partly because they disapproved of a non-Arsenite patriarch. Bishops became chary. The tome was finally signed by only 41 bishops and 30 officials besides the Emperor and the Patriarch, a very small number compared with the total number of bishops, especially as several of them were new creations of the anti-unionist factions. Some of the signatories had collaborated with Beccus when he was Patriarch.[10] They moved with the times.

Gregory's enemies in the hierarchy took their chance. After a great deal of intrigue and maneuvering they made him resign. He did it only when he had extorted from them a public recognition of his orthodoxy, which effectively cleared him of the charges alleged for his removal. A committee set up later by the Emperor to amend the "tome" could find no satisfactory solution of the difficulties raised by the quotation from St. John Damascene. In the end they deleted the phrase altogether.

Gregory died shortly afterwards and was given simple, not patriarchal, burial. His successor was Athanasius I, a monk long practised in the ascetical life of the monastery but devoid of secular learning. Nicephorus Gregoras remarked about him: "Had he remained a hermit all his life, he would have been a happier man." On the patriarchal throne he remained the monk. Himself changing as little as possible the austere habits of his earlier days, he imposed regularity of life on the monks of Constantinople, sent bishops away from the capital to look after their dioceses, frequently advised the Emperor of malpractices of his officials, asked his help to enforce Church discipline and admonished him to set an example to his subjects. He was a friend of the poor and organised soup kitchens and the distribution of wheat in time of famine to the crowds of resourceless refugees who poured into Constantinople from Asia Minor ravaged by the Turks and Thrace laid waste by the Catalans. Inevitably he made enemies of nearly all of those whose lives he tried to amend. He was forced to resign his office but he returned, not without guile on his part. He had laid an excommunication on all who had had any hand in his abdication, so that the scrupulous Andronicus was not happy till he was restored to office to lift it and, when he did return, it was on his own conditions confirmed by an oath from the Emperor. Be that as it may, Gregoras regretted that his successors on the patriarchal throne did not follow his example of integrity and preserve his high standards.[11]

Andronicus, who had grown up in an atmosphere of religious tension, was never free from it during the whole of his reign. Superstitious and scrupulous, he aimed at bringing the squabbling factions of the Church into harmony. It led him to neglect pressing political needs. His father's policy and reconquest of lost territories had been costly, and the money he had spent furthering his political aims in Italy, Aragon and Sicily had further depleted the treasury. To win popular support Andronicus lowered the heavy taxes that Michael had imposed. The results were tragic. He could afford only small armies to defend his frontiers; he let the navy lapse altogether; the landowners on whom his father had relied were disaffected and tended to make for themselves local independent princedoms. Piracy in the Aegean was rife and he could do nothing to check it. In Asia Minor, at one time the arsenal of the Empire, the Ottoman Turks made steady progress, so that by 1300 only a few of the larger towns still remained in Greek hands. The money he might have employed to hire troops he had to use to buy off enemies.

In the last decades of the thirteenth century the West was still trying to settle the problems left by the Sicilian Vespers. Neither Charles I of Sicily nor Martin IV was content to leave the island of Sicily in Aragonese hands. Papal exhortations and censures had no effect, but papal money helped Charles to maintain the stalemate of Angevin and Aragonese troops facing each other in southern Italy. Peter of Aragon returned to Spain to look after the kingdom there and to prepare it against eventual reprisals. Charles of Anjou went to France to raise money and troops. To persuade him to make war on Aragon, Pope Martin, in collusion with Charles, played on the susceptibilities of King Philip of France, who felt himself outraged at the dishonour done to the French name by the disaster of Sicily. It was proposed that King Peter should be deposed and Philip's younger son, Charles, Count of Valois, should be invested with the thrones of Aragon and Valencia. Assured also of the support of Peter's brother, James, king of Majorca, on 2 February 1284 Philip accepted the offer in his son's name. The relevant papal Bull was issued on 5 May following.[12] The campaign was to be a crusade.[13] Tenths over a period of three years were granted to Philip by Martin.[14]

Charles of Anjou returned to Naples on 6 June 1284 only to learn that on the previous day his only son, Charles of Salerno, had been defeated at sea and captured by a Sicilian fleet. With his new army and a large number of ships he went south, attacked Messina and was repulsed, besieged Reggio without success, and then retired. The next year, 1285, was a fateful one. Charles I died on 7 January. On 29 March died Pope Martin IV who had pledged the honour and prestige of the Holy See to the success of Angevin arms and lost. In May, Philip III of France launched his campaign against Aragon. He besieged the fortress of Gerona from 25 June till 5 September. His fleet was destroyed on 4 September by Roger of Lauria, the Italian admiral in the pay of Aragon, who had captured Charles of Salerno. His army was ravaged by malaria. He retreated and himself died at Perpignan on 5 October, whereupon the retreat became a flight. Peter of Aragon died on 10 November.

Charles Martel, eldest son of Charles of Salerno, a minor, was to rule in Naples as long as his father languished in prison in Catalonia. Philip IV the Fair succeeded to the throne of France. In Aragon, Peter's eldest son, Alfonso, became king; in the island of Sicily his second son, James, succeeded. On the papal throne there sat Honorius IV, a Roman, elected on 2 April 1285. The stage was set in much the same way as it had been three years earlier, but the actors were different. The play being performed, however, had not changed much. Four popes, Honorius IV (3 April 1287), Nicholas IV (the Franciscan Jerome of Ascoli, who previously had been ambassador to the Greeks, 22 February 1288–April 1292), St. Celestine V (5 July–12 December 1294) and Boniface VIII, elected on 24 December 1294, were all of them adamant that the Aragonese should not retain Sicily. Charles II, released from captivity against payment of a large sum of money and the surrender of hostages, kept wars going to recover the island. In this he was encouraged and helped by the popes. Alfonso of Aragon died young on 18 June 1291. James from Sicily succeeded him on the Spanish throne. His brother, Frederick, in spite of an agreement made by James with the King of France and the Pope, had himself crowned King of Sicily on 25 March 1295. More campaigns followed without producing any significant change in the political situation. A settlement was finally reached at Caltabellotta on 31 August 1302. Frederick would remain king of the island of Sicily and would marry Charles's daughter, but at his death his realm would revert to the Angevins. Pope Boniface accepted the treaty and at last the south of Italy was at peace.

Meanwhile the Greek Emperor Andronicus II also had been aiming at peace. To forestall any western inclinations to restore the Latin Empire, he sought for his son and heir, Michael, the hand of Catherine of Courtenay, only child of Philip of Courtenay and Beatrice of Anjou and so heiress to the Latin throne in the east. At that time Catherine was residing at the court of Naples. A papal letter of 3 June 1288 records that Andronicus had approached the Regent of Naples with respect to the marriage.[15] On 13 January 1289 Pope Nicholas in a very friendly spirit wrote to Andronicus, whom he still regarded as being in the unity of the one Church, apologising for not having notified him of his election to the papal throne and referring to the passing of an embassy.[16] In 1291 envoys from Naples were in Nymphaeum and Greeks were expected in Naples.[17] Nothing came of these various missions and so Andronicus renewed his request again in 1294.

Pope Nicholas was favourable to the project and so at first was King Philip of France. But in 1294 Philip, seeing no advantage to his country from it, had the girl brought to his court. Michael Palaeologus finally married an Armenian princess. But Catherine was a prize of sorts. Pope Boniface tried to persuade Frederick of Aragon to turn his eyes from the throne of Sicily to the throne of Constantinople by accepting Catherine's hand, with the promise that Charles II of Naples, James of Aragon and he himself would all support his claims and his arms.[18] But Frederick and Catherine decided that they were not suited to each other, so that scheme fell through. Finally, in 1301 Catherine of Courtenay married Charles of Valois, brother of the King of France. At one time he had been promised the crown of Aragon. Now he could aspire to that of Constantinople.

Charles of Valois had no land of his own. His brother, the King of France, gave him moral but not material support. Popes Benedict XI (1303–1304) and Clement V were generous to him with crusading money and tried to persuade Venice and Genoa[19] and the King of Serbia, Milutin, to join his expedition, which, if successful, would (they wrote) facilitate the liberation of the Holy Land. On 3 June 1307, Clement excommunicated Andronicus, "who calls himself Emperor of the Greeks," and forbade all commerce with him.[20] Charles II of Naples should by treaty have given Valois support, but his interest lay elsewhere. He had since 1294 handed over to his brother Philip, Prince of Taranto, all Angevin rights in Greece and the Morea. Philip's position there had been improved by his marriage with the daughter of Nicephorus of Epirus (1294) and by the spontaneous surrender to him of Durazzo. With papal help in 1306 he launched an expedition to defend his interests, without success. One other powerful aid was possible to Valois, alliance with the Catalan Grand Company.

The Catalan Grand Company, a mercenary army, had been part of the Aragonese forces in Sicily, but after the peace of Caltabellotta it was disengaged. Andronicus II, pressed by continuous Turkish conquests in Asia Minor, invited the Catalans to Constantinople (1303). They conducted a victorious campaign against the Turkish forces (1304), then, undisciplined, they raided Turks and Greeks impartially. Andronicus managed to bring them back west of the Bosphorus. Soon, at a banquet given by his son Michael, the Catalan chief Roger di Flor was murdered (April 1305). The Company wanted revenge. It ravaged Thrace for a couple of years before descending to desolate Thessaly. While it was there, Valois thought to obtain its services for his own ends. In 1308 it seemed that he had succeeded. Constantinople, surrounded by enemies (Turks, Catalans, French, Venetians and Serbs were all allied against it) and despaired of by some of its own nobles (John Monomachos, governor of Thessalonica, and Constantine Ducas Lampidenus of Sardis had expressed to Charles their readiness to receive him) could apparently hardly escape falling again into Latin hands. Charles, however, was not the only one who was aiming at Constantinople. The Catalans owed a primary allegiance to Frederick, King of Sicily, and could not forget loyalty to their native Spain and James, King of Aragon. Charles, Frederick, James and the Catalans all claimed to be fighting a crusade for Holy Mother Church—Muntaner flew the papal flag over Gallipoli where the Company's booty was stored. Each of the three western princes sent out reinforcements and representatives to Greece. But, in the event, the Grand Company, intent only on its own advantage and unreliable, disappointed them all.[21] Philip the Fair turned Valois's eye from Greece to the vacant German throne. So Constantinople survived. Charles of Valois, not elected king of the Germans, seemed to become disillusioned. He did not renew his treaty with Venice, which consequently made a truce for ten years with Andronicus and took no further part in western schemes against Byzantium.

With danger threatening on all sides Andronicus tried to find a solution in a judicious marriage. In 1311 he sent an embassy to the Pope, the King of France and Charles of Valois, asking the hand of Catherine, Charles's only child (and heir to the Latin Empire) for one of his sons by his second wife.[22] Though he offered for himself, his heir and his people acknowledgement of the Catholic faith and obedience to the Holy See,[23] nothing came of his request. The girl had been promised to Philip of Taranto, who married her in 1313, thereby becoming the protagonist of the Latin claims to the Byzantine throne. Andronicus's envoy persevered with his quest for a Latin alliance. He tried the court of Aragon, but was no more successful there.[24]

The Popes, in spite of their involvement in the Sicilian question, did not lose sight of larger issues. Nicholas IV in particular, who as simple Fra Jerome of Ascoli had known the East, was very active in promoting relations with eastern powers. He sent several letters to the Mongol King of Persia, Argon, expounding Christian doctrine, and he thought that in the end Argon, like his mother,[25] had received baptism (wherein he was mistaken).[26] To the Catholicos of the Nestorians of Persia he sent a copy of the profession of faith drawn up by Pope Clement, inviting him to subscribe to it, and to a Greek bishop of the same country who had already accepted the Catholic faith he sent a copy of the same.[27] A year later, 7 July 1289, he wrote to all the heads of all the Oriental Churches he could think of, repeating his invitation and the profession of faith.[28]

This outburst of apostoliç activity, the continuation doubtless of his earlier missionary zeal, was occasioned by promising contacts closer at hand. To Uros II Milutin, whose mother was a Latin Catholic, he sent a letter by two Franciscans to remind him that, "as no one can come to this Truth [Christ] except by the Catholic faith delivered by God and the Apostles, which the holy Roman Church professes and conserves," he should adopt it.[29] His mother was urged to bring up her two sons in the faith.[30] Some years later he took the king and his realm under papal protection.[31] Soon after, at the suggestion of Queen Helena, he wrote to Terter, King of the Bulgars, exhorting him also to return to the Latin Church,[32] and to the Bulgarian Patriarch reminding him that they had once met at the court of the Emperor of Constantinople, when Joachim had promised submission to the Holy See.[33] Benedict followed up Nicholas's initiative with similar letters, and the fruits of these endeavours were reaped by Clement V. A letter of his dated 1 April 1308 to King Uros welcomes the Serbian envoys who had announced the readiness of king and people to join the Latin Church. They were given the usual Profession of Faith, warned to chant the *Filioque* in the Creed of the Liturgy and to profess obedience to the Holy See.[34] Instructions to the papal nuncios insist on sincerity as a condition of reception into the Church and allow the use of leavened bread in the non-Latin Liturgy, especially so that "the King may assist at such Liturgies."[35] The Church of Serbia, to judge from a report of the archbishop of Antivari, stood in dire need of reform. Benedict XI empowered the archbishop to institute reform measures in Serbia and the adjacent parts subject to King Uros and the Emperor Andronicus.[36]

Armenia was another object of papal solicitude. Nicholas wrote friendly letters to King Het'um II and his Catholic aunt, thanking them for their benevolence to a Franciscan missionary.[37] The capture of Acre by the Saracens on 18 May 1291 added a new urgency to relations with Armenia. A letter from Nicholas to Het'um and other kings laments the tragedy and exhorts them to a crusade.[38] Boniface consoled the Catholicos of the Armenians, who had sent to inform the Pope that he had submitted himself to the Holy See, that a crusade was in active preparation in the West and that the kings of France and of England were both engaged to participate in it, though at war with each other at the moment. As soon as peace between them and in the kingdom of Sicily had been obtained, the "passagium" would be effected.[39]

The crusade that Boniface wrote about was a genuine and serious project. The Council of Lyons had enacted that all should give a tenth for six years for the Holy Land and the collections had on the whole been steadily made. In some places, of course, war conditions caused it temporarily to lapse, and the popes diverted money in France and Italy to their local wars about Sicily, which obviously militated against a concentrated preparation for the crusade. But the general interest and desire to defend the Holy Land were there, so much so that Nicholas had established the year 1293 as the time for the "passagium."[40] By that date, however, there was nothing left to defend; everything would have to be reconquered, for the last Christian possessions had been lost. Armenia and Cyprus were now the outposts of Christianity, and they made appeals for protection.

In the West there was a spate of literature analysing the causes of past failures, suggesting right methods to be adopted and indicating the best routes to follow. A few of the tracts were from theorists or from politicians who had never seen the Holy Land. Most were from people of experience—missionaries, old crusaders, Armenians, Cypriots. All were agreed on the faults—dissension among Christians and in Syria itself, wars between Christian countries, the unscrupulous commerce with the Mamluks of Christians, chiefly Venetians and Genoese, who freely sold war-material and slaves to the infidel. Unfortunately none of these causes of failure was cured or likely to be.[41] But in the Council of Vienne (1311), because of the general feeling of the Church that the Holy Land should not be left in infidel hands, the bishops agreed to pay a tenth for six years, and this was solemnly decreed on 3 April 1312. The King of France with his two sons, the King of England and many knights received the Cross at the hands of the papal legate in the Church of Notre Dame. Philip the Fair was given by the pliant French Pope the six years' tenth in France with five years more, i.e., eleven years in all, "without having to give any account of its use." Neither he nor Edward II of England ever set out for the East.[42]

Not a few of the many pamphlets on the recovery of the Holy Land advocated as a preliminary requisite the capture of the Greek Empire. In 1310 Andronicus had managed to settle the Arsenite schism. It was done in a picturesque ceremony in the church of St. Sophia, presided over by the corpse of Arsenius seated on the patriarchal throne with the form of absolution in his hand, while the living patriarch Niphon read the formula of union from the pulpit. Concord had been reached by accepting the Arsenite conditions, two of which were that Joseph's name should be deleted from the list of Patriarchs and that all clergy ordained under Beccus should be permanently deposed and suspended.[43]

With the ecclesiastical peace, Andronicus enjoyed also a short period free from grave anxieties in his European relations, though the Turks were beginning to raid the mainland of Greece. His influence in the Peloponnesus had been considerably strengthened by the wise administration of its governors. The victories of the Catalans over the Latins of Athens had eliminated danger from that quarter and had put a barrier to Angevin expeditions organised from Italy. Epirus and Thessaly were friendly. But the calm lasted only a short time. As a protest against the dissolute life led by his grandson Andronicus, the son of the dead Michael († 12 October 1320), the Emperor passed him over as heir to the throne in favour of an illegitimate cousin. Prince Andronicus gathered together his friends, the chief of whom was a rich landowner, John Cantacuzenus, to assert his rights by force of arms. He gained easy support by promising all kinds of relief from taxes, and the imposing forces he raised intimidated Andronicus II in 1321 and again in 1322 to make concessions and to come to terms. The third outbreak of hostilities (1327) ended with the forced abdication of the old Emperor (1328), who two years later became a monk and died on 13 February 1332.

Whatever chance the Greek Empire of Byzantium had of surviving when Andronicus II came to the throne, it had less when he died. The civil war not only impoverished the already poor people. It threw open the frontiers everywhere to inroads from external enemies. Worse, the enemies were invited in. Andronicus II and Andronicus III allied themselves with Bulgars and Serbs, who were most willing to accelerate the weakening of the Byzantine Empire, to facilitate their taking it over themselves. The country folk, weighed down with taxes in kind, could not even cultivate the land ravaged by contending arms. They flocked to the towns and the discontent increased.

In one of the intervals in the spasmodic hostilities between the two Andronici, the Emperor made contact with the West, where a crusade was in preparation. Philip V of France had got as far as commissioning a fleet of twenty ships intended to relieve Armenia (1321), but the Captain General showed himself interested in Greece and Achaia. Andronicus was alarmed. Through the Dominican bishop of Caffa, who passed through Constantinople on his way to Avignon, he sent messages of goodwill, peace and Church union to the pope and to Charles the Fair (1323). He had an able advocate in a Venetian well known to both Pope and King. That was Marino Sanudo, author of a treatise on how best to help the Holy Land and indefatigable letter-writer in favour of a crusade, who assured his many Latin correspondents of the goodwill of the Greek Emperor and deprecated any idea of an attack on Constantinople. He told them to judge by past experience, that by conquest they would get from the Greeks "obedience only of word, not of heart." Nothing, in fact, came of the royal project. As Sanudo wrote to the bishop of Mende and Count Gabalatani, organisers of the "passagium," "they intended to arm twenty galleys but did not allow enough money to do it well and so nothing was effected."[44]

Three years later (1326) Andronicus II again opened communication with the West. He sent to Pope John and the King of France letters by the Genoese Simone Doria requesting union and peace.[45] The king with the cognizance of the Pope sent Benedict of Como, O.P., to Constantinople to bid (rather than to request) Andronicus to fulfil what he was promising. Pope John gave the envoy the usual faculties of reconciling schismatics and heretics[46] and sent him to talk with Robert of Sicily and Prince Philip of Taranto (Latin claimants to territories in Greece). He was to inform the Pope of their views to help His Holiness more fully to decide on his own action.[47] In May 1327 Andronicus replied to Pope and king by the same messenger, who on arriving in Byzantium had found a state of civil war. In the circumstances Andronicus dared not prejudice himself in the eyes of his subjects by negotiating openly for Church union or making territorial concessions. So the Pope, writing to Charles IV, concluded: "We gathered that there was nothing at all that We could do to promote the business in question."[48]

Writing to the King of France from Venice on 4 April 1332, Sanudo reported the capture of Nicaea by the Turks and referred to rumours current in Venice that a new crusade was being prepared.[49] Sanudo was right. King Philip VI on 18 November 1331 had enquired from the Signoria about the hiring of a fleet. This new enterprise stimulated to action Andronicus III, who by his third rebellion had taken the throne from his grandfather on 24 May 1328. He sent one embassy to the court of Naples to speak of peace (before 4 April 1332, the date of Sanudo's letter that mentions it) and two to the Pope. One of these, composed of two Dominican bishops passing through Constantinople from the Crimea, was to express his desire for union; the other was to ask for learned men to effect the conversion of his subjects to the Roman faith.[50]

There may have been more behind this second request than a thinly veiled desire to prevent at all costs any western enterprise involving Greek territories. In a letter to Philip VI of 13 October 1334, Sanudo, who had lately returned from Constantinople, recounts that there was still among the Greeks a nucleus of people loyal at heart to the union of Lyons. He encouraged the king to promote union. "And this could easily be done and accomplished by what I perceived in Constantinople when last year I was talking with abbots of monasteries and with some priests, and particularly with Chernuf [Kyr Niphon?] who, wise, very rich and old, was at one time Patriarch of Constantinople and who is thoroughly hand-in-glove with the Emperor of the Greeks who is now reigning. So it seems to me certain that the time is ripe to bring it to a conclusion." He advised that the Pope should send sufficient good preachers. When Benedict of Como went to Constantinople there was a state of civil war. "Now it is the opposite. For the Greeks themselves cannot see any other means or way of escaping from the hands of the Turks and of the infidel Tartars except union in the above-mentioned faith. So, if anyone has the Emperor Andronicus and the ex-Patriarch Chernuf on his side, all other Greeks and other nations [i.e., countries ecclesiastically dependent on Constantinople, e.g., Trebizond] will straightway return to the Catholic faith and with God's help never leave it." But, if they will not, "then one must deal with them as with heretics and traitors," i.e., by war, but even so be understanding and lenient after victory.[51]

Sanudo was not letting his goodwill distort his judgement. There are other witnesses to a readiness among the Greeks to accept union, the result, at least in part, of the hopelessness of their situation. Two Dominicans, used by Andronicus as messengers, assured the Pope that both Emperor and prelates were well disposed to union: John XXII sent letters to them welcoming them and encouraging them to accept Roman faith and primacy. He sent a letter also to a certain John Pisano, who had written to tell him of the goodwill of the Greeks in general and in particular of the abbots of the monasteries of St. Basil and St. Demetrius who wanted union. The Pope ordered the two Dominican bishops, Francis of Camerino, archbishop of Vospri (Kertsch), and the Englishman Richard, bishop of Cherson, to go to Greece to work for union, inciting the Greeks to it by indicating the loss, both spiritually and temporally, that resulted from schism and the gain that would accrue from unity.[52] Nicephorus Gregoras records that two bishops (they were the two mentioned above) came to Constantinople from the Pope "to discuss peace and harmony of the Churches." The populace was eager for a public disputation and pressed the Patriarch to arrange one. He, "not having his tongue sharpened in the practice of speaking and realising that most of the bishops were deeply ignorant," held back. Finally he asked Gregoras himself, a layman, to undertake the task, but he addressed a small gathering of bishops at great length and convinced them of the uselessness of such a proceeding.[53] What Gregoras did not do was done by Barlaam, a Calabrian monk (of whom more will be said soon), but without any positive result.

The Pope continued correspondence with the Greeks. By the hands of the two Dominican bishops he sent letters to Andronicus and to the Patriarch and the people.[54] He wrote again to Andronicus the next year.[55] At the same time he wrote to the Empress Anna, the daughter of the Latin Count Amadeus V of Savoy, inciting her to work for union, for "The unbelieving husband will be saved through his wife" (I Cor. VII 14).[56]

It is possible that Andronicus was "saved." A Franciscan chronicle records: "In the year of the Lord 1332. Fra Garcias Arnaldi, from Aquitaine in the Custody of Auch, remaining in Constantinople and attaching himself to the Latin Empress of the Greeks of the House of Savoy brought the Emperor of the Greeks and converted him to the true faith and the unity of the Church. The Emperor despatched Fra Garcia to my Lord the Pope begging that he would send Catholic teachers to convert his people."[57]

This simple statement has a ring of truth about it. There are a number of factors that add credibility to it, though they do not amount to a proof. The conversion, of course, would have been private and kept secret. In 1332, the presumed date of the conversion, there was, in Constantinople, as has been noted, a certain inclination towards union remarked upon by several sources, and, to judge from a statement of Gregoras, an enquiring attitude about the theological questions controverted between the Churches.[58] At that time Andronicus was entering into a pact with Venice and the Hospitallers to oppose the Turks; it was signed in Rhodes on 6 September. There was, too, far more communication than usual between the West and Constantinople on three diverse questions—Church union, co-operation of Byzantium in the "passagium" and, when that project yielded place to the League, participation in the greater League of maritime powers against the Turk—this last in itself a purely political business, whereas the other two were ecclesiastical. On 7 March 1333 the Pope urged King Philip to write to Andronicus again. On 8 March the pact for the greater League, comprising the Venetian group and the French group, was signed in Avignon. On 14 March John XXII again wrote to Philip (the letter is synopsised, not quoted *verbatim,* by Raynaldus) suggesting that, if he intended "sending anyone about his return to the unity of the Roman Church, it would be better that that embassy should be secret; the one about the 'passagium' and the Turks could be public."[59] At about the same time, John, writing to another correspondent, referred to secret information about Greece. Why was it all so hush-hush? A hint of an answer may be found in another letter of the Pope to Philip of France, dated 18 July 1334. Its exact sense is obscure because of an abundance of confusing pronouns. The king should intimate that he would have invited him (Andronicus) to the *passagium,* "But since he [Andronicus] was being said to be divided from the unity of the holy Roman Catholic Church, he [the king] had not been able to do that, wherefore he [Andronicus] besought you in the Lord and asked that he might return to the bosom and unity of the said Church; which done, he

[Andronicus] asked the same [king] to prepare him [Andronicus] for the said *passagium* to be done at a predetermined time and Your Excellency to arrange that the Cross and the indulgence should be preached also in those parts."[60] In this quotation it is not always clear who the pronouns are referring to (the names in brackets are my suggestion), but the "this having been done" seems to apply to the "return to the bosom and unity of the said Church." From these considerations no definite conclusion can be drawn. That Andronicus was converted to the Roman Church is in the nature of things very unlikely, but not utterly impossible. In any case it had no consequences.

The League of 1334, of which Byzantium was a member, was designed to clear the Aegean sea of Turkish pirates, a political enterprise to make the seas safe for commerce. It would have also its happy repercussion for the projected crusade: the seas would be safer also for the "passagium." The immediate object was to destroy a large Turkish fleet that was massed in the Gulf of Adramyttium. The French, papal, Venetian, Hospitaller and Cypriot ships (but not, as had been hoped, also Greek) held the Turkish fleet immobile for some months and finally destroyed it in a series of encounters, the last of them in the Gulf of Adramyttium (17 September 1334).[61] It was a good beginning of concerted action, but it was not followed up because members of the League became involved in wars, and Pope John XXII died on 4 December 1334. His successor, Benedict, continued propaganda for the great crusade, timed to set out on 1 August 1336.[62] It never took place for it was impossible without the participation of France and England and they were on the point of starting their Hundred Years' War.

Andronicus again made overtures to the West about union in 1337. He sent a Venetian, Stephen Dandolo, offering to discuss the ecclesiastical differences. He promised the Pope that, if the Greeks were shown to be in error, they would amend, and proposed that both parties should send spokesmen to the court of Naples and there confer. From the Pope he received a benevolent reply, but Benedict recommended Avignon as the scene of the meeting and wrote to Robert of Naples asking him to encourage the Greek Emperor.[63] Two years later Stephen Dandolo was back again, this time accompanied by the monk Barlaam.

Barlaam was a monk of Greek rite from Calabria, who had gone to Constantinople. There he had attracted the attention and patronage particularly of John Cantacuzenus, the Emperor's right-hand man, and had been made abbot of the monastery of the Saviour. He had in word and writing attacked the Latin doctrines of the Procession of the Holy Spirit and of the primacy of the Roman See and had also fallen foul of the Greek Church by becoming embroiled in a bitter controversy connected with an ascetical practice, the prayer of hesychasm.

To the Pope and the cardinals the envoys declared that they had been sent by Emperor Andronicus to achieve two aims: the first, the holding of a general council for discussion and settlement of the *Filioque* question; the other, to recover three or four of the biggest cities that the Turks had taken from the Empire. Challenged to show their credentials, they replied that they had none. Nevertheless they were allowed to make their proposals. Barlaam was the speaker. This, in brief, is what he said.

There are two ways to obtain union, one by force, the other by persuasion leading to a voluntary acceptance. No one approves of the first way. The second way could be effected and easily by discussion between thirty or forty orientals and as many Latins. When, however, the orientals returned home, they would be rejected by the people, for they would be accused of having accepted union from unworthy motives. It would be better to lead the mass of the people by a general council, for the people would recognise that the decisions of a general council are right and sound. It is no use replying that the Council of Lyons was such a general council. The Greeks there did not represent the four patriarchs but only the Emperor "who tried to conclude union with you by force and not freely." So Your Holiness should send to the East religious and God-fearing men, humble and patient, who should courteously invite the Emperor and the patriarchs to a council. Then there would be a council in which union would be made and the people would concur.

Turning, then, to the question of the cities, Barlaam told the Pope and the cardinals that the population of those cities—"Greeks, by force become Turks"—had informed the Emperor that they wished to return to the Christian faith, if he would recapture the cities. Barlaam and his companion had gone to the King of France, who had sent them on to Avignon. Two main reasons recommended action—Latin help would win Greek minds; the Emperor would not be able to devote himself to a council while he was at war with the Turks nor would the patriarchs be able to come to it. It was a mistake for the Latins to retort, Union first and then help, for even if they were disinclined to help Greeks, they should help Armenians, Cypriots and Rhodians, who were their own subjects. They should help also Greeks, if not as Greeks, at least as venerators of the Cross of Christ. The continued existence of the Greek Empire was their own best defence; it would certainly be easier for them to oppose the Turks with the aid of the Greeks even if disunited than without them. "Fifthly, realise also this, that it is not so much difference in dogma that alienates the hearts of the Greeks from you, as the hatred that has entered their souls against the Latins, because of the many great evils that at different times the Greeks have suffered at the hands of Latins and are still suffering every day. Until this hatred has been removed from them, there cannot be union. In truth, until you have done them some very great benefit, neither will that hatred be dispelled nor will anyone dare to breathe a word to them about union. Sixthly, know this too, that it was not the people of Greece that sent me to seek your help and union, but the Emperor alone and secretly. Until help is sent to these parts, he cannot let his people see that he wants union with you."

In case the proposals he had made were not acceptable, Barlaam offered another, but less secure, way to union. To dissolve the Greek hatred he asked three things: that the King of France should be allowed to send help to the places named; that the Pope should grant (the crusade) indulgence to all willing to go to the aid of the Greeks, to all ready to help materially and to all who died in war against the Turks; and thirdly, "that all Greeks who have been sold [into slavery] by Latins, wherever they are, should be freed, and that for the future Greeks should not be sold but that anyone selling or buying" them should be excommunicated. Then let preachers come to teach the people and perhaps the people may accept union even without a general council.

The Pope and the cardinals considered Barlaam's words carefully and replied briefly, that since this article of faith, that the Holy Spirit proceeds from the Son as from one principle and one operation, had been defined by the Councils of Ephesus, Toledo, Lyons and other councils approved by the popes, it would be neither fitting nor expedient to call it in question by new disputations, especially as the Greeks in the days of Hormisdas and of Patriarch John professed it and latterly John Beccus and Emperor Michael had written accepting it.

Barlaam, therefore, suggested that each Church should retain its own faith in respect of the Holy Spirit and still unite,[64] but the Pope rejected that solution outright. Instead he proposed that the Emperor and the Greek Patriarch should summon a synod of the eastern patriarchates to send a select group to the West, not for disputation, but for instruction. On their return they would enlighten the rest. In any case, a council was very costly both in time and money and, especially in a period of political disturbances, a very difficult undertaking.

Barlaam parried the arguments for rejecting a council, proposing once again in slightly different form his compromise solution. When the Pope did not accept it, as a last resort he presented in writing a final observation.

> Most holy Father, although I have received from you a complete answer, yet I beg Your Holiness to deign to listen to these last few words, for I must say them and you should ponder them. In regard to union with the orthodox Church, Your Holiness said that legates should come from those parts with imperial and synodical letters—I pray God that He will make it possible. In itself it is extremely difficult and that for a variety of reasons. The Emperor dare not disclose that he wants to unite with you, because if he did many of his nobles and of the people, afraid that perhaps he might want to act as

Michael Palaeologus acted, would seek occasion to kill him.[65] Further, the Church of Constantinople would not send its legates for this undertaking without the counsel and consent of the patriarchs of Alexandria, Antioch and Jerusalem. So these would have to meet and that, because of wars, would be difficult. Besides, it is by no means certain that they would come, even if invited. Then, allowing that they came and that they were all agreed on sending legates for that purpose, they would never grant full powers for that to such legates, except under such conditions as you would never tolerate. So, it seems to me that such legates in the end would not arrive, since they would realise that you would not acquiesce in some of the articles of the eventual agreements. Wherefore, should it be that such legates come to Your Holiness, may you have what God, to whom nothing is impossible, can grant. If they should not come, do not blame the Emperor or imagine that negligence on his part is the cause, for he has for a long time been intent on union.[66]

Chapter XI

The Decline of Byzantium

Before he went as ambassador to Avignon, the Calabrian monk Barlaam had been involved in Byzantium in a bitter controversy that was to have momentous consequences. On the occasion of his discussions with the two Latin bishops who had visited Constantinople in the Pope's name, he had written several tractates against the Latin doctrine of the *Filioque*. His method did not recommend itself to a monk, Gregory Palamas, who thought fit to remonstrate with him. Barlaam riposted by criticizing a style of prayer practised in monasteries. By this method the monk, after a long preparation of ascetism and mortification, was said to attain to communion with God and even to see glowing within himself a light that was no other than the effulgence that enveloped Christ on Mount Thabor. As a help to this, he regulated his bodily functions, controlling his breathing and concentrating his attention on his own interior (the heart being the centre of the spirit), while rhythmically repeating the Jesus-prayer. Barlaam thought it ridiculous, criticised it openly and denounced it to the Patriarch of Constantinople, John XIV Calecas. Palamas took up the cudgels in its defence.

Gregory Palamas after a good education became a monk on Mount Athos (c. 1316) at the age of about twenty. He came immediately under the influence of the ascetic Nicodemus, who taught him the hesychastic method and theory. Both on Mt. Athos and, when Turkish attacks made Athos unsafe, in Thessalonica, Palamas lived the life of a hermit for five days of the week in solitary prayer, rejoining the monastic community only on Saturdays and Sundays to participate in the Liturgy. He was ordained priest in Thessalonica in 1326. Five years later, disturbed this time by the Serbs, he moved back to Athos (1331), where he was when Barlaam began his attacks on the monks. It was Palamas who in 1338 started the war of the written word by a Triad of treatises, explaining the hesychastic method.

Barlaam was in Avignon when Palamas's second Triad appeared. In that the monk of Athos put forward a theological defence of hesychasm, wherein it was stated that the light of Thabor, hence also the light experienced in prayer, was a divine energy, eternal, really distinct from the divine essence—a "divinity." The title of Barlaam's reply, *Against the Messalians,* implied an accusation of heresy, that God can be seen with human, bodily eyes. In a third Triad Palamas further expounded his hesychastic theology. Barlaam denounced him in Constantinople and, to settle the issue and stifle the growing controversy, the Patriarch summoned Palamas to the capital to give an account of himself. Before leaving the Holy Mountain the monk armed himself with a document, the "Hagioretic (i.e., monastic) Tome," giving a categorical statement of the hesychastic position. It was signed by the "Protos" of the monastic colony, three abbots and sixteen monks, and was witnessed by the Bishop of Herissos.[1]

The synod was held in Constantinople on 10 June 1341. It was presided over by Emperor Andronicus himself. Barlaam was censured for confusing theology by the introduction of a secular philosophy, having spoken "blasphemously and evilly" about the Light of Thabor and for having "blasphemously and evilly" calumniated the monks. It was forbidden to all and sundry to discuss dogma. On 15 June Andronicus died, leaving as heir his son, John, only nine years old. At this point Palamism became involved in politics. The regency for the boy John was claimed by his mother, Anna, with the Patriarch John Calecas and a rather unsavoury politician, Alexis Apocaucus. The Great Domestic, John Cantacuzenus, lifelong companion of the dead Andronicus, competent general and able administrator during his friend's reign, also claimed to be regent. He presided at a synodical gathering in August 1341, in which Gregory Akindynus, a layman, was condemned for continuing the Palamite controversy, because, though he utterly disapproved of the Calabrian's attacks on the monks, he could not accept the theology with which his friend, Palamas, defended them. Barlaam had already gone back to Italy. The gathering issued a "tome," recording the proceedings of the synod of the previous June and the condemnation made against Barlaam. Patriarch Calecas signed. Palamas had won.[2]

The political tension led to civil war. Cantacuzenus had himself proclaimed emperor at Didymotichus on 26 October 1341. So the boy John was hurriedly crowned on 19 November. Anna with the support of the people and Cantacuzenus with that of the landowners faced each other. Cantacuzenus allied himself with the Seljuq Emir Omur. Anna made a treaty with Venice for seven years and pledged the crown jewels for 30,000 ducats (they were never redeemed). The Czar of Serbia, Dusan, first helped Cantacuzenus, then the regent Anna, but retained for himself the towns he conquered, and on 16 April 1346 he had himself crowned in Skoplje "Emperor of the Serbs and the Greeks." Omur lost his port of Smyrna captured by the Western League on 28 October 1344, and was henceforward of less use to Cantacuzenus, who in May 1346 gave his second daughter in marriage to the Ottoman Emir Orkhan. His help and that of the Serbs forced Anna, who by 1347 retained power over only Constantinople, to compromise with Cantacuzenus, who, having been crowned at Adrianople on 21 May 1346 by the Patriarch of Jerusalem, was crowned again in Constantinople by the Patriarch of Constantinople on 21 May 1347.

The Patriarch who crowned John VI Cantacuzenus in Constantinople was not John Calecas but Isidore. When the civil war broke out in 1341, Palamas and the monks had supported Cantacuzenus. Patriarch John Calecas tried but failed to persuade Palamas to silence, so he had him tried on an ecclesiastical charge and imprisoned. He remained in confinement till 1347, when Anna released him to act as go-between with Cantacuzenus. By now she was ruling alone, for Apocaucus had been murdered in 1345 and, when Calecas did not fall in with her inclinations to make peace with Cantacuzenus, he was deposed on 2 February 1347. Cantacuzenus entered Constantinople on 3 February. A Palamite, Isidore, was elected Patriarch on 17 May. Cantacuzenus was crowned on 21 May and John V Palaeologus married his daughter a week later.[3]

So there were two emperors to rule a very diminished and impoverished Empire. It was divided into segments whose only communication was by sea. Dusan's realm stretched from coast to coast cutting off Greek Thessaly from Thrace. The Catalan domains divided Greek Morea from Thessaly. Thrace, that had been a battlefield for six years, overrun by two Greek armies, pillaged and ravished by Turks and Serbs, much of its population carried off as slaves by the Turks and the rest drastically reduced by the Black Death,[4] lay uncultivated and could pay no taxes. The civil unrest led to a Zealot movement in Thessalonica, where a popular rising took over the city and preserved an uneasy autonomy from 1342 to 1349. Cantacuzenus restored imperial rule there in 1350, when Gregory Palamas, made archbishop of that city in 1347 (one of thirty-two new bishops, all Palamites, promoted by Emperor John VI Cantacuzenus and the Palamite Isidore), was able to take possession of his See.

In spite of the prohibition of the synodal "tome," the Palamite controversy had never ceased. Palamas himself, though confined in a monastery, and Akindynus, released from prison by Calecas, had continued writing. On 2 February 1347, when Anna needed Palamas's diplomatic services, the synod that deposed the Patriarch approved the Palamite doctrine again and condemned Akindynus, who fled and shortly afterwards died. His mantle was taken up by Nicephorus Gregoras, historian, philosopher and theologian. Patriarch Isidore, too, had his opponents. He was excommunicated by a group of dissident bishops, who were, of course, excommunicated in their turn by him. So in 1351 Emperor John Cantacuzenus held a synod for free discussion of the question. All except two of the twenty-seven metropolitans and seven bishops present, with the Emperor, were Palamites. Afterwards the anti-Palamites claimed with some justice that, though in the earlier sessions they had been allowed liberty to state their case, later they were silenced. The "tome" of 1341 was re-affirmed. The two dissident metropolitans were deposed and the other opponents of Palamas condemned and excluded from the meetings. At a fifth session, in the absence of all opposition, six statements of Palamite theology were put to the gathering and all six were approved. These were incorporated into a synodal "tome," which also decreed excommunication for all who would not accept them.[5] The Emperor Cantacuzenus, having signed the "tome," laid it solemnly on the altar of St. Sophia on 15 August 1351. The Emperor John Palaeologus added his signature some time later.

Already before the synod of 1351, Palamism had been introduced into the profession of faith required of bishops before their consecration. The year after the synod, Patriarch Callistus added to the *Synodicon* recited from the pulpit each year on the Sunday of Orthodoxy a series of anathemas against Barlaam, Akindynus and their followers, and of acclamations in honour of Palamas and his doctrines. Palamism was now triumphant.

Even so, it was not unopposed. Its critics were not Barlaamites. Their objections were against the theology proposed by Palamas, which they regarded as a dangerous innovation, a departure from the tradition of the Fathers and suspect in itself. Most of them were as hostile to the Latins as was Palamas, and to call them *Latinophrones* (Latin-minded) was a complete misinterpretation of their position. Yet it was freely done. In truth, they meant to be rigidly conservative Greeks.

The aim of Palamas was to find a solution of a real theological problem. He was trying to explain in theological terms, as far as that was possible, God's deification of man. The occasion for this was Barlaam's attack on the monks, and so the solution had to have particular application to the light that the hesychasts said they experienced within themselves as a fruit of their prayer. The explanation that Palamas offered was on these lines. The essence of God is absolutely invisible and incommunicable to any creature. So if man is to be "a partaker in the divine nature" (II Peter I 4), some operation or attribute of God that is inseparable from God and indivisible from his essence, but really distinct from it, must affect man. Such operations are "energies." They are not substance, for they subsist not of themselves but in the divine essence; nor are they accidents. They are visible and communicable; they are really distinguished among themselves and from the essence, though always united to the essence. As being of God, they are eternal and uncreated, and can rightly be called "divinities." The Light of Thabor is one of the divine energies. It is the beauty of God, deifying grace, that makes men participators in the divinity; it is eternal and uncreated, and reaches men's souls directly, though in different degrees according to the capacity of each. It is also the reward that the blessed enjoy in heaven, for even there the essence of God will remain hidden from men's eyes.

Palamas and his followers claimed that this theory was founded on the teaching of the early Church. Certainly much had been written by the Fathers on the transcendence of God and much poetic diction expended on the Light of Thabor. But his opponents flatly denied any place in tradition to his theory of energies. The synodal "tome" of 1351 rebutted the charge that this "should rightly be called an addition to," but allowed that "it is a development of, the sixth council." The introduction to the "Hagioretic Tome" of 1341 suggested that, as the revelation of the Old Testament was the preparation for that of the New, so the New Testament was the preparation for the revelation of the mysteries revealed in prayer.[6] Perhaps, then, the critics of Palamas had a case. They objected also, especially the later critics, on dogmatic grounds, that the exigencies of the theory involved two Gods, indeed a multiplicity of Gods. Nicephorus Gregoras, imprisoned after the synod of 1351, attacked Palamism in a series of writings precisely because he held that hesychastic theology impugned the unicity of the Godhead. Procorus Cydones, priest-monk of Mt. Athos, wrote a long and incisive treatise founded on Thomistic theology to the same effect, and was excommunicated and perpetually suspended by a synod in 1368, whose synodical "tome" ended with a decree canonising Gregory Palamas.[7]

The Palamite controversy was a purely domestic dispute, internal to the Greek Church. Barlaam was not a Roman Catholic, but coming from Italy and arguing in a western manner, for eastern minds he implicated the Western Church. In consequence, opposition to Palamism was for them associated with the Latin Church. Its proponents were called *Latinophrones*—Latin-minded—and anti-Latin sentiment was deepened. Palamism became the touchstone of orthodoxy and dissidents were excommunicated and persecuted. Procorus Cydones, who died shortly after his condemnation, was at his death refused viaticum, religious obsequies and religious burial, as were other anti-Palamites.[8] The corpse of Gregoras († c. 1360) had been dragged through the streets.

The civil war between the rival Emperors was a golden opportunity to both their enemies and their allies to enrich themselves at their expense. Between 1327 and 1359 the Turkish troops of Cantacuzenus's son-in-law, Orkhan, raided European territory no less than sixteen times—on some of these occasions by invitation—even attacking Constantinople itself with a fleet of thirty-six ships. To check such Turkish aggression and to secure safety of movement in the Aegean, Pope Clement began negotiations for another Naval League. Its great success was the capture on 28 October 1344 of the port of Smyrna, the base of Omur, Cantacuzenus's ally. But the League's fleet was small and the Genoese ships, to the distress of the Pope, used the opportunity when Byzantium was embroiled in civil war, to retake the island of Chios and the town of Phocaea not from the Turks, but from the Greeks.[9]

The Naval League continued in Aegean waters ineffectively under the leadership of the Dauphin Humbert. When he at last resigned, it gained a resounding victory off Imbros (1347).[10] But it was ill-supported; papal money was running out, the Mediterranean powers were unenthusiastic, the Black Death struck a blow at all multiple enterprises. By 1348 the League, Pope included, was seeking a truce with the Turks. In 1350 war broke out between Venice and Genoa. Though the League was renewed for ten years from 1 January 1351, all the Latins with interests in the Aegean were involved on one side or the other in the Venetian-Genoese war. So in September 1351 Pope Clement dissolved it.[11]

In this Naval League there was no question of a Greek contingent, for Byzantium was locked in civil war. There was, however, communication with Avignon. On 21 October 1343 the Pope replied to a request made by an envoy of John V Palaeologus for ships against the Turks that in pity for them he had already ordered the preparation of a fleet, adding that, if only the Greeks would abandon "their execrable and damnable schism," they would get help not only against the Turks but against Tartars as well and all other enemies.[12] These messages were taken by Bartholomew, a canon of Negroponte, who went to Constantinople with the returning envoy of the Empress, Philip of Saint-Germain, one of the many Savoyards in her suite.

When Cantacuzenus entered Constantinople triumphantly in 1347, he found Bartholomew at the royal court, and he lost no time in utilising his services. Cantacuzenus sincerely aimed at union of the Churches. He had also at that time need to destroy in western eyes the image of himself as a rebel against legitimate authority and as friend and ally of the infidel Turk.[13] In 1347 he sent Bartholomew with two Greeks, George Spanopoulus and Nicholas Sigerus, and a Frenchman, Francis of "Pertuxo," on a mission to the Pope. Before they set out, all four had an audience with the Emperor to be briefed on their task. Cantacuzenus told them that he had already, with the assent of the co-Emperor, subscribed a formal chrysobull giving the Pope his title and recognising the primacy and universality of the Roman Church. He was ready to show the same obedience to the Pope as did the King of France and to unite the Empire with the Pope and the Roman Church as the kingdom of France was united with them, and that not just nominally but really. To settle the question of faith there should be a synod in Constantinople, Negroponte or Rhodes. For this he would need financial assistance and he hoped for help also against his enemies. He was ready to combine his troops with those of the Pope and of the League and to campaign in person—indeed to assume the captaincy, for he would achieve more in a month than Humbert had done in a year.

The credentials given to his ambassadors are dated 22 September 1347, but it was only on 5 March 1348 that the Greeks presented a mémoire to the Pope in Avignon. Cantacuzenus was ready to participate in a "great passagium" (crusade) personally with fifteen to twenty thousand men, or in a "small passagium" (League) personally and with 4,000 men. If either of these enterprises should help Constantinople, it would heal the ecclesiastical schism and bring the Churches under one head, the Pope. Union should be by means of a synod, but the envoys were not empowered to arrange details for one; the Pope should send an embassy quickly to treat of that with the Emperor, remembering that the Greek Church was vaster by far than the Greek empire. Cantacuzenus asked help to pay the expenses of summoning the oriental Patriarchs and representatives, and aid to protect Greek frontiers, so that he might not be engaged in their defence when the crusade was set in motion. He asked also that Clement would write to the Czar of Serbia bidding him restore to the Empire the territories he had occupied.[14]

When the Greek envoys returned home, they were accompanied by two Latin bishops, bearers of only a brief note of thanks and a promise that the Pope would shortly send an embassy. It was two years, however, before the promised embassy set out. The reasons for the delay are not known, but perhaps Clement was not sure what line to take with a usurper turned Emperor and, while he was engaged in negotiating peace with the Turks, he might have felt it wiser to have as little to do as possible with Orkhan's father-in-law. For his part Cantacuzenus persisted, writing to the Pope three times in the course of 1349[15] and getting one brief acknowledgement back.[16] However, in the account he gives in his *History* of these negotiations he does not mention these letters nor advert to the long delay before the Holy See sent its promised embassy. He dilates at length on his interview with the two Latin bishops, William, O.F.M., and Hugo de Spert, O.P., who had accompanied his returning envoys, Spanopoulus and Sigerus. To them he explained the pressing needs that had led to his friendship with the

Turks and spoke persuasively of the utility of a general council. They, he says, were convinced and, on their return to Avignon, spoke highly of him and of his plan, to such effect indeed, that Pope Clement "said that he was favourably inclined to a synod and sent with all speed to tell the Emperor that the advice seemed to him to be extremely good and that he thought that a meeting of the bishops was of the utmost importance." All his bishops should meet together and a time and place be fixed. Then, continues Cantacuzenus, within a short time other letters came from the Pope warning him that the project of the synod should not be allowed to languish. The Pope told him that he was putting union of the Churches in the first place and thought it of primary importance, but that, as Italy was convulsed with wars, he was fully engaged negotiating peace. When that was achieved, his most urgent action would be to determine a time and a place for the meeting. Cantacuzenus, therefore, sent a Dominican friend of his, John, to say how much he reciprocated the Pope's zeal. Then Clement VI died.[17]

There is some doubt whether this account of events from the pen of the Emperor is accurate. As regards chronology, it is not, for Clement did not answer "with all speed." He waited two years and it is doubtful if at the end of that time he favoured a council. It would have been completely contrary to papal attitudes both before him and after him. What private instructions he may have given his envoys, William Emergavi, O.F.M., bishop of Kisamos in Crete, and Gasberto de Orgoglio, O.P., bishop of Ceneta in northern Italy, is not recorded. The letters, at any rate, concerning the embassy that are preserved do no more than recommend the envoys and in general terms encourage various people to co-operate in the good work of union.[18]

Clement, in fact, died on 6 December 1352, and his successor, Innocent VI,[19] was on the throne when Cantacuzenus's next envoy arrived.[20] Innocent replied promptly and enthusiastically, not only to the Emperor, but also to two of his relatives, John and Manuel Asen. Also he told the King of Cyprus, the Governor of Genoa and the Grand Master of the Hospitallers of Cantacuzenus's good dispositions and asked them to respond to any request for help.[21] Yet another letter came from Cantacuzenus carried by a Latin bishop, John, and again Innocent replied extolling union.[22] But Byzantium was once more in the throes of civil war.

In the few years of peace after 1347 Cantacuzenus had striven against heavy odds to lead the Empire back to some sort of prosperity, but he could achieve little against the entrenched Genoese. Then in 1351 the young Emperor, John V, decided to vindicate his claim to be sole *Basileus*. Cantacuzenus's Turkish allies at first crushed John's troops and his Serb and Bulgar helpers. Cantacuzenus then had his son Matthew crowned Emperor (1354). But Turkish atrocities and loyalty to the Palaeologan dynasty gave John the support of public opinion. With the aid of a Genoese corsair, Francesco Gattilusio, he entered Constantinople on 21/22 November 1354, whereupon Cantacuzenus retired to a monastery as the monk Joasaph (10 December). He lived another thirty years with an influence almost as great as if he had still been actively Emperor.

Pope Innocent, having received letters only from Cantacuzenus, had replied only to Cantacuzenus and had paid no attention to John V. With Cantacuzenus dethroned and Byzantium still desperately unsettled (John V did not dispose of Matthew Cantacuzenus till 1357), he sought to satisfy elsewhere his zeal for Church union and for warring against the Turk, who in the course of the civil war, had inflicted a mortal wound on Byzantium. Cantacuzenus's Turkish allies had seized Gallipoli (1354) and refused an offer of forty thousand ducats to evacuate it. They now possessed an open door to the conquest of Europe. It was to the Serbs that Innocent turned, or rather Stephen Dusan, the eminently successful Czar of the Serbs, turned to him. Dusan had sent an embassy asking to be made the Church's Captain General against the Turks. He claimed to have restrained the opponents of the Latin Church in his kingdom and to have restored ruined churches and monasteries,[23] and he asked for nuncios to unite his people to Rome, since he acknowledged the Latin faith. Innocent's first reply of 28 August 1354 was non-committal.[24] A later letter of 24 December of the same year announcing as his nuncios the local Apostolic Legate Bartholomew and the Carmelite Peter Thomas, bishop of Patti in Sicily, was warm and effusive.[25] Letters to Dusan's wife and father, to the Patriarch, to the hierarchy and to the barons of Serbia were despatched also.[26] To his nuncios Innocent repeated the instructions given by his predecessor three years before, indicating the multiple errors and abuses rampant in Serbia, for which they were to find a cure.[27] Bartholomew and Peter Thomas met Dusan early in 1355, but by that time the Serbian King's zeal for Catholicism had waned, probably because the end of the civil war in Byzantium had reduced his opportunities for conquests there and because King Louis[28] no longer threatened him from Hungary. Dusan died on 20 December 1355 and the ensuing anarchy rendered any unionist activity there impossible.

Innocent's disappointment over Serbia was abruptly changed when in the summer of 1356 he received a chrysobull from the Emperor of Byzantium, John V.[29] It was brought by Paul, Latin archbishop of Smyrna, and Nicholas Sigerus. Paul, a Calabrian by birth, speaking both Latin and Greek, had been in Smyrna for some ten years and knew the East well. He had had friendly relations with both Emperors. Sigerus had several times before been at Avignon as the messenger of John Cantacuzenus. The document they presented to Pope Innocent was no less than the Greek Emperor's scheme for procuring ecclesiastical union. Dated 15 December

1355, the chrysobull began: "I, John, in Christ God faithful Emperor and ruler of the Romans, Palaeologus, swear on the holy Gospels of God . . . that I will steadfastly and wholly observe and fulfil each and all of what follows, which I promised to Paul . . . in the place of Innocent VI, Pope of the holy Roman and universal Church." John professed obedience to Innocent and his successors and pledged to bring all his subjects to the same, according to a detailed and considered plan evolved in consultation with Paul and Sigerus.

According to this scheme the Pope should send the envoys back in three galleys. In one of them the Emperor would despatch his second son, Manuel, to Avignon, the other two would remain under his command. On receipt of the hostage, Innocent should quickly provide fifteen transport vessels, five lighter vessels, 500 knights, and 1000 infantry. While these were fighting the Turks under imperial command for six months, a papal legate should nominate various selected persons to office in the Greek Church to bring the Church back to union. If within six months after the arrival of the papal expedition the Greeks had not of their own accord embraced union, "which We do not credit, We promise that they shall be completely obedient." He undertook to allot a palace and a church to the Legate, that his heir should learn Latin and that three schools would be set up to teach Latin to the children of the magnates. If he should fail in any of this, John promised to abdicate in favour of his eldest son, who should then be subject to the Pope as to a father, the Pope acting as regent and ruling the Empire. In the event that Innocent despatched the original three galleys and John failed to send Manuel, he promised a forfeit of 4000 florins per galley to be raised on his and his people's property. If, however, he fulfilled all his obligations, he hoped that a major expedition would be mounted in the West to drive the Turks out of Byzantine territory and that His Holiness would bear the cost of some part of it—such expedition to be under the Byzantine Emperor as captain and standard-bearer of holy Mother Church. If John faithfully did his part, his son Manuel should be returned with due honours. If, however, through no fault of his he should fail to implement these promises and should personally present himself to the Pope, Innocent should defend and help him to regain his throne and he should not be visited with any penalty.

This chrysobull is a document at the same time fantastic and realistic. Fantastic in implying that the Greeks at large would accept union within six months and put up with nominations to Greek bishoprics and ecclesiastical offices by a Latin Legate. It was realistic in that it did not start off demanding a world-crusade, but only three ships and a small force, not enough to take the offensive, but sufficient to defend and to show the Greeks that the Latin Church was alive to their needs and was helping.[30]

The proposal to teach Latin was sound, even if practical only after preparing people's minds to receive the idea. The sanctions proposed for his failures were a guarantee of sincerity, though it may be doubted whether any Pope could have asserted the right given him of acting *in loco parentis* to the heir to the throne. The hope for a major expedition should have been reasonable, but was not. The western powers were far, far too concentrated on themselves and their own advantages to look beyond the immediate future and to bother about the crumbling Byzantine Empire.

What Innocent and his cardinals thought about the imperial plan, explained and advocated by its envoy-architects, there is no knowing. The Pope, however, did not send Paul and Sigerus back with an armed expedition. At that moment he was trying to renew the League against the Turks with Venice, Rhodes, Cyprus and Genoa, and King Louis of Hungary was threatening war against Venice, the key partner in the papal schemes. With commendable speed (the imperial embassy had taken six months to reach Avignon, for it arrived only between 12 and 19 June 1356) he nominated in July 1356 two nuncios to go to Constantinople, Peter Thomas, bishop of Patti, and William, bishop of Sozopolis in Thrace. *En route* Peter Thomas was to try to prevent war between Hungary and Venice. His parleys with the one side and the other consumed much time and he arrived in Constantinople only in April 1357. John V was away campaigning. The envoys went to meet him in the field and returned with him later to the capital. The letter they carried from the Pope was full of joy and gladness, praise and encouragement, but it was not a detailed reply to John's detailed proposal. He was only counselled to give a benevolent hearing to the nuncios and to follow their advice.[31]

The nuncios carried other letters too. Innocent told the Patriarch that "perhaps from the negligence of the messengers or from some other chance" no letter from him had come with the imperial proposal. He chided him gently but not very tactfully and recommended his envoys to him.[32] Letters of the same date were sent to half-a-dozen Italian notables and to seven Greek personages, inviting their help.[33]

It seems as if Innocent was not quite sure of the sincerity of the Emperor. No sooner had he decided to send an embassy than he wrote to the members of the League announcing the joyful news of John's offer and the names of his nuncios. "And since We trust . . . that the Emperor will confirm by the attestation of his own spoken word what by the same nuncios he has proposed," he exhorted the members of the League to give him all the help they could when "by his word of mouth he has ratified and approved" what the nuncios said in his name; and when one or the other of these had assured them of it.[34]

Peter Thomas was a persuasive advocate. While he was in Constantinople he was instrumental in bringing John Lascaris Calopherus and Michael Angelus (knight of Thessalonica) into the Latin fold. He met also the more famous Demetrius Cydones, who later became a Catholic, possibly owing to his influence. With the Emperor he was equally successful. Palaeologus wrote to the Pope on 7 November 1357:

> Be assured, most holy Father, that with all the care We can We have striven and are striving that our Church should be united with the holy Roman Church. With the counsel and considered advice of Our barons We replied to Brother Lord Peter that, just as We promised, so do We wish to be obedient and faithful and devoted to the Roman Church, and indeed We do promise and swear. For my part, I promise faithfully and hold in its entirety everything that the holy Roman Church holds, and in that faith I wish to live and die, and never will I depart from it. In that way I promised to Brother Lord Peter, and in the presence of many bishops I swore in his hands, and I will from this time forward preserve faith and fidelity to my Lord the sovereign Pontiff, as other princes of the Roman Church preserve it.

He could not, he continued, at the moment win over all his people, but the appearance of a papal fleet would do that. As Peter Thomas had advised him not to send his son, Manuel, to Avignon, he was not doing so. He hoped that it might soon be possible, and even that he might come himself. He would substitute a pro-Roman patriarch for the anti-Roman Callistus.

So John did "by the attestation of his own spoken word" do what he had promised and became a Roman Catholic, accepting the faith on oath and making the manual act of obedience. Philippe de Mézières, companion and biographer of St. Peter Thomas, records that after his reconciliation with the Church, John received Holy Communion at the hands of the legate.[35]

Despite the drastic limitations imposed on him by the perpetual wars between Catholic States, Innocent managed to do something to show his goodwill to the newly converted John. In 1357 he was able to renew the League for the defence of Smyrna, appointing as Captain a Hospitaller, Nicolo Benedetti, and as Apostolic Legate Peter Thomas, by this time bishop of Corone. The legate had entire supervision over all the Latin Church of the East, including the patriarchate of Constantinople in things both spiritual and temporal, especially in the prosecution of the war against the Turks.[36] The force at his disposal was small—eight galleys in addition to the two maintained for the defence of Smyrna. The expedition, however, was given crusaders' privileges. Following papal instructions, it went first to Constantinople to give John V the moral support of its presence. It then was successful in various encounters, its greatest exploit being the capture of Lampsacus, on the eastern side of the Dardanelles (1359). That, however, was a flash in the pan. Peter Thomas fell seriously ill. The League fleet dissolved.[37]

The political situation in Greece soon deteriorated. The Sultan Murad occupied much of Thrace, captured Didymotichus in 1361, and took Philippopolis in 1363. Venetians, Genoese and Greeks talked of pacts and agreed on nothing. The Byzantine Emperor then approached his Christian neighbours. Patriarch Callistus led an embassy to Serbia, but died there. On the Latin side, King Peter left Cyprus on 24 October 1362 to tour Europe with the aim of getting men and money for a crusade. On 31 March 1363 Pope Urban proclaimed the crusade and the king of France and many nobles took the Cross. When Crete revolted, Venice refused to give the crusaders its promised assistance, but was repersuaded by Peter Thomas. The King of Cyprus failed to appear in Venice at the appointed time. Many of the troops that had gathered there departed, and finally Peter with only his own force returned to Cyprus. He left Venice on 27 June 1365 together with Peter Thomas, now Patriarch of Constantinople, who had been nominated papal legate for the crusade.[38] This, however, was not the crusade that Pope Urban had originally planned. He had meant to launch a bigger one under King John II of France, but John had died in April 1364. Rendered perhaps somewhat uneasy by the movement for a crusade, the Byzantine Emperor John V offered to take part in it and asked only that his Empire should not suffer at Latin hands. Pope Urban reassured him and urged union.[39]

Not long afterwards (18 April 1365) the Pope addressed an affectionate and helpful letter to the Byzantine Emperor. "Although Your Serenity, the clergy and the people of the Greeks are damnably separated from the bosom of the sacrosanct Roman and universal Church, outside whose obedience there is no salvation, nevertheless, because We look on you as sons of that same Church, though prodigal of your own salvation," we await your filial return. The Pope told John that the crusade had fallen through, but that, because the Turks had occupied most of the Greek Empire, he had, precisely "to drive out the Turks from the said Empire," organised help from the Hospitallers, the House of Montferrat and Genoa, which, when peace had been restored between Genoa and Cyprus, would take the field. John should consider how advantageous union of the Churches would be. Should he, as he had once wished and as Urban desired, visit the Apostolic See, he would be royally and warmly welcomed.[40]

Through the good offices of Peter Thomas peace between Genoa and Cyprus was made on 18 April 1365, but the projected expedition never materialised. Peter of Cyprus directed his crusade against Alexandria, which he took and held for six days, when his allies made him retire. On 25

January 1366 Pope Urban again addressed himself to Emperor John V to announce still another scheme to assist the Empire. This time the prime helpers would be Louis, King of Hungary, Peter of Cyprus and Palaeologus's own cousin, Amadeus of Savoy. Amadeus would carry the papal letter himself. Urban hoped that this gesture would win the Greeks to union. If not, "the Holy See will deem you publicans and sinners, and if you should be harassed by Christian or infidel, We shall not be able, as indeed We ought not, to aid you, severed as you are from the body of the universal Church."[41] Louis had so far directed his armies only against Christians. Profiting by the disturbances in Bulgaria on the death of its king, John Alexander, he had occupied the fortress and region of Vidin and taken Prince Stracimir prisoner.

Before ever the papal letter left Avignon, John V with two of his sons, Manuel and Michael, his Catholic chancellor, Manicaites, and a very small suite, in the middle of winter 1365-6, "went off to the illustrious King of Hungary to persuade him to fight with me [so John later declared in a public announcement] against the infidel, because I was convinced that it was incumbent on me to face that danger on behalf of all, since he would not yield to persuasions from others." The meeting between the monarchs seems to have been very harmonious and successful at first, for Louis wrote off to Venice asking them to prepare for him at his expense two to five galleys, since it was his intention "to go in person with a great army by land and sea to the defence of the Empire of Romania against the Turks and [he said] that was at the request of my Lord the Emperor of Constantinople."[42] Not much later Louis and John sent a combined embassy to Avignon, composed of the Hungarian Bishop of Nyitra and the Greek Manicaites. From the Pope's answers one can deduce the purpose of the mission.

Three papal letters dated 1 July 1366 were addressed to John Palaeologus. They all deal with a promise John had made on oath to the Hungarian King "that you and your noble sons, Manuel and Michael, would accept, do and fulfil . . . everything that We shall enjoin on you and your sons regarding reconciliation" with the Latin Church. Two of the letters detailed what they had to do. By one of them, John, his clergy and people should make a profession of faith in the form accepted by Michael VIII Palaeologus. Formulae for the attestation on oath of acceptance of Roman faith and obedience and for an abjuration of schism were contained in a second letter. In addition prelates should show their obedience by the ceremony of the manual act.[43] The third letter was short and formal. It acknowledged John's embassy and informed him that nuncios were being sent from the Curia to Louis who would communicate to him what was relevant. With words to encourage him to persevere in his good intent, the Pope ended: "We have with a fatherly eye seen the requests put forward in your name by George [Manicaites] and We intend . . . once your return has been effected, to grant these and other deserving petitions from you and yours."[44] Urban, it is worth noting, sent his nuncios to the Catholic Louis, and John was to be informed of their message through Louis and at his discretion.[45]

The Pope, naturally, wrote also to Louis, thanking him for his part in the prospective union of Churches and encouraging him to continue his co-operation. Both the King and his mother, whose influence with her son was great, were informed of the requirements asked of John.[46] With the briefs on the ecclesiastical project went a sheaf of others connected with the military expedition. Urban stressed the danger to Christians from the Turks and congratulated Louis on his intention of opposing them "with a great multitude of his own subjects and of other faithful." The expedition was made into a crusade of which Louis was appointed Captain General. An encyclical and letters to various notables were sent to create enthusiasm for the enterprise aimed not immediately at operations in the Holy Land or against the Mamluks, but at defending against the ravages of the Turks "all faithful continuing in the unity of the Church." To reach the Turks Louis would have to penetrate into the Balkans and the Empire, which would consequently gain (so Urban hoped) by a successful campaign.

There can be no reasonable doubt that Pope Urban was genuine and sincere in urging Louis of Anjou to attack the Turks and thereby to relieve the pressure on the Eastern Empire. Yet, while the double embassy was still in Avignon, he wrote to Louis sounding a note of caution. The Greeks, he warned, in the past have deceived the Church and what has happened once can happen again. At present "the same Greeks do not seem to be motivated by zeal of devotion and a pure intention, but they want to obtain this union from the necessity of gaining help from you. So you should proceed in their regard only after much consideration and with studied caution." In case Louis had already pledged himself to act within a fixed, short time, Urban dispensed him from his bond for the period of one year, but would be pleased if, meantime, the king gave John and his sons, "returned to unity," help on a small scale.[47]

It is, indeed, a strange-sounding letter, and some historians have seen in it only another proof of Roman intransigence, and indeed duplicity.[48] Halecki proposes several other lines of explanation. The crusade against the Turks was primarily to help the *faithful* of the East, who were not Greeks but Latin subjects: the campaign was not dependent on any condition of a previous conversion of the Greek people; the spate of letters, written in July (*after* the hesitating Brief of June) to the hierarchy and many notables recommends and publicises it unconditionally: the letter in question is the only one of all those dealing with this project of union of the Churches and the crusade that is registered among the *litterae patentes et de curia,* i.e., those of lesser importance, and not with the *litterae secretae,* which suggests that it was not a letter *motu proprio* of the Pontiff proposing new ideas of his own, but an answer to a detailed plea acceding to ideas proposed by the client—Louis. It may be significant that Louis's ambassador, the Bishop of Nyitra, was still in Avignon when the letter was approved. If this whole supposition is correct, it implies that Louis had bound himself on oath to a quick expedition and then on second thoughts wanted to evade his obligation. It may be that so speedy a *volte face* caused the rupture in negotiations and John's unhonoured departure.

Whether that was the cause or not, something certainly happened in Buda to upset the harmony between the monarchs. In the event, John had to leave one of his sons as hostage and he, himself, was refused transit at the Bulgarian border, admittedly by the Bulgarians who would not let him cross their country, but Louis made no move to free him from his impasse, nor did he send any "help on a small scale" to Constantinople. What is more, he abandoned his intention of leading the crusade and of taking any part in it at all. On 20 September 1366, he cancelled his acceptance of the Venetians' offer to provide him with two to five vessels manned and armed at their expense and asked only for empty hulls. It turned out that he wanted them, not to combat the Turks, but to pursue his plans of conquest in the Balkans at the expense of the Serbs, the Bulgars and perhaps of the Greeks.[49]

Of the other partners in Urban's proposed enterprise, Peter Lusignan had shot his bolt in Alexandria, but Amadeus of Savoy, the "Green Knight," though late in his preparations, fulfilled his obligations. With the force he had collected he took Gallipoli from the Turks on 23 August 1366, after a three months' campaign he forced the Bulgars to let Palaeologus return home, and he restored to the Empire a number of towns on the litoral of the Black Sea. In the following winter (when fighting was in abeyance) he had long conversations with his cousin, the Emperor.[50] With Amadeus was the Latin Patriarch of Constantinople, Paul, who, born in the kingdom of Naples, both spoke Greek and was sympathetic towards the Greeks. As archbishop of Smyrna, he had influenced Emperor John to make his offer of union in 1355 and had taken it in the Emperor's name to the Pope. He became metropolitan of Thebes on 15 May 1357 and was engaged in organising a Naval League. On the death of Peter Thomas he was nominated Latin Patriarch of Constantinople and his place in Thebes was taken by another lover of union, Simon Autumano, born of a Turkish father and a Greek mother, an anti-Palamite who joined the Latin Church.[51]

Paul and Amadeus were both enthusiastic promoters of Church union.

When they first met John in Sozopolis and in later contacts in Constantinople, they used their persuasions on him, and Paul tried to broach the subject officially with the Greek Patriarch, Philotheus. He had to be content with a meeting with the ex-Emperor, the monk Joasaph, at which the Church was represented by three members of the synod, and there were present also Emperor John V Palaeologus, his wife and his two eldest sons, Andronicus and Manuel. Paul proposed union by imperial decree after agreement with the Pope. Joasaph rejected that outright. No Emperor could command dogma without a council and even a council was not final, for the convictions of the faithful must be taken into account. A united Church must have unity of faith if there were to be an end of discussion, and that could be achieved only by a council in which the whole Church—all the patriarchates with the Serbs, Bulgars, Georgians, Russians, etc.—should take part. The conclusions of such a council would, indeed, be final. Even Paul ended by admitting: "Before Christ and the truth, I say again now what I said before, that what you say is holy, good and true. So I also accept and agree that there should be a council." It was arranged that the council should be held in Constantinople between 1 June 1367 and 31 May 1369.[52]

In the course of the discussion Joasaph produced a curious bit of information. He said that, when John was in Buda, King Louis had insisted that he and his sons should be rebaptised as a condition of getting help. If that were so, it could explain why the early harmony between them so rapidly deteriorated into hostility. Meyendorff suggests that the main purpose of the double embassy to the Curia was in this connection of rebaptism.

One may, however, doubt the accuracy of Joasaph's information. There is no hint in any surviving document that this question was, in fact, raised in Avignon. The Pope's conditions for John were exactly those laid down in all proposals for union and for all countries and by all his predecessors since Clement IV a hundred years earlier, without there being a hint of any extra stress on baptism and the sacraments to suggest that there was conflict on that point between the two monarchs. On the other hand it is true that the Hungarians had found an undesirable confusion as regards baptism and confirmation in Vidin when they had occupied it, and zealous Franciscan missionaries were consequently baptising by the thousand people who flocked to them for that purpose. But Vidin was part of Bulgaria with a heterogeneous population of Latins and oriental Christians, Vlachs, infidels, and Bogomils. It was not the Greek Empire with its single Christian rite. It is most unlikely that Louis ever tabled the suggestion of rebaptism, let alone that he maintained it as a necessary condition.[53]

Emperor John V Palaeologus referred the conclusions arrived at in the meeting of Paul with Cantacuzenus to Patriarch Philotheus, who discussed them with the Patriarchs of Alexandria and Jerusalem then in Constantinople, and with his synod of bishops. They all welcomed the proposal but insisted on there being a council and they meant that council to be at full oriental strength. The two eastern Patriarchs wrote off to their Churches to summon their bishops and they agreed to inform the Patriarch of Antioch. Philotheus sent letters to the chief Churches under his jurisdiction. One such letter, addressed to the Bishop of Ochrida and All Bulgaria, is preserved. The Patriarch told his correspondent: "The synod will be universal and general, for, whereas the Church here possesses its orthodox beliefs and its sound and blameless faith, lately there has been talk about orthodox beliefs and faith, so it is essential that you come . . . for we do not wish even one syllable or one tittle of the established dogmas to suffer diminution." Nothing should be allowed to stand in the way of attendance. No credit should be paid to rumours that in Constantinople the ancient, traditional doctrines were being forsaken; that was not true. Come, "for we have reached an agreement with the counsellors of the Pope, that if our dogma shall be shown in the synod to be more in accordance with the holy Scriptures than the Latins', they will accede to us and profess what we profess and, by God's help, we do not doubt that so it will be, by his grace and aid."[54]

With this confidence in the superiority of their faith, it was little wonder that the Patriarchs agreed to send their own representatives with the royal embassy, with Amadeus and Paul, to Pope Urban. Amadeus's contract with his troops ran out in June 1367 and he had to return to Italy. Before he left, an agreement had been drawn up and signed by the Emperor (on 29 May), that he would present himself in his own person or by the person of his son, Andronicus, before the Pope in the course of the next month of March. As a guarantee of his good faith, he gave in pledge certain jewels (which were deposited with the Genoese in Pera) and 20,000 ducats to Amadeus for the Pope. Clauses were included allowing for legitimate delays either by Pope or Emperor.[55]

The Count's returning expedition reached Venice with the eight Greeks towards the end of July.[56] Amadeus informed the Pope of their arrival. Urban was no longer in Avignon. He had come to Viterbo in Italy and so was very much more available for the Greeks. In the company of Amadeus and Paul the ambassadors met the Pope on 7 October and seven days later went with him to Rome. Negotiations continued for four weeks. But unfortunately there is no record of them. Certainly the main subject must have been union of the Churches and the means to achieve it. To judge by results, one must conclude that the negotiations failed. The Pope wrote at least twenty-three letters, all dated 6 November 1367, to personages or groups interested in the project. In not one of them was the word "council" mentioned nor, beyond a pious wish, was there word of any practical military help. The most important Brief, the one that must have been addressed to the Emperor himself, is lost. The rest, sent to the Queen, to the heir Andronicus, to his younger brothers Manuel and Michael, to the citizens of Constantinople, to the barons, to certain individuals both Greek and Latin, declare the Pope's joy, thank them for their co-operation and invite them to help the Emperor keep his promise and to effect the union, which would be of benefit to the Empire. The three Patriarchs he thanked for their letter and exhorted them to "persist unswervingly in their declared purpose" letting their light shine to all from the candlestick. John Cantacuzenus, the monk Joasaph, also received a special Brief. Urban asked him to use his great influence with his son-in-law and (interestingly) with the monks, the clergy and the people to prosper the union about which "you say you were concerned in the recent negotiations in Constantinople." The Commune of Pera, the Genoese community of Chios, the Queen of Sicily, Venice and many others—all received letters.[57] The central idea of all of them was the visit of the Emperor "with many of the nobles and the clergy" to the Holy See.

Patriarch Paul, whose zeal had contributed so much to making the imperial visit a probability, was entrusted with the task of turning it into a reality. He went with the Greeks back to Constantinople, the bearer of some of the papal letters.[58] He faced an arduous task, for he brought no message of comfort—he could not assure the Emperor of western help or the Church of a general council. His mission was rendered even more difficult when Venice sent a truculent ambassador to demand from the Emperor the 26,663 hyperpers they said he owed, who, if John was not compliant, should arrange with Sultan Murad the establishment of a commercial base on the other side of the Bosphorus to rival Constantinople. Even the zealous and optimistic Paul, it seems, lost heart as the months passed without the promised visit of Palaeologus to the Holy See. On 26 October 1368 Urban sent him a letter to console and encourage him. It ended: "As long as there is any hope remaining, do not desist from so praiseworthy an enterprise, but persist in urging the illustrious Emperor of the Greeks for his own salvation and that of his subjects to fulfil what he has promised, and if (may it not so happen) you do not achieve the desired result, you will nevertheless receive from God the reward of your zeal and labors."[59]

Urban's optimism and Paul's patience were not in vain. Towards the end of August 1369 Paul, accompanied by Demetrius Cydones, a Greek converted a dozen years before to the Roman faith by his study of St. Thomas Aquinas,[60] went to Viterbo to announce to Pope Urban the proximate arrival of the Emperor John Palaeologus. The Pope wrote to John on 2

September 1369 to inform him that he had arranged with the imperial messengers the details of their future meeting and that he had appointed one of his cardinals to visit and to stay with him until they met.[61] This letter addressed Palaeologus as *Carissimo in Christo filio,* the salutation used for the faithful of the Roman Church, the first time it was employed by Pope Innocent for John. The Emperor arrived with four ships at Naples on 7 August and reached Rome in mid-September with his suite. No eminent Greek ecclesiastic was with him, no representative of the Greek nobility, the clergy or the people.

On 7 October the Pope nominated four cardinals to receive the Emperor's profession of faith. He himself arrived in Rome on 13 October. Four days later John V made his profession of Roman faith in the Hospital of the Holy Spirit, situated in the shadow of St. Peter's, in the apartment of the aged Cardinal Nicholas de Bessia. There were present those of his suite who were Catholics and various Latin ecclesiastics. He signed it and sealed it with his golden seal. It was the Clementine formula that Michael VIII Palaeologus had accepted nearly a century before.[62] After this private ceremony there followed the public manifestation. On Sunday, 21 October, Pope Urban, seated on the steps before the church of St. Peter's and surrounded by the cardinals and the prelates then in Rome, received the Emperor's homage. John genuflected three times and then kissed the Pope's foot, knee and cheek. Urban rose, embraced him and intoned the *Te Deum.* There followed a papal Mass in the church with the Emperor present. Afterwards he dined with the Pope and the cardinals. A few days later Urban informed Amadeus of the happy issue of his initiative and reminded him of his obligation to restore to the Emperor the 20,000 florins that he held as pledge.[63] A short letter to the Church announced the Emperor's genuine conversion[64] and the Genoese of Pera were notified that they should return to their owner the jewels that had been deposited with them. All of them were firmly exhorted to help the stricken Empire.[65]

Emperor John remained in Rome for some five months, not leaving for Naples and Venice till March 1370. Meantime he had close contact with the Pope who remained in the eternal city till 17 April. In January 1370, probably to satisfy the doubts of some scrupulous Latin canonist, Palaeologus was called upon to sign a document stating that when in his profession he had declared his acceptance of the faith preached by the Roman Church he had meant the Church presided over by the Pope.[66] Presumably it was thought by some that the *imperator Romaeorum* was cunningly intending to hold the faith of the *Romaei* (Greeks) and not that of the *Romani* (Latins). Strange! On 13 February, probably at his own request, he was given a general permission to have Mass celebrated in his presence on a portable altar—but only by a Latin priest and in the Latin rite.[67] The Venetians and the Genoese were reminded by the Pope that the Emperor was now a Catholic and were asked, therefore, to help "his Empire brought almost to the point of destruction by the savage pillaging and occupation by the Turks, those monstrous enemies of the Cross."[68] The Venetians had sent an embassy to John in Rome to settle their differences. They renewed their treaty with him on 1 February 1370 and easier arrangements were made for the repayment of his debt.

When the Greek Emperor began his preparations to return home, Pope Urban despatched a Brief "To all the prelates of the churches and monasteries, by whatever name they go, and to the clergy and the monks of the city of Constantinople and of other parts of Greece, grace in the present by which they may obtain glory in the future." The letter reads like this. The Roman Church rejoiced because John, the Emperor of the Greeks, had come to its bosom, "from which by the execrable division of damnable schism he had been astray," and it was hoped that his example like that of Constantine the Great would influence others. "But the said Church would have been filled with an excess of greater joy, if you, who are dedicated to the care of souls and in other ways to the service of God, who are equipped with knowledge and consecrated to religion, would abandon the ancient schism to which you damnably and pertinaciously cling, and return to the one, holy, catholic and apostolic Church, outside which there is no salvation, and to the true and pure obedience of the Vicar of Christ and successor of the Prince of the Apostles, in order that, as he is the one and chief pastor, there might be one fold." Would that God would grant this union in this day when the Greek people, deceived by diabolic fraud and overwhelmed by the impious and foul nation of the Turks, might be freed by their western brethren, and the Turks themselves either driven from Romania or, what is more desirable, converted to the faith. The Church not only awaits the Greeks with the yearning that comes from delay, but in the fervour of its love it also goes out to meet them and invites them in with maternal loving-kindness.

> Moreover, for many serious reasons We have not granted the convocation of a synod of Latin and Greek ecclesiastical prelates, which many people, as We have heard, vainly request, in order that those points in which you differ from the westerners and from some easterners (since, in accordance with what the holy Roman Church holds and teaches, these are known to be certain, seeing that they are proved by the witness of the sacred Scriptures and by the words and decisions of the holy Doctors both Latin and Greek and from apostolic faith) may not be brought to the sifting of doubt and of prying discussion and that by useless debate we may not replace the old faith by a new. We shall, however, be graciously ready humbly to instruct any who are in doubt, if they will come to this See, about the witness, words and decisions in question. Given in Rome . . . .[69]

If any uncertainty had remained about the calling of a council, this letter dispelled it. There would not be one. Union could come about only by the imitation of the Emperor's example, by submission to the Latin Church.

The journey to Rome of the Emperor Palaeologus culminating in his acceptance of Roman faith and obedience was a purely personal act, the fulfilment of what the son of Anna of Savoy had had in mind for a number of years. It in no way implicated the Church of Greece. At that time there were many Roman Catholics living in Constantinople, besides the large number of Venetians, Genoese and others established there for their own concerns. How many, it is impossible to say, for it is only by chance that here and there their names are recorded, chiefly in papal documents. At the court there were many, for Anna at her marriage had brought with her from Savoy an entourage of her own compatriots that had grown as the years went by. The Emperor, too, was in close relations with many Italians like Francis Gattilusio, his loyal supporter and a witness in Rome of his profession of faith. Greeks, also, became Catholics either because they could not accept Palamism or for other reasons. There must have been many from every rank of life, now unknown because not in the forefront of events. The names of others are recorded because they were in public life or had contact with the Pope or figured in curial documents. John Lascaris Calopherus, in exile because he had aspired to the hand of a daughter of Cantacuzenus,[70] was a faithful servant of the King Peter of Cyprus and a frequent envoy of the Popes. His brother Maximus, protosyncellus of the patriarchal curia of Constantinople and abbot of the monastery of St. Diomede received the thanks of Pope Innocent for inciting "by his ministry" the Emperor John to make his proposal for union in 1355. With him the Megastratopedarch George Tagaris, the Megadomesticus Alexius Metochites Palaeologus, the Megalogothetes Nicephorus Metochites, the Megastratopedarch Demetrius Angelus Metochites, and Thomas of Vanezo, Captain of the city of Constantinople, received like letters of thanks.[71] George Manicaites was ambassador to Buda and Avignon. Demetrius Cydones, who was shielded from the full rigour of Palamite persecution because he was the friend and minister of three Emperors, Cantacuzenus, John V Palaeologus and Manuel II Palaeologus, translated Aquinas's *Summa contra gentiles* and part of the *Summa theologiae*. He was so pestered by both sympathetic and hostile enquirers about his conversion that he wrote a long account and explanation of it, unhesitatingly affirming papal primacy and the *Filioque* and giving reasons for his faith.[72] His brother Procorus shared his admiration for St. Thomas and he too (without becoming a Catholic) translated some of St. Thomas's works. These translations with Demetrius's *Apologia* brought the living thought of Latin theology to the notice of Greek intellectuals and won their respect, though not always their agreement. Whereas the three brothers Chrysoberges and Manuel Calecas became Dominicans and Thomists, Nilus Cabasilas wrote against Aquinas, as did Matthew Angelus Panaretus at roughly the same time and, later, Joseph Bryennius.[73] Manuel Angelus accompanied John V to Italy in 1369 and (perhaps his brother) Demetrius Angelus was an associate of John Calopherus. Witnesses to the Emperor's profession of faith in Rome, with Cydones, were the knight Michael Strongilo and Philip Tzycandyles. Cassianus, "*civis Constantinopolitanus,*" was used as a messenger by the monk Joasaph (Cantacuzenus). Many ecclesiastics of Constantinople were made abbots of monasteries in Italy.

Besides these known Catholics and the greater number of unknown ones, there were many, not Catholics, who were not opposed to the Latin Church and who favoured union. The two Emperors Andronicus and Cantacuzenus used these as envoys to the Holy See. Demetrius Palaeologus, son of Andronicus II, accompanied John V to Rome. If one may believe the Dominican Filippo Incontri of Pera, when he first went to Greece in the days of Andronicus III, there were many educated Greeks who were in favour of union, but who were afraid to say so openly.[74]

So much talk about Catholicism and union led to a reaction. The Patriarch Philotheus, anti-Latin and ardent Palamite, not unnaturally led the forces of resistance in his Church. It was when Emperor John was on the point of going to Rome that Procorus Cydones was excommunicated for his anti-Palamism—an attack nearly as much on his more famous and influential brother Demetrius as on himself, and one that could be interpreted as a condemnation of St. Thomas's teaching, which Procorus had defended against Palamism. The patriarchal registers record abjurations made by Latins of the *Filioque* and reconciliations of some guilty of the error of Barlaam and Akindynus.[75] The contact with the oriental patriarchates, manifested in regard of the proposed council, was maintained.[76] Philotheus's invitation to the metropolitan of Ochrida led to happier relations with Serbia, whose Church Dusan in 1346 had made independent. In 1368 the ruler of eastern Serbia, John Ugljesa, formally declared that such independence was illegitimate, and promised to restore to Constantinople its rights.[77] The promise was fulfilled in May 1371. In the course of 1370 Philotheus had sent a series of letters to Russia and Lithuania deciding matters there with a high hand. What Cantacuzenus pointed out to Pope Clement, that the Byzantine Church was vastly bigger than the Byzantine Empire, was manifestly true, and, as the Empire's prestige dwindled with the loss of its territory and independence, the authority of the Church increased.

The shrinking of the Empire, however, inevitably caused a shrinking of the Church. Asia Minor, which over the centuries had been "the political, economic, as well as the ecclesiastical center of gravity of the Byzantine Empire," in the course of the fourteenth century was occupied by the Turks. In 1204 there were subordinate to the Church of Constantinople 48 metropolitanates in Anatolia and 37 in Europe, 421 bishops in Anatolia and 190 in Europe. By the fifteenth century Anatolia had only 17 metropolitans to Europe's 54 and 3 bishops to Europe's 115, and those few that remained in Anatolia were in a sad state. Matthew, Metropolitan of Ephesus, described his situation in 1339/1340. After immense difficulties, he told a correspondent, he managed to reach his See only to find that the conquerors had taken all his church's property and that the famous cathedral church was a mosque. Only after bribes and much insistence, in return for his yielding all claim to his metropolitan cathedral, an old woman was evicted from her cottage to give him a place of shelter. There with a little land for cultivation he had to maintain himself "and all the six priests—no more—that the metropolitanate could boast of," and besides, he had to pay taxes. His flock was composed of prisoners and slaves in thousands, among whom were priests and monks. Indeed over the whole of Anatolia the distribution of the population had changed. Massacres and enslavements had denuded many areas. Transplantation of local populations from one region, usually fertile, to another, usually arid, left people without roots. Flight before victorious Turks left many towns and villages desolate—Manuel II towards the end of the fourteenth century on his way with Sultan Bayezid to reduce the last free Greek city, Philadelphia, recorded: "There are many cities to be seen here, but they have no inhabitants . . . not even their names survive." In such towns as weathered the first storm of conquest, the victorious took the churches, mansions and other properties that had any value, while the original citizens, if they had not fled, were held in subservience. The surest way to hold on to life and property was to become a Muslim. Deprived of their churches, without pastors and the help of religious practices, very many of the Greeks in Asia Minor publicly apostatised, even though in their hearts they meant to remain faithful to their creed: not only individuals but whole communities yielded. Barlaam in 1339 pleaded before Pope Benedict XI the cause of "four large and rich cities which . . . were Christian, but have been forced to become Turkish [i.e., Muslim]. Wishing to return to the Christian faith they begged the Emperor" to help them. A Christianity conforming exteriorly to the regular practises of Muslim prayer and customs with difficulty could survive the passing of generations. The missionary zeal of fiery Dervishes, marriages, military service, the ubiquity of victorious Islam, time itself, were in favour of the Muslim religion as the Greek language in Anatolia yielded to Turkish.[78]

Ugljesa's gesture of reconciliation with the Church of Constantinople was not unconnected with his political aims. He wanted Byzantium to combine with him and the other Serbian princes to halt the Turkish advance. At the same time a Turkish embassy was offering peace to the Greeks in return for the cession of Gallipoli.[79] There was a great debate in Constantinople when Cydones, who had just returned from Rome, made a long speech in favour of alliance with the Serbs and of retaining Gallipoli. Perhaps after his insight into the West he had no longer any hope of help from that quarter. But while they talked the Turks fought and crushed the Serbs near the Marica river on 26 September 1371, killing Ugljesa and King Vukasin. Manuel Palaeologus took advantage of the Serbian plight to retake some Greek towns lately held by the Serbs. Vukasin's son, Marko, had to pay tribute to the Sultan and perform military service as to his suzerain.

When John V left Naples he went to Venice, where he was detained for a year for debts owed to Venetian citizens.[80] He reached Constantinople again only in the autumn of 1371 with his ships and 4,000 ducats, an advance payment from the 25,000 ducats and his jewels that would be given to him when he handed over to the Signoria the island of Tenedos. When Pope Gregory heard of the calamity on the Marica he wrote round to rouse the Latins to a defence against the Turks, especially Louis, reminding him of the danger that now lay at his own door.[81] At the instigation of the archbishop of Neopatras, he invited Venice and Hungary and other interested parties, including John V, to a meeting in Thebes on 1 October 1373 to agree on combined action against the common threat.[82] In the late spring of 1373 he sent John Lascaris Calopherus round the courts to press on the authorities the urgent need for action[83] and wrote a letter to John V with a promise of assistance. He told the Emperor that he had heard of the tight ring drawn by the Turks round his territories. So, "moved with paternal compassion for the Catholics who are in those parts and also for the peoples of the Greeks and of Romania, though separated from the holy, catholic and apostolic Church by inveterate schism, but in the hope that they would return to the fold of the Lord and unity of the holy, apostolic See," he was arranging a League of ships against the Turk and, if union should result, he hoped to organise an even stronger force of resistance. John might use Calopherus and Demetrius Cydones to negotiate union, and the Pope asked to be informed "what Your Highness and also the clergy mean to do, by letters both from you and them."[84] Union was stressed in his letter, but it was not a condition of help. But the help did not materialise. No one attended the projected meeting in Thebes.

Gregory, however, did not give up his efforts to raise a western force against the Turks. In the beginning of 1374 he sounded the Venetians only to get back the usual non-committal answer. Nevertheless he decided on an embassy to Constantinople and nominated as his nuncios Thomas de Bozolasco, O.P., and Bartholomew Cheraccio, O.F.M., with two Knights Hospitallers, who were furnished with the usual wide faculties and a copy of the Clementine profession of faith for would-be converts. Safe-conducts addressed to various courts and letters to Latins and Greeks, Catholic and non-Catholic, were despatched, seeing that the pope "with paternal solicitude was minded to promote the spiritual and temporal welfare of our most dear son in Christ, John, illustrious Emperor of the Greeks, and yours too, and that of the peoples subject to the same Emperor, and to check the impiety of the savage Turks, enemies of the sacred Christian name."[85] Once again he was counting on King Louis to play a major role and once again Louis refused, this time flatly. The embassy, however, went on its way in October 1374. It had not reached its destination before the Pope received an envoy of the Emperor, the nobleman Philip Tzycandyles, who had been in Rome at the imperial profession of faith. The answer to the Emperor's letter and to the oral message that Tzycandyles delivered discloses the reason for the embassy. John wanted to explain two events which could very easily be misunderstood.

On his return from Venice[86] with his hands practically empty he had had no choice, after the resounding Turkish victory over the Serbs and their consequent more complete grip on Thrace, but to become a vassal of the Sultan. In 1373, therefore, he had had to accompany Murad on one of his expeditions. In his absence, his heir Andronicus had combined with Murad's son Saudzi Celebi and both had revolted against their parents. They were defeated (25 May 1373) and the Sultan insisted on both being blinded. His son died under the operation. Andronicus was only partially blinded and was imprisoned. On 25 September 1373 John V had made his second son, Manuel, his heir and had had him crowned. That was the story Tzycandyles had to tell—the impossibility of not "making a treaty" with the Turk and of not being able to avoid mutilating his own son.

Gregory's answer was most understanding. "It does not become Us to reply [with human judgement] otherwise than to offer you our sympathy and condolences over both actions." John should not, however, put any trust in the perfidious Turk but should place his hopes only in a sincere and strong union of Latins and Greeks, about which papal nuncios, already on their way, would treat.[87] Gregory's hopes for union were increased by what a companion of Tzycandyles, Cassian,[88] told him—that the ex-emperor Cantacuzenus and his son, Manuel, the Despot of Morea, were very favourable. He wrote a letter to the latter to recommend his envoys to him.[89]

Philip Tzycandyles had not left the port of Venice before John had sent still another letter, an autograph, with a Latin translation, by the hand of the Latin Bishop of Tabris, in transit through Constantinople. Once again the Emperor's message has to be divined from the papal replies. Gregory wrote to Emperor John, Emperor Manuel, to the ex-Emperor Cantacuzenus and to King Louis on the same day, 28 January 1375. To the two Greek Emperors he complained of persecution of Greeks converted to the Roman faith, who "are deprived of their goods, their offices and their ranks and that vexations of many kinds are inflicted on them by other Greeks who maintain the schism." Such behaviour did not encourage help from the West. Also Turks after the making of the treaty with the Emperor were found in no small numbers in Constantinople and there they were guilty of great excesses. The letter to Cantacuzenus was occasioned by a report of the Bishop John. He had told Gregory that, during a public debate held in the previous October between a group of Dominicans on their way to Armenia and Cantacuzenus with some other Greeks, Cantacuzenus had declared that "he believed and held that the holy Roman Church . . . possessed the primacy over all the Churches of the world and that he would willingly suffer death in defence of that truth, if it would help." The Pope urged him to use his erudition and influence to promote union and to protect Greek Catholics from molestation.[90]

In his autograph letter Emperor John V had appealed to the Pope to bring pressure to bear on Louis of Hungary to make him fulfil the compact they had made together in Buda some ten years before. John claimed that by returning to the obedience of the Roman Church he had fulfilled the conditions they had agreed on for Louis to defend Constantinople. Despite the truce between Emperor and Sultan, Constantinople was still in dire peril and Gregory did not hesitate, in the light of what he had learnt from other sources, to confirm the Emperor's statement on that. He bade Louis think of the danger that the Turkish victories spelt for Hungary itself and for Sicily, and so, even if there had been no bargain between him and the Emperor, he should use what the generosity of God had given him for the defence of the Empire and of Christianity. It would hasten the union that the papal envoys were then negotiating and for which Constantinople was becoming "more ready, to judge from the outcome of the Dominicans' debate."[91]

After the return of his four nuncios from Constantinople and enlightened by the information they brought, Pope Gregory wrote again to King Louis on 25 September 1375. With perhaps a little irony he began by reminding the monarch that, not long before, he had with almost breathless haste begged letters authorising the preaching of a crusade against the Turks. These had been granted, yet so far no such preaching had been done. He should know that "the Turks had been allowed to prevail far too much over the Christians, schismatics though they were, and that the Emperor of the

Greeks, overwhelmed by the Turk and without resources, had become his tributary." The Pope had raised men and galleys in some quantity to be sent as quickly as possible. "And we have been told that, as regards the obedience and reconciliation of the Greeks, if adequate aid is sent them, We shall be satisfied with the result." So, in order to conquer or repress the Turks "who are in Romania or other areas on this side of the sea, quite near to your own realm," despatch as quickly as you can the large army you promised so as to take the enemy between your force and the other expedition coming from the seaward side and so gain the desired victory.[92]

The Pope had the Hospitallers supply a fixed number of knights from each national priory.[93] With them Sicily, Genoa and Venice were to form the naval expedition. But only the Hospitallers furnished a contingent: they were obeying orders. Sicily and Hungary seem never even to have replied to the Pope's letter. Venice certainly sent a fleet to Constantinople, but it was to force the Emperor to pay his debts. In consequence John surrendered Tenedos to them. Thereupon the Genoese helped Andronicus, who had just escaped from prison to Pera, to fight his father, whom after a thirty-two days' siege, he imprisoned with the co-Emperor Manuel. He gave Tenedos to the Genoese. Genoa used 25,000 florins granted them by the Pope to fit out a fleet—but to fight the Venetians, to stop them getting possession of Tenedos.[94] On 18 October 1378 Andronicus had himself crowned and, to keep the goodwill of the Turks who had helped him secure the throne, he surrendered to them the invaluable Gallipoli. John and Manuel escaped from prison in June 1379 to take refuge with Murad, and in July the Turks aided them to dispossess Andronicus, who fled to Pera. "Byzantium was now only a pawn in the political game of the great powers who had interests in the East—the two Italian republics and the Ottoman empire."[95] The rival claims to the island of Tenedos were settled by a compromise, one condition of which was, apparently, that Andronicus should be given an appanage on the Black Sea and recover his right of succession to the imperial throne. Manuel, put out, betook himself to his old Despotate of Thessalonica in late 1382 and from there defied the Turks by retaking various towns and securing Serres.

Meantime Pope Gregory had died in Rome on 27 March 1378. On 8 April, after a conclave invaded by Roman citizens clamouring for a Roman as pontiff, Urban VI was elected. By 20 September the cardinals who had elected him had declared his election invalid because of intimidation by the mob, and had elected Clement VII. The Great Schism of the West had begun.

The Latin Orient, like the rest of the Latin Church, was involved in its rivalries.[96] Each pope tried to attach it to his obedience. Both appointed collectors. Both nominated bishops. Both tried to ensure the adherence of the local rulers. For example, in 1387, since the Hospitallers in Achaia had taken the side of Clement, Urban nominated a canon of Patras his general vicar and governor of Achaia and wrote to the Navarrese (a type of Catalan Grand Company) for their support. Even though the Latin Patriarch of Constantinople, James of Itro, had opposed Urban, on the whole Greece remained loyal to the Roman line, partly at least because that was the policy also of Venice. Nicholas de Mercadantibus, canon of Patras, was Urban's faithful collector for many years. A Bull of 1 June 1383, addressed to him, mentions the areas of his activity—all under Venetian influence—Patras, Crete, Rhodes, Durazzo, Corfu, Athens, Thebes, Corinth, Neopatras and Nisyros—and those who did not pay their tenths were to be excommunicated.[97]

Apart from allowing the Hospitallers to use the proceeds of the tenths collected in Greece for the defence of Smyrna, before the year 1405 the popes of Avignon seem to have done little directly to help the countries oppressed by the Turks.[98] The Roman line was more active. On 23 May 1383 Urban gave a safe-conduct to Simon Atumano for *partes Constantinopolitanas,* apparently for private business,[99] but there may have been more behind it than that, for in 1384 he sent the Franciscan William, bishop of Daulis, to Constantinople as his nuncio to convey some message about union of the Churches and of sympathy for the situation of Constantinople. Patriarch Nilus received him benevolently, but wrote in answer that, as William had no letters of credence, he could give no official reply. When he knew Urban's purpose better he would answer accordingly. "For we are very ready to accept peace and union of the Churches, provided they are brought about as God wills and as it was before the schism. It is a libel to suggest that we want the first place for ourselves and so will not accept union. That is not true, for we profess that you hold the first place according to the canons of the holy Fathers." Though the Turks cause much annoyance, the Patriarch added, they do not interfere in Church administration.[100]

Manuel in Thessalonica was soon being besieged by the Turks (autumn 1383) and in dire straits. By early 1385 he was planning to appeal to Venice for arms[101] and to the papacy for help.[102] He sent an embassy led by the anti-Latin Euthymius (later Patriarch) who found Urban probably in Genoa. The result was the despatch of a papal envoy who went first to Constantinople, where he was coldly received.[103] He embarked for Thessalonica in 1386. What happened when he got there is not known. Rumours were rife in Constantinople of lamentable concessions made to him about the *Filioque* and the primacy in return for a promise of help. Whatever was agreed, it had no effect. Urban was not in a position to raise an expedition and, in any case, Manuel had to escape from Thessalonica to

Constantinople on 9 April 1387. While he had been away his brother Andronicus had again taken up arms against his father, but had been defeated. Andronicus died on 28 June 1385 and bequeathed to his son, John VII, his rights to the imperial throne. The old Emperor, after having survived an armed insurrection by his grandson John VII, died on 16 February 1391.[104]

In 1388 Venice, becoming more and more alarmed at the Turkish aggression, had begun to talk about a defensive league.[105] Pope Urban ordered two galleys to be armed at the Church's expense and he commissioned the Bishop of Castellano to preach in the provinces of Venice and Ferrara the granting of crusaders' indulgences for those who helped in the enterprise.[106] Nothing came of the league. In any case, it was too late. Sultan Murad struck first. At Kossovo on 15 June 1389 he destroyed the Serbs. In the battle he met his own death but, with another enemy eliminated, he left his more cruel and more aggressive son, Bayezid, freer to concentrate on the Greeks. The new Sultan determined to liquidate the last pocket of Greek resistance in Asia Minor. He organised a campaign against Philadelphia and summoned the heir to the Greek throne of Byzantium, Manuel, who was his vassal, to assist him in person and with an army. It was while Manuel was engaged on that campaign that he heard of his father's death. He escaped secretly from the Sultan's army to return with all speed to claim the throne. Bayezid let him keep it, but on conditions imposed by himself.

When Manuel showed signs of resisting Turkish pressure, the Sultan began a siege of Constantinople which continued with greater or lesser intensity from 1394 to 1402. Manuel appealed to the Venetians. They advised him to write to the Pope, to the Emperor of Germany and to the kings of France and England.[107] Unfortunately, concerted action between those powers was difficult for they were divided by the ecclesiastical schism. The result was a double effort. Without (as far as is known) having received any appeal from Constantinople, Boniface IX (Urban had died on 15 October 1389) sent the bishop of Naupactus to preach a crusade against the Turks in favour of "Hungary, Dalmatia, Croatia, Bosnia and the kingdoms of Slavonia, also the principality of Achaia and the Duchy of Athens."[108] The Byzantine Empire was not mentioned, but it would benefit. This papal initiative, reinforced by another preacher commissioned on 15 October 1394,[109] did in fact assist the movement that shortly afterwards was set afoot by Sigismund of Hungary and the Duke of Burgundy, with the help of others, to send an army to relieve Constantinople.

A large force mainly of Hungarians with French, Wallachian, German and English knights and soldiers, set off by land in 1396. After a small initial success, this luxurious but disorderly army about 10,000 strong was faced at Nicopolis by Bayezid with a slightly bigger force (25 September). Superior discipline won the day, and hardly any of the knights escaped with King Sigismund. The noblest prisoners were saved by the payment of very high ransoms. Some others were made slaves, while the rest of the survivors were massacred. Bayezid also lost many men, but he retained his hold on Europe and continued his siege of Constantinople.[110]

Pope Boniface reacted immediately to the news of the defeat of Nicopolis. He sent envoys to Venice to propose co-operation not merely to restrain the Turks but precisely to defend Constantinople. The Signoria, however, by answers of 12 and 24 February 1397, declined on the grounds that their united forces would not suffice.[111] Still he persevered. On 1 April 1398, not in response to an appeal from the Emperor, but spontaneously, "with a heart full of compassion for the illustrious Prince Emmanuel Palaeologus, Emperor of Constantinople, and for his subjects who, though they are not in full obedience and devotion to Us and in agreement of faith and the unity of the holy Roman Church, and whom that monstrous and awful beast, the inveterate enemy of Jesus Christ, Baisetus, prince of the Teucrans who are commonly called Turks, hastens with the vast multitude of men and arms that he has brought together to invade, exterminate, grind down and, to the utmost of his power, to subject to himself," wishing to instigate and animate a Christian effort, the Pope sent Paul, (titular) bishop of Chalcedon and Apostolic Legate, to preach with the usual indulgences a crusade "in each and every city, region, town, fortress and place of note" within his Obedience and to incite high and low to take part.[112]

Boniface had occasion to help also Greeks who were "in agreement of faith and the unity of the holy Roman Church." Towards the end of 1397 Maximus Chrysoberges petitioned Boniface for permission to found a convent "in partibus Graecis de quibus oriundus existis," because "the faithful who profess the faith of the holy Roman and universal Church grow lax in their faith and slip into the errors of the Greeks, precisely because there are found there few to propound in due season the word of God and to strengthen and confirm them in fidelity to that faith."[113] Maximus had been a monk of the monastery of Our Lady of Peribleptos, Constantinople. After his conversion he was made abbot of the monastery of Saints Peter and Paul *in Agro* of the Order of St. Basil in the diocese of Messina.[114] When he made his request to the Pope in 1397 he was a Dominican. His petition was granted on 25 February 1398.

On the same day another petition of his was granted, so as "to meet the malpractice of some Catholics living in Greece who frequent churches of the Greeks and there assist at Masses and other services on the plea that, when the epistles and gospels are read or chanted in the Greek language according to the custom of those parts, they can understand them better than if they are read or recited in Latin; and so such Catholics here and there slip into the errors of the Greeks." Maximus had asked to be allowed to have the Latin Mass and the offices of the Dominican rite translated into Greek and to use these in his church to be a counter-attraction for local Catholics.[115]

He asked his friend, Manuel Chrysoloras (who, as a pioneer of Greek teaching in Italian universities, began to lecture in the Studio of Florence in 1397), to make the translation, which Chrysoloras did. Later Chrysoloras himself asked Pope Innocent VII for permission "to be promoted to all the sacred Orders according to the Roman rite" and to celebrate or have celebrated by a suitable priest the divine offices in the Greek translation he himself had made. Innocent granted his request on 19 February 1406. As far as is known Manuel was never ordained. Copies of his translation still remain in some libraries.[116]

News of the Pope's persistent efforts to raise men and money for the relief of the Greeks must have reached the ears of Emperor Manuel Palaeologus. In late 1398 he sent a confidant of his own, the Genoese Ilario Doria, to Boniface to describe his parlous state. The result was another papal appeal to the Church. The Pope again commissioned Paul, bishop of Chalcedon, to preach the crusade everywhere except in Hungary. Once more he wrote of the excesses of the Turks and the consequent danger not only to Greece but (as Emperor Manuel had warned him) to Hungary and Wallachia and the rest of the Christian world. "Behold, the foundations of the Catholic faith are shaking under the blows of the battering rams that the infidel rains upon them. See, if no one moves to their aid, the Christians who still remain in those parts are surrendered to destruction. Further, if (may it not happen) the said Emperor should fall into the power of Bayezid (as, alas, We see is likely, unless the Christian people makes a determined effort to send strong and speedy help to the Emperor), Christians should consider how great will be the danger to the whole of Christendom."[117] Unfortunately, Boniface was ill served by his agents. Doria demanded too much for his individual expenses. In England he and Paul fell out: the latter was accused of peculation and was replaced by the Benedictine, Augustine de Undinis (12 January 1400). Doria, however, was not in disgrace. On 21 February 1400 he was authorised to collect money in Genoese territories, at home and overseas, in a Bull that implored and commanded all the faithful to help generously in return for indulgences on the usual conditions. "Even if it should happen that the said Emperor should by chance meantime leave the city of Constantinople or should already have left or by the fortunes of human destiny have departed this life, still the preaching and the indulgences must go on in favour of his heir and the city of Constantinople."[118]

France, the stonghold of the Avignonese Benedict XIII, did not ignore the needs of the Greek Emperor. In 1398 Venetian ships delivered to Constantinople 7000 ducats sent from France.[119] In the next year Charles VI organised a small expedition of about 1200 men. Under the command of Marshal Boucicaut it set out in June 1399 and gave Constantinople a feeling of temporary relief. Clearly it was no final solution. To find that, Emperor Manuel at Boucicaut's suggestion put Constantinople in the charge of his nephew, John VII, left his wife and children with his brother in the Morea and himself set off to tour the courts of Europe to obtain assistance. He sailed from Constantinople on 10 December 1399. He arrived in Venice in April 1400.

There is no record that he visited Boniface in Rome. His plight, however, moved the Pope to show once more his deep concern. This time it was to be no mere local effort entrusted to a single preacher, but an appeal to the whole Church transmitted in an encyclical addressed "To my venerable brethren the patriarchs, archbishops, bishops and my beloved sons, wheresoever they are." The Pope dilated on the Turkish danger, because of which "the Emperor . . . has left the city of Constantinople and goes from place to place begging the help of the faithful of the Church." The Christian people must react zealously, strongly and quickly. So Boniface raised his voice to rouse the faithful "to the help of the aforesaid Emperor and, consequently, of the Christian religion," by the granting of the crusading indulgences. Therefore, he ordered that in every large church there should be placed a triply-locked chest to receive the alms of the faithful; on Sundays and feast days the crusade should be preached from the pulpits; collectors should be appointed and accounts kept; and the papal encyclical was to be translated into the vernacular and promulgated so as to reach the notice of everyone.[120]

The Bull was prepared. Copies were engrossed ready for transmission to the many dioceses. But, in the margin of the papal register it is noted: "Cancelled at the order of my Lord the Treasurer, when the Bulls were torn up by the same Lord Treasurer." Not one of the Bulls was despatched, and in the remaining four years of Boniface's reign there is no record of any further papal action in favour of Emperor or Constantinople.

No certain reason, but only conjectures, can be assigned for the drastic change of papal policy towards Byzantium. It has been suggested that Emperor Manuel, while he was in France, visited, or at least contacted, Benedict XIII in Avignon and that resentment at such a recognition of his rival moved Boniface to cancel the Bull. There is no evidence, let alone proof, of any such visit or contact, and so an explanation founded only on a supposition must be purely hypothetical. The truth is simply, that we do not know.

Chapter XII

The Fourteenth Century
Occasional Contacts

The story of the many contacts and initiatives for union of the Eastern and the Western Churches over the thirteenth and fourteenth centuries has now been told. To produce a consecutive narrative as one event led into and explained the next, many details had to be omitted that, if inserted in their chronological place, would have distracted attention from the main line of historical development with bits of information on disparate and unconnected incidents. These, however, were all parts woven into the tale of history as it unfolded and, because they indicate attitudes and exemplify practices, deserve at least mention to complete the account. They are, therefore, grouped together and briefly described in this chapter, which is, perhaps, a kind of appendix to what has gone before.

A multitude of Latin missionaries, men of indefatigable zeal, swarmed over all the Christian East. Sent by the popes, they kept up a steady communication with the Holy See. Hence the papal registers contain innumerable documents concerned with their activities—answers to queries, directives, exhortations, authorizations, enactments—that disclose the situations in the areas where they laboured and the purposes they were meant to pursue. They reflect also developments in papal organisation and practice in the West, not least in respect of the collation of benefices.

Under the Avignon popes things came to such a pitch that few benefices could be granted without papal approval. "The last stage in this development [i.e., of special and general reservations to the pope] occurred when Gregory XI retained during his lifetime the right to appoint to all patriarchates, archiepiscopal and episcopal churches, as well as to all houses of monks and friars regardless of their revenues wherever and however they fell vacant."[1] What the popes were doing in the West, they applied also to the East, and increasingly in the fourteenth century as the years went by the documents of appointment to Sees and abbeys more and more often declare that for one reason or another the pope has reserved the provision of the dignity to himself, that he quashes any other attempted nomination and appoints his own candidate. In such a way, for example, Innocent made a monk of Mt. Athos abbot of a monastery near Durazzo,[2] and Gregory appointed a Latin to the old Greek diocese of Kisamos in Crete.[3] But John XXII in the Brief appointing by reservation an archbishop to the Latin See of Nicosia expressly notes that he does not reserve any Greek benefice or office in Cyprus.[4]

In the eyes of Roman pontiffs, the Greeks were schismatics, not so much heretics, and, though in papal letters the combined phrase, "schismatics and heretics" often occurs, both words should not lightly be taken as applying to the Greeks.

In most eastern countries there usually existed such a mixture of beliefs—monophysites or bogomils or others mingled with a majority of the local Church—that both words were applicable. But schism put men out of the Church, and often enough the popes intimated that to the Greeks. The way back was by abjuration "according to the form of the Church by Our authority and so thus absolved to bring them back and incorporate them into the unity of the Church."[5]

The canonical consequences of schism were felt most acutely in places where Latin powers ruled over ethnically Greek areas, like Crete. In such places no schismatical bishop was allowed to function. When Naupactus (in Epirus) came again into Latin hands the Greek incumbent was ejected to make way for a Latin.[6] Thirty years later Pope Benedict XII heard that a Greek bishop, sent by the Patriarch of Constantinople, was in Crete "where many Latins live, celebrating Orders [ordaining?] according to the Greek rite and dispensing from the prohibited degrees in respect of marriage . . . to the displeasure of the Divine Majesty, disrespect to the Roman Church, weakening of the Catholic faith and the danger of souls, when rather it should be that the Greeks are invited by Catholics to the saving observances of the sacrosanct Roman Church." The papal letter, addressed to the Doge and the commune of Venice, ordered that the bishop should be expelled forthwith from the island.[7]

In Crete not only no episcopal See, but no benefice at all, could be held by schismatics. A certain Cretan convert priest, Rampanus, was made archpriest of the city and of the diocese of Candia. He was given also a canonry in the church of St. Michael and a benefice in another Church. Twelve schismatical canons of St. Michael's used to employ twelve schismatical carriers to take an icon of our Lady in procession through the streets each Tuesday, for which office the carriers were exempt from the corvée. Archpriest George Rampanus complained of this to the Pope, who ordered the ecclesiastical authorities of the island to deprive the canons and the carriers of their offices and to substitute, if possible, Catholics who should enjoy the same civil immunities as had the schismatics.[8] At the same time the church of St. Michael was taken over for Catholic use. That was not the end of the story. George Rampanus was possibly too successful. At any rate, he managed to antagonise not only his fellow countrymen, especially the evicted canons and carriers, but also the Latin ecclesiastical authorities, so much so that Gregory XI withdrew him from their jurisdiction and put him under the Bishop of Methone in the Morea.[9] Antony, archbishop of Crete, and his Vicar General reinstated four of the deposed schismatical canons, though they had categorically refused to accept Roman faith and obedience. These had the icon borne in procession by Catholic carriers and they accompanied it themselves. They had "Masses and other divine services solemnly celebrated or rather profaned in the same church as schismatical priests, after and contrary to the return of that church to the Catholic rite. . . . To these same and to other schismatics leave had been given to celebrate or rather profane divine offices in the church of St. Michael, according to the Greek and schismatical rite," though the carriers and other Catholics who took part in them fell thereby under the excommunications promulgated by that same (Latin) archbishop, who, however, absolved them. Pope Gregory ordered the removal of the four schismatics and the installation of four convert priests, as canons, two of whom bore the same surname as George Rampanus.[10]

The net result was a constitution sent on 7 May 1375 to the hierarchy of Crete, beginning solemnly: *Gregorius episcopus, servus servorum Dei, ad perpetuam rei memoriam.* "It has come to our ears that certain churches with and without cure of souls on the island of Crete, which is inhabited by both Catholics and schismatics, churches that belong to clerics and faithful of the Catholic Church of the said island, have hitherto been granted and leased to schismatical priests and other clerics and are still thus being granted and leased. In them divine services are profaned by those schismatics in contempt of the Apostolic See, to the danger of souls and the maintenance of the damnable schism." All such collations and leases were forthwith "cancelled, quashed and declared invalid and void" by the Pope, and all ecclesiastics, whether secular or regular, were forbidden under pain of excommunication to give or favour such. The schismatical holders, if they wanted to retain their benefices, were allowed one month in which to make the usual profession of faith.[11]

Innocent III had allowed Greek converts to retain their rite.[12] The only change that he had insisted on was the addition of the anointing ceremonies used in the Latin Church in conferring baptism and orders, and in certain circumstances even those could be omitted. His practice became the norm and Alexander repeated it in his Instruction for Cyprus. In 1326 Pope John XXII, in conformity with the decree of the Fourth Lateran Council, insisted on a Catholic Greek bishop, "obedient in everything to the archbishop and the Church," being appointed by the Archbishop of Crete to administer the sacraments to and instruct Catholics of Greek rite "according to the customs of the Roman Church." He was "to minister to them all orders, Confirmation and other sacraments" in their own rite. Thereafter no schismatical prelate was to be allowed to exercise his office on the island.[13]

The same Pope wrote sympathetically to the Greeks of Cyprus. There had been dissension between the Latin and the Greek hierarchies over their respective jurisdictions, in the course of which there had been a lively popular demonstration in front of the Apostolic Legate's palace. In consequence, two Greek bishops had been deemed responsible and imprisoned. They appealed to the Pope. From the Latin side there were accusations of heresy on the grounds that the Greek faithful made a very deep reverence to the elements of bread and wine when in the Liturgy these were brought in processionally at the Great Entry. The Latins interpreted this as adoration of the as yet unconsecrated species. The Pope was very gentle in his replies. In the end he appointed Baldwin, bishop of Famagusta, to instruct the Greeks. His letter to him begins: "Although like our predecessors . . . We wish to allow (*tolerare*), as far as in the Lord We can, the customs and rites of the Greeks of the kingdom of Cyprus, provided they are not contrary to Catholic faith, still We consider it salutary that the Greeks and the Syrians of that realm, observing the same customs and rites as the Greeks of old . . . should often be besprinkled with the dew of the preaching of the word of God." So Baldwin was to teach them that at the Great Entry the Body and Blood of Christ were not yet present to be adored. The letter ended: "But We do not mean to prevent the said Greeks and Syrians from reverently and devoutly begging in a seemly fashion the priest who carries the elements to the altar after their custom and rite, to pray to God for them."[14] A few years later he instructed the Legate in Cyprus to act against certain errors. Besides Nestorians and Jacobites, there were certain Greeks "who do not communicate in the Sacrament of the Altar unless it has been brought from Constantinople and some others who dare to feed this sacrament as a medicine to their cattle."[15] When there was question of the union of the Serbian Church with Rome, Pope Clement had specifically allowed the use of fermented bread in the Liturgy to facilitate participation by the king.[16] But that was no exceptional concession, for the Latin Church had always acknowledged the validity of the Greek use of leavened bread in their Liturgy.[17]

There were few practices in the oriental rite considered illicit and perhaps invalid by the Latins, though probably they disapproved in a general way of a large number more. Confirmation was to be performed only by a bishop (though, as we shall see, exceptions were allowed), and the oils used for the sacraments should be blessed only by a bishop. Pope John requested the Armenians to observe these two rites and also to put a little water in the wine they consecrated in the Liturgy.

It was strictly forbidden to Latins to take part in Greek religious services. King Peter of Cyprus asked Urban V to put a stop to abuses in his kingdom, where nobles and commoners frequented Greek services or had Mass and the sacraments celebrated in their private houses, with the result that the parish churches were largely deserted. The Pope ordered the Archbishop of Nicosia to end the abuses. He was to forbid also the hiring of mixed groups of Latin and Greek women to wail at funerals, "which secular priests, Mendicants and others, motivated by the love of gain, openly allow in their churches."[18]

Pope Urban was harsher in respect of rites than his predecessors. The Greek Emperor, John V, was granted the use of a portable altar, but it was only for the Latin rite with a Latin celebrant. The same restriction was placed on the permission given for the celebration of Mass before dawn.[19] In the turbulent island of Crete, where the Venetians were nearly overcome twice in the fourteenth century by successful rebellions, religion and politics reacted one on the other and opposition to Rome went hand in hand with opposition to Venice. In 1368, after one of the more serious uprisings, Urban wrote to the Latin hierarchy bidding them extirpate heresy from the island—"where your churches are situated, where the Doge and the Commune of Venice rule more firmly than ever [i.e., after the repression of the rebellion] over Latins and Greeks, and where better than in most places ecclesiastical censures can be duly enforced with the help of the secular arm." The bishops, therefore, were to ensure that no student, that is, literate Greek layman, was given clerical status or promoted to any orders except by a Latin bishop or a Greek Catholic (i.e, a "uniate") bishop. Those ordained to the priesthood must "celebrate Masses and other religious services according to the rite used by the Roman Church [i.e., the Greek rite as modified by Latin popes] . . . No Greek monk or priest who does not follow that rite may in future hear confessions or preach."[20]

There was on the island a certain Macarius, with the title of Archbishop of Crete, "sent by the anti-Patriarchs of Constantinople, heretics and schismatics," apparently with the cognizance of the Venetian authorities.[21] On his death, a Governor of Crete had forbidden the entrance of any other Greek prelate and also had enacted that candidates for Greek orders should not be allowed to go for ordination to bishops outside the island. His decree dealing with the bishops had been observed, wrote Pope Gregory on 27 October 1373 to the Doge of Venice, but the part of it concerned with the ordination of priests had soon been relaxed. He asked for it to be strictly enforced as a means not only to ecclesiastical but also to civil peace.[22]

The Latin Church insisted on unctions in ordinations and on the reception also of minor orders. It did not challenge the validity of Greek orders.[23] Occasionally deacons or priests were re-ordained when they entered the Latin Church, but, as far as I can check, that was done only when the individual himself demanded it, either because of scruples about the efficacy of his ministrations to others or to ensure that there was no canonical obstacle to his holding a benefice. For example, in 1344 an Armenian, before being consecrated bishop of the Armenians in Cyprus by the (Latin) Cardinal Archbishop of Tusculum, asked to be rebaptised and re-ordained, which was done.[24] A Greek from Constantinople, on being given a canonry in the church of Patras, had himself reconfirmed and, "belonging to the clerical order only according to the rite of the Greeks," was given the "clerical character" at the hands of a Latin bishop.[25]

Repetition of the sacraments of baptism and orders was fairly common with the Armenians and Bulgarians. Missionaries, finding practices different from the observances of the Roman rite, appealed to the Holy See for counsel. John XXII in 1333 bade them, if in doubt, to rebaptise conditionally and repeated to them the formula usual in such cases: "If you are baptised, I do not baptise you; but if you are not baptised, I baptise you in the name of the Father and of the Son and of the Holy Ghost." A like prescription was made for re-ordination.[26] In all its replies about baptism the Curia offered normal Church discipline—that any one may be the minister of the sacrament, which is not to be repeated unless there is serious doubt about its validity, and then conditionally.

When Benedict XI in 1303 had hopes of the conversion of King Uros of Serbia, he authorised the archbishop of Antivari to find remedies for the abuses rife in neighbouring territories subject to Uros or to Andronicus of Greece. The chief abuses mentioned were simony, bad customs respecting marriage and alienation of church property. Some fifty years later King Stephen Dusan made overtures to the Holy See, professing readiness to accept its faith and primacy. His envoys to Innocent VI told the Pope of how much the king had already done to give justice to the Latin Church in his realm and how much more he would do. From his remedies one can diagnose the ills from which Serbia suffered. Dusan had stopped (so he said) the forcible rebaptism and reconfirmation of Catholics; he had restored prelates, abbots and monks to their properties (except in the case of six specially circumstanced monasteries), and had given them freedom to perform their religious services and to preach: he himself acknowledged the Catholic faith, asked for legates and for nomination as Captain General of the Church against the Turks.[27] Dusan, however, died shortly afterwards (20 December 1355).

In 1365 Louis of Hungary occupied the province of Vidin and took the Bulgarian prince, Stracimir, prisoner. With him went Franciscan missionaries. Fra Bartholomew of Alverna, Vicar of Bosnia, sent a list of queries to the Curia.[28] It gives a fair idea of the religious confusion they found there. The missionaries had so many applications for baptism that they got help from the local clergy and then they had scruples. "Since the Friars are not numerous enough for the baptism of so great a multitude and in so vast a country, it is asked if they should allow priests of those parts to baptise who are willing to employ our formula, even though they do it for gain and though they are not really priests, but uneducated and schismatics, ordained according to the custom of these parts, namely, not canonically ordained." They were reassured by the Curia.

That there was a real doubt about the validity of the baptisms of the area is uncontrovertibly shown by the examples that the Vicar quoted of the words that the local priests used as the sacramental form. "One recites [the psalm] 'Blessed are those'; another, 'Thou shalt sprinkle me with hyssop'; another says 'As many of you as are baptised have put on Christ'; another repeats three times 'Alleluia'; another, 'The servant of God is baptised in the name of St. Peter or St. Demetrius,' according to the name the child is given. And you will find barely two in twenty who agree in their baptisms."[29]

A little later the same Fra Bartholomew wrote a letter to his Friars to persuade them of the wisdom of using the secular arm to promote conversions, in accordance with a directive issued by Pope Urban.[30] Some of the Friars, it seems, disapproved of it on principle. As one of many reasons in its favour the Vicar instanced the confusion about baptism for peoples like the Slavs and the Vlachs, who were so docile and who readily embraced the true faith if they were not misled. He told his missionaries: "If they [the indigenous priests] followed the form of the Greeks, namely, 'The servant of God N. is baptised in the name etc.' we should never baptise any one of them. But we find without the shadow of a doubt after many enquiries and by various means that those priests of the Slavs from ignorance and lack of training observe no proper and true form and they do not apply the form they use to the matter. Indeed last year, when the king baptised 400,000, there was found no single one among the 400 priests who could observe the form."[31]

Other questions in the list of queries disclosed that in Bosnia chrism was kept for twenty years; that only a priest might baptise; that the elements used in the Liturgy were considered consecrated by prayers recited long before the anaphora (canon); that wine from grapes, wine from herbs, cider and other liquids were used in the Liturgy. The curial answer gave solutions to all these *dubia* and had many sage replies besides. The simple faith of uneducated Greeks should not be disturbed; they would save their souls.

Marriage with a condition, "If you are good to me," was invalid; a schismatical priest, converted and with scruples about his baptism, must be also ordained conditionally; adult converts need not confess their sins if they are to be baptised.[32] All this was current discipline. There was no sign of vindictive legislation against Greek or infidel.

Surprisingly there was no query in the list about confirmation. The question must have arisen there. It certainly arose elsewhere. The Church's regulations were many times repeated. Confirmation, like the blessing of oils, was reserved to a bishop, as Pope John informed the Armenians in 1319.[33] His predecessor, however, in the long list of faculties he had given to missionaries in the East had authorised simple priests to confirm their converts if there was no bishop available for this.[34] Several popes in the course of their reigns issued similar general faculties, usually repeating verbatim the lists of their predecessors. So John himself promulgated one on 23 October 1321, and it contained the permission for priests to confirm.[35] Clement VI in a special faculty for Armenians allowed priests to *chrismare in fronte iuxta ritum et formam sanctae Romanae Ecclesiae,* when no bishop was available.[36] Urban V repeated the permission in a general list of faculties.[37]

Another unusual faculty, of ordaining people to be clerics and acolytes, was given by Pope Boniface to simple priest missionaries in a document of 10 April 1299.[38] A like permission was included in many of the lists of subsequent popes. Of much wider application was the special faculty granted to missionaries to dispense from certain impediments to marriage. The reason for this was because it was difficult for Latins to find suitable partners of their own rite for marriage in missionary countries where Latins were relatively few, and the Church would not countenance marriage with schismatics. On that it was adamant, no matter the rank of the applicant, whether prince or commoner.

Still extant is the reply that Pope John XXII gave to Edward of Savoy, brother of Joanna, who had asked for a dispensation for his sister to marry the heir to the Byzantine throne, Andronicus.

> We reply briefly that, for your honour as for that of your sister, it would have given Us great pleasure if she had been united in such a marriage as is fitting for a Catholic, with a prince of rank suitable to hers—especially since she cannot be united in marriage with him to whom, it is said, she is engaged and who is a non-Catholic. And though, son, hope (so it is reported to Us) of her husband being brought into our faith through her led you to accede to this, still We greatly fear that the husband will more likely draw her to his rite, (may it not be so) than the opposite. But let us beg the Lord to give your sister the grace of converting her husband to the Catholic faith and of abiding steadfastly in it herself.[39]

Joanna married Andronicus. A dozen years later she was reminded of her brother's unfulfilled hope by the Popes. John XXII and later Clement VI, optimistic at a message of goodwill for union from her husband, sent a letter also to her, "that the unfaithful husband shall be saved by the faithful wife."[40] It seems, however, that John XXII's first pessimistic reaction was right. She is commemorated in the *Synodicon* of the Sunday of Orthodoxy in the Eastern Church as a faithful supporter of Palamism (for it was she who convoked the synod of 1347 that approved Palamism again and opened the door to Cantacuzenus's return), who became the nun Anastasia before she died.[41]

John XXII put the case clearly to the King of Sicily seeking papal approval for some mixed marriage. He told his royal client that he did not know precisely what he wanted: "It would be useless to grant a dispensation for that impediment [of consanguinity or affinity] when from the other side the disparity of religion *(disparitas cultus)* seems to bar a marriage. The religions of Greeks and Latins seem to be disparate, seeing that the former are heretics and the latter are classed as Catholics. Between these, so it seems, there cannot be marriage."[42]

That rule was followed by John and succeeding popes without exception. They gave dispensations to Latins from various other impediments to enable them to marry among themselves, but not with Greeks.[43] Before long, the Pope included in the faculties granted to missionaries authority to dispense in the marriages of converts from impediments in degrees of consanguinity and affinity not forbidden by divine law.[44] They were authorised also to permit priests converted from schism who had married after receiving orders or simply who were married when they were converted to retain their married state, even though they might be related to their wives in the third or fourth degree of consanguinity. They should still enjoy the privileges attaching to the clerical state.[45]

The Armenians had special ties with the Latin Church, for they were formally united with it. The loss of all Christian territories in the Holy Land and Syria left the kingdom of Little Armenia unsupported against the infidel. Appeals to the West for help brought no worthwhile result. They offered, however, occasion to the popes to press for effective ecclesiastical union. Under King Het'um II (1289–1305) the unionist party prevailed. The Catholicos, Gregory VI Apirat, had proclaimed union of the Churches in 1198 and that union with some vicissitudes continued till 1375 when the kingdom succumbed to the Mamluks.

About the year 1330 there was a strong movement towards union among the monks, many of whose monasteries combined among themselves and shortly afterwards put themselves under the rule and direction of the Dominicans, to form the "Unionist Brethren." A little too zealous and not sufficiently prudent, they disparaged their own rite (they began to rebaptise baptised Armenians) in favour of Latin practices.[46] One of the most severe critics of the national Church was Nerses Palientz, bishop of Ourmia, who had—and retained—the ear of the Holy See. Because of the accusations he levelled against the united Armenian Church, Benedict XII asked the Catholicos to summon a synod to correct errors and abuses. Of these he sent for consideration a list of one hundred and seventeen. They covered most of Christian doctrine, with stress on Christology and on sacramental belief and usage. There were twelve sections on baptism alone. The Armenians were said not to recognize Latin or Greek baptisms and to rebaptise Latins and Greeks who entered their Church; they had no stable form of baptism but each minister made up his own—some used wine, not water, with the words: "I wash you in wine that you may be strong and not suffer cold."[47]

James, the Catholicos, gave an interim reply in "Faith of the Armenians" which is completely orthodox. More than that, he asserts in the document that the current practice of the Armenian Church already included a number of points introduced to satisfy papal injunctions—confirmation conferred only by a bishop and with the western ritual, the infusion of a little water into the wine of the Liturgy, the use of minor orders, renewed use of Extreme Unction after the Latin manner, and the *Filioque* recited in the Creed.[48]

A fuller reply was produced by a synod of six archbishops, fifteen diocesan and other bishops, ten abbots, officials and priests. Each of the one hundred and seventeen accusations was quoted and discussed.[49] If here and there the document allowed that there had been abuse in the past and might still be in remote places, it made it quite clear that the papal accusations were in general a gross exaggeration and some of them (for example, the one about baptising in wine or milk) pure calumnies. The synod did not mince its words about Nerses in whom the Holy See put such trust. Nevertheless, Pope Clement, who received this answer, was not fully satisfied. He sent another series of queries ranging over the length of the synod's long reply. Fourteen of his items were to extract acknowledgement of the full primacy of the Roman Church, that all Roman pontiffs possess "all positive jurisdiction which Christ as Head in the form of his human life possessed."[50] To this screed there was no immediate answer for lack of qualified interpreters.[51] So Innocent VI sent as his nuncios to Armenia bishop Nerses with the Dominican provincial of the province of the Holy Land.[52] No account of the activities of this embassy is extant. Soon the kingdom was beset by enemies from outside and anarchy from within. Its end came when King Leo VI was defeated by the Mamluk viceroy of

Aleppo with the help of local rebellious barons. On 13 April 1375 Sis fell and Leo and his family were taken prisoner. Leo died in Paris in 1393.

The prospects facing Christianity at the end of the fourteenth century were bleak indeed—Jerusalem lost forever; Armenia liquidated; Constantinople besieged by the Turks with little hope of survival; the Latin Church rent by schism. Projects of union, certainly, seemed at an end. Yet they did not end. Timurlane the Mongol defeated Bayezid the Turk and gave Constantinople relief. The Latin Church regained peace in the Council of Constance, and contacts for union began again which led to the Council of Florence and ceased only in 1453 when the Byzantine Empire also came to an end.

Chapter XIII

Epilogue

The course of the thirteenth and fourteenth centuries brought little change in the basic attitudes of the Eastern and Western Churches. Each believed the other wrong on the *Filioque,* the chief dogmatic issue between them. The Latin Church was convinced of the primacy of the See of Rome; the Greek Church of the principle of the pentarchy. Each thought its rite superior and each had no small contempt for the other, as it noted this or that abuse or quaint (and different) custom. Throughout this period the western world—the Church and the various States—was fighting an offensive action; the Greeks were on the defensive. The Fourth Crusade, Manfred, Charles of Anjou, the commercial grip of Genoa and Venice on trade in the Black Sea and the Aegean moulded the history of Byzantium in the thirteenth century. In the fourteenth century western pressure increased as the Turk ate up Greek territory and forced the Emperors to look more and more to the West for salvation. The Latin Church was involved in all these coercions, even if it did not approve them. For the most part it was attempting to restrain them and, over at least much of the fourteenth century, trying to mobilise western strength to protect the Christian East. But it had its own method of pressure—the ecclesiastical organisation that was set up wherever Latin influence was established, with the personnel drawn from the new Mendicant Orders, active and learned men of high aspirations, aflame with zeal to convert all and sundry to the Latin faith. They were in all territories of oriental rite—Greece, Crete, Cyprus, Palestine, the Balkans, Lithuania, Hungary, Poland, Russia, the Crimea—everywhere including the land of the Tartars. The Greek Church was, as it were, at the receiving end. Its representatives could only sit tight and offer a passive resistance. It had no element like the industrious Mendicants to throw into an attack, even had its own ethos and its political circumstances made such a policy possible. In consequence, it is not difficult to draw an outline of papal attitudes and actions, whereas there is no little difficulty in attempting to do the same for the Greeks.

On the Latin side, Innocent III established the conditions for union of the Churches—acceptance of Latin faith and Roman primacy, the latter to be shown by an oath and (usually) the manual act. These conditions were more clearly specified when Clement IV produced the formula of a profession of faith. Thereafter in proposals for union and in ceremonies of conversion that formula always figured. With it went an abjuration of errors.

There can be no reasonable doubt that the popes throughout the whole period seriously desired and aimed at union of the Greek and Latin Churches. The zeal of some of the pontiffs is more immediately striking than that of others, but there was none who did not work for it. More than that—they all jumped at every chance of an ecclesiastical union wherever it appeared. Most of these were motivated on the non-Roman side by political and material aims, and one cannot escape the conclusion, so often was that fact verified in the subsequent history of such unions, that the popes themselves suspected their doubtful nature. But they felt that they could not in conscience repel anyone seeking the fuller truth that the Catholic Church professed, and they were, perhaps, not sorry to increase Rome's sphere of influence at the expense of Constantinople. However that may be, the sad conclusion, at the close of a study of the relations of the two Churches over a period of two centuries, is that union was as remote, perhaps even more remote, at the end than it was at the beginning. Why?

The root reason was the ecclesiology of the medieval Latin Church. There could be only one Church with one faith and one supreme authority. That faith was the bond of unity of the whole Christian community and the one authority was that of the keeper of the faith, the pope. Heresy and schism were denials of that unity, and heretics and schismatics, therefore, put themselves outside the pale of the Christian community. They were excommunicates with whom the faithful should have no contact and who had no rights against the faithful. The Greeks were schismatics and, in so far as they denied the *Filioque* defined in Lyons, also heretics, and so under excommunication with all its consequences. In their case, however, there was always a divergence between theory and practice. Contacts with them were constant; commerce was continual; popes had regular diplomatic correspondence. The theory showed itself rather in official papal documents dealing with unity, for there the matter was theological. The Greeks were called "schismatics and heretics"; their schism was "damnable" and "leading to damnation"; they were not of the one Church "outside of which there is no salvation." The one and only solution for them was to enter that one Church by professing its faith and acknowledging its authority. "If they chose to persist in their hard obstinacy, the Holy See would consider them as publicans and gentiles, and, if they should be assailed by any of the faithful or by infidels, We shall not be able, as we ought not, to help people cut off from the body of the universal Church''—so wrote Pope Urban V. Entry into the Roman Church was what Innocent III proposed and after him all his successors. That was what the Greeks would not do, because they were not convinced that the Roman Church was what it claimed to be, the one Church of Christ ''outside of which there is no salvation.''

Acceptance was not made easier for them by the fact that the Latins did not restrict their demands to the doctrinal minimum. Doctrine was thought to cover some things that were no more than liturgical practices: authority was conceived of as so absolute that, e.g., all rights and privileges of bishops and even of patriarchs were judged to be concessions of the Holy See. This was a principle embodied in the profession of faith of Clement IV. It was given exaggerated application in the fourteenth century when the bureaucratic centralization of the papal Curia reached its peak in the Avignonese pontificates.[1] In these ways the age-long traditions of the East were assailed and opposition was intensified.

In respect of rites the Latins were less insistent. But rites enshrine beliefs and so the Latin Church looked on all rites but its own with suspicion. It allowed them ''in so far as they did not offend against the faith and the canons,'' but where opposition was less—Bulgaria and Armenia—it tended to impose some of its own practices. In this respect, however, it was at least as liberal in outlook as the Greeks. If it insisted on anointing in certain sacraments, it made no difficulty about the use of leavened bread in the Eucharist, whereas the Greeks condemned outright the Latin sacrament in unleavened bread. Pope Urban's mandate that new priests in Crete should be ordained by, and use, the Greek rite as modified according to papal instructions would, if it could have been universally and rigidly enforced, have resulted in the elimination of the use there of the pure Greek rite. No such restriction by Urban or any other pope was imposed on Cyprus or on other areas under Venetian rule, and one wonders if the difficult political situation in Crete was not somehow connected with the prohibition.

It is alleged that papal zeal for union was more or less a cloak for papal aggrandisement, that the main motive of one pope after another was world politics. W. Norden argues in this way in his deservedly well-known book, *Das Papsstum und Byzanz.* That political motives were mingled with religious ones in papal policies is beyond doubt. That the desire to achieve a world domination, ''to pursue a political end,'' namely, ''to govern and to wield influence,''[2] was the deeper and chief motive is by no means certain and I think not true. The words quoted above from Norden refer to Innocent III. Innocent certainly believed wholeheartedly in the *plenitudo potestatis* of the successor of St. Peter, a *potestas* primarily over things spiritual and secondarily and, as it were, contingently over the temporal. Such was his conviction in general and his actions within the western Church were based on that. If this is to be judged as aiming at world domination and as "pursuing a political end" as his overall purpose, then he can justly be said to have done that in respect also of the Greek Church, because he acted towards it precisely as he did towards the Latins—for both he was head of the Church, successor of St. Peter, Vicar of Christ.

His immediate successors were more caught up in resisting the threat that Frederick II posed to the Church than in making capital out of the Greeks. They used spiritual as well as physical arms to combat Frederick and began the degradation of the ideal of the crusade by giving their wars against him crusading privileges. It was very undesirable, but it did not touch the Greeks. In their regard the popes continued Innocent's general policy—they had the same convictions of the primacy of the See of Rome—and had not the courage to abandon a dying Latin Constantinople to its fate. In the thirteenth century Innocent IV was the most implacable of the popes towards Frederick and the most open and large-minded with the Greeks, insisting like his predecessors on Roman faith and primacy, but being conciliatory about the rest, without giving any sign that this was for any other motive than the evangelical precept of unity.

With Frederick's death the backdrop of the stage changed, but the plot being played was much the same—the political position, and therefore the spiritual freedom, of the papacy was still being challenged. Constantinople was now back in Greek hands. Its Emperor meant it to remain so. The papacy was dependent upon and also threatened by, first Manfred, and then its own protégé Charles. It did not want either of them to become more powerful by conquering Byzantium. Protection of Michael Palaeologus lessened the threat; Michael also kept the prospect of union to the fore. As long as there was some hope of ecclesiastical union the popes held up military action against the East. But no pope offered Michael union on easy terms—a watered-down faith, a nominal obedience. On the contrary, when the Greek Emperor was plainly just playing for time, Pope Clement faced him with his detailed, uncompromising profession of faith and the need to accept unfeignedly the supreme jurisdiction of Rome. Even Gregory, wholly sympathetic and understanding, kept the same standards though he allowed, as it were, payment by installments. The popes after Lyons, becoming increasingly skeptical of Michael's good faith, turned the screw to make the Greek Church declare itself. It had to answer, "Yes" or "No." It said "No."

The Sicilian Vespers and the death of Michael VIII, occurring almost simultaneously, changed the situation completely. In Greece there was an immediate end of the union; not so in the West. For the Latin Church the Council of Lyons was a general council, in which the Greeks had participated and whose decrees they had approved. Its definition of the Procession of the Holy Spirit from Father and Son was valid for all time. The union of the Churches was a juridical fact, which the Greek Church had accepted and which it should acknowledge. The Curia must quickly have learnt of the official repudiation of the union by Andronicus and of the persecution of unionists by the Greek Church. Yet Nicholas IV in 1289 was still writing in friendly terms to his "beloved son" Andronicus, as to a member of the Roman Church. The Sicilian Vespers had eliminated all possibility of a western conquest of Constantinople, so for many years after 1282, though there were occasional movements to retain or regain Latin possessions in the East, there was no serious project to attack Constantinople. Attention was concentrated on the other after-effect of the Vespers, the possession of Sicily by Aragon. The popes continued the unhappy custom of devoting crusading money to their private wars; the contending princes fought to assert their rights.

The popes went to Avignon.[3] There they were independent in a little independent state. They were all French, their cardinals nearly all were French and Avignon was an enclave in the Comtat-Venaissin, itself an enclave belonging to the Holy See in France. Not unnaturally the popes in Avignon were very much under the influence of France. Till the beginning of the Hundred Years' War it was always to the King of France that they turned to ask advice and to have put into practical effect what they proposed, and, if he did not concur, no action was taken. Likewise the Emperors of Constantinople addressed their envoys to France as well as to the popes. In Avignon the popes had a relative peace. The wars they carried on in Italy to save the Papal States they paid for, but, being far away, they were not in danger of attack or exile. They had other affairs that dominated their minds—for Clement V harassment by Philip the Fair and the question of the Templars; for John the quarrel with Louis of Bavaria and the revolt of the Fraticelli; for all, the perfecting of the papal financial machine. The Greek question was less urgent. In the first half of the fourteenth century it was taken up only when appeals came from Constantinople. In the second half, appeals were more frequent and the situation in the East was more ominous not only for the Greeks but for the rest of Europe. Then the popes were more energetic in trying to raise help.

For this they depended on the civil powers. It is true that the Avignon popes in general managed to amass wealth. Part of this treasure was squandered on nepotism and high-living, part was spent admirably on the poor, but more than a half went to the wars to recover the Papal States.[4] Only one of the popes, Benedict XII, left a moderately full treasury to his successor. Avignon had no army, and only limited financial resources. In any expedition the papal treasury could help; it could not sustain the whole burden. The popes had to appeal to others. After 1337 it was no use approaching France or England which were bleeding themselves to death in their own war. Venice and Genoa, each by itself, and certainly both together, could have protected Byzantium, but neither had any other aim than its own enrichment. Innocent VI, Urban V and Gregory XI appealed time and again to Louis of Hungary, who was most zealous to Latinise the subjects of Hungary and of territories he conquered, for it made for a greater unity in his realm, but who disappointed the popes every single time they asked him to fight for the survival of Christians.

Yet in spite of the continuous rebuffs they received when they asked the various Catholic authorities to co-operate to save the Eastern Empire, the popes seemed to remain optimistic. They forever promised the Emperors abundant help if only they would procure union of the Churches. Yet it was most unlikely that Venice, Genoa or Hungary would have done more for a united Empire than they did for it when separated. Nevertheless the popes seemed to believe that they would and with a crescendo of insistence they spared no labour to persuade them to do so. Apart from Nicholas IV the popes from Honorius IV to Clement V seem to have been uninterested in Constantinople and, if anything, inclined to approve projects for its reconquest. John XXII and Benedict XII responded to overtures from the Emperors with courtesy but little enthusiasm. Innocent VI, however, and his successors showed a growing concern and produced continuous schemes to organise aid.

Urban tried to unite the Hospitallers, the House of Montferrat and Genoa in an expedition in 1365. That failing, he approached Hungary, Cyprus and Savoy: only Amadeus of Savoy responded. In 1373 Gregory proposed the congress of Thebes. Still in 1373 he sent round to organize help. In 1374 a four-man embassy spread the Pope's concern. In 1375 he begged Louis to rally to the aid of John V now that he had made his submission to the Church. In the same year he tried Louis again, enticing him with the announcement that he himself had already enrolled an embryo force. Then he attempted to bring Sicily, Genoa, Venice, Hungary and the Hospitallers into a combined action, and failed.

In the early days, the popes made union a condition of military assistance. In the second half of the century, when they wrote to the Emperor, they announced aid unconditionally and added an exhortation to union and the promise of spontaneous assistance from the western Christian powers if union should be made. To the western powers, on the other hand, they held out as an incentive to generosity the prospect of a willing union of the Greeks. They were too optimistic in their promises of help, and they were too ready to believe every report of goodwill in Greece and to generalise from individual cases.

The popes admittedly varied on their personal attitudes towards Byzantium. Their policy, however, from Innocent III to Gregory XI never changed. Curial letters were written by curial officials who had in their hands all the previous correspondence, which they had certainly read and remembered. There are constant references in the letters of later popes to the instructions of their predecessors. Clement's profession of faith was the standard for later conversions and was used also in the Council of Florence. Legatine privileges for apostolic legates were repeated in stock phrases. The same faculties for missionaries were issued by nearly every pope. The purpose of it all was the "reduction," i.e., the bringing back, of the Eastern Church to the mother and mistress of all Churches, the See of Rome. The means—profession of the same faith and obedience to the same authority.

Though the Eastern Church of oriental rite probably extended over a larger area than the Latin Church—from Russia, through Lithuania, Hungary, the Balkans, the Black Sea region, Trebizond, the Crimea to Greece and, in theory at least, from Greece through Asia Minor to Cyprus, Egypt, and the Holy Land—the negotiations about union were almost confined to Constantinople. Most of the Emperors during the thirteenth and fourteenth centuries at some time in their reigns favored union. Theodore I Lascaris and John Vatatzes made overtures. Theodore II provoked a meeting and rejected union. Michael Palaeologus united the Churches. His son, Andronicus II, as Emperor, hardly dare breathe the word "union," but Andronicus III and John VI Cantacuzenus both made promising proposals. John V Palaeologus made his personal submission. The Church, however, was steadily opposed to union. The most promising negotiations were those between Vatatzes and Innocent IV. The holy synod of Constantinople considered the Greek proposition before it was presented and approved it. But even those prelates excepted the Latin doctrine of the Procession, maintaining that it should be settled only according to "the authentic testimony of Scripture."

The Greek opposition to union in the thirteenth and fourteenth centuries was not a sudden upsurge of anti-Latin sentiment. It was the consequence, heightened by political circumstances, of divergence of outlook and development that dated from the earliest centuries of the Church's life. In the sub-apostolic age Christianity was carried rapidly to all parts of the Roman Empire and it naturally took its configuration from it. The faith spread from the more important centers of civic administration outward to the areas round about, and the political divisions of the Empire with their central townships set the plan also for the Church. From the point of view of orthodoxy of doctrine, appeal was made to origins—an apostle as founder of a Church was a guarantee of purity of faith. These trends were verified in both East and West. In the West, Rome, the very capital of the Empire and possessor of the tombs of two such apostles as Peter and Paul, tended as the years went by to stress apostolic origin as an evidence of pre-eminence; the Eastern Church, outstanding political importance. The transference of the residence of Emperor and Senate to Byzantium in 330 suddenly made a small episcopal town the administrative center of the Empire. Its Church rose in status with it. Quickly Alexandria, which hitherto had ranked second after Rome, felt the effects and reacted; and Rome also became apprehensive. The Council of Chalcedon with its "Twenty-eighth Canon" was a significant stage in development. Alexandria was humiliated and ultimately rejected the council. Pope Leo refused to confirm the canon and insisted on the apostolicity of the Churches of Rome and Alexandria.

Of the 506 years that intervened between the death of Constantine (337) and the Feast of Orthodoxy (11 March 843), 217 were years of schism between Rome and Constantinople, usually provoked by Emperors trying to secure political unity by formulae compromising dogma. On most of these occasions Constantinople finally yielded to Roman firmness. The Roman Church became more assured in the security of its apostolic origin, its pope the successor of St. Peter and Vicar of Christ, commonly called the "Apostolic." In the East political importance was still the norm for ranking in the ecclesiastical organisation and it gave rise to the conception of the Church as a Pentarchy of five equal patriarchates. Rome insisted on its primacy. The forced abdication in 858 of Patriarch Ignatius in favour of Photius brought these two outlooks into more direct conflict.

In his riposte to Pope Nicholas, Photius censured the Western Church for introducing without reference to the other patriarchates into the sacrosanct form of the liturgical Creed the word *"Filioque,"* which moreover was doctrinally erroneous. So began another controversy between the East and West. The Latins had for centuries been reciting the *Filioque* in the Creed without contradiction, originally to counter the Arianism of the invaders who overran Western Europe in the fifth century. Again there is question of a divergence in the development of theological thought. The Greeks in their reply to Arianism sought an explanation and defense of the Mystery of the Blessed Trinity in metaphysical terms, beginning from the unity of the Godhead anchored in the prime source of divinity, the Father; the Latins thought more on psychological lines, beginning rather with the trinity of Persons in the one God. Neither approach to the Mystery is of faith, but once controversy had broken out criticism sharpened. The West saw danger of a diminution of the Son's full Godhead if the Spirit was from the Father only; the East, a danger of derogation from the Father as prime source of divinity if the Spirit was also from the Son. Photius, who started this controversy, founded his arguments in metaphysics. But at some time between the ninth and the thirteenth centuries all Greek thinking about it had become patristic, expressed in long catenae of quotations from the Fathers. The unionist Beccus excelled in that, but he could not persuade his fellow-bishops, who were furious with him for trying to make them pronounce on the doctrinal issue.[5] They wanted to wait till the storm of the Emperor's wrath had passed. Not so the monks.

Whether Michael's project of Church union would have stood any chance of success if there had never been any Arsenite schism, no one can say. Probably not. It is, however, certain that with rancour and hatred filling the hearts of countless monks, union was doomed. For many at that time the rightness or wrongness of the *Filioque* came second to fanatical loyalty to the deposed Patriarch. But these were combined into one cause, crystallised externally into opposition to the Emperor. The union question was not judged purely on its own merits. It was seen as the policy of the usurper Emperor. When he died, the cause and its chief upholders, the monks, emerged trimphant.[6] They held trials; they deposed bishops. They bullied Emperor Andronicus for thirty years and, as he adopted one ineffectual means after another to appease them, the crown's hold upon the Church was weakened.

When Barlaam attacked the monks, he automatically lost the sympathy of the Greeks, for the monks were held in veneration as spiritual guides and examples. They had come out of the unionist controversy with enhanced confidence and prestige, and they were very numerous. That fact colored the early stages of the Palamite controversy to Barlaam's disadvantage, and Palamas won the day. Palamism was lucky in having the support of John Cantacuzenus. Without him it might not have survived Barlaam's attack and Calecas's opposition. Both Palamas and Cantacuzenus profitted by the alliance. Thereafter religious controversy in Byzantium centered on the "uncreated energies." But it had been provoked by a Calabrian; the opponents of Palamism relied on Latin methods and they took their arguments from the Latin Aquinas. In consequence, Palamism tended to replace the *Filioque* as the epitome of opposition to Latinism and henceforward the *Filioque* appeared only as a background to demands for a council of union and in the abjurations of Latin converts to the Greek faith. There was, however, no direct confrontation on the Palamite issue between the Latin Church and the Greek Church. Yet the steady campaign to stifle "Barlaamism" in the East, while it was primarily to preserve the Palamite doctrine from attack, inevitably had an anti-Latin overtone. Palamism had become another obstacle to union, and loyalty to it implied repudiation of union.

At various times Andronicus III, Cantacuzenus and John V in overtures to the papacy proposed a general council as a necessary means of union. There never was one. The popes replied: "First union—fulfill the promise of Lyons—then help." The Greeks: "Help and then union—by a council." It was stalemate and in retrospect seems to have been the futile fruit of mutual obstinacy. But, however excellent in theory, one wonders whether at that time a council was possible in practice. Neither Church would have been content to send only a few representatives to the other's territory, there to be completely outnumbered, and, with the popes in Avignon and Constantinople never securely at peace, there was no neutral and convenient site for a prolonged meeting of hierarchies.

Several of the Emperors held out high hopes for union, if only the West would give tangible help that would earn the gratitude and goodwill of the Greek people. As such help was never forthcoming, it is impossible to say if they were right. Such, however, was the plight and despair of the Greeks, oppressed by civil wars and Turkish victories, that substantial Latin success might have produced a great change also in the ecclesiastical situation.[7] Be that as it may, it would have needed another pope with the understanding of Gregory X to take advantage of it. The popes of the fourteenth century, like most of those of the thirteenth, were not capable of that. They had no appreciation of the character of the Greek Church, its loyalty to tradition, its conviction of the purity of its own faith, its legitimate attachment to its rite and customs, its pride in its independence, and the extent of its influence and leadership over Christians of so many different nations and countries. Though they had sympathy for the plight of the afflicted Greeks, when it was a question of union of Churches they had only one answer, Clement's profession of faith that made all patriarchal rights and privileges stem from Rome, to be swallowed whole.

As the fourteenth century progressed there was less and less likelihood of the Greek Church acquiescing in that. In the first half of the century it went from strength to strength culminating in the victory of Palamism.[8] Thereafter it was left to direct its own way without interference from the Emperor. John V, from the time he proposed his scheme of union in 1355, probably thought of himself as a Latin Catholic and felt disinclined to intervene—almost disbarred from intervening—in the affairs of the Greek Church. In November 1367 he did ask the Patriarch's consent to alienate two monastic properties "for soldiers," but with little courtesy he was refused, and the synod declared that it was beyond the Church's power to give away what had been donated for pious purposes.[9] After the battle of Marica (1371), however, John confiscated the half of monastic properties, if not the actual possession, at least the revenues. But, as regards the policy of the Church, till almost the end of his reign[10] he stood aside and left it to its own devices with Philotheus at its head, the most active and effective opponent of union.

In the fourteenth century it was, in fact, the Church more than the crown that upheld Byzantine prestige.[11] It had emerged from the Palamite controversy stronger than before and certainly much more united (for it ruthlessly put down all opposition), firmly anti-Latin and self-confident. Till the end of the century all the Patriarchs were monks and Palamites, and they were all able and far-seeing men. Monasteries had multiplied in the Balkan countries and in Russia, and nearly all of them had drawn inspiration from the monastic foundations in the Empire and had adopted "typica"—constitutions—modeled on those of Mt. Athos or of the monastery of Studios in Constantinople. With the growth of monastic life, the practice of hesychasm spread and it was soon firmly established throughout the eastern Christian world, where it both strengthened local religious life and created a bond of spiritual unity between the various branches of the oriental Church, while at the same time it emphasised the pre-eminence of the Church of Constantinople.

When Stephen Dusan was crowned "Emperor of the Serbs and the Greeks" in 1346 by the patriarchs of Serbia and Bulgaria, Callistus of Constantinople replied with an excommunication. He had been trained in hesychasm in the monastery of Paroria in Bulgaria. In his action against the head of the Bulgarian Church, he was supported by Abbot Theodosius of the Bulgarian monastery of Kilifarevo, who had been a fellow pupil of his in Paroria.[12] It was Callistus, also, who was able in 1359 to set up as a bastion against the influence of the Latin Church in Wallachia a new metropolitan See, that of Oungrovlachia, directly subject to Constantinople in territories that hitherto had been within the jurisdiction of the Bulgarian hierarchy.[13]

His successor on the patriarchal throne was Philotheus (1353–4, 1364–1376), a bitter enemy of all anti-Palamites and author of a *Life* of Palamas, for whose canonisation he was responsible. He welcomed back into communion the Church of south-east Serbia, ruled over by Ugljesa, one of the several princes who shared the Serbian Empire after Stephen Dusan's death.[14] When as part of the maneuvering for political hegemony in Russia, Lithuania wanted the metropolitan of Kiev and All Russia to reside in Kiev or at least to share his vast territory with another metropolitan for Lithuania, the Byzantine authorities yielded for a time to the pressure of events and finally favoured Moscow. Thereafter Philotheus used no uncertain language. In June 1370 he wrote to the Grand Duke Demetrius: "I, as the common father established from on high by God for Christians wherever they are found in the world."[15] He informed the Russian princes that the Metropolitan of Kiev stood in his stead.[16] They would be excommunicated if they did not fight for Demetrius[17] and the

Prince of Smolensk was in fact excommunicated.[18] But the waning power of the Imperial throne contrasted with the vigorous actions of the Patriarch. In the last decade of the century Basil I of Moscow instructed his metropolitan to cease commemorating the Emperor of the Rhomaioi in the Liturgy. He drew down on himself a stern rebuke from Patriarch Antony, who, as "teacher of all Christians" and "holding the place of Christ," repeated and re-asserted the old "faith" of the God-crowned emperor, head of the State-Church kingdom of God on earth: "The Emperor is ordained Emperor and *autocrator* of the Romans, that is, of all Christians. . . . It is not possible for Christians to have a Church and not to have an Emperor, for Empire and Church are bound together in an indissoluble unity and affinity, and they cannot be reft asunder."[19]

Popes and Patriarchs both attributed the plight of Byzantium to the sins of its people. But, whereas by "sins" the popes meant only the sin of schism, the patriarchs meant the low general level of Christian living. Whatever may have been the moral standard of individuals of East and West, particularly in the fourteenth century the public morality of the States of East and West was alike at least in one respect—the complete lack of Christian charity in their relations. Kingdoms, princedoms, republics behaved with utter selfishness, aiming always to promote for themselves conquest and gain. The only exceptions were Peter de Lusignan, King of Cyprus—and he was murdered—and the Green Knight, Amadeus of Savoy. In the West the kings of England and France would not make peace. Genoa and Venice, having sacrificed the Holy Land to their rivalries, battened on the Byzantine Empire. Louis of Hungary fought to acquire Christian territories, not to protect them.

The East was no better. The Christian countries of Byzantium, Bulgaria and Serbia united could have resisted the Turks. Instead, they were ever at war with each other and took every advantage of one another's misfortunes to attack and rob. While the Turk made himself more and more secure in Europe, they still continued their incessant in-fighting, till, one by one, they were all engulfed. Internally, too, they were divided into warring factions, diminishing the power of the nation to resist an external foe. Byzantium which most needed internal unity was the most divided. From 1322 till the end of the century there was almost continuous civil strife. Andronicus III revolted three times against his grandfather and finally deposed him. John VI Cantacuzenus, and later his son Matthew, took up arms against the rightful Emperor, John V Palaeologus. John V three times had to defend his throne against his son Andronicus IV and once against his grandson John VII, and twice nearly lost it. It is a sad story, this complete eclipse of Christian charity in the relations of Christian nations. And so the infidel prevailed.

Notes

Preface

1. A. Luchaire, *La Question d'Orient* (Paris, 1907, reprinted 1969).
   H. Tillman, *Papst Innocenz III* (Bonn, 1954).
   L.E. Binns, *Innocent III* (London, 1931).
2. S. Runciman, *A History of the Crusades* III (Cambridge, 1954).
   The Later Crusades, 1189–1311, ed. R.L. Wolff and H.W. Hazard as vol. II of *A History of the Crusades,* ed. K.M. Setton (Madison, 1969).
   H.E. Mayer, *The Crusades* (Oxford, 1972).
   J.-F. Michaud, *Histoire des Croisades* III (Paris, 1970).
   The latest and by far the most thorough account of the Latin crusades is K.M. Setton, *The Papacy and the Levant,* vol. I, *The Thirteenth and Fourteenth Centuries* (Philadelphia, 1976).
3. H. Roscher, *Papst Innocenz III, und die Kreuzzüge* (Göttingen, 1969).
   D.E. Queller, *The Latin Conquest of Constantinople* (New York, 1971) recapitulates the various opinions on the several controversies about the Fourth Crusade.
4. *L'Empire Latin de Constantinople et le Principauté de Morée* (Paris, 1949).
5. *Die Union zwischen der griechischen und der lateinischen Kirche auf dem II. Konzil von Lyon (1274)* (Bonn, 1962).
6. Some items from the patriarchal archives are preserved in a MS in Vienna, published by F. Miklosich and J. Müller, *Acta et diplomata graeca medii aevi sacra et profana,* vols. I and II (from 6 vols.) (Vienna, 1860, 1862). A new edition is in preparation: cf. J. Darrouzès, *Le Registre synodal du patriarcat byzantin au XIV*[e] *siècle* (= *Archive de l'Orient Chrétien* 12) (Paris, 1971).

Chapter I

1. Cf. below, chapter VIII.
2. G. Ostrogorsky, *History of the Byzantine State,* ed. J. Hussey (New Brunswick, N.J., 1969), p. 377.
3. Cf. C.M. Brand, *Byzantium Confronts the West 1180–1204* (Cambridge, Mass., 1968), pp. 141–2.
4. Cf. J.K. Fotheringham, "Genoa and the Fourth Crusade," in *The English Historical Review,* XXV (1910), pp. 26–57.
5. *De capta Thessalonica,* ed. S. Kyriakidis (= Ist. Sicil. Test. V) (Palermo, 1961), pp. 112–20.
6. Brand, *Byzantium,* p. 156.
7. To fill out the sketch of events given in this introductory chapter, the following books could be consulted:
   F. Chalandon, *Histoire de la domination normande en Italie et en Sicile,* 2 vols. (Paris, 1907).
   B. Leib, *Rome, Kiev et Byzanze à la fin du XI*[e] *siècle* (Paris, 1924).
   J. Hussey, *Church and Learning in the Byzantine Empire 867–1185* (London, 1937).

CMH, vol. IV (Cambridge, 1966) ch. V.
Ostrogorsky, *History,* ch. V.
S. Runciman, *A History of the Crusades,* 3 vols. (Cambridge, 1951–1954).
K. Setton, *A History of the Crusades,* 2 vols. (Philadelphia, 1955–1962).
G. Buckler, *Anna Comnena* (London, 1929).

Chapter II

1. J. Gill, "Innocent III and the Greeks: Aggressor or Apostle?" *Relations between East and West in the Middle Ages,* ed. D. Baker (Edinburgh, 1973), pp. 95–108.

2. *MPL* 214 779BC. A new edition of those of Innocent's letters that deal with the oriental Churches has been produced by T. Haluscynskyj, *Acta Innocentii III (1198–1216) (= Pont. Comm. III, II)* (Città del Vaticano, 1944). I have used this improved edition in writing this book, but I have preferred to give my reference to the edition of Migne, which has many useful letters not included in the *Acta Innocentii* and is more readily available to students.

3. *MPL* 217 665B.

4. *MPL* 215 262A.

5. *MPL* 215 281B.

6. *MPL* 214 680B.

7. *MPL* 215 767B.

8. *MPL* 215 1358D. 214 871B.

9. *MPL* 216 1162ABC.

10. *MPL* 214 377AB.

11. Whereas Innocent legitimised the children of the King of France who had no liege-lord, he refused a like office to a noble who had; *MPL* 214 1132BC.

12. Cf. M. Maccarone, *Chiesa e stato nella dottrina di Papa Innocenzo III* (= *Lateranum* nova series An. VI n.3–4) (Roma, 1940).

13. *Gesta Innoc., MPL* 214 pp. clxxii-clxxv. On the high historical value of the *Gesta* cf. Y. Lefèvre, "Innocent III et son temps vus de Rome," in *Mélanges d'archéologie et d'histoire,* 61 (1949), pp. 242–5.

14. *Regesta Innocentii III* (in *MPL* 214–217; hereafter = *Reg*) I 353: *Die Register Innocenz III.,* eds. O. Hageneder and O. Haidacher, Bd. I (Graz-Köln, 1964) n. 353.

15. *MPL* 214 327A, "cum per Dei misericordiam tempus acceperimus iustitiam iudicandi," a vague phrase in which Norden (p.138f.) sees a very sinister meaning.

16. *Reg,* 1354, esp. *MPL* 214 328B: Hageneder, n. 354.

17. February 1199. Greek text, A. Papadakis and A.M. Talbot, "John X Camaterus Confronts Innocent III: An Unpublished Correspondence," in *Bslav.,* 33 (1972), pp. 33–5. Latin text, *Reg,* II 208. Camaterus was elected Patriarch on 5 August 1198.

18. *Reg,* II 210, esp. *MPL* 214 768C.

19. *Reg,* II 211, esp. *MPL* 214 771BC.

20. Innocent's letter, *Reg,* II 209, esp. *MPL* 214 765A. The Patriarch's reply, Papadakis-Talbot, *Art. cit.* pp. 35–41. It is reported (Grumel, *Regestes pat.* III n. 1197) that Camaterus promised on oath to submit the Church of Constantinople to the Roman Church and to go to Rome to receive the pallium at the hands of the Pope. But this is hardly credible in view of the letters analyzed here and of his leaving Constantinople with other wretched refugees after the capture.

21. He took the Greek threat to conquer Cyprus seriously, for he asked the kings of France and England to intervene to prevent it; cf. *Reg,* II 251.

22. *Reg,* I 355, esp. *MPL* 214 330A.

23. There is controversy over the date of the arrival in Italy of Alexius, whether in 1201 before the crusaders congregated in Venice (which would have allowed time for concerting a plan to divert the crusade to Constantinople) or in 1202 when they were already there (which would have given no time for that) (cf. infra n. 47). The weight of opinion favors autumn 1201. D.E. Queller, *The Latin Conquest of Constantinople* (New York, 1971) pp. 75–83, and H.E. Mayer, *The Crusades* (Oxford, 1972) pp. 188–9 outline the different views with references; to which add Brand, *Op. cit.*, App. II, pp. 275–6 for a fresh argument for September-October 1201.

24. *MPL* 1124B.

25. *Gesta,* p. lxxxiii.

26. *Gesta,* p. lxxxv; *Reg* VI 48.

27. *Devastatio Constantinopolitana,* ed. G.H. Pertz, in *MGH SS* XVI (Hanover, 1859), p. 10.

28. Ibid.

29. *Gesta episcoporum Halberstadensium,* ed. L. Weiland, in *MGH SS* XXIII (Hanover, 1874), p. 217.

30. *Guntheri monachi historia Constantinopolitana sub Balduino, anna 1210,* in *Thesaurus monumentorum ecclesiasticorum Henrici Canisii,* ed. J. Basnage, Tom. IV (Amsterdam, 1725), p. ix.

31. *MPL* 214 1179B.

32. Conrad of Halberstadt: "Veneti. . .ad deditionem coegerunt, licet quedam lettere apostolice ibidem apparuerint, que sub excommunicationis interminatione id fieri vetuissent" (*Gesta Halberstadensium,* p. 117). Robert of Clari: Letters came from Rome threatening excommunication if they made war or damaged Zara: "Quant li message vinrent a l'ost, si lut on les letres devant le duc [i.e. Doge] et devant les pélérins [i.e. crusaders]." The Doge defied the threat and the barons agreed to help him (Robert De Clari, *La Conquête de Constantinople,* ed. P. Lauer [Paris, 1924], p.14). Villehardouin's account tallies. According to him the order of events was: arrival at Zara; deputation of citizens persuaded by anti-diversion group that the French would not fight them; then "A certain Abbot of Vaux . . . rose to his feet and said: 'My lords, in the name of the Pope of Rome I forbid you to attack this city; for the people in it are Christians, and you wear the sign of the cross.' " The Doge appealed to the barons who decided to fulfill their promise. "The next morning the troops encamped in front of the gates of the city. They set up their petraries . . ." (Villehardouin, pp. 47–8). The *Gesta* relate that Capuano returned to Innocent with news of the project of Zara. The Pope commissioned the Abbot of Locedio to promulgate his prohibition and himself informed Montferrat of it *viva voce* (MPL 214 p. cxxxix). Montferrat arrived at Zara a fortnight after the siege (Villehardouin, p. 50).

33. The sources give various dates for the capture of Zara: Villehardouin, 17 November (pp. 47–8); Conrad of Halberstadt, 24 November (p. 117); the *Devastatio,* 25 November, which also explains (and it is the only source that does) why the fleet took so long to travel from Venice to Zara: "Veneti cum peregrinis ascendentes mare in Ystriam venerunt, Triestum et Muglam ad dedicionem compulerunt, totam Ystriam, Dalmatiam Slaviniam tributa reddere coegerunt. Iadram navigaverunt" (p. 10).

34. *Reg,* V 122, esp. *MPL* 214 1125B.

35. Villehardouin names 4 messengers—two ecclesiastics, Névelon, bishop of Soissons, and Jean de Noyon, with two knights, Jean de Friaize and Robert de Boves: Gunther

mentions three—the Bishop of Soissons, the Abbot Martin and Master John, i.e., the ecclesiastics (p. x); while Robert of Clari gives 2, Soissons and de Boves (p. 15). Both Villehardouin and Clari record that Robert de Boves did not return to the army, but went off straight to Syria.

36. *Reg,* V 161, 162; esp. *MPL* 214 1180D. H. Tillmann, *Papst Innocenz III.* (Bonn, 1954) on the grounds of these two letters suggests that Innocent would have been ready to turn a blind eye to the *fait accompli* of Zara, had the French crusaders not been conscious of their guilt, and H. Roscher, *Papst Innocenz III. und die Kreuzzüge,* (Göttingen, 1969), p. 107, seems to agree with her. I do not think that the letters warrant such an explanation. *Alioquin vos excommunicationis sententiam subjacere* means "Otherwise realize that you are [already] under sentence of excommunication."

37. Gunther, p. x.

38. *MPL* 215 262B.

39. pp. 51–3.

40. *MPL* 214 1124C.

41. *Reg,* VI 48.

42. *Reg,* VI 99.

43. *Reg,* VI 100, esp. *MPL,* 215 105B, 104C.

44. Villehardouin pp. 55–6. How serious it was can be gauged from the fact that "Indeed, it is only true to say that more than half the men in the army were of the same mind" (p. 55). Count Hugh of St. Pol in a letter to the Duke of Brabant relates the same crisis: "Super hoc autem fuit inter nos maxima dissensio et ingens tumultus; omnes enim clamabant ire apud Accaron; pauci fuerunt plus quam 20 qui Constantinopolim collaudassent" (*Annales Colonienses Maximi,* ed. K. Pertz on MGH SS XVII (Hanover, 1861), p. 812.

45. "Et se vous ensi nel faites, sachiés que vous ne vous moverés de cheste isle devant la que nous serons paié, ne ne troverés qui vous port ne que boire ne que menger" (Robert de Clari, p. 10). Cf. also *Devastatio,* p. 10; Conrad of Halberstadt, p. 117.

46. Gunther, p. x.

47. *Reg,* VI 101. There is great diversity of opinion about responsibility for the diversion of the crusade to Constantinople, whether it was just the result of a fortuitous build-up of circumstances, or a plot organised primarily by Philip of Swabia or by Venice, with the co-operation of the leaders of the crusade willingly or under duress: cf. Queller, *Op. cit.,* pp. 19–75 for a review of opinions and references. In my view, the project, since it admirably suited the ambitions of Alexius, Philip of Swabia and the Venetians and was attractive to Montferrat, may have been concocted by them. This is the opinion of McNeal and Wolff in K. Setton, *The Crusades* II, pp. 172–3.
A further question concerns the attitude of Innocent III towards the diversion. F. Cognasso tried ingeniously to show that Innocent III was fully cognizant of the crusaders' intention to go to Constantinople but "he pretended to know nothing about it" and foresaw without revulsion the possibility of having to take it by force (*Storia delle crociate* [Varese, 1967], pp. 697–727 passim, 740–1). D.M. Nicol states: "The Fourth crusade set out for Constantinople with the connivance if not with the blessing of Innocent III." (*CMH* IV, p. 280). S. Runciman (*A History of the Crusades* III [Cambridge, 1954], p. 117) would probably agree with him. McNeal and Wolff (*Op. cit.,* p. 176), after a little unsound argumentation, concur also. I think that they are wrong and I have worked out my opinion from the sources in an article: "Franks, Venetians, and Pope Innocent III 1201–1203," in *Studi Veneziani* XIII (1970), pp. 85–106. H.E. Mayer (*Op. cit.,* pp. 188–9) notes that Innocent, so that their voyage might not be abruptly terminated, did not forbid the French to continue relations with the excommunicated Venetians (he is using a subsequent letter to make this point and

referring it to a time when Innocent did not know what attitude the Venetians would adopt to the excommunication) and concludes: "Now [at Zara] as later the pope's attitude to the Fourth Crusade remained ambiguous." A. Frolow (*La déviation de la IVe croisade vers Constantinople* [Paris, 1955] pp. 42–4) is definite that Innocent opposed the diversion to Constantinople. I think that he overstresses attraction for the acquisition of relics as a cause of the diversion. It is not mentioned in that connection in any of the major sources of the Fourth Crusade.

48. *Reg,* VI 102, esp. *MPL* 215 109AB.

49. *Reg,* VI 210, 211.

50. Villehardouin, p. 78. Clari, p. 56. These figures are taken from Clari and are possibly inaccurate. It will be noticed that they amount, not to 100,000 marks, but to 106,000.

51. *Reg,* VI 229, esp. *MPL* 215 259C. The reason for the long interval between the despatch of the crusaders' letters and Innocent's answer was because the ship carrying the bearer of the letters (and of rich gifts for the Pope) was captured by a Genoese pirate. The Pope later protested and demanded restitution of the gifts. He never got them. Cf. J.K. Fotheringham, "Genoa and the Fourth Crusade," in *English Historical Review,* XXV (1910), pp. 20–57.

52. *Reg,* VI 230, esp. *MPL* 215 260D.

53. *Reg,* VI 231, 232, esp. *MPL* 215 261C.

54. *MPL* 215 261B.

55. *Reg, MPL* 214 II 176, 177.

56. *Reg,* V 155, esp. *MPL* 214 1113BC. Cf. R.L. Wolff, "The 'Second Bulgarian Empire': Its Origin and History to 1204," in *Speculum,* XXIV (1949), pp. 167–206.

57. *Reg,* VII 4.

58. *Reg,* VII 8, esp. 293C.

59. *Reg,* VII 2, esp. *MPL* 215 281A. Kalojan had asked for a patriarch: "I beg you to send cardinals to crown me emperor and to make in my country a patriarch" (*MPL* 215 156A, 291A). He told the Pope that when the Greeks had heard of the negotiations, "the Patriarch and the Emperor sent to me: 'Come to us, we will crown you as Emperor and will make a patriarch for you, since an empire would not stand without a patriarch.' " (*MPL* 215 156A).

60. *MPL* 215 282A; *Reg,* VII 3.

61. *Reg,* VII 12.

62. *Reg,* VII 2. Canon 5 of the Lateran Council held under Innocent III in 1215 decreed the privileges of patriarchs in a similar way except that they could be preceded by the Cross anywhere except in Rome and in the presence of a papal legate, and could hear appeals from any part of their patriarchate (Mansi 22 991).

63. *Reg,* II 220.

64. Gregory IV was disinclined to make his submission to Rome and so was replaced.

65. *Reg,* II 220.

66. *Reg,* II 252.

67. *Reg,* II 253, 255, 17 December 1199.

68. *Reg,* V 153, 1 October 1201.

69. *Reg,* VI 158, 157.

70. *Reg,* V 156, esp. 1012BA; 1 June 1202.

Chapter III

1. *Reg,* V 122.
2. *MPL* 215 237B.
3. Letter of St. Pol, *MGH SS* XVII p. 814.
4. *MPL* 215 238D, 237B.
5. Villehardouin, p. 75. The conditions were 1. to place the whole Empire under the jurisdiction of Rome; 2. to give 200,000 silver marks to the army and provisions for a year; 3. to convey 10,000 men in his own ships to Egypt and to keep them there for a year; and 4. during his lifetime to maintain at his own expense 500 knights overseas to keep guard.
6. *Nicetae Choniatae historia* (Bonn, 1835), p. 729.
7. Clari, p. 60.
8. *Reg.* VII 215. Cf. S. Borsari, *Studi sulle colonie veneziane in Romania nel XIII secolo* (Napoli, 1966), pp. 15–25. For the texts of the Pact cf. TT 119/120, I, pp. 445–52.
9. Clari, pp. 63, 65.
10. Nicetas Choniates, *Op. cit.*, pp. 757–61. Nicetas himself left Constantinople on the fifth day after the capture. Just in front of him in the throng of fugitives escaping from the city, on a little donkey, was the Patriarch of Constantinople, John Camaterus.

    The new Emperor Baldwin merely wrote: "There was taken a vast quantity of horses, gold and silver, silken and precious garments and gems; and so incalculable a quantity of everything that is esteemed by men as riches was found there as all the Latin world seemed not to possess" (*MPL* 215 451B). The ecclesiastics exulted in the vast number of precious and curious relics that they grabbed and took back with them to the West. Only Clari touches on a more sombre note and even that lightly. He reported with some bitterness that the barons hastened to seize the best mansions and when the poorer crusaders realised it "they went each one as best he could and took what they could lay hands on. They found a lot; they took a lot; a lot they left behind because the city was very big and densely populated" (p. 80). But after the capture of Baldwin: "So verily the Lord God avenged Himself on them for their pride and for the bad faith they had shown to the poorer members of the host and for the horrible sins that they committed in the city after they had captured it" (p. 106).

    That a city as strongly fortified as Constantinople should be captured in a week needs explanation. In the past it had resisted attacks from Arabs, Russians and others and, when it was in a more ruinous state than it was in 1204, it would keep at bay for several months Mehmet the Conqueror though he disposed of a very large army and fleet and had the most enormous cannon employing gunpowder that the world had ever yet seen. E. Frances suggests that the reason was that the mass of the population was so oppressed by taxes that it despaired of any relief being given by its own ruling classes, and so would not and did not raise a finger to defend the city. The Latins (he thinks) knew this and so, when they agreed on the division of the spoils before they had even attacked, they did so with a reasonable prospect of success (E. Frances, "La Conquête de Constantinople par les Latins," in *Bslav,* 15 [1954], pp. 21–6).
11. "This is the city that had dared on many occasions to cement savage friendships with the infidel with mutual drinking of blood in a filthy pagan usage instead of with brotherly association, and for long has nourished them with the milk of a free-flowing breast and raised them to the height of worldly pride by providing them with arms, ships and victuals. What, on the other hand, it has done to pilgrims the history of every Latin nation can declare better than words. This is the city that in hatred of the apostolic primacy could hardly bear to hear spoken the name of the Prince of the Apostles and never granted even one single church among the Greeks to him who

received from the Lord Himself the first place among all the churches. This is the city which had inculcated the honouring of Christ only with pictures and, among the execrable usages which to the contempt of Scripture she had devised for herself, very often dared to impugn by repeating it even the baptism of salvation. This is the city that considered that all Latins should be dubbed not men but dogs, the shedding of whose blood was deemed almost meritorious and not thought to need any penitential satisfaction from laymen or monks, in whose hands in contempt of the priesthood all powers of binding and loosing lay. These and other frenzies of the kind . . . has divine judgement visited with a worthy vengeance by our instrumentality" (*MPL* 215 452BC).

"Mutual drinking of blood" refers to a Cuman ceremony of alliance in which blood taken from the allying parties was mingled in a bowl and drunk. The Greeks did it when in urgent need of peace and the Latins in similar circumstances did the same (Joinville, *The Life of Saint Louis,* trans. M.R.B. Shaw [= Penguin Classics L 124] [London, 1963], p. 290). The sentiment that Latins were dogs and deserved to be murdered is attributed to the Patriarch Dositheus apropos of the crusade of Frederic I: "Besides, they recounted how the Patriarch of Constantinople, that pseudo-apostle, at that period in his sermons to the people on feast days used to call the pilgrims of Christ dogs and how he was accustomed to proclaim from the pulpit that, if a Greek was guilty of the deaths of ten men, he would be free and absolved from the guilt of his previous murders and of all his crimes if he killed a hundred pilgrims" (Ausbert, *Historia de expeditione Friderici Imperatoris,* ed. A. Choust in *MGH SS* nova series V, [Berlin, 1928], p. 49). The German Emperor specifically insisted on the signature of Dositheus to the treaty he later made with the Greek Emperor Isaac II. Cf. C.M. Brand, *Byzantium Confronts the West,* pp. 182–3.

12. Anno 1204 plus mille Cremonenses Constantinopolim profecti sunt eam defensuri et rebus suis consulturi, sicut innumeri homines ex aliis terris tunc Constantinopolim confluxerunt (*Sicardi Episcopi Cremonensis cronica,* ed. O. Holder-Egger, in *MGH SS* XXXI, [Hanover, 1903], p. 43).

13. *Reg,* VII 102. This letter is so laced with biblical quotations and allusions, especially from St. Paul—just the style to appeal to Innocent III, who did precisely the same—that it must have been written for Baldwin by a cleric, perhaps the Bishop of Soissons.

14. 7 Nov. 1204, *Reg,* VII 153. 7 Nov. is long after the probable date of Baldwin's letter, which was carried by Barozzi, a Templar. How long it took him to reach Rome is unknown for he was captured en route by Genoese pirates (J.K. Fotheringham, "Genoa and the Fourth Crusade," in *English Historical Review,* 25 [1910], pp. 42–3). The Pope wrote to Genoa remonstrating on 4 November (*Reg,* VII 147).

15. 13 November 1204, *Reg,* VII 154.

16. 7 December 1204, *Reg,* VII 164.

17. *Reg,* VII 203.

18. "the peoples of the Greeks, departing from the unity of the Apostolic See and the Roman Church which by the disposition of God is mother and mistress of all the faithful fashioned for themselves another church—if indeed that which is other than the one should be called a church" (To Emperor Alexius III, 1198; *MPL* 214 326C). "The people of the Greeks . . . fashioned for itself another Church . . . and departed from the unity of the Apostolic See, following neither what was established by the Lord nor what was authoritatively taught by Peter, and endeavours even until now, though in vain, to rend the seamless garment of the Lord, which the hands of the crucifiers spared even when they were dividing up the other garments" (to the Patriarch, *MPL* 214 328B). Cf. also *MPL* 214 763A, 764C; 215 513D, 623, 634C; 216 557B etc.

19. "Strive also—rather, as indeed you can, bring it about—that the Church of the Greeks returns to the unity of the Apostolic See and the daughter comes back to her mother" (To Emperor Alexius III, *MPL* 214 327A). The Patriarch "invited to the council should

come at the appointed time to offer to the Apostolic See reverence and obedience as befits his canonical status, lest if this is not done (which we do not credit) We be forced to take action both against the Emperor himself, who can, if he will, effect what We enjoin, and against you and the Church of the Greeks" (*MPL* 214 765A = 771D).

20. "After the kingdom of the Greeks went astray from the obedience of the Apostolic See, it steadily sank down from bad to worse until by a just judgment of God it was transferred from the proud to the humble, from the disobedient to the faithful, from schismatics to Catholics, so that by the virtue of obedience that kingdom, which by the vice of disobedience declined into evil, might rise again to good" (*MPL* 215 455C). "Indeed that is the work of God and it is wonderful to our eyes" (*MPL* 215 456A). In a letter to Theodore Lascaris: "Even though they [the crusaders] are not altogether blameless, nevertheless We believe that through them the Greeks, who have striven to rend the seamless garment of Christ, have been punished by a just judgment of God" (*MPL* 215 1373D). Cf. *MPL* 215 515B, 635AB, 959B, 1374BC.

21. "By God's grace they came because, after the Empire of Constantinople was transferred at this present time from the Greeks to the Latins, the Church also of Constantinople came back to obedience to the Apostolic See like a daughter to a mother" (*MPL* 215 514A). "The Lord called his own . . . when the Empire of the Greeks was transferred from the disobedient and the superstitious to the sons of obedience and the faithful," who offer their praise. "With, then, the transference of the Empire, the rite of the priesthood was necessarily transferred [the Pope is here using an Old Testament analogy] . . . and Rome will instruct them" (*MPL* 215 623C). Cf. also *MPL* 215 514D, 595A, 636D, 957C, 1388C; 216 557B.

22. (To the Patriarch) "If invited you come [to the council We intend to summon] to pay due reverence and obedience to the Roman Church, since these are the truths which We required by Our letters, namely that the member should return to the head and the daughter to the mother, We shall receive you with kindness and joy as a most dear brother and chief member" (*MPL* 214 764CD = 771CD). Alexius IV would show his sincerity towards Rome if he should "succeed with the patriarch in getting him to recognise by envoys of consequence the primacy in jurisdiction and teaching of the Roman Church and to promise reverence and obedience to Us and to seek from the Apostolic See the pallium taken from the body of St. Peter, without which he cannot validly exercise the patriarchal office" (*MPL* 215 260D = 262A).

23. "Seeing then . . . that the Roman Church is the head and mother of all Churches not by the decision of some council but by divine ordinance, so, because of difference neither of rite nor of dogma, should you hesitate to obey Us as your head generously and devotedly in accordance with ancient custom and the canons, since what is certain is not to be abandoned in favour of what is doubtful" (To the Patriarch, *MPL* 214 764C = 771B).

24. "The Apostolic See . . . so elevated [the See of Constantinople] as to place her before the Churches of Alexandria, Antioch and Jerusalem in dignity of rank" (*MPL* 215 575A). "The oriental Church [i.e. of Constantinople] as the chief member" (*MPL* 215 711BC) Cf. 215 522B, 623C; 216 676C. "The Church of Constantinople second to that of Rome" (*MPL* 215 728A, 960A).

25. Letter of reprimand to Capuano for releasing crusaders in Constantinople from their vow: "When the Empire of Constantinople is consolidated and the Church there established in devotion to the Apostolic See, the Emperor may be able to drive forward to overcome the barbarous peoples who hold in their power the land in which God, our King, centuries ago deigned to effect the salvation which our sins necessitated" (*MPL* 215 636AB). Cf. *MPL* 215 455B, 516A, 708CD; 216 354A etc.

26. *Gesta Innoc. MPL* 214, p. xciii; *Reg,* VII 205.

27. End of May, *Reg,* VIII 69–71.

28. 16 Aug. 1205, *Reg,* VIII 130.

29. *Gesta Innoc. MPL* 214 pp. cvi-cviii.

30. *MPL* 215 957C.

31. *Gesta Innoc. MPL* 214 p. xcv.

32. 18 Feb. 1205, *Reg,* VII 208.

33. 12 July 1205, *Reg,* VIII 126. The full text of his description of the sack of Constantinople reads as follows: "Indeed (and this We relate with sadness and shame) We fail where there seemed to be the greatest promise of success, and where We thought We had the most freedom of action, there We are held in check. For how will the Church of the Greeks return to unity of the Church and devotion to the Apostolic See, no matter what afflictions and persecutions it suffers, when it has beheld in the Latins nothing but an example of perdition and the works of darkness, so that now rightly it abominates them more than dogs? For the men, who were reputed to be seeking not what was their own but what was Jesus Christ's, bathed in Christian blood the swords that they should have wielded against the infidel. They spared neither religion nor age nor sex; they committed incest, adultery and fornication in the eyes of men and delivered over matrons and virgins, even those dedicated to God, to the vileness of their camp-followers. It was not enough for them to empty the imperial treasury and to scatter the spoils of great men and small; they stretched their rapacious hands out to the treasures of the Church and, what is worse, to Church properties, wrenching silver plating even from altars, smashing it up into pieces for division, violating sanctuaries, carrying off crucifixes and reliquaries" (*MPL* 215 701AB).

    The sharpness of this reprimand to Capuano was owning to Innocent's anxiety at that time about the Holy Land, which was without king, without patriarch, and without legates. Cf. H. Roscher, *Papst. Innozenz III und die Kreuzzüge* (Göttingen, 1969), p. 127.

34. 20 May 1205, *Reg,* VIII 62. Cf. Borsari, *Studi,* pp. 99–105.

35. *Reg,* VIII 136; IX 100, 148; XII 113; XIII 18–19.

36. 21 June 1206, IX 130; 24 April 1208, XI 76; 21 Dec. 1209, XII 105.

37. *Reg,* IX 142. R.L. Wolff, "Politics in the Latin Patriarchate of Constantinople, 1204–1261," in *DOP,* 8 (1954), pp. 255 ff. TT, II, pp. 31-34. P. Charanis, *"The Monastic Properties and the State in the Byzantine Empire,"* in *DOP,* 4 (1948), pp. 51–118, esp. 93ff.

38. *Reg,* XIII 44.

39. 20 Dec. 1210, *Reg,* XIII 192.

40. 16 April 1208, *Reg,* XI 52.

41. *Reg,* XI 120, one of eleven letters on similar subjects dated 14 July 1208.

42. 24 Jan. 1209, *Reg,* XI 245.

43. 3 Oct. 1210, *Reg,* XIII 161; 26 Aug. 1213, *Reg,* XVI 98.

44. *Reg,* XIII 98; XV 76.

45. Venetians *Reg,* IX 140; Kingdom of Thessalonica *Reg,* XI 116–9; Constantinople *Reg,* XII 141; Morea *Reg,* XIII 161.

46. *Reg,* XI 153; XIII 23.

47. *Acta Honorii III et Gregorii IX* (Pont. Comm., III, III), ed. A.L. Tautu, (Città del Vaticano 1950), no. 115 (= P. Pressutti, *I regesti del Pontefice Onorio III dall'anno 1216 all'anno 1227,* (Roma, 1884), II, no. 4480).

48. 13 Nov. 1199, *MPL* 214 764D, 771B.

49. *MPL* 215 260D, 262A.

50. H. Heisenberg, *Neue Quellen zur Geschichte des lateinischen Kaisertums und der Kirchenunion* (Sitzungsberichte der bayerischen Akademie der Wissenschaften, philos,-histor. Klasse)I, (Munich, 1922), pp. 48–50.

51. Letter of recommendation to Emperor Baldwin 15 May 1205, *MPL* 215 623C.

52. S. Lambros, *Michael Akominatou tou Choniatou ta sozemena,* II (Athens, 1880), p. 312.

53. 27 Nov. 1206, *Reg,* IX 190.

54. 8 Dec. 1208, *Reg,* XI 179.

55. 20 March 1210, *Reg,* XIII 25.

56. Norden, p. 184, n. 1.

57. Heisenberg, *Neue Quellen* 1, pp. 9–11. J.M. Hoeck und R.-J. Loenertz, *Nikolaos-Nektarios von Otranto Abt von Casole* (Ettal, 1965), pp. 34–52.

58. Heisenberg, *Neue Quellen* II, Die Unionsverhandlungen von 30 August 1206, (Munich, 1923).

59. Heisenberg, *Neue Quellen* I, pp. 52–53.
According to B. Sinogowitz ("Uber das byzantinische Kaisertum nach dem vierter Kreuzzuge [1204–5]" in *BZ,* 45 [1952], pp. 345–56) Lascaris had assumed the purple and claimed to be Emperor as early as 1205. R.L. Wolff (*A History of the Crusades,* ed. K. Setton, 2nd ed. [Madison, 1969], p. 201 n. 11) does not agree.

60. Heisenberg, *Op. cit.,* I, pp. 63–6: J.B. Cotelerius, *Ecclesiae Graecae Monumenta,* III (Paris, 1686), 514–20.
Though the letter as published by Cotelerius is completely different in style and to some degree also in content from the text reported by Mesarites as from his brother's pen, I think that both letters refer to the same occasion and not to different occasions. Others (e.g., Norden, *Op. cit.,* pp. 227ff.; Setton, *The Crusades* II, p. 211; W. de Vries, "Innocenz III. [1198–1216] und der christliche Osten," in *ArchHP,* 3 [1965], pp. 120ff.) consider them as different and as prompted by different circumstances, dating the Cotelerius version as from 1213/1214, though the Greeks then had their Patriarch in Nicaea. Any argument, therefore, to the benevolent attitude of the clergy of Constantinople towards the Latin Church in c. 1214, founded on Cotelerius's version, is of very doubtful value.

61. Letters to Nicaea with the Emperor's answer. Heisenberg, *Op. cit.* III, pp. 25–35. Charlemagne in the ninth century and the Czar of Bulgaria in the tenth were given the title of *Basileus.* Only the Emperor of Constantinople was called *Basileus kai autocrator.*

62. August 1205, *Reg,* VIII 133.

63. *Reg,* XI 47, addressed to "Nobili viro Theodoro Lascari." When this letter was written Lascaris had not yet been crowned, but in any case Innocent would not have recognized two emperors.

64. Besides the Patriarch John Camaterus, also Michael Choniates, archbishop of Athens; Euthymius Tornikes, archbishop of Patras; Emanuel, archbishop of Thebes; and Constantine Mesopotamites, archbishop of Thessalonica; with the archbishop of Corinth, abandoned their Sees. A decision of the *Synodus endemousa,* dated 4 June 1209, in Nicaea, was signed by 17 bishops, of whom 4 were of mainland European Sees (K. Hadjipsaltis, "Scheseis tes Kyprou pros to en Nikaia byzantinon kratos," in *Kypriakai Spoudai,* 28 (1964), pp. 135–68.

65. 8 March 1208, *Reg,* XI 23.

66. 14 July 1212, *Reg,* XV 134, 135.

67. 4 Oct. 1208, *Reg,* XI 152.

68. *Reg,* XIII 103.

69. J.B. Pitra, *Analecta sacra et classica spicilegio Solesmensi* VII (Roma, 1891), pp. 447–62, esp. 454, 459.

70. 18 Sept. 1207, *Reg,* X 128.

71. 19 April 1207, *Reg,* X 51.

72. Tautu, *Op. cit.,* no. 115 (= Pressutti, *Op. cit.,* no. 4480 = *MPL* 216 968B).

73. Instruction to Morosini, 2 August 1206, *Reg,* IX 140. R.L. Wolff, "The Organisation of the Latin Patriarchate of Çonstantinople, 1204–1261," in *Trad,* VI (1948) pp. 33–60. J. Longnon, "L'Organisation de l'Eglise d'Athènes par Innocent III," in *Mémorial Louis Petit* (Bucharest, 1948), pp. 336–46.

74. *MPL* 215 963D; *Reg,* XI 214, 215.

75. *Reg,* XVI 97.

76. *Reg,* IX 140.

77. 8 March 1208, *Reg,* XI 23, 155.

78. 8 Dec. 1208, *Reg,* XI 179.

79. *Reg,* IX 140.

80. *Reg,* XI 155.

81. *Reg,* XIII 34.

82. *Reg,* IX 192; XIII 40.

83. 17 Jan. 1214, *Reg,* XVI 168.

84. Lambros, *Op. cit.,* esp. II, pp.238, 252–7, 311, 240. G. Stadtmüller, *Michael Choniates, Metropolit von Athen* (= *Orientalia Christiana Analecta* 33) (Rome, 1934), esp. p. 196 ss.

85. The metropolitan of Patras substituted canons regular for the secular clergy who had abandoned their posts (*Reg,* XIII 159), but the latter came back, and with the aid of the secular arm invaded the canonry and ejected the others (*Reg,* XV 21).

86. *Reg,* XIII 16.

87. *MPL* 216 969ABC (= Tautu, *Op. cit.,* no. 115).

88. *Reg,* XIII 41.

89. *Georgii Acropolitae annales,* ed. I. Bekker (Bonn, 1836), pp. 32, 35. Of Henry, Acropolites wrote: "Henry, though a Frank, nevertheless had most pleasant relations with Greeks and the natives of Constantinople. To many he gave high office either in the State or in the armed forces and he cherished the Greek populace as he did his own" (Ibid. p. 31).

90. J.B. Cotelerius, *Ecclesiae graecae monumenta* III (Paris, 1686), p. 519. It was "exactly similar to that given to the Emperor."

91. Tautu, no. 97 (= Pressutti, II no. 3914).

92. J.B. Papadopoulos-Kerameus, "Théodore Eirénicos, patriarche oecuménique de Nicée," in *BZ,* X (1901), pp. 182–92.

93. Nicholas of Otranto commented on this discussion: "But the Cardinal, even though he was learned and well-versed in the Holy Scriptures and experienced in the art of dialectics, did not wish to make any answer, even the slightest, in this matter. He said to me: 'Both fermented and unfermented bread are pleasing to God.' " (Quoted by Heisenberg, *Neue Quellen* I, p. 11).

94. The only source for these events is a sermon preached in Ephesus by Mesarites probably on 27 February 1216, the Sunday of Tyrophagou. It is published by A. Heisenberg, *Neue Quellen* III: *Der Bericht des Nikolaos Mesarites über die politischen und kirchlichen Ereignisse des Jahres 1214* (München, 1923). Cf. Hoeck-Loenertz, *Nikolaos-Nektarios von Otranto,* pp. 56–61.

95. Cotelerius, *Op. cit.,* III pp. 495–514. According to A.E. Bakalopoulos, *Historia tou neou Hellenismou. I Arches kai diamorphosi tou,* (Thessalonica, 1961), p. 57. "It is estimated that the half, or even the majority, of the refugees from Constantinople found asylum in Epirus." This book has been translated into English, which is not available to me.

96. 29 April 1213, *Reg,* XVI 30.

97. "Im Fruhjahr 1207 hatte der 4. Kreuzzug auch im Denken seines Initiators, Papst Innocenz' III., sang-und klanglos sein Ende gefunden," H. Roscher, *Op. cit.,* p.131.

98. A. Luchaire, "Un document retrouvé," in *Journal des Savants,* N.S. 3 (1905), pp. 557–67: R. Foreville, *Latran I, II, III et Latran IV* (= Histoire des Conciles Oecuméniques 6) (Paris, 1963), p. 391.

99. *Conciliorum Oecumenicorum Decreta* (Basel, etc.), pp. 206, 208, 211; J.D. Mansi, *Sacrorum Conciliorum nova et amplissima Collectio* XXII, 989.

100. *Conciliorum Decreta* p. 212; Mansi XXII, 990–1.

101. *Conciliorum Decreta* p. 215; Mansi XXII, 998.

102. *Conciliorum Decreta* p. 218; Mansi XXII, 1003.

103. *Conciliorum Decreta* p. 243–7; Mansi XXII, 1057–68.

104. Alexius IV was resisted by the inhabitants of Constantinople because they thought "that the Latins had come to destroy their ancient liberties and to hasten to give their realm and nation over to the Roman Pontiff and to subject the Empire to the laws of the Latins" (from a letter of Alexius—*MPL* 215 237AB—and a letter of the crusaders—*MPL* 215 238D—to the Pope).

    Murtzuphlus, who deposed Alexius IV and his father, is reported by Baldwin as being determined on this point. "But he so firmly refused the obedience to the Roman Church and the aid for the Holy Land that Alexius had guaranteed by oath and an imperial rescript, that he would prefer to lose life itself and that Greece should be ruined rather than that the Oriental Church should be made subordinate to Latin prelates" (Letter of Baldwin to Innocent, MPL 215 450A). Most of the Greek prelates who fled the country apparently agreed with him.

105. de Vries, *Op. cit.*

106. "Since, therefore, it is by the marvellous translation of the Empire that the Lord has deigned to open the way to the recovery of the Holy Land and the possession of the former is practically the restoration of the latter," Innocent bade the crusaders stay in Constantinople for one year. (Letter addressed probably in May 1205, to "The Totality of the Clergy and the People in the Christian Army in Constantinople," ed. L. Delisle, "Lettres inédites d'Innocent III," in *B Chartes,* 39 [1873], p. 408.)

107. After 1207 he no longer wrote of help to Constantinople being help to the Holy Land; money and men were to go directly to the Holy Land; he addressed his letters no longer to the "crusaders" or to the "Christian army," but to "the Emperor of

Constantinople," or to the "Inhabitants of Constantinople," or to the "clergy among the pilgrims." Cf. Roscher, *Op. cit.*, pp. 130–1.

108. A.E. Bakalopoulus, *Op. cit.*, pp. 56–92.

109. N. Oikonomides, "Cinq actes inédites du Patriarche Michel Autôrianos," in *REB,* 25 (1967), pp. 113–45, esp. nos. II, III, IV pp. 117–24.

Chapter IV

1. On 9 December 1210 Innocent wrote to the prelates of the Empire informing them that Michael Doucas had broken his truce with Henry, that he tortured and killed Latin prisoners and beheaded all priests (Latin) that he could lay hands on. Yet Latins fought in his army, because they got better pay. They were to be excommunicated ((*MPL* XIII 184).

2. Laurent *Reg,* n. 1225 (shortly before Easter 1220).

3. The letters that passed between Apocaucus and the patriarchs have been edited by V.G. Vasilievsky in *Byzantina Chronica,* 3 (1896), pp. 233–99. Here letters 14, 15, 16, 17 and 26 have been synopsised. Letters of Chomatianus to Germanus and a reply of the Patriarch are in J.B. Pitra, *Op. cit.*, cc. 481–98 The decision of the synod of Thessalonica written by Bardanes is to be found edited by R.-J. Loenertz in *EEBS,* 33 (1964), pp. 484–501. Cf. also D.M. Nicol, "Ecclesiastical Relations between the Despotate of Epirus and the Kingdom of Nicaea in the Years 1215–1230," in *Byz* 22 (1952), pp. 207–28; A.D. Karpozilos, *The Ecclesiastical Controversy between the Kingdom of Nicaea and the Principate of Epirus* (1217–1233) (= Byzantine Texts and Studies 4) (Thessalonica, 1973).

4. 14 Nov. 1216, Pressutti, op. cit., n. 111. Similar letters to 52 metropolitans are recorded as of this date, and later many others were sent.

5. Frederick II, King of the Romans, had claimed that coronation in St. Peter's was the privilege of the Emperors of the Holy Roman Empire. Honorius wrote on 12 April 1217 to the Latin Patriarch of Constantinople to explain that his coronation of Peter was not intended to prejudice his patriarchal rights in that matter—Pressutti, n. 497.

6. Norden, p. 298, is less than just to Honorius in suggesting that the Pope was so much more concerned for his legate than for the Emperor that he invoked aid only for the release of the former. Honorius wrote to the secular powers for the release of both (Pressutti, nn. 684, 685, 688, 689): to Theodore himself and to bishops for the Legate (Pressutti, nn. 687, 690, 691).

7. *Acta Honorii III et Gregorii IX,* ed. A.L. Tautu (= Pont. Comm., III, III) (hereafter cited as Tautu, *Hon.*) (Roma, 1950), n. 25.

8. 11 Dec. 1220, Tautu, *Hon.* n. 73; 13 May 1223, Tautu, n. 112.

9. L. Brehier, *L'Eglise et l'Orient au Moyen Age: Les Croisades,* 3rd. edit. (Paris, 1911), p. 200.

10. Tautu, *Hon.*, n. 17.

11. Tautu, *Hon.*, n. 122.

12. 16 May 1224, Tautu, *Hon.*, n. 124; 25 Dec. 1225, Tautu, *Hon.*, n. 146; 12 Jan. 1226, Tautu, *Hon.*, n. 147.

13. 20 Jan. 1226, Tautu, *Hon.*, n. 148.

14. 15 Jan. 1218, Tautu, *Hon.*, n. 22; 28 Sept. 1218, Tautu, *Hon.*, n. 42; 1 Oct. 1218, Tautu, *Hon.*, n. 43; etc.

15. 13 April 1217, Tautu, *Hon.*, nn. 9, 10.

16. 20 May 1217, Tautu, *Hon.*, n. 13; 13a, 13b, 13c.

17. 19 Feb. 1222, Tautu, *Hon.*, n 90.

18. 29 April 1222, Tautu, *Hon.*, n. 97. Cf. E.A.R. Brown, "The Cistercians in the Latin Empire of Constantinople and Greece 1204–1276," in *Trad.* 14 (1958), pp. 63–120, esp. pp. 78–96.

19. Tautu, *Hon.*, nn. 99, 100.

20. 7 April 1225, Tautu, *Hon.*, n. 133.

21. 18 August 1218, Tautu, *Hon.*, n. 39.

22. 8 August 1220, Tautu, *Hon.*, n. 71. Under Innocent III the Greeks objected rather to the "hominium."

23. 17 Jan. 1217, Tautu, *Hon.*, n. 6.

24. 14 Feb. 1217, Tautu, *Hon.*, n. 7; 9 Jan 1218, Tautu, *Hon.*, n. 21; 13 August 1218, Tautu, *Hon.*, n. 37. By planting a cross behind the altar during the construction of a monastery, a Patriarch indicated that he took that monastery under his exclusive jurisdiction (du Cange, *Glossarium ad scriptores mediae et infimae graecitatis* [Lugduni, 1588], cc. 1432–3).

25. 31 March 1218, Tautu, *Hon.*, n. 30. Cf. Brown, "The Cistercians," pp. 96–103.

26. 18 August 1218, Tautu, *Hon.*, n. 38.

27. 29 Oct. 1218, Tautu, *Hon.*, n. 45; 8 Feb. 1221, Tautu, *Hon.*, n. 74.

28. 6 June 1222, Tautu, *Hon.*, n. 101. The Vicariate was originally set up by Pope Siricius in the last decade of the fourth century.

29. 19 May 1218, Pressutti, n. 1354; cf. also 28 Nov. 1224. Tautu, *Hon.*, n. 128.

30. 21 March 1222, Pressutti, n. 3877.

31. 14 Oct. 1222, Pressutti, n. 4134.

32. 9 Oct. 1223, Pressutti, n. 4529.

33. E.g. 11 April 1219, Tautu, *Hon.*, n. 57 (Crete); 11 March 1222, Tautu, *Hon.*, n. 93, various suffragan dioceses of Greece.

34. A suffragan of Ephesus given to Mitylene, 9 March 1222, Tautu, *Hon.*, n. 92: Chios given to Mitylene, 1222, Tautu, *Hon.*, n. 92a.

35. Charanis, "Monastic Property and the State," p. 97.

36. 14 May 1223, Pressutti, n. 4360.

37. 7/8 Feb. 1224, Pressutti, nn. 4754, 4758.

38. 28 Nov. 1224, Tautu, *Hon.*, n. 128; Jan. 1225, Pressutti, nn. 5270, 5277, 5279.

39. May 1217, Pressutti, n. 584.

40. Letter to the legate 11 June 1218, Pressutti 1428, 1434.

41. 19 Jan. 1219, Tautu, *Hon.*, n. 48; 21 Jan. 1219, Tautu, *Hon.*, n. 49.

42. The pact was dated Gaudete Sunday 1219; was sealed by Robert in May 1221; was confirmed by the Pope on 17 March 1222, Tautu, *Hon.*, n. 95. The Venetians, after remaining for some time under a ban of excommunication and interdict imposed by the legate, Cardinal Colonna, accepted the convention; cfr. 11 April 1223, Tautu, *Hon.*, n. 109. Geoffrey of Achaia and Othon de la Roche of Athens, after a long period under ecclesiastical censures for outrages against ecclesiastics and the Church, followed suit in the same year; cf. 4 Sept. 1223, Tautu, *Hon.*, n. 115.

43. 15 March 1219, Tautu, *Hon.*, n. 59.

44. 13 Sept. 1223, Tautu, *Hon.*, n. 118.

45. 8 Nov. 1222, Tautu, *Hon.*, n. 89.

46. To Queen Alice, Tautu, *Hon.*, n. 85. A similar letter was sent to the Latin hierarchy, Pressutti, n. 3628.

47. J.L. La Monte, "A Register of the Cartulary of the Cathedral of Santa Sophia of Nicosia," in *Byz,* V (1929-1930), pp. 441-522, under date Oct. 1222; J. Hackett, *A History of the Orthodox Church of Cyprus* (London, 1901), p. 81; G. Hill, *A History of Cyprus* III (Cambridge, 1948) chap. XVI (closely dependent on Hackett).

48. 3 Jan. 1222, Tautu, *Hon.*, n. 87.

49. 20 Jan. 1222, Tautu, *Hon.*, n. 88.

50. La Monte, *Op. cit.*, under date 8 March 1222.

51. The document is dated 14 Sept. 1222. If Honorious had by his action of 3 Jan. 1222 intended to banish all Greek bishops from Cyprus, this agreement was a compromise solution. At any rate, he confirmed it on 21 Jan. 1223 in letters to Queen Alice and the Latin hierarchy; Tautu, *Hon.*, n. 108; La Monte, *Op. cit.*, under date 14 Sept. 1222; Pressutti, n. 4212.

52. 10 May 1224, 5 March 1225, Pressutti, nn. 4998, 5361.

53. While the tithes still belonged to the Greeks, Philip d'Ibelin had commuted those due from his estates for a lump sum. The change over to the Latins made him liable again. Cf. Hackett, *Op. cit.*, p.86.

54. "Indeed where there is implicated no abandonment of the canons, tradition, rites, the very faith, if adroitly and with no offence to the Church of Christ the Cypriot bishops can carry on and, by seeming to submit, uphold the churches which in truth are collapsing and save them from the soul-destroying pressure that hangs over them, I think that such economy, or rather such pretence, can be pardoned and, with St. Paul on their side, they should be deemed blameless" (*MPG* 140 601-13, esp. 608D-609A).

55. The Church of Cyprus was autocephalous. Its head was appointed by the Emperor of Constantinople selecting one from three names submitted to him by the electors in Cyprus, in the same way as he appointed the Patriarch of Constantinople.

56. *MPG* 140 613-21. Cf. H.J. Magoulias, "A Study in Roman and Greek Orthodox Relations on the Island of Cyprus between the years A.D. 1196 and 1360," in *The Greek Orthodox Theological Review,* 10 (1964), pp. 75-106.

57. K. Hadjipsaltis, *Op. cit.*, pp. 135-68. Cf. also *idem,* "He ekklesia tes Kyprou kai to en Nikaia oikoumenikon patriarcheion," in *Kypriakai Spoudai* 15 (1951), pp. 63-82.

58. F. Thiriet, *Délibérations des Assemblées Vénitiennes concernant la Romanie,* I (Paris, 1966), n. 23, 11 December 1228, p.30.

59. J.M. Hoeck and R.-J. Loenertz, *Nikolaos-Nectarios von Otranto, Abt von Casole* (Ettal, 1965), p. 166.

60. Tautu, *Hon.*, 1 April 1232, n. 176.

61. MM, III, nn. 13, 14, 15.

62. Dölger, *Reg.*, nn. 1744, 1746. Laurent *Reg.*, (spring 1235) nn. 1282, 1285.

63. M. Roncaglia, *Georges Bardanès, métropolite de Corfou et Barthélémy de l'Ordre Franciscain* (= Studi e Testi Francescani 4) (Rome 1953). The date of this mission, 1231, as proposed by Roncaglia should be corrected to 1235-6 as indicated by Hoeck-Loenertz, *Op. cit.*, p.155; of this book App. II (pp. 148-235) is a detailed study of the correspondence of Bardanes.

64. Tautu, *Hon.*, nn. 179a, 179b. The letter to the Pope is in Greek and Latin, which do not always coincide. Matthew of Paris gives Latin versions of both letters which contain phrases of a less courteous tone, not found in those of the papal register.

65. Tautu, *Hon.*, n. 179.

66. 18 May 1233. Tautu, *Hon.*, n. 193. "Both swords, therefore, are given to the Church but one is to be wielded by the Church, the other is to be drawn for the Church by the secular prince: one is to be utilised by the priest, the other by the soldier at the will of the priest."

67. Their choice of the Eucharist for discussion was due to an incident, when a Greek priest excommunicated a Latin layman for assisting at the Friars' Mass. The Friars remonstrated with the Patriarch and the priest was punished. This incident and all the account given here of the discussion in 1234 are drawn from the report officially presented to the Pope by the four Friars. This report is tersely and factually written and gives every impression of being trustworthy. It has been edited by G. Golubovich, "Disputatio Latinorum et Graecorum," in *ArchOFM*, XII (1919), pp. 428–65. Happily Nicephorus Blemmydes in his *Curriculum Vitae* (ed. Heisenberg, Leipzig, 1896) written some thirty years afterwards (1264) recounts the part he took in the debates. It supports substantially the Latin document.

68. Blemmydes gives his name—Demetrius Karykes.

69. *Ad Amphiloch* c. 18 - Lib. *De Spiritu Sancto* XVIII, *MPG* 32, 151.

70. In Joan. Evang. *MPG* 74, 443.

71. Ep. XXXVIII, *MPG* 32, 331.

72. The account of the debate given here follows the Latin report which is fully confirmed by the Greek text published by P. Canard, "Nicéphore Blemmyde et le mémoire adressé aux envoyés de Grégoire IX" (Nicée, 1234), in *OCP*, XXV (1959), pp. 310–25. Blemmydes's version written in 1264 differs in detail but is substantially the same. It will be utilised more fully when the development of his thought, so influential on John Beccus, is discussed.

73. Report to the Pope, *BBTS* pp. 442–3.

74. *MPG* 76 307; Mansi XXIII, 290–1.

75. Golubovich, *Op. cit.*, p. 446.

76. Presumably, since Vatatzes called them emperors, Manuel I Comnenus and Theodore Lascaris.

77. *Symb. de fid. cath.*, *MPG* 28, 1582–3: *Expos. fid.*, *MPG* 25, 199.

78. *Expos. fid.*, *MPG* 10 983–6.

79. *Quod non sint tres Dei*, *MPG* 45 133.

80. *Lib. de recta in D.N.J.C. fid.*, *MPG* 76 1187; *Scholia de Incarn. Unigen.*, *MPG* 75 1370, 1374, 1383; *Explic.* XII cap., *MPG* 76 307, 307–10: Mansi IX, 375ss, about Theodoretus: Ep. 40. *MPG* 77 183: Ep. 48. *MPG* 77 250.

81. I Cor. XI 23.

82. Mansi 23, 307–20 in Latin. Greek texts exist but they are drawn up in dialogue form and seem to be versions written for local Greek use. The Latin text is a straightforward statement and more like what one would expect of a document to be transmitted to the Pope and the West as an official profession of faith. Allatius asserts that Germanus wrote two tractates on the Holy Spirit and made a collection of patristic quotations from both Greek and Latin Fathers, which he says was more exhaustive than any other he knew. It may be that, utilising his previous writings, Germanus composed this profession of faith. Blemmydes in his *Curriculum vitae* makes no claim to its authorship.

83. He was probably taken to task by Frederick II for his negotiations with the Pope, as being contrary to the spirit of the brotherly love that obtained between himself and Vatatzes. Cf. M.A. Dendias, "Epi mias espistoles tou Friderikou II pros Ioannen Doukan Batatzen," in *EEBS* 13 (1957), pp. 400–411.

84. The Pope on 21 May 1237 before he learnt of Brienne's death wrote to Vatatzes threatening him with an army "whose number is well-nigh infinite," that could be diverted against him from its aim of going to the Holy Land, if he harassed John the Emperor. Rather he should help, counsel and support him. Vatatzes's answer was equally haughty and ended by telling Gregory that he would acknowledge papal rights when the Pope did his. Dölger, Reg. n. 1757; Auvray, n. 3693. Cf. V. Grumel, "L'authenticité de la lettre de Jean Vatatzès Empereur de Nicée au Pape Grégoire IX," in *EO,* 29 (1930), pp. 450–8.

85. Auvray, nn. 2909–11.

86. Auvray, n. 3382.

87. Tautu, *Hon.,* n. 217.

88. Tautu, *Hon.,* n. 252.

89. Auvray, n. 4035.

90. Auvray, nn. 4209–17. The Crown of Thorns had been given to the Venetians in lieu of 13134 hyperpers already borrowed and spent. Cf. TT vol. XIII doc. xxxcvi.

91. 50,000 troops for Constantinople reached Venice, but while they were held up there by Frederick, their leader died, the troops melted away and very few ever reached Greece. (Cf. J. Longnon, *L'Empire Latin de Constantinople et le Principauté de Morée* [Paris, 1949], pp. 179–80). Gregory wrote to Frederick, 17 March 1238: "We sent Dominican and Franciscan Friars to Vatatzes . . . to the said Patriarch of Nicaea and the prelates and bishops under him . . . urging them with paternal warnings and supplications . . . to return to Catholic union. But they, as we learnt from the trustworthy report of the Friars, put forward a variety of errors against orthodox faith and, stopping their ears like the asps, could by no warnings be induced to come back to the way of ecclesiastical unity. At this We were very much saddened, and that the power of plucking up and planting might not have been given to Us from on high in vain, against the said schismatical Vatatzes and his supporters, whose excommunication once every year We publicly renew, since their wounds cannot be healed by that kind of medicine, We encouraged many princes, barons and soldiers to take the Cross, not so much to aid Constantinople as to strengthen and defend the Catholic faith in the regions of the East." Frederick should, therefore, assist, not hinder. (Tautu, *Hon.,* n. 236).

92. Auvray, nn. 3717–9, 3720.

93. 21 May 1237, Tautu, *Hon.,* n. 226.

95. 27 Jan. 1238, Tautu, *Hon.,* n. 229. The Council of Lyons had decreed this punishment for princes who failed to rid their territories of heresy; Hefele-Leclercq, *Histoire des Conciles,* vol. V, p. 1331.

95. 7 June 1238, Tautu, *Hon.,* n. 248b.

96. 9 Aug. 1238, Tautu, *Hon.,* nn. 248, 248a.

97. Auvray, nn. 4484–90.

98. Patriarch Nicholas in the Council of Lyons; Matthew of Paris, *Chronica Majora,* ed. H.R. Luard, Rolls Series (London, 1874), Bk. IV, pp. 431–2.

99. 18 July 1231, Tautu, *Hon.,* n. 167.

100. 12 Nov. 1231, Tautu, *Hon.,* n. 170.

101. Tautu, *Hon.,* n. 173.

102. Their only argument may have been that the Greek formula attributed the action of baptism to the Holy Spirit, whereas the Latin formula attributed it to the Church and men. Cf. C. Giannelli, "Un documento sconosciuto della polemica tra Greci e Latini intorno alla formula battesimale," in *OCP* X (1944), pp. 150–67.

103. Tautu, *Hon.*, nn. 178, 178a. Cf. Hoeck-Loenertz, *Nickolaos-Nektarios von Otranto*, pp. 63–7, 194.

104. The Dominicans were active among the Cumans (Tautu, *Hon.*, n. 159) and neighbouring tribes (Ibid., nn. 224, 225). A Dominican was made bishop of Bosnia (Ibid., nn. 238, 251). They were working also in Morocco (Ibid., n. 149), Poland and Kiev (Ibid., nn. 186, 188), Russia (Ibid., n. 189), in the Holy Land, Armenia, Egypt (Ibid., n. 227a), in Greece; and in 1240 eight of them went to evangelise Georgia (Ibid., n. 261).

105. 22 Feb. 1234, Ibid., n. 201. Bela swore: "We will endeavour in good faith according to our strength to expel from the lands subject to our jurisdiction and from such as shall be so, God granting, in the future, all heretics and other Christians who, abandoning the Christian faith, are perverted to the superstition of the Israelites or the Jews, by whatever name they may go, and false Christians. We will compel those who in our land do not obey the Roman Church to obey that Church according to the rite of each nation that [i.e. rite] is not opposed to the Catholic faith."

106. He was also to endow the diocese sufficiently: 14 Nov. 1234, Tautu, *Hon.*, n. 209.

107. 9 March 1238, Tautu, *Hon.*, n. 230. The emphasis on unleavened bread probably reflects the controversy in the synod of Nymphaeum.

108. 13 April 1240, Tautu, *Hon.*, n. 262.

109. 26 June 1238, Tautu, *Hon.*, n. 241.

110. 26 June 1238, Tautu, *Hon.*, nn. 242, 243.

111. 31 July 1238, Tautu, *Hon.*, nn. 245, 246, 247.

112. R.L. Wolff, "Politics in the Latin Patriarchate of Constantinople," *DOP*, 8 (1954), pp. 225–303.

113. Th. Uspenskij, *Organisation du second Empire bulgaire* (Odessa, 1879), pp. 75–8.

Chapter V

1. Encyclical, *Eger cui levia*, 1245.

2. 13 July 1243, *Registres d'Innocent IV (1243–1254)*, ed. E. Berger, (Paris, 1884–1921), n. 22.

3. 24 July 1243, *Acta Innocentii PP. IV (1243–1254)* (= Pont. Comm. III, IV), ed. T.T. Haluscynskyj and M.M. Wojnar (Rome, 1962) (hereafter = Wojnar), n. 2; repeated 2 September 1243, Ibid., n. 6.

4. 17 Sept., Berger, n. 123.

5. 16 May 1244, Wojnar, no. 12.

6. 30 May 1244, Wojnar, n. 13.

7. This decree was applied for the full three years in France and Italy; was suspended immediately in Germany owing to the political upheavals consequent on Frederick's deposition; was vigorously resisted in England, and had good results in Poland and Portugal; cf. H. Wolter, *Lyon I et Lyon II* (= Histoire des Conciles Oecuméniques, 7) (Paris, 1966), p. 95.

8. Cf. Berger, n. 3468, 3 Dec. 1246: "Licet imperii constantinopolitani tranquillum statum ei prosperum affectemus, non tamen nostre intentionis existit post constitutionem in

Lugdunensi concilio a nobis super hoc editam importabilem imponere sarcinam humeris subjectorum."

There is one exception. On 20 August 1252 Innocent ordered bishops in the Morea to provide 1000 silver marks for Venice and Achaia provided that these supplied sufficient defence of Constantinople for one year (Wojnar, n. 82). Earlier, in 1246, he had encouraged the Master of the Spanish Order of St. James, in return for certain concessions and a sum of money, to go with a strong contingent to establish a house of the Order in Constantinople. In the event the project fell through, for Baldwin could not pay (R.L. Wolff, "Mortgage and Redemption of an Emperor's Son," in *Spec,* 29 [1954], pp. 83–4).

9. 22 March 1244, Wojnar, n. 8; 21–22 March 1245, Ibid., n. 19.

10. 21 March 1245, Wojnar, n. 20; 25 March 1245, Ibid., n. 21.

11. Wojnar, nn. 52–56.

12. 3 March-3 May, Wojnar, nn. 26–29a. For the part that the Franciscan, John of Pian Carpino, played in this, cf. C. Dawson, *The Mongol Mission* (London, 1955), pp. xvii, 70.

13. 27 August 1247, Wojnar, n. 43.

14. Wojnar, nn. 46, 48.

15. 7 July 1246, Wojnar, n. 31. Two weeks later the Pope answered a letter of the Archbishop of Nicosia complaining of the disorders in some Greek monasteries. He told him that he already had the necessary powers to deal with the situation, but strengthened his hand by not allowing appeals (25 July 1246, Wojnar, n. 30).

16. 4 June 1247, Wojnar, n. 35.

17. 3 August 1247, Wojnar, n. 37.

18. Symeon II was the Greek Patriarch of Antioch from c. 1206 to c. 1240. At one time he had given obedience to Rome, for in 1217/8 he was formally received back into communion by the Patriarch and synod of Nicaea (Laurent, *Reg,* n. 1220). "His successor was David, who in 1245 submitted to the Pope and for two years was the only patriarch in Antioch, the Latin, Albert, having retired to Europe to complain of the arrangement at the Council of Lyons, where he died. The next Latin patriarch, the pope's nephew Opizon, reached Antioch in 1248. Soon afterwards he quarreled with David's successor, Euthymius, who rejected papal supremacy and was banished from the city" (Setton, *Crusades,* II p. 566).

19. 7 Aug. 1247, Wojnar, n. 40.

20. Wojnar, nn. 60–63.

21. 21 July 1250, Wojnar, n. 74. The Archbishop who was recalled by Brother Lawrence was Neophytus. In exile since c. 1240, he appealed to Vatatzes. The Greek Emperor and his queen both wrote to Henry I, King of Cyprus. Henry replied saying that Neophytus, too, had written and that one of his priests, Constantine, had spoken with him, recounting the kindness shown to them by Vatatzes. So in Cyprus the way was prepared for Lawrence's pacific activity. (Hadjipsaltes, "The Relations of Cyprus to the Empire of Nicaea").

22. Wojnar, n. 78. This would be a yearly event. The Pope did the same each Maundy Thursday; Cf. Tautu, *Hon.,* n. 236.

23. 20 December 1251, Wojnar, n. 79. The papal document gives the name of the elect as "George"; it is probably a mistake for "Germanus."

24. Same date, Wojnar, n. 80.

25. 25 February 1254, Wojnar, nn. 103, 103a.

26. 6 March 1254, Wojnar, n. 105.
27. Tautu, *Hon.*, n. 260.
28. Wojnar, n. 17.
29. 22 November 1248, Wojnar, n. 67. Cf. P. Pelliot, "Les Mongols et la Papauté," in *Revue de l'Orient Chrétien,* 23 (1923), pp. 1–33, 24 (1924), pp. 225–335. C. Dawson, *Op. cit.*, contains translations of Pian Carpini's report, of Innocent's letters, of the Khan's replies, of William Rubuck's report (which is known as the *Itinerary*), as well as of reports of other missionaries.
30. 20 February 1253, Wojnar, n. 86.
31. 14 May 1253, Wojnar, n. 89; 21 May, ibid. n. 89a.
32. Cf. Wojnar, p.154, n. 6.
33. 29 August 1254, Wojnar, n. 109; cf. p.187, n. 1.
34. Frederick's messenger in these negotiations was Fra Elias, companion of St. Francis and second Minister General of the Order. He was excommunicated by Gregory in 1240 and by Innocent in 1244 for his support of Frederick.
35. Dölger, *Reg.* n. 1760. Vatatzes would become a vassal of Frederick, if the latter would eject the Latins, with Baldwin and his family, from Constantinople. (The source of this information, however, is not altogether above suspicion, at least as regards details.)
36. Wojnar, n. 34.
37. 28 May 1249, Wojnar, n. 70.
38. 28 May 1249, Wojnar, n. 71.
39. Frederick, informed by Vatatzes, refers to it with indignation in his reply dated September 1250: the Friars "as is their usual custom were sowing cockle between father and son." But they found "the bond of affection solid and unshaken": N. Festa, "Le lettere greche di Federigo II," in *Archivio Storico Italiano,* 13 (1894), n. III.
40. John XVI. 14.
41. N. Blemmydes, *Curriculum vitae,* ed. Heisenberg, pp. 74–80.
42. Frederick wrote, probably in February 1250, to the Despot of Epirus, Michael, asking him for the safe passage of these troops to Durazzo, whence Sicilian ships would take them on to Sicily: Festa, *Lettere,* no. I.
43. Festa, *Lettere,* no. III.
44. "Vita eiusdem Innocentii Papae IV scripta a Fratre Nicolao de Curbio Ordinis Minorum, postmodum episcopo Assinatensi," in L. Muratori, *Rerum Italicarum Scriptores,* vol. III 1 Milan 1723, 592e, 592k. Fra Nicholas was the Pope's chaplain.
45. 8 August 1250. Wojnar, n. 76. "Oh! If in our day this grace might be granted from on high that among these waves, by which the invincible barque of St. Peter is buffeted, the longstanding fissure of division, which manifestly spells peril to the Christian faith, might be welded firm by the timely re-uniting of the parts. . . . Hence it is that We await your arrival with the joyous approval of apostolic congratulation, hoping that your feet may bring and carry back the hoped-for peace, and with suppliant prayer begging the mercy of divine goodness that it may crown with the desired result the efforts of your labours and the goodwill of your intention."
46. Wojnar, App. pp. 195–9. This document is not dated. It is possible that it was brought by the embassy of 1253, but the reference in it to Innocent's envoys suggests a more immediate connection with the mission of 1251.
47. *Theodori Ducae Lascaris Epistulae CCXVII,* ed. N. Festa (Florence, 1898), n. XVIII, p. 24.

48. Curbio, p. 592k.

49. 22 August 1252, Wojnar, n. 82.

50. June-11 July 1253, Wojnar, nn. 93–99.

51. At some date, possibly as early as 1248, Baldwin mortgaged his son and heir, Philip, to a merchant in Venice, where the boy lived till June 1259, when he was redeemed by Alfonso, King of Castile, his parents being still unable to repay the loan (of 24,000 hyperpers?) (R.L. Wolff, "Mortgage and Redemption of an Emperor's Son," in *Spec.*, 29 [1954], pp. 45–84).

52. Curbio, p. 592m.

53. Fortunately they are preserved, though not in the registers of Innocent IV, but in those of his successor, Alexander IV, to whom it fell to continue the negotiations. In his letters about these Alexander states what the proposals were and what Innocent had agreed to, and he records some of his predecessor's judgments. The account given in this book is based on Alexander's documents to be found in *Acta Alexandri PP IV (1254–1261)* (= Pont, Comm., III, IV, II) ed. T.T. Haluscynskyj and M.M. Wojnar (Rome, 1966) (hereafter = H. & W.), n. 28; also in Raynaldus, 1256, 48–53. Pachymeres (Pach. I, pp. 366, 374) twice briefly mentions this Greek initiative. V. Laurent (Laurent *Reg.* n. 1223) mistakenly attaches these references to an action of the Church of Nicaea in December 1219. Laurent's n. 1223 should be cancelled.

54. "Super hoc igitur praefati praedecessoris iudicium non mutantes . . . te providimus" (Alexander to Constantine, H. & W., n. 28a), Innocent "statuerit ad illas partes celebres nuntios destinare" (ibid., repeated in a letter to Theodore II Lascaris, H. & W., n. 28b).

55. Wojnar, n. 70.

56. "That all should live and go forward within the profession of the catholic faith and culture, this We desire beyond all else. We long for it with a deeper yearning and as what would most satisfy our desires, and with the deepest longing We look to this as to the chief instrument of salvation. This, I say, union or bond would flood our heart with the dew of an inestimable joy, if adherence to the same faith should unite together the nations of the different races into one people worthy of acceptance by Christ" (Beginning of Innocent's letter to his legate Châteauroux, Wojnar, n. 105).

57. W. de Vries, "Innocenz IV. (1243–1254) und der christliche Osten," in *Ostkirchliche Studien,* 2 (1963), pp. 113–31.

Chapter VI

1. Greg, pp. 53–4; Georgius Acropolites, *Annales* ed. I. Bekker (Bonn, 1836), p.113. Apropos of the election of Arsenius, Acropolites wrote: "Rulers prefer patriarchs to be of low station and of mediocre talent, to yield easily to their wishes as if they were orders."

2. H. & W., App. n. 1, taken from N. Festa. *Theodori II Ducae Lascaris Epistolae CCXVII,* (Firenze, 1898), pp. 202–3.

3. H. & W., n. 28a.

4. This we have freely used above in the section on Innocent IV and Vatatzes.

5. H. & W., n. 28.

6. H. & W., n. 28b.

7. H. & W., n. 28c.

8. Acropolites *Annales,* p.149.

9. "A Letter of the Most Holy Metropolitan of Thessalonica. Lord Manuel Dishypatus to the Pope of the Elder Rome, Lord Alexander, as from the person of the All-holy Patriarch Arsenius." The Greek text—very defective—taken from Vat. Gr. 1409 268v-269v, is to be found in H. & W., App. n.6. The last section reads something like this: ". . . and an indelible proof of this, the worthy legate sent by Your Holiness to my God-governed, holy and wise King and to My Mediocrity, and the Brothers with him, approved men, adorned with prudence and piety, and distinguished for secular and religious knowledge, who were received, welcomed and worthily honoured by our most mighty and holy King and God-crowned Emperor, and by Our Mediocrity. They conveyed to us the message given them by Your Holiness and we replied in a suitable manner in so far as the occasion offered and the nature of the business demanded. Especially the God-honoured and God-crowned, holy Emperor and King, brilliantly endowed with ready wit, honoured them in word and deed, and returned cautious words to their words. He was set on examining the scheme of the negotiations (what they had to say, I mean) and on bringing it to completion in act, if the legate of Your Holiness was empowered for a full and effective exercise of your authority. He had, indeed, some of the authority of Your Holiness—nay, rather, not even some; for to receive he was the complete legate, but to give in return he had no power, not the slightest. Hence the words remained words, without acquiring the cover of a deed. Your mandataries, then, returned home to Your Holiness with their authority to receive, to supplement what they lacked—either for themselves or others—so that so arduous a mission of words only, divorced from deeds, might not be dubbed pointless and useless, and that, having returned bearers of the intentions of my holy Emperor and of Our Mediocrity, they might receive the [necessary] authority from the Holiness of Your Majesty. Hasten, therefore, most holy Lord, with all possible goodwill and zeal to the longed-for accomplishment of this good work and give a portion to the seven held by us as good, and even the eight, with the fraternal honours of Your Holiness and your proclamations, just as you see us too not cast down (?) or losing heart [sitting inactive] with hands folded (according to the proverb of Solomon), but for our part zealous and active, and lifting our hands towards God praying for the unity of the Church and indeed choosing that all the most holy brethren, I mean the archbishops, of our eparchy, in number five hundred, should be gathered together, when we shall hear that the apocrisiarii on their return have arrived back to us; but now not more than thirty have convened with Our Mediocrity and these for an affair of my holy Emperor and of a well-defined purpose concerned with our province.

   "By the power of Him who gathers together what is scattered and who unites the divided, the omnipotent Christ, our veritable God, let all of us, in what place soever separated, be united quickly and by the communication of the Holy Spirit let us go forward with one mind and one voice, according to the mouthpiece of Christ, Paul the apostle and [?], and let us not utter the phrase of division: 'I am of Paul, another of Cephas', but all of Christ and of the same Spirit, fitted together into the substance of one body and acknowledging the head, Christ, who is glorified exceedingly in the aspirations of love and the peaceful institutions for piety.

   "Farewell in the Lord, most holy and blessed Lord-bishop."

   Arsenius had been a member of the embassy sent to Innocent IV in 1253.

   Constantine, bishop of Orvieto, died in the east towards the end of 1256, i.e. before he returned to report on his mission. His body was brought back to Italy for burial: cf. Th. Käppeli, "Kurze Mitteilungen über mittelalterliche Dominikanerschriftsteller," in *ArchOP,* X (1940), p. 289.

10. Cf. V. Laurent, "Le Pape Alexandre IV (1254–1261) et L'Empire de Nicée," in *EO,* 34 (1935), pp. 26–55.

11. "Historia dogmatum," in A. Mai. *Patrum nova bibliotheca* VIII, (Roma, 1871), p. 28. Pachymeres reports that the proposals of Vatatzes were a "synodical action." He goes on to say "It would have been done, if they had accepted." Later he writes that Michael had the official, written, ecclesiastical record (to kodikion tes ekklesias) with the prelates' signatures produced in proof. Pach. I, pp. 366, 367, 374–5.

12. H. & W., n. 4.

13. H. & W., n. 19.

14. 22 April 1258, H. & W., n. 39; 22 June 1248, ibid., n. 39a.

15. 3 July 1260, H. & W., n. 46.

16. H. & W., n. 46a. There is no certainty when this Raphael held his synod of Nicosia nor, apart from this document, is there evidence that he existed. Some authorities place him shortly after 1260, others between 1270 and 1280, E.C. Furber (in Setton, *Crusades* II, p. 628) as from 1278 to 1286; others later still. It is likely, however, that the Constitution was composed shortly after the last of its sources saw the light, viz. 1260. There is no mention in it of a Greek metropolitan, and so probably Germanus had already ceased to hold office; but there is no information as to when that was.

17. *Acta Urbani IV, Clementis IV, Gregorii X (1261–1276)* (= Pont. Com. III, V, I) ed. A. Tautu, (Roma, 1963), n.4. (Hereafter cited as Tautu, *Urban IV*) 23 January 1263.

18. 13 April 1264, Raynaldus, 1264, n. 66.

19. Tautu, *Urban IV,* n. 14.

20. S. Runciman, *The Sicilian Vespers* (Pelican Books, London, 1960), pp. 52–3.

21. The main sources for the Greek history of this period are
    a) G. Acropolites, *Annales,* ed. I. Bekker (Bonn, 1836) (for the Kingdom of Nicaea), who barely mentions ecclesiastical events;
    b) G. Pachymeres, *De Michaele Palaeologo,* ed. I. Bekker (Bonn, 1835); and
    c) N. Gregoras, *Byzantina historia,* ed. L. Schopenus (Bonn, 1829), the last two treating of ecclesiastical events at length. For the years under review in this chapter, cf. Acropolites, pp.170ss, Pachymeres, pp. 1–105 passim, and Gregoras, pp. 61–95.

22. D.M. Nicol, "The Date of the Battle of Pelagonia," in *BZ,* 19 (1956) pp. 68–71; D.J. Geanakoplos, *Emperor Michael Palaeologus and the West* (Cambridge, Mass., 1959), pp. 47–74.

23. Norden, App. 13. The pact, probably of May 1260, was perhaps never implemented; may be, never agreed upon.

24. Agreed on in Nymphaeum 13 March 1261, ratified in Genoa 10 July 1261.

25. It was composed of 800 men, according to Greg., I, p. 87.

26. Pach. I, pp. 163–4.

27. *Les registres d'Urbain IV (1261–1264),* ed. J. Guiraud, (Paris, 1901 ff.), n.131. No date, but probably June 1262.

28. 19 January 1263, Tautu, *Urban IV,* n. 3.

29. According to Innocent IV's chaplain, Nicholas of Curbio, Charles had offered as early as 1252 or 1253 to take over Sicily (Muratori, *RIS,* III, I, p. 592k).

30. Pach. I, p.168. Their names were Nicephoritzes and Alourbades. The former was captured and flayed in southern Italy by followers of the Latin ex-Emperor. The latter managed to escape and may even have managed to deliver his message to Rome (R.-J. Loenertz, "Notes d'histoire et de chronologie byzantine II," in *Byzantina et Franco-graeca* [Roma, 1970], pp. 432–4).

31. A Dondaine, "Nicholas de Cotrone et les sources du Contra Errores Graecorum de Saint Thomas," in *Divus Thomas,* 28 (1950), pp. 313–40.

32. Tautu, *Urban IV,* n. 6.

33. *Annales Minorum . . . auctore L. Waddingo*[3], IV, p. 204.

34. "Noviter enim tunc fuerat cervicibus nostris impositium iugum apostolicae servitutis et in illo nostrae novitatis initio tot et tantis fuimus sollicitudinibus et curis obsessi, quod ad sustinendos inundantium super nos negotiorum impetus reputabamus nos quasi penitus impotentes. Sed quantumcumque essemus negotiorum varietatibus occupati, semper tamen cogitabamus . . ." (Guiraud, *Reg.*, n. 295).

35. Dölger, *Reg.*, n. 1911.

36. R. Roberg, *Die Union zwischen der griechischen und der lateinischen Kirche auf dem II. Konzil von Lyon (1274)* (= Bonner historische Forschungen 24) (Bonn, 1964), p. 31, n. 7.

37. Tautu, *Urban IV,* n. 6, p. 20. Palaeologus's actions should correspond with his words.

38. Guiraud, *Reg.*, nn. 231, 232, dated 27 April 1263.

39. Ibid., nn. 228–30 of 7 May 1263.

40. Ibid., n. 94, 26 April 1262.

41. Ibid., n. 151, 11 November 1262.

42. It is clear that no papal letter on union with the Greeks was written without reference to all the previous correspondence.

43. William of Villehardouin had regained his liberty only at the end of 1261 or the beginning of 1262 by paying a large ransom and surrendering four key fortresses of his territories. Michael meant to use these to conquer the whole. A campaign in 1263 ended with the defeat of the Greeks.

44. On 1 August 1263 Urban asked Villehardouin to abstain from attacking Byzantine possessions as long as negotiations for a truce were in progress (Guiraud, *Reg.*, n. 325).

45. Tautu, *Urban IV,* n. 6, p. 23.

46. Cotrone's book was sent by the Pope to Thomas Aquinas for examination. Aquinas utilised some of it in his *Contra errores graecorum* and, since Nicholas had garbled some of his Greek quotations to suit his thesis, Aquinas was led into mistakes (A. Dondaine, "Nicholas Cotrone. . .").

    Dondaine has summarised the conclusions of several of his articles about Cotrone and Saint Thomas in the introduction of *Sancti Thomae de Aquina, Opera omnia* (Editio Leoniana) Tom. XL, pars A, *Contra errores graecorum* (Rome, 1967), pp. A1–A65, where he has also published on pp. A109–A151 a critical edition of the Latin text of Cotrone's *Libellus de fide Trinitatis ex diversis auctoritatibus sanctorum grecorum confectus contra grecos.* No manuscript of the Greek text is known to be extant.

47. Tautu, *Urban IV,* n. 10a.

48. Tautu, *Urban IV,* n. 10, p. 36. Cotrone remained in Constantinople afterwards. According to Pachymeres (I, p. 360), he was allowed to adopt Greek religious dress and would have obtained a church for his own use, had he not lost the favour of the Emperor. He was exiled to near Heraclea, always professing his readiness to help. He died probably in Viterbo between 2 October and 21 May 1276 (Loenertz, *Art. cit.*, p. 436).

49. Pach. I, p. 375.

50. Roberg, *Op. cit.*, p. 28.

51. He was not to know that Cotrone had changed some of the Greek texts. But the texts, unchanged, sufficed to convince a whole series of later theologians.

52. Similarly George Metochites († 1328) and Constantine Meliteniotes († 1307) both died still imprisoned, after enduring 45 and 24 years respectively of prison for their faith. For an account of the evolution of Greek opinion about the Procession of the Holy Spirit, cf. chapter VIII.

53. 23 May 1264, Tautu, *Urban,* n.10.

54. Geanakoplos (pp. 175–6) makes the letter carried by Cotrone the result of the defeat in the Morea. Allowance being made for a prolonged campaign, the journey of the embassy from Constantinople to Orvieto, the necessary interval between the delivery of the letter and the inditing of the reply which is dated 23 May, and the organising of an embassy of two suitable Friars to return with Cotrone to Constantinople—that seems impossible.

    He states also that Palaeologus, to win the Pope's sympathy more effectively, offered aid for a crusade. Neither Palaeologus's letter nor Urban's reply mentions any such offer or says anything at all about a crusade.

55. 13 May 1264, Guiraud, *Reg,* nn. 577–9, i.e., while he was preparing his answer to the letter of the Emperor Michael (dated 13 May), which may account for the conservatism of its content, despite the warmth of its tone.

56. Guiraud, *Reg,* nn. 375–97, 468 ss.

57. Ibid., nn. 758–9, 778, 853–4, 857, 870.

58. Ibid., nn. 804, 805.

59. 8 May, Ibid., n. 800.

60. *Les registres de Clément IV (1265–1268),* ed. E. Jordan (Paris, 1893–1945), n. 216.

61. 19 March, Jordan, *Reg,* n. 217.

62. The imperial letter is not extant. It was accompanied by a letter from the Patriarch written either before 14 September 1266, when Germanus abdicated (Pachymeres, I. p. 299) or after 28 December 1266 when Joseph was elected. The latter alternative is the more unlikely. For information on the content of the Emperor's letter one must rely solely on the papal answer, dated 4 March 1267, Tautu, *Urban,* n. 23.

63. Apparently the Curia knew nothing of these proposals till they were produced by the Greek envoys. It seems as though the four Friars, finding a new Pope on the throne when they returned, never reported their mission. Roberg (p. 52, n. 61) is mistaken in referring *in nostra protulerunt praesentia* to the Latin envoys; it refers to the Greek apocrisiarii.

64. 4 March 1267, Tautu, *Urban,* n. 24. The patriarch who wrote to the Pope was Germanus (cf. n. 42 above): the Patriarch who received the answer was Joseph.

65. The two Friars who accompanied Cotrone to Constantinople returned after a protracted stay *(qui apud te [Palaeologum] moram diutius contraxerunt),* but as far as is known with no positive result—not even information about the written proposals that, "it is said," the four Friars of the earlier embassy had agreed to; cf. Tautu, *Urban,* n. 23, p. 65.

66. While Pope Clement was trying to arrange that Manfred's widow should marry Henry of Castile and that Henry should be given Corfu, Charles appointed Gazo Echinard, the son of the murdered ruler of Corfu, as his Captain General, and within two months he had the island organized; cf. S. Borsari, "La politica bizantina di Carlo d'Angio dal 1266 al 1271," in *Archivio storico per le Provincie Napoletane,* NS 35 (1956), p. 322; D.M. Nicol, "The Relations of Charles of Anjou with Nikephorus of Epirus" in *BForsch,* IV (1972), pp. 170–94.

67. 24 May 1267, Geanakoplos, *Op. cit.,* p. 197.

68. *in presentia . . . domini Clementis . . . papae IV ac ipso consentiente.*

69. 27 May 1267, Geanakoplos, *Op. cit.,* pp. 197–200; Runciman, *Op. cit.,* pp. 153–4.

70. 9 June 1267, Tautu, *Urban,* n. 26.

71. Ibid. It is not clear why Clement makes this flat statement. Had the bearers of the profession of faith so declared before leaving for home? Or had the "legate" with another letter from the Emperor (to be discussed immediately) brought this assurance? In this case it looks as if Palaeologus had already received the profession of faith and authorised the statement.

72. Letter of the Conclave to the Apostolic Legate in France; 15 May 1270, Tautu, *Urban*, n. 29, p. 81. Charles of Anjou had facilitated their return. He gave a safe-conduct for Thomas Meliteniotes and others dated 21 March 1267.

73. I.e. ten days before the anti-Greek pact of 27 May; Tautu, *Urban*, n. 25.

74. This does not necessarily mean that he had not received it. He had been absolved from his excommunication by Patriarch Joseph only a few months before (2 February 1267) and, till his relations with his hierarchy had settled a little more, he would not have been so imprudent as to demand the bishops' acceptance of the Latin faith.

75. *si affectui responderet effectus;* 17 May 1267, Tautu, *Urban*, n. 25.

76. *Pach.* I, pp. 251–317; Greg., pp. 93–108.

77. Borsari, *Op. cit.*, p. 339.

78. TT, n.CCCLXX (III, p.159ss) *Judicum Venetorum in causis piraticis contra Graecos decisiones, A.D. 1278 mense martio* gives the names of 90 pirates of all races (mainly Italians and Greeks) operating from islands, Monemvasia, Smyrna and a variety of other places, who *durante treugua et existente inter ipsum [Palaeologum] et commune Veneciarum* attacked Venetian ships or colonies, for which the Signoria demanded compensation from the Emperor. In the treaties of 1265, 1268 and 1277 (hence the judicial process of 1278) there were clauses about this. As the Emperor recovered the Greek islands piracy increased, because many of the pirates sailed under the Greek flag. Some (the Genoese) preyed particularly on Venetian shipping. Cf. P. Charanis, "Piracy in the Aegean during the Reign of Michael VIII Palaeologus," in *Annuaire de l'Institut de Philologie et d'Histoire Orientales et Slaves,* X (1950), pp. 127–36.

79. Runciman, *Op. cit.*, p. 121.

Chapter VII

1. Signed 14 September 1269.

2. This is now in the Bibliothèque Nationale of Paris with written in it a note to say who gave it and when.

3. 15 May 1270. Tautu, *Urban*, n. 29. This letter is the sole source of knowledge of the communications the Emperor Michael sent to King Louis. What it reports is not at first hand, but through the medium of Louis's account.

4. Most of the cardinals as members of the Curia had personal knowledge of them.

5. Tautu, *Urban*, n. 29a.

6. Mansi, 24, 39.

7. Pachymeres, I, pp. 369–70.

8. Cf. the letter of the conclave to King Louis. "We were on the point of sending letters and envoys to Your Magnificence [the Emperor Michael] but at their [the cardinals'] advice we delayed the despatch"; Gregory to Michael, 24 October 1272, Tautu, *Urban*, n. 32, p. 93.

9. Charles accompanied Gregory to Viterbo and was in Rome from 29 March till 4 June: Gregory was in Rome from mid-March till early April.

10. The quotation in note 8 continues: "while with some anxiety We waited for messengers from you in regard to what . . . Pope Clement had recently written, so that We might send Our envoys more fully instructed for action."

11. J. Guiraud, *Les registres de Grégoire X (1272–1276).* (Paris, 1892), n. 220, 11 March 1273.

12. Since his document was divided into three parts, dealing respectively with the crusade against the Saracens, the union with the Greeks, and abuses to be reformed in the Church, it has come to be called the *Opus Tripartitum*. The second part concerning the Greeks is to be found in Mansi 24, 125B-132D, of which large sections have been translated into French in H. Wolter & H. Holstein, *Lyon I et Lyon II* (= Histoire des Conciles Oecumèniques 7) (Paris, 1966), pp. 268–72; and in E. Brown, *Appendix ad Fasciculum rerum expetendarum et fugiendarum* (London, 1690), pp. 207–23, finely analysed by B. Roberg, *Op. cit.*, pp. 85–95.

13. He had made a pilgrimage to the Holy Land. Cf. D.A. Mortier. *Histoire des Maîtres Généraux de l'Ordre des Frères Prêcheurs* I (Paris, 1903), pp. 415–664; II, pp. 89–93.

14. John Parastron was a Franciscan, a Greek, who had made himself an apostle of union in Constantinople. An admirer of the Greek rite, in which he participated as much as he could, he was in constant communication with the Patriarch and the synod, persuading them of the necessity and ease of union. Cf. Pachymeres, I, p. 371. Cf. G. Golubovich, "Cenni storici su Fra Giovanni Parastron," in *Bess.*, X (1906), pp. 295–304.

15. This description of Palaeologus's letter is taken from Gregory's answer to it; Tautu, *Urban,* n. 32.

16. Tautu, *Urban,* n. 32, of rather more than 3000 words, in addition to the text of Pope Clement's profession of faith.

17. Tautu, *Urban,* p. 99.

18. 25 October, Tautu, *Urban,* n. 33.

19. 25 October 1272, Tautu, *Urban,* n. 34.

20. Before 26 October 1272 when Charles gave orders for the safety of the papal envoys.

21. E. Martène, and U. Durand, *Veterum scriptorum . . . amplissima collectio* VII (Paris, 1733), ep. VIII, pp. 229–30.

22. Ibid., ep. XI, pp. 232–3.

23. Pach. I, p. 368. Apropos of the Emperor's relations with Pope Gregory, Pachymeres wrote: "It was obvious that the Emperor was striving for [ecclesiastical] peace only because of fear of Charles and that without this he would never for a moment have considered it; whereas the Curia was bent on the good itself of concord and union." (p. 370).

24. Pach. I, p. 193.

25. Pach., pp. 337–8. Cf. V. Laurent, "L'excommunication du patriarche Joseph par son prédecesseur Arsène," in *BZ,* 30 (1929–30), pp. 489–96, who concludes that it was very improbable.

26. Pach., p. 368.

27. Ibid., pp. 374–8.

28. Ibid., pp. 378–83. Cf. V. Laurent, "Le serment antilatin du patriarche Joseph I (juin 1273)," in *EO,* 26 (1927), pp. 396–407.

29. Ibid. pp. 380–1, 383–4; Greg. I, pp. 129–30. Both authors dilate on the high reputation, the ability and the honesty of Beccus, and state clearly that his change of mind was the

result of his study of the Greek Fathers and of only Greek Fathers. He was not "plied with select passages from the Latin fathers . . . carefully chosen to illustrate the basic identity of belief between Orthodox and Catholics" (D.M. Nicol, *The Last Centuries of Byzantium 1261–1453* [London, 1972], p. 59). Beccus knew little or no Latin and had no knowledge of Latin patristic literature beyond a few texts (probably only four) available to him in translation. G. Hofmann, "Patriarch Johann Bekkos unde die lateinische Kultur," in *OCP,* 11 (1945), pp. 140–161.

30. Tautu, *Urban,* n. 36.

31. Tautu, *Urban,* n. 37. Similar letters went to ex-Emperor Baldwin, and to many prelates and barons.

32. Martène, *Op. cit.,* ep. XVIII, pp. 237–8.

33. Ibid., ep. XVI; Tautu, *Urban,* n. 39.

34. *"mandatis* [papae] . . . *contrariis mentis nostre."*

35. Tautu, *Urban,* n. 38.

36. "economy" — not to insist on the rigour of the law, so as to meet some particular situation.

37. Pach. I, pp. 393–4. "These events occurred at the beginning of the year, on 6 October, Patriarch Arsenius having died on that island six days previously, on 30 September [1273]." (The Byzantine year began on 1 September.)

38. J. Gill, "The Church Union of the Council of Lyons (1274) Portrayed in Greek Documents," in *OCP,* 40 (1974), pp. 5–45, esp. doc. I.

39. Pach. I, p. 396. Cf. J. Gill, "Notes on the 'De Michaele et Andronico Palaeologis' of George Pachymeres," in *BZ,* 68 (1975), pp. 295–303.

40. Pachymeres (p. 384) says they were "elected" or "selected."

41. *aliarum ecclesiarum sive aliorum praelatorum:* in English with or without the definite article?

42. Roberg, *Op. cit.,* App. I, n.1, pp. 227–9. Jerome in this letter writes that the ship was sunk off Negroponte; Pachymeres, p. 396, reports that it was on the "ship-devouring Cape Malea."

43. A. Franchi, *Il Concilio II di Lione (1274) secondo la "Ordinatio Concilii Generalis Lugdunensis"* (Rome, 1965), pp. 72–3. This *Ordinatio* is a record of the ceremonies, to which the writer added information about events. Contemporaneous (written between 17 July and 1 November 1274), in the absence of any written Acts of the council it is a primary source for the history of the council. An earlier edition, but dependent on less accurate MSS, was first printed under the title *Brevis Nota* in 1612 in the *Editio Romana* of the General Councils, and it has been repeated in later collections of councils. Cf. S. Kuttner, *L'édition romaine des conciles généraux et les actes du premier concile de Lyon* (= Miscellanea Historiae Pontificiae 5) (Rome, 1949).

44. Ibid., p. 75. There has long been confusion over the number and identity of the decrees of this council of Lyons, because, though most of them were read out publicly in the sessions (which ended on 17 July), they were not officially promulgated till 1 November, when the texts of some and their "incipits" were slightly modified. The situation has been completely clarified by S. Kuttner. "Conciliar Law in the Making. The Lyonese Constitutions (1274) of Gregory X in a Manuscript at Washington" in *Lateranum* n.s. XV (= Miscellanea Pio Paschini II) (Rome, 1949), pp. 39–81.

45. Franchi, *Op. cit.,* pp. 79–81.

46. *Desiderium erat,* Tautu, *Urban,* n. 43; Roberg, App. I, n. 7. They carried also an imperial letter giving them plenipotentiary powers, Tautu, *Urban,* n. 45.

47. "The profession of faith which the Apostolic Throne holds and teaches, which was expounded to Us in writing by Your Great Holiness, We confess to be *eusebes,* that is, pious and trustworthy and in every detail orthodox, and there is nothing in it that does not contain the truth. In the same way our Greek Church also believes and thinks in an orthodox manner . . . and there is no conflict between both the Churches in respect of faith and *eusebia* and true dogmas; certain small words—and these because of differences of language—caused in these difference and diversity." Cf. Tautu, *Urban,* n. 43 p. 128.

48. Ibid., p. 129.

49. *Ex aliis quidem,* Tautu, *Urban,* n. 46.

50. This is indicated by Jerome of Ascoli; C. Giannelli, "Le récit d'une mission diplomatique de Georges le Métochite (1275–1276) et le Vat. Gr. 1716" (= App. IV in M.H. Laurent, *Le bienheureux Innocent V [Pierre de Tarentaise] et son temps)* (= ST 129) (Città del Vaticano, 1947), p. 442.

51. Franchi, *Op. cit.,* p.83. There is no documentary evidence to suggest that Theophanes either was not present or did not chant the "From the Son" as did the rest—*cum omnibus Grecis* includes him. In the fourth session, when "From the Son" was sung twice by the Greeks, he is specifically mentioned (Ibid. p. 91). Similarly, there is no evidence to suggest that "The Greek clergy were required to repeat the offensive doctrine on the Procession of the Holy Spirit three times" (D.M. Nicol, "The Byzantine Reaction to the Second Council of Lyons, 1274," in *Studies in Church History,* vol. 7 [Cambridge, 1971], pp. 113–4). Jerome of Ascoli described them as unionists of long standing, to whom the doctrine, therefore, was not "offensive": they would not have been in Lyons, if they had not been unionists.

52. Franchi, *Op. cit.,* pp. 86–7.

53. Whether the translation was made in Constantinople by the imperial interpreters or in Lyons by perhaps John Parastron or some other is not certain. Franchi (p. 88, n. 36) favours translation in Constantinople; Roberg (pp. 261–3) translation in Lyons. The words of the *Ordinatio, que tres erant bullate bulla aurea et translate in lictera latina* (presuming that the semi-colon inserted in the printed text after *aurea* is due to the modern editor and is not in the MS), seeming as they do to imply both actions as from the same source, suggest Constantinople.

54. Cf. supra pp. 114–15.

55. *Quoniam missi,* Tautu, *Urban,* n. 41; Roberg, App. I, n. 6.

56. *Non solum nunc,* Tautu, *Urban,* n. 42. Roberg, pp. 255–63 examines the MSS tradition of this document at length and the sources of the Latin translation, of which he concludes to two main ones. In App. I, n. 5 he gives a critical edition of the text in which there are 30 metropolitans with their synods and 9 archbishops mentioned in the preamble. Some of the names in Tautu are not included in this list. A letter of Gregory (Tautu, *Urban,* n. 53) is addressed to still another list of 33 metropolitans and 9 archbishops, which coincides with neither of the other two lists, though it is nearer that of Tautu, n. 42. The Sees of the 9 archbishops are the same in all three lists, though with different spellings.

The account written by G. Metochites of the attitude of the bishops at this early stage to the proposed union supports what is said in this letter. The Emperor, in the light of the canons and history, was stressing and clarifying union. Then "some bishops adhered to the proposal as soon as it was made; others consented to it after some little discussion; and others finally, trusting in their colleagues' judgment, agreed to approve the 'economy' and added their signatures to what had been decided" (*Historia dogmatica,* in Mai, *Patrum nova bibliotheca* VIII pp. 40–1).

57. *Quoniam cum placuit,* Tautu, *Urban,* n. 44.

58. *Nos qui missi,* Tautu, *Urban,* n. 47.

59. Franchi, *Op. cit.*, pp. 88–9.

60. Tautu, *Urban,* n. 48. Acropolites specifically associated himself with the Emperor as bound by the oath.

61. Franchi, *Op. cit.*, pp. 91–2.

62. *Cum sacrosancta,* Roberg, App. I, p. 247, promulgated on 1 November as *Fideli ac devota.*

63. Tautu, *Urban,* n. 49.

64. Tautu, *Urban,* n. 50. Written in Latin, it reads like a rather too literal translation from a Greek original.

65. In 1220 the Greeks conceded autonomy to the Church of Serbia, in 1235 to that of Bulgaria. In 1272 Emperor Michael declared them subject to the (Greek) archbishop of Ochrida, which See claimed privileges granted by Pope Virgilius and Justinian I. The Primate of Bulgaria was at Michael's court while Jerome of Ascoli was there and then professed submission to Rome, as Jerome, after becoming Pope Nicholas IV, reminded him: *Acta Romanorum Pontificum ab Innocentio V ad Benedictum XI (1276–1304)* (= Pont. Comm. III, V, II) eds. F.M. Delorme and A.L. Tautu, (Rome, 1954), n. 100.

66. Tautu, *Urban,* nn. 51, 52.

67. A reference to the *Song of Solomon* VI, 9.

68. Tautu, *Urban,* n. 53.

Chapter VIII

1. Greek lists: 1. J.B. Cotelerius, *Ecclesiae graecae monumenta* III (Paris, 1686), pp. 495–520; J. Darrouzès, "Le Mémoire de Constantin Stilbès contre les Latins," in *REB,* 21 (1963) pp. 50–100. 2. *Tractatus contra errores Graecorum* (Constantinople 1252) in *MPL* 202 227–396 which utilises the writings of Ugo Eteriano (Hugo Aetherianus), an Italian Latin, who spent some 20 years in a post of responsibility in the court of Manuel I Comnenus; his chief theological work, *De sancto et immortali Deo* was written probably in 1176. Cf. A. Dondaine, " 'Contra Graecos.' Premiers écrits polémiques des Dominicains d'Orient," in *ArchOP,* 21 (1951), pp. 320–446; "Hugues Ethérien et Léon Toscan," in *Archives d'Histoire doctrinale et litteraire du Moyen Age,* 27 (1952), pp. 67–125. 3. Humbertus de Romanis, "Opus tripartitum" II, in E. Brown, *Appendix ad Fasciculum rerum expetendarum et fugiendarum* (London, 1690), pp. 207–223, who depends in part on Leo Tuscan, i.e., Leo Eteriano, brother of Ugo; cf. above.

   Latin lists: 1. *Tractatus contra errores Graecorum,* cf. above. 2. Letter of Pope Innocent IV *De ritibus Graecorum,* in Wojnar, n. 105. 3. St. Thomas Aquinas, *Summa contra errores Graecorum.* 4. Humbertus de Romanis, cf. above. 5. Report of Fra Jerome of Ascoli to Pope Gregory X, in Roberg, *Die Union* etc. App. I, n. 2 pp. 229–30.

2. Causes nn. 2 and 3 are historically baseless—the *Filioque* was never formally added to the Creed in a council of the Roman Church and chrism was not sent annually to Constantinople. But they reflect an attitude—resentment at the addition to the Creed without the consent of a general council and disgust at the avarice attributed to the Church of Rome. Beccus said much the same thing as Humbert: "Must we go on fighting to uphold the schism just because it is ancient?" (*MPG* 141 24A).

3. F. Dvornik, *Early Christian and Byzantine Political Philosophy. Origins and Background* II (Dumbarton Oaks Center, Washington, 1966), p. 617.

4. [The political world of ideas of the Byzantines] "rests, not on assertions of philosophy or theories, but in the first place on a FAITH, which binds together the next world and this, the religious and the secular, in a vast vision seen from a single viewpoint" (F. Dölger, "Die Kaiserurkunde der Byzantiner als Ausdruck ihrer politischen Anschauungen," in *Byzanz und der europaische Staatenwelt* [Ettal, 1953], p.10).

5. *The Works of Liutprand,* trans. F.A. Wright (London, 1930), p. 263. "The silly blockhead of a pope does not know that the sacred Constantine transferred to this city the imperial sceptre, the senate and all the Roman knighthood, and left in Rome nothing but vile slaves, fishermen, confectioners, poulterers, bastards, plebeians, underlings" (Ibid., p. 265).

6. C. Mango, "The Conciliar Edict of 1166," in DOP, 17 (1963), pp. 317–30, esp. p. 324.

7. MM, II, n. 447. Most of this letter has been translated by J.W. Barker, *Manuel II Palaeologus 1391–1425* (New Brunswick, 1969), pp. 106–109.

8. Conclusion of a lecture by R. Jenkins entitled "The Byzantine State—Its Essential Qualities," in *Byzantium and Byzantinism* (Univ. of Cincinnati, 1963), p. 20. For a wider picture cf. K. Vogel, "Byzantine Science" which is chapter XXVIII in the *CMH* IV, pt. II, pp. 264-305. A Pertusi, "L'atteggiamento spirituale della più antica storiagrafia bizantina," in *Aevum,* 30 (1956), pp. 138–66, is more benign in his judgement than Jenkins.

9. E.g., Blemmydes in the discussions in Nymphaeum (cf. supra): Barlaam discountenanced the use of syllogisms whereas Palamas challenged him in their favour (cf. G. Schirò, *Barlaam Calabro, Epistole greche* [Palermo, 1954], p. 7); Greg., p. 507 ss.; the Greeks in the Council of Florence (cf. J. Gill, *The Council of Florence* [Cambridge, 1959], p. 227).

10. H. Wolter in the *Handbook of Church History,* ed. H. Jedin and J. Dolan, vol. IV (London, 1970), p. 108.

11. *Guntheri monachi historia Constantinopolitana sub Balduino, anno 1210,* in P. Riant, *Exuviae sacrae constantinopolitanae,* I (Geneva, 1877), pp. 104–106.

12. N. Choniates, *Historia,* ed. I. Bekker (Bonn, 1835), p. 391, apropos of the sack of Thessalonica in 1185 by the Normans.

13. *Acta Benedicti XII (1334–1342)* (= Pont. Comm., III, VIII) ed. A. Tautu (Città del Vaticano, 1958), n. 43, p. 90; *MPG* 151, 1336B. Barlaam doubtless had in mind not only the sufferings endured by the Greeks under the Latin Empire, but also the miseries inflicted by Genoese and Venetians and by the Catalans.

14. Humbert de Romanis, in Brown, *Op. cit.,* p. 215.

15. Letter of Innocent III to the clergy of Constantinople, 9 December 1210, *Reg.* XIII 184 (MPL 216, 353).

16. Lampros, *Sozomena,* p. 151.

17. *BBTS* I, p. 407.

18. William of Adam, O.P., quoted by M. Viller, "La question de l'union des Eglises entre Grecs et Latins depuis le Concile de Lyon jusqu'à celui de Florence (1274–1438)," in *Revue d'Histoire Ecclésiastique,* XVII (1921), p. 286.

19. Antony of Massa, O.F.M., c. 1422, ibid.

20. T. Kaeppeli, "Deux nouveaux ouvrages de Philippe de Péra," in *ArchOP,* 23 (1953), pp. 163–94, esp. p. 179.

21. *The Chronicle of Muntaner,* trans. Lady Goodenough, II (London, 1921), p. 489. Muntaner's reason was that the co-Emperor Michael with 12,000 horse and 100,000 foot had not dared fight the Turks whom the Catalans defeated with 1,500 horse and

4,000 foot. The Greek lack of charity he illustrated by narrating that Greek refugees from Asia Minor "lived and lay among rubbish heaps" unassisted by Greeks. The Catalan soldiers gave them food and so 2,000 of the destitute Greeks followed them on their campaigns (Ibid. p. 491).

22. Quoted by D. Obolensky, *The Byzantine Commonwealth* (London, 1971), p. 283.

23. Letter written between 1 September 1189 and 31 August 1190; text in C.M. Brand, "The Byzantines and Saladin 1185–1192: Opponents of the Third Crusade," in *Spec.*, 37 (1962), pp. 167–81, esp. p. 175.

    After he had had to let Barbarossa through his territory, he wrote in explanation to Saladin: "He [Frederick] has experienced every type of deception on the way; the sufferings he has endured and the shortage of his supplies have weakened and troubled him. He will not reach your country in any shape useful to himself or his army; he will find his grave there without being able to return and will fall victim to his own trap" (Ibid., p. 176).

24. Pach., I, p. 307.

25. Writing of a period some seventy years later, Gregoras asserts that, whereas the Genoese of Pera collected 200,000 hyperpers in customs duties, the Greeks of Constantinople could collect barely 30,000 (Greg., II, p. 842). Cf. J. Chrysostomides, "Venetian Commercial Privileges under the Palaeologi" in *Studi Veneziani,* 12 (1970), pp. 267–356.

26. Cf. Roberg, *Op. cit.*, App. II, pp. 248ss. For a more general treatment cf. A. Michel, "Sprache und Schisma," in *Festschrift Kardinal Faulhaber* (München, 1949), pp. 37–69.

27. Palaeologus deplored the incapacity of interpreters in theological matters and attributed some of the misunderstandings to this: cf. Tautu, *Urban IV* n. 10a, p. 38. To the Pope in Lyons he sent his chief interpreter Berrhoiotes, unfortunately drowned en route. (Ibid., n. 45, p. 131).

28. Jerome of Ascoli; cf. Roberg, *Op. cit.*, p. 230. This same "error" is found also in the Cypriot list, Wojnar, *Innocent IV,* n. 105, p. 174.

29. "They [the Greeks] do not understand arguments from reason but they cling to certain councils and to opinions they have received from their fathers"—Humbert de Romanis.

30. *MPG* 140 487–574.

31. Beccus—*MPG* 141 972C–975C, 976D, 977A, 978AB. Nicetas, *De processione Spiritus Sancti, MPG* 139 169–221. According to M. Jugie, Nicetas lived and wrote under the Emperor Manuel Comnenus (1143–80) and died c.1145 ("Nicétas de Maronée et Nicétas de Mitlyène," *EO,* 26 [1927], pp. 408–416). Corrado Giorgetti, in his book, *Niceta de Maronea e i suoi dialoghi sulla processione dello Spirito Santo anche dal Figlio,* dates his writings in the year 1177–9 (reviewed in *REB,* 28 [1970], p. 293).

32. Loosely expressed as a "Finger of the hand of the person," but the first "of" does not mean cause, whereas the second does.

33. *MPG* 142 604–5, especially 604D. G. Mercati "Blemmidea," in *Bess.*, 31 (1915), pp. 226–38. The date of this reply to Vatatzes is uncertain. It probably was closely connected with the events of 1250–1254.

34. *MPG* 142 533–65.

35. *MPG* 142 565–84.

36. *MPG* 142 557CD.

37. *MPG* 142 553B.

38. *MPG* 142 577B-D.

39. Blemmydes, *MPG* 142 544D; S. Cyril, *Thesaurus, MPG* 75 585A.

40. Beccus wrote two recensions of this treatise, one during his patriarchate "with economy" i.e., a certain reticence, the other compiled in prison, without "economy." *MPG* 141 16–157 gives the second recension.

When Beccus begain writing polemical literature is not certain. Soon after his elevation to the patriarchal throne he agreed with Xiphilinus that it would be a mistake to seem to call the truth in question by entering into the (often ignorant) pamphlet controversy then in full progress (Pach., I, pp. 415–6). Later he changed and, if the order of Pachymeres's narrative has chronological significance (which it does not always have), that was shortly after the accession of Pope Nicholas IV, 26 December 1278 (Pach., I, p. 476).

Cf. H.-G. Beck, *Kirche und theologische Literatur im byzantinischen Reich* (Munich, 1959), pp. 681–3.

41. *MPG* 141 17C.

42. *MPG* 141 25BC.

43. *MPG* 141 44A.

44. *MPG* 75 585A.

45. *MPG* 141 61D.

46. *MPG* 141 64A. Cf. Blemmydes: "The mission of the Holy Spirit is half-way between an hypostatic and an essential property," *MPG* 142 577C.

47. *MPG* 141 64C.

48. In this treatise Beccus confined his comments on Photius to a refutation of each of the syllogisms that Photius had proposed against the *Filioque.* In several other writings he treats of the historical origin of the Photian schism. According to his account, Photius was reserved in reaction to, and still courteous in his relations with, Pope Nicholas I, hoping that things would turn out well for him in the end. When Adrian II condemned him and linked his name with those of earlier heretics, he reacted violently, produced his encyclical letter and denounced as abuses and heresies what he had long before known about without feeling any need to take action. After Ignatius's death, Pope John VIII was more benevolent, and Photius in the presence of three hundred bishops made a complete recantation of his acts and attacks on the Holy See. To the council of 879 "he brought the canons and delivered in anathema everything that in the period of discord he had done or said against the Roman Church" (*MPG* 141 328B).

Beccus's conclusion is that it was not doctrine—the *Filioque*—that was the cause of the schism, but Photius's ambition. Hence to uphold a schism only because it was traditional was to support a schism that had no justification.

In writing about the history of Photius, Beccus quotes at length three letters not found in other sources. It is to be noted that as Chartophylax he had free access to the patriarchal archives and could have found them there. Also it is significant that Beccus wrote this version of Photian history openly and in several contexts—*III Ep. ad Theodorum Sugd. MPG* 141 322–37; *Refutatio lib. Phot. de Spir. S.*, Ibid. 728–864; *De pace eccles.* Ibid. 925–37. As far as is known, it was not challenged, but the documents he quotes have since disappeared. Cf. V. Laurent, "Le cas de Photius dans l'apologétique du patriarche Jean XI Beccos (1275–1282) au lendemain du deuzième concile de Lyon," in *Echos d'Orient,* 29 (1930), pp. 396–415.

George Metochites held the same view of Photian history as Beccus, perhaps dependently on Beccus. "The documents that Photius himself when patriarch had destroyed, men who later wanted to reopen the controversy brought to light again. Then others in succeeding generations receiving them [as part of tradition] and thinking them incontrovertible and as not having been destroyed by fire, continued to preserve them and made the schism stable, believing in the end that the antiquity that comes with the passage of time was sufficient warranty for their truth" (*Historia dogmatica,* in A. Mai. *Patrum nova bibliotheca* VIII [Rome, 1871], p.44).

49. *MPG* 141 157A.

50. *MPG* 141 1017D.

51. *II Ad Theodorum Sugd. MPG* 141 319C.

52. *MPG* 141 400B.

Chapter IX

1. Tautu, *Urban,* n. 54.

2. Runciman, *Op. cit.,* pp. 186–8.

3. D.M. Nicol, "The Relation of Charles of Anjou with Nikephorus of Epirus," in *BForsch,* IV (1972), pp. 180–94, esp. p. 180.

4. Dated 1 May 1275, M.-H, Laurent, *Innocent V et son temps* (ST 129, Città del Vaticano, 1947), p. 269.

5. Ibid., p. 141. In the document the two others are called "Calada et Ioannis Paganus."

6. C. Giannelli, "Le recit d'une mission diplomatique de Georges le Métochite (1275–1276) et le Vat. Gr. 1716," = Appendix IV in M.-H. Laurent, *Op. Cit.,* pp. 419–43. The envoys found the Pope probably in Beaucaire negotiating with Alfonso of Castile and went with him to Lausanne, where he arrived on 6 October 1275 to treat with Rudolph of Habsburg.

7. I.e., Abaga, son of Hülegü, Khan of the Mongols.

8. This is known from a letter of Gregory's successor, Innocent V, who dealt with the two embassies: *Acta Romanorum Pontificum ab Innocentio V ad Benedictum XI (1276–1304)* (= Pont. Comm., III, V, II), ed. F.M. Delorme, O.F.M. and A.L. Tautu (Città del Vaticano, 1954) (quoted hereafter as Delorme), n. 2, dated 23 May 1276. The Greek Emperor was suspicious of western crusades: one of them had captured Constantinople.

9. 23 May 1276, Delorme, n.2.

10. It recounted the imprisonment and the freeing of St. Peter taken from the Acts of the Apostles; Pach. I p. 399. The celebrant of the Liturgy was not the Patriarch, for the patriarchal throne was vacant, and so the place of the celebration was not the patriarchal Great Church; hence this promulgation of the union was unimpressive.

11. Pach. I p. 401.

12. Pach. I pp. 409–410. "Consummation of the business" probably refers to promulgation of the union through the Liturgy in the Blachernae palace. The only Pope who blandly refused Charles's pleas would have been Gregory X. His successors restrained him somewhat but with a barely disguised sympathy towards him. Charles, however, was never at Gregory's court at the same time as Greek envoys. This description may refer to Innocent's reign. Charles was at Innocent's side from 7/8 February till the end of May.

13. M.-H Laurent, *Op. cit.,* pp. 441–2.

14. Gill, "The Church Union of Lyons etc.," doc. V.

15. Ibid., doc. VI. The name of the historian George Pachymeres is among the signatures.

16. Ibid., doc. VII.

17. Ibid., doc. IV. The Latin preposition "ek" is translated by the Greek "apo" or "para." The title of this text in the manuscript runs: "Synodical decree which the bishops of that time in Constantinople made about the Holy Spirit." This title is the work of the compiler of the collection of texts or of a copyist, and may or may not be correct.

18. Most of the statements made in this paragraph are taken from an *aide-mémoire* given by Ogerius, "protonotary of Latin interpreters of the Curia of My Lord the most holy Emperor of Romania," to two papal envoys, Marcus and Marchetus, about whom no detail is known. The text is in Delorme, n. 23, and in R.J. Loenertz, "Mémoire d'Ogier," in *OCP,* 31 (1965), pp. 374–408.

The two envoys went to Constantinople probably in early 1278. The *aide-mémoire* was written probably in late spring 1278. Its purpose was to remind the envoys of what the Emperor had said to them *viva voce,* so the authority behind it is the Emperor's. At one point it states that Michael sent to the "apostates," Nicephorus and John, "the excommunication accounced by the nuncios of the holy Apostolic See." Certainly no nuncio excommunicated any of Palaeologus's political enemies by name. They may have made known the general excommunication of all enemies of the union.

Cf. D.M. Nicol, "The Report of Ogerius," in *Proceedings of the Royal Irish Academy* LXIII, sect. C, I (Dublin, 1962); V. Grumel. "Concile anti-unioniste contre Michel et Beccos," in *EO,* 24 (1925), pp. 321–4.

19. So the letter was written in late February or early March.

20. For the Greek text with an English translation cf. Gill, *Art. cit.,* doc. VIII. A French translation has been published by V. Laurent, "Lettre inédite de Jean XI Beccos, patriarche de Constantinople (1275–1282) au Pape Grégoire X (1271–1276)," in *L'Unité de l'Eglise,* XII (1934), pp. 268–70.

21. Giacomo, bishop of Ferentino; Goffrido, bishop of Turin; Rainone, prior in Viterbo; and Salvo, lector in Lucca.

22. Safe-conduct from Charles, 26 November 1276.

23. *soliditate roboris plenioris:* Delorme, nn. 4, 5; to Patriarch, n. 6.

24. ". . .chiefly because our most dear son in Christ, Philip, Emperor of Constantinople, claims that the Empire of Constantinople belongs to him and that it is common knowledge that his father of glorious memory, Baldwin, Emperor of Constantinople, to whose place and right he succeeded, was by violence despoiled of the city of Constantinople; and Charles, illustrious King of Sicily, claims rights over certain parts of that Empire. These, trusting in their rights, their illustrious blood, their title of victory and the strength of their valiant race, declare that they will not be sluggish in enforcing their claims, but with all their might, with fixed intent and with the combined forces of themselves and their friends, will prosecute it with determined purpose" (Delorme, pp. 5–6).

25. Delorme, n. 3, dated 23 May 1276. "May 28: By agreement with Innocent V Charles sends Brother Jerome of Ascoli to Michael VIII Palaeologus to treat with a view to a truce between [Charles] and Palaeologus"; M.-H. Laurent, *Op. cit.,* p. 483, n. 163.

26. Michael called himself "Emperor of the Romans," i.e., of the whole Christian world.

27. Delorme, n. 8.

28. Delorme, nn. 9, 11.

29. Pach. I, p. 410.

30. Delorme, n. 14.

31. Delorme, nn. 15, 16, 17. Four copies of Michael's profession in Latin with his signature in Greek and three copies of Andronicus's profession, two in Latin, one in Latin and Greek, all with his signature in Greek, are still preserved in the Vatican archives.

32. Greek text in A. Theiner and F. Miklosich, *Monumenta spectantia ad unionem ecclesiarum graecae et latinae* (Vindobonae, 1872), pp. 21–8. Latin text in Delorme, n. 18.
33. That is, the tomographia, as described above.
34. "But in her the plenitude of power consists in this, that what privileges the other Churches and especially patriarchal ones, acquired at different times by acts of the illustrious and holy emperors of yore and by canonical decisions and enactments of holy and divine councils, these the Roman Church approved and confirmed, and in no other way did such prerogatives of the Churches obtain approval, if the same Roman Church had not expressed on them its judgement and sentence, its own privileges, however, both in general councils and in all others remaining unimpaired" (pp. 23–4 of the Greek text, p. 38 of the Latin text). This is not quite what Pope Clement wrote, but the result is the same.
35. The Greek text uses the technical term "proceeds from" (ekporeuetai) in respect only of the Father, for this had a special significance, viz., "proceed from as from the primary source." With relation to the Son it employs "is poured forth from" (ekcheitai). That does not, however, imply any hesitation in belief of the *Filioque* doctrine, for the whole context reads as follows: "For he is poured forth, that is, he proceeds from God and Father as from a source; he is poured forth too from the Son himself as from a source, exactly as from God himself and Father. But, both the Father is the source of the Spirit and the Son is source of the Spirit, nevertheless the Father and the Son are not two sources, but the orthodox mind holds Father and Son as one source of the Spirit, and for that reason the luminaries and doctors of the Church have always taught that the Holy Spirit is common to Father and Son. For just as the Spirit is from the substance of the Father by nature, so the Spirit is from the substance of the Son by nature, and just as in respect of substance he is from God and Father, so according to substance he is of the Son, and just as he is properly of the substance of the Father and not coming forth into being apart from him, so he is properly of the substance of the Son, and not coming forth into being outside of him too" (Theiner and Miklosich, *Op. cit.*, pp. 25–6).

    This profession of faith was a "more personal" act of the Patriarch. Probably few of the bishops would have subscribed to it in its entirety. On the other hand, incidents like the persecution of the bishops of Trikkala and Kitros (whose metropolitan of Thessalonica is reported as also having signed the profession) for loyalty to their signatures given at this synod and the fact that, in Pachymeres's narrative, bishops do not figure among those who were exiled or mutilated for their faith but that, on the contrary, they were still at large and in communication with the Emperor (which they would not have been, had they boycotted the synod or openly refused to subscribe to its document) imply a certain loyalty to the union.

    Of two bishops in particular, Pachymeres, with perhaps a little sarcasm, wrote that when Beccus in synod (probably c. 1280) was urging the equivalence of "Through" and "From," "the friends of the Metropolitan of Ephesus and of Meletius of Athens and very many more were scandalised, preferring the lesser evil of their own sin in making peace with people who erred in divine dogmas to the greater evil of seeming to call dogmas in question." He goes on to relate that Meletius got very worked up and threatened to go into exile (but does not say that he went), whereas "Isaac of Ephesus and his friends were more prudent, keeping in mind the Emperor and not wishing to seem to embroil the situation further with scandals" (p. 483). So Ephesus and Meletius and their friends with very many others "made peace" with the Latins—and signed the synodical document.
36. Delorme, n.20.
37. Latin text dated 16 July 1277, Delorme, n. 19.
38. Delorme, n. 23. The treachery of Michael's generals occurred in early summer 1277.
39. The anti-unionist "synaxis" in 1450 argued precisely on these lines when it refused to

acknowledge Constantine Palaeologus as Emperor: cf. J. Gill, *The Council of Florence* (Cambridge, 1959), p. 373 with n. 5.

40. The anti-unionists, inspired by the devil, "deceived and corrupted the more guileless and simple and taught them what perverts the Christian way and manner of life, that is, not to frequent the holy and divine churches, to boycott [unionist] priests, to shun the sacrifices celebrated by them, and moreover to reject and set aside the baptisms performed by them. In other words, by all this they tried to the best of their power to bring Christianity to an end" (Gill, "The Church Union of Lyons, etc.," p. 25).

The Arsenites held a council in Thessaly in 1278 where they condemned by name the patriarchs Nicephorus, Germanus and Joseph, i.e., all those who had held office during the lifetime of Arsenius; Cf. V. Grumel, "Un concile arséniste en 1278," in *EO,* 24 (1925), pp. 324–5.

41. Pach. I, p. 449–52.

42. Delorme, nn. 21, 22.

43. 1, 5, 7 April 1278, Delorme, nn. 24, 25, 27. Raynaldus, 1278, 18–22.

44. 18 August 1278, Delorme, n. 26. The papal letter also states that there were no Latin faithful in the diocese in need of his ministrations.

45. 7 October 1278, Delorme, n. 28.

46. Safe-conducts, dated October 1278, Delorme, nn. 32, 40, 41, 42.

47. 7 October 1278, Delorme, n. 29.

48. 7 October 1278, Delorme, n. 30.

49. Delorme, n. 20. Nicholas wrote to Philip, Emperor of Constantinople: [Pope John had treated with Palaeologus about political relations with Philip and Charles.] "At length We, called to the supreme See of the apostolate, since We find that the envoys sent on the part of Palaeologus had no mandate to treat of political questions, We mean to reply to him by our letters to send within five months" authorised ambassadors as desired by John XXI: he asked Philip and Charles to co-operate: (no date, but clearly before October 1278): M.J. Gay, *Les registres de Nicholas III,* I–V, (Paris, 1898–1938), n. 709. Cf. also nn. 708, 710 and (dated 18 October 1278) n. 378.

50. 7, 8 October 1278, Delorme, nn. 31, 34.

51. 9 October 1278, Delorme, n. 35.

52. Gay, *Registres,* n. 711.

53. 9 October 1278, Delorme, nn. 36, 37, 38.

54. 11, 18 October 1278, Delorme, nn. 40, 41, 42.

55. The letters and instructions given to the four Franciscan nuncios were the answer to the letters and professions of faith, dated April 1277, of the Greek Emperors and Patriarch, entrusted to the papal envoys sent by John XXI for transmission to the same Pope. They reached the Curia, *sede vacante,* after John's death and before the election of Nicholas. This is stated in the letters that Nicholas gave his own envoys and is manifest also from their general content. In these letters there is absolutely no reference, either direct or indirect, to the Greek letters of congratulation on his elevation to the papacy or to the *aide-mémoire* of Ogerius carried by the messengers, Marcus and Marchetus.

Hence R.-J. Loenertz is mistaken in asserting that these latter letters and the *aide-mémoire* "played a decisive role in the mission of the four apostolic nuncios of autumn 1278" ("Memoire d'Ogier, protonotaire, pour Marco et Marchetto nonces de Michel VIII Paléologue auprès du pape Nicholas III. 1278, printemps-été," in *OCP,* 31 [1965], p. 376), and has no grounds for stating that they reached the Pope either "before July [1278]" (Ibid. p. 375) or (here followed by V. Laurent, *Reg.,* n. 1439, p. 231) before 8

October 1278 ("Notes d'histoire et de chronologie byzantines," in *REB,* 20 [1962], p. 179). The Greek letters, being in answer to the announcement of Nicholas's crowning (26 December 1277), were written probably in 1278. There is no indication when they arrived at the papal Curia apart from their place in the papal registers—which suggests the year 1278—and their lack of influence on the papal embassy, which received its safe-conduct from Charles of Anjou some time after 7 January 1279, when he ordered his port officials to facilitate their journey (*BBTS* I p. 299)—which suggests 1279.

56. Pp. 455ss.

57. Pach. I, pp. 461–2, is the sole source for knowledge of this letter. He describes it, but does not transcribe the text.

58. Delorme, nn. 45, 46.

59. Here Pachymeres insists on the sufficiency of western sacraments, "baptism, priesthood, matrimony, the monastic state and the rest" (p. 463). The "tomographia" quoted in note 40 reflects the rejection of these by the anti-unionists.

60. Pach. I, pp. 472ss., 494–5.

61. Pach. I, pp. 483–93.

62. Pach. I, pp. 475–6, the only source of information about this embassy.

63. Pach. I, p. 505, Dölger, *Reg,* n. 2049, Geanakoplos, *Op. cit.,* p. 344, and Roberg, *Op. cit.,* pp. 214–5 date the departure of this embassy from Greece as before 9 January 1281, because 1) Pachymeres (the sole source of more precise information) seems to say that Palaeologus anticipated Martin's accession (ephthase), and 2) Dölger and Geanakoplos connect it with the capture of two Greek envoys, Philip and Constantine, by an Angevin war galley; the order for their release given by Charles was dated 9 January 1281 (Norden, *Op. cit.,* p. 621 n. 2). The connection, at any rate, between Philip and Constantine and the Greek bishops is purely conjectural.

64. Pach. I, p. 505.

65. *TT.* III, pp. 287–95. When the treaty was being made Pope Martin was ill and knew nothing of it—Roberg, *Op. cit.,* p. 216 n. 14.

66. Delorme, n. 53.

67. Delorme, n. 54.

68. For a more detailed account of this diplomatic activity cf. Geanakoplos, *Op. cit.,* pp. 344–57 and Runciman, *Op. cit.,* pp. 222–35 and App. pp. 313–18. These excellent books, the one treating events as western history, the other as eastern history, happily complement each other. Runciman's study covers a wider field. Dölger, *Reg,* n. 2059.

69. D.M. Nicol, "The Relations of Charles of Anjou with Nikephorus of Epirus," p. 191.

70. *Les registres de Martin IV (1281–1285)* par Les Membres de l'Ecole Française de Rome, I-III (Paris, 1901–1935), nn. 116, 117, dated 18 March 1282.

71. Runciman, *Op. cit.,* pp. 251–303.

72. 18, 21 November 1282, Delorme, nn. 58, 59, 59a.

73. Pach. I. p. 506.

Chapter X

1. Dölger *Reg,* n. 2086.

2. Pach. II, p. 19. The description of Constantinople after 1282 here given is founded on Pachymeres, *Op. cit.,* pp. 12ss.

3. There seems to be no doubt that Beccus (as well as Metochites and Meliteniotes) did give way on the union in the first trial of 1283. Pachymeres records that he signed a "profession of orthodox faith, a rejection of whatever error had been made and a resignation from the priesthood" (p. 36). Metochites recounts that, surprised and overwhelmed by the sudden vehemence of the raging mob, "since there was no hope, we yielded to their senseless fury" (*Historia dogmatica,* in Mai, *Pat. nova biblio.* VIII, p. 93). Gregoras says Beccus "openly renounced the union" (I, p. 171). The text of the document that Beccus signed is incorporated "word for word" in the *tomos* that Patriarch Gregory the Cypriot evolved in 1285 to refute him (*MPG* 142, 237–8) and it is very complete. After that trial Beccus was exiled to Brusa.

   Beccus later declared that he then bowed before the storm because there was no possibility of having a hearing for his defence, but with the firm intention, which he expressed at the time to Metochites, "as soon as the storm had died down a little of coming into the open before those responsible and the instigators to defend the truth openly." The result was the trial of 1285, which Beccus provoked—Pachymeres says by a public challenge given viva voce in Brusa when he was in exile (pp. 88–9); Metochites says by an encyclical letter circulated some little time before the Arsenite meeting in Adramyttium (p. 121). A letter of Patriarch Gregory complaining to the Emperor of Beccus's action confirms the statement of Metochites (Laurent, *Reg.,* n. 1474). At the trial of 1285 Gregory used the confession to challenge Beccus's honesty. The ex-Patriarch replied: "When we advanced the sayings of the Fathers and requested occasion to discourse on these, realising that the right time for such an exposition was not then, and with the one idea of being conciliatory, we let it go and did what we did, but assuredly not with the intention of admitting or incurring a charge of heresy" (Pach. II p. 90). Already in 1283 the dying Patriarch Joseph, "when he learnt of the violence done to a man of right faith," with regard to the abdication, condemned it as uncanonical (Ibid. p. 36).

4. In early 1285 rumours were reaching Venice of an impending change of Emperor. On 22 March Venetian envoys setting out for Constantinople were empowered, if they found another Emperor on the throne, to treat with him (F. Thiriet, *Délibérations des Assemblées Venétiennes concernant la Romanie,* I, 1160–1363 [Paris, 1966], n. LXXXXVI).

5. V. Laurent, "La fin du schisme arsénite," *in Bull. sect. hist. Acad. Roum.* XXVI 2, (1945), pp. 225–313.

6. Greg. I, pp. 171–3; Metochites, *Hist. dogm.,* pp. 99ss; describe this trial.

7. V. Laurent, "La vie et les oeuvres de Georges Moschabar," *EO,* 28 (1929), pp. 129–58.

8. Pach., II, p. 91. Cf. J. Gill, "Notes on the De Michaele et Andronico Palaeologis of George Pachymeres" in *BZ,* 69 (1975), pp. 295–303.

9. Pach., p. 113.

10. V. Laurent, "Les signataires du second synode des Blachernes (1285)," in *EO,* 26 (1927), pp. 128–49.

11. Greg. I, pp. 180–1, 184. One hundred fifteen letters of Athanasius have been published: *The Correspondence of Athanasius I Patriarch of Constantinople,* text, translation, and commentary by Alice-Mary Maffry Talbot (= Corpus Fontium Historiae Byzantinae VII) (Washington, 1975). V. Laurent gives résumés of most of them in *Reg.,* nn. 1589–1782 (pp. 372–563). Cf. also V. Laurent, "Le serment de l'empereur Andronique II Paléologue au patriarche Athanase Ier, lors de sa seconde accession au trône oecuménique (Sept. 1303)," in *REB,* 23 (1965), pp. 124–39.

   Theodore Metochites, in his "First Imperial Oration" (unpublished) dilates on Andronicus's religiosity, which manifested itself in his assiduity at religious vigils, prayers and processions "beyond what the nature of things demands and much beyond what customary indulgence allowed to Emperors in the past" (Cod. Vindob. Philol. Gr. 95, f. 93v).

12. *Les registres de Martin IV* (1281–1285), n. 455 (27 August 1283); nn. 580, 581.

13. 13 January 1283 for Sicily, *Reg. Martini,* n. 301.

14. 2 September 1283, *Reg. Martini,* n. 457; for 4 years, 13 May 1284, *Reg. Martini,* n. 583, on the plea that this campaign impeded the crusade to the Holy Land.

15. *Les registres de Nicholas IV,* ed. E. Langlois (Paris, 1886–1893), 3 June 1288, n. 954.

16. Delorme, n. 81.

17. G.I. Bratianu, "Notes sur le projet de mariage entre l'Empereur Michel IX Paléologue et Catherine de Courtenay (1288–95)," in *RHSE,* I (1924), pp. 59–63.

Pope Nicholas never rejected Andronicus as a schismatic. In August 1291 he asked his good will for travelling missionaries and after the capture of Acre in 1291 he appealed to him with other princes to aid the Holy Land: Delorme, nn. 110, 113.

18. *Les registres de Boniface VIII,* ed. G. Degard, M. Faucon, A. Thomas, R. Fawtier (Paris, 1884–1939), nn. 794, 874, 809, 857, 858.

19. 14 January 1306, *Acta Clementis PP. V. (1303–1314)* (= Pont. Comm. III, VII, I) ed. F.M. Delorme and A.L. Tautu (Citta del Vaticano, 1955), nn. 1, 2; Raynaldus, 1306, 2. Venice acceded in December of that same year.

20. Delorme, *Clement,* n. 15.

21. For accounts of the Catalans in Greece and of the Catalans' relations with Valois, cf. the detailed study of A. Lowe, *The Catalan Vengeance* (London-Boston, 1972); A. Laiou, *Op. cit.,* chapters VI and VII; R.I. Burns, "The Catalan Company and the European Powers 1305–1311," in *Spec,* 29 (1954), pp. 751–71.

22. She was Yolande, niece of Boniface of Montferrat, whom Andronicus II married as his second wife.

23. It was so reported by the Franciscan who accompanied the Greek bishop on his mission to the courts (H. Finke, *Acta Aragonensia* II [Berlin, 1908], p. 748).

24. C. Marinescu, "Tentatives de mariage de deux fils d'Andronique II Paléologue avec des princesses latines," in *RHSE,* (1924), pp. 139–43.

K.M. Setton traces in detail the complicated relationships, family and feudal, of Latin claimants to territories in Greece, in *The Papacy and the Levant (1204–1571),* I, chapters 8 and 16.

25. Delorme, n. 68.

26. Delorme, nn. 66, 67, 71, 90, 112.

27. 7 April 1288, Delorme, nn. 69, 70.

28. Delorme, nn. 83, 86.

29. Delorme, n. 76.

30. 7 August 1288, Delorme, n. 77.

31. 15 March 1291, Delorme, n. 96.

32. 23 March 1291, Delorme, nn. 98, 99.

33. 23 March 1291, Delorme, n. 100.

34. The interest of Uros in Catholicism was purely political. When Charles of Valois's expedition failed to materialise, Uros dropped his contacts with Avignon; Raynaldus, 1308, 29. John XXII wrote of him as "that treacherous King of Serbia, nay, a schismatic and a thorough enemy of the Christian religion"; Raynaldus, 1318, 35.

35. 1 April 1308, Delorme, *Clement,* nn. 25–9.

36. 18 November 1303, Delorme, n. 147. The frontiers between the Byzantine Empire,

Serbia, Bulgaria and Albania were constantly changing as one or other of the countries was victorious in war. Physical desolation and moral decadence of the areas were the inevitable consequence.

37. 7 July 1289, Delorme, n. 85; 14 July 1289, n. 88.

38. 13 August 1291, Delorme, n. 113. Copies went also to the kings of the Hyberi (tributaries of Argon), of Georgia, of Trebizond and to Andronicus.

39. 26 October 1298, Delorme, n. 125.

40. Raynaldus, 1290, 30.

41. In obedience to papal prohibitions Venice sent no ship to Alexandria between 1323 and 1345, J. Gay, *Le pape Clément VI et les affaires d'Orient (1342–1352)* (Paris, 1904), p. 83.

42. J. Lecler, *Vienne* (= Histoire des Conciles Oecuméniques 8) (Paris, 1964), pp. 68–76, 143–5. The Council also ordered four universities to establish chairs in Hebrew, Syriac and Arabic.

43. During Andronicus's reign there were nine patriarchs: Beccus, Joseph, Gregory, Athanasius elected in 1289, a monk who "n'avait qu'un tort, c'était de considérer Byzance comme un vaste monastère" (R. Guilland, "La correspondance inédite d'Athanase"' in *Mélanges Charles Diehl* [Paris, 1930], I, p. 137; cf. also J. Gill, "Emperor Andronicus II and Patriarch Athanasius I," in *Byzantina,* 2 [1970], pp. 13–19); John XII Cosmas, a monk "advanced in years . . . completely devoid of secular learning" (Greg., I, p. 193) reigned from 1294 to 1303, before Athanasius returned 1303–1309. There followed Niphon I, "a man not merely with little, but with absolutely no, education either secular or religious, unable to write with his own hand even the alphabet" (Greg., I, p. 259), but with a strong acquisitive instinct 1310–1314; John XIII Glykas, a married man, became patriarch from being Logothete, a man of first class ability who shortly abdicated for reasons of health 1315–1319 (Greg., I, p. 270). He was succeeded by Gerasimus, a monk, deaf, "who had never touched Greek learning even with his little finger, but because of his ignorance and simplicity of character an apt instrument for the Emperor's purposes" (Greg., I, p. 292), 1320–1321. The last was a monk, who for various alleged crimes had not been ordained priest, uneducated, a septuagenarian, Isaias (1323–1332), who was not as subservient as Andronicus II wished, for he openly supported his rebellious (and victorious) grandson (Greg., I, p. 360). Of these patriarchs one abdicated genuinely for health, the rest (apart from Isaias who died in office under Andronicus III) abdicated under pressure.

44. "Marini Sanuto dicti Torselli epistolae," ed. J. Bongars in *Gesta Dei per Francos* II (Hanover, 1611), pp. 289–316, esp. epp. IV, VIII.

45. Sanudo refers also to a Dominican Andrew at the papal court on Andronicus's behalf (Ibid., ep. XIII).

46. Norden, p. 690, seems to suggest that they were very unusual.

47. Raynaldus, 1326, 26.

48. H. Omont, "Projet de réunion des Eglises grecque et latine sous Charles le Bel en 1327," in *BChartes,* 53 (1892), pp. 254–7. Norden, App. XVI, papal letter to King Charles dated 21 October 1327; Dölger, *Reg.,* n. 2557 s.d. At the end of her excellent book on the foreign policy of Andronicus A.E. Laiou treats of his "Unionist Approach" and is of the opinion that he was serious in his overtures for union (pp. 308–29).

49. F. Kunstmann, "Studien über Marino Sanudo der Alteren," in *Abh. der hist. Cl. der kgl. bayer. Akad. der Wiss.,* VII (1855), pp. 695–819, ep. V. Nicaea fell on 2 March 1331, which Sanudo refers to as "this year."

50. Both probably in 1333; Dölger, *Reg.*, n. 2792, Francis, bishop of Vospri, and Richard, an Englishman, bishop of Cherson; Ibid., n. 2796, Grazia Arnaldi.

51. Kunstmann, *Op. cit.*, ep. VI.

52. 4 August 1333, Raynaldus, 1333, 17–19; *Acta Ioannis XXII (1317-1334)* (= Pont. Comm., III, VII, II) ed. A.L. Tautu (Città del Vaticano, 1952), n. 134 (cited hereafter as Tautu, *John XXII).*

53. Greg., I, pp. 501–20.

54. 4 August 1333, Tautu, *John XXII,* nn. 135, 136.

55. 22 February 1334, Tautu, *John XXII,* n. 141.

56. 22 February 1334, Tautu, *John XXII,* n. 141a. In October 1326 Andronicus III had married Joanna, princess of Savoy, whose name was changed to Anna on her marriage.

57. *BBTS,* III, p. 294, U.V. Bosch (*Andronicus III. Palaeologos* [Amsterdam, 1965], p. 121, n. 4), discussing this text notes that the Empress was a member of the Third Order of St. Francis. The same author also (*Op. cit.*, pp. 121–8, 194) is inclined to accept this testimony as true.

58. When the two Dominican bishops returned from the Pope to Constantinople, "immediately one could see many from the people, full of zeal though not according to knowledge, with ready but uncalculating tongues urging on the Patriarch himself to discussion" (Greg., I, p. 501).

59. Raynaldus, 1334, 3.

60. "Si autem serenitas regia interim sibi intendat scribere, salva deliberatione regia, expediens videretur, quod sibi insinuet quomodo ipsum ad transmarinum passagium invitasset, cum multum desideret ipsum magnifice aggredi et prosequi negotium antedictum. Sed quia ab unitate sancte romane ecclesie catholice dicebatur divisus hoc non potuerat adimplere, quare hortabatur te in domino et rogabat ut in gremium et unitatem dicte rediret ecclesie, quo facto ipse rogabat eundem, ut ad dictum passagium se disponeret in prefixo termino faciendum, tuaque procuraret excellentia quod crux deberet in illis partibus et indulgentia predicari" (Reg. Vat. 117 204r. Raynaldus, 1334, 6 omits "te" after "hortabatur").

Bosch, apparently as a further reason for accepting Andronicus's conversion, argues that Andronicus must have fulfilled his obligation to supply ships and that his ships must have fought with the other partners against the Turks. But that does not seem to have been the case. Sanudo's letter recounting the victories is addressed to the Pope, the King of France and the Grand Master of the Knights Hospitallers, and is sent to the King of Cyprus—he was writing from Venice. It was not addressed to Andronicus (with whom he was on friendly terms) and, when describing the division of the fleet, he mentions the contingents of all the above, but no Greek one.

61. C. de la Roncière and Léon Dorez, "Lettres inédites et mémoires de Marino Sanudo l'Ancien (1334–1337)," in *BChartes,* 56 (1895), pp. 21–44; Sp. Theotokis, "He prote symmachia ton kyriakon kraton tou Aigaiou kata tes kathodou ton Tourkon archomenon tou 14th aionos," in *EEBS* 7 (1930), pp. 283–98.

P. Lemerle, *L'Emirat d'Aydin, Byzance et l'Occident* (Paris, 1957), pp. 89–101. V. Laurent, "Action de grâces pour la victoire navale remportée sur les Turcs à Atramyttion au cours de l'automne 1334," in *Eis mnemen K. Amantou 1874–1960* (Athens, 1960), pp. 407–20. Fr. Laurent is right in locating the last victory of September in the gulf of Adramyttium, instead of Smyrna, but mistaken, I think, in postulating a second victory there later. When Sanudo wrote from Venice to the Duke of Borboni on 22 October, he probably had not the latest stop-press news. Incidentally, the panegyrist has no word of thanks to say to the Latins for their successful and useful enterprise and no praise of any Greek prowess in the fight, which he would have had, had the Greeks been engaged.

62. Raynaldus, 1335, 30.

63. Raynaldus, 1337, 31, 32.

64. Already before his embassy to Avignon, Barlaam had made a similar proposal in Constantinople—that each Church should retain the ancient "proceed from the Father" and forbid any addition either of "only" or of "from the Son"; C. Giannelli, "Un progetto di Barlaam Calabro per l'unione delle Chiese," in *ST,* n. 123 (1946), pp. 157–208.

65. In view of the reports of a few years previously of a friendlier attitude in Constantinople to the Latins and union, it might be thought that here Barlaam, to impress the Curia, is exaggerating more than a little.

66. *Acta Benedicti XII (1334–1342)* (= Pont. Comm., III, VIII) ed. A.L. Tautu (Città del Vaticano, 1958), n. 43; Raynaldus, 1339, 19–31. A very exact résumé of these speeches was sent to the King of France on 5 September 1339—Tautu, *Benedict XII,* n. 42; Raynaldus, 1339, 32–7. If the account and quotations here given seem disproportionately long, in excuse one may plead their interest and the insight they give of the Greek mentality. What Barlaam forecast for his own day was fulfilled almost to the letter a hundred years later in connection with the Council of Florence.

Chapter XI

1. *MPG,* 150, 1225–36. In the first half of the Palaeologan period there was a revival of philosophical and other writings, notably by George of Cyprus († c. 1290), Maximus Planudes († 1310), George Pachymeres († 1310), the monk Joseph (c. 1330) and, in particular, by Theodore Metochites and Nicephorus Choumnus who from 1315 to 1327 vied with each other as polymaths. Metochites's protégé, Nicephorus Gregoras († 1360), continued the tradition of learning, which then tended to be lost in the theological controversy about the Light of Thabor. All these writers were familiar with the works of both Aristotle and Plato and tied to neither, especially when the ancient philosophies conflicted with Christian tenets. Palamism was in part a reaction to dangers inherent in the old philosophies. Cf. H.G. Beck, *Theodoros Metochites. Die Krise des byzantinischen Weltbildes im 14. Jahrhundert* (Munich, 1952); J. Verpeaux, *Nicéphoros Choumnos. Homme d'état et humaniste byzantin (cc. 1250/1255–1327)* (Paris, 1959); I. Sevcenko, *Etudes sur la polémique entre Théodore Métochite et Nicéphore Choumnos* (Brussels, 1962); R. Guilland, *Essai sur Nicéphore Grégoras* (Paris, 1926).

   At that time there were certainly fourteen, probably fifteen, major monasteries on Mt. Athos, so the signatures of only three abbots is not impressive.

2. *MPG,* 151, 679–92. Literature about Palamism tends to be polemical. Of the sources, Nicephorus Gregoras is anti-, Cantacuzenus pro-Palamism, and the other sources are either frankly polemical treatises or the life of Palamas written by the Patriarch who canonised him. Of modern authors, J. Meyendorff, *Introduction à l'étude de Grégoire Palamas* (Paris, 1959), translated as *A Study of Gregory Palamas* (London, 1964) is sympathetic to Palamas. J. Bois, "Le synode hésychaste de 1341," in *Echos d'Orient,* 6 (1903), pp. 50–60 with a good short outline of Palamitic theology; and M. Jugie, arts. *Palamas, Grégoire* and *Palamite (controverse)* in the *Dictionnaire de Théologie Catholique,* XI, 1735–1818 are less sympathetic to him. G. Weiss, *Joannes Kantakuzenos—Aristokrat, Staatsmann, Kaiser und Mönch—in der Gesellschaftsentwicklung von Byzanz im 14. Jahrhundert* (Wiesbaden, 1969), esp. pp. 103–37, challenges many accepted views.

   Fr. Meyendorff thinks that the synodal "tome" of July 1341 clearly approved Palamas's theology. Weiss agrees that it contains it, but insists that the "tome" added to the purely disciplinary conclusions of the synod of June a theological element not approved there, and that Cantacuzenus was responsible, who "unscrupulously exploited the religious controversies for his own political ends" (pp. 107, 110, 112). The same author describes Cantacuzenus's role in the synod of 1351 as anything but impartial.

The most complete bibliography on Palamism is D. Stiernon, "Bulletin sur le Palamisme," in *REB*, 30 (1972), pp. 231–341.

3. There is confusion in the sources about these dates. The "Chronique brève de 1352," pt. III, ed. P. Schreiner (*OCP*, 31 [1965], p. 368) gives 17 May and 21 May as above, but for the marriage 24 May. Cantacuzenus *History* III (Bonn, 1832), p. 28, records his coronation by Isidore on 13 May (before Isidore was patriarch?) and the marriage eight days later on the feast of Saints Constantine and Helen. Gregoras (*Op. cit.*, p. 788) dates the coronation as on 21 May and the marriage seven days later. Cantacuzenus dates his coronation in Adrianople as on 21 May 1346, the feast of Saints Constantine and Helen. It would have been surprising if he had not been struck by the coincidence of day, month and feast of his second crowning, if coincidence there was. Perhaps the date of Isidore's election is at fault, though it is given as 17 May in all lists of patriarchs of Constantinople; cf. D.M. Nicol, *The Byzantine Family of Kantakouzenos (Cantacuzenus) ca. 1100–1460* (Dumbarton Oaks, 1968), p. 65, n. 82.

4. It is said that Constantinople lost eight-ninths of its inhabitants by the plague; R. Guilland, *L'Europe Orientale de 1081 à 1453* (Paris, 1945), p. 317.

5. *MPG* 151, 717–63.

6. *MPG* 151, 722B. *MPG* 150, 1225D–1228C.

7. *MPG* 151, 693–716.

8. The story of Procorus Cydones can be gathered from the synodical "tome" of 1368, composed by his bitterest enemy, the Patriarch Philotheus, and from letters in his defence written by his brother, Demetrius. Needless to say, there is a vast difference between these sources. Cardinal G. Mercati utilised both in "Cenni sulla vita di Procoro" in *Notizie di Procoro e Demetrio Cidone . . . ed altri appunti* (= *ST* 56) (Città del Vaticano, 1931), pp. 44–55. The same volume gives the text of Demetrius's letters, pp. 285–335, and a wealth of other information about hesychastic and anti-hesychastic writers, pp. 192–282.

Weiss, *Op. cit.*, pp. 123–37 enumerates and evaluates the leading Palamite and anti-Palamite personalities c. 1351.

9. 18 September 1344, Tautu, *Clement VI*, n. 46. The Genoese family Zacharia had established itself in Phocaea in 1275 and had occupied Chios in 1304. Andronicus III had retaken Chios in 1329 and set at liberty its Duke, Martin Zacharia, only when he had solemnly sworn in a public ceremony that "he would never enter into a pact with the Roman Church or any king or prince or community or person against the Emperor of the Greeks, or by word or deed indirectly act against him." Pope Clement dispensed him from this oath as having been extorted under duress (12 October 1343, Tautu, *Clement VI*, n. 23). He also made him captain of the papal ships of the League because of his intimate knowledge of Greek waters, but thought that he had made any private venture impossible for him by deliberately subordinating him to the papal Legate. Cf. K.M. Setton, *The Papacy and the Levant* I, pp. 190–1, 206–7. Before taking Smyrna the League ships had defeated a Turkish fleet off Pallene on 13 May 1344.

10. Cf. P. Lemerle, *L'Emirat*, pp. 180–203.

11. The combined fleets of the Leagues never consisted of more than 40 ships and usually of about 25 begrudged vessels. Gay comments: "The great naval powers of the Mediterranean have no difficulty in arming against each other fleets of 30 to 40 galleys, whereas the Naval League formed by the Holy See, after having with great difficulty had a combined fleet of 25 ships, rapidly fell to a derisory number" (J. Gay, *Le Pape Clément VI et les affaires d'Orient (1342–1352)* (Paris, 1904), p. 124.

12. Tautu, *Clement VI,* n. 25. Other letters of the same date to the Patriarch and hierarchy of the Greeks, to the monks of Mt. Athos, to the lay magnates (Ibid., nn. 26–8). A letter to Apocaucus of 27 October authorises a confessor of his choice to absolve him when he enters the Roman Church, as he says he will (Ibid., n. 29). The Despot Demetrius (son of Andronicus II and Irene of Montferrat) had sent to express his devotion to the Church: Clement replied (15 November) encouraging him to "put his desire into effect" (Ibid., n. 30) and wrote to the authorities of Pera asking them to assist him (Ibid., n. 30a).

13. Cantacuzenus, *History* IV, p. 54.

14. R.-J. Loenertz, "Ambassadeurs grecs auprès du pape Clément VI (1348)," in *OCP,* 19 (1953), pp. 178–96.

15. Dölger, *Reg,* 2937, 2942, 2943, and perhaps again towards the end of the year, 2957.

16. Gay, *Op. cit.,* p. 104.

17. Cantacuzenus, *Op. cit.,* IV, pp. 55–62.

18. Dated 13 February 1350 faculties for the envoys, Tautu, *Clement VI,* nn. 161, 163; letters to Francesco "de Pertuxo," to Kalogianni Asen, father-in-law of Cantacuzenus and Captain General of Constantinople, and to the "Patriarch of the Greeks"; Ibid., n. 162; to Cantacuzenus, Ibid., n. 164.

19. Cf. G. Mollat, *The Popes at Avignon 1305–1378* (London, 1963), pp. 45, 46. Innocent was the most unworldly of the Avignon popes and somewhat unrealistic in his external policy.

20. Nicholas Sigerus again.

21. 15 March 1353, Tautu, *Innocent VI,* nn. 8, 9; 1 April, n. 10.

22. 27 October 1353, Tautu, *Innocent VI,* n. 21.

23. "In Serbia itself Dusan showed not the least toleration towards the Roman Catholics. According to his Code of Law every attempt to convert his Orthodox subjects to the 'Latin heresy' was severely punished"—M. Dinić in *Cambridge Medieval History* IV (Cambridge, 1966), p. 540.

24. Tautu, *Innocent VI,* n. 43.

25. 24 December 1354, Ibid., n. 28.

26. Ibid. nn. 29, 30.

27. 27 December 1354, Tautu, *Innocent VI,* n. 31, repeating 1 September 1351, Tautu, *Clement VI,* n. 189. Something will be said later about the ecclesiastical confusion in Serbia.

28. Louis, King of Hungary, the grandson of Charles Martel (son of Charles II of Anjou, king of Sicily) became titular king of Hungary when his mother, heiress to the Hungarian crown, transferred her rights to him.

29. Tautu, *Innocent VI,* n. 84; Raynaldus, 1355, 33–7.

30. It is worth remembering that Venice thought 40 ships enough for the Latin League to control the Aegean and actually 25 ships did it. The regular defence force of Smyrna was 3 ships.

31. 21 June 1356, Tautu, *Innocent VI,* n. 84a.

32. 18 August 1356, Tautu, *Innocent VI,* n. 91.

33. Tautu, *Innocent VI,* nn. 92, 92a. Cf. O. Halecki, *Un Empereur de Byzance à Rome* (Warsaw, 1930), pp. 43–9.

34. Halecki, Appendix n. 1 addressed to Hugo of Cyprus dated 17 July 1356.

35. The Emperor's letter, dated 7 November 1357, is recorded in *The Life of Saint Peter Thomas by Philippe de Mézières,* ed. J. Smet (= Textus et Studia Historica Carmelitana, II) (Rome, 1954), pp. 76–9. The reference to Holy Communion is on p.75. Cf. also App. III and IV, pp. 197–206.

Halecki (pp. 61–3) considers that the Greek Emperor did not fulfil the condition laid down in the papal letters to the members of the League and doubtless communicated to him *viva voce* by the nuncios, a) because he wasted more than a year before replying, b) because his action did not amount to the required "ratification officielle et publique de l'union." Halecki did not know that Peter Thomas, though despatched in summer 1356, did not, owing to his diplomatic activities for Venice and Hungary, arrive in Constantinople till April 1357. To end a campaign, discuss and make a profession of faith within six months (April to November) does not argue undue delay. His second reason is too narrow. The Pope did not demand (as far as we know) a public declaration of union, but a personal and sincere profession, and he said nothing about it being public. John's profession was, in fact, public and complete, and Pope Innocent in a letter of 11 May 1359 refers to him as *carissimus in Christo filius noster,* which phrase the Curia used only of members of the Church (Reg. Aven. 141 f. 20v).

36. 11 May 1359, Tautu, *Innocent V,* n. 122–4.

37. *Philip de Mézières,* pp. 74–89, 206–212 where Fr. Smet utilises many unpublished documents. During this period Peter Thomas was called to Crete to deal with heresy. As legate, he had the usual very wide faculties in respect of heretics and schismatics and most other kinds of aberrations and ecclesiastical crimes. The heresy in Crete, however, was among the Latins, not the Greeks, and the legate's inquisition, ending in the burning of one of them, tried only Latins. Halecki has misread the source (*Philip de Mézières,* pp. 7–9 in Smet's edition) and his "Les persuasions et les négociations ayant échoué, il fallait, à son avis recourir à la force" (p. 70) with what follows is quite out of place.

J. Meyendorff, "Projets de concile oecuménique en 1367," in *DOP,* 14 (1960), p. 152, quotes Halecki with approval.

38. *Philip de Mézières,* pp. 102–24 with Smet's footnotes.

39. Halecki, pp. 86–7. The envoy from Greece was the Genoese Michael Malaspina, one of the many Italians in the service of the Greek Emperor.

40. Tautu, *Urban V,* n. 74. This letter begins *gratiam in praesenti, per quam obtineat gloriam in futuro*—the form used for non-Catholics. So Urban either knew nothing of or discounted John's act of submission of 1355. In this letter the Pope does not make union a condition of aid; he offers aid and suggests union.

41. Raynaldus, 1366, 1–2; Tautu, *Urban V,* n. 90. Urban utilised the services of a Greek nobleman, John Lascaris Calopherus, to carry his message to various courts and to exhort them to help the Greeks; Ibid., n. 75a–75e. Cf. A.K. Eszer, *Das abenteuerliche Leben des Johannes Laskaris Kalopheros* (Wiesbaden, 1969).

42. K.E. Zacharias von Lingenthal, "Prooemien zu Chrysobullen von Demetrius Cydones," in *Sitzungsberichte der Pruss. Akad. d. Wiss.* (Berlin, 1888) II, p. 1419. G. Wenzel, *Monumenta Hungariae historica* II (Budapest, 1875), doc. 479. Venice answered on 10 March agreeing to lend the ships even free of charge.

43. Tautu, *Urban V,* nn. 107, 108. No. 107, besides giving the text of the profession of faith, expresses also the Pope's joy and his congratulations to the Emperor.

44. Tautu, *Urban V,* n. 111. George Manicaites had made various requests for minor benefices for several simple priests (examples in Halecki, App. n. 6). Halecki interprets in the phrase, *Huiusmodi reductione completa, eas et alias tuas et tuorum honestas preces . . . proponimus exaudire,* the word, *eas,* as referring to the minor requests of

Manicaites and *alias tuas* as demands by John for help against the Turks. He concludes that Urban's reply was the old "Union first and then (and only then) help." This differentiation is, I think, unjustified because a) there is no suggestion of it in the text, b) it takes no account of *et tuorum,* and c) it is not reflected in the papal letters sent on this same occasion to Louis.

45. Letter to Louis, 23 July 1366, Tautu, *Urban V,* n. 112; letter to Palaeologus of same date, Ibid., n. 113.

46. Tautu, *Urban V,* nn. 109, 110.

47. 22 June 1366, Tautu, *Urban V,* n. 105.

48. Norden, p. 703, n. 1, interprets it as a "categorical discussion" from undertaking a full-scale campaign, in order to force the Greeks to union.

49. Halecki, pp. 129–34.

50. E.L. Cox, *The Green Count of Savoy: Amadeus VI and Transalpine Savoy in the Fourteenth Century* (Princeton, 1967), esp. pp. 204–39. It is a pity that in so excellent a book the author has made no use of papal archives, even when dealing with events connected with the popes.

51. G. Fedalto, *Simon Atumano, monaco di Studio, arcivescovo latino di Tebe* (Brescia, 1968); Eszer, *Kalopheros,* pp. 115–7; G. Mercati "Se la versione dall'ebraico del codice veneto greco VII sia di Simone Atumano, arcivescovo di Tebe" in *ST* 30 (Roma, 1916), pp. 26–45.

52. J. Meyendorff, "Projets de concile oecuménique en 1367," in *DOP,* 14 (1960), pp. 147–79.

53. Meyendorff, *Op. cit.,* p. 154. For more information on this subject, cf. the next chapter.

It should be noticed that John V after his profession of faith in Rome demanded that Louis should fulfill the pact agreed on in Buda by sending an army to help Constantinople. Louis refused. John appealed to the Pope, who wrote to Louis reminding him firmly of his obligation (28 January 1375, Tautu, *Gregory IX,* n. 137). John was not rebaptised in Rome. One may, therefore, conclude that in Buda, in return for military assistance, John promised no more than his own entry into the Roman Church.

Another dissuasive from taking the condition of rebaptism too seriously is furnished by a letter of the Franciscan Vicar of Bosnia, written to his own Friars in 1379. In it he states categorically that he and they never wittingly rebaptised anyone baptised by the Greek formula: "If they [i.e., the local priests] preserved the form of the Greeks, 'The servant of Christ is baptised in the name etc.,' we should never baptise any one of them," and he further records: "Also John, the Emperor of the Greeks, when he came to the King said in the hearing of many: 'The King acts rightly in baptising these Slavs, because they follow neither the Greek nor the Roman form' " (D. Lasić, "Fr. Bartholomaei de Alverna, Vicarii Bosnae, 1367–1407 quaedam scripta hucusque inedita" in *ArchOFM,* 55 [1962], pp. 74, 75).

J. Gill, "John V Palaeologus at the Court of Louis I of Hungary (1366)," in *Bslav* 38 (1977), pp. 31–38.

54. MM I, n. 234. Philotheus's explanation to Ochrida is the source of the account given above.

55. 16 November 1369, Tautu, *Urban V,* n. 172. Halecki, App. 15; also pp. 149ss.

For the Bulgarian expedition Amadeus had received 12,000 hyperpers and ships from the Byzantine Empress. He refused to hand over the Greek cities on the Black Sea that he had taken till John V promised him 15,000 more. To return home in June 1367 he got from John V 35,000 hyperpers, 20,000 of them being a loan as a kind of pledge, and he borrowed 28,000 more from Italian bankers in Pera. His whole crusade cost 225,000 florins *boni ponderis:* (Cox, *The Green Count,* p. 222).

56. The Greek envoys were the Chamberlain Theophylactus for the Emperor; the Metropolitan Nilus and the Great Chartophylax Theodore for the Church; the representatives of the city of Constantinople, Theodore, Proximus and Constantine Metasopoulus, with two others. Nilus was probably the ardent Palamite metropolitan of Rhodes, very hostile to the Latin Church, who had been ejected from the island by the Knights (Halecki, pp. 164–5). The names of the envoys are taken from the letters later addressed to them by the Pope.

57. Tautu, *Urban V,* nn. 124–132a, pp. 201–15.

58. Tautu, *Urban V,* n. 138.

59. 26 October 1368, Halecki, App. n. 11.

60. A chronology of the life of Cydones is offered by R.-J. Loenertz, *Les receuils de lettres de Démétrius Cydonès* (= ST, 131) (Città del Vaticano, 1947), pp. 108–22.

61. Halecki, App. n. 12.

62. The original document is still preserved, Tautu, *Urban V,* n. 167. For the notarial instrument with details of authorities, interpreters, witnesses, etc., cf. Ibid. n. 168.

63. 4 November, Tautu, *Urban V,* n. 169.

64. 13 November, Ibid., n. 170.

65. It is this papal letter that gives what details are known of this whole transaction of 1367. It has been utilised earlier in this chapter. 16 November, Tautu, *Urban V,* n. 172.

66. Tautu, *Urban V,* n. 181.

67. Tautu, *Urban V,* n. 183.

68. 29 January 1370, Tautu, *Urban V,* n. 182.

69. 22 February 1370, Tautu, *Urban V,* n. 184.

70. Eszer, *Kalopheros,* pp. 17 ss.

71. 18 August 1356, Tautu, *Innocent VI,* n. 92a.

72. "Ai Greci Ortodossi," c. 1363, in G. Mercati *Notizie di Procoro e Demetrio Cidone,* pp. 359–403.

72. St. G. Papadopoulos, Hellenikai metaphraseis thomistikon ergon, thomistai kai antithomistai en Byzantio, (Athens, 1967).

74. T. Kaeppeli, "Deux nouveaux ouvrages de Fr. Philippe Incontri de Péra O.P.," in *ArchOP,* 23 (1953), p. 176.

75. MM, I nn. 243, 275 of the year 1369; 251 of 1370; 310 of 1371; 293 of 1374.

76. 1370, MM, nn. 260, 277.

77. Ibid., I, nn. 306, 300.

78. S. Vryonis, Jr., *The Decline of Medieval Hellenism in Asia Minor and the Process of Islamization from the Eleventh through the Fifteenth Century* (Berkeley, 1971), esp. chaps. VI and VII.

79. *De non reddenda Gallipoli, MPG* 154 1009–36. R.-J. Loenertz dates this speech to 1371 (*Les Receuils de lettres de Démétrius Cydonés* [= ST 131], p. 112); J.W. Barker (*Op. cit.,* p. 16), following P. Charanis ("The Strife among the Palaeologi and the Ottoman Turks, 1370–1402," in *Byz* 16 [1942–3], p. 297) to 1376/7.

80. John sent a message home to raise money to save him from his embarrassing situation. It was his second son, Manuel, Despot of Thessalonica, who brought him relief. Cf. E. Voordeckers, "Un Empereur Palamite à Mistra en 1370," in *RHSE,* IX (1971) pp. 607–15.

81. Tautu, *Gregory XI,* n. 30.

82. 13 November 1372, Tautu, *Gregory XI,* nn. 48a, 48b, 48.

83. 29 June 1373, Tautu, *Gregory XI,* n. 78. Louis of Hungary refused (Raynaldus, 1374, 6).

84. 21 June 1373, Tautu, *Gregory XI,* n. 77.

85. From the letter addressed to the prelates and rectors of major churches and monasteries in Constantinople, 25 July 1374, Tautu, *Gregory XI,* n. 116.

86. Probably in October 1371, i.e., after the battle on the Marica; cf. Barker, *Op. cit.,* p. 14. Cf. O. Iliescu, "Le montant du tribut payé par Byzance à l'Empire Ottoman en 1379 et 1424," in *RHSE,* 9 (1971), pp. 427–32.

87. 12 December 1374, Tautu, *Gregory XI,* n. 128.

88. A convert to Catholicism; cf. (3 November 1374) Tautu, *Gregory XI,* n. 102a.

89. Raynaldus, 1374, 5.

90. Tautu, *Gregory XI,* nn. 136, 134, 135.

91. Tautu, *Gregory XI,* n. 137. The Pope sent a note also to the Dominicans of Constantinople to congratulate them (13 February 1375, Ibid., n. 138); and at the request of the Venetian Baillie gave leave for them to build a convent in Constantinople as a base for the work of conversions (13 February 1375, Ibid., n. 139).

92. 27 October 1375, Tautu, *Gregory XI,* n.173.

93. In a letter to the Hospitallers of Bohemia Gregory fixed the date of the expedition as spring 1377. The knights were to fight for Christians as Christians. "It is common knowledge that already the impious Turks, persecutors of the Christian name, not being opposed by a sufficient resistance from the faithful, first ravaged many of the islands, which were fertile and inhabited by Christians, then they invaded, captured and pillaged almost the whole of the glorious Empire of Romania and made it their tributary, stripping it of innumerable inhabitants of both sexes whom they led off to a wretched slavery. Now they are said to have savagely attacked the Empire of Bulgaria and the kingdom of Serbia and other Christian areas. The glorious city of Constantinople, also, and its illustrious Emperor are so straightened by those same Turks that not only are they rendered tributary but they are practically within their grasp, unless they receive speedy help from the faithful of the West. The kingdom of Lesser Armenia, that too Christian, wedged between the Saracens and the Turks, for a long time now has seen no help at all from western Christians, and so slowly and nearly completely it is falling into the hands of the infidel"; Raynaldus, 1375, 9.

94. The archbishop of Genoa had requested this money. The Pope replied that he was glad to learn that Genoa was going to help Constantinople and other regions, "which are inhabited by people who, though not quite of sound faith, are nevertheless worshippers of Our Lord, Jesus Christ" (Raynaldus, 1376, 23).

It was the friction over Tenedos that sparked off the Chioggia war between Genoa and Venice which ended only in 1381 with Genoa's exhaustion and decline.

Tenedos was important for its position near the southern entrance to the Dardanelles. In the hands of the Venetians it would have largely offset the grip on commerce that the possession of Pera gave to the Genoese.

95. G. Ostrogorsky, *History of the Byzantine State,* vol. 2. Eng. trans. by J. Hussey (Oxford, 1968), p. 543.

96. O. Halecki, "Rome et Byzanz au temps du Grand Schisme d'Occident," in *Collectanea Theologica* (Lwów), 18 (1937), pp. 477–532.

97. *Acta Urbani VI, Bonifacii IX, Innocentii VII et Gregorii XII* (Pont. Comm. III, XIII, I), ed. A. Tautu (Roma, 1970), n. 6. It is to be noted that the registers of the Roman line of popes, particularly of Urban VI, are very defective. Also, to assess rightly the generosity of these popes, one should remember that they were involved in opposition to the popes of Avignon and harassed on all sides—"like being on the high seas buffeted by the four winds of heaven," in the words of Pope Boniface.

98. *Acta pseudopontificum Clementis VII, Benedicti XIII, Alexandri V et Ioannis XXIII.* (= Pont. Comm. III, XIII, II) ed. A.L. Tautu (Roma, 1971), n. 25, 19 January 1380.

99. G. Mercati, *Simone Atumano,* pp. 50–1.

100. MM, II, n. 379, September 1384. Nilus was prepared to treat of union, but on the old conditions. Converts from Latinism to the Greek Church still had to abjure the *Filioque* doctrine, e.g. Ibid., nn. 359 (December 1382), 333 (September 1383), 376 (March 1384).

101. R.-J. Loenertz, *Démétrius Cydonès correspondance II* (= Studi e Testi 208) (Città del Vaticano, 1960), App. D. 5, pp. 436–8.

102. For all this episode cf. G. Dennis, *The Reign of Manuel II Palaeologus in Thessalonica 1382–1387* (= Orientalia Christiana Analecta 159) (Rome, 1960), esp. pp. 132–50.

103. Knowledge of this embassy is drawn from Cydones's letters, nn. 314, 334, 327 in Loenertz, *Op. cit.* Translations of large parts of nn. 334 and 327 are to be found in Dennis, *Op. cit.,* pp. 144–7.

Manuel's brief reign in Thessalonica was in despite of his father. He had left Constantinople secretly and John V had never approved. So the papal envoy was not likely to get a warm welcome from either State or Church.

104. Historians pass scathing judgments on John V Palaeologus, I think unfairly. There is room for a sympathetic biography of him.

105. F. Thiriet, *Régestes des Délibérations du Sénat de Venise concernant la Romanie* I (Paris, 1958), n. 739, 8 June 1388.

106. Raynaldus, 1388, 4, 18 April 1388.

107. Thiriet, *Op. cit.,* n. 851, 21 May 1394.

108. Raynaldus, 1394, 23, 3 June 1394.

109. Raynaldus, 1394, 24.

110. A.S. Attiya, *The Crusade of Nicopolis* (London, 1934), synopsised in chap. XVIII, pp. 435–62, of *The Crusades in the Later Middle Ages* (London, 1938). K.M. Setton, *The Papacy and the Levant* I, pp. 342–69.

111. Halecki, *Rome e Byzanz* etc., p. 505.

112. 1 April 1398, Tautu, *Urban VI,* n. 55. The diocese and province of Mayence were excepted. To these he sent another nuncio.

113. 25 March 1398, Tautu, *Urban VI,* n. 51.

114. 25 June 1376, Tautu, *Gregory XI,* n. 206.

115. Tautu, *Urban VI,* n. 52. G. Mercati, "Fra Massimo da Constantinopoli e l'uso del greco coi Greci uniti di Oriente," in *SBN,* 4 (1935), pp. 311–15.

116. A. Mercati, "Una notiziola su Manuele Crisolora," in *Stoudion,* 5 (1928), pp. 65–9.

117. 6 March 1399, Raynaldus, 1399, 2–4. Hungary was excluded probably because it had suffered badly from the disaster of Nicopolis.

118. Tautu, *Urban VI,* n. 85. Manuel, it seems, foresaw that he might have to leave Constantinople, in which case he wanted to entrust it to the Venetians: Venice refused; Thiriet, *Op. cit.,* n. 932 (7 April 1397).

119. Thiriet, *Op. cit.,* n. 946.

120. 27 May 1400, Tautu, *Urban VI,* n. 90; Raynaldus, 1400, 8. Manuel sent a relic to Benedict XIII at the latter's request, but on 20 June 1402.

Chapter XII

1. G. Mollat, *Op. cit.,* pp. 336–7.

2. 20 July 1356, Tautu, *Innocent XI,* n. 83.

3. 3 March 1371, Tautu, *Gregory XI,* n. 4.

4. 20 July 1327, Tautu, *John XXII,* n. 93; Nostrae tamen nequaquam intentionis existit ecclesias quas Graeci tenent in civitate et diocesi Nicosiensi per tenorem praesentium reservasse.

5. Faculty given to the Apostolic Legate in the East, 23 August 1326, Tautu, *John XXII,* 88a.

6. 14 September 1307, Delorme, *Clement V,* n. 20.

7. 25 July 1335, Tautu, *Benedict XII,* n. 3.

8. 23 July 1368, Tautu, *Urban V,* nn. 149–52.

9. 13 September 1373, Tautu, *Gregory XI,* nn. 86, 87.

10. 7 April 1375, Tautu, *Gregory XI,* n. 153; 25 April 1375, Ibid., n. 156. A month later another Rampanus received a canonry and other offices of the church of St. Michael, Ibid., n. 157. On 4 July 1379 the Senate of Venice advised the Cretan authorities to take measures against a Protopapas Rampanus and his son, who were "sowing schism and error among the Greeks of Crete"; F. Thiriet, *Régestes des Délibérations du Sénat de Venise concernant la Romanie,* I (Paris, 1958), n. 599, p. 147.

11. 7 May 1375, Tautu, *Gregory XI,* n. 159. For a brief appreciation of the Venetian pragmatic approach to religion in its colonies, cf. F. Thiriet, *La Romanie Venitienne au Moyen Age* (Paris, 1959), pp. 283–91; F. Thiriet and P. Wirth, "La politique religieuse de Venise à Négropont à la fin du XIVe siècle," in *BZ,* 56 (1963), pp. 297–303.

12. The Latin word, *tolerare,* which Innocent and many of his successors used in respect of the Greek rite, did not mean "tolerate," which in English often has an overtone of contempt. It meant "permit" or "allow."

13. 1 April 1326, Tautu, *John XXII,* n. 81.

14. January-February 1321, Tautu, *John XXII, nn.* 35, 36, 37.

15. 1 October, Ibid., n. 89.

16. 1 April 1308, Delorme, *Clement V,* n. 26.

17. "In the celebration of solemn and other Masses . . . provided they retain the form of words used and transmitted by the Lord . . . they are allowed to follow their own custom": 6 March 1254, H. & W., *Innocent IV,* n. 105.

18. 29 May 1368, Tautu, *Urban V,* nn. 143, 144.

19. Tautu, *Urban V,* n. 191. In the opinion of G. Mercati these permissions are not to be understood as implying that the Emperor was at all times and everywhere to follow the Latin liturgical rite, but he was to do so whenever he took advantage of these special privileges.

Further, G. Mercati (quite correctly) insists that the word "rite" in papal documents often means no more than "customs" or even "Church" (Mercati, *Notizie di Procoro e Demetrio Cidone,* pp. 491–2).

E.g., Halecki quotes a papal letter to "Maximus Lascaris, Abbot of the monastery of St. Diomede in Constantinople," that because "having already long before rejected the schism of the Greeks, you stand firm and constant in the faith, rite and devotion of the holy Roman Church," the pope hopes and trusts that "you will incite other Greeks to the faith, rite and devotion of the same." Halecki interprets this as an order to Lascaris to abandon altogether the Greek liturgical rite and practise the Latin (Halecki, p. 294). The rest of the letter, however, shows that Halecki's interpretation is mistaken. The letter is nothing more than a recommendation to Lascaris of the papal envoys, mentioned by name, who were its bearers: "So, We exhort Your Reverence in the Lord, putting full trust in the said nuncios in respect of what they think good to explain to you from Our part, to give them your help, counsel and favour" (Reg. Vat. 270 f. 58r, 26 September 1374).

Ten years earlier, Lascaris had received a letter from the same Pope Urban in nearly the same words: "To our dear son, Maximus, protosyncellus in Constantinople." He told him: "Realising that the inveterate schism of the Greeks would lead to damnation and separation from divine grace, you abandoned it entirely and following (*imitando*) the rite of the holy Roman Church" etc. Again the Pope hoped for the conversion of others from Maximus's example (18 April 1365, Tautu, *Urban V,* n. 76; Halecki, pp. 363–4: at the same time Urban wrote similar letters to two others).

Maximus's brother, John, had also abandoned the "inveterate schism" and meant "to persist in the rite and devotion of the Latin faithful and under the *magisterium* and obedience of the holy Roman Church" (Tautu, *Urban V,* nn. 75a, 75b).

20. 28 July 1368, Tautu, *Urban V,* n. 153. Cf. J. Gill, "Pope Urban V (1362–1370) and the Greeks of Crete," in *OCP,* 39 (1973), pp. 462–8: Pope Urban was implementing the decree of John XXII about Crete (Tautu, *John XXII,* n. 153), who in turn was applying the decree of the Fourth Lateran Council. His purpose was to strengthen the "uniate" Church on the island.

    For more information on the state of the Greek Church in Crete after 1204 cf. N.B. Tomadakis, "Orthodoxoi archiereis en Krete epi Henetokratias," in *"Orthodoxia,"* 27 (1952), pp. 63–75: S. Borsari, *Il dominio veneziano a Creta nel XIII secolo* (Naples, 1963), esp. pp. 105–25; App. II and III: Z.N. Tsirpanlis, "Nea stoicheia schetika me ten ekklesiastike historia tes benetokratoumenes Kretes (13th–14th centuries) apo anekdota benetika eggrapha," in *Hellenika* 20 (1967), pp. 42–106, esp. 42–62.

    For information on the Latin Church in Crete, cf. G. Fedalto, *La Chiesa Latina in Oriente,* I, (Verona, 1973), pp. 312–52.

21. Gregory was very sympathetic to John V and the Greeks of the Empire; obviously (to judge from this letter) less so to the Greeks in Latin territory. It is surprising to find from him "heretic" applied to the Patriarch of Constantinople. In this same letter he calls Macarius "bishop, or rather anti-bishop, heretic and schismatic."

    Besides Macarius, who was in Crete in 1357 but had died considerably before 1373, there was also Anthemius, nominated in 1365/6, died 1370 (V. Laurent, "Le Synodicon de Sybrita et les métropolites de Crète aux Xe–XIIIe siècles," in *EO,* 32 [1933], pp. 385–412).

22. 27 October 1373, Tautu, *Gregory XI,* n. 91. Insistence on ordination according to the Roman ritual was the result (a) of the belief that the anointings which figured in the Latin rite had an apostolic origin and therefore should not be omitted; and (b) belief that the minor orders, customary in the Latin rite but not in the Greek, were in some sense obligatory. So, not infrequently clerics of the Greek rite were ordained by Latin bishops, e.g. Leo of Solia (Cyprus) cf. 1 February 1301, Delorme, *Boniface VIII,* n. 133.

23. To the query, "Since Greeks and schismatics have already lost sound Catholic faith and knowledge, and their patriarchs are created at the whim and will of their Emperors, it is

asked whether their bishops can make chrism, as they indeed do make it, and if their priests consecrate the Body of Christ." The answer was given: "We reply that Greek bishops can make chrism and Greek priests consecrate the Body of Christ, provided only that they are rightly ordained"; Tautu, *Gregory XI,* n. 34a.

24. 19 April 1344, Tautu, *Clement VI;* n. 41.

25. In both rites, it appears, he was not a priest; Tautu, *Gregory XI,* n. 129.

26. 3 October 1333, Tautu, *John XXII,* n. 139, repeated verbatim by Urban V (12 March 1370) Tautu, n. 189, and again by Gregory XI (6 March 1374) Tautu, n. 101.

27. 24 December 1354, Tautu, *Innocent VI,* n. 28. Cf. also 1 September 1351, Tautu, *Clement VI,* n. 189.

28. 1373, Tautu, *Gregory XI,* n. 34a.

29. From a slightly longer form of the queries, though by the same proponent; D. Lasić, "Fr Bartholomaei de Alverna, Vicarii Bosnae, 1367–1407, quaedam scripta hucusque inedita," in *ArchOFM,* 55 (1962), pp. 59–81, esp. p. 66.

30. 22 December 1378, *Dilectionis sinceritas.*

31. Lasić, *Op. cit.,* p. 74. The same letter then records John V's reaction to the situation, quoted earlier in this chapter, and continues: "Besides, yesterday, in Ceni some monks coming from Greek territories said in the presence of our Friars about those priests, 'Those are not priests, they are dogs; and they do not really baptise. So we baptise them conditionally because what was done without knowledge cannot be said to be repeated.' " Fra Bartholomew adds that some Slav priests had been taught correctly by monks from Mt. Athos, but they were so few that it was hard to know who they were.

32. Queries, Gregory XI, n. 34a.

33. 29 April 1339, Tautu, *John XXII,* n. 20.

34. 23 July 1307, Delorme, *Clement V,* n. 17.

35. Tautu, *John XXII,* n. 48.

36. 31 August 1346, Tautu, *Clement VI,* n. 100.

37. 28 January 1369, Tautu, *Urban V,* n. 159.

38. Delorme, n. 127.

39. 31 December 1325, Tautu, *Benedict XII,* n. 15b.

40. 22 February 1334, Tautu, *John XXII,* n. 141a; 17 January 1337, Tautu, *Benedict XII,* n. 15a. "Indeed, daughter, because in the first place it concerns you, who have your origin from a house and family hitherto all Catholic, to draw by diligent and effective means your husband to union and reconciliation with the Church which is the mother of all the faithful and head of all Churches, especially as Sacred Scripture invites you in the words of St. Paul: 'The unfaithful husband shall be saved by the faithful wife'—this for your own sake as well as for him who is one flesh with you, and also that your children and their issue may not be removed from and in a sense strangers to the Catholic faith and the unity of Mother Church."

41. G. Mercati, *Notizie di Procoro e Demetrio Cidone,* p. 150, n. 4. Cardinal Mercati seems a bit dubious about the historical value of this.

42. 8 May 1332, Tautu, *John XXII,* n. 127.

43. 28 March 1318, Tautu, *John XXII,* n. 11 to the bishop of Caffa, where Latin men were marrying Greek women and following the Greek rite, promising themselves that they would return to their own Church before they died; cf. Ibid., n. 9. Similarly for Constantinople, Ibid., n. 9a; Benedict XII, nn. 11, 11a. Forbidden also in Poland and Slav countries, Clement VI, n. 106 etc.

44. Delorme, *Clement V,* n. 17.
45. Delorme, *Clement V,* n. 17; *John XXII,* Tautu, n. 14.
46. Cf. R.-J. Loenertz, *La Société des Frères Pérégrinants* (Rome, 1937), esp. pp. 141–50.
47. 1341, Tautu, *Benedict XII,* n. 57.
48. Ibid., n. 58.
49. Sent to Pope Clement, 1345, Tautu, *Benedict XII,* n. 59.
50. 29 September 1351, Tautu, *Clement VI,* n. 192.
51. 1 October 1353, Tautu, *Innocent VI,* n. 20.
52. 18 January 1355, Ibid., n. 59.

Chapter XIII

1. For an analysis of the documents of the Avignonese popes, cf. W. deVries, "Die Päpste von Avignon und der christliche Osten," in *OCP,* 30 (1964), pp. 85–128.
2. Norden, pp. 195–6.
3. The popes went to Avignon because they could not go to Rome. Conditions were such in Rome itself and in the papal States that it would have been unsafe for them to return and, returned, they could not have ruled the Church. The situation was not new, it was only worse. "In the 204 years from 1100 until 1304, the popes spent 122 away from Rome and 82 in Rome; that is, 40 years more away from Rome than in it"; L. Gayet, quoted by Mollat, *The Popes at Avignon,* p. xiv.
4. "Whereas John XXII's total expenditure amounted to about 4,200,000 florins, the maintenance of the papal forces in Italy between 1321 and 1331 cost 2,390,433 florins. Karl Heinrich Schäfer, who has set himself the task of balancing the pope's accounts, estimates that the cost of the war in Italy amounted to 63.7 per cent of the whole expenses of the reign. The conquest of the Papal States during the reigns of Clement VI, Innocent VI, Urban V and Gregory XI involved equally heavy sacrifices. The Apostolic Camera was always in debt, and to remedy this the popes were compelled to raise large loans and extort money from ecclesiastical benefices"; Mollat, *Op. cit.,* p. 316. For details of the extreme poverty of Gregory XI and of the means he adopted to alleviate it, cf. A. Pélissier, *Grégoire XI ramène la Papauté à Rome* (Tulle, 1962), pp. 163–72.
5. Pach. I, pp. 480–3.
6. H. Evert-Kappesowa has written four interesting articles on the events of just before and just after 1282 in Constantinople, in *Bslav,* 10 (1949), pp. 28–41; 13 (1952), pp. 68–92; 16 (1955), pp. 297–317; and 17 (1956), pp. 1–18.
7. Note, however, should perhaps be taken of the fact that the "Hymn of Thanksgiving" after the western League's victory near Adramyttium had no word of thanks for the victors.
8. Cf. L.-P. Raybaud, *Le gouvernement et l'administration centrale de l'Empire Byzantin sous les premiers Paléologues (1258–1354)* (Paris, 1968), pp. 85–6, 100–111.
9. MM, I., n. 252.
10. In 1380 nine articles were agreed to and signed by the synod acknowledging the Emperor's rights to a control over nominations to bishoprics and the higher offices of the Church and to his immunity and that of his officials from ecclesiastical penalties: cf. V. Laurent, "Les droits de l'empereur en matière ecclésiastique. L'accord de 1380–82," in *REB,* 13 (1955), pp. 5–20.

11. "Now that the political fabric of the Byzantine State was irretrievably shattered, the Patriarch of Constantinople was the only force capable of championing the traditional claims of the East Roman Empire to hegemony over the whole of Eastern Christendom"—D. Obolensky, "Byzantium, Kiev and Moscow. A Study of Ecclesiastical Relations," in *DOP,* 11 (1957), pp. 21–78, esp. p. 40.

12. Cf. D. Obolensky, *The Byzantine Commonwealth* (London, 1971), pp. 301–308.

13. MM. I, May 1359, n. 171; November 1370, n. 281. Cf. J. Meyendorff, *Society and Culture in the Fourteenth Century. Religious Problems:* paper read at the XIVth Internat. Byzantine Congress, Bucharest 6–12 September 1971, p. 62.

14. MM, March 1368, n. 306; May 1371, n. 300.

15. June 1370, Ibid., n. 264.

16. Ibid., n. 266.

17. Ibid., n. 268.

18. Ibid., n. 269.

19. Ibid., n. 447.

Bibliography

General Accounts

Barraclough, G. *The Medieval Papacy*. London, 1968.

Beck, H.-G. *Kirche und theologische Literatur im byzantinischen Reich*. Münich, 1959.

Cambridge Medieval History. Vol. IV. 2 pts. Cambridge, 1966–7.

Fliche, A., and Martin, V., eds. *Histoire de l'église*. Vols. X–XIV. Paris, 1950–62.

Guilland, R. *Histoire du Moyen Age* (= *Histoire Général*, ed. Glotz, vol. IX, pt. 1). Paris, 1939.

Hackett, J. *History of the Orthodox Church of Cyprus*. London, 1901.

Hill, G. *A History of Cyprus*. Vol. II. Cambridge, 1948.

Ostrogorsky, G. *History of the Byzantine State*^{2}. Translated by J. Hussey. Oxford, 1968.

Vasiliev, A.A. *History of the Byzantine Empire*. Madison, 1952.

General Sources

Boissade, J.F. *Anecdota graeca*. Vols. I–V. Paris, 1829–33.

______. *Anecdota nova*. Paris, 1844.

Brown, E. *Appendix ad fasciculum rerum expetendarum et fugiendarum*. London, 1690.

Cotelerius, J.B. *Ecclesiae graecae monumenta*. Vol. III. Paris, 1686.

Dölger, F. *Regesten der Kaiserurkunden des oströmischen Reiches*. Pt. III: 1204–82; pt. IV: 1282–1341; pt. V: 1341–1453. Münich and Berlin, 1931–65.

Karayiannopoulos, I.E., *Sources of Byzantine History*. In Greek. Thessalonica, 1970.

Lambros, Sp. *Palaeogeia kai Peloponnesiaka*. 4 vols. Athens, 1912–30.

Laurent, V. *Les regestes des actes du patriarchat de Constantinople*. Vol. I, *Les actes des patriarches*; fasc. IV, *Les regestes de 1208 à 1309*. Paris, 1971.

Mansi, J.D. *Sacrorum conciliorum nova et amplissima collectio*. Florence and Venice, 1759–98.

Migne, J.P. *Patrologiae cursus completus*. *Series graeco-latina:* Paris, 1857–66. *Series latina*: Paris, 1844–55.

Miklosich, F., and Müller, J. *Acta et diplomata graeca medii aevi sacra et profana*. Vols. I and II. Vienna, 1860, 1862.

Potthast, A. *Regesta pontificum romanorum inde ab anno post Christum natum MCXCVIII ad annum MCCCIV*. Berlin, 1875.

Raynaldus, O. *Annales ecclesiastici*.

Rohricht, R. *Quinti belli sacri script. min.* 3 vols. Geneva, 1879.

Sathas, K.N. *Mesaionike bibliotheke. Bibliotheca graeca medii aevi.* 7 vols. Venice and Paris, 1872–94.

Sbaralea, J. *Bullarium franciscanum.* Rome, 1759.

Tafel, G.L.F. and Thomas, G.M. *Urkunden zur älteren Handels- und Staatsgeschichte der Republik Venedig* (= Fontes Rerum Austriacarum, II, xii–xiv). Vols. I–III. Vienna, 1856–7.

Theiner, A., and Miklosich, F. *Monumenta spectantia ad unionem ecclesiarum graecae et romanae.* Vienna, 1872.

Thiriet, F. *Délibérations des Assemblées vénitiennes concernant le Romanie.* Vol. I. Paris/La Haye, 1966.

______. *Régestes des délibérations du Sénat de Venise concernant la Romanie.* Vol. I. Paris/La Haye, 1958.

Particular Sources

Greek

Acropolites, George. *Annales,* edited by I. Bekker (Bonn: CSHB, 1836); *Historia,* edited by A. Heisenberg (Leipzig, 1903).

Akindynus, Gregory. "De essentia et operatione," *MPG* 151:1192–1242; "Dix-huit lettres de Grégoire Acindyne analysées et datées," edited by R.-J. Leonertz, *OCP* 23 (1957): 114–44. "Gregorii Acindyni epistulae selectae IX," edited by R.-J. Loenertz, *EEBS* 27 (1957): 89–109.

Alexander IV, Pope. "Constitutio cyprica." In Greek and Latin. *MPG* 140: 1533–60.

Apocaucus, John. Works edited by V.G. Vasilievsky. "Epirotica saeculi XIII." *Vizantijsk; Vremennik* 3 (1896): 233–99.

Anthanasius I. *The Correspondence of Athanasius I, Patriarch of Constantinople,* text, translation and commentary, by Mary-Alice Maffrey Talbot (= Corpus Fontium Historiae Byzantinae VII) (Washington, 1975); "La Vie d'Athanase Patriarche de Constantinople," edited by R.P.H. Delahaye, in *Melanges d'archeologie et d'histoire de l'Ecole Francaise de Rome* 17 (1897): 39–75.

Bardanes, George. E. Kurtz, "Georgios Bardanes Metropolit von Kerkyra," *BZ* 15 (1906):603–613; J.M. Hoeck and R.-J. Loenertz, *Nikolaos-Nectarios von Otranto Abt von Casole* (Ettal, 1965), app. II, pp. 148–235.

Barlaam de Seminaria. *Opera, MPG* 151:1255–1364; C. Gianelli, "Un progetto di Barlaam Calabro per l'unione delle Chiese," *Miscellanea Giovanni Mercati* III (= *ST* 123) (Città del Vaticano, 1946), pp. 154–208.

Beccus, John. *Opera, MPG* 141:16–1032.

Blemmydes, Nicephorus. *Opera, MPG* 142:533–1622; A. Heisenberg, *Curriculum vitae et carmina* (Leipzig, 1896).

Cabasilas, Nilus. "De causis dissensionis in ecclesia et de papae primatu." *MPG* 149: 684–730.

Calecas, John, Patriarch of Constantinople. *Decrees, MPG* 152:1215–84; P.

Joannou, "Joannes XIV Kalekas Patriarch von Konstantinopel unedierte Rede zur Krönung Joannes' V.," *OCP* 27 (1961): 32–45.

Calecas, Manuel. *Opera, MPG* 152: 11–661; "Contro Giuseppe Briennio," edited by G. Mercati, *Notizie di Procoro e Demetrio Cidone, etc.* (= *ST* 56) (Città del Vaticano, 1931), pp. 450–73; *Correspondance de Manuel Calecas,* edited by R.-J. Loenertz (= *ST* 152) (Città del Vaticano, 1950).

Callistus and Philotheus, Patriarchs of Constantinople. *Letters. MPG* 152:1303–1460.

Cantacuzenus, John. *Historiarum libri IV*, edited by I. Schopen and B.G. Niebuhr (Bonn: CSHB, 1828–32); *The History of John Cantacuzenus*, book IV, text, translation and commentary by T. Miller (Ann Arbor, Michigan: Univ. Microfilm International, 1975).

Chomatianus, Demetrius. *Letters*. Edited by J.B. Pitra. *Analecta sacra et classica Spicilegio Solesmensi parata*. Vol. VII (VI). Paris/Rome, 1891.

Choniates, Michael (Acominatus). *Extant Works*. Edited by S. Lambros. 2 vols. Athens, 1879–80.

Choniates, Nicetas. *Historia*. Edited by I. Bekker. Bonn: CSHB, 1835.

Cydones, Demetrius. *Letters*, edited by R.-J. Loenertz, *Démétrius Cydonès, Correspondance*, 2 vols. (*ST* 186, 208) (Città del Vaticano, 1956, 1960); G. Cammelli, (Paris, 1930); Letters about his brother Procorus, An Account of his Faith to the Greeks, A Vindication of his Sincerity, and Religious Testament in G. Mercati, *Notizie di Procoro e Demetrio Cidone* (*ST* 56) (Città del Vaticano, 1931), pp. 293–335, 359–435.

Speeches: Occisorum Thessalonicae monodia, *MPG* 109:639–52; De admittendo Latinorum subsidio, *MPG* 154:961–1008; De non reddenda Gallipoli, ibid., 1009–36.

Dossier grec de l'Union de Lyon (1273–1277) (= Archives de l'Orient Chrétien 16), edited by V. Laurent and J. Darrouzès (Paris, 1976).

Ephraem Monachus. *Imperatorum et patriarcharum recensus,* edited by A. Mai (Bonn: CSHB, 1840).

Frederick II Hohenstaufen. N. Festa, "Le lettere greche di Federigo II," *Archivio Storico Italiano*, ser. 5, 13 (1894):1–34; M.A. Dendias, "About a Letter of Frederick II to John Doucas Vatatzes" (in Greek), *EEBS* 13 (1937): 400–411.

Georgius Cyprius. *Vita et opera*. *MPG* 142:20–470.

Germanus II, Patriarch of Constantinople. *Opera*, *MPG* 140:601–757; 119: 797–808; Letters: in A. Tautu, *Acta Honorii III et Gregorii IX* (Città del Vaticano, 1950), pp. 240–9; to the cardinals, ibid., pp. 249–52; to John Apocaucus, in J.B. Pitra, *Analecta sacra,* etc., Vol. VII (Rome, 1891), pp. 483–6; J. Nicole, "Bref inédit de Germain II Patriarche de Constantinople avec une recension nouvelle de l'Empereur Jean Ducas Vatatzès," *Revue des Etudes Grecques* 7 (1894):68–80; J. Gill, "An Unpublished Letter of Germanus Patriarch of Constantinople (1222–1240)," *Byz* 44 (1974): 138–51.

Gregoras, Nicephorus. *Byzantina Historia*, edited by L. Schopen, 3 vols. (Bonn: CSHB, 1829–55); R. Guilland, *La correspondance de Nicéphore Grégoras* (Paris, 1927).

Isidore, Patriarch of Constantinople. *Opera, MPG* 152:1285–1302.

John Camaterus, Patriarch of Constantinople. A. Papadakis, "John Camaterus Confronts Innocent III: An Unpublished Correspondence," *Bslav* 33 (1972): 26–41.

Makrembolites, Alexius. "Dialogue between Rich and Poor." Edited by I. Ševčenko, *Zbornik Radova* 6 (1960):187–228.

Meliteniotes, Constantine. *Opera, MPG* 141:1032–1273.

Metochites, George. *Opera, MPG* 141:1276–1424; *Historia dogmatica*, in A. Mai, *Nova patrum bibliotheca*, tom. VIII, pt. 2, (Rome, 1871), pp. 1–227.

Metochites, Theodore. *Miscellanea philosophica et historica*. Edited by G. Müller and Th. Kiessling. Leipzig, 1821.

Michael Autoreianus, Patriarch of Constantinople. N. Oikonomidès, "Cinq actes inédites du patriarche Michel Autôrianos." *REB* 25 (1967):113–45.

Michael Palaeologus. "Imperatoris Michaelis Palaeologi de vita sua," edited by H. Grégoire, *Byz* 29–30 (1959–60):447–75; N. Festa, "Lettera inedita del imperatore Michele VIII Paleologo al Pontefice Clemente IV," *Bess* 6 (1899–1900):42–57.

Nicetas, Metropolitan of Manronea. *Sermones. MPG* 139:170–221.

Pachymeres, George. *De Michaele et Andronico Palaeologis*. Edited by I. Bekker. 2 vols. Bonn: CSHB, 1835.

Palamas, Gregory. *Opera, MPG* 150: 909–1225; 151: 9–550; *Writings*, edited by P. Chrestou et al, 3 vols. to date (Thessalonica, 1968–72).

Philotheus, Patriarch of Constantinople. Cf. *Callistus*.

Schmitt, J. *The Chronicle of the Morea*. London, 1904.

Theodore II Lascaris, Emperor. *Theodorus Lascaris junior, De Processione Spiritus sancti apologetica*, edited by H.B. Swete (London, 1875); *Theodori Ducae Lascaris epistolae* CCXVII, edited by N. Festa (Florence, 1898).

Latin

Bartholomaeus de Alverna, OFM. "F. Bartholomaei de Alverna vicarii Bosniae, 1367–1407, quaedam scripta hucusque inedita." *ArchOFM* 55 (1962): 59–81.

Clari, Robert de. *La Conquête de Constantinople*. Edited by P. Lauer. Paris, 1924.

Finke, H. *Acta aragonensia*. Vol. II. Berlin, 1908.

Franchi, A. *Il concilio II di Lione (1274) secondo la "Ordinatio Concilii Generalis Lugdunensis*." Rome, 1965.

Guntherus. "Guntheri monachi historia Constantinopolitana sub Balduino„ anno 1210." *Thesaurus monumentorum ecclesiasticorum . . . Henrici Canisii*. Edited by J. Basnage. Vol. IV (Amsterdam, 1725), pp. v–xxii.

John of Joinville. *The Life of St. Louis*. Translated by M.R.B. Shaw. London: Penguin Classics, 1963.

Liber censuum, de censuis Camerarius (= Honorius III). Edited by P. Fabre, L. Duchesne, et G. Mollat. 3 vols. Paris, 1905–52.

Longnon, J. *Histoire de l'Empereur Henri de Constantinople*. Paris, 1948.

Muntaner, Ramon. *The Chronicle of Ramon Muntaner*. Translated by Lady Goodenough. London, 1920–1.

Monumenta Germaniae Historica.

Devastatio Constantinopolitana. Edited by G.H. Pertz. SS. XVI (Hanover, 1859), pp. 9–12.

Annales Colonienses Maximi. Edited by K. Pertz. SS. XVII (Hanover, 1861), pp. 729–847.

Gesta episcoporum Halberstadensium. Edited by L. Weiland. SS. XXIII (Hanover, 1874), pp. 73–123.

Chronica Albrichi monachi Trium Fontium. Edited by P. Scheffer-Boichorst. SS. XXIII (Hanover, 1874), pp. 631–950.

Sicardi episcopi Cremonensis cronica. Edited by O. Holder-Egger. SS. XXXI (Hanover, 1903), pp. 1–183.

Salimbene di Adam, cronica. Edited by P. Holder-Egger. SS. XXXII. Hanover/Leipzig, 1905–13.

Chronica regia Coloniae continuatio IV. Edited by G. Waitz. *MGH* in usum scholarum, n. 18. Hanover, 1880.

Ausbert, Historia de expeditione Friderici Imperatoris. Edited by A. Choust. *MGH*, SS., nova series V. Berlin, 1928.

Registers of Papal Letters.

Innocent III. *Opera omnia*, *MPL* 214–217; Die Register Innocenz III., I Band, 1 Pontifikatsjahr: Text eds. O. Hageneder and A. Haidacher (Graz/Kôln, 1964).

Honorius III. *I regesti del Pontefice Onorio III dall'anno 1216 all'anno 1227*. Edited by P. Pressutti. Rome, 1884.

Gregory IX. *Les Registres de Grégoire IX*. Edited by L. Auvray. Paris, 1896, 1907.

Innocent IV. *Les registres d'Innocent IV*. Edited by E. Berger. Paris, 1884–1911.

Alexander IV. *Les registres d'Alexandre IV*. Edited by Bourel de la Roncière, J. de Loye, and A. Coulon. Paris, 1895–1959.

Urban IV. *Les registres d'Urban IV (1261–1264)*. Edited by J. Guiraud. Paris, 1892–1958.

Clement IV. *Les registres de Clément IV (1265–1268)*. Edited by E. Jordan. Paris, 1893–1945.

Gregory X. *Les registres de Grégoire X (1272–1276)*. Edited by J. Guiraud. Paris, 1892–8.

Nicholas III. *Les registres de Nicholas III (1277–1280)*. Edited by M.J. Gay. Paris, 1898–1938.

Martin IV. *Les registres de Martin IV (1281–1285)*. Edited by Membres de l'Ecole Française de Rome. 1901–1935.

Honorius IV. *Les registres d'Honorius IV (1285–1287)*. Edited by M. Prou. Paris, 1888.

Nicholas IV. *Les registres de Nicholas IV (1288–1292)*. Edited by E. Langlois. Paris, 1886–1893.

Boniface VIII. *Les registres de Boniface VIII (1292–1303)*. Edited by G. Degard, M. Faucon, A. Thomas, and R. Fawter. Paris, 1884–1939.

Clement V. *Regestum Clementis Papae V*. Cura monachorum Ordinis S. Benedicti. Rome, 1885–92, 1948.

John XXII. *Jean XXII (1316–1334): Lettres communes*, edited by G. Mollat (Paris, 1904–46); *Lettres secrètes et curiales*, edited by A. Coulon (Paris, 1906–).

Benedict XII. *Benoit XII (1334–1342): Lettres communes*, edited by J.-M. Vidal (Paris, 1903); *Lettres closes et patentes* (not concerning France), edited by J.-M. Vidal (Paris, 1913); *Lettres closes et patentes* (concerning France), edited by G. Daumet (Paris, 1920).

Innocent VI. *Innocent VI (1352–1362): Lettres secrètes et curiales*. Edited by P. Gasnault and M.-H. Laurent. Paris, 1959–68.

Urban V. *Urbain V (1362–1370): Lettres communes*, edited by M.-H. Laurent and others (Paris, 1954–); *Lettres secrètes et curiales*, edited by P. Lecacheux and G. Mollat (Paris, n.d.–1955).

Gregory XI. *Grégoire XI (1370–1378): Lettres secrètes et curiales* (concerning France), edited by L. Mirot and H. Jassemin; (concerning other countries), edited by G. Mollat (Paris, 1962–5).

Pontificia Commissio ad Redigendum Codicem Iuris Canonici Orientalis: Fontes, Series III (= Pont. Comm.).

Vol. II. *Acta Innocentii PP. III (1198–1216)*, edited by P. Theodosius Halušĉynskyj (Città del Vaticano, 1944).

Vol. III. *Acta Honorii III (1216–1227) et Gregorii IX (1227–1241),* edited by A.L. Tautu (Città del Vaticano, 1950).

Vol. IV, tom. I. *Acta Innocentii PP. IV (1243–1254),* edited by T.T. Halušĉynskyj and M.M. Wojnar (Rome, 1962).

Tom. II. *Acta Alexandri PP. IV (1254–1261),* edited by T.T. Halušĉynskyj and M.M. Wojnar (Città del Vaticano, 1966).

Vol. V, tom. I. *Acta Urbani IV, Clementis IV, Gregorii X (1261–1276),* ed. A.L. Tautu (Città del Vaticano, 1953).

Tom. II. *Acta Romanorum Pontificum ad Innocentio V ad Benedictum XI (1276–1304),* edited by F.M. Delorme and A.L. Tautu (Città del Vaticano, 1954).

Vol. VI. *Excerpta ex actis synodorum oecumenicorum* (Città del Vaticano, 1954).

Vol. VII, tom. I. *Acta Clementis PP. V (1303–1314),* edited by F.M. Delorme and A.L. Tautu (Città del Vaticano, 1955).

Tom. II. *Acta Ioannis XXII (1317–1334),* edited by A.L. Tautu (Città del Vaticano, 1952).

Vol. VIII. *Acta Benedicti XII (1334–1342),* edited by A.L. Tautu (Città del Vaticano, 1958).

Vol. IX. *Acta Clementis PP. VI (1342–1352),* edited by A.L. Tautu (Città del Vaticano, 1960).

Vol. X. *Acta Innocentii PP. VI (1352–1362),* edited by A.L. Tautu (Città del Vaticano, 1961).

Vol. XI. *Acta Urbani PP. VI (1362–1370),* edited by A.L. Tautu (Città del Vaticano, 1964).

Vol. XII. *Acta Gregorii PP. XI (1370–1378),* edited by A.L. Tautu (Città del Vaticano, 1966).

Vol. XIII, tom. I. *Acta Urbani PP. V (1378–1389), Bonifatii PP. IX (1389–*

1404), Innocentii PP. VII (1404–1406) et Gregorii PP. XII (1406–1415), edited by A.L. Tautu (Rome, 1970).

Tom. II. *Acta pseudopontificum Clementis VII (1378–1394), Benedicti XIII (1394–1417), Alexandri V (1409–1410) et Johannis XXIII (1410–1415)*, edited by A.L. Tautu (Rome, 1971).

Sanudo Torsello, Marino. "Marino Sanuto dicti Torselli epistolae." Edited by J. Bongars in *Gesta Dei per Francos*, II (Hanover, 1611).

Smet, J. *The Life of Saint Peter Thomas by Philippe de Mézières* (= *Textus et Studia Historica Carmelitana* 2) (Rome, 1954).

Tractatus contra Graecorum errores de processione Spiritus Sancti, de animabus defunctorum, de azymis et fermentato, de obedientia Romanae Ecclesiae, anno 1252, In *Thesaurus monumentorum ecclesiasticorum et historicorum Henrici Canisii*. Edited by J. Basnage IV (Amsterdam, 1725).

Villehardouin, Geoffroy de. *The Conquest of Constantinople*. Translated by M.R.B. Shaw (London: Penguin Classics, 1963).

Modern Works

Altaner, B. *Die Dominikanermission des 13. Jahrhunderts*. Habelschwerdt, 1924.

Andrea, A.J. "Pope Innocent III and the Diversion of the Fourth Crusade Army to Zara." *Bslav* 33 (1072): 6–25.

Angold, M. *A Byzantine Government in Exile*. Oxford, 1974.

Attiya, A.S. *The Crusade of Nicopolis*. London, 1934.

Bakalopoulos, A.E. *Origins of the Greek Nation: The Byzantine Period, 1204–1461*. New Brunswick, N.J., 1970.

Baldwin, M.W. *Alexander III and the Twelfth Century* (= *The Popes Through History* 3). Glen Rock, 1968.

Barker, J.W. *Manuel II Palaeologus 1391–1425: A Study in Late Byzantine Statesmanship*. New Brunswick, N.J., 1969.

Beck, H.-G. *Theodore Metochites. Die Krise des byzantinischen Weltbildes im 14. Jahrhundert*. Münich, 1952.

Berger de Xivrey, M. "Mémoire sur la vie et les ouvrages de l'Empereur Manuel Paléologue." In *Mémoires de l'Institut de France*, XIX, 2e partie, pp. 1–201. 1853.

Beyer, H.-V. "Nikephoros Gregoras als Theologe und sein erstes Auftreten gegen die Hesychasten." *JOBG* 20 (1971): 171–88.

Binns, L.E. *Innocent III*. London, 1931.

Bois, J. "Les débuts de la controverse hésychaste." *EO* 5 (1902): 353–62.

______. "Le synode hésychaste de 1341." *EO* 6 (1903): 50–60.

Borsari, S. *Il dominio veneziano a Creta nel XIII secolo*. Napoli, 1963.

______. "La politica bizantina di Carlo d'Angiò dal 1266 al 1271." *Archivio storico per le Provincie Napolitane*, NS 35 (1956): 39–62.

______. *Studi sulle colonie veneziane in Romania nel XIII secolo*. Napoli, 1966.

Bosch, U.V. *Andronikos III. Palaeologos*. Amsterdam, 1965.

Bradford, E. *The Great Betrayal: Constantinople 1204*. London, 1967.

Brand, C.M. "The Byzantines and Saladin 1185–1192: Opponents of the Third Crusade." *Spec* 37 (1962): 167–81.

______. *Byzantium Confronts the West 1180–1204*. Cambridge, Mass., 1968.

Bratianu, G.I. "Notes sur le projet de mariage entre l'Empereur Michel IX Paléologue et Catherine de Courtenay (1288–93)." *RHSE* 1 (1924): 59–63.

Brehier, L. "Attempts at Reunion of the Greek and Latin Churches." *CMH* IV^1 (1923): 594–626.

______. *L'Eglise et l'Orient au moyen âge*[5], pp. 144–81. Paris, 1928.

______. *Les Institutions de l'Empire Byzantin* (= *Le Monde Byzantin* II), pp. 431 ss. Paris, 1949.

______. "Notes sur l'histoire de l'enseignement supérieur à Constantinople." *Byz* 3 (1926): 73–94; 4 (1927–8): 13–28.

Brown, E.A.R. "The Cistercians in the Latin Empire of Constantinople and Greece 1204–1276." *Trad* 14 (1958): 63–120.

Burns, R.I. "The Catalan Company and the European Powers, 1305–1311," *Spec* 29 (1954): 751–71.

Cahen, C. *La Syrie du Nord*. Paris, 1940.

Canart, P. "Nicéphore Blemmyde et le mémoire adressé aux envoyés de Grégoire IX (Nicée 1234)." *OCP* 25 (1959): 310–25.

Carile, A. "La Partitio Terrarum Imperii Romanie del 1204 nella tradizione storica dei Veneziani." *SBN* 2–3 (1965–1966): 167–79.

______. "Partitio Terrarum Imperii Romanie." *Studi Veneziani* 7 (1965): 125–305.

Cessi, R. "Venice to the Eve of the Fourth Crusade." In *CMH* IV^2, pp. 251–74. Cambridge, 1966.

Chalandon, F. *Histoire de la domination normande en Italie et en Sicilie*. 2 vols. Paris, 1907.

Chapman, C. *Michel Paléologue restaurateur de l'Empire Byzantin (1261–1282)*. Paris, 1926.

Charanis, P. "An Important Short Chronicle of the Fourteenth Century." *Byz* 13 (1938): 335–62.

______. "Internal Strife in Byzantium during the Fourteenth Century." *Byz* 15 (Boston, 1940–41): 208–30.

______. "The Monastic Properties and the State in the Byzantine Empire." *DOP* 4 (1948): 51–118.

______. "The Monk as an Element of Byzantine Society." *DOP* 25 (1971): 61–84.

______. "A Note on the Population and the Cities of the Byzantine Empire in the XIIIth Century." In *Joshua Starr Memorial Volume*, pp. 135–48. New York, 1953.

______. "On the Date of the Occupation of Gallipoli by the Turks." *Bslav* 16 (1955): 113–117.

______. "On the Social Structure and Economic Organization of the Byzantine Empire in the Thirteenth Century and Later." *Bslav* 12 (1951): 94–153.

______. "Piracy in the Aegean during the Reign of Michael VIII Palaeologus." *Annuaire de l'Institut de Philologie et d'Histoire Orientales et Slaves* 10 (1950): 127–36.

______. "The Strife among the Palaeologi and the Ottoman Turks 1370–1402." *Byz*

16 (1942–43): 286–314; 17 (1944–45): 330.

Charitakis, G. "Catalogue of the Dated Manuscripts of the Patriarchal Library of Cairo." In Greek. In *EEBS* 4 (1927): 109–204.

Chrysostomidis, J. "John V Palaeologus in Venice (1370–1371) and the Chronicle of Caroldo: a Re-interpretation." *OCP* 31 (1965): 76–84.

______. "Venetian Commercial Privileges under the Palaeologi." *Studi Veneziani* 12 (1970): 267–356.

Clugnet, L. *Dictionnaire grec-français des noms liturgiques en usage dans l'Eglise grecque.* London: Variorum Reprints, 1971.

Cognasso, F. *Storia delle Crociate.* Varese, 1967.

Cohn, N. *The Pursuit of the Millennium*[3]. London, 1970.

Constantelos, D.J. "Intellectual Challenges to the Authority of Tradition in the Medieval Greek Church." *Greek Orthodox Theological Review* 15 (1970): 56–84.

Cox, E.L. *The Green Count of Savoy: Amadeus VI and Transalpine Savoy in the XIVth Century.* Princeton, 1967.

Darroutzes, J. "Conférence sur la primauté du pape à Constantinople en 1357." *REB* 19 (1961): 76–109.

______. "Lettre inédite de Jean Cantacuzène relative à la controverse palamite." *REB* 17 (1959): 7–27.

______. *Recherches sur les "Offices" de l'Eglise Byzantine* (= *Archives de l'Orient Chrétien* 11). Paris, 1970.

Dawson, C. *The Mongol Mission.* London, 1955.

Delaville le Roulx, J. *La France en Orient au XIV*[e] *siècle.* 2 vols. Paris, 1886.

Demetrakopoulos, A. *Graecia Orthodoxa.* Leipzig, 1872.

Dennis, G.T. "The Deposition of the Patriarch John Calecas." *JOBG* 9 (1960): 51–5.

______, ed. and trans. *The Letters of Manuel II Palaeologus* (= Dumbarton Oaks Texts 4). Dumbarton Oaks, 1977.

______. *The Reign of Manuel II Palaeologus in Thessalonica 1382–1387* (= *Orientalia Christians Analecta* 159). Rome, 1960.

DeVries, W. "Innocenz III. (1198–1216) und der christliche Osten." *ArchHP* 3 (1965): 87–126.

______. "Innocenz IV. (1243–1254) und der christliche Osten." *Ostkirchliche Studien* 2 (1963): 113–31.

______. "Die Päpste von Avignon und der christliche Osten." *OCP* 30 (1964): 85–128.

Diehl, C. *Byzance. Grandeur et Décadence* (Paris, 1919), translated by N. Walford, *Byzantium, Greatness and Decline* (New Brunswick, N.J., 1957).

______. "L'Empire byzantin sous les Paléologues." In *Etudes Byzantines.* Paris, 1905.

Diller, A. "Byzantine Lists of Old and New Geographical Names." *BZ* 63 (1970): 27–42.

______. "Directorium ad litteras imperatorum Orientis quae in Archivo Arcis S. Angeli exstabant, nunc in Vaticano etc." *Bess 6* (1899): 249–57.

Dölger, F. *Byzanz und die europäische Staatenwelt.* Ettal, 1934.

______. "Johannes VII., Kaiser der Rhomaer, 1390–1408." *BZ* 31 (1931): 21–36.

______. "Zum Aufstand des Andronikos IV. gegen seinen Vater Johannes V. im Mai 1373." *REB* 19 (1961): 328–32.

Dondaine, A. " 'Contra Graecos.' Premiers écrits polémiques des Dominicains d'Orient." *ArchOP* 21 (1951): 320–446.

______. "Hugues Ethérien et Léon Toscan." *Archives d'Histoire doctrinale et littéraire du Moyen Age* 27 (1952): 67–125.

______. "Nicholas de Cotrone et les sources du 'Contra Errores Graecorum' de Saint Thomas." *Divus Thomas* 28 (1950): 313–40.

Duggan, A. *The Story of the Crusades 1097–1291*. London, 1969.

Dvornik, F. *Byzantium and the Roman Primacy*. New York, 1966.

______. *Early Christian and Byzantine Political Philosophy: Origins and Background* (*Dumbarton Oaks Studies* IX, 1966).

Erickson, J. "Leavened and Unleavened." *St. Vladimir's Theological Quarterly* 14 (1970): 155–76.

Erriquez, L. "I legati pontifici in Oriente dal 1261 al 1334." *Apollinaris* 38 (1965): 307–47.

Eszer, A.K. *Das abenteuerliche Leben des Johannes Laskaris Kalopheros*. Wiesbaden, 1969.

Eustratides, S. "Patriarch Arsenius Autoreianus." In Greek. *Hellenika* 1 (1928): 78–94.

______. "The Letters of Patriarch Gregory the Cypriot." In Greek. *Ekklesiastikos Pharos* 1 (1908): 195–211.

Evert-Kappesowa, H. "La société byzantine et l'union de Lyon." *Bslav* 10 (1949): 28–41.

______. "Une page de l'histoire des relations byzantino-latines." *Bslav* 13 (1952): 68–92; 16 (1955): 297–317; 17(1956): 1–18.

Every, G. *The Byzantine Patriarchate 451–1204*². London, 1962.

______. *Misunderstandings between East and West*. London, 1965.

Failler, A. "La déposition du patriarche Callistus 1er (1353)." *REB* 31 (1973): 5–163.

Faral, E. "Geoffrey de Villehardouin: La question de sa sincérité." *Revue Historique* 177 (1936): 530–82.

Fedalto, G. *La Chiesa latina in Oriente*. 3 vols. Verona, 1973, 1976, 1978.

______. *Simone Atumano, monaco di Studio, arcivescovo latino di Tebe, secolo XIV*. Brescia, 1968.

Ferrard, Ch. G. "The Amount of Constantinopolitan Booty in 1204." *Studi Veneziani* 13 (1971): 95–104.

Fliche, A. "Innocent III et la réforme de l'Eglise." *Revue d'Histoire Ecclésiastique* 44 (1949): 87–152.

______. "Le problème oriental au second concile oecuménique de Lyon (1274)." *OCP* 13 (1947): 475–85.

Folda, J. "The Fourth Crusade 1201–1203: Some Reconsiderations." *Bslav* 26 (1965):277–90.

Foreville, R. *Latran I, II, III, et Latran IV* (= *Histoire des Conciles Oecuméniques* 4). Paris, 1965.

Fotheringham, J.K. "Genoa and the Fourth Crusade." *English Historical Review* 25 (1910): 20–54.

Frances, E. "Sur la Conquête de Constantinople par les Latins." *Bslav* 15 (1954): 21–26.

Frolow, A. *Recherches sur la déviation de la IVe croisade vers Constantinople.* Paris, 1955.

Gardner, A. *The Lascarids of Nicaea.* London, 1912.

Garitte, G. "Une tentative de suppression du rite grec en Calabre en 1334." In *Miscellanea Giovanni Mercati* (= *ST* 123) pp. 31–40. Città del Vaticano, 1946.

Gautier, P. "Récit inédit sur le siège de Constantinople (1394–1402)." *REB* 23 (1965): 100–117.

Gay, J. *Le Pape Clément VI et les affaires d'Orient (1342–1352).* Paris, 1904.

Geanakoplos, D.J. *Byzantine East and Latin West.* Oxford, 1966.

______. *Emperor Michael Palaeologus and the West.* Cambridge, Mass., 1959.

______. *Interaction of the "Sibling" Byzantine and Western Cultures in the Middle Ages and Italian Renaissance (330–1600).* New Haven and London, 1976.

Gianelli, C. "Le récit d'une mission diplomatique de Georges Métochite (1275–1276) et le Vat. Gr. 1716." In M.-H. Laurent, *Le Bienheureux Innocent V*, pp. 419–43.

______. "Un progetto du Barlaam Calabro per l'unione delle Chiese." In *Miscellanea Giovanni Mercati* (= *ST* 123) pp. 157–208. Città del Vaticano, 1946.

______. "Un documento sconosciuto della polemica tra Greci e Latini intorno alla formula battesimale." *OCP* 10 (1944): 150–67.

Gill, J. "John Beccus, Patriarch of Constantinople 1275–1282." *Byzantina*, 7 (1975): 251–66.

______. "John V Palaeologus at the Court of Louis I of Hungary (1366)." *Bslav* 38 (1977).

______. *The Council of Florence.* Cambridge, 1959.

______. "The Church Union of the Council of Lyons (1274) portrayed in Greek Documents." *OCP* 40 (1974): 5–45.

______. "Emperor Andronicus II and Patriarch Athanasius I." *Byzantina* 2 (1970): 13–19.

______. "Franks, Venetians and Pope Innocent III 1201–1203." *Studi Veneziani* 3 (1970): 85–106.

______. "Innocent III and the Greeks: Aggressor or Apostle?" In *Relations between East and West in the Middle Ages*, pp. 95–108. Edited by D. Baker. Edinburgh, 1973.

______. "Notes on the 'De Michaele et Andronico Palaeologis' of George Pachymeres." *BZ* 68 (1975): 295–303.

______. *Personalities of the Council of Florence.* Oxford, 1964.

______. "The Tribulations of the Greek Church in Cyprus 1196–c. 1280." *BForsch* 4 (1977): 73–93.

______. "An Unpublished Letter of Germanus, Patriarch of Constantinople (1222–1240)." *Byz* 44 (1974): 138–51.

______. "Pope Urban V (1362–1370) and the Greeks of Crete." *OCP* 39 (1973): 461–68.

Giunta, F. "Sulla politica orientale di Innocenzo VI." *Storia e Letteratura* 71 (1958): 305-20.

Golubovich, G. *Biblioteca bio-bibliografica della Terra Santa e dell'Oriente francescano* (= *BBTS*). 5 vols. Quaracchi, 1906-27.

______. "Cenni storici su Fra Giovanni Parastron." *Bess* 10 (1906): 295-304.

______. "Disputatio Latinorum et Graecorum seu relatio apocrisiariorum Gregorii IX de gestis Nicaeae in Bithynia et Nymphaeae in Lydia, 1234." *ArchOFM* 12 (1919): 418-70.

Gouillard, J. "Le Synodikon de l'orthodoxie: Edition et commentaire." *Travaux et Mémoires* 2 (1967): 1-316.

Grégoire, H. "The Question of the Diversion of the Fourth Crusade." *Byz* 15 (1940-41): 152-66.

Grégoire, J. "La relation éternelle de l'Esprit au Fils d'après les écrits de Jean de Damas." *Revue d'Histoire Ecclésiastique* 64 (1969): 713-55.

Grumel, V. "Les ambassades pontificales à Byzance après le IIe Concile de Lyon (1247-1280)." *EO* 23 (1924): 437-47.

______. "L'année du monde dans l'ère byzantine." *EO* 34 (1935): 319-26.

______. "L'authenticité de la lettre de Jean Vatatzès empereur de Nicée au Pape Grégoire IX." *EO* 29 (1930): 450-8.

______. "Un concil arséniste en 1278." *EO* 24 (1925): 324-25.

______. "Concile anti-unioniste contre Michel et Beccos." *EO* 24 (1925): 321-22.

______. "Une correction proposée à la relation d'Ogerius." *EO* 24 (1925): 323-24.

______. "En Orient après le Concile de Lyon." *EO* 24 (1925):321-5.

______. "Une identification—Jean évêque de Tricola." *EO* 24 (1925): 322-23.

______. "Lyon, Le concile de." In *Dictionnaire de Théologie Catholique,* IX: 1374-1410.

______. "Nicéphore Blemmyde et la procession du Saint-Espirit." *Revue des Sciences Philosophiques et Theologiques* 18 (1929): 636-56.

______. "Saint Thomas et la doctrine des Grecs sur la procession du Saint-Esprit." *EO* 25 (1926): 257-80.

Guilland, R. *Essai sur Nicéphore Grégoras*. Paris, 1926.

______. "Remarques sur la vie monastique à Byzance." *EEBS* 30 (1960-61): 39-53.

Hadjipsaltis, K. "The Church of Cyprus and the Oecumenical Patriarchate in Nicaea." In Greek. *Kypriakai Spoudai* 15 (1951): 63-82.

______. "The Relations of Cyprus to the Byzantine Empire of Nicaea." In Greek. *Kypriakai Spoudai* 28 (1964): 135-68.

Halecki, O. "La Pologne et l'Empire Byzantin." *Byz* 7 (1932): pp. 41-67.

______. "Rome et Byzance au temps du grand schisme d'Occident." *Collectanea Theologica (Lwów)* 18 (1937): 477-532.

______. *Un Empereur de Byzance à Rome*. Warsaw, 1930.

Heisenberg, A. *Neue Quellen zur Geschichte des lateinischen Kaisertums und der Kirchenunion.* I. *Der Epitaphios des Nikolaos Mesarites auf seinem Bruder Johannes;* II. *Die Unionsverhandlungen vom 30. August 1206;* III. *Der Bericht des Nikolaos Mesarites über die politischen und kirchlichen Ereignisse des Jahres 1214. Sitzungsberichte der bayer. Akad. der Wissenschaften, phil.-hist. Klasse*

(Münich, 1922), Abh. V; (1923), Abh. II and III.
Helfer, W. "Das Testament des Patriarchen Isidorus (1347–1349/50)." *JOBG* 17 (1968): 73–84.
Hoeck, J.M., and Loenertz, R.-J. *Nikolaos-Nektarios von Otranto, Abt von Casole*. Ettal, 1965.
Hofmann, G. "Johannes Damaskenos, Rom und Byzanz (1054–1500)." *OCP* 16 (1950):177–90.
_____. "Patriarch Johann Bekkos und die lateinische Kultur." *OCP* 11 (1945): 141–61.
Hunger, H. "Kaiser Johannes V Palaeologos und der heilige Berg." *BZ* 45 (1952): 357–79.
Hussey, J. *Church and Learning in the Byzantine Empire 867–1185*. New York, 1963.
Iliescu, O. "Le montant du tribut payé par Byzance à l'Empire Ottoman en 1379 et 1424." *RHSE* 9 (1971): 427–32.
Jacoby, D. "Jean Lascaris Calophèros, Chypre and la Morée." *REB* 26 (1968): 189–263.
Janin, R. "Au lendemain de la conquête de Constantinople. Les tentatives d'union des Eglises (1204–1208)." *EO* 32 (1933): 5–21.
_____.· L'Eglise latine à Thessalonique de 1204 à la conquête turque." *REB* 16 (1958): 206–16.
_____. "L'Empereur dans l'Eglise byzantine." *Nouvelle Revue Théologique* (1955), pp. 49–60.
_____. "Le monachisme byzantin au moyen âge; commende et typica (X–XIV siècle)." *REB* 22 (1964): 5–44.
_____. "Les sanctuaires de Byzance sous la domination latine (1204–1261)." *REB* 2 (1944): 134–84.
Jenkins, R.J.H. *Byzantium and Byzantinism*. Cincinnati, 1963.
John, E. "A Note on the Preliminaries of the Fourth Crusade." *Byz* 28 (1958): 95–103.
Jugie, M. "Barlaam est-il né catholique?" *EO* 39 (1940–42): 100–25.
_____. "La controverse Palamite (1341–1368). Les faits et les documents conciliaires." *EO* 30 (1931): 397–421.
_____. Démètrius Cydonès et la théologie latine à Byzance aux XIVe et XVe siècles." *EO* 27 (1928): 385–402.
_____. "Nicétas de Maronée et Nicétas de Mitylène." *EO* 26 (1927): 408–16.
_____. "Palamas Grégoire" and "Palamite (controverse)." In *Dictionnaire de Théologie Catholique,* XI: 1735–1818.
_____. "Le voyage de l'Empereur Manuel Paléologue en Occident (1399–1403)." *EO* 15 (1912): 322–32.
Kaeppeli, T. "Benedetto di Asinago da Como († 1329)." *ArchOP* 11 (1941): 83–88.
_____. "Deux nouveaux ouvrages de fr. Philippe Incontri de Péra, O.P." *ArchOP* 23 (1953): 163–83.
_____. "Kurze Mitteilungen über mittelaltliche Dominikanerschriftsteller." *ArchOP* 10 (1940): 282–96.

Karpozilos, A.D. *The Ecclesiastical Controversy between the Kingdom of Nicaea and the Principality of Epirus (1217–1233) (= Byzantine Texts and Studies* 7). Thessalonica, 1973.

Kemp, F. *Papsttum und Kaisertum bei Innocenz III* (= *Miscellanea Historiae Pontificiae* 19). Rome, 1954.

Konstantinidi-Bibikou, H. "*Yolande de Montferrat impératrice de Byzance*." *L'Hellénisme Contemporain* 4 (1950): 425–42.

Krekić, B. "Deux notes concernant le patriarcat latin de Constantinople au XIV siècle." *REB* 20 (1962): 202–9.

Kunstmann, F. "Studien über Marino Sanudo der Alteren." In *Abh. der hist. Cl. der kgl. bayer. Akad. der Wissen*. VII (1855): 695–819.

Kurtz, E. "Christophoros von Ankyra als Exarch des Patriarchen Germanos II." *BZ* 16 (1907): 120–42.

Kuttner, S. "Conciliar Law in the Making." In *Miscellanea Pio Paschini*, II: 39–81.

______. *L'édition romaine des conciles généraux et les actes du premier Concile de Lyons* (= *Miscellanea Historiae Pontificiae* 3). Rome, 1940.

Labarge, M.W. *St. Louis IX*. London, 1968.

Lagopates, S.P. *Germanos II, Patriarch of Constantinople-Nicaea*. In Greek. Tripoli, 1913.

Laiou, A.E. *Constantinople and the Latins: The Foreign Policy of Andronicus II (1282–1328)*. Cambridge, Mass., 1972.

______. "Marino Sanudo Torsello, Byzantium and the Turks; Background to the Anti-Turkish League of 1332–1334." *Spec* 45 (1970): 374–92.

______. "The Provisioning of Constantinople during the Winter of 1306–1307." *Byz* 37 (1967): 91–113.

La Monte, J.L. "A Register of the Cartulary of the Cathedral of Santa Sophia in Nicosia." *Byz* 5 (1929–30): 441–522.

Langer, W.L., and Blake, R.P. "The Rise of the Ottoman Turks and its Historical Background." *American Historical Review* 37 (1932): 468–505.

Laurent, M.-H. *Le Bienheureux Innocent V et son temps* (= *ST* 129). Città del Vaticano, 1947.

______. "Georges le Métochite, ambassadeur de Michael VIII Paléologue auprès du B. Innocent V." In *Miscellanea Giovanni Mercati* III (= *ST* 123), pp. 136–53. Città del Vaticano, 1946.

Laurent, V. "Action de grâces pour la victoire navale remportée sur les Turks à Atramyttion au cours de l'automne 1334." In *Eis Mnimim K. Amantou 1874–1960*, pp. 407–20. Athens, 1960.

______. "Le cas de Photius dans l'apologétique du patriarche Jean Beccos (1275–1282) au lendemain du deuzième concile de Lyon." *EO* 29 (1930): 396–415.

______. "La chronologie des patriarches de Constantinople de la première moitié du XIVe siècle (1294–1350)." *REB* 7 (1949–50): 145–55.

______. "Les crises religieuses: le schisme antiarsénite du métropolite Théolepte de Philadelphie († 1324)." *REB* 18 (1960): 45–54.

______. "La croisade et la question d'Orient sous le pontificat de Grégoire X." *RHSE* 22 (1945).

______. "La date de l'entrée de Jean VI Cantacuzène à Byzance et la déposition du patriarche Jean Calécas." *EO* 36 (1937): 169–71.

______. "Les dates du second patriarcat de Joseph 1er (31 XII 1282–av. 26 IV 1283)." *REB* 18 (1960): 205–08.

______. "Les droits de l'empereur en matière ecclésiastique. L'accord de 1380/82." *REB* 13 (1955): 5–20.

______. "Ecrits spirituels inédits de Macaire Choumnos († 1382) fondateur de la 'Néa Moni' à Thessalonique." *Hellenika* 14 (1955–56): 40–86.

______. "L'excommunication du patriarche Joseph par son prédecesseur Arsène." *Bz* 30 (1929/30): 489–96.

______. "Les grandes crises religeuses à Byzance: la fin du schisme Arsénite." *Bulletin de l'Academie Romaine, sect. hist.* 26, 2 (1945).

______."Grégoire X (1271–1276) et le projet d'une ligue antiturque." *EO* 37 (1938): 257–73.

______. "Lettre inédite de Jean XI Beccos, patriarche de Constantinople (1275–1282) au pape Grégoire X (1271–1276)." *L'Unité de l'Eglise* 12 (1934): 266–70.

______. "Notes de chronologie byzantine." *REB* 27 (1969): 209–28.

______. "Le Pape Alexandre IV (1254–1261) et l'Empire de Nicée." *EO* 34 (1935): 26–55.

______. "Le rapport de Georges le Métochite apocrisiaire de Michel VIII Paléologue auprès du Pape Grégoire X (1275–76)." *RHSE* 23 (1946): 233–47.

______. "Le serment antilatin du patriarche Joseph 1er (juin 1273)." *EO* 26 (1927): 396–407.

______. "Le serment de l'Empereur Andronique II Paléologue au Patriarche Athanase I lors de sa seconde accession au trône oecuménique (sept. 1303)." *REB* 23 (1965): 124–39.

______. "Les signataires du second synode des Blachernes (été 1285)." *EO* 26 (1927): 129–49.

______. "Les Vêpres Siciliennes et les dessous de la politique byzantine." *SBN* 7 (1953): 407–11.

______. "La vie et les oeuvres de Georges Moschabar." *EO* 28 (1929): 129–58.

______. "Un théologien unioniste de la fin du XIIIe siècle. Le métropolite d'Adrianople Théoctiste." *REB* 11 (1953): 187–96.

Lefèvre, Y. "Innocent III et son temps vus de Rome." *Mélanges d'archéologie et d'histoire* 61 (1949): 242–45.

Lemerle, P. *L'Emirat d'Aydin, Byzance et l'Occident.* Paris, 1957.

Lilla, S. "Un opuscolo polemico anonimo contro il patriarcha Becco di Costantinopoli (1275–1282)." *Bess* 40 (1970): 75–86.

Loenertz, R.-J. "Ambassadeurs grecs auprès du Pape Clément VI (1348)." *OCP* 19 (1953): 178–96.

______. *Byzantina et Franco-Graeca.* Articles parus de 1935 à 1966 réédités avec la collaboration de Peter Schreiner (= Storia e Letteratura: Raccolta di Studi e Testi). Rome, 1970.

______. "Démétrius Cydonès, I: De la naissance à l'année 1373." *OCP* 36 (1970): 42–47; "De 1373 à 1375." *OCP* 37 (1971): 5–39.

______. "Manuel Calécas, sa vie et ses oeuvres d'après ses lettres et ses apologies inédites." *ArchOP* 17 (1947): 195–207.

______. "Manuel Paléologue et Démétrius Cydonès. Remarques sur leurs correspondances." *EO* 36 (1937): 270–87, 474–87; 37 (1938): 107–24.

______. "Mémoire d'Ogier, protonotaire, pour Marco et Marchetto nonces de Michel VIII Paléologue auprès du Pape Nicholas III, 1278 printemps-été." *OCP* 31 (1965): 374–408.

______. "Notes d'histoire et de chronologie byzantines." *REB* 17 (1959): 158–67; 20 (1962): 171–80.

______. "La première insurrection d'Andronique IV Paléologue (1373)." *EO* 38 (1939): 334–45.

______. *La Société des Frères Pérégrinants.* Rome, 1937.

______. "Théodore Métochite et son père." *ArchOP* 23 (1953): 184–94.

Longnon, J. "L'Empereur Baudouin II et l'ordre de Saint Jacques." *Byz* 22 (1952): 297–99.

______. *L'Empire Latin de Constantinople et la Principauté de Morée.* Paris, 1949.

______. "L'Organisation de l'Eglise d'Athènes par Innocent III." In *Mémorial Louis Petit,* pp. 336–46. Bucharest, 1948.

Lowe, A. *The Catalan Vengeance.* London-Boston, 1972.

Luchaire, A. "Un document retrouvé." *Journal des Savants* N.S. 3 (1905): 557–67.

______. *Innocent III. La Question d'Orient.* Paris, 1907. Reprint. 1969.

Lunt, W.E. "The Sources for the First Council of Lyons, 1245." *Engl. Historical Review* 33 (1918): 72–78.

Maccarrone, M. *Chiesa e Stato nella dottrina di Papa Innocenzo III* (= *Lateranum,* N.S. an 6, nn. 3–4). Rome, 1940.

______. "La ricerca dell'unione con la Chiesa greca sotto Innocenzo III." *Unitas.* Italian Edition. 19 (1964): 251–67.

Magoulias, H.J. "A Study in Roman Catholic and Greek Orthodox Church Relations on the Island of Cyprus between the Years A.D. 1196 and 1360." *Greek Orthodox Theological Review* 10 (1964): 75–106.

Mango, C. "The Conciliar Edict of 1166." *DOP* 17 (1963): 317–30.

Matteucci, G. *La missione francescana di Costantinopoli* (= *Bibl. di Studi Francescani* 9). Florence, 1971.

Mayer, H.E. *The Crusades.* Oxford, 1972.

Mercati, G. "Fra Massimo da Costantinopoli e l'uso del greco coi Greci uniti di Oriente." *SBN* 4 (1935): 311–15.

______. *Notizie di Procoro e Demetrio Cidone, Manuele Caleca e Teodoro Meliteniote ed altri appunti* (= *ST* 56). Città del Vaticano, 1931.

______. *Se la versione dall'ebraico del codice veneto greco VII sia di Simone Atumano arcivescovo di Tebe* (*ST* 30). Rome, 1916.

Merendino, E. "Quattro lettere greche di Federico II." In *Atti Accad. Sc. Lett. e Arti di Palermo,* s.IV, 34, p. 11 (1974–1975), pp. 293–344.

Meyendorff, J. "Alexis and Roman: A Study in Byzantino-Russian Relations (1352–1354)." *St. Vladimir's Theological Quarterly* 2 (1967): 139–48. Reprint. *Bslav* 28 (1967): 277–88.

______. "Humanisme nominaliste et mystique chrétienne à Byzance au XIVe siècle." *Nouvelle Revue Théologique* 79 (1957): 905–14.

______. *Introduction à l'étude de Grégoire Palamas.* Paris, 1959. Translated without notes as *A Study of Gregory Palamas.* London, 1964.

______. "Projet de concile oecuménique en 1367: un dialogue inédit entre Jean Cantacuzène et le légat Paul." *DOP* 14 (1960): 147–77.

______. "Society and Culture in the Fourteenth Century: Religious Problems." In *Reports of the XIVth Internat. Byz. Congr.*, 1:51–65. Bucharest, 1971.

______. "Le tome synodal de 1347." In *Mélanges Ostrogorsky,* pp. 209–27. Belgrade, 1963.

Michaud, J.-F. *Histoire des Croisades.* Vol. 3. Paris, 1970.

Michel, A. "Sprache und Schisma." In *Festschrift Kardinal Faulhaber,* pp. 40–47, 1949.

Miller, W. *Essays on the Latin Orient.* Cambridge, 1921.

______. *The Latins in the Levant: A History of Frankish Greece 1204–1566.* London, 1908.

Mollat, G. "Jean XXII et Charles IV le Bel (1322–1328)." *Journal des Savants* (1967), pp. 92–106.

______. *The Popes at Avignon 1305–1378.* London, 1963.

Moranville, H. "Les projets de Charles de Valois sur l'empire de Constantinople." *BChartes* 51 (1890): 63–86.

Morris, C. "Geoffrey de Villehardouin and the Conquest of Constantinople." *History* 53 (1968): 24–34.

Nicol, D.M. "The Abdication of John VI Cantacuzenus." *BForsch* 2 (1967): 269–83.

______. "The Byzantine Church and Hellenic Learning in the Fourteenth Century." *Studies in Church History* 5 (Leiden, 1969): 23–57.

______. *The Byzantine Family of Kantakouzenos (Cantacuzenus) ca. 1100–1460* (= *Dumbarton Oaks Studies* XI). Washington, D.C., 1968.

______. "The Byzantine Reaction to the Second Council of Lyons 1274." *Studies in Church History* 7 (Cambridge, 1971): 113–47.

______. "Byzantine Requests for an Ecumenical Council in the Fourteenth Century." *Annuarium Historiae Conciliorum* 1 (1969): 69–75.

______. *The Despotate of Epirus.* Oxford, 1957.

______. "Ecclesiastical Relations between the Despotate of Epirus and the Kingdom of Nicaea in the years 1215 to 1230." *Byz* 22 (1952): 207–28.

______. "The Greeks and the Union of Churches: The Preliminaries to the Second Council of Lyons, 1261–1274." In *Medieval Studies Presented to A. Gwynn, S.J.*, edited by J.A. Watt and others, pp. 454–80. Dublin, 1961.

______. "The Greeks and the Union of Churches: The Report of Ogerius, Protonotarius of Michael VIII Palaeologus, in 1280." In *Proceedings of the Royal Irish Academy LXIII, sect. C,1.* Dublin, 1962.

______. *The Last Centuries of Byzantium 1261–1453.* London, 1972.

______. "Mixed Marriages in Byzantium in the Thirteenth Century." *Studies in Church History* 1 (London, 1964): 160–72.

______. "The Relations of Charles of Anjou with Nikephorus of Epirus." *BForsch* 4 (1972): 170–94.

Norden, W. *Das Papsttum und Byzanz: Die Trennung der beiden Mächte und das Problem ihrer Wiedervereinigung.* Berlin, 1903.

Obolensky, D. *The Byzantine Commonwealth.* London, 1971.

———. "Byzantium, Kiev and Moscow: A Study of Ecclesiastical Relations." *DOP* 11 (1957): 21–78.

———. "The Principles and Methods of Byzantine Diplomacy." In *Reports of the XIIth Internat. Byz. Congr. I Belgrade,* 1963, pp. 45–61.

Oeconomos, L. "L'Etat intellectuel et moral des Byzantins vers le milieu du XIVe siècle d'après une page de Joseph Bryennios." In *Mélanges Charles Diehl* 1 (Paris, 1930): 227–33.

Omont, H. "Lettre d'Andronique II Paléologue au Pape Jean XXII." *BChartes* 67 (1906): 587.

———. "Projet de réunion des Eglises grecque et latine sous Charles le Bel en 1327." *BChartes* 53 (1892): 254–57.

Ostrogorsky, G. "The Byzantine Empire and the Hierarchical World Order." *Slavonic and East European Review* 35 (1956): 1–14.

———. "Observations on the Aristocracy in Byzantium." *DOP* 25 (1971): 1–32.

Pall, F. "Considerazioni sulla partecipazione veneziana alla crociata antiottomana di Nicopoli (1396)." *RHSE* 7 (1969): 187–97.

———. "Encore une fois sur le voyage diplomatique de Jean V Paléologue en 1365/66." *RHSE* 9 (1971): 535–40.

Papadakis, A. "Gregory II of Cyprus and an Unpublished Report to the Synod." *Greek, Roman and Byzantine Studies* 16 (1975): 227–39.

———. "Gregory Palamas at the council of Blachernae 1351." *Greek, Roman and Byzantine Studies* 10 (1969): 333–42.

Papadopoulos, Ch. "Athanasius II of Alexandria (1276–1316)." In Greek. *EEBS* 6 (1929): 3–13.

———. "The State of the Orthodox Church of Alexandria in the XIVth and XVth Centuries." In Greek. *EEBS* 13 (1937): 143–54.

Papadopoulos, I.B. *Theodore II Lascaris, empereur de Nicée.* Paris, 1908.

Papadopoulos, S.G. *Greek Translations of Thomistic Works: Philo-Thomists and Anti-Thomists in Byzantium.* In Greek. Athens, 1967.

Papadopoulos-Kerameus, A. "Documents grecs pour servir à l'histoire de la quatrième croisade." *Revue de l'Orient Latin* 8 (1893): 540–55.

———. "Theodore Eirénikos, patriarche oecuménique de Nicée." *BZ* 10 (1901):182–92.

Parisot, V. *Cantacuzène homme d'état et historien.* Paris, 1845.

Pasini, R. *Un sommo conciliatore Gregorio X.* Milan, 1962.

Pears, E. *The Fall of Constantinople: The Story of the Fourth Crusade.* London, 1885.

Pelissier, A. *Grégoire XI.* Tulle, 1962.

———. *Innocent VI.* Tulle, 1961.

Pelliot, P. "Les Mongols et la Papauté." *Revue de l'Orient Chrétien* 23 (1922–23): 3–30; 24 (1924): 225–335; 28 (1931–32): 3–84.

Petridès, S. "Sentence synodique contre le clergé unioniste (1283)." *EO* 14 (1911): 133–36.

Polemis, D.J. "La querelle de Grégoras et de Barlaam, 'La Réfutation.' " *Hellenika* 18 (1964): 44–72.

Previale, L. "Un panegirico inedito per Michele VIII Paleologo." *BZ* 42 (1942): 1–19.

Primov, B. "The Papacy, the Fourth Crusade and Bulgaria." *Byzantinobulgarica* 1 (1962): 182–211.

Purcell, M. *Papal Crusading Policy: The Chief Instruments of Papal Crusading Policy and Crusade to the Holy Land from the final Loss of Jerusalem to the Fall of Acre, 1244–1291.* Brill, Leiden, 1975.

Queller, D.E. "Innocent and the Crusader-Venetian Treaty of 1201." *Medievalia et Humanistica* (1963), pp. 31–34.

_____. *The Latin Conquest of Constantinople.* New York, 1971.

Rachewiltz, Igor de. *Papal Envoys to the Great Khan.* London, 1971.

Raybaud, L.-P. *Le gouvernement et l'administration centrale de l'Empire Byzantin sous les premiers Paléologues (1258–1354).* Paris, 1968.

Riant, P. *Exuviae sacrae constantinopolitanae.* Vol. 1. Geneva, 1877.

Richard, J. "Le royaume de Chypre et le grand schisme." In *Compt rendu Acad. Inscript. et Belles Lettres,* pp. 498–507. 1965.

Roberg, B. *Die Union zwischen der griechischen und der lateinischen Kirche auf dem II. Konzil von Lyon (1274)* (= *Bonner historische Forschungen* 24). Bonn, 1964.

_____. "Die Tartaren auf dem Konzil von Lyon 1274." *Annuarium Historiae Conciliorum* 5 (1973): 241–302.

Rochcau, G. "Innocent IV devant le péril Tatar: Ses lettres à Daniel de Galicie et à Alexandre Nevsky." *Istina* 6 (1959): 167–86.

Roncaglia, M. "Les Frères Mineurs et l'Eglise grecque orthodoxe au XIIIe siècle, 1231–1274." In *Bibl. bio-biblio,* series 4. *Studi* 2 (Cairo, 1954): 23–120.

_____. *Georges Bardanès, métropolite de Corfou et Barthélémy de l'Ordre Franciscain* (= *Studi e Testi Francescani* 4). Rome, 1953.

Roscher, H. *Papst Innocenz III. und die Kreuzzüge.* Göttingen, 1969.

Rouillard, G. "La politique de Michel VIII Paléologue à l'égard des monastères." *REB* 1 (1943): 73–84.

Runciman, S. *The Eastern Schism.* Oxford, 1955.

_____. *A History of the Crusades.* Vol. 3. Cambridge, 1954.

_____. *The Sicilian Vespers.* Cambridge, 1958.

Salaville, S. "Cabasilas le sacellaire et Nicolas Cabasilas." *EO* 35 (1936): 421–27.

_____. "Deux documents inédits sur les dissensions religieuses byzantines entre 1275 et 1310." *REB* 22 (1964): 222–37.

_____. "La vie monastique grecque au début du XIVe siècle d'après un discours inédit de Théolepte de Philadelphie." *REB* 2 (1944): 119–25.

Santifaller, L. *Beiträge zur Geschichte des lateinischen Patriarchats von Konstantinopel (1204–1261) und der venezianischen Urkunde.* Weimar, 1938.

Schillmann, F. "Zur byzantinischen Politik Alexanders IV." *Römische Quartalschrift* 22 (1908): 108–31.

Schirò, G. *Barlaam Calabro, epistole greche.* Palermo, 1954.

_____. *Barlaam and Philosophy in Thessalonica in the XIVth Century.* In Greek. Thessalonica, 1959.

Setton, K.M. "The Avignonese Papacy and the Catalan Duchy of Athens." *Byz* 17

(1944–45): 281–303.

———. "The Byzantine Background to the Italian Renaissance." In *Proceedings of American Phil. Soc.* 100 (1956): 1–76.

———. *Catalan Domination in Athens, 1311–1388.* Cambridge, Mass., 1948.

———, general editor. *A History of the Crusades.* Vols. 1, 2 (1969); Vol. 3 (1975). Madison, Milwaukee, and London.

———. *The Papacy and the Levant (1204–1571).* Vol. I. *The Thirteenth and Fourteenth Centuries.* Philadelphia, 1976.

Ševčenko, I. "Alexios Makrembolites and his 'Dialogue between the Rich and the Poor.' " *Zbornik Radova* 6 (1960):187–228.

———. "The Decline of Byzantium Seen through the Eyes of its Intellectuals." *DOP* 15 (1961): 167–86.

———. *Etudes sur la polémique entre Théodore Métochites et Nicéphore Choumnos* (= *Corpus Brux. Hist. Byz. subsidia* III). Brussels, 1962.

———. "Nicholas Cabasilas 'Anti-Zealot' Discourse: a Reinterpretation." *DOP* 11 (1957):81–171.

———. "Theodore Metochites, the Chora, and the Intellectual Trends of His Time." In *The Kariye Djami,* edited by P.A. Underwood, vol. 4, *Studies in the Art of Kariye Djami and its Intellectual Background* (= Bollingen Series LXX). Princeton University Press, 1975, pp. 19–91. Also in French in *Art et Société à Byzance sous les Paléologues,* pp. 15–39. Venice, 1971.

Sinogowitz, B. "Uber das byzantinische Kaisertum nach dem vierten Kreuzzuge (1204–1205)." *BZ* 45 (1952): 345–56.

Souarn, R. "Tentatives d'union avec Rome: Un patriarche grec catholique au XIIIe siècle." *EO* 3 (1900): 229–37.

Soulis, G.C. "Czar Stephen Dušan and the Holy Mountain." In Greek. *EEBS* 22 (1952): 82–96.

Stadtmüller, G. "Michael Choniates Metropolit von Athen (ca. 1138–ca. 1222)." *Orientalia Christiana* 133 (Rome, 1934): 125–325.

Stănescu, E. "Autour d'une lettre de Démétrius Kydonès expediée en Valachie." *RHSE* 7 (1969): 221–50.

Stiernon, D. "Bulletin sur le Palamisme." *REB* 30 (1972): 231–341 (up to January 1971).

Stiernon, L. "Les origines du Despotat d'Epire." *REB* 17 (1959): 90–126.

Sykoutris, I. "On the Schism of the Arsenites." In Greek. *Hellenika* 2 (1929): 267–332; 3 (1930): 15–44; 5 (1932): 107–26.

Talbot, A.M.M. "The Patriarch Athanasius and the Church." *DOP* 27 (1973): 11–28.

Thiriet, F. *La Romanie vénetienne au moyen âge.* Paris, 1959.

———. "La situation religieuse en Crète au début du XVe siècle." *Byz* 36 (1966): 201–12.

Thiriet, F., and Wirth, P. "La politique religieuse de Venise à Négrepont à la fin du XIVe siècle." *BZ* 56 (1963): 297–303.

Tillman, H. *Papst Innocenz III.* Bonn, 1954.

Tomadakis, N.B. "Orthodox Prelates in Crete under the Domination of the Venetians." In Greek. *Orthodoxia* 27 (1952): 63–75.

______. "Studies on Joseph Bryennios, I: The Question of the 'Virtue-testers.' " In Greek. *EEBS* 29 (1959): 1–12.

Trapp, E. "Die Metropoliten von Nikaia und Nikomedia in der Paleologen Zeit." *OCP* 35 (1969): 183–92.

Tsirpanlis, Z.N. "New Factors for the Ecclesiastical History of Crete under the Venetians." In Greek. *Hellenika* 20 (1967): 42–106.

Ullmann, W. "The Constitutional Significance of Constantine the Great's Settlement." *Journal of Ecclesiastical History* 27 (1976): 1–16.

______. *Medieval Papalism*. London, 1949.

Uspenskij, T. *Organisation du second empire bulgaire*. Odessa, 1879.

Van Moe, E.-A. "L'envoi des nonces à Constantinople par les papes Innocent V et Jean XXI (1276)." In *Mélanges d'archéologie et d'histoire de l'Ecole franç. de Rome* 47 (1930): 30–62.

Vasiliev, A.A. "The Foundation of the Empire of Trebizond." *Spec* 11 (1936): 3–37.

______. "Mesarites as a Source." *Spec* 13 (1958): 180–82.

______. "Il viaggio di Giovanni V Paleologo in Italia e l'unione di Roma nel 1369." *SBN* 3 (1931): 153–92.

Verlinden, C. "Orthodoxie et esclavage au bas Moyen-Age." In *Mélanges Tisserant* (= *ST* 235), pp. 427–56.

Verpeaux, J. *Nicéphoros Choumnos, Homme d'état et humaniste byzantin (ca. 1250/1255–1327)*. Paris, 1959.

Voordeckers, E. "Quelques remarques sur les prétendus 'Chapitres Théologiques' de Jean Cantacuzène." *Byz* 34 (1964): 619–21.

______. "Un Empereur Palamite à Mistra en 1370." *RHSE* 9 (1971): 607–15.

Vryonis, Sp. Jun. "Byzantine Attitudes toward Islam during the Late Middle Ages." *Greek, Roman and Byzantine Studies* 12 (1971): 263–86.

______. *The Decline of Medieval Hellenism in Asia Minor and the Process of Islamisation from the Eleventh through the Fifteenth Century*. Berkeley, Los Angeles, London, 1971.

Waas, A. *Geschichte der Kreuzzüge*. Freiburg, 1956.

Waley, D. *The Papal States in the Thirteenth Century*. London, 1961.

Watt, J.A. *The Theory of Papal Monarchy in the Thirteenth Century*. London, 1965.

Weiss, G. *Johannes Kantakuzenos—Aristocrat, Staatsmann, Kaiser und Mönch—in der Gesellschaftsentwicklung von Byzanz im 14. Jahrhundert*. Wiesbaden, 1969.

Wirth, P. "Die Haltung Kaiser Johannes'V. bei den Verhandlungen mit König Ludwig I. von Hungarn zu Buda im Jahre 1366." *BZ* 56 (1963): 271–73.

Wittek, P. *The Rise of the Ottoman Empire*. London, 1938.

Wolff, R.L. "Baldwin of Flanders and Hainault, First Latin Emperor of Constantinople: His Life, Death and Resurrection 1172–1225." *Spec* 27 (1952): 281–322.

______. "Footnote to an Incident of the Latin Occupation of Constantinople: The Church and the Icon of the Hodegetria." *Trad* 6 (1948): 319–28.

______. "Hopt's so-called 'Fragmentum' of Marino Sanudo Torsello." In *The*

Joshua Starr Memorial Volume (= N.Y. *Jewish Social Studies,* Publication 5, 1953), pp. 149–59.

______. "The Latin Empire of Constantinople and the Franciscans." *Trad* 2 (1944): 213–37.

______. "Mortgage and Redemption of an Emperor's Son: Castile and the Latin Empire of Constantinople." *Spec* 29 (1954): 45–84.

______. "The Organization of the Latin Patriarchate of Constantinople, 1204–1261: Social and Administrative Consequences of the Latin Conquest." *Trad* 6 (1948): 33–60.

______. "Politics in the Latin Patriarchate of Constantinople 1204–1261." *DOP* 8 (1954): 225–303.

______. "Romania: The Latin Empire of Constantinople." *Saeculum* 23 (1948): 1–34.

Wolff, R.L., and Hazard, H.W. *The Later Crusades 1189–1311* (= *A History of the Crusades,* edited by K.M. Setton, vol. 2). Madison, Milwaukee, and London, 1969.

Wolter, H., and Holstein, H. *Lyon I et Lyon II (= Histoire des Conciles Oecuméniqes* 7). Paris, 1966.

Zacharias von Lingenthal, K.E. "*Prooemien zu Chrysobullen von Demetrius Cydones.*" In *Sitzungsberichte der preuss. Akad. d. Wiss.*, vol. 2, p. 1419. Berlin, 1888.

Zakythinos, D.A. "Archbishop Antelmos and the First Years of the Latin Church of Patras." In Greek. *EEBS* 10 (1933): 401–17.

______. *Le Despotat de Morée.* Vol. 1, *Histoire politique* (Paris, 1932); vol. 2, *Vie et institutions* (Athens, 1953).

Index

A

Abaqa, il Khan, 135, 172
Achaia, 36, 54, 61
Acre, 52, 190
Acropolites, George, in Thessalonica, 99; suppresses unrest, 118; in Council of Lyons, 132, 135, 138, 140
Adramyttium, 184, 196
Adrianople, 6, 171, 175
Agnes-Anna, 4, 5
Aide-mémoire, see Ogerius
Akindynus, Gregory, 201, 202, 203, 222
Albania, 120, 161
Alexander III, pope (1159–81), 3–4
Alexander IV, pope (1254–61), 92, 97–104 passim
Alexandria, 2, 43, 44, 212
Alexius I Comnenus, emp. of Constantinople (1081–1118), 1–2, 148
Alexius II Comnenus, emp. of Constantinople (1180–3), 4, 5
Alexius III Angelus, emp. of Constantinople (1195–1203), 7, 11, 15, 16, 19
Alexius IV Angelus, emp. of Constantinople (1203–04), prince, 14, 16, 17, 258 n.23; emperor, 19, 24–5, 147
Alexius Comnenus, emp. of Trebizond, 170, 171
Alfonso, kg. of Castile, 130, 161
Alice, queen of Cyprus, 57, 58, 59
Allage, 180
Amadeus of Savoy, 213, 215, 217, 219
Amalric, kg. of Cyprus, 61
Ambrose, St., 144
Anatolia, 186, 223
Andrew of Longjumeau, O.P., 87
Andronicus I Comnenus, emp. of Constantinople (1183–5), 5, 7, 8
Andronicus II Palaeologus, emp. of Constantinople (1282–1328), 106, 182–92 passim; and union of Lyons, 136, 137, 141, 165, 172–3, 176, 182; and Catalans, 148, 189; contacts with west, 188, 189, 192, 193; buries his father, 180; political policy, 186; ecclesiastical policy, 183–4; deposed, 192
Andronicus III Palaeologus, emp. of Constantinople (1328–41), 192–201 passim; rebels, 192; contacts with west, 193, 198; convert to Latin Church (?), 195–6; at synod of 1341, 201
Andronicus IV Palaeologus, emp. of Constantinople (1376–9), 216, 217, 218; rebels, 225, 227, 229
Angelo, O.F.M., envoy, 172
Anna of Savoy, empress of Constantinople, 195; regent, 201–02, 221, 241
Anointings, sacramental, 21, 37, 85, 103, 238, 246
Anselm, bp. of Havelberg, 151
Antioch, 1–2, 3, 22, 44, 76, 82–3, 93, 96, 148
Antony IV, pat. of Constantinople (1380–90, 1391–7), 144, 255
Apocaucus, Alexius, Grand Admiral, 202
Apocaucus, John, bp. of Naupactus, 49–50

Apulia, 74
Archives, papal, ix, 109
Argon, Mongol prince, 190
Argyrus, Isaac, 149
Armenia (Little), 9, 75, 82, 190, 191; Church rite, 241–2
Arnaldi, Fra Garcias, O.F.M., 195
Arsenites, 111, 118, 128, 171, 191, 252
Arsenius Autorianus, pat. of Constantinople (1255–9, 1261–4), 97–100 passim, 277 n.9; crowned Michael VIII, 104, 106; deposed, 118; vindicated, 184, 191
Ascelin, O.P., 87
Asen, John, czar of Bulgaria, 62, 63; ally of Vatatzes, 72, 73–4; died, 79
Asen, John, relative of John VI Cantacuzenus, 207
Asen, Manuel, relative of John VI Cantacuzenus, 207
Athanasius I, pat. of Constantinople (1289–93, 1303–09), 185
Athanasius, pat. of Alexandria, 184
Athanasius, bp. of Sardis, 183–4
Athens, 54
Athos, Mount, 38, 200, 201
Augustine, St., 149, 151
Augustine de Undinis, 231
Autumano, Simon, bp. of Thebes, 215, 228
Avignon, 248–9

B

Baichu, khan, 87
Baldwin I, Latin emp. of Constantinople, 26, 27, 261 n.10, 262 n.11
Baldwin II, Latin emp. of Constantinople, minor, 51, 63; reigning, 73, 74, 79, 80; refugee, 106–07, 108, 115, 116
Baldwin, bp. of Famagusta, 236
Baptism, doubts about rite of Greeks, 74–5, 216; of Bulgarians, 216, 238–40, 302 n.53, 308 n.31; and of Armenians, 238, 242
Bardanes, archbp. of Corfù, 50, 64, 75
Barlaam of Calabria, envoy to Avignon, 147, 149, 196–9; against papacy, 194; against Hesychasm, 200–01, 204, 222
Bartholomew of Alverna, O.F.M., 239–40
Bartholomew, O.F.M., bp. of Grosseto, 172–5
Bartholomew, canon of Negroponte, 205
Bartholomew of Otranto, O.F.M., 64
Basil, primate of Bulgaria, 21, 63
Batu, khan, 87
Bayezid, Sultan of Ottoman Turks, 223, 230
Beccus, *see* John XI Beccus, pat. of Constantinople
Bela, kg. of Hungary, 73–4, 75, 88
Benedict XII, pope, (1334–42), 147, 196–9, 234
Benedict XIII, antipope, 231
Benedict, card. of St. Susanna, 30, 32, 33–4, 38, 39
Benedict of Como, O.P., 193, 194
Benefices, 233
Benevento, Battle of, 113
Berat, Siege of, 177
Bernard, St., 11
Bernard, abbot of Monte Cassino, 130, 133, 140, 161, 162
Berrhoiotes, interpreter, 132
Black Death, 202, 205
Blemmydes, Nicephorus, discussions at Nicaea, 66–7; with John of Parma, 89–90; relations with emperor, 91, 97; treatises on *Filioque*, 111, 129; influence on Beccus, 152–7
Boethius, 149
Bohemond of Antioch, 148
Bohemond of Sicily, 1–2, 22
Bonagrazia of San Giovanni in Persiceto, O.F.M., 125, 132, 134
Bonaventura of Mugello, O.F.M., 125
Bonaventure, St., O.F.M., 134, 139, 146
Boniface VIII, pope (1294–1303), 103, 187, 188, 190, 191
Boniface IX, pope (1389–1404), 229–32 passim
Boniface of Ivrea, O.F.M., envoy, 109
Boniface of Montferrat, 14, 15, 17, 18, 26, 27, 36
Boucicaut, marshal, 232
Bryennius, Joseph, 149
Buda, 213, 216, 226
Bulgaria, 37, 64, 143. *See also* Asen, John; Vidin
Butrinto, 177

C

Cabasilas, Nilus, 149, 222
Calabria, 74
Callistus, pat. of Constantinople (1350–3, 1355–63), 211, 212, 254
Calopherus, John Lascaris, 221, 222, 224
Calopherus, Maximus, monk, 221, 306 n.19
Caltabellotta, Peace of, 187, 189
Camaterus, Andronicus, 158
Cantacuzenus, Manuel, 225
Cantacuzenus, *see* John VI, Matthew Cantacuzenus
Capuano, Peter, card., 15, 16, 17, 20, 30
Cassianus, 222, 225
Catalan Grand Company, 148, 186, 189
Catherine of Courtenay, 188
Catherine (of Valois), 189
Celestine III, pope (1191–8), 9, 57, 101
Celestine V, pope (1294), 187
Chalcedon, Council of, 143
Charlemagne, 144, 145
Charles IV, kg. of France (1322–8), 192
Charles VI, kg. of France (1380–1422), 232
Charles Martel, 187
Charles of Anjou, I of Sicily, 113–41, 161–87 passim; kg. of Sicily, 106, 112, 113, 120, 123, 130; activities in Italy, 119, 164, 166, 168, 174; treaties against Constantinople, 115–6, 178; activities in the east, 115–6, 120–1, 122, 161, 172, 174, 177; gives safe-conducts, 127, 129–30, 162, 175; 'Sicilian Vespers,' 179–80, 186; death, 187
Charles of Salerno, 187
Charles of Valois, 187–9
Chios, 205, 299 n.9
Chomatianus, Demetrius, archbp. of Ochrida, 49–50
Choniates, Michael, archbp. of Athens, 32, 38, 148
Choniates, Nicetas, historian, 25, 147
Chrysoberges brothers, O.P., 222
Chrysoberges, Maximus, O.P., 230–1
Chrysoloras, Manuel, 231
Church property, 25, 30–1, 38–9, 42, 53, 55
Clement IV, pope (1265–8), 112–19 passim; proposes a profession of faith, 114–5
Clement V, pope (1305–14), 188, 236
Clement VI, pope (1342–52), 205, 206, 207, 242
Clement VII, antipope, 227, 228
Clementine Profession of Faith, 114–5, 121, 126, 136, 168, 190, 213, 216, 219, 225, 246, 247, 250, 253
Colonna, John, Latin pat. of Constantinople, 53, 54
Commercial privileges, 1, 4–5, 8, 105, 149, 244
Confirmation, Sacrament of, in Bosnia, 239; reserved to bps., 74, 237, 239–40; allowed to priests, 240
Conrad III, kg. of Germany, 3
Conrad IV, kg. of Germany, 92, 97
Conrad, archbp. of Helmstadt, 15
Conradin, 97, 113, 119
Constance, daughter of Manfred, 179
Constantine Mesopotamites, archbp. of Thessalonica, 55
Constantine, bp. of Orvieto, 95, 98–100, 277 n.9
Constantinople, passim throughout the book; 1, 8; massacre of Latins, 5; captured, 18, 19, 24–6, 261 n.10; in Latin hands, 25–105; growing weakness, 52, 56, 68, 74; attacked, 72–3; assisted by Holy See, 55, 79, 100; regained by Greeks, 105; besieged by Turks, 229
Corfù, 3, 18, 104, 106
Crete, 56, 234–6, 237–8
Crown of Thorns, 73
Crusades, second, 3; third, 6; fourth, chapters II and III; fifth, 51; other projects, 191, 192, 195, 214, 229; decreed in councils, 44–5, 80–1, 191; literature about, 191; abuse of, 112, 187, 189, 247, 248
Cumans, 6, 29, 75
Cydones, Demetrius, 149, 218, 221, 222, 224
Cydones, Procorus, 149, 204, 221, 222
Cyprus, ecclesiastical organization, 57–9, 75; relations with Nicaea, 59–60; decrees on rite, 82–6, 101–03, 236, 237
Cyzicus, archbp. of, 92

D

Damietta, 52
Dandolo, Enrico, Doge, 15, 25, 26, 29
Dandolo, Stephen, envoy, 196

Daniel, prince of Galicia, 74, 82, 88
Dardanelles, 211
Devol, Treaty of, 2
Didymotichus, 212
Dieux de Beaumont, general, 127
Discussions, theological, 32–3, 38, 40–3, 65–72. *See also Filioque*
Dokianus, Theodore, 98
Dominicans, 61, 65, 75, 81, 146, 244
Donation of Constantine, 79
Doria, Ilario, envoy, 231
Doria, Simone, envoy, 193
Doucas, John, "The Bastard," 164–5, 169–70, 171
Doucas, Lampidenus Constantine, 189
Doucas, Manuel, despot of Thessalonica, 62, 63, 79
Doucas, Michael Angelus Comnenus I, prince of Epirus, 26, 48–9
Doucas, Michael II, despot of Epirus, 104–05, 120
Doucas, Nicephorus I, despot of Epirus, 99, 165, 169–70, 177, 179
Doucas, Theodore, emp. in Thessalonica, 48–50, 54–6, 62, 77, 79
Durazzo, 6, 161, 188, 234
Dusan, Stephen, czar of the Serbs, 202, 208, 222, 238, 300 n.23

E

Emergavi, William, O.F.M., bp. of Kisamos, 207
Epirus, 42, 48–50, 99, 104
Eucharist, bread for, discussions on, 65, 67, 68–72; permissions, 82, 96, 190, 239
Eude de Châteauroux, 83, 95
Eulogia Palaeologina, 164, 182
Eusebius, bp. of Caesarea, 143
Eustathius, archbp. of Thessalonica, 5
Eustorgius, archbp. of Nicosia, 75–6
Euthymius, envoy, 228

F

Filioque, 143, 145, 221, 228, 245; historical background, 151, 251–2; discussed, 13, 41–2, 88–90; excluded, 93–5; mentioned in 4th Lateran Council, 43; chanted and defined in 2nd Council of Lyons, 135, 138, 139, 140, 164; to be inserted in Creed, 167, 168, 169, 173, 175; exposition of Beccus, 151–9
Florence, Council of, 111, 139
Francis of Camerino, bp. of Vospri, 194
Francis of 'Pertuxo,' envoy, 205
Francis William, bp. of Daulis, 228
Franciscans, 61, 65, 81, 88, 146, 244
Frederick I Hohenstaufen (Barbarossa), 3, 4, 6, 9, 148
Frederick II, kg. of Germany, I of Sicily, 86; crusades, 52, 61–2; relations with popes, 62, 73, 78, 80; with Vatatzes, 88, 90
Frederick II, kg. of Sicily, 187–8

G

Galaction, monk, 176, 182
Gallipoli, 72, 189, 208, 215, 227
Gasberto de Orgoglio, O.P., bp. of Ceneta, 207
Gattilusio, Francis, 221
Gelasius, pope (492–6), 10
Genoa, 5, 100, 105–08, 118
George of Cyprus, *see* Gregory III, pat. of Constantinople
Georgia, 86
Gerard of Prato, O.F.M., envoy, 112
Germanus II, pat. of Constantinople (1222–40), 50, 59–61, 63, 64, 65–72, 77
Germanus III, pat. of Constantinople (1365–6), 132, 134, 135, 140
Germanus, archbp. of Cyprus, 84, 101–03
Germany, 86
Gervasius, Latin pat. of Constantinople, 53, 54, 76
Giustiniani, Pantaléon, Latin pat. of Constantinople, 92
Gratian, 146
Gregoras, Nicephorus, historian, viii, 186, 194, 195, 203, 204
Gregory VII, pope (1073–85), 1, 10
Gregory IX, pope (1227–41), 61, 63, 65, 73–6
Gregory X, pope (1261–76), 120–41 passim, 142, 160, 161, 162, 172

Gregory XI, pope (1370–8), letters, 224–6; benefices, 233, 234–5; Crete, 237; death, 227
Gregory III, pat. of Constantinople (1283–9), 128, 182, 183–5
Gregory VI Apirat, Catholicos of Armenia, 241–3
Guiscard, Robert, 1
Gunther, 16
Guy de Lusignan, kg. of Cyprus, 57

H

Halecki, Oscar, historian, 214, 301, n.44, 306 n.19
Haymo of Faversham, O.F.M., envoy, 65–72
Helena, queen of Serbia, 190
Helena, wife of John V, 202, 216
Helena, wife of Manfred, 177
Henry of Flanders, Latin emp. of Constantinople, 29, 31, 34, 39, 48, 51–2
Henry VI Hohenstaufen, kg. of Sicily, 6, 7, 9
Hesychasm, 200–01
Het'um II, kg. of Armenia, 190, 241
Holobolus, rhetor, 128, 131, 182
Honorius I, pope (625–38), 34
Honorius III, pope (1216–27), 50–61 passim, 79
Honorius IV, pope (1285–7), 187
Hugh, kg. of Cyprus, 57
Hugh of St. Pol, 259 n.44
Hugo, O.P., envoy, 65–72
Hugo Aetherianus, 146, 152
Hugo le Rousseau de Sully, general, 177
Hugo le Spert, O.P., envoy, 206
Huguccio, 11
Humbert, dauphin, 151, 206
Humbert de Romanis, O.P., 124, 134, 143, 150
Humbert of Silva Candida, card., 145

I

Incontri, Philippo, O.P., 222
Innocent III, pope (1198–1216), chapters II and III passim, 52, 55, 76, 245; attitude to Greek Church, 11, 20, 28–31, 258 n.32, 259 n.47, 264 n.33; to Bulgarian Church, 21, 22, 29; to diversions, 15–18, 18–20; acclamations of, 39; appreciation of, 45–6
Innocent IV, pope (1243–54), 78–95 passim; in Council of Lyons, 80; on Cyprus, 85–6; discussions with Greeks, 88–90; and proposals of Vatatzes 92–5; death, 95
Innocent V, pope (1275–6), 139, 162–5 passim
Isaac II Angelus, emp. of Constantinople (1185–95), 6, 7, 14, 19, 24–5; and Saladin, 148, 287 n.23
Isaac, archbp. of Ephesus, 175, 291 n.35
Isidore, pat. of Constantinople (1347–50), 202

J

Jacobites, 82, 236
James I of Aragon, 107, 133
James II of Aragon, 187
James of Itro, Latin pat. of Constantinople, 228
James, Catholicos of Armenia, 242
Janes, archbp. of Bulgaria, 153, 155
Jerome, St., 149
Jerome of Ascoli, O.F.M., *see* Nicholas IV, pope
Jerusalem, 2, 9, 61–2, 80
Job Jasites, monk, 129, 131, 163
John of Damascus, St., 153, 157, 184–5
John XXI, pope (1276–7), 165–170 passim
John XXII, pope (1316–34), 193–6 passim, 237, 238
John II Comnenus, emp. of Constantinople (1118–43), 2
John III Vatatzes, emp. of Constantinople (1222–54), 46, 54, 59, 97, 111, 128, 153; proposals for union, 66, 67–72, 88–90, 92–5; attacks on Constantinople, 62, 79, 80, 88; relations with Frederick II, 88, 90; death, 95
John IV Lascaris, emp. of Constantinople (1258–61), 104, 105, 106, 128
John V Palaeologus, emp. of Constantinople (1341–91), 201–29

passim; fights for the throne, 207–8; requests aid from popes, 205, 208, 211, 225; from Louis of Hungary, 213, 215–8; goes to Rome, 219, 222; goes to Venice, 224; wars with son, 225, 227, 229; has portable altar, 237
John VI Cantacuzenus, emp. of Constantinople (1347–54), 201–07 passim; and Palamism 201–03, 204; relations with papacy, 205–07, 208, 216, 218, 225, 226
John VII Palaeologus, emp. of Constantinople (1390), 229, 232
John of Brienne, regent of Constantinople, 61, 63, 68, 72, 73
John II, kg. of France (1350–64), 212
John XI Beccus, pat. of Constantinople (1275–1282), 122, 128, 131, 137, 180, 294 n.3; made patriarch, 163, 164; conversion to *Filioque* doctrine, 129, 152–9, 283 n.29; writer, 155–9, 176; meets legates, 175–6; professions of faith, 165, 168–9; centre of hostility, 171, 182, 183, 184–5, 192
John X Camaterus, pat. of Constantinople (1198–1206), 12–13, 31, 34, 35, 257 n.17
John XIV Calecas, pat. of Constantinople (1334–47), 200–01, 202
John, pat. of Antioch, 2
John of Parma, O.F.M., 88–90, 154
John of Pian Carpino, O.F.M., 87
John of Procida, 179
Joseph I, pat. of Constantinople (1266–75), 111, 118, 180; against union, 128, 129, 131, 132; abdicates, 163; restored to throne, 183–4; rejected, 179, 191
Josephites, 171

K

Kalojan, czar of Bulgaria, 7, 63; conversion to Rome, 21–2, 25, 26; defeats crusaders, 26, 29
Karakorum, 88
Karukes, 66
Khan, The Great, 86–8
Kisamos, 234
Kitros, bp. of, 170, 291 n.35
Koloman, kg. of Bulgaria, 79, 80, 81
Kossovo, Battle of, 229

L

Lampsacus, 211
Lascaris, *see* Theodore, John
Lateran, Fourth Council of, 42, 75, 236
Lawrence, Fra, O.F.M., 82–3, 95
Leo II, kg. of Armenia, 22, 24
Leo VI, kg. of Armenia, 243–4
Leo, bp. of Heraclea, 178
Leo Tuscan, 142, 143
Leuca, Cape of, 132
Licario, admiral, 127, 177
Light of Thabor, 200, 201, 204
Livonia, 57
Louis I, kg. of Hungary, and John V, 213–6; and other Christians, 208, 210; and popes, 224, 225, 226
Louis IX, kg. of France (1226–70), 73, 78, 118; on crusade, 80, 83, 87, 88, 122; relations with Michael VIII, 121, 122
Lyons, First Council of, 78, 80
Lyons, Second Council of, 123, 133–41, 164

M

Makriplagi, Battle of, 112
Mandas (or Mercurius), 178
Manfred, kg. of Sicily, dominates Italy, 97, 104, 112; in Epirus, 105; the papacy, 106, 107, 112; death, 113
Mangana monastery, 175
Manicaites, George, 213, 214, 221
Manuel I Comnenus, emp. of Constantinople (1143–80), 2–4, 143, 144
Manuel II Palaeologus, emp. of Constantinople (1391–1425), 221; hostage, 209, 213, 215; relations with the West, 218, 229, 230, 232; in Thessalonica, 227–8; in wars, 227, 229; made heir, 225, 227
Manuel I Sarantenus, pat. of Constantinople (1217–22), 49, 51
Manuel II, pat. of Constantinople (1244–54), 89–91, 95
Margaret, queen in Thessalonica, 36, 39
Marica River, Battle of, 224
Marino Sanudo, 192, 193
Maronites, 96
Marriage, 85, 103, 240–1
Martin IV, pope (1281–5), 178, 179, 186, 187

Martin of Pairis, abbot, 15, 147
Matthew Cantacuzenus, emp. of Constantinople (1354–7), 207, 208
Matthew, archbp. of Ephesus, 223
Maximus Planudes, 149
Meletius, monk, 177
Meliteniotes, 122, 128, 180, 182, 184–5
Mendicant Orders, 61, 87, 244. *See also* Dominicans, Franciscans
Mercurius (or Mandas), envoy, 178
Mesaites, John, 32–4
Mesaites Nicholas, archbp. of Ephesus, 32–4, 35, 40–2
Messina, 179, 180, 187
Metochites, Alexius Palaeologus, 221
Metochites, Demetrius Angelus, 221
Metochites, George, 100, 162, 164, 180, 182, 184–5
Metochites, Nicephorus, 221
Meyendorff, John, 216
Michael Angelus, ruler of Epirus, 79–80
Michael VIII Palaeologus, emp. of Constantinople (1258–82), 104–41, 161–81 passim; before 1274 relations with papacy, 106–12, 113–7, 121, 123, 129; relations with Greek Church, 111, 117–8, 128, 131, 132; Council of Lyons, 125, 136; after 1274, to impose union, 165–8, 172–5, 176–7, 178; excommunicated, 178, 180; commercial privileges to Latins, 149; wars, 112, 161, 177; character, 110, 111, 180–1; death, 180
Michael IX Palaeologus, emp. of Constantinople (1294–1320), 148, 188
Michael I Cerularius, pat. of Constantinople (1043–58), 145, 152
Michael IV Autorianus, pat. of Constantinople (1208–14), 35, 40, 46–7
Milutin, czar of Serbia, 188, 190, 236
Moerbeke, William of, *see* Morbecca
Monasteries, 37, 52, 53; *see also* Athos, Sinai
Mongols, 74, 80, 82, 86–8, 172
Monks, 37, 39, 40, 42, 52, 53, 55, 59; *see also* Athos, Sinai
Monomachus, John, 189
Monomachus, Theodore, 162
Morbecca, William of, 135
Morea, *see* Peloponnesus
Morosini, Latin pat. of Constantinople, 27, 28, 30, 31, 33–4, 37, 39, 76
Moschabar, George, chartophylax, 184
Moscow, 254–5
Muntaner, Roger, 148
Murad, sultan, 218, 225, 229
Muzalon, George, 104
Myriokephalon, Battle of, 4

N

Naples, 219
Naupactus, 234
Naval Leagues, 195–6, 205, 210, 211, 215, 224
Nektarios-Nicholas, abbot, 32, 75
Neophytus, archbp. of Cyprus, 59, 60, 83–4, 274 n.21
Nestorians, 82, 190, 236
Nicaea, city, 193
Nicaea, kingdom of, 39, 42, 48, 59
Nicephorus of Epirus, 188
Nicetas of Maronea, 111
Nicetas, bp. of Nicomedia, 151
Nicetas, archbp. of Thessalonica, 152
Nicholas III, pope (1277–80), 171–5, 177
Nicholas IV, pope (1288–92), envoy in Constantinople, 125, 163–4; letter from Leuca, 132, 134, 137, 142; pope, 187–90
Nicholas de Bessia, card., 219
Nicholas, bp. of Cortone, 109–11, 112, 152, 180
Nicholas of Curbio, 91, 92
Nicholas de Mercadantibus, 228
Nicholas of Methone, 158
Nicholas of Santo Arquarto, Latin pat. of Constantinople, 77
Nicomedia, 54
Nicopolis, Battle of, 229–30
Nicosia, 57
Nilus, pat. of Constantinople (1379–88), 228
Niphon, pat. of Constantinople (1310–14), 191, 194
Norden, W., historian, vii, 246, 268 n.6
Nyitra, bp. of, 213, 215

O

Obedience, Oath of, 31, 42, 75

Ogerius, 170–1, 178
Omur, Emir of Aydin, 201–02, 205
Ordinations, 33, 238, 239, 240, 246
Orkhan, Emir of Ottoman Turks, 202, 205
Othon de la Roche, 31, 54, 56
Otto of Brunswick, 13–4, 16
Ovid, 149

P

Pachymeres, George, historian, viii, 123, 128, 148, 175, 176, 178, 180
Palaeologus, *see* Michael, Andronicus, John
Palaeologus, Demetrius, 222
Palamas, Gregory, archbp. of Thessalonica, 149, 200–04
Palamism, 203, 221, 252–4
Palermo, 179, 180
Palienz, Nerses, Armenian bp., 243
Pallium, 21, 22, 23
Panaretus, Matthaeus Angelus, 149
Pantaléon, James, pat. of Jerusalem, 100
Parastron, John, O.F.M., 121, 124, 126, 128, 134, 135, 161
Parlement of Ravennica, 30, 31, 38–9, 56
Paul, Latin pat. of Constantinople, 208, 210, 215–8
Paul, bp. of Chalcedon, 231
Pelagius, card., 39, 40–1, 52, 57, 58, 84, 85
Pelagonia, Battle of, 105
Peloponnesus, 31, 100
Pentarchy, 151, 160
Pera (Galata), 175, 219
Peter, St., 11, 12, 22, 27, 33, 41, 108, 247
Peter, pat. of Antioch, 152
Peter, kg. of Aragon, 179, 180, 186
Peter of Cézanne, O.P., 65–72
Peter of Courtenay, Latin emp. of Constantinople, 51, 55
Peter of Cresta, O.F.M., envoy, 109
Peter, kg. of Cyprus, 212
Peter Lombard, 146
Peter of Moras, O.F.M., envoy, 109
Peter Thomas, O. Carm., Latin pat. of Constantinople, 208, 210–12, 215
Philadelphia, 223, 229
Philip of Anjou, 115, 122, 123, 177
Philip II Augustus, kg. of France (1180–1233), 9, 13, 14
Philip III, kg. of France (1271–85), 186, 187
Philip IV, kg. of France (1286–1314), 188, 189
Philip VI, kg. of France (1328–50), 193, 195
Philip II of Burgundy, 229
Philip of Courtenay, Latin emp. of Constantinople, 116, 161, 166, 172, 178, 276 n.51
Philip d'Ibelin, 57
Philip of Swabia, 7, 13–4, 15, 16, 17
Philip of Saint-Germain, envoy, 205
Philip, prince of Taranto, 188
Philip, O.F.M., envoy, 172
Philippe de Mézières, 211
Philippopolis, 212
Philotheus, pat. of Constantinople (1353–4, 1364–76), 216, 217, 222, 254
Photius, pat. of Constantinople (858–67), 143, 145, 151, 158, 288 n.48
Phurnes, John, 158
Pisano, John, 194
Plenitudo potestatis, 10, 246–7
Poland, 86
Profession of Faith, Clement's, 114–5, 121–6, 136. *See also* Clementine profession of faith
Purgatory, 64

R

Ralph of Rheims, O.F.M., envoy, 65–72
Rampanus, George, archpriest, 234–5, 306 n.10
Raniero of Siena, O.F.M., envoy, 112
Raphael, archbp. of Nicosia, 102–03
Raymond Berengario, O.F.M., envoy, 125
Re-ordination, 238
Richard Lionheart, kg. of England (1189–99), 9, 13, 57
Richard, bp. of Cherson, 194
Rites, 96, 246; equality of rite, 21, 37, 44, 173; in Bulgaria, 21; in Cyprus and Crete, 85–6, 101–03, 235–42; Latin privileges, 219–20, 230–1; Ruthenian, 74, 75, 82
Robert of Courtenay, Latin emp. of Constantinople, 51, 52, 56
Robert of Sicily, 193

Roger II, kg. of Sicily, 3
Roger de Flor, Catalan leader, 148, 189
Roger of Lauria, admiral, 187
Rudolph of Hapsburg, 130, 161, 174
Russia, 222, 254-5

S

Sacraments, *see* Baptism, Confirmation, Eucharist, Marriage, Ordination
St. Sophia, 26, 28, 30, 33, 182, 183
Saladin, 6, 9, 287 n.23
Sardis, archbp. of, 91, 92
Sartach, khan, 88
Saudzi Celebe, 225
Schism, Great of the West, 227-32 passim
Serres, archbp. of, 162
Sgouros, Leo, 7
'Sicilian Vespers,' 179-80, 247-8
Sigerus, Nicholas, envoy, 205, 206, 208, 210
Sigismund, kg. of Hungary, 229-30
Simon of Auvergne, O.F.M., envoy, 109
Simon of Tyre, Latin pat. of Constantinople, 76
Sinai, 52, 57
Smyrna, 202, 205, 211, 228
Spanopoulus, George, envoy, 205, 206
Spartenus, Demetrius, 98
Stracimir, prince of Bulgaria, 213, 239
Strongilo, knight, 222

T

Tagaris, George, 221
Tagliacozzo, Battle of, 119, 120
Tarentaise, Peter, *see* Innocent V, pope
Tartars, *see* Mongols
Tenedos, 224, 227
Thebes, 224
Theodora, empress of Constantinople, 184
Theodore, bp. of Sugdaia, 158
Theodore, bp. of Negroponte, 32, 36, 37, 43
Theodore I Lascaris, emp. of Constantinople, (1204-22), 26, 35-6, 42, 49, 50, 51
Theodore II Lascaris, emp. of Constantinople (1254-8), 97-100 passim; 91, 153, 155
Theodore II Irenicus, pat. of Constantinople (1214-16), 40
Theophanes, archbp. of Nicaea, 132, 134, 135, 178
Theophylactus of Bulgaria, 158
Theophylactus, Great Interpreter, 92
Thessalonica, 5, 202, 227-8
Thibaut of Champagne, 14
Thomas Aquinas, St., 146, 149, 221, 222
Thomas de Bozolasco, O.P., envoy, 225
Thomas of Vanezo, 221
'Tomographia,' 164, 165, 180
Tractatus contra errores Graecorum, 143
Trebizond, 48
Trikkala, bp. of, 170, 291 n.35
Tunis, 122, 123
Tzycandeles, Philip, 222, 225

U

Ugljesa, John, ruler in Serbia, 222, 223-4
Ugo da Fagiano, archbp. of Nicosia, 84, 101
Unctions, *see* Anointings
Urban II, pope (1088-99), 1
Urban IV, pope (1261-4), 104, 106-12 passim, 113
Urban V, pope (1362-70), urged crusades, 212-3; and John V, 213-5, 216, 217-20; and rites in Crete, 237
Urban VI, pope (1378-89), 227, 228, 229

V

Valona, 120
Venice, 215, 221, 225; before 1204, 1, 2, 3, 4, 8; and Fourth Crusade, 14-5, 17, 18, 19, 23, 25; Pact, 25, 26; Latin Empire, 29, 30-1, 48, 56, 68, 92, 105; relations with Palaeologi, 107, 118, 127, 149, 177, 189, 212, 218, 224; with Genoese, 100, 205; with religion, 27, 30, 76, 191, 234, 237, 246; with Naval Leagues, 195-6, 205, 210, 211; response to papal appeals, 224, 227, 228, 230, 234
Victor IV, antipope, 3
Vidin, 216, 239

Vienne, Council of, 191
Villehardouin, Geoffrey of, chronicler, 16
Villehardouin, Geoffrey II, prince of Achaia, 54, 56, 73, 79
Villehardouin, William II, prince of Achaia, 105, 107, 109, 112, 115–6, 177, 279 n.43
Viterbo, 107, 116, 120–1, 130, 139, 178, 217
Vlachs, 6, 7, 75, 216

W

Wallachia, 254
William of Barres, general, 127
William of Montferrat, 56
William I, kg. of Sicily, 3
William II, kg. of Sicily, 4, 5–6, 7
William of Rubruck, 88
William, bp. of Sozopolis, envoy, 210

Y

Yolanda, regent in Constantinople, 51, 52

Z

Zaccaria, 179
Zara, 14–24 passim, 258 n.33